Magill's
Cinema
Annual
2003

Magill's Cinema Annual 2003

22nd Edition
A Survey of the Films of 2002

Christine Tomassini, Editor

Carol Schwartz, Contributing Editor

A VideoHound® Reference

GALE®

THOMSON

GALE

Detroit • New York • San Diego • San Francisco • Cleveland • New Haven, Conn. • Waterville, Maine • London • Munich

Magill's Cinema Annual 2003

Project Editor
Christine Tomassini

Editorial
Carol Schwartz

Editorial Support Services
Wayne Fong

Manufacturing
Evi Seoud
Rhonda Williams

Product Design
Tracey Rowens

For permission to use material from this product, submit your request via Web at http://www.gale-edit.com/permissions, or you may download our Permissions Request form and submit your request by fax or mail to:

Permissions Department
The Gale Group, Inc.
27500 Drake Rd.
Farmington Hills, MI 48331-3535
Permissions Hotline:
248-699-8006 or 800-877-4253, ext. 8006
Fax: 248-699-8074 or 800-762-4058

ISBN 1-55862-459-7
ISSN: 0739-2141

Printed in the United States of America
10 9 8 7 6 5 4 3 2 1

Table of Contents

Preface

M*agill's Cinema Annual 2003* continues the fine film reference tradition that defines the VideoHound series of entertainment industry products published by Gale. The twenty-second annual volume in a series that developed from the 21-volume core set, *Magill's Survey of Cinema*, the *Annual* was formerly published by Salem Press. Gale's ninth volume, as with the previous Salem volumes, contains essay-reviews of significant domestic and foreign films released in the United States during the preceding year.

The *Magill's* editorial staff at Gale, comprising the VideoHound team and a host of *Magill's* contributors, continues to provide the enhancements that were added to the *Annual* when Gale acquired the line. These features include:

- More essay-length reviews of significant films released during the year
- Obituaries and book review sections
- Trivia and "fun facts" about the reviewed movies, their stars, the crew, and production
- Quotes and dialogue "soundbites" from reviewed movies, or from stars and crew about the film
- More complete awards and nominations listings, including the American Academy Awards®, Golden Globe, New York Critics Awards, Los Angeles Film Critics Awards, and others (see the User's Guide for more information on awards coverage)
- Box office grosses, including year-end and other significant totals
- Publicity taglines featured in film reviews and advertisements

In addition to these elements, the *Magill's Cinema Annual 2003* still features:

- An obituaries section profiling major contributors to the film industry who died in 2002
- An annotated list of selected film books published in 2002
- Nine indexes: Directors, Screenwriters, Cinematographers, Editors, Art Directors, Music Directors, Performers, Subject, and Title (now cumulative)

Compilation Methods

The *Magill's* editorial staff reviews a variety of entertainment industry publications, including trade magazines and newspapers, as well as online sources, on a daily and weekly basis to select significant films for review in *Magill's Cinema Annual*. *Magill's* staff and other contributing reviewers, including film scholars and university faculty, write the reviews included in the *Annual*.

Magill's Cinema Annual: A VideoHound Reference

The *Magill's Survey of Cinema* series, now supplemented by the *Annual*, is the recipient of the Reference Book of the Year Award in Fine Arts by the American Library Association.

Gale, an award-winning publisher of reference products, is proud to offer *Magill's Cinema Annual* as part of its popular VideoHound(R) product line, which includes *VideoHound's Golden Movie Retriever and The Video Source Book*. Other Gale film-related products include the *St. James Film Directors Encyclopedia*, *The St. James Women Filmmakers Encyclopedia* and the *Contemporary Theatre, Film, and Television* series.

Acknowledgments

Thank you to Judy Hartman, GGS Information Services, for her typesetting expertise, and Wayne Fong for his invaluable technical assistance. The *VideoHound* staff is thanked for its contributions to this project, especially Carol Schwartz for her generosity, hard work, and goodwill, as well as Peter Gareffa for his guidance and direction. Also, the following producers, distributors, and publicists were gracious enough to provide screeners and other materials that helped in the writing of some of the reviews in this edition: Susan Norget and Anne Crozat of Susan Norget Public Relations and Marketing; Sophie Gluck of Sophie Gluck and Associates; Brooke Travis of Weber Shandwick/Rogers Cowan; Rodrigo Barando of Kino International; the publicity office of Samuel Goldwyn Films; and the Press Office of the Film Society of Lincoln Center.

The Year in Film: An Introduction

My Big Fat Greek Wedding made some $225 million in domestic boxoffice in 2002. And why is this so notable? Because the story behind the low-budget indie release is a "dreams can come true" Hollywood-style fairytale in the best tradition of "let's put on a show!" Greek-American actress Nia Vardalos wrote a one-woman play about the trials and tribulations of belonging to an exuberant, loving, and sometimes overwhelming, immigrant family and the consternation of said clan when she married a non-Greek. The production just happened to delight Greek-American actress Rita Wilson, who told her husband Tom Hanks what a great movie it would be. (Their production company helped back the film.) Of course, the unknown Vardalos would have to play the lead and, of course, no Hollywood studio would take that chance, no matter how low the budget. The film finally gets made and then the studios pass on releasing an ethnic romantic comedy, leaving it to IFC Films to give *Wedding* a slow, platform release. For the most part, film critics dismiss the movie as fluff (when not using more disparaging terms) but word-of-mouth from those who actually pay for their tickets is nothing less than wonderful and *My Big Fat Greek Wedding* becomes a big fat hit and even gets the suddenly hot Vardalos an Oscar nomination for original screenplay. Only in Hollywood.

The year's boxoffice champ, released in early May at the start of the new summer movie season, just happened to be about a popular comic book character. That would be director Sam Raimi's *Spider-Man,* which brought Sony studios a coffer-filling $400 million plus and saw actor Tobey Maguire joining the ranks of superhero franchises, whose sequel is set for 2004. Following the web-slinger in both release date and boxoffice was another franchise picture—*Star Wars: Episode II—Attack of the Clones.* A scroll caught viewers up on the saga so far but it was a disappointment, with weak performances and stilted dialogue. About the most exciting thing the movie had to offer was a CGI-created Yoda kicking butt, but even that character was somehow more endearing back in his '70s puppet days.

Peter Jackson offered no such introduction to viewers of *his* continuing saga, *The Lord of the Rings: The Two Towers.* It began exactly where the first film left off and woe to anyone who couldn't keep the members of the Fellowship straight. Besides deepening the peril for our heroes, the second film also offered its own remarkable CGI character—Gollum, as voiced by actor Andy Serkis. Jackson also filmed Serkis's movements in character and then translated them (via computer) to the screen. A marvelous technical feat but the character itself turned out to be both terrifying and touching. *The Two Towers* moved the Tolkein saga relentlessly forward, leaving its fans yearning for the end of the trilogy, *The Return of the King,* which won't make an appearance until late in 2003.

And speaking of late, critics may have wondered where all their Top 10 releases and potential Oscar nominees were hiding. As it turns out, and as usual, studios flooded the last weeks of December by releasing four of the five Oscar-nominated films for Best Picture: *Chicago, Gangs of New York, The Hours,* and *The Lord of the Rings: The Two Towers.* The fifth nomination was Roman Polanski's Holocaust-drama, *The Pianist,* which had already won the Palme d'Or at the Cannes Film Festival. Polanski also received an Oscar nomination for Best Director while star Adrien Brody was nominated for Best Actor.

The big winner in the Oscar race was the long-aborning *Chicago,* which received 13 nominations. Since its Bob Fosse Broadway days in 1975, the musical was a contender for the big screen but no one could seem to overcome its stage restrictions until director Rob Marshall and screenwriter Bill Conden (both of whom received Oscar nominations). Marshall made studio Miramax happy by casting movie stars Renee Zellweger, Richard Gere, and Catherine Zeta-Jones in the lead roles. Zellweger and Zeta-Jones received Best Actress and Supporting Actress nominations respectively while co-stars Queen Latifah and John C. Reilly also got supporting nominations. Oscar may have ignored Gere but the Golden Globes thought he was worthy of *their* Best Actor in a Musical/Comedy award.

From a musical about murder in the 1920s to a drama about murder (and many other things) in the 1840s—director Martin Scorsese's *Gangs of New York.* This was another film with a long-gestation period, as Scorsese first announced that it would be his next directorial effort back in 1977. The film went through numerous and well-publicized trials and was originally scheduled for release in 2001. Many critics found the plot uneven as were the performances of Leonardo DiCaprio and Cameron Diaz. But all agreed on the skill of Daniel Day-Lewis in the leading role of Bill "the Butcher" Cutting for which he received a Best Actor nod. It was Scorsese who persuaded Day-Lewis to break his five-year screen hiatus to film *Gangs.* The director received his fourth Best Director nomination and some think he may be the Academy's sentimental favorite even if the film is not considered his best.

The Hours was the sort of literary drama that Oscar and the critics love and it's well-worth the acclaim. An adaptation of Michael Cunningham's Pulitzer Prize-winning novel, which concerns author Virginia Woolf and her novel *Mrs. Dalloway,* the film was a showcase for three powerhouse actresses: Nicole Kidman, Julianne Moore, and Meryl Streep. The film, director Stephen Daldry, screenwriter David Hare, and Kidman (Best Actress), Moore (Best Supporting Actress), and Ed Harris (Best Supporting Actor) all received nominations. While Streep did not receive a nomination for *The Hours,* she did for portraying author Susan Orlean in the quirky Spike Jonze film *Adaptation.* This is the actress's 13th record-breaking Oscar nomination.

Actor Jack Nicholson also broke the Oscar nomination record on the male side by receiving his 12th nomination, this time as Best Actor in Alexander Payne's film *About Schmidt.* Nicholson loses his familiar acting tics—the smirky smile and raised eyebrow—to play a sudden widower who finds his life empty after he retires so he decides to make a road trip. His route takes him into contact with Kathy Bates (a Best Supporting Actress nominee) who has a brief hot tub nude scene with Nicholson.

No film probably had a more interesting "creation" story than *Adaptation.* Writer Charlie Kaufman found it impossible to adapt Susan Orlean's non-fiction book *The Orchid Thief* into a viable screenplay so, instead, he wrote about screenwriter Charlie Kaufman (played by Nicolas Cage) finding it impossible to adapt Orlean's book while his (fictional) twin brother Donald (also Cage) finds screenwriting comes a lot easier when you write with a blockbuster in mind. Meanwhile, parts of Charlie's screenplay come to life as he depicts Orlean (Streep) writing *her* book. (Chris Cooper, who portrays orchid thief John Laroche, received a Best Supporting Actor nomination.) And if this isn't confusing enough, *Adaptation's* screenplay is credited to both Charlie and Donald Kaufman, although the Academy has stated that if it wins for Best Adapted Screenplay only one statue—to Charlie—will be handed out.

Julianne Moore is this Oscar race's double-dipper. Besides her Supporting Actress nomination for *The Hours,* she received a Best Actress nod for her portrayal of another unhappy 1950s housewife in Todd Hayne's beautifully artificial *Far from Heaven.* Her co-star, Dennis Quaid, won critical plaudits as Moore's equally unhappy spouse—a far cry from his other well-regarded film role of 2002, the Disney release *The Rookie.*

Of course, neither Streep nor Moore nor Quaid were the only actors to see themselves on the big screen more than once in 2002. *Chicago's* Richard Gere began his year as the cuckholded husband to Oscar nominee Diane Lane in Adrian Lyne's *Unfaithful.* Leonardo DiCaprio not only starred in *Gangs of New York* but Steven Spielberg's *Catch Me If You Can* as a youthful con man. DiCaprio's FBI nemesis in that film was Tom Hanks who played the role of a 1930s hitman in the elegiac *Road to Perdition. Perdition* also offered the pleasure of seeing Hanks opposite 77-year-old Paul Newman, who received a Best Supporting Actor nomination as the patriarch of an Irish gang. Spielberg himself had double directing duty with *Catch* and the future cop thriller *Minority Report,* starring Tom Cruise.

Another director with double credits this year was Steven Soderbergh. After the commercial pleasures of 2001's *Ocean's Eleven,* Soderbergh came back to more indie fare with the ensemble *Full Frontal.* Despite the cast, which included Julia Roberts and Blair Underwood, the film was a puzzlement to most. Even more puzzling was Soderbergh's next choice, a remake of the 1972 Russian film, *Solaris,* starring production partner George Clooney. A science fiction tale more angst than alien, it proved to be a boxoffice downer. Clooney had better luck, at least critically, with his own directorial debut, *Confessions of a Dangerous Mind.* This oddball comedy was based on the autobiography of game-show maven Chuck Barris, who claimed to also be an assassin for the CIA. Sam Rockwell took on the Barris part and Clooney himself had a role as a CIA handler.

Clooney wasn't the only actor to decide to try his talents behind the camera. Bill Paxton made a feature-length debut with the haunting *Frailty,* a study in religious madness and family ties. Denzel Washington, who starred in the polemic *John Q.,* also took his turn in the director's chair with the life-affirming *The Antwone Fisher Story.* The lead was well-played by newcomer Derek Luke, from whom more will no doubt be heard. Probably the most startling acting debut was that of Eminem in Curtis Hanson's Detroit-set drama *8 Mile.* While the rapper may have been playing a variation of his own persona, in Hanson's hands there was a vulnerability behind the rage. At least Em was better served than Britney Spears, who made her debut in *Crossroads,* a forgettable teen movie about friendship and romance during a road trip. Singer Mandy Moore offered a more-winning presence in the teen romantic drama *A Walk to Remember.* Meanwhile, Madonna, no newcomer to the screen, displayed zero ability in husband Guy Ritchie's *Swept Away,* a remake of Lina Wertmuller's 1974 film. Perhaps they should both stick to what they do best.

Adam Sandler actually showed he had acting talent with his lead turn in P.T. Anderson's *Punch-Drunk Love.* However, he gained critical brickbats for the egregious animated Hanukah film *Adam Sandler's 8 Crazy Nights* as well as for the misbegotten remake *Mr. Deeds.* Also misbegotten was the remake of *Charade;* the 2002 release was *The Truth About Charlie,* which had Mark Wahlberg and Thandie Newton in the roles first played by Cary Grant and Audrey Hepburn. Anthony Hopkins once more donned the role of Hannibal Lecter in *Red Dragon.* Thomas Harris's novel had been previously filmed in 1984 as *Manhunter.* The title role of the serial killer in *Red Dragon* was played by Ralph Fiennes who tried his hand at romantic comedy with the forgettable *Maid in Manhattan* in the type of role usually played by Hugh Grant. As a matter of fact, Grant did play his patented romantic leading man, opposite Sandra Bullock, in the equally forgettable *Two Weeks Notice.* Grant had earned much better notices earlier in the year with his role as a man who refuses to accept adult responsibilities in *About a Boy.*

Since Hollywood loves sequels, prequels and their ilk, they flooded the cineplexes with a third Austin Powers film, *Austin Powers in Goldmember;* a 20th James Bond, *Die Another Day,* which featured Halle Berry in what could turn out to be the spinoff role of spy Jinx; a second *Harry Potter* (the third film won't be out until 2004); *Blade II, Men in Black II, The Santa Clause 2, Spy Kids 2,* and *Stuart Little 2; Jason X* and the 10th film in the *Star Trek* franchise, *Star Trek: Nemesis;* as well as the third of the *Friday* films, *Friday After Next,* a prequel to the *Mummy* movies, *The Scorpion King,* and a sequel to *Analyze This* cleverly entitled *Analyze That.* Not to mention more versions of *The Count of Monte Cristo, The Four Feathers, The Importance of Being Earnest,* and *The Time Machine.*

Paramount tried to revive its Jack Ryan franchise by radically altering the Tom Clancy novel *The Sum of All Fears* (with the author's consent). Suddenly, Ryan is 30 years younger than his last portrayer (Harrison Ford) and a green-horn CIA analyst embodied by Ben Affleck. The film was successful enough that Affleck may be portraying Ryan in the future as buddy Matt Damon will no doubt be asked to reprise the role of Jason Bourne in the even-more successful thriller *The Bourne Identity.*

The affable Affleck also got to bear the overwhelming media scrutiny of his relationship with Jennifer Lopez. If 2001 was the year when star gossip focused on the Tom-and-Nicole breakup, 2002 was the year for Ben and J.Lo frenzy. The photogenic twosome filmed two movies set for release in 2003 and we will then see if their offscreen chemistry (at the moment the two are engaged) translates into onscreen heat and boffo boxoffice. After all, what is Hollywood without gossip to keep the public interested?

2002 also saw the deaths of some beloved and respected performers, both in front of and behind the scenes. These included tough guys Rod Steiger and Lawrence Tierney, Irish hell-raiser Richard Harris, James Coburn of the shark's smile, comic actor Eddie Bracken, diminutive comedian/composer Dudley Moore as well as "Mr. Television" Milton Berle, songbirds and occasional actresses Peggy Lee and Rosemary Clooney, notable Mexican actress Katy Jurado, English actress Katrin Cartlidge, and young Russian actor/director Sergei Bodrov Jr. Julia Phillips, the first woman producer to win an Oscar, celebrity photographer Herb Ritts, lyricist and writer Adolph Green, animator extraordinaire Chuck Jones, directors Chang Cheh, Ted Demme, John Frankenheimer, George Roy Hill, Karel Reisz, George Sidney, and the incomparable Billy Wilder are also among those profiled in the Obituaries section, located in the back of this book.

As the screen fades upon another year of moviemaking, the *Magill's* staff looks forward to preparing the 2004 *Annual.* We invite your comments. Please direct all questions and suggestions to:

Christine Tomassini
Editor, *Magill's Cinema Annual*
Gale
27500 Drake Rd.
Farmington Hills, MI 48331-3535
Phone: 248-699-4253
Toll-free: 800-347-GALE
Fax: 248-699-8062

Contributing Reviewers

Laura Abraham
Freelance Reviewer

Michael Adams
Graduate School, City University of New York

Vivek Adarkar
Long Island University

Michael Betzold
Freelance Reviewer

David L. Boxerbaum
Freelance Reviewer

Beverley Bare Buehrer
Freelance Reviewer

Jim Craddock
Freelance Reviewer

Peter N. Chumo II
Freelance Reviewer

Beth Fhaner
Freelance Reviewer

David Flanagin
Freelance Reviewer

Jill Hamilton
Freelance Reviewer

Patty-Lynne Herlevi
Freelance Reviewer

Eric Monder
Freelance Reviewer

Michael J. Tyrkus
Freelance Reviewer

James M. Welsh
Salisbury State University

Hilary White
Freelance Reviewer

User's Guide

Alphabetization

Film titles and reviews are arranged on a word-by-word basis, including articles and prepositions. English leading articles (A, An, The) are ignored, as are foreign leading articles (El, Il, La, Las, Le, Les, Los). Other considerations:

Acronyms appear alphabetically as if regular words.

Common abbreviations in titles file as if they are spelled out, so *Mr. Death* will be found as if it was spelled *Mister Death*.

Proper names in titles are alphabetized beginning with the individual's first name, for instance, *Gloria* will be found under "G."

Titles with numbers, for instance, *200 Cigarettes,* are alphabetized as if the numbers were spelled out, in this case, "Two-Hundred." When numeric titles gather in close proximity to each other, the titles will be arranged in a low-to-high numeric sequence.

Special Sections

List of Awards. An annual list of awards bestowed upon the year's films by the following associations: Academy of Motion Picture Arts and Sciences, Directors Guild of America Award, Golden Globe Awards, Los Angeles Film Critics Awards, National Board of Review Awards, National Society of Film Critics Awards, New York Film Critics Awards, the Screen Actors Guild Awards, and the Writer's Guild Awards.

Obituaries. Profiles major contributors to the film industry who died in 2002.

Selected Film Books of 2002. An annotated list of selected film books published in 2002.

Indexes

Film titles and artists are arranged into nine indexes, allowing the reader to effectively approach a film from any one of several directions, including not only its credits but its subject matter.

Directors, Screenwriters, Cinematographers, Editors, Art Directors, Music Directors, and *Performers* indexes are arranged according to artists appearing in this volume, followed by a list of the films on which they worked.

Subject Index. Films may be categorized under several of the subject terms arranged alphabetically in this section.

Title Index. The title index is a cumulative alphabetical list of films covered in the twenty-two volumes of the *Magill's Cinema Annual,* including the films covered in this volume. Films reviewed in past volumes are cited with the year in which the film was originally released; films reviewed in this volume are cited with the film title in bold with a bolded Arabic numeral indicating the page number on which the review begins. Original and alternate titles are cross-referenced to the American release title in the Title Index. Titles of retrospective films are followed by the year, in brackets, of their original release.

Sample Review

Each *Magill's* review contains up to sixteen items of information. A fictionalized composite sample review containing all the elements of information that may be included in a full-length review follows the outline below. The circled number preceding each element in the sample review designates an item of information that is explained in the outline on the next page.

(1) **Title:** Film title as it was released in the United States.

(2) **Foreign or alternate title (s):** The film's original title or titles as released outside the United States, or alternate film title or titles. Foreign and alternate titles also appear in the Title Index to facilitate user access.

(3) **Taglines:** Up to ten publicity taglines for the film from advertisements or reviews.

(4) **Box office information:** Year-end or other box office domestic revenues for the film.

(5) **Film review:** A signed review of the film, including an analytic overview of the film and its critical reception.

(6) **Reviewer byline:** The name of the reviewer who wrote the full-length review. A complete list of this volume's contributors appears in the "Contributings Reviewers" section which follows the Introduction.

(7) **Principal characters:** Listings of the film's principal characters and the names of the actors who play them in the film.

(8) **Country of origin:** The film's country or countries of origin.

(9) **Release date:** The year of the film's first general release.

(10) **Production information:** This section typically includes the name(s) of the film's producer(s), production company, and distributor; director(s); screenwriter(s); cinematographer(s) (if the film is animated, this will be replaced with Animation or Animation direction, or it will not be listed);

editor(s); art director(s); production designer(s); music composer(s); and other credits such as visual effects, sound, costume design, and song(s) and songwriter(s).

(11) **MPAA rating:** The film's rating by the Motion Picture Association of America. If there is no rating given, the line will read, "Unrated."

(12) **Running time:** The film's running time in minutes.

(13) **Reviews:** A list of citations of major newspaper and journal reviews of the film, including publication title, date of review, and page number.

(14) **Film quotes:** Memorable dialogue directly from the film, attributed to the character who spoke it, or comment from cast or crew members or reviewers about the film.

(15) **Film trivia:** Interesting tidbits about the film, its cast, or production crew.

(16) **Awards information:** Awards won by the film, followed by category and name of winning cast or crew member. Listings of the film's nominations follow the wins on a separate line for each award. Awards are arranged alphabetically. Information is listed for films that won or were nominated for the following awards: American Academy Awards®, British Academy of Film and Television Arts, Directors Guild of America, Golden Globe, Los Angeles Critics Association Awards, National Board of Review Awards, National Society of Film Critics Awards, New York Critics Awards, Writers Guild of America, and others.

(1) The Gump Diaries
(2) (Los Diarios del Gump)

(3) *Love means never having to say you're stupid.*
—Movie tagline

(4) **Box Office:** $10 million

(5) In writer/director Robert Zemeckis' *Back to the Future* trilogy (1985, 1989, 1990), Marty McFly (Michael J. Fox) and his scientist sidekick Doc Brown (Christopher Lloyd) journey backward and forward in time, attempting to smooth over some rough spots in their personal histories in order to remain true to their individual destinies. Throughout their time-travel adventures, Doc Brown insists that (8) neither he nor Marty influence any major historical events, believing that to do so would result in catastrophic changes in humankind's ultimate destiny. By the end of the trilogy, however, Doc Brown has revised his thinking and tells marty that, "Your future hasn't been written yet. No one's has. Your future is whatever you make it. So make it a good one."

In *Forrest Gump*, Zemeckis once again explores the theme of personal destiny and how an individual's life affects and is affected by his historical time period. This time, however, Zemeckis and screenwriter Eric Roth chronicle the life af a character who does nothing but meddle in the historical events of his time without even trying to do so. By the film's conclusion, however, it has become apparent that Zemeckis' main concern is something more than merely having fun with four decades of American history. In the process of re-creating significant moments in time, he has captured on celluloid something eternal and timeless—the soul of humanity personified by a nondescript simpleton from the deep South.

The film begins following the flight of a seemingly insignificant feather as it floats down from the sky and brushes against various objects and people before finally coming to rest at the feet of Forrest Gump (Tom Hanks). Forrest, who is sitting on a bus-stop bench, reaches down and picks up the feather, smooths it out, then opens his traveling case and carefully places the feather between the pages of his favorite book, *Curious George*.

In this simple but hauntingly beautiful opening scene, the filmmakers illustrate the film's principal concern: Is life a series of random events over which a person has no control, or is there an underlying order to things that leads to the fulfillment of an individual's destiny? The rest of the film is a humorous and moving attempt to prove that, underlying the random, chaotic events that make up a person's life, there exists a benign and simple order.

Forrest sits on the bench throughout most of the film, talking about various events of his life to others who happen to sit down next to him. It does not take long, however, for the audience to realize that Forrest's seemingly random chatter to a parade of strangers has a perfect chronological order to it. He tells his first story after looking down at the (16) feet of his first bench partner and observing, "Mama always said that you can tell a lot about a person by the shoes they wear." Then, in a voice-over narration, Forrest begins the story of his life, first by telling about he first pair of shoes he can remember wearing.

The action shifts to the mid-1950's with Forrest as a young boy (Michael Humphreys) being fitted with leg braces to correct a curvature in his spine. Despite this traumatic handicap, Forrest remains unaffected, thanks to his mother (Sally Field) who reminds him on more than once occasion that he is no different from anyone else. Although this and most of Mrs. Gump's other words of advice are in the form of hackneyed cliches, Forrest whose intelligence quotient is below normal, sincerely believes every one of them, namely because he instinctively knows they are sincere expressions of his mother's love and fierce devotion.

(6) —*John Byline*

CREDITS (7)

Forrest Gump: Tom Hanks
Forrest's Mother: Sally Field
Young Forrest: Michael Humphreys

Origin: United States
Language: English, Spanish (9)
Released: 1994
Production: Liz Heller, John Manulis; New Line Cinema; released by Island Pictures
Directed by: Scott Kalvert (10)
Written by: Bryan Goluboff
Cinematography by: David Phillips
Music by: Graeme Revell
Editing: Dana Congdon
Production Design: Danny Nowak
Sound: David Sarnoff
Costumes: David Robinson
MPAA rating: R (11)
Running time: 102 minutes (12)

REVIEWS

Entertainment Weekly. July 15, 1994, p. 42. (13)
The Hollywood Reporter. June 29, 1994, p. 7.
Los Angeles Times. July 6, 1994, p. F1.
New York Times Online. July 15, 1994.

QUOTES

Forrest Gump (Tom Hanks): "The state of existence may be likened unto a receptacle containing cocoa-based confections, in that one may never predict that which one may receive."

TRIVIA (15)

Hanks was the first actor since Spencer Tracy to win back-to-back Oscars for Best Actor. Hanks received the award in 1993 for his performance in *Philadelphia*. Tracy won Oscars in 1937 for *Captains Courages* and in 1938 for *Boys Town*.

AWARDS AND NOMINATIONS

Academy Awards 1994: Film, Actor (Hanks), Special Effects, Cinematography
Nomination:
Golden Globes 1994: Film, Actor (Hanks), Supporting Actress (Field), Music

New York Times wrote that the "sentimental climax (is) more repellent than any of the crude effluvia the film is drenched with." In a strange way, though, the odd mix fits Sandler's pattern. He's always been somewhat of a man-child character. The grossness would appeal to this immaturity as would the overly simplistic view of the world. There is a love story in the film, but as usual in Sandler films (not including the non-Sandler-penned *Punch-Drunk Love*), the romance is perfunctory and without depth. Jennifer (voiced by Jackie Titone) loves Davey even though he would strike anyone with an ounce of sense as being a very bad catch. This is another Sandlerism: the overly understanding woman who inexplicably can see some sort of decent boyfriend within Sandler's boorish exterior.

Eight Crazy Nights was being touted as some sort of Hanukkah holiday film and it was released just before the beginning of Hanukkah. There were probably some pretty surprised families who took the kids to this film expecting a nice change of pace from the usual Christmas films. Maybe Rankin-Bass, the people who did the animated holiday specials like *Rudolph the Red-Nosed Reindeer* could get on a Hanukkah project fast so that *Eight Crazy Nights* is not the only one out there.

In the film, Sandler's Davey is the menace of the small New England town of Dukesberry. (Sandler came from a similar small New England town.) He likes to do things like moon Christmas carolers, then pass gas on them. In the first few minutes of the film, he skips out of a Chinese restaurant without paying the bill, but not before letting out the world's longest burp. To add that extra oomph of tastelessness, the guy who runs the Chinese restaurant (voiced by Rob Schneider) is the type of character who says stuff like "I no likee you." This is followed by a scene of Davey humping his car and whispering endearments in its ear. That's entertainment.

Davey's antisocial behavior always gets worse right before Hanukkah. Even though the film tips us off that Davey has something in his past that's made him such a bad guy, it's hard to feel sympathetic for such a boorish jerk. Davey's latest crime ends with him in front of a judge (Norm Crosby) that he's been before many times. The unsympathetic judge wants to throw Davey in jail for 10 years, but Davey's old basketball coach Whitey offers to hire Davey and keep him in line. If Davey misbehaves, he'll go to jail.

Even though Whitey has saved Davey, Davey is mean to the old man (see the first paragraph). But Whitey is the sort of simple, kindhearted man who does odd jobs around the town for a dollar. He remembers the younger, nice Davey and thinks he can bring him back.

Even though Davey is going to turn nice and all, the movie enjoys lingering on the parts where he's not so nice. When an overweight young boy on the basketball team has the misfortune to catch Davey's eye, Davey taunts him and tells him he needs a bra. When Davey's being mean to

people is not enough, there are plenty of other immaturities to get the fifth-grade-level laughs off. There is a woman with three breasts who, get this, nurses three kids at the same time, and a Davey competitor who has to eat a sweaty fat man's jock strap. There are also some fairly lame jokes from the narrator (Schneider, again) like "He's so behind the times, he thinks Viagra is a waterfall."

And amazingly, Sandler and company were able to squeeze even another smidgen of reprehensible content into the movie. In a scene where Davey decides to change his ways, he heads to the local mall. The drunken Davey hallucinates that the logos of the various stores come alive and urge him to cry. Thus we have a scene where, say, the Foot Locker referee is telling Davey that crying will help him to face his emotions. Ross Anthony of Hollywood Report Card wrote that the film "gives into product placement advertising so blatantly that one wonders who conceived the film— Sandler or some mall association of merchants."

There are some bright spots in the film. Whitey's relationship with his sister Eleanore (voiced by Sandler as well) is promising. Eleanore, especially, is a good character. She wears a series of bad wigs and is obsessed with anyone getting any footprints on her floor. Usually Sandler's voices sound just like him trying to make a funny voice but Eleanore is her own person. There are also some clever songs in the film. In "Technical Foul," Whitey and Eleanore list out the things that Davey is not to do while a guest in their house.

Critics, who despite popular belief, will give Sandler credit when they think it's due (*The Wedding Singer, Punch Drunk Love*), mostly did not like this film. Elvia Mitchell wrote, "He's come back with a forgettable, soggy and dumb take on the syndicated holiday specials he probably grew up watching." Mark Caro of the *Chicago Tribune* gave the film one star (out of four) and wondered who would watch the film. "Who is this movie for? Not kids, who don't need the lesson in repugnance. It's also not smart or barbed enough for older viewers—not everyone thinks poo-poo jokes are 'edgy.'" And Sean Axmaker of the *Seattle Post-Intelligencer* wrote that the film was "a truly flabbergasting movie that careens from bullying insults and scatological sight gags to a barrage of product placements playing the ghost of Christmas past in a soppy sentimental lesson."

—*Jill Hamilton*

CREDITS

Davey/Whitey/Eleanore/Deer: Adam Sandler (Voice)
Mayor: Kevin Nealon (Voice)
Chinese Waiter/Narrator: Rob Schneider (Voice)
Judge: Norm Crosby (Voice)
Jennifer: Jackie Titone (Voice)

Benjamin: Austin Stout (Voice)
Tom Baltezor: Jon Lovitz (Voice)

Origin: USA
Released: 2002
Production: Jack Giarraputo, Adam Sandler, Allen Covert; Happy Madison Productions; released by Columbia Pictures
Directed by: Seth Kearsley
Written by: Adam Sandler, Allen Covert, Brooks Arthur, Brad Isaacs
Music by: Marc Ellis, Ray Ellis, Teddy Castelucci
Sound: Gabe Veltri
Editing: Amy Budden
Production Design: Perry Andelin Blake
MPAA rating: PG-13
Running time: 71 minutes

REVIEWS

Chicago Sun-Times Online. November 27, 2002.
Entertainment Weekly. December 6, 2002, p. 70.
Los Angeles Times Online. November 27, 2002.
New York Times Online. November 27, 2002.
USA Today Online. November 27, 2002.
Variety Online. November 26, 2002.
Washington Post. November 29, 2002, p. WE44.

Adaptation

Box Office: $4.9 million

Spike Jonze's *Adaptation* is perhaps the most self-reflexive movie ever made, one that ultimately chronicles its own creation. It is also the ultimate Hollywood insider's movie, full of in-jokes about the screenwriting process and satiric jabs at the cliché-ridden scripts that commonly get the green light. Written by screenwriter Charlie Kaufman but credited to him and his fictional twin brother, Donald, the story follows Charlie's attempt to adapt Susan Orlean's *The Orchid Thief,* a nonfiction book about orchid poachers and the enthusiasts who make orchids their passion. *Adaptation,* however, is not a traditional adaptation of a book but rather a meditation on adaptation itself. The film at first is very funny and even poignant in odd ways, but unfortunately, for all of its initial cleverness, it finally takes a disastrous twist that makes a mockery of writing and fails to say anything new about the struggle to create art.

Much of *Adaptation* follows two separate but related story lines, which alternate in a free-floating time structure—Charlie Kaufman (Nicolas Cage) attempting to adapt *The Orchid Thief* and Susan Orlean (Meryl Streep) researching the book itself three years earlier. Charlie is a scared, socially inept, balding screenwriter who, in a rambling voice-over at the beginning, lays out all of his insecurities regarding his appearance, his talent, indeed his entire self-image. He is based on the real-life Charlie, who scored a critical hit in 1999 with *Being John Malkovich* and then, for a follow-up, struggled in vain to turn Orlean's book into a script. In a meeting with a young, attractive studio executive, Valerie (Tilda Swinton), Charlie tells her that he wants to be faithful to Orlean's vision and not write a conventional Hollywood tale filled with sex, guns, chase scenes, and important life lessons.

At the same time, Charlie's twin brother, Donald, also played by Cage, is living in his brother's apartment and has decided to become a screenwriter. Unlike his morose, indecisive brother, Donald is cheerful and confident. Far from rejecting Hollywood formula, he revels in it and chooses the serial killer thriller as his genre. In one of his best performances, Cage expertly handles both roles and creates, with very little change in physical appearance, two distinct characters. The brothers' exchanges, which are the best aspect of the script, are seamless and often hilarious. Donald routinely asks for advice on his script, only to be given sarcastic answers that he takes with good cheer. In one of *Adaptation*'s best lines, Charlie mockingly proposes a thriller about a literature professor who cuts off his victims' body parts one at a time and calls himself the Deconstructionist. Donald, however, takes the idea seriously.

In the second story line, *New Yorker* writer Susan Orlean becomes fascinated by larger-than-life orchid poacher John Laroche (Chris Cooper), who was brought up on charges of stealing orchids deemed endangered species in Florida's Fakahatchee Strand State Preserve. Because he went as an advisor with three Seminole Indians whom he thought the law protected in the taking of endangered species, he did not believe that he would be prosecuted. Laroche has a scraggly, rough-and-tumble demeanor but considers himself "probably the smartest person I know." He lost his front teeth in a car accident that took the lives of his mother and uncle and put his wife in a coma before she left him. Then a hurricane destroyed everything he had, including his nursery, effectively ending his interest in orchids until the Seminoles hired him. Cooper balances Laroche's cockiness with a poetic appreciation for the wonders of orchids. Laroche may be a big dreamer and braggart, constantly hopping from one get-rich-quick scheme to another and making himself the hero of all his grand stories, but Cooper, with the subtlest gesture or look, lets us see his underlying sadness.

Streep is moving as Susan, who seems vaguely dissatisfied and lonely in her posh New York life and is drawn to Laroche's tall tales and the whole orchid subculture that thrives in Florida. *The Orchid Thief* is not just a book about flowers but also a lengthy exploration of how people cling to such an interest like orchids because it gives shape to their lives in an otherwise big, impersonal world. Orlean herself longs to experience the kind of passion that orchid collectors like Laroche feel, and Streep's beautiful voice-over musings convey this deep longing.

Charlie and Donald are opposite in every way. Charlie fumbles his relationship with a woman named Amelia (Cara Seymour), who likes him, and his flirtations with a cute waitress (Judy Greer) go nowhere except in his masturbatory fantasies. Meanwhile, Donald effortlessly attracts the attention of a pretty makeup artist, Caroline (Maggie Glyllenhaal), when he visits his brother on the set of *Being John Malkovich*.

Professionally, Donald has no problem writing his trite genre piece, a thriller of multiple personalities called *The 3*, in which the criminal, hostage, and cop turn out to be the same person. Even though Charlie points out that a hostage locked in a basement cannot also be the police officer investigating the crime, Donald is undeterred. He even uses the guidance of famed, real-life screenwriting teacher Robert McKee (Brian Cox), whose emphasis on basic storytelling structure Charlie scorns. Charlie, meanwhile, engages in a series of false starts on his screenplay. One begins with Laroche. Another goes back to the beginning of time to trace the history of evolution. Developing a kind of crush on Susan as he looks at her photo on the book's dust jacket, he tries to write about her. He finally writes himself into the script because that is the only subject he knows, which may be an unintentional comment on the narcissism at the heart of the movie. Donald recommends that Charlie meet Susan personally, but, when he travels to the offices of *The New Yorker* and sees her in an elevator, he is too scared to talk to her. Finally throwing his principles aside, Charlie takes one of McKee's classes, even getting advice from him afterwards. No matter what Charlie writes, McKee advises that it is important for him to wow the audience with a great ending.

Adaptation has some very funny moments, most at the expense of the beleaguered Charlie, who cannot bring himself to sell out to the mediocrity that the industry seems to want. (Incidentally, he hates it when Donald uses the word "industry" and other show business jargon that seems to denigrate the craft of screenwriting.) But the brothers' relationship is also sweet. No matter how much Charlie dismisses Donald's screenplay ideas, he remains good-natured and in awe of Charlie's talent.

Donald hits the jackpot with his serial killer script, and, out of desperation, Charlie finally enlists his brother's help in finishing his own script. Pretending to be Charlie, Donald interviews Susan and concludes that she is hiding something. The brothers decide to investigate, and, as the two story lines converge, *Adaptation* takes a disastrous turn that is self-indulgent in the extreme.

The Orchid Thief ends on a bittersweet note. Susan goes with John on an expedition through the swamp in the hope of seeing a ghost orchid, but they finally give up, and, having never seen one, she concludes that it is better that she live with a sense of yearning. In *Adaptation,* Susan's disappointment is acknowledged as the ending of the book, but the brothers in the film discover that was not the end of the story. John and Susan find the ghost orchid, and Susan begins snorting a drug derived from the flower—Streep is hilarious in scenes when Susan gets high and tries to imitate a dial tone over the phone—and has an affair with John. The brothers travel to Miami and find Susan and John together along with a huge laboratory, where they manufacture the drugs from the orchids. When Susan and John find out that Charlie and Donald know what they are up to, Susan decides that they must kill them, and she and John end up chasing them through the Fakahatchee Strand. In a respite from the chase, Donald delivers a poignant life lesson on love to his brother, but, as they are trying to escape John and Susan the next morning, their car crashes into another vehicle, and Donald dies after being thrown from the car. John is attacked by an alligator before he can shoot Charlie and then dies in Susan's arms as she cries over his body.

The last section of the film, then, employs all of the standard Hollywood clichés—drugs, sex, chases, a touching life lesson, tragic death scenes—that Charlie loathes. So the big joke is that the movie we have been watching all along is the movie Charlie was struggling to write. When everything goes crazy and becomes a purely fictionalized account of John and Susan post *Orchid Thief,* we are seeing Donald's contribution to the screenplay, which is meant to save the film by turning it into a standard Hollywood genre piece.

The most obvious problem with the ending is that it is a copout. Almost any writer can throw his hands in the air and simply resort to cliché. The fact that it is being done self-consciously does not make the last part of the film less annoying. If anything, the ending is more annoying because it turns everything that came before it into a big goof. Charlie's fascination with Susan and the tender way he falls in love with his ideal notion of her through her prose is actually a real tribute to the power of writing. The relationship between the cultured Susan and the hillbilly Laroche, which moves from condescension to admiration to genuine affection, is also complex. At the end, however, we are made to feel like fools for having taken an interest in these characters when they suddenly become pawns manipulated in a hackneyed genre flick. Admittedly, Meryl Streep gives one of her funniest performances in years as she goes from straitlaced *New Yorker* writer to loopy drug addict and even a crime boss of sorts barking orders to kill the Kaufmans. But Susan's transformation takes place within the context of nonsense; her character changes are completely arbitrary, motivated only by the script's phony third act.

By the end of the movie, the title has taken on more than one meaning. It does not just refer to the act of turning a book into a screenplay but also refers to the process in evolutionary theory whereby living things take on the characteristics they need to survive. The ending, then, suggests that selling out in Hollywood is a form of adaptation for Charlie, but this is the easy way out when one considers that many screenwriters succeed by making unique films within the confines of genre and even adapt very difficult, seemingly unadaptable books. The real-life Kaufman's own idea of adaptation is just as cynical and narcissistic as his alter ego's. Instead of being true to the book he supposedly admires and agreed to adapt, he has made a movie about himself (albeit a fictionalized, sometimes unattractive version of himself), paying tribute to his own ego. Extending the self-reflexive joke beyond the narrative itself by sharing screenwriting credit with the fictional Donald and then dedicating the film "In Loving Memory of Donald Kaufman" at the end is not cleverness but rather a celebration of cleverness that takes the narcissism to a new level.

—Peter N. Chumo II

CREDITS

Charlie/Donald Kaufman: Nicolas Cage
Susan Orlean: Meryl Streep
John Laroche: Chris Cooper
Valerie: Tilda Swinton
Amelia: Cara Seymour
Robert McKee: Brian Cox
Alice the waitress: Judy Greer
Caroline: Maggie Gyllenhaal
Marty: Ron Livingston
Ranger Steve Neely: Stephen Tobolowsky
Matthew Osceola: Jay Tavare
Russell: Litefoot
Buster Baxley: Gary Farmer
Defense attorney: Peter Jason
Orlean's husband: Curtis Hanson

Origin: USA
Released: 2002
Production: Edward Saxon, Jonathan Demme, Vincent Landay; Intermedia Films, Clinica Estetico, Magnet; released by Columbia Pictures
Directed by: Spike Jonze
Written by: Charlie Kaufman
Cinematography by: Lance Acord
Music by: Carter Burwell
Sound: Drew Kunin

Editing: Eric Zumbrunnen
Art Direction: Peter Andrus
Costumes: Casey Storm
Production Design: K.K. Barrett
MPAA rating: R
Running time: 114 minutes

REVIEWS

Boxoffice. January, 2003, p. 56.
Chicago Sun-Times Online. December 20, 2002.
Entertainment Weekly. December 6, 2002, p. 65.
Los Angeles Times Online. December 6, 2002.
New York Times Online. December 6, 2002.
People. December 6, 2002, p. 47.
USA Today Online. December 6, 2002.
Variety Online. November 11, 2002.
Washington Post. December 20, 2002, p. WE43.

QUOTES

Donald to Charlie (both Nicolas Cage): "You are what you love, not what loves you."

TRIVIA

Despite being given screenplay credit, Charlie Kaufman does not have a twin brother named Donald.

AWARDS AND NOMINATIONS

British Acad. 2002: Adapt. Screenplay
Golden Globes 2003: Support. Actor (Cooper), Support. Actress (Streep)
L.A. Film Critics 2002: Support. Actor (Cooper)
Natl. Bd. of Review 2002: Screenplay, Support. Actor (Cooper)
N.Y. Film Critics 2002: Screenplay
Nomination:
Oscars 2002: Actor (Cage), Adapt. Screenplay, Support. Actor (Cooper), Support. Actress (Streep)
British Acad. 2002: Actor (Cage), Support. Actor (Cooper), Support. Actress (Streep)
Golden Globes 2003: Actor—Mus./Comedy (Cage), Director (Jonze), Film—Mus./Comedy, Screenplay
Screen Actors Guild 2002: Actor (Cage), Support. Actor (Cooper), Cast
Writers Guild 2002: Adapt. Screenplay.

The Adventures of Pluto Nash

The MAN on the Moon.
—Movie tagline

 Box Office: $4.4 million

It's not a good sign when, at a 7:30 p.m. show on a Saturday night of the opening weekend of a movie starring a major star, there are only a handful of people in the theater. The latest Eddie Murphy vehicle, *The Adventures of Pluto Nash,* was dead on arrival when it was finally released in August 2002. It was one of three Murphy films scheduled for release late in 2002, along with *Showtime* and *I Spy.*

Murphy used to be one of Hollywood's most bankable stars as a leading man in action pictures such as *48 Hrs.* or comedies such as *Trading Places.* But since then he has made a number of poor choices in roles (in movies such as *Boomerang, Vampire in Brooklyn,* and *Holy Man*) and has concentrated most of his considerable talents on multiple-character comedies of the *Dr. Doolittle* and *Nutty Professor* series. He remains a skilled impersonator, capable of transforming himself into any shape, sex, gender, or form. Murphy, one of the busiest actors on any planet, was so good at the voice of the donkey in *Shrek* that he received a supporting actor nomination at the British Academy Awards. And he remains a likeable actor.

The Adventures of Pluto Nash, a science-fiction comedy starring Murphy as the owner of a nightclub on the moon in the year 2087, was shot in Montreal during the spring and summer of 2000. Halle Berry was originally signed to star as Murphy's love interest, but she backed out and was replaced by Rosario Dawson. Filming was finished by September, and the Nov. 2, 2000, issue of *Hollywoof Reporter* featured Murphy jumping over the moon in an orange spacesuit. But the original release date of Easter 2001 was moved back to early 2002, and then pushed back again to late summer, and when the film was finally released, it had the musty aroma of a release that its studio, Warner Bros., had no faith at all in.

Pluto Nash, written by Neil Cuthbert (*Hocus Pocus, Mystery Men*) and directed by Ron Underwood (*City Slickers, Mighty Joe Young*), has an unremarkable plot set in an exotic locale. Nash is an ex-smuggler who owns the hottest club on an American moon colony, Little America. He is threatened with extinction by a crime boss who wants to take over the colony and set up casinos. That's all there is, really, to the plot, so the movie must have been sold on the premise that the sets—strange colonies on the moon—and the sci-fi gadgets, vehicles, and special effects would, along with a bankable major star, carry the day.

This might have been sufficient to make such a film fly thirty years ago, but audiences wooed by *Star Wars, Star Trek,* and countless other vehicles for outer-space adventure are not going to get automatically charged up by a motion picture on the moon. And they aren't going to go gaga over the limited imagination shown by the creators of this film in concocting life on the moon in the future. There is actually a sequence in which Dawson's character, Dina Lake, is shown gleefully bouncing about the lunar surface in a spacesuit, as if audiences in the 21st century would still be amazed by the effects of lower gravity on the moon. And what fantastic gadgets are there at Nash's disposal in this futuristic saga? There are computers, picture phones, hovercraft cars, body-part replacement surgery, and quite ordinary guns—and that's about it, certainly nothing much to stir the imagination. Civilization doesn't appear to have advanced very far from the present day.

In fact, in this film, the moon is simply a comic-book version of early 21st century Earth—a little cheaper, a little more lawless, and a lot more gaudy. The sets look like they were designed by Planet Hollywood—everything is painted in bright colors, and everything looks like it was constructed on the cheap.

The producers of *Pluto Nash* were obviously trying to create a frontier feel to the moon milieu, but if this moon is merely an updated, transplanted version of the Old West, why would casinos be such a sinister concept? It's explained at one point that casinos were recently outlawed on Earth—no reason is given for this, because what plausible reason could there be?—and the villain, the mysterious Rex Crater, may have been a mobster on Earth who has cloned himself and relocated to the moon.

Of course, it's best not to think too much about *Pluto Nash,* but just try to sit back and enjoy the ride—there's some cheap eye candy and some even cheaper jokes, and an interesting supporting cast. The redoubtable Peter Boyle is along for the ride as Nash's pal Rowland, a retired cop who knows his way around the moon's criminal information system. Pam Grier has a small role as Nash's mother, but she makes the most of it. Comedian Jay Mohr plays a lounge singer whom Nash rescues at the beginning of the film. Nash not only saves his life, but suggests he change his routine and name from that of a kilted, according-playing Polish entertainer to a Sinatra-style Italian crooner. He makes it big, and the joke is supposed to be that a 1950s-style lounge act is now considered to be an innovative new thing. It doesn't make sense, but much of *Pluto Nash* doesn't. It's just a string of skits run together.

One of the better ones involves Luis Guzman as Felix Laranga, a Puerto Rican devotee of Nash. He is driving a hover-craft version of a 1980s-style gauchely decorated van when he happens upon Nash, Dina, and Nash's robot Bruno room has two phone lines so the couple can both be calling at the same time.) Fisher finds his mother, Eva (the wonderful Viola Davis of *Solaris* and *Far from Heaven*), living in squalor and pours his heart out to her. She can't bring herself to look at him and says nothing. More satisfying is his reunion with his father's family, which brings him a houseful of cousins, grandparents and a delighted Auntie (Vernee Watson Johnson).

Critics liked the film and even those who were careful to note that it was a bit sappy were willing to accept the sap in such a well-made movie. Roger Ebert of the *Chicago Sun-Times* wrote that the film "ends with scenes so true and heartbreaking that tears welled up in my eyes both times I saw the film," adding that, "I don't cry easily at the movies; years can go past without tears." Stephen Holden of the *New York Times* wrote that Washington's direction had "a hearty meat-and-potatoes style" and that Luke's performance was "hands down the year's most auspicious acting debut." "If the movie's sugar-coated ending leaves a hint of saccharine, its beautifully balanced performances and faith in its characters keep it honest despite itself." And Kenneth Turan of the *Los Angeles Times* wrote, "There are moments when issues resolve too tidily or do not resolve at all. But because you'd have to be a stone not to be moved by *Antwone Fisher*'s story of hope, forgiveness and love, its focus on the power of the family to heal what it once destroyed, those difficulties seem insignificant and beside the point compared to the good things that are going on."

—Jill Hamilton

CREDITS

Antwone Fisher: Derek Luke
Jerome Davenport: Denzel Washington
Cheryl Smolley: Joy Bryant
Berta: Salli Richardson
James: Earl Billings
Slim: Kevin Connolly
Eva: Viola Davis
Grayson: Rainoldo Gooding
Mrs. Tate: Novella Nelson
Annette: Vernee Watson-Johnson
Kansas City: Kente Scott
Nadine: Yolonda Ross
Berkley: Stephen Snedden

Origin: USA
Released: 2002
Production: Todd Black, Randa Haines, Denzel Washington; Mundy Lane Entertainment; released by Fox Searchlight
Directed by: Denzel Washington

Written by: Antwone Fisher
Cinematography by: Philippe Rousselot
Music by: Mychael Danna
Sound: Willie Burton
Editing: Conrad Buff
Art Direction: David Lazan
Costumes: Sharen Davis
Production Design: Nelson Coates
MPAA rating: PG-13
Running time: 113 minutes

REVIEWS

Boxoffice. November, 2002, p. 124.
Chicago Sun-Times Online. December 20, 2002.
Entertainment Weekly. January 3, 2003, p. 45.
Los Angeles Times Online. December 20, 2002.
New York Times Online. December 19, 2002.
People. December 23, 2002, p. 36.
USA Today Online. December 20, 2002.
Variety Online. September 15, 2002.
Washington Post. December 20, 2002, p. WE43.

QUOTES

Jerome Davenport (Denzel Washington): "I understand you like to fight." Antwone (Derek Luke): "That's the only way some people learn." Jerome: "But you pay the price for teaching them."

AWARDS AND NOMINATIONS

Nomination:
Ind. Spirit 2003: Actor (Luke), Support. Actress (Davis)
Writers Guild 2002: Orig. Screenplay.

Ararat

In a world full of denial, how do you determine who's telling the truth?
—Movie tagline

Uncover the shocking secret of the movie they don't want you to see. Ararat *. . . is where it all happened.*
—Movie tagline

Box Office: $1.4 million

For writer-director Atom Egoyan, a Canadian of Armenian descent, the genocide committed by Turkey against the Armenian people during World War I was a subject he felt compelled to tackle. Unlike the Holocaust, the Armenian genocide is not widely known, yet the entire Armenian population of Eastern Turkey, over a million citizens, was eliminated by the Turkish government, which, to this day, does not acknowledge its guilt. In the press notes for *Ararat,* Egoyan focuses on denial as his key theme, "how something which is so evident and which so many people understand to be true can be denied, and how that affects the psychology of the present day."

Egoyan, however, has not simply made a historical epic but also has tried to question the efficacy of film itself for remembering the past by telling the story of a Canadian film crew making a movie about the genocide. He creates yet another level of narrative by delving into the family conflicts among the characters to explore questions of personal memory. Unfortunately, Egoyan stuffs his film with so many themes and subplots that it ends up feeling like a clumsy history lesson as well as a pretentious attempt to deconstruct the nature of memory itself.

As he has done in the past, Egoyan employs an elliptical narrative style that allows him to move freely among different time frames, locations, and groups of characters, many of whom are connected to each other in odd, coincidental ways. This approach worked beautifully in the haunting *The Sweet Hereafter* but is far less effective in *Ararat* because the connections feel tenuous and random. Ani (Arsinée Khanjian) is an art historian who is publishing a book on Arshile Gorky (Simon Abkarian), a famous Armenian painter who survived the genocide. Because of her expertise on Gorky, she is enlisted by a movie director, Edward (Charles Aznavour) and screenwriter, Rouben (Eric Bogosian), to be a consultant on their historical epic on the genocide.

Very soon Gorky as a boy is being worked into the screenplay and emerging as a hero of the Armenian resistance, even though he had not played such a role. Perhaps Ani is merely being used to justify historical inaccuracies that make for more exciting drama. At the same time, she faces problems at home—her stepdaughter, Celia (Marie-Josée Croze) thinks that Ani is responsible for her father's death, either killing him or driving him to suicide when he learned that Ani was being unfaithful to him. Celia spends her free time interrupting her stepmother's lectures on Gorky to embarrass her and get her to admit guilt. Ani's son by her first marriage, Raffi (David Alpay), is sleeping with his stepsister, thus complicating his loyalties.

Through his mother, Raffi has a job as a production assistant on Edward's film and later travels to Turkey on his own to shoot footage of some important cultural sites. When he is returning to Canada with some film cans, Raffi is stopped at the airport by David (Christopher Plummer), a customs agent on his last day of work before retirement. He suspects the cans may contain heroin and begins a lengthy interrogation. David himself is facing strained relations with his son, Philip (Brent Carver), because he cannot accept Philip's homosexuality. Philip just happens to be a guard in the museum where a Gorky retrospective is being held and Ani lectures, and his lover, Ali (Elias Koteas), is an actor of Turkish descent who gets the part of Jedvet Bey, the Turkish villain in Edward's film.

Ararat, then, is very densely layered and filled with characters whose interconnectedness is convoluted and strains credulity. To complicate further what is quickly becoming a confusing movie, the contemporary stories are inter-cut with re-creations of historical events, such as the slaughter of the Armenians at Van in Eastern Turkey in 1915 and the adult Gorky painting in his New York studio in 1934. The connection from past to present remains vague at best, and the only overarching theme seems to be that everyone's lives have been affected in one way or another by the atrocities in Armenia.

But the characters do not seem to be Egoyan's main concern. They are merely props for educating the audience about the Armenian genocide. Raffi, under interrogation by David, spouts off historical facts and narrates horrifying stories of his people's suffering and slaughter. Ani lectures on Gorky and his most famous painting, "The Artist and His Mother," an artistic interpretation of a photograph that she sees as a key Armenian touchstone, a way for Gorky to preserve his mother's memory and rescue her from death.

Unfortunately, Ani's lectures feel like purely academic exercises, especially her analysis of the painting, which is so cerebral that one almost needs to be a student of art history to understand the nuances, like a discussion of why Gorky erased his mother's hands from his painting. Egoyan may feel that he is doing for his ancestors what Gorky did for his mother, using his art to save them from oblivion. Without a coherent framework, however, his screenplay is very fragmented, filled with historical re-creations that are sometimes hard to follow and do not build any dramatic momentum.

But if Egoyan has failed to bring history alive, he also seems to suggest that any attempt to do so would be a distortion. Edward's film, also called *Ararat,* is based on the eyewitness account of the genocide by a real-life American physician named Clarence Ussher, played in Edward's film by Martin (Bruce Greenwood). But when the filmmakers put Gorky in the film, the historical truth is compromised. Gorky is transformed into a freedom fighter who, as a little boy, delivers an important letter for Ussher, is captured by the Turks, hears his friend being tortured to death, and later picks up a Turkish rifle and fights the Turkish aggressors.

The film within the film, which is supposedly trying to tell a true story, actually mythologizes Gorky, the most famous genocide survivor. Incensed that the actor Ali is skeptical that the Turks were guilty of genocide, Raffi challenges his ignorance and makes the case that the world needs to remember what really happened, but the very film they are making seems to lie even as it presents much truth. If Egoyan is consciously commenting on the difficulties of presenting history in a completely honest way, it is not a very original point.

The personal stories do not shed light on Egoyan's themes—they just further muddle his ideas and diffuse the film's dramatic energy in too many directions. Both Celia and Raffi live in the shadows of their late fathers, but Celia's died in a supposed freak accident, while Raffi's died as a kind of hero (or terrorist, depending on one's point of view) trying to assassinate a Turkish ambassador. Celia's insistence that Ani admit to her complicity in her father's death leaves us wondering what really happened. Is Celia just trying to make her father's death mean something? Is she in denial about the truth? Or is Ani's refusal to remember the death the way Celia wants her to meant to parallel the Turks' unwillingness to admit their own guilt? Egoyan's intentions are not clear, but Celia and Ani are such one-dimensional characters that we hardly care what really happened. The climax of Celia's story is unsatisfying—she attacks Gorky's "The Artist and His Mother" in the museum, presumably because she is frustrated that her stepmother will not admit any culpability, but it is not clear why attacking the painting will make Celia feel better.

Raffi, on the other hand, seeks closure in a different way. To make his father's death matter to him, Raffi follows Celia's advice to visit their ancient homeland. The story Raffi has told David about going to Turkey to get process shots for Edward's film is a lie; in fact, Edward's film has already been completed and is set to premiere. When David finally discovers the truth, he grows more suspicious of Raffi's cans of film, which, it turns out, do not even belong to Raffi. He agreed to bring them back to Canada as a favor for someone who helped him shoot footage of Mount Ararat. But despite David's suspicions that the cans are full of heroin and that Raffi was used as a patsy to import drugs, Raffi maintains that they contain film. He cannot believe that he could be a drug smuggler. Does his belief in his own innocence make him as blind as Ali when he denies the genocide? Is Egoyan showing us denial on both individual and collective levels? It is a tantalizing idea, but the connections are tenuous at best and ultimately feel like a huge stretch. Rather than complementing the larger historical themes, then, Raffi's story is just one more subplot in an already overloaded film.

David opens a can in the dark (to avoid exposing the film if it indeed exists) and discovers heroin. However, he frees Raffi anyway and explains to Philip that he was thinking of him when he let Raffi go. In an inexplicable twist, then, David takes mercy on Raffi as a way of building a bridge with his own son. This resolution makes no sense, especially given David's tenacity throughout the interrogation and the fact that his family conflict has nothing to do with his work. Raffi's sense of closure is just as puzzling. He tells Celia that he did not find clarity in the old country but did feel his father's ghost when the can was opened. This moment is probably meant to be a great epiphany, but it really says nothing about the journey he has taken and where he has ended up.

For a film that delves into a deeply emotional subject, it is surprising how cold *Ararat* feels. The characters are reduced to abstractions assuming certain political positions, and, despite the horrors we see in the film within the film like mass murder and rape, the whole project has the tenor of a muted history lesson. Egoyan may have felt strongly about telling a story of the Armenian genocide, but, to move us emotionally as well as intellectually, he needed to find a more compelling dramatic framework in which to tell it.

—*Peter N. Chumo II*

CREDITS

Edward Saroyan: Charles Aznavour
Rouben: Eric Bogosian
Philip: Brent Carver
Raffi: David Alpay
Celia: Marie Josee Croze
Ani: Arsinee Khanjian
Martin/Clarence Ussher: Bruce Greenwood
Ali/Jevdet Bey: Elias Koteas
David: Christopher Plummer
Arshile Gorky: Simon Abkarian

Origin: Canada
Released: 2002
Production: Robert Lantos, Atom Egoyan; Alliance Atlantis, Serendipity Point Films; released by Miramax Films
Directed by: Atom Egoyan
Written by: Atom Egoyan
Cinematography by: Paul Sarossy
Music by: Mychael Danna
Sound: Steven Munro, Ross Redfern
Editing: Susan Shipton
Art Direction: Katherine Climie
Costumes: Beth Pasternak
Production Design: Phillip Barker
MPAA rating: R
Running time: 116 minutes

REVIEWS

Boxoffice. July, 2002, p. 78.
Chicago Sun-Times Online. November 27, 2002.
Entertainment Weekly. November 22, 2002, p. 54.
Los Angeles Times Online. November 15, 2002.
New York Times Online. November 15, 2002.
New York Times Online. November 17, 2002.
Variety. May 13, 2002, p. 14.
Variety. June 3, 2002, p. 26.
Washington Post. November 29, 2002, p. WE44.

AWARDS AND NOMINATIONS

Genie 2002: Actress (Khanjian), Costume Des., Film, Support. Actor (Koteas), Score
Nomination:
Genie 2002: Actor (Alpay), Actor (Plummer), Art Dir./Set Dec., Orig. Screenplay.

Austin Powers in Goldmember

The Good. The Bad. The Dad.
—Movie tagline
What do you call a swinger old enough to be your father? Daddy!
—Movie tagline

 Box Office: $213.1 million

Austin Powers in Goldmember is definitely bigger and badder, if not funnier, than ever. Like the Bond franchise it spoofs, Austin Powers movies now come with increasingly higher expectations, resulting in more action and bigger stars, but fewer laughs, in this case. Along with the title character, producer/writer/star Myers revives the usual suspects: Robert Wagner's Number Two, Mini-Me (Verne Troyer), Scott Evil (Seth Green), Basil Exposition (Michael York), Frau Farbissina (Mindy Sterling), along with Myers' Dr. Evil and Fat Bastard. New additions to the frenzied mix include the somewhat disappointing new villain, Goldmember, and bright, new "Powers" Girl, Foxxy Cleopatra (Beyonce Knowles). Though definitely a worthy addition to the previous two Myers efforts, *Goldmember* tries a little too hard and packs a little too much in.

Goldmember starts in true Bond style with a souped up action sequence jam packed with A-list guest stars and cameos, including Steve Spielberg, Tom Cruise, Gwyneth Paltrow and the traditional opening credits chorus-line style dance number. The unabashed, star-filled spectacle sets the pace for the rest of the film, which continues to parade celebrities from Michael Caine as Austin's father to TV news darling Katie Couric as a prison guard. Former TV child star Fred Savage even turns up in an amusing role as the mole with a glaringly obvious facial mole that Austin is obsessed with. Despite the title's suggestion, Dr. Evil is still Austin's real nemesis and Powers must journey back to 1975 to rescue his father Nigel (Michael Caine) from the two-time Powers movie villain who, along with his cloned sidekick Mini-Me, have escaped from a maximum security prison (complete with *Silence of the Lambs* spoof) and gone back to the 70's.

Ditching the "Shaguar" for a seventies-style ride and sporting his finest disco-era regalia, Austin time-warps back to Studio 69, a trendy roller disco in New York. Austin soon meets Dr. Evil's new partner in crime, Goldmember, an idiosyncratic hot-pants clad Dutchman with a penchant for gold and eating his own flaking skin. It seems Johann van der Smut acquired his unusual (and quite literal) moniker as a result of a smelting accident that necessitated the replacement of his genitalia with a gilded prosthetic. Other than his amusing name and an excuse to mock the Dutch, Goldmember's presence is largely ignorable. However, former flame Foxxy Cleopatra (modeled on the blaxploitation babes of the 70's like Pam Grier) is impossible for Austin to ignore with her free-flowing Afro and kick-ass attitude. The two soon hook up to get the bad guys and rescue the world. Austin must again foil the autocratic plans of Dr. Evil, who plans to flood the earth using a beam from a giant, brassiere-shaped satellite. The first order of business, however, is finding Nigel.

Amid all the usual comedic chaos that ensues, the theme of father/son relationship manages to weave its way throughout the film. A casting coup, none better than Caine, with his Harry Palmer spy series that began with *The Ipcress File*, evokes the swinging 60's-era, suave bachelor on which the ever-randy Austin was based and is the perfect father figure for the shag happy super-spy. Despite their obvious similarities and a thorough knowledge of Cockney slang (shown in an amusingly subtitled scene) the affable Nigel, also a renowned secret agent, bears little respect for his son. What with his booming spy career, Nigel was an absentee parent and Austin secretly resents his father and the two definitely have some matters to work out to patch up the relationship. On the other side of the moral spectrum, Dr. Evil also has issues with his son Seth, who is quickly warming to the idea of becoming part of his dad's evil empire, and Mini-Me, his always ill-tempered junior-sized clone, who is increasingly jealous of Scott's new and improved relationship with his dad. Mini-Me begins to get short shrift from his usually doting DNA double when Scott lovingly bestows his dad with the much hoped for sharks with laser beams attached to their heads. Not missing a beat, the dastardly doctor notices the rising tensions and pits the two against one another for his own amusement.

The film is generously peppered with the trademark double entendre and sight gags, all which are up to the usual hilarious Myers standards. Ironic positioning still takes the comedic center stage as Austin, posing as a bad guy, awaits a requisite physical exam and disappears behind a screen to give a urine sample. With Mini-Me in tow, positioned just right, the silhouetted results give a new meaning to mojo. A quasi-familiar scene has Austin doing his best as a stand-in for a broken statue that tinkles into a fountain conveniently located within Dr. Evil's lair. Another clever play on positioning sets our mod superspy against nefarious Japanese businessman, Mr. Roboto (real life Los Angeles restaurateur Nobu Matsuhisa) complete with subtitles that unfortunately get blacked out in all the wrong places, turning the phrase, "Please eat some shitake mushrooms" into a more objectionable gastronomic offering. The requisite gross-out humor, supplied chiefly by obese Scotsman, Fat Bastard, however, has surpassed even the usually strained limits of the franchise. Scatological humor of every shape and form passes with unashamed glee from his chubby orifice with mixed results.

Powers adds an interesting plot twist as the talented Troyer's Mini-Me has had enough of his manipulative full-size twin and decides to join forces with the other side. Unaware that the tiny replica has flipped, Austin gets to have one last go at the tiny terror, who is forced to undergo quite a beating until his true mission is revealed. Although not as successful a comedic team as Dr. Evil/Mini-Me, who perform a brilliant gangsta rap of artist Jay-Z's "It's a Hard Knock Life," from the musical *Annie* while in prison, Austin and the clone still get their fair share of laughs. Meanwhile Dr. Evil, in a flamboyantly outrageous submarine shaped like himself, plots away with Number Two and Scott to carry out their scheme. Continuing on the theme of rampant spoofing of pop culture, the *Star Wars*-esque surprise ending forgives even the worst of the offensive humor, not to mention leaves the door conveniently wide open for the possibility of future appearances of the Powers pack.

Myers still makes it look like great fun playing the same characters for the third time and Austin seems as fresh he did in his debut. Myers almost seems able to perform the role of Dr. Evil in his sleep, however, and is perhaps getting a little too comfortable in his evil shoes and unable convey quite the same relish at wiping out humanity as he once did. A new side to Dr. Evil is explored, however, that will certainly prove fruitful in future installments. Bastard has come into his loathsome own, finding his niche filling the lowest brow humor. He also is allowed a dramatic character change

with a surprise ending, though there is no heart-felt revealing scene which almost made him palatable in the previous *Powers*. Among the most inspired and enlightening scenes, are the flashbacks to a young Powers, Evil, and Nigel, which chronicle the budding character development that guides their various life choices.

For her part, Knowles character isn't as fleshed out as Elizabeth Hurley's or Heather Graham's, in their respective *Powers's*, but there is much more going on in *Austin III* than in the others with far more comedic ground being covered. Other more established characters are also given less screen time, including Number Two and the Frau, but much like Moneypenny and Q, they become the familiar faces that help hold things together. Director Jay Roach keeps things in full tilt throughout, certainly at home in this familiar territory, and allowing writer/producer/star Myers plenty of room, once again, to do his brilliant and zany thing.

—*Hilary White*

CREDITS

Austin Powers/Dr. Evil/Fat Bastard/Goldmember: Mike Myers
Nigel Powers: Michael Caine
Scott Evil: Seth Green
Foxxy Cleopatra: Beyonce Knowles
Mini Me: Verne Troyer
Basil Exposition: Michael York
Number Two: Robert Wagner
Frau Farbissina: Mindy Sterling
The Mole: Fred Savage
Cameo: Steven Spielberg
Cameo: Gwyneth Paltrow
Cameo: Tom Cruise
Cameo: Kevin Spacey
Cameo: Danny DeVito
Cameo: John Travolta
Cameo: Susanna Hoffs

Origin: USA
Released: 2002
Production: Suzanne Todd, Jennifer Todd, Demi Moore, Eric McLeod, John Lyons; Team Todd, Moving Pictures Company Ltd., Gratitude International; released by New Line Cinema
Directed by: Jay Roach
Written by: Mike Myers, Michael McCullers
Cinematography by: Peter Deming
Music by: George S. Clinton
Sound: Kenneth McLaughlin
Music Supervisor: John Houlihan
Editing: Jon Poll, Greg Hayden

Betty: Mary Jo Deschanel
Harold: Scott Wilson
Rebecca: Aimee Graham
Tom: Wade Andrew Williams

Origin: USA
Released: 2002
Production: Tom Reed, Alicia Allain; High Wire Films, Propaganda Films; released by First Look Pictures
Directed by: Kasia Adamik
Written by: Heather Morgan
Cinematography by: Irek Hartowicz
Music by: Eric Colvin
Sound: Itamar Ben-Jacob
Editing: Jim Makiej
Art Direction: Michelle J. Goode
Production Design: Kaija Vogel
MPAA rating: Unrated
Running time: 100 minutes

REVIEWS

Boxoffice. April, 2002, p. 177.
Variety. January 21, 2002, p. 40.

QUOTES

Harold (Scott Wilson) about his daughter Lucy (Heather Morgan), who thinks she's a dog: "All the women in our family are eccentric, but they sure are fun!"

TRIVIA

Debuting director Kasia Adamik is the daughter of veteran helmer Agnieszka Holland.

Bartleby

"I would prefer not to."
—Movie tagline

Jonathan Parker's *Bartleby* couldn't hit the theatres at a better time. Given the state of unrest and layoffs in the corporate arena, many current or former employees would be happy uttering Bartleby's infamous phrase, "I would prefer not to." On one hand, Herman Melville's novella, *Bartleby the Scrivener,* from which Parker adapted

his film, proves irritating at best; on the other hand, the story's sentiments still ring true in contemporary society. Those among us that have worked as office drones might also have rebelled against spending one's life in total drudgery, if not for fear and societal constraints. Yet, day after day, in office buildings across the world many poor souls are trapped in office monotony and unable to simply say no. Bartleby, although a tragic character, could at least put his foot down—even if he placed it in a different sort of trap.

Parker and co-writer Catherine DiNapoli, who also acted as a co-producer on the film, created subplots to flesh out the story. However, the film's characters appear as one-dimensional office stereotypes. Stereotypes can often lead to comical situations, Melville's intentions were less comical and more about irony. In Parker's version, the boss/narrator (David Paymer) reflects the original story while undergoing a transformation from a brain-numbed employer to a man that bleeds for humanity. By the end of the story, the boss pleads with a publisher to tell Bartleby's story despite the fact that very few readers would actually care. Although Crispin Glover's Bartleby falls on the droll and dry side, the actor does manage to convey his silent suffering and elicits our sympathy despite his annoying tenacity.

At the beginning of the film we see Bartleby standing on a walkway above a freeway clinging to a chain link fence. In a sense he's trapped and we begin to feel his claustrophobia. Later, after he's hired to work as a file clerk, we feel the office walls closing in around him. Parker shoots Glover in the narrow walkway of a windowless file room where Bartleby is surrounded by file cabinets of deeds and contracts. Later on, Bartleby tries to open a window but is unable to get fresh air. The secretary, Vivian (Glenne Headly), points to a dusty vent on the ceiling and tells Bartleby that if he listens closely he can hear the ocean. To further get his point across, Parker sets the story in a futuristic building set away from the city, on top of a hill. Although we are told an employee can take the bus to get to the building, they have to catch three buses and wake up at 4:45 a.m.

And if that's not hell enough, Bartleby is trapped in an office with three other desperate souls. Vixen Vivian flirts with men as validation that she exists and from flat-out boredom. Yet, when she fears that Bartleby will replace her, she makes a desperate attempt to please her boss so that she won't lose her job. The womanizing Rocky (Joe Piscopo) stays at a job he hates but is commitment-phobe in his relationships with women. Former Vietnam vet (and office klutz) Ernie (Maury Chaykin) takes on the role of the office complainer and keeps himself entertained by sharing his problems with his uninterested co-workers. When Rocky asks Ernie how he is, he receives a long list of troubles that at least bring a sense of drama to the mundane office.

Bartleby received mixed reviews from the national press. Jessica Winter, of the *Village Voice*, criticized *Bartleby:* "You'd think Melville had drafted a *Saturday Night Live* skit . . ." Roger Ebert admired the film, but preferred not to recommend it citing, "The Melville short story was short because it needed to be short . . . to make its point and then to stop dead without compromises or consideration." *Los Angeles Times* critic Kevin Thomas claimed that the film lacked energy and felt dead, while A. O. Scott of the *New York Times* praised its director: "Parker has done his job beautifully, using literature from the past to make the present look as strange as it is." The *San Francisco Chronicle*'s Mick LaSalle agreed with Scott in claiming that the 19th century novella translated well into contemporary times.

—*Patty-Lynne Herlevi*

CREDITS

Bartleby: Crispin Glover
The Boss: David Paymer
Vivian: Glenne Headly
Rocky: Joe Piscopo
Ernie: Maury Chaykin
Frank Waxman: Seymour Cassel
Book Publisher: Carrie Snodgress
Mayor: Dick Martin

Origin: USA
Released: 2001
Production: Jonathan Parker; Parker Film Co.; released by Outrider Pictures
Directed by: Jonathan Parker
Written by: Jonathan Parker, Catherine Di Napoli
Cinematography by: Wah Ho Chan
Music by: Jonathan Parker, Seth Asarnow
Sound: Dan Gleich
Editing: Rick Lecompte
Art Direction: Deborah Stairs Parker
Costumes: Morganne Newson
Production Design: Rosario Provenza
MPAA rating: PG-13
Running time: 83 minutes

REVIEWS

Boxoffice. August, 2002, p. 63.
Chicago Sun-Times Online. May 24, 2002.
Los Angeles Times Online. May 31, 2002.
New York Times Online. March 23, 2001.
San Francisco Chronicle Online. June 7, 2002.
San Francisco Examiner Online. June 7, 2002.
Variety. March 19, 2001, p. 34.

Village Voice Online. May 22, 2002.

QUOTES

Bartleby (Crispin Glover) announces: "I've given up working."

Beijing Bicycle (Shiqisuide Danche)

Two men and one bicycle tough it out in Chinese independent filmmaker Wang Xiaoshuai's first commercial release, *Beijing Bicycle.* The film itself, with its bicycle symbol and centerpiece recalls both the Italian classic, *Bicycle Thief,* and Italian neo-realism of a bygone era. According to the film's informative press kit, the second generation of Chinese filmmakers, a group of left-wing Shanghai-based artists, created a melodramatic style of filmmaking that was later termed neo-realism. Chinese cinema has arrived at its sixth generation of filmmakers and traveled through the Cultural Revolution and epic cinema; now returning to a style akin to social realism and greatly influenced by contemporary Iranian cinema. Here, too, we see a simple story leaning against the backdrop of a social message and the bicycle in the film's title merely becomes the symbol that delivers the message.

"The bicycle has a special meaning in China. We all went through the time when we were jubilant about getting a bike and heartbroken over losing one," says director Wang Xiaoshuai in the film's press kit. For country boy Guei (Cui Lin), the shiny metal and rubber represents a means of support as he tries to succeed in the city. After being employed as a bike messenger, Guei's wages are deducted until his bicycle is paid off. For city boy Jian (Li Bin) the same bicycle becomes a status symbol in which the high school boy is able to impress his biker friends and even a local beauty Qin (Zhou Xun) who quickly becomes his sweetheart. However, the bike also represents loss for both men. On a fateful day, Guei's bike is stolen—leading to the loss of his economic means and right to live in Beijing. Jian buys the same bike at a flea market and is unaware of future complications.

Xiaoshuai creates two protagonists and fleshes out the characters by showing us the details of both young men's circumstances. Therefore, when the conflict arises between the two young men, we can't choose sides since they both have a valid argument. Tension builds as we wonder how they will solve their conflict. At first, they try subterfuge, then violence, and finally a compromise. In fact, the boys decide to share the bicycle. We are reminded of two children sharing a single pair of shoes in Majid Majidi's *The Children of Heaven* as they meet in an alley where the bike swaps hands each day.

Beijing Bicycle also ties in a couple of subplots involving two women and another subplot involving a gang of toughs who will use any excuse to perform violent acts against their peers. The subplots are successfully woven in with the main plot, leaving us with a snapshot of contemporary urban Chinese life. One of the subplots involves the relationship that unfolds and disintegrates between Qin and Jian. After Jian loses his bicycle, he takes his frustration out on Qin, so she eventually leaves him for a hotshot biker (played by former bicycle champ, Li Shuang). This leads Jian to seek revenge on the biker, but then the biker and his gang pursue both Jian and innocent bystander Guei, which results in a bloody climax.

A second subplot involves a mysterious woman, Xiao (Gao Yuanyuan), who lives in a mansion next door to Guei's brother's store. At first, the men have the impression that she's a bored rich girl with nothing better to do than dress in fashionable clothing, but we later learn her true identity and the odd circumstances involving the theft of her employer's clothing. Obviously, people aren't who they appear to be on the surface, which leads to intriguing narrative.

While many viewers familiar with classic world cinema will make comparisons between *Beijing Bicycle* and Vittoria de Sica's *Bicycle Thief*, Xiaoshuai's film can stand on its own as an original story. While it's true that bicycles represent economic means in certain parts of the world, as well as a status symbol for youth and an asset for sports enthusiasts, in Xiaoshuai's film the bicycle represents all three. *Beijing Bicycle*, with its country/city mouse and working-to-get-ahead themes, might also be compared to Eric Rohmer's *Four Adventures of Reinette and Mirabelle* and Chinese director Zhou Sun's *Breaking the Silence*. Sixth generation filmmaker Xiaoshuai shares a love for life with his characters and can look forward to a rewarding career.

—*Patty-Lynne Herlevi*

CREDITS

Guei: Cui Lin
Jian: Li Bin
Qin: Zhou Xun
Xiao: Gao Yuanyuahn
Da Huan: Li Shuang
Father: Zhao Yiwel
Mother: Pang Yan

Origin: Taiwan, France

Language: Chinese
Released: 2001
Production: Peggy Chiao, Hsiao-Ming Hsu; released by Sony Pictures Classics
Directed by: Xiaoshuai Wang
Written by: Xiaoshuai Wang, Danian Tang, Peggy Chiao, Hsiang-Ming Hsu
Cinematography by: Jie Liu
Music by: Wang Hsiao Feng
Editing: Ching-Song Liao
Art Direction: Chao-Yi Tsai, Anjun Cao
MPAA rating: PG-13
Running time: 113 minutes

REVIEWS

Boxoffice. November, 2001, p. 129.
Boxoffice. December, 2001, p. 39.
Los Angeles Times Online. January 25, 2002.
New York Times Online. January 25, 2002.
Sight and Sound. July, 2002, p. 38.
Variety. February 26, 2001, p. 43.
Washington Post. February 8, 2002, p. WE42.

Big Fat Liar

Two friends are about to cut one Hollywood big shot down to size.
—Movie tagline

 Box Office: $47.8 million

There was a joke going around during the time that the cast of *Friends* were again negotiating whether or not they would return for another season. The joke was that they had to stay with TV because they couldn't afford the pay cut of becoming movie stars. What was unsaid was that by becoming movie stars, they'd also be taking quite a cut in the quality of material that they'd be working on. The cast members had a few nice movie projects that they worked on—as well as some stinkers (Matthew LeBlanc in *Lost in Space*, anyone?)—but nothing reached the consistent level of quality that their TV show reached week after week.

The usual Hollywood wisdom is that TV is on some sort of lower quality plane than movies, but more often that not, TV actors find far more interesting work on the boob tube than on the more highly regarded movie screen. *Big Fat Liar* is one example. When the film was released, its star

Frankie Muniz was appearing on sitcom *Malcolm in the Middle*. The show was expectably funny and won awards for its actors. *Big Fat Liar* is not a terrible movie, but it's not nearly the quality of Muniz's day job. It's hard to imagine why he would have picked the project unless he bought into the idea that doing a movie would be a career promotion. Maybe he'd realized the shelf life of child stars and was trying to grab all the projects he could while he was still employable.

Muniz's participation, as well as the talents of the other major actors in the film, are what make *Big Fat Liar* more interesting on the screen than it probably was on the page. Muniz is Jason Shepherd, a 14-year-old kid from that bland upper-level income strata that movie teens populate, who is a big liar. When the film opens, he's starting the day with his usual casual, and not so casual, lies. He tells his dad he's been up for hours when he hasn't and tells his mother he's eaten his oatmeal, when in fact he's fed it to the dog.

His lies get more complex when he gets to school. When he hasn't done his homework for English class, Jason tells his teacher that he wasn't able to do it because he was busy taking his father to the Emergency Room. His teacher, who has a good idea about Jason's trustworthiness, announces that she's going to call Jason's father. Jason tells her to go ahead. He gives her his own cell phone number so that when the teacher leaves the room to call dad, Jason can answer his own phone and impersonate the dad.

Jason ends up getting caught and has to write a short story that night. Jason becomes inspired and writes a tale called "Big Fat Liar," about a liar who literally turns big and fat. On the way to school the next morning, he and his bike collide with the limousine of big Hollywood producer Marty Wolf (Paul Giamatti), who is in Jason's Michigan hometown filming his latest bad movie. (The movie is a horrendous creation called *Fowl and Whitaker* and stars former *Family Matters* Urkel portrayer Jaleel White in a buddy comedy about a man and chicken crime fighting duo. It is one of the many pretty clever Hollywood digs peppered throughout the film.) Jason accidentally leaves his paper in Wolf's limo and when he tries to explain what happened, naturally no one believes him. Jason feels horrible when he realizes that his father no longer trusts him.

Months later, when watching a film with his best buddy, Kaylee (Amanda Bynes of Nickelodeon's *The Amanda Show*), he sees a preview for a film called *Big Fat Liar*. Wolf has stolen his idea. Jason should be miffed but, instead, he sees it as an opportunity. If he can go to Hollywood and get Wolf to call his dad and admit that he's stolen the paper, then Jason can win back his dad's trust. Using his babysitting money (how much does babysitting in Michigan pay, anyway?) he buys airplane tickets for Kaylee and himself and sets off for Hollywood.

Wolf is so devoid of human empathy that he refuses Jason's request and laughs in his face. Jason decides that he

and Kaylee will make Wolf's life a living heck (this is a kids' movie, after all) until Wolf fesses up. The bulk of the movie focuses on the way the kids torture Wolf. The most elaborate of their gags is putting blue dye in Wolf's pool so that he is forced to attend his big Hollywood meetings looking like one of the uglier Smurfs. Jason and Kaylee also rig Wolf's car so that all the controls operate the wrong things. When he honks his horn, the windshield wipers turn on and so forth. This leads to a nice sequence where Wolf tailgates the souped truck of a muscle-bound guy and when Wolf tries to put on the brakes, instead he repeatedly honks at the hot-headed guy.

To fill space between the pranks, the movie relies a bit too heavily on an idea films are so fond of—that Hollywood is a special magical place. Because Jason and Kaylee don't have that much money, they camp out in a wardrobe department. In a boring montage, they try on various costumes. Younger kids might like the scenes where the pair walk around the back lot and see a bunch of cowboys, circus clowns, etc., mingling in the streets, but older viewers will remember seeing the same thing done with way more humor in movies like *Pee Wee's Big Adventure* and *Blazing Saddles*.

And speaking of self-aggrandizement, a lot of the movie seems to be dedicated to furthering the idea that *Big Fat Liar*'s studio, Universal, is a super duper company. Most of the movie takes place around Universal Studios and the theme park there. In addition to being a way to advertise themselves, it must have lightened the locations budget considerably.

The best part of the film is Giamatti's hamming it up as Wolf. He embodies the sleazy egotism that's not exactly rare in Los Angeles. He casually abuses his eager assistant, Monty Kirkham (Amanda Detmer) by giving her impossible tasks, then yelling, "I don't care how you do it. Just do it!" Later he barks at her, "I am producing a major motion picture. I don't have time to work on the script!" His crowning achievement in character might be the scene where he wakes up in his hilltop mansion and goes for a swim. Singing along to the Duran Duran song "Hungry Like a Wolf," he preens and prances on his way to the pool. Despite his lumpy body and balding pate, Wolf obviously sees himself as the Alpha Male.

Also good is Bynes as Jason's best friend, who proves herself to be adept at playing various characters. In one scene, she needs to answer phones at Wolf's office and she does a dead-on impersonation of an entry-level Hollywood would-be player. Besides Jaleel White's cameo, Lee Majors also shows up as Vince, an aging stunt man who is one more person for Wolf to abuse. "Out of my way, Methuselah!" is the usual way Wolf addresses Vince.

Film critics gave *Big Fat Liar* mixed reviews. Owen Gleiberman of *Entertainment Weekly* gave the film a D and called it "a noisy, frantic dud." Steven Rea of the *Philadelphia Inquirer* called it "a harmless and mildly amusing family comedy." Roger Ebert liked the film and wrote that it was a "surprisingly entertaining movie—one of those goodhearted comedies like *Spy Kids* where reality is put on hold while bright teenagers outsmart the best and worst the adult world has to offer." And Stephen Holden of the *New York Times* makes the point: "As a moral fable about honesty, it's completely weightless. Its putative message—that honesty is the best policy—is continually undercut by the sheer exuberance with which Jason and Kaylee carry out their deceptions."

—*Jill Hamilton*

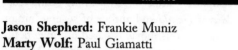
CREDITS

Jason Shepherd: Frankie Muniz
Marty Wolf: Paul Giamatti
Kaylee: Amanda Bynes
Monty Kirkham: Amanda Detmer
Frank Jackson: Donald Adeosun Faison
Vince: Lee Majors
Mrs. Caldwell: Sandra Oh
Marcus Duncan: Russell Hornsby
Carol Shepherd: Christine Tucci
Leo: Sean O'Bryan
Jocelyn Davis: Amy Hill
Harry Shepherd: Michael Bryan French

Origin: USA
Released: 2002
Production: Mike Tollin, Brian Robbins; Tollin/Robbins Productions, Mediastream Film; released by Universal Pictures
Directed by: Shawn Levy
Written by: Dan Schneider
Cinematography by: Jonathan Brown
Sound: David Obermeyer
Music Supervisor: Gary Jones, Dave Jordan
Editing: Stuart Pappe, Kimberly A. Ray
Art Direction: Francis J. Pezza
Costumes: Sanja Milkovic Hays
Production Design: Nina Ruscio
MPAA rating: PG
Running time: 87 minutes

REVIEWS

Chicago Sun-Times Online. February 8, 2002.
Entertainment Weekly. February 15, 2001, p. 46.
New York Times Online. February 8, 2002.
People. February 18, 2002, p. 32.
USA Today Online. February 8, 2002.

Variety. February 4, 2002, p. 33.
Washington Post. February 8, 2002, p. WE41.

QUOTES

Jason Shepherd (Frankie Muniz) to Marty Wolf (Paul Giamatti): "You taught me a valuable lesson. The truth is not overrated."

Big Trouble

They have forty-five minutes to save the world. They need forty-six.
—Movie tagline

Box Office: $7.2 million

There is no way to recount the plot of *Big Trouble* without encountering, well, big trouble. It is an incredibly complex, but not hard to follow, tangle of story lines all woven together into a fairly funny story . . . although it may be a while before the giggles begin. The reason for this is that the filmmakers have to spend precious time at the start of the film just setting up the intricate plot and characters before they can let loose with some of the funniest gags. Consequently *Big Trouble* is a bit slow on the uptake, but if one is willing to give the filmmakers the benefit of the doubt, some laughs will eventually come your way.

Trying to untangle the plot of this story may be more easily done by describing the characters and their function in the story, and oddly enough, they seem to come in pairs. For example there are the pair of disgruntled parents who will eventually fall in lust with each other. Eliot Arnold (Tim Allen) is a recently divorced, Pulitzer Prize-winning writer with the *Miami Herald.* Or at least he was until the day he put his foot through his editor's computer screen. Now he owns his own advertising agency, doing hack work for overbearing loudmouths like the owner of Fishhook Beer who demands more big-breasted women in his ad. Anna Herk (Rene Russo) is the discontented wife of wealthy sleazeball Arthur Herk (Stanley Tucci). While she likes all that Arthur's money can buy, Arthur himself is beginning to wear very thin.

This brings us to the pair of children. Eliot's son, Matt (Ben Foster), has no respect for his dad, mostly it seems because he drives a nerdy Geo. Matt also has a school "assignment" that is going to bring him into contact with Anna and Arthur's daughter Jenny (Zooey Deschanel). According to the rules of the school game "Killer," one student must "shoot" a fellow student with a water gun, and Matt's assignment is to "kill" Anna.

When Matt tries to soak Anna in her own home, however, the result is the arrival of a pair of police officers: Monica Romero (Janeane Garofalo) and Walter Kramitz (Patrick Warburton). What the officers stumble on, though, is that Ben's attempted assassination of Jenny with non-lethal H2O was going on at the same time as a pair of hit men, Henry (Dennis Farina) and Leonard (Jack Kehler), were trying to kill Arthur Herk with real, lethal bullets. (All they kill, though, is Arthur's television set.)

So, to protect himself, Arthur now tries to purchase a nuclear bomb from a pair of unscrupulous Russian arms merchants, Leo (Lars Arentz Hansen) and John (Daniel London), who use the seediest bar in film history as their front. However his transaction is put on hold when a pair of totally inept petty crooks, Snake (Tom Sizemore) and Eddie (Johnny Knoxville), decide to take Arthur hostage along with the bomb—although they have no idea what it is, but it must be valuable because Arthur wants it. However, Arthur, Snake, and Eddie are not the only ones interested in possessing the nuclear weapon, because hot on their trail are a pair of FBI agents, Seitz (Omar Epps) and Greer (Dwight "Heavy D" Myers).

Even the two remaining characters, who seem to be loners, can be paired up. Puggy (Jason Lee) is an innocent, Christ-like homeless man who ends up living in a tree in the Herk's back yard and doing odd jobs for the two Russian arms dealers. He is discovered by the Herk's maid, Nina (Sofia Vergara), who is lusted after by her employer Arthur Herk but who finds herself falling in love with Puggy. There, we've even managed to pair them up, although Puggy seems only to be in love with Frito corn chips, but that's another story. Oh, and there's also a pair of twin security guards both played by Andy Richter.

By the way, did I mention the toad that spits hallucinogenic juices or the goats? How about the dog with Martha Stewart's head that barks "arugilla"? What's amazing about all this is that the story is not hard to follow and even makes sense—in a warped kind of way. Similarly, even with all the characters involved, somehow the filmmakers have managed to flesh them out to the point where we eventually even understand their motivations. Something movies with many fewer characters and much simpler story lines often fail to do.

Big Trouble features a wonderful ensemble cast, with each actor's character given a balanced amount of screen time. And considering the number of actors and the film's short running time (less than 90 minutes) that is quite a feat. Much of the richness of the characters comes from the details: Eliot's desire to write a column on pelicans trained to drop bombs on Castro; Officer Kramitz's unfulfilled lust for Officer Romero just because he once saw her blouse open—revealing her red bustier from Victoria's Secret's desire col-

lection; hitman Henry's running problems with an annoying automatic seatbelt; and the evident stupidity of Gators fans. And for anyone who has ever panicked at all the signs for traffic when driving to an especially busy airport, Eddie's quandary about arrivals and departures is especially funny; he is, after all, arriving in his car but he plans on departing on a plane, so which road should he take?

Throwaway lines abound in *Big Trouble*. One can actually feel the audience miss a beat before they laugh at the incompetent Eddie's line "Let's go, I think I hear the silent alarm." Or hitman Henry watching through the sights of his rifle as the crooks take the Herk household captive. "We have a Die Hard situation in the Kitchen," he says, followed soon by the line "this is better than pay per view."

Dave Barry, popular Pulitzer Prize-winning humor columnist for the *Miami Herald* and author of several humor books, including the one this movie is based on, invests his story with a wealth of details and popular references: Martha Stewart and her magazine, the Discovery channel, talk radio, stupid sports fans, beer commercials featuring big breasts, and snack foods barely touches on them. *Big Trouble* is Barry's first attempt at fictional humor—although some could argue that even his non-fictional humor is so over the top that it could pass as fiction. As a book it was a best seller, but as a movie it may not fare as well. That, however, shouldn't keep people from sampling this cinematic translation of his work nor should it keep moviemakers from again trying to bring Barry's uproarious humor to the screen.

What may keep some audiences away is that *Big Trouble* is one of those movies whose original release was postponed in the wake of the events of September 11, 2001. In fact, it was scheduled to hit theaters September 21st but suddenly smuggling bombs past inept airport security officers and hijacking planes didn't seem quite so funny. Now, with more than a six month buffer zone between that tragic event and the movie's release, it still feels a bit awkward, but if that can be overlooked, *Big Trouble* truly is a charming, funny movie that just takes a little time to get up to speed.

Director Barry Sonnenfeld has a penchant for off-the-wall comedies, sometimes the more frantic the better. Sometimes it produces a fun and popular product like *Men in Black* or *Get Shorty,* but sometimes it misses the mark as did his remake of *Wild Wild West. Big Trouble* is a little bit of both. It's an old-fashioned kind of comedy with a great ensemble cast, most of whom are not known as comedians, in a Byzantine plot with screwball situations a la *It's a Mad Mad Mad Mad World.* It's silly, light and fun to watch. It's chock-a-block with plot and details without ever being confusing. And best of all, it's a comedy that doesn't rely on sex, drugs, violence, swearing or scatological humor. Now that's a real treat. 🎬

—*Beverley Bare Buehrer*

CREDITS

Eliot Arnold: Tim Allen
Anna Herk: Rene Russo
Arthur Herk: Stanley Tucci
Snake: Tom Sizemore
Eddie: Johnny Knoxville
Henry: Dennis Farina
Leonard: Jack Kehler
Monica Romero: Janeane Garofalo
Walter Kramitz: Patrick Warburton
Matt Arnold: Ben Foster
Jenny Herk: Zooey Deschanel
Greer: Dwight Myers
Seitz: Omar Epps
Puggy: Jason Lee
Jack/Ralph Pendick: Andy Richter
Nina: Sofia Vergara

Origin: USA
Released: 2002
Production: Barry Sonnenfeld, Tom Jacobson, Barry Josephson; released by Touchstone Pictures
Directed by: Barry Sonnenfeld
Written by: Robert Ramsey, Matthew Stone
Cinematography by: Greg Gardiner
Music by: James Newton Howard
Sound: Peter Kurland, Steve Bowerman
Editing: Steven Weisberg
Art Direction: J. Mark Harrington
Costumes: Mary Vogt
Production Design: Gareth Stover
MPAA rating: PG-13
Running time: 84 minutes

REVIEWS

Chicago Sun-Times Online. April 5, 2002.
Chicago Tribune Online. April 5, 2002.
Entertainment Weekly. April 12, 2002, p. 49.
Hollywood Reporter Online. April 3, 2002.
Los Angeles Times Online. April 5, 2002.
New York Post Online. April 5, 2002.
New York Times Online. April 5, 2002.
People. April 15, 2002, p. 35.
USA Today Online. April 2, 2002.
Variety. April 1, 2002, p. 31.
Washington Post. April 5, 2002, p. WE39.

QUOTES

Officer Romero (Janeane Garafalo) about crooks Snake (Tom Sizemore) and Eddie (Johnny Knoxville): "I think you guys should turn yourselves in and plead not guilty on grounds of stupidity."

Birthday Girl

Before they share a future, they have to survive her past.
—Movie tagline
Somebody's in for a big surprise.
—Movie tagline

 Box Office: $4.9 million

Many of us have at some time ordered something we saw advertised and then found upon receipt of the item that it was not quite what we had in mind. Perhaps it was the latest gizmo or potion touted on a late-night infomercial promising to make our lives blissful and complete, often at a fabulously-low bargain price. In *Birthday Girl,* a diffident English bank employee gets more than he bargained for when he resorts to seeking wedlock on the Web in this quirky, moderately successful hybrid of a film.

Even before the end of the opening credits, we get a highly effective sketch of the aforementioned John Buckingham (Ben Chaplin): decent, reticent and, most of all, lonely. He agonizes over a video profile of himself that might pique the interest of one of the fetching foreigners at a site called "From Russia, With Love." After clearing his throat nervously, he comes up with the following description of his hobbies: "running, reading, going out, staying in . . ." Clearly unsure of himself and anxious to please, one cannot help but feel for him (as well as question the advisability of such a pursuit). He sits and stares forlornly at his computer screen, clicking away to find out more about woman after woman and not quite seeing what he is looking for until he comes across Nadia (a convincing Nicole Kidman, who learned Russian for this role), who meets two vital prerequisites: she does not smoke and she has a command of the English language which will give John someone to talk to.

When he goes to meet her at the airport, he looks on enviously as passengers disembark and dash into the waiting arms of their loved ones. It initially looks as if John is going to once again be left out in the cold, but then he turns and sees Nadia with her long coat and short skirt, succeeding in looking attractive despite dark eye makeup that makes it look like there might have been raccoons somewhere on her family tree. Their first meeting, while awkward, goes well enough, but it becomes clear as John drives her home in his sputtering car that his dreams of bliss are going to pieces as rapidly as his vehicle appears to be.

Before arriving, John is startled to see that she is a smoker, and is even more dismayed when he quickly comes to realize that she only knows a single word of English. ("Are you a giraffe," he tests her. "Yes," she answers warmly.) As if things are not going poorly enough, she also vomits along the way. Distressed that she has not arrived as advertised, John urgently tries to contact the people at "From Russia, With Love," but his messages go unanswered. It soon becomes apparent to John that while Nadia has less-than-expected language skills, she possesses some amorous talents that clearly speak to him. After she comes across—and learns from—John's stash of pornography, which reveals the mild-mannered man to be an enthusiast of kinky sex, it is clear that John is now rather glad to be bound with Nadia in more ways than one.

What looked like a romantic film about an unlikely couple finding love abruptly changes tone after two men who knew Nadia from the old country crash the quiet and sweet little birthday celebration John is throwing for her. John's confusion, frustration and suspicion of these interlopers is clear, with close ups emphasizing his discomfiture and sense of being shunted aside while the other three jabber away in Russian. (Subtitles are used throughout the film when necessary.) There are hints that jovial guests Yuri and Alexei (French actor/director Mathieu Kassovitz and his countryman Vincent Cassel) might be bad news, such as when Alexei surprises John while jogging and exhibits some kickboxing ability, or when he roughhouses a little too roughly with Nadia while the four are swimming in a pond.

John wants time alone with Nadia (apparently not turned off by her continued vomiting), and politely asks the men to leave. They seem to take their eviction notice well, until the next morning when, in a harrowing scene, Alexei tears apart the kitchen, ties up Nadia and threatens to pour scalding water on her unless John coughs up some cash. As John was given the key to the bank's vault as a consolation prize when he was recently passed over for a big promotion, he commits grand theft , risking all to save Nadia. While he is now wanted by the police (his coworkers shake their heads about "good old John"), at least Nadia will be released. However, while John is breathing easier about Nadia as they all speed away in his car, Nadia is breathing heavily while making out with Alexei in the back seat, and another telling close up shows John sweating and in utter disbelief. The group heads to a hotel, where John is gagged and tied up on a toilet, while Yuri shows him photographs of all the other lonely men the three have scammed. When John gets loose while the men are away and finds that Nadia has been roughed up and tied up by her partners in crime, he is in for

more shocking revelations: she speaks English and is pregnant with brutal Alexei's child.

On the run from the Russians and the police, John is wondering whether to protect her or turn her in, deciding on the former for the time being. They lash out at each other, both physically and verbally, pointedly pointing out the shortcomings of each other's less-than-perfect situations in life. Finally, John just stops his car and sits silently by the side of the road, his world turned upside down and at a complete loss as to what to do next. Still in the vehicle, Nadia finds a love note he had carefully written for her with the help of a Russian-English dictionary, and we see that she is moved that he had gone to such trouble. Around a fire in the woods, the two begin to relax and open up to each other. Ditching the car, they proceed on foot to put Nadia on a plane back to Russia. We get some beautiful shots of the two of them traipsing through lush, peaceful countryside, a couple of odd, misguided people trying to find their way in the world. The film switches back to its grimmer, violent tone once more when, to John's horror, Alexei and Yuri grab Nadia at the airport and take her to a nearby hotel. Reticent John now bursts into action to save her, nearly getting his throat cut by Alexei in the process. Back at the airport, John and Nadia say goodbye to each other but then decide to head off to Russia together, two virtual strangers united meaningfully within the frame, glancing shyly at each other and smiling.

Birthday Girl is the second film from writer-director Jez Butterworth and his brother and co-writer Tom, who initially teamed on *Mojo* (1997). Jez has stated that the naughtiness in the film was toned down considerably before its release in theaters, cuts which will be included in the film's DVD release. Filmed on a budget of $13 million in 1999 before Kidman shot *Moulin Rouge* and *The Others* and then shelved until she was available to reshoot some scenes, *Birthday Girl* grossed $4.9 million on no more than 1000 screens. Critical reaction was mixed, often with praise for the performances but gripes about the screenplay. No one can complain that the film is typical cinematic fare. However, it is hard to know exactly how to feel about it. *Birthday Girl* puts dark comedy, romance and thriller elements together in an interesting but not fully successful manner.

While the film may have more twists and turns and shifts of tone than the rather thin story can support, what keeps us with *Birthday Girl* are the solid performances of Chaplin and Kidman. Chaplin has played the shy guy before in such films as 1996's *The Truth About Cats and Dogs* but the note of vulnerability he strikes from the start keeps us with him throughout. Proving her range, Kidman is sexy and edgy and eminently watchable, but all that poor John is put through makes her a less palatable character than the Butterworths seem to have counted on. As John and Nadia walk off together, it is hard to feel that it is an especially good thing. It is difficult to see what these two really have together, beyond titillation, turmoil, and an equal need to start over. They are certainly a quirky combination, much like *Birthday Girl* itself.

—*David L. Boxerbaum*

CREDITS

Nadia: Nicole Kidman
John: Ben Chaplin
Alexei: Vincent Cassel
Yuri: Mathieu Kassovitz
Clare: Kate Evans

Origin: USA, Great Britain
Released: 2002
Production: Eric Abraham, Stephen Butterworth, Diana Phillips; Portobello Pictures, FilmFour, Mirage Enterprises; released by Miramax Films
Directed by: Jez Butterworth
Written by: Jez Butterworth, Tom Butterworth
Cinematography by: Oliver Stapleton
Music by: Stephen Warbeck
Sound: Ian Fuller
Editing: Christopher Tellefsen
Art Direction: Diann Wajon
Costumes: Phoebe de Gaye
Production Design: Hugo Luczyc-Wyhowski
MPAA rating: R
Running time: 93 minutes

REVIEWS

Boxoffice. November, 2001, p. 129.
Chicago Sun-Times Online. February 1, 2002.
Entertainment Weekly. February 15, 2002, p. 44.
Los Angeles Times Online. February 1, 2002.
New York. February 11, 2002, p. 67.
New York Times. February 1, 2002, p. E20.
People. February 11, 2002, p. 31.
Sight and Sound. July, 2002, p. 40.
Variety. September 17, 2001, p. 24.
Wall Street Journal. February 1, 2002, p. W1.
Washington Post. April 19, 2002, p. WE47.

QUOTES

John (Ben Chaplin) figures out Russian Nadia (Nicole Kidman) only knows one word of English: "Are you a giraffe?" "Yes."

Blade II

Last time he fought against his sworn enemies. This time he will fight with them . . .
—Movie tagline
This time he will lead his sworn enemies against a new breed of terror.
—Movie tagline

Box Office: $81.6 million

Back in 1998, a film based on a black superhero from Marvel Comics came to the big screen. Starring cool incarnate Wesley Snipes as a half-vampire, half-human killing machine called *Blade,* this New Line Cinema release scored an impressive $70 million in domestic boxoffice. The film was fast-paced, filled with thumping techno, stylized to the max, gory, and flagrantly entertaining. Could the sequel be anything less? Of course not—the sequel is more, much more, and that's the problem. If one fight is good, then 10 are better; they can't be two minutes long, they have to be extended ad infinitum (and frankly, ad nauseum); Blade can't kill one or two, he has to kill dozens; and the plot, well, let's just say the unexpected *doesn't* happen.

At a Prague blood bank (which looks like some sort of underground Nazi torture chamber), a strange-looking man, Nomak (Luke Goss), is taken to donate blood. He's informed by the vampires who run the place that his blood has some anomaly, but instead of becoming the prey, he's the hunter. He slaughters everyone around him. Meanwhile, Blade is giving us a quick rundown (via voiceover) about his past—how he became the daywalker, how he hunts and kills vampires, and what happened to his mentor and friend, Whistler (Kris Kristofferson), who was bitten by vamps and presumably killed himself rather than turn into a "suck head." Only he didn't die; vampires captured him and kept him alive in a blood stasis tank and Blade has been tracking his whereabouts every since.

Of course, hunting leads to lots of tedious vampire slaughter (you've seen one exploding vampire, you'll see many, many more before the film is over) until Blade manages to rescue Whistler and take him back to his hideout, where a scruffy slacker called Scud (Norman Reedus) makes weaponry and generally serves as Blade's sidekick. Blade gives Whistler a shot of a viral d-tox and locks him up. If he survives the sunlight the next morning, he should be cured of his vampire cravings although Scud doesn't seem too sure. Whistler does survive and promptly resents being treated as an old fart by the upstart. (Kristofferson's can't-be-bothered attitude and his frequently profane dialogue, spoken in a sarcastic drawl, are character highlights.)

Blade's lair is invaded by a couple of martial-arts vampires, Nyssa (Leonor Varela) and Asad (Danny John Jules), who offer Blade a truce from the vampire nation. They need his help to eradicate something "worse than you" that is out on the streets. Blade, Whistler, and Scud accompany the two to vampire headquarters where, it turns out, Nyssa is the daughter of vampire overlord Damaskinos (Thomas Kretschmann), who happens to resemble the rat-like vampire from F.W. Murnau's silent classic *Nosferatu* for no discernible reason.

The overlord offers a temporary truce so Blade and the other vampires can hunt the "reapers" (more Nosferatu lookalikes), who are led by Nomak. It seems that the virus that causes vampirism has evolved into a new strain and Nomak is the carrier. These creatures feed on both vampires and humans and their victims don't always die, instead they become infected and turn into reapers themselves. And since they must feed daily, their numbers are growing exponentially. Blade reluctantly agrees to work with a vampire tactical unit, known as the Bloodpack, which includes Nyssa and the shifty Reinhardt (Ron Perlman), who would just as soon kill Blade and get it over with.

Blade informs them that if "you want to catch the hunter, start with the prey," so the team heads to a vampire hangout that seems a likely reaper feeding ground. Sure enough, the reapers show up and the team springs into action but none of the usual weapons work. These fiends aren't stopped by garlic, silver, stakes to the heart, or any of the other methods familiar to Blade. The only thing that does seem to work is daylight or its equivalent (some of the weapons are equipped with UV lights). They manage to capture one injured reaper and Nyssa learns that their metabolism burns too fast—if they don't have a steady supply of fresh blood, they begin to feed on themselves.

Oh yes, the reapers also don't have fangs. Their lower jaws expand into insectlike mandibles that they wrap around their victims. Then they paralyze them and the virus is injected through barbs in the reaper's tongue (very nasty and shown much too often) as they feed. Since the reapers are occupying the sewer system, Blade has his team split up to go a-hunting. Whistler is separated and meets up with Nomak, who doesn't kill him but does give him a ring and a message for Blade about figuring out the truth. Most of the team is killed by reapers and Nyssa is injured. Blade gives Nyssa his own blood to survive. While they've survived the reapers, Blade, Whistler, and Nyssa are captured by a bunch of the overlord's goons.

Back at Damaskinos' headquarters, Blade learns that the overlord has been recombining DNA in an effort to engineer a pure vampire race that is immune to the usual methods of killing (as the reapers are) but who can also withstand daylight. The reapers are a failed experiment and

Nomak is actually Damaskinos' son (the ring is the family crest). Scud is the turncoat who has betrayed Blade and Whistler because he would rather be a vampire "pet" than someone's food source in the new world order. Blade manages to kill the traitor before they take him away. It seems that Damaskinos intends to harvest Blade's blood and find the missing link to creating more daywalkers. He has hundreds of fetuses in jars in a lab just waiting.

Whistler escapes from Reinhardt's clutches and rescues Blade, who gets his strength back by taking a dive into the overlord's blood-filled pool. He then defeats endless numbers of minions before killing Reinhardt while Whistler destroys the lab. In the meantime, Nomak has also made an appearance to get revenge on his father. He kills Damaskinos and feeds on Nyssa before Blade finally kills him (in a four-minute thumping). Blade has to kill Nyssa since she's infected. She tells him: "I want to die while I'm still a vampire. I want to see the sun." He takes her out into the daylight and holds her as she disintegrates. As happened in the first film, there's a short coda that shows Blade back at work, hunting vampires and ready for another sequel.

Unlike Stephen Dorff's Deacon Frost from the first film, Blade doesn't have a particularly worthy opponent. Actually, he has too many. There's Nomak, Damaskinos, Reinhardt, the other vampires, the rest of the reapers, turncoat Scud—none of whom are particularly memorable. Whistler warns Blade about getting too fond of Nyssa but she's only eye candy with an attitude; you don't seriously consider her and Blade as an item. Although Blade gets the stuffing kicked, punched, cut, etc., out of him by Nomak, he appears invulnerable, unlike in the first film. He doesn't appear to be half-human; he appears to be half-machine. Cool is good but Blade is an iceberg.

Snipes certainly has the look and the moves but his character hasn't progressed much, Kristofferson's reappearance is welcome, but the rest of the cast are so much filler; and, as happened in *Highlander: Endgame,* Hong Kong martial arts master and fight choreographer Donnie Yen has a too-brief co-starring role. Since opening weekend boxoffice came in at more than $33 million, screenwriter David S. Goyer (who also wrote the original) has a third script waiting to go and a willing star in Snipes. Let's hope next time they try the "less is more" approach and not the overkill that is *Blade II.*

—*Christine Tomassini*

CREDITS

Blade: Wesley Snipes
Whistler: Kris Kristofferson
Reinhardt: Ron Perlman
Nyssa: Leonor Varela

Scud: Norman Reedus
Damaskinos: Thomas Kretschmann
Nomak: Luke Goss
Chupa: Matt Schulze
Snowman: Donnie Yen
Asad: Danny John Jules
Lighthammer: Daz Crawford
Kounen: Karel Roden
Priest: Tony Curran
Rush: Santiago Segura
Verlaine: Marit Velle Kile

Origin: USA
Released: 2002
Production: Peter Frankfurt, Wesley Snipes, Patrick Palmer; Amen Ra, Imaginary Forces; released by New Line Cinema
Directed by: Guillermo del Toro
Written by: David S. Goyer
Cinematography by: Gabriel Beristain
Music by: Marco Beltrami, Danny Saber
Sound: Mark Holding
Music Supervisor: Happy Walters
Editing: Peter Amundson
Costumes: Wendy Partridge
Production Design: Carol Spier
MPAA rating: R
Running time: 116 minutes

 REVIEWS

Boston Globe. March 22, 2002, p. C4.
Chicago Sun-Times Online. March 22, 2002.
Detroit Free Press. March 17, 2002, p. F1.
Detroit Free Press Online. March 22, 2002.
Entertainment Weekly. March 29, 2002, p. 47.
Los Angeles Times Online. March 22, 2002.
New York Times Online. March 22, 2002.
San Francisco Chronicle. March 22, 2002, p. D3.
USA Today Online. March 22, 2002.
Variety. March 25, 2002, p. 36.
Washington Post. March 22, 2002, p. WE38.

QUOTES

Blade (Wesley Snipes): "Forget what you think you know. Vampires exist."

 TRIVIA

Filmed on location in and around Prague, Czech Republic.

Blood Work

The key to catching a killer is only a heartbeat away.
—Movie tagline
A serial killer is just a heartbeat away.
—Movie tagline

 Box Office: $26.2 million

"**9**03 472 568." Those are the numbers written on the wall at the murder site of victims five and six. These numbers have been written at other murder locations and for that reason the serial murderer has been dubbed "The Code Killer." So far, no one has been able to decipher the meaning of the code, not even FBI profiler Terry McCaleb (Clint Eastwood). But since Terry has been on the case these numbers are not the only message The Code Killer is leaving at murder sites. He also writes, "McCaleb catch me." Now it's personal.

While touring the latest murder scene with detectives John Waller (Dylan Walsh) and Ronaldo Arrango (Paul Rodriguez), a bloody sneaker footprint is pointed out. Later, outside the scene, McCaleb sees exactly that type of sneaker in the crowd and takes off after the wearer who runs off. As they chase through darkened streets and alleys, the older McCaleb struggles to keep up, tripping over trash cans and just gasping for breath. When the person he is chasing easily jumps a chain link fence, McCaleb tries to follow but immediately grabs his chest and arm. He is having a heart attack.

The hooded figure he has been pursuing notices that Terry is in trouble and turns around to get a closer look at the man he has been taunting on crime scene walls. But even though McCaleb can't climb the fence to catch the murderer, he can muster enough effort to draw his gun and shoot him. The murderer is wounded, but he escapes as Terry descends into the darkness of his failing heart.

Two years later, Terry McCaleb has retired and lives peacefully on his boat. It was a close call, though, for Terry was in desperate need of a heart transplant and his unusual blood type, AB negative, meant that matching hearts were hard to come by. However, just recently a miracle must have happened because he has had his transplant. Under the care of cardiologist Dr. Bonnie Fox (Angelica Huston) he is doing well, but he is warned to take it easy. That will soon prove difficult to do.

One day Graciella Rivers (Wanda De Jesus) shows up at his boat. She knows about Terry's reputation as a profiler and she wants him to help find her sister Gloria's murderer. Gloria was shot during a convenience store robbery. Terry insists that he is retired and can't help her, but Graciella reveals a piece of information that will lay a guilt trip on Terry and force him to help. What connection could Terry possibly have with Gloria? It is her heart that beats in his chest. Although reluctant to take on the case, after all, he's no longer in law enforcement and his transplant was only a few months ago, Terry feels obliged to help. "I'm just going to have a look," he tells Graciella. "I owe your sister that much."

He starts by asking Detectives Waller and Arrango for the case files on the robbery at Kang's Valley Market where Gloria was killed. And even though he has brought along a traditional offering to the police, a box of doughnuts, Arrango, especially, does not want to help him. Arrango is an Hispanic officer with a huge chip on his shoulder and he resents McCaleb's expertise and publicity . . . and possibly the Mexican heart that has kept McCaleb alive.

Eventually, however, Terry does get access to the crime information and even discovers a connection between Gloria's murder and the killing of another man at an ATM machine a week earlier. To get information on that crime he asks for help from a much more willing detective, Jaye Winston (Tina Lifford), who to some extent owes her law enforcement career to Terry and who may have been romantically involved with him in days gone by.

It soon becomes apparent to McCaleb that the two murders are connected, but how? And could they even be connected to his previous involvement with The Code Killer? This is what he attempts to uncover with the unlikely help of Buddy Noone (Jeff Daniels), his slacker next-boat neighbor. "Starsky and Putz," Buddy calls their team, but what the two discover will eventually connect everything.

All throughout *Blood Work,* Clint Eastwood's 18th film as producer, his 23rd film as director, and his 44th film as star, people keep telling him how bad he looks. And it's true. The one-time Dirty Harry looks incredible fragile. We wince and hurt as he falls over obstacles during his chase after the serial killer. We inhale deeply for him as his breathing seems more and more labored. We worry as he seems to always, unconsciously, rest his hand on his chest above his frail heart. This is an action hero? Yes, only now Dirty Terry uses his mind as much as his body to catch the criminal. And that's why Eastwood's character seems even more enfeebled than he is. We see where the plot is going long before the profiler does. His heart isn't the only thing that may be working at a sub par capacity.

Based on the novel by Michael Connelly, the first in his mystery series featuring the ex-FBI profiler Terry McCaleb, and with a condensed screenplay by Brian Helgeland, *Blood Work*'s most obvious change is making the central character the 70-plus-year-old Eastwood instead of the 46-year-old he was written as by Connelly. This brings a totally different dynamic to the character of Terry McCaleb, especially when he ends up in bed with the ever-so-much-younger Graciella. As played by Wanda De Jesus, Graciella is a strong character

in search of justice. However, when she falls in bed with McCaleb, it sabotages her character's believability.

Blood Work may be sold as a suspenseful mystery, but in reality it is a story about characters. Believability is essential. We have no problem with Eastwood's enfeebled McCaleb. Similarly Jeff Daniel's Buddy Noone is just an interesting take on the character he played in *Dumb & Dumber.* No problem there. While Paul Rodriguez's Arrango is an unusually hostile character for the comedian, one can understand where his anger comes from. That, however, does not prevent his character from being terribly annoying.

But it all still comes back to Clint Eastwood. It is his character, his senior citizen McCaleb, that we are interested in. The mystery becomes secondary. Eastwood expertly shows us how this character faces not only the dark force of the killer he is tracking but also the even darker force of his own mortality. We are rooting for him not necessarily to catch the killer, but just to live through the end of the movie.

Like other Eastwood works, *Blood Work* is tough and tries to be smart. It has sharp dialogue confidently delivered. It has a top notch cast, even if all the primary actors may not be that well known. It has a solid style that some may find a little old-fashioned and maybe even a bit too leisurely. The story may be too easy to figure out, but we enjoy watching a very old friend, Eastwood, work his way through it. There is no doubt, however, that he should have left out the love story.

—Beverley Bare Buehrer

CREDITS

Terry McCaleb: Clint Eastwood
Dr. Bonnie Fox: Anjelica Huston
Buddy Noone: Jeff Daniels
Graciella Rivers: Wanda De Jesus
Det. Ronaldo Arrango: Paul Rodriguez
Jaye Winston: Tina Lifford
Det. John Waller: Dylan Walsh
Mr. Toliver: Gerry Becker
Mrs. Cordell: Alix Koromzay
Raymond: Mason Lucero
James Lockridge: Rick Hoffman

Origin: USA
Released: 2002
Production: Clint Eastwood; Malpaso Productions; released by Warner Bros.
Directed by: Clint Eastwood
Written by: Brian Helgeland
Cinematography by: Tom Stern
Music by: Lennie Niehaus
Sound: Walt Martin
Editing: Joel Cox

Art Direction: Jack G. Taylor Jr.
Costumes: Deborah Hopper
Production Design: Henry Bumstead
MPAA rating: R
Running time: 111 minutes

REVIEWS

Chicago Sun-Times Online. August 9, 2002.
Entertainment Weekly. August 16, 2002, p. 46.
Los Angeles Times Online. August 9, 2002.
New York Times Online. August 9, 2002.
People. August 19, 2002, p. 33.
USA Today Online. August 9, 2002.
Variety. August 5, 2002, p. 19.
Washington Post. August 9, 2002, p. WE34.

QUOTES

Terry (Clint Eastwood): "I got a new heart but I didn't necessarily get a new life."

TRIVIA

Reporter No. 1 is Dina Ruiz, Clint Eastwood's wife.

Bloody Sunday

On January 30, 1972, British troops clashed with civil rights demonstrators from the Catholic ghetto of Bogside in the city of Derry in Northern Ireland. The stunning outburst of lethal violence was an iconic moment in the 30-year-plus civil war known as "The Troubles," ratcheting up the level of tension and laying waste to hopes of a peaceful and just settlement to the religious, economic, and political conflict in the British province. "Bloody Sunday," as the incident became known, exposed the violence behind the British military presence in the north and turned many Catholics and Republicans into recruits for the paramilitary Irish Republic Army. More than 3,000 people eventually died during the Troubles, as Bloody Sunday set the pattern for a long orgy of violence and retribution, attack and counterattack.

To make a film about the events of the day, until recently, may have been seen as simply more provocation, and, despite the uneasy truce in the conflict in recent years, some Unionists may be incensed by Paul Greengrass's ex-

traordinary *Bloody Sunday*. That's because Greengrass, a little-known writer-director (*The Theory of Flight*), pulls few punches in portraying the events of that day and the complicity and duplicity of the British soldiers and their commanders, who managed to gun down 13 unarmed civilians and escape any retribution. But Greengrass's film is all the more remarkable because it isn't simply a piece of Republican agitprop. It is refreshingly free of rhetoric, and Greengrass sees no need to pile on with propagandistic moralizing.

In the best traditions of journalism, Greengrass seems wholly dedicated to depicting realistically what happened that day, and he cares not if he exposes any warts on the side of the victims. In the great traditions of the kind of cinemaverite expressed in such disparate films as *Battle of Algiers,* *Z,* even *Black Hawk Down, Bloody Sunday* immerses the viewer in the horrifying truth about this particular landmark political clash—and in so doing, with great particularity and precision, achieves universal impact. Few political films have more stunningly torn into the guts of the age-old argument about violence versus non-violence in the service of a just cause, and few films of any kind have left such lasting and disturbing images about what human beings are capable of doing to one another.

Though it has not nearly the range, the special effects budget, nor the sweeping scope of Ridley Scott's masterpiece about the U.S. intervention in Somalia, *Bloody Sunday* is 2002's *Black Hawk Down.* It drags the viewer into the heart of a confrontation, without any of cinema's usual distancing mechanisms. In fact, *Bloody Sunday* is much more raw than Scott's picture, and, in its insistence on showing the conflicting views of participants on both sides of the conflict, it gives a fairer and more thorough account of the confrontation.

That it does all this without sacrificing edge-of-the-seat tension, gripping immediacy, and unrelenting realism is a measure of how far *Bloody Sunday* exceeds expectations. Before viewing this film, I could not have conceived a depiction so free of didacticism yet so powerful. *Bloody Sunday* makes history come alive in an extremely disturbing, haunting, and wonderfully instructive way.

It is an uncompromising film on every level, and it demands much of the viewer. Those unfamiliar with recent Irish history may have trouble understanding all of what goes on, since Greengrass has chosen not to provide the story with any preliminary explanation or background. Instead, he plunges you into the knife-thick tensions of the day, introducing characters who are already carrying a lot of political baggage and personal dilemmas.

The casual American viewer's task is made doubly difficult because the actors—many of whom are non-professionals from the Bogside—speak in authentic Irish and British brogues, and the dialogue is often not separated out from the rest of the ambient sound of the film. Instead, the words of the characters are part of the general cacophony. There have been few movies, in fact, where sound has played such a vivid role with such jarring impact. Rude sounds come at you from everywhere—the drone of tanks in the streets, the punchy punctuation of guns firing rubber bullets, the shrill shriek of a phone, the shouts and murmurs of humans caught in confusion and terror.

Greengrass uses a hand-held camera, repeated abrupt fades to black, jarring close-ups, and scenes unusually framed through doorways or alleys, to add to the documentary feel. Sometimes, the camera jerks and lurches, sometimes it follows characters in a mad rush, but it rarely intrudes, and Greengrass doesn't overuse these cinema verite tricks. The overall effect is to thrust the viewer, over and over again and unrelentingly, into the thick of messy situations. Nothing is neat and cut-and-dried, nothing is slick and produced, and that is why there is a nary a moment in the entire 107-minute film where the audience is allowed the relaxing take-a-breath distancing provided by the routine and customary signals that remind viewers they are only watching a film. With tinting designed to make the film look old and sometimes grainy, with natural lighting, with extraordinary performances by individual actors, and with crowd scenes that look spontaneous and unrehearsed, Greengrass has gone farther than almost any filmmaker in making his reenactment look like a pure documentary. It's impossible to stop at any point in this film, gather your wits, and remember that you are watching a movie rather than real events—and yet Greengrass has paced and edited the story so well that it moves along in as dramatic a fashion as any work of fiction.

It's not always clear what's going on, but the chaotic rush of the day's events is palpable and totally involving. All the confusion, the surprise, the terror of Bloody Sunday rush in—and there is no refuge from it. For here is a day that the main actors on both sides have imagined but have not fully prepared for, and everything is done on the fly. No one can ever get their bearings for long—things are moving at too breakneck a pace and over such totally uncharted territory.

In all this, Greengrass has managed to focus on a few characters. One is a young Bogside man who has been in trouble in the past and is now tempting further trouble by seeing a young Protestant girl. We first see them, through a doorway, repeatedly trying to get romantic as they are interrupted by a baby crying, and at first it's easy to mistakenly assume the baby is theirs. Instead, it's the boy's younger sibling. The young man is part of a hot-tempered and impressionable but fairly decent and typical group of young Catholic men who are galvanized and radicalized by the day's events.

A more central character is Ivan Cooper (James Nesbitt), a Protestant member of the British Parliament who, inexplicably, represents the Bogside. He is the leader of the Derry civil rights movement, and his goal is to lead a peaceful march to protest the British government's internment of Irish political prisoners and to push for rights for the beleaguered Catholic minority in northern Ireland. At his side at times, and arguing against him at others, is the more famous Bernadette Devlin, a co-leader of the movement.

Greengrass was criticized by some for giving Cooper such a prominent role, but Nesbitt is simply mesmerizing, and Cooper's leadership perspective gives the film a way to show the various factions on the Republican side of the chasm and how they push and pull at the movement. Cooper must navigate an incredibly tricky course, fending off and feeding the media, leafleting his constituents to get them to come out for the march, negotiating with British soldiers blocking the street, signaling his intentions to a sympathetic local police officer, trying to defuse angry young rock-throwers manning a stone barricade at the entrance to what the Catholics call "Free Derry," and trying, without success, to get the lurking Irish Republican Army operatives to make good on their vow not to engage in violence. To top it all off, he has to soothe the ruffled feelings of a lady friend; their relationship, like the rest of Cooper's life, is repeatedly put on hold because of Cooper's activism. In a brilliant scene, they wearily talk of their dashed hopes for a normal life in a hotel room that is Cooper's headquarters, as activist lieutenants dash in and out. At one point, they kiss, and the woman lays her head on Cooper's shoulder, and then the shrill phone shrieks again—the violent intrusion of the Cause.

Cooper is a well-drawn, iconic character, unlike almost any ever scene on film. Rarely do movies give portraits of activist leaders and, when they do, they are likely to be romanticized. Cooper is seen as a man desperately trying to pick up the legacy of Gandhi and Martin Luther King but continually thwarted by circumstances and forces that are larger than his political abilities. Try as he might to avoid a confrontation with the British forces—after the British government has enacted a new ban on parades—yet to satisfy his followers' demands for a meaningful march, Cooper is caught in a political vice and squeezed. In a defining moment, he tries to steer the march away from a police trap but is flabbergasted when many of the marchers break off and walk into a confrontation.

In a moment that is emblematic of the largest challenges of that era—and of today—Cooper gives a speech to the main marchers at the planned rally upholding the importance of a commitment to non-violence even as, behind his crowd, he can see and hear the battle raging between the rump marchers and their armed foe. Then, when the gung-ho soldiers, firing real bullets, chase their quarry towards the peaceful rally, the nightmare of violence overtakes the rhetoric of non-violence. It is a moment of great and terrible truth—one of many in *Bloody Sunday*.

It is fair to say that the characters on the British side are more crudely drawn, but there is ambiguity there as well, in the role of Brigadier General Patrick MacLellan (Nicholas Farrell), who is caught between his hope for restraint and pressures for violence from above and below. From above there are the cold rhetorical urgings of visiting British Major General Ford (Timothy Pigott-Smith). From below there is the urge for action by the trigger-happy, Irish-hating paratrooper unit whose job is to move in and arrest the "hooligans"—the alleged ringleaders of the Republican cause. Within that unit is one frightened soldier who questions the rationale for violent retribution, but in the end he, too, must save his neck by helping to cover up what really happened that day.

Greengrass cuts skillfully back and forth between his characters throughout the preparations for the march and as the march begins and takes a sickening turn. The scenes of the violence—which leave 13 dead and 14 others wounded—are horrifying and almost impossible to believe to be inauthentic. Never has the "you are there" ethos been more skillfully followed—down to the wailing of kin for the victims who lie dying on the street or dumped on the floor of an overcrowded hospital. Brilliant, unforgettable scenes abound, and nothing important is omitted, though Greengrass must, in the interests of not attenuating his story too much, cut short the matter of how the whole affair was whitewashed.

At the end of the long day, again there is Cooper, a man changed by events beyond his imaginings, a man who has seen his worst nightmares come true, speaking at a press conference and warning that the British soldiers' slaughter that day has "unleashed a whirlwind," killed the civil rights movement, and been a glorious day for recruiters for the IRA. Amid haunting scenes of loved ones who don't come home, Greengrass emphasizes the overriding irony—among those most wounded and changed are a young Protestant girl waiting in vain for her lover to return, and a Protestant politician who has seen his world and his vision of non-violent civil rights activism torn asunder. *Bloody Sunday* leaves you with much more to contemplate that I would have thought possible from a reenactment of an event that is long over and done.

Remarkable it must have been for Greengrass to shoot this film in Derry, covering the same ground where the events of January 30, 1972, occurred, using friends and relatives of the actual victims as extras. It is hard to say what is most extraordinary about *Bloody Sunday*—the considerable technical achievements of sound, editing, and cinematography; Greengrass's risk-taking directing and lucid, daring script; the political touchstones that the film unearths and reveals in all their gripping drama; or the very fact that the film was done at all. In the end, though, what remains is the ripping open of human hearts and souls, and the image of a bug-eyed, half-shocked Ivan Cooper prophesying the whirlwind to come and questioning his own deepest held beliefs. Rarely if ever has a film been made that so deftly and dramatically shows the impact of violence on human beings.

—Michael Betzold

CREDITS

Ivan Cooper: James Nesbitt
Major General Ford: Tim Pigott-Smith
Brigadier Maclellan: Nicholas Farrell
Chief Supt. Lagan: Gerard McSorley
Frances: Kathy Kiera Clarke
Kevin McCorry: Allan Gildea
Eamonn McCann: Gerard Crossan
Bernadette Devlin: Mary Moulds
Bridget Bond: Carmel McCallion
Gerry Donaghy: Declan Duddy
Colonel Wilford: Simon Mann

Origin: Ireland, Great Britain
Released: 2001
Production: Mark Redhead; Granada Film Productions, Hell's Kitchen, Irish Film Board, Portman Film; released by Paramount Classics
Directed by: Paul Greengrass
Written by: Paul Greengrass
Cinematography by: Ivan Strasburg
Music by: Dominic Muldowney
Sound: Albert Bailey
Editing: Clare Douglas
Art Direction: Padraig O'Neill
Costumes: Dinah Collin
Production Design: John Paul Kelly
MPAA rating: R
Running time: 110 minutes

REVIEWS

Boxoffice. September, 2002, p. 140.
Chicago Sun-Times Online. October 25, 2002.
Entertainment Weekly. October 11, 2002, p. 54.
Los Angeles Times Online. October 18, 2002.
New York Times. September 29, 2002, p. AR25.
New York Times Online. October 2, 2002.
Sight and Sound. March, 2002, p. 39.
Variety. January 28, 2002, p. 27.
Washington Post. November 1, 2002, p. WE41.

QUOTES

Ivan Cooper (James Nesbitt): "We just want a peaceful march. This is our day."

should remake "That Girl is Mine" as "That Ho is Mine" and, to his horror, his boss enthusiastically agrees. Dre realizes that he's exactly what he's always hated about hip-hop music—he's a sellout. For Dre, street credibility is the only thing that matters.

When he decides to leave his high-paying job to start his own label, he confides first in Sidney. She loves the idea and gives Dre a large sum for seed money. When Reese finds out about Dre's decision, she is worried over their family's finances and mad that Dre has confided in Sidney first.

What makes this movie different from the usual romantic comedy is that the side characters have a bit more depth than usual. As Roger Ebert of the *Chicago Sun-Times* points out about Reese's character: "In a less thoughtful movie, she'd be the shallow, bitchy life-wrecker. Here, she is blameless and basically reasonable: mad at Dre for quitting his job without talking it over with her, jealous of Sidney because she (correctly) suspects Sidney and Dre have always been in love but lied to themselves about it." Similarly, Sidney's love interest also isn't a one-dimensional loser. He's an attractive, kind man who treats Sidney well.

The actors in the second-banana roles shine, too. As Francine, Queen Latifah, is the Rosie O'Donnell character of the film. She's the large, wisecracking friend of the lead. When Sidney says that she is working too much to have time for love, Francine cracks, "You're turning into a Terry McMillan character." But better is Mos Def as Dre's first authentic rapper client Chris V. Mos Def has an appealing, easy-going quality as the talented rapper who would prefer driving a taxi to selling out his music. In one of the film's more successful jokes, Chris tries to get Dre to make his move with Sidney. He compares the two's plight to the characters in *Casablanca* and urges Dre not to be like Humphrey Bogart who "punks out and lets that fine Ingrid Bergman get on that plane." When Dre retorts that maybe Chris should follow his own advice and ask out Francine, Chris answers, "I'm not the Humphrey Bogart. I'm the Peter Lorre character. I'm the sidekick."

Hip-hop lovers will also appreciate the authenticity offered by several cameo appearances. Russell Simmons, Big Daddy Kane, Kool G. Rap, Jermaine Dupri, Pete Rock and Black Thought are among the rap heavyweights who show up to answer Sidney's question about falling in love with hip-hop.

And Famuyiwa adds some creative flourishes here and there. To show the disintegrating marriage between Dre and Reese, the director borrows the breakfast sequence from *Citizen Kane*. Early in their marriage, the two cuddle and kiss over a quick breakfast as they start their day. Later in their relationship, they pass each other with silence reproach in the kitchen.

Still, the film, written by Famuyiwa and Michael Elliot (*Like Mike* and the former publisher of *Krush Rap*), has some problems. The movie bangs on the hip-hop-as-the-

metaphor-for-love too long and too hard. Sidney and Dre are continually talking about their love of hip-hop in a sort of code for how they feel about each other. Once or twice would have been clever, but it's hammered in so often, it becomes tiresome. Plus, it's nice to be passionate about something, but don't these two ever have anything else to talk about? And, as endings of romantic comedies often are, the ending is cheesy. It involves Dre declaring his love in a cute way that is neither particularly cute, or, for that matter, surprising to anyone but Sidney.

Critics liked the movie. Many recognized it was formulaic, but credited the movie for working well within the formula. Ebert wrote, "*Brown Sugar*, which charts romantic passages in these lives, is a romantic comedy, yes, but one with characters who think and talk about their goals and are working on hard decisions." Kevin Thomas of the *Los Angeles Times* called it a "sly and sophisticated romantic comedy" and wrote, "It's a mainstream movie in the best sense: an all-too-infrequent big-screen depiction of successful, affluent African-Americans facing complex personal and professional choices." Dave Kehr of the *New York Times* wrote that the film "sustains the charm of an early 60's New York romance." And Sean Axmaker of the *Seattle Post-Intelligencer* wrote, "You don't need to recognize the references to feel [Dre and Sidney's] investment in the culture. Famuyiwa finds the universal chords in their unique anthems."

—*Jill Hamilton*

CREDITS

Dre: Taye Diggs
Sidney: Sanaa Lathan
Chris V: Mos Def
Reese: Nicole Ari Parker
Francine: Queen Latifah
Simon: Wendell Pierce
Kelby: Boris Kodjoe
Ren: Erik Weiner
Ten: Reggi Wyns

Origin: USA
Released: 2002
Production: Peter Heller; Heller Highwater, Magic Johnson Entertainment; released by Fox Searchlight
Directed by: Rick Famuyiwa
Written by: Rick Famuyiwa, Michael Elliot
Cinematography by: Enrique Chediak
Music by: Robert Hurst
Sound: William Sarokin
Music Supervisor: Barry Cole, Christopher Covert
Editing: Dirk Westervelt
Art Direction: David Stein

Costumes: Darryle Johnson
Production Design: Kalina Ivanov
MPAA rating: PG-13
Running time: 109 minutes

REVIEWS

Boxoffice. September, 2002, p. 34.
Boxoffice. October, 2002, p. 58.
Chicago Sun-Times Online. October 11, 2002.
Entertainment Weekly. October 18, 2002, p. 24.
Entertainment Weekly. October 18, 2002, p. 92.
Los Angeles Times Online. October 11, 2002.
New York Times Online. October 11, 2002.
Variety Online. October 6, 2002.
Washington Post. October 11, 2002, p. WE46.

QUOTES

Francine (Queen Latifah) to Sidney (Sanaa Lathan): "You're turning into a Terry McMillan character."

TRIVIA

Taye Diggs and Sanaa Lathan previously worked together in director Rick Famuyiwa's "The Wood" (1999) and Malcolm D. Lee's "The Best Man" (1999).

The Business of Fancydancing

W hile many Seattle-based filmmakers have been complaining about the lack of filmmaking opportunities in the Emerald City, Native American author/poet/screenwriter Sherman Alexie (*Smoke Signals*) not only transformed one of his books into a digital video feature, but also employed local crew and talent. Alexie touted the fact that his debut feature, *The Business of Fancydancing*, was shot, edited and distributed by locals when he spoke at a screening for his film. One would think that the best-selling author and celebrated Seattlelite would have dazzled us with a spectacular gem. But, in fact, *The Business of Fancydancing* sports blurry footage and uneven performances amongst a lot of anti-white sentiment, including a scene in which two Native American men beat a white motorist just because he's white.

On one hand, Alexie should be applauded for not making a New Age-friendly film where white people pretend to be Native. This is not *Dancing with Wolves* and the Native Americans in this film do not connect with Mother Nature and wise elders do not lecture us about saving the planet for the next seven generations. On the other hand, Alexie's heavy-handed approach could only further alienate whites from whatever message he presents with his film. Alexie, known for his sarcastic wit and guilt-ridden lectures, lets it all hang out with this almost plot-less script. *The Business of Fancydancing* at times feels more like a performance art piece since the director combines dance sequences, poetry readings, and on-camera interviews. The film proves to be confusing as it jumps back and forth through time and tells its story in segments much like Francois Girard's *32 Short Films About Glenn Gould.* The film, based on a collection of poetry, *The Business of Fancydancing,* also recalls the Canadian feature, *Hard Core Logo,* which was constructed from Michael Turner's fragmented novel. Did Alexie look to Canadian filmmakers for inspiration?

Alexie might have streamlined his script, added a bit of tension, and cut back on the rhetoric. However, all is not lost because the script does contain humor, refreshing dialogue, and scenes at the "rez" that portray documentary realism. Alexie doesn't shy away from telling his truth about growing up a Yakima Indian on a Spokane reservation. He doesn't hide the poverty or alcohol and drug addiction and he even pokes fun at himself through his autobiographical character, Seymour Polatkin (Evan Adams of *Smoke Signals*). His characters are angry, volatile, and desperate. They are gay, alcoholics, liars, dropouts, and suicidal. Even celebrated poet Seymour realizes that he will always be an outsider, on the reservation and also in an urban setting. This is a dilemma that indigenous people from around the world face after they graduate from college and assimilate into the dominant culture.

"Affirmative Action" and flavor-of-the-day poet Seymour promotes his poetry books to an eager white audience while sharing an assortment of lies with his fans. Other characters, his cousin Mouse (Swil Kanim) and best buddy Aristotle (Gene Tagaban), later reveal that Seymour lifted his poetic inspiration from others' lives. When Seymour shares poetry about his days battling with alcoholism, he is in fact talking about Aristotle's experiences and not his own. And as the film moves along and more dirt is revealed about our charming celebrity, we see that he is weighed down by his own self-preservation attitude. But just as we peek through his façade, the illusions that Seymour built crash around him in a powerful scene in which the character sheds a fancydancing costume one layer at a time until we see his glass house shatter when he confronts his true image, that of an outsider.

Alexie practices several devices in this brazen feature with varying degrees of success. A black intellectual woman (Rebecca Carroll) grills Seymour about the source of his inspiration. Eventually, after being asked too many questions about reservation life, Seymour lashes out at the journalist by telling her a painful story about his childhood. Was Alexie aiming for irony here having a detached African-American woman interviewing a Native American poet? Alexie also employed another device by portraying the ghost of Mouse at several of Seymour's readings as Mouse mocks Seymour's attempts to fit into mainstream society.

Sean Axmaker, *Seattle Post Intelligencer,* gave Alexie's film a mixed review: "The pieces don't all fit together and some of the performances are out of tune, but *Fancydancing* is more than the sum of its awkward parts.". In the meantime, the celebrated Seattle writer-turned-filmmaker will return to the drawing board while his loyal fans await his next project.

—*Patty-Lynne Herlevi*

CREDITS

Seymour Polatkin: Evan Adams
Agnes Roth: Michelle St. John
Aristotle Joseph: Gene Tagaban
Mouse: Swil Kanim
Interviewer: Rebecca Carroll
Teresa: Cynthia Geary
Mr. Williams: Leo Rossi
Steven: Kevin Phillip
Kim: Elaine Miles

Origin: USA
Released: 2002
Production: Larry Estes, Scott Rosenfelt; FallsApart; released by Outrider Pictures
Directed by: Sherman Alexie
Written by: Sherman Alexie
Cinematography by: Holly Taylor
Sound: Scot Charles
Editing: Holly Taylor
Production Design: Jonathan Saturen
MPAA rating: Unrated
Running time: 103 minutes

REVIEWS

Boxoffice. April, 2002, p. 183.
New York Times Online. October 18, 2002.
San Francisco Chronicle. August 30, 2002, p. D5.
Seattle Post-Intelligencer Online. May 10, 2002.
Seattle Times Online. May 10, 2002.
Seattle Weekly Online. January 10, 2002.
Seattle Weekly Online. May 9, 2002.
Variety. January 28, 2002, p. 33.

QUOTES

Steven (Kevin Phillip) warns his Native American lover Seymour (Evan Adams), who's going home for a funeral: "They're not your tribe anymore. I'm your tribe now."

Butterfly

Butterfly recounts the newsworthy story of a courageous young woman who climbed up a thousand-year-old redwood tree in order to save it from logging. Viewers may remember the occasion, in December 1997, when Julia Butterfly Hill started her two-year tree sit-in. In case they don't, Doug Wolens's straightforward documentary reviews how Hill, the daughter of an evangelical preacher, fell in love with a California redwood she nicknamed "Luna," and, in order to protect the tree from being cut down, created a makeshift treehouse in which to live.

Charles Hurwitz, President of the Pacific Lumber Company and owner of the land, tried to remove Hill, but realized he was on the losing side of a public relations war. Environmentalists capitalized on the occasion by making a martyr out of Hill, although they themselves didn't always agree with her tactics. Despite the hazards of living in the tree, including harassment by Pacific Lumber, Hill stayed on much longer than she—or anyone else—thought she would. Finally, the weary Hill climbs down from Luna, but only after Pacific Lumber agrees to protect the tree and many others in the three-acre area.

Doug Wolens perfectly complements Hill's story with a simple, scrappy hand-held video style. Wolens also proudly declares (in his presskit) that *Butterfly* was "edited entirely on my home PC." This now-familiar social documentary format gives the film an immediate quality and engages the viewer more greatly than the slicker network news approaches to the same material (ABC News is captured in Wolens' film doing their own piece).

Given the title of the film and its "grassroots" look, one would expect Wolens to favor Hill over her opponents, and, yes, the young heroine is compared to Gandhi when not being called "special" and "magical;" yet Wolens makes a dedicated and sincere effort to show more than one side of the issue. He alternates talking head interviews with Hill (he lived in her treehouse for several days), the environmentalists, the loggers, the other members of the Humboldt County community, and the media.

Some of the interviews are quite revealing, particularly when the subjects show their disingenuousness. Charles Hurwitz claims he is "concerned about [Hill's] welfare," yet a helicopter attack on her treehouse is clearly directed by

Pacific Lumber. Just the same, environmentalist Mickey Hart (of the rock group, The Grateful Dead) doesn't feel Hill is being "romantic" in her ambitions, yet Hill's idealism is downright palpable, and members of Earth First call Hill arrogant for not agreeing with all their decisions, yet they show some smugness themselves. In the end, still, the "tree-huggers" (Hill, Hart, Peter Yarrow [of Peter, Paul, and Mary], Earth First!, The Sierra Club), come off much better than the "lumberers" (Hurwitz, a spokeswoman from Maxaam [Pacific Lumber's public relations firm], and the conservative rural neighbors).

The flaws in Wolens' account are more expositional: one might ask why Hill got as devoted as she did to her cause, how she survived day-to-day in the tree, and at what point the helicopter attack and deadly storms (courtesy of El Nino) occurred (the brief snippets of striking footage are inserted in odd, achronological moments). The lack of narrative development saps some of the drama from the overall story, but at least the feature film of *Butterfly* gives more detail than the truncated public television version shown on *P.O.V.* in 2000.

—*Eric Monder*

CREDITS

Origin: USA
Released: 2000
Production: Doug Wolens; released by Open City Films
Directed by: Doug Wolen
Cinematography by: Doug Wolen
Sound: Robert Donald
Editing: Doug Wolen, Zack Bennett
MPAA rating: Unrated
Running time: 79 minutes

REVIEWS

Guardian Online. October 18, 2000.
New York Magazine Online. June 26, 2000.
Variety Online. October 30, 2000.

Catch Me If You Can

The true story of a real fake.
—Movie tagline

 Box Office: $71.6 million

Catch Me If You Can is a story that is told in flashbacks: the early to mid 1960s alternating with the late 1960s and 1970s and ending with the present day. It begins with a television show, *To Tell the Truth* in which three men dressed as airline pilots all claim to be Frank Abagnale Jr. who posed as an airline pilot for Pan Am from 1964–67, but who also posed as an assistant district attorney, a doctor and passed millions of dollars worth of phony checks all before his 19th birthday. Seamlessly edited into this vintage television footage is the Frank Abagnale of the film, Leonardo DiCaprio.

Next it is 1969 and we're in a prison in Marseilles, France where a very ill Frank is being held in deplorable conditions and from which American FBI agent Carl Hanratty (Tom Hanks) is trying to get him extradited. The film now flashes back six years earlier to 1963 New Rochelle, New York where a young Frank is attending a Rotary Club dinner honoring his father, Frank Sr. (Christopher Walken), by making him a lifetime member. Frank Jr. obviously adores Frank Sr. and admires the marriage of love his father has to Paula (Nathalie Baye), a French war bride.

It soon becomes apparent, however, that Frank Sr. may be a bit of a con man himself. He has gotten himself in trouble with the IRS (tax fraud) and his stationers store could go under if he doesn't get a bank loan. All the local banks have turned him down so he cons a clothing store owner into lending him a black suit for his son who then acts as his chauffeur as he approaches banks in New York City for the money. The con fails, however, and soon the family has to sell their car and suburban home and move into a seedy apartment. It is a humiliation that will drive Frank Sr. and Paula apart and will forever scar Frank Jr.

Frank Jr.'s drift into being a con man himself starts small and funny. Pulled from his private school and enrolled in a public one, Frank is looking for his French classroom when a jock bully slams him in the hall. When Frank finally finds the classroom he discovers that the bully is enrolled in the class, too. Instead of cowering, though, Frank immediately pretends to be the French substitute teacher and picks unmercifully on the jock. It is every high school student's idea of the perfect revenge and audiences love the scene. Indicating shades of the chameleon to come, Frank manages to keep this charade up to the point of holding parent-teacher conferences and scheduling a field trip to a French bread factory in Trenton! When he is finally stopped, his parents are called in, but a congratulatory smile can't help but cross his father's face.

The poverty, however, takes its toll on the Abagnale's marriage and soon Paula is fooling around with the president of the Rotary Club, Jack Barnes (James Brolin), and divorce papers are drawn up. All this hits Frank Jr. very hard, but when he is told that he must chose which of his parents he will live with it is too much for the young man and he runs away.

In New York City Frank soon runs out of money and his checks are bouncing. But then one day he notices the special way everyone treats airline pilots. They are the golden boys who can get and do anything they want. So Frank pretends to be a high school reporter doing a story on Pan Am, interviews someone who tells him everything he needs to know about being a pilot, and sets out to get himself a fake ID, a fake FAA license and even a uniform. Thus is born Frank Taylor, a Pan Am co-pilot who can cash his checks anywhere. Soon he is perfecting his check passing skills by creating Pan Am paychecks using decals from model airplanes, discovering details of the banking process, and perfecting his fake "piloting" skills by discovering the art of deadheading (getting a lift on an airplane) to other cities where he cashes more checks.

Eventually the law catches up to Frank in the form of the ever serious Carl Hanratty, an FBI agent working on bank fraud cases. Carl isn't taken very seriously by his fellow agents, in fact it soon becomes apparent that being assigned to the bank fraud division is a punishment. Carl manages to track Frank down to a motel in Hollywood complete with all his incriminating check-making paraphernalia scattered about the room. But since Carl doesn't have a clue as to what the check pusher he is chasing looks like and since Frank is such a young kid, Frank manages to convince Carl that he is really Barry Allen of the U.S. Secret Service and makes his escape before Carl is any the wiser.

The movie now alternates between Frank and Carl's life. Frank is buying James Bond clothing and sports cars and "dating" high-cost prostitute Cheryl Ann (Jennifer Garner) while Carl is doing his own laundry and turning all his whites pink. But on Christmas Eve, the lonely Frank places a phone call to the just-as-lonely, job-obsessed and divorced Carl. It is an act that will become something of a tradition between the hunted and the hunter and make a very human connection between the two.

Carl soon discovers the true identity of his check passer but Frank has now become Dr. Connors, a graduate of Harvard Medical school and a doctor in Atlanta, Georgia. There he meets a young candy striper, Brenda (Amy Adams), and proposes to her. Just as Carl catches up to him in Atlanta, Frank moves on to New Orleans where he becomes an assistant prosecutor working under Brenda's father (Martin Sheen). Unfortunately for Frank, Carl will eventually catch up with him here, too, on the night of his engagement party. Now Frank takes his check forgery schemes overseas and Carl will again eventually catch up with him, the French police will arrest him, and we are again at the opening scenes of the film. It does not, however, end there,

but to tell you more would ruin some of the more interesting plot twists to this true story.

Based on the real Frank Abagnale, Jr's 1980 biography, there are, nonetheless, several times the script roams away from reality. For example, while Frank is a real character, Carl is said to be a composite created from several FBI agents who tried to crack Frank's case. This compression into the character of Carl, however, is what allows the filmmakers the fiction of making a more personal connection between the chased and the chaser and creating a more enjoyable story. Similarly, Abagnale has admitted that he was more sexually addicted than the movie would indicate, but Spielberg wisely realized that all that sex would detract from the film's breezy tone. And while time is questionably extended to heighten suspense at several points in the movie, in reality, Frank was a doctor in Atlanta only for about two weeks and spent even less time as a lawyer in Louisiana

In the film's press kit Abagnale calls himself an opportunist, "The more I got away with, the more of a game it became—a game I knew I would ultimately lose, but a game I was going to have fun playing until I did." And it is this sense of fun—not the sense of criminality—that dominates the film and the characters.

Catch Me If You Can may be one of Steven Spielberg's most light-hearted films. That does not make it light weight, however. Intensely character driven, Spielberg has chosen two lead actors well up to the job. With all his Oscar nominations and wins, no one doubts Tom Hanks' ability to create convincing characters, to win audience approval and to carry a film. Leonardo DiCaprio, however, might have been a bit harder sell. Known primarily for his role in *Titanic,* he is nonetheless quite winning as the ultimate con man . . . and a 17-year-old at that. Combined, they are a perfect cat and mouse team.

Looking like yet another dour Blues Brother, Hanks' serio-comic FBI agent is played straight but inadvertently leaks humor at his edges such as when he flashes his badge upside down and backwards (he obviously doesn't do it very often) or when he tries to tell a knock-knock joke (jokes being something else he is not too familiar with). It is interesting, then, that Carl will eventually become the father figure Frank lost when he ran away from his crumbling real family.

Frank on the other hand is smarter than his chronological years would imply. He is innocently daring, amazing even himself as he pulls off bigger and bigger cons. He is charming, precocious, nervy, fast thinking, cool, and ultimately a lonely man. DiCaprio, who was 27 when the film was made, perfectly captures the heart of this 17-year-old who is both innocent and worldly.

Although the psychological underpinnings of his life of crime are shown to be in the life he lost because of his father's incautious business dealings, they are offered only to give a degree of motivation and poignancy to Frank's acts.

We sense that he wants nothing more than to use his new-found wealth to bring his parents back together again, buy back their house and car and return to the way things were. We see this in several moving scenes when the two Franks meet. They are heart-breaking.

One of the reasons for this is that Christopher Walken, playing the part of Frank Sr., gives an understated and sly performance. Even though it is just a small role, his charming but ultimately sad scoundrel may be one of his most poignant characters in Walken's career. Because of these three strong performances, audiences are won over to a story that has an admittedly over-the-top plot. Who'd believe it if it weren't based on fact?

Believe it or not, *Catch Me If You Can* was shot in a whirlwind 56 days with more than 140 sets in Los Angeles, New York, Montreal and Quebec City. Despite this fast pace, the movie never sacrifices its ambiance for expediency. It flawlessly captures the feeling of the 1960s.

For example, perennial Spielberg composer John Williams again provides a pitch-perfect score that impeccably reflects the times. As it plays against the catchy, animated opening credits, we are immediately transported back to the days of innocent crime capers like *The Pink Panther*. Written in the progressive jazz style so popular back then, William's seems to be paying homage to the *Panther*'s composer Henry Mancini, which is entirely possible since Williams was the pianist in Mancini's orchestra when both their careers were just starting. The score, therefore, not only enhances the feeling of suspense of the film, but also captures its setting in an age of innocence; it was a time when someone like Frank could get away with these kinds of things, not like our paranoid post-September 11th America. Along with the score is the use of colors and costumes and details: bright yellow bikinis, harvest gold appliances, black suits and ties, Mitch Miller sing-a-longs, and fondue pots all add to the film's faultless authenticity.

Some may object that *Catch Me If You Can* celebrates Frank's criminal activities, makes a hero out of a felon, but it does so in the almost carefree style of *Butch Cassidy and the Sundance Kid*. Both films present a cat-and-mouse game that is relaxed yet fast-paced, that is true and engaging. They are both also technically superior films containing brilliant performances, infectious humor and just a touch of tenderness. And as we watch the story unfold in front of us, we're also in awe because it's basically true.

—*Beverley Bare Buehrer*

CREDITS

Frank Abagnale Jr.: Leonardo DiCaprio
Carl Hanratty: Tom Hanks
Frank Abagnale: Christopher Walken
Paula Abagnale: Nathalie Baye
Roger Strong: Martin Sheen
Brenda Strong: Amy Adams
Jack Barnes: James Brolin
Cheryl Ann: Jennifer Garner
Earl Amdursky: Frank John Hughes
Paul Morgan: Steve Eastin
Special Agent Witkins: Chris Ellis
Assistant Director Marsh: John Finn
Tom Fox: Brian Howe

Origin: USA
Released: 2002
Production: Steven Spielberg, Walter F. Parkes; Amblin Entertainment, Kemp Company, Splendid Pictures; released by Dreamworks Pictures
Directed by: Steven Spielberg
Written by: Jeff Nathanson
Cinematography by: Janusz Kaminski
Music by: John Williams
Sound: Ronald Judkins
Editing: Michael Kahn
Costumes: Mary Zophres
Production Design: Jeannine Oppewall
MPAA rating: PG-13
Running time: 140 minutes

REVIEWS

Chicago Sun-Times Online. December 25, 2002.
Chicago Tribune Online. December 25, 2002.
Entertainment Weekly. January 3, 2003, p. 46.
Los Angeles Times Online. December 6, 2002.
Los Angeles Times Online. December 25, 2002.
New York Times Online. September 8, 2002.
New York Times Online. December 25, 2002.
People. January 13, 2003, p. 37.
USA Today Online. December 23, 2002.
Variety Online. December 13, 2002.
Washington Post. December 25, 2002, p. C1.

QUOTES

Frank (Leonardo DiCaprio): "Stop chasing me." Carl (Tom Hanks): "I can't stop. It's my job."

AWARDS AND NOMINATIONS

British Acad. 2002: Support. Actor (Walken)
Natl. Soc. Film Critics 2002: Support. Actor (Walken)

The Cat's Meow

A Triangle . . . A Murder . . . A Secret . . . Don't Tell.
—Movie tagline
Some secrets won't stay buried.
—Movie tagline
"The Whisper Told Most Often . . ."
—Movie tagline

 Box Office: $3.2 million

An imaginative speculation on the events leading up to the death of Hollywood producer Thomas Ince during a weekend cruise aboard media mogul William Randolph Hearst's yacht in November 1924, *The Cat's Meow* would appear to be ideal material for director Peter Bogdanovich. Perhaps more than any of his contemporaries, Bogdanovich has always maintained a fascination with Hollywood history and the mystique of old Hollywood. He began his career as a writer interviewing legendary directors and learning from them before making his own breakthrough as a director with *The Last Picture Show.* Moreover, as a personal friend of Orson Welles, Bogdanovich must have relished the thought of bringing his own version of Hearst to the screen, thus following, in some small way, in the steps of *Citizen Kane.*

Despite the seemingly perfect melding of director and subject in *The Cat's Meow,* however, the result is decidedly mixed. Adapted by Steven Peros from his own play, the film gives us an entertaining peek into the lives of the rich and powerful, and the period details, from the art direction to the costumes, are beautiful. But there is also a curious remoteness to the whole production, whose mechanical plot turns and sometimes lackluster direction prevent us from getting truly involved with many of the characters.

The truth about the death of Thomas Ince has never been ascertained and is shrouded in mystery. There are even conflicting reports about who was on Hearst's yacht, the *Oneida,* that fateful weekend, and only the doctor on ship was questioned afterwards. Official reports state that Ince died from heart failure due to indigestion, but Hollywood lore suggests that Hearst, mistaking Ince for Charlie Chaplin, with whom Hearst suspected his mistress, Marion Davies, of having an affair, shot him and then covered up the crime. This is the version presented in *The Cat's Meow,* which the film's narrator, novelist Elinor Glyn (Joanna Lumley), calls "the whisper told most often."

Edward Herrmann portrays Hearst as a towering man with jovial spirits that barely mask deep jealousy and paranoia. We first see him eavesdropping via hidden recording devices on his guests as they board his yacht. The cast of characters includes Ince (Cary Elwes), a legendary producer whose past triumphs cannot hide the fact that he has hit on hard times, and his mistress, Margaret Livingston (Claudia Harrison). His goal for the weekend is to get Hearst to agree to a merger of their interests that will keep him afloat. Also on board is Charlie Chaplin (Eddie Izzard), who has recently impregnated his 16-year-old leading lady, Lita Grey, and is on the brink of imminent scandal. He is smitten by Hearst's young mistress, Marion Davies (Kirsten Dunst), and trying to make her his own. Rounding out the key players is Louella Parsons (Jennifer Tilly), a movie reviewer for Hearst; hoping to wield more power as a writer, she wants to persuade her boss to expand her role in his empire.

Out of the clash of these personalities spin the classic Hollywood elements of obsession, jealousy, and scandal. The story itself, however, is fairly thin, and the script feels bound to its stage roots, with characters being moved around the ship as if they were chess pieces. We are treated to scene after scene of famous people clashing with each other and jockeying for position in the Hollywood hierarchy, but there is little energy moving the story forward. Ince constantly pursues Hearst for his business deal, Charlie chases Marion, and Louella snoops in everyone's business. Ince is determined to get Hearst to commit to a merger that could secure his future but finds himself rebuffed every time he tries. Hearst even cavalierly calls him a cripple to his face—a jab at his diminished place in the Hollywood system. Meanwhile, Margaret desperately wants to be acknowledged as Tom's girl, even though he has a wife back home. Tom's preoccupation with his wheeling and dealing, however, prevents him from taking her seriously, and finally the frustrated Margaret begins blurting out to everyone that she is his lover.

The most compelling performance in the film belongs to Dunst. While Marion can be girlish and in thrall to larger-than-life men, Dunst lets us see the intelligence and authenticity at the core of Marion. She is no mere object but rather an intelligent woman torn between Hearst's obsessive devotion and Chaplin's constant flattery. She is forthright when she needs to be, telling Chaplin, for example, that he is more in love with himself than with her, but she never loses her essential charm.

Indeed, Dunst shows us a playful, silly side of Marion early in the film when the guests gather to watch recent rough footage of Marion in one of Hearst's movies, and, between takes of the serious costume drama, she clowns around on the set and mugs for the camera. Her behavior confirms Chaplin's words to Hearst that Marion would excel in comedies, but Hearst, bristling at the idea of people laughing at her, insists on her acting in serious films. And yet, as the audience aboard ship enjoys Marion's comic bits, Chaplin gives a knowing, I-told-you-so look at Hearst, as if confirming that he understands Marion better than Hearst does. It is a subtle moment that speaks volumes about their rivalry over Marion's future and the way Chaplin, the true genius, can see in Marion the talent that Hearst cannot.

Charlie does his best to win Marion, who knows that he is a notorious womanizer and is reluctant to surrender to him, even though she is clearly drawn to his rakish charm. While the heavyset Izzard looks nothing like the real-life Chaplin, Izzard gives us a fresh take on this very familiar screen legend by focusing on his inner turmoil. He can be sardonic and sure of himself when he is the center of everyone's attention, yet he seems like a helpless suitor when he is attempting to woo Marion. Given his reputation with the women, however, it is never clear how much Marion really means to him. Is she one more potential conquest, or does he really want to run away with her? Marion does her best to resist him but is gradually drawn to him, first in a game of charades that takes on a sexual connotation and then later in a fight during which passions heat up and she finally gives in to him.

As time goes on, Ince gets more and more desperate and, seeing the closeness between Charlie and Marion, tries to use it to his advantage. He tells Hearst that his proposed merger would be beneficial because he could keep an eye on Marion for him in Hollywood. Ince finds a discarded love letter Charlie wrote to Marion (but never gave her) and shows it to Hearst, which feels like an easy theatrical gimmick that, along with a news story suggesting an intimacy between Charlie and Marion, ultimately pushes Hearst over the edge.

Soon the panicked Hearst is scurrying around the ship like a madman and searching Charlie's room, where he finds a brooch he recently gave Marion, which confirms that Charlie and Marion have indeed been together. Hearst also finds in Marion's room a love note and gift that Marion intended for him but that he thinks is meant for Charlie. Finally mistaking Tom for Charlie, he shoots Tom in the back of the head, where the bullet remains lodged. The ship's doctor treats Tom, but he obviously needs urgent care, and the ship docks in San Diego, where the comatose Tom is rushed off the yacht.

Marion reassures Hearst of her love for him, something that the powerful magnate seems to need to keep going and finally stays with him instead of fleeing with Charlie. An emotionally insecure yet cunning man, Hearst cries in Marion's arms one minute but then is figuring out how to cover his crime the next. He is ruthless in the way he creates a story

about ulcers sending Tom off the ship and getting everyone onboard to acquiesce to silence regarding Tom's mysterious departure. While Hearst sometimes comes close to acting more like a buffoon than a powerful newspaper tycoon, Herrmann does his best to make all the sides of Hearst believable.

Jennifer Tilly, on the other hand, plays Louella Parsons with the same squeaky voice and overly artificial expressions she often uses. Her performance grows tiresome quickly and is ultimately not very persuasive. Having witnessed the shooting, Louella suddenly becomes a formidable foe sweetly blackmailing Hearst into a lifetime contract for her silence, but it is not believable that this dingy woman-child could suddenly become shrewd enough to pull off such a deal.

The Cat's Meow succeeds more in evoking a world gone by—the opulence of old Hollywood and the secret shenanigans of some Hollywood luminaries—than in telling a dark, gripping Hollywood story. Bogdanovich's direction is often sluggish, and the tale does not build the dramatic momentum it needs for the ultimate tragedy to be truly shocking. Moreover, the cover-up, involving the sheer exercise of Hearst's influence through his media machine, feels like yet another tale of the rich and powerful getting away with murder and not the dark revelation it should be.

Perhaps the biggest disappointment is that the film, while workmanlike in laying out all the conflicts among the players, is not clear on what it all means. Glyn's voice-over narration at the end tries to raise the theme to a commentary on these supposedly frivolous people, who are constantly seen dancing the Charleston so they do not have to take a hard look at themselves. But this idea feels like a tacked-on commentary, not an insight that has grown out of the drama. *The Cat's Meow* is an entertaining spin on infamous Hollywood lore but ultimately does not carry the dramatic weight or social significance it needs to serve as a metaphor critiquing this whole group of people.

—*Peter N. Chumo II*

CREDITS

William Randolph Hearst: Edward Herrmann
Marion Davies: Kirsten Dunst
Thomas Ince: Cary Elwes
Charlie Chaplin: Eddie Izzard
Elinor Glyn: Joanna Lumley
Louella Parsons: Jennifer Tilly
George Thomas: Victor Slezak
Dr. Goodman: James Laurenson
Joseph Willicombe: Ronan Vibert
Margaret Livingston: Claudia Harrison

Origin: Great Britain, Germany
Released: 2001
Production: Julie Baines, Kim Bieber, Carol Lewis, Dieter Meyer; Dan Films, CP Medien; released by Lion's Gate Films
Directed by: Peter Bogdanovich
Written by: Steven Peros
Cinematography by: Bruno Delbonnel
Sound: Paul Oberle
Editing: Edward Norris
Art Direction: Christian Eisele
Costumes: Caroline De Vivaise
Production Design: Jean-Vincent Puzos
MPAA rating: PG-13
Running time: 112 minutes

REVIEWS

Boxoffice. December, 2001, p. 57.
Chicago Sun-Times Online. April 26, 2002.
Entertainment Weekly. April 19, 2002, p. 47.
Hollywood Reporter. December 4, 2001, p. 18.
Los Angeles Times Online. April 12, 2002.
New York Times Online. April 12, 2002.
USA Today Online. April 12, 2002.
Variety. July 13, 2001, p. 47.
Washington Post. May 3, 2002, p. WE43.

TRIVIA

Kirsten Dunst was 19 when she filmed her role; Marion Davies was actually 27 in 1924.

Changing Lanes

One wrong turn deserves another.
—Movie tagline

Box Office: $66.8 million

There is no doubt that Hollywood is capable of putting out a thriller about road rage in which the parties involved exact retribution through a series of increasingly gory and violent confrontations complete with frenzied car chases, deafening fireball explosions, and numerous bullets and body parts flying through the air. That would be a much easier movie to make than *Changing Lanes,* an excellent, gripping, complex, thoughtful and thought-provoking film which, while unquestionably full of rage, thankfully chooses to take a much different road. The film is driven by an always intriguing character study of two men who have little in common at first glance, but when both are at a loss for what to do next, we see that they are equally capable of resorting to poor and inflammatory choices which, in the end, make them as much in disbelief at their own behavior as that of the other man.

Changing Lanes is impressive in its storytelling from the start, beginning with parallel scenes that effectively sketch these two main characters for us. Both of the film's main characters are on vitally important missions when their cars accidentally clip each other while vying for the same lane on New York City's FDR Parkway. First there is Doyle Gipson (flawless Samuel L. Jackson), an average-Joe insurance salesman and loving father who has apparently been waging a successful battle with the bottle. We see him speaking with other recovering alcoholics at an A.A. meeting, exuberantly optimistic about the future. Although his wife Valerie (Kim Staunton) has asked for a separation and plans to move all the way to the West Coast with their two young sons, Doyle has gone to great pains to purchase another home in New York City that he hopes will keep them all closer together, facilitating visitation and a desired reconciliation with his wife. He heads to the courthouse, adding to his carefully crafted notes to effectively plead his case at a custody hearing.

Then there is Gavin Banek (impressive Ben Affleck), a young hotshot attorney for a prestigious Wall Street law firm who we see speaking at a much glitzier gathering than Doyle's, singing the praises of the late philanthropist Simon Dunne, a former client. Dunne's granddaughter Mina (Jennifer Dundas Lowe) is clearly seething, which Gavin cannot fathom and which Stephen Delano (Oscar-winning director Sydney Pollack), his father-in-law and head of the firm, tells him to ignore. Gavin, on orders from his boss, had taken the questionable step of getting elderly Mr. Dunne to sign over control of his foundation's finances to Delano and his partner shortly before his death, and Mina smells a rat. So Gavin, talking on his cell phone and running late, is also racing to the courthouse with papers to support his position.

It is a minor traffic accident they get into, which appears incapable of causing either man much grief. However, when Doyle tries to deal with the situation properly and exchange information, Gavin breezily brushes him off with an offer of a blank check, and hurries back into his car. Doyle, his own vehicle disabled, asks for a ride, but only gets a cheerful but dismissive "Better luck next time!" as Gavin leaves him stranded. We get a telling shot of Doyle standing alone as traffic streams around him, his world having come to a sudden, unexpected halt while everyone else seems to be going about their merry way. It even starts to rain on the poor guy. When he finally gets to the courthouse, he is beside himself to learn that the hearing has gone ahead without him, his wife and kids are now free to move away, and the judge makes some undeservedly-harsh, dismissive comments.

Gavin's best-laid plans have also gone awry, as he walks in with great confidence but without the all-important power of appointment Dunne had signed, and realizes he must have left it with Doyle amidst the confusion and haste. In discussing his situation with his mistress, Michelle (Toni Collette, also good in this year's *About a Boy*), Gavin blames Doyle instead of his own hastiness, baffled by the man's appeal to do things by the book instead of just gratefully accepting the blank check. He happens upon Doyle and apologizes for his uncharacteristic bad behavior, offers a brand new car, and asks for the file back. Doyle, feeling dehumanized and disgusted, is not in any mood to let bygones be bygones. Grabbing Gavin by the lapel, he explosively asserts that all he needs or wants is a restoration of the crucial minutes Gavin's abandonment on the highway cost him, which in turn cost him a great deal more. Informed that Doyle threw the file away, Gavin now also walks hunched through the rain, not knowing what to do next.

The complexity of characterization in *Changing Lanes* is unusual and fascinating. We see alternating flickers of the best and worst in both men. Even though Gavin seems to ridicule Doyle's actions, we also see him lost in thought and questioning his own. It seems promising when Doyle retrieves the file Gavin desperately needs from the trash, but then he uses the first page to send an inflammatory fax to Gavin. He finally decides to do the right thing and send the whole file back, but by then Gavin, uneasy about the extremes he is going to but determined to gain the upper hand, has sought out a highly-recommended hacker (Dylan Baker) who ruins Doyle's credit and throws him into bankruptcy. Doyle sinisterly removes the bolts from a wheel on Gavin's car, causing what could have been a fatal crash, and yet he is also capable of a touching moment with Valerie soon after. Gavin in turn puts a cruel plan into motion that ends with Doyle being dragged out of his children's school in handcuffs, and the lawyer feels like a big man until the sight of Doyle's distraught sons clearly deflates him.

Even the supporting characters are complex and multi-layered. Stephen turns out to indeed be pocketing money he really should not be from Dunne's foundation, but justifies himself by saying that, overall, he does more good than harm. He points out that the business that gave Simon Dunne the millions now helping so many people was not without its share of blemishes. Michelle sounds high-minded, questioning Gavin's ethics since joining the firm, and yet she is the one who recommends the hacker. Gavin's wife Cynthia (Amanda Peet), who reveals that she knows about Gavin's infidelity, pushes him to illegally submit a forged power of appointment before the court's deadline as her father has requested, saying that she accepts his playing fast and loose with the truth as the necessary price she pays to be the well-to-do wife of a prominent attorney.

As the war of wills winds down, Gavin and Doyle show signs of wising up. Valerie gives Doyle a tongue-lashing in jail about his being "addicted to chaos" and accepting responsibility for his own actions, and he realizes that she is right. His own bad choices put him in that cell. Meanwhile, Gavin can only chuckles to himself at the idealism of a young attorney who speaks of the innate goodness of people and the rule of law as a buffer against vendetta, violence and chaos which keeps us civilized. When Gavin and Doyle meet again, equally exhausted and stunned by what they have let themselves become, they apologize, and Doyle returns the file. Both would clearly like to forget the day ever happened, but they are forever changed, now better people, or at least better able to see their way forward. It has been an eye-opening ride up a steep learning curve for both. The film's ending, in which Gavin tries to pay for his sins by getting Valerie to stick around and give Doyle another chance seemed like a tacked-on happy ending to some, but it comes as a welcome, reassuring note of healing after all the destructiveness that went before.

Filmed on a budget of $45 million, *Changing Lanes* grossed $66.79 million at the boxoffice. It was quite a departure for director Roger Michell, previously best known for his 1999 romantic comedy *Notting Hill*. The idea for the screenplay came from a production assistant named Chap Taylor, who was given the chance to write a script that was then reworked by veteran scribe Michael Tolkin. Both Affleck and Jackson are well-cast, and do some of their best work to date. Affleck ventures into difficult emotional territory far more successfully than some might have expected. By film's end, when Gavin lays the law down to his father-in-law and wife about how things are going to be from now on, Affleck is believable as a changed man—and his own man—who is committed to putting some hard-gained new insights into practice. Jackson shows off his immense skill and a great emotional range, running the gamut from tenderness with his children, to glee upon purchasing the house, to bewilderment at the break-up of his family, and then to smoldering anger turning to intense, roaring rage as the day's testosterone level contest escalates The two are admirably supported, especially by Pollack, Collette, Peet, Staunton, and William Hurt as Gavin's A.A. sponsor, who clearly recognizes the man's penchant for excess before he does.

There is no simplistic good guy versus bad guy battle in *Changing Lanes,* but an exploration of the mixture of good and evil in all of us. We are all capable of making reasonable, moral, ethical choices, but sometimes, especially when pushed to the brink and with emotions running high, we can make some less attractive, ill-advised ones. Perhaps they would not be as extreme as what these two characters stoop to, but the potential to veer into the wrong lane in life is always there.

—David L. Boxerbaum

CREDITS

Gavin Banek: Ben Affleck
Doyle Gipson: Samuel L. Jackson
Michelle: Toni Collette
Delano: Sydney Pollack
Sponsor: William Hurt
Cynthia Banek: Amanda Peet
Walter Arnell: Richard Jenkins
Valerie Gipson: Kim Staunton
Carlyle: John Benjamin Hickey
Mina Dunne: Jennifer (Jennie) Dundas Lowe
Finch: Dylan Baker
Ron Cabot: Matt Malloy

Origin: USA
Released: 2002
Production: Scott Rudin; released by Paramount Pictures
Directed by: Roger Michell
Written by: Michael Tolkin, Chap Taylor
Cinematography by: Salvatore Totino
Music by: David Arnold
Sound: Danny Michael
Editing: Christopher Tellefsen
Art Direction: Steven Graham
Costumes: Ann Roth
Production Design: Kristi Zea
MPAA rating: R
Running time: 98 minutes

REVIEWS

Chicago Sun-Times Online. April 12, 2002.
Entertainment Weekly. April 19, 2002, p. 44.
Los Angeles Times Online. April 12, 2002.
New York Times Online. April 12, 2002.
People. April 22, 2002, p. 35.
Rolling Stone. May 9, 2002, p. 79.
USA Today Online. April 12, 2002.
Variety. April 8, 2002, p. 29.
Washington Post. April 12, 2002, p. WE37.

QUOTES

AA sponsor (William Hurt) to Doyle Gipson (Samuel L. Jackson): "Booze isn't really your drug of choice. You're addicted to chaos."

TRIVIA

The film is set during a 36-hour period around Good Friday but it was filmed from December through early March and shooting was adjusted so no snow would appear on screen.

Charlotte Gray

The story of an ordinary woman in an extraordinary time.
—Movie tagline

Australian director Gillian Armstrong, who burst on the international scene with the feminist historical drama *My Brilliant Career* in 1977 and later directed *Little Women* in 1994, specializes in adaptations of historical novels. But she hadn't directed anything since *Oscar and Lucinda* in 1997 when she made *Charlotte Gray*. Based on a best-selling novel by Stephen Faulks about an Scottish woman who goes underground to help the French Resistance in World War II, it seemed like a good bet for Armstrong, especially when Cate Blanchett was cast in the starring role. The film, however, experienced many delays in production and release scheduling, and it finally was dumped on the U.S. market early in 2002 with little fanfare. It never even was shown in many cities.

Blanchett is a pro, one of the most talented and versatile actresses around, and she has shown her ability for drama (*The Gift* and her scene-stealing role in *The Talented Mr. Ripley*), historical roles (*Elizabeth*), and even comedy (*Bandits*). She starred in *Oscar and Lucinda*. From the start of *Charlotte Gray*, it's clear how much Armstrong loves Blanchett's porcelain, old-fashioned face. Her camera adores it, dwells on it, and comes back to it time and again when it's unclear how to proceed—and unfortunately, there are many such moments in this muddled drama.

It's as if Armstrong is straining to make Blanchett and her character encapsulate an era and a sentiment—just as Judy Davis did in *My Brilliant Career*. At the start, Blanchett is allowed an opening narration (though she never narrates again), where she says, "Looking back, it all seemed so simple. . . . Good must triumph over evil." The problem is that the story is not simple, nor clear, despite the lines of morality drawn by the war.

Charlotte Gray is a spunky woman, living in London though raised in Scotland, who is eager to do something to aid in the war effort against the Nazis. Her knowledge of French, gained when her World War I-veteran father took her to France to visit sites from that war, is helpful to the Allies. As the film opens, Charlotte has a whirlwind love affair with a Royal Air Force flyer named Peter (Rupert

Penry-Jones). Armstrong truncates the romance to a couple of pregnant glances—in one frame the two, who have barely met, are staring at each other across a balcony at the party, and the next they are naked in bed. True, this is wartime, but it's almost as if the director finds the preliminaries uninteresting. It's also unnerving how the pair instantly behave as if they were long-time lovers. The scenes play like an editor got out of hand, but they aren't the only such passages in the film.

Soon, Peter flies off the war and Charlotte learns that he has been shot down in France. This development stiffens her resolve to become an agent working with the French Resistance. After a few scenes in which Charlotte goes through training—alternating obstacle courses and word-association tests, for no apparent reason—she is sent on her mission. She is to be a courier, and her tasks won't be clear, even to her. She is told that "Charlotte Gray is dead" as long as she is in France, and she assumes a new identity—that of a Parisian woman named Dominique. Blanchett's hair goes from blonde to black, and she is parachuted into a field outside a village in the south of France, where she is welcomed by members of the Resistance, first and foremost a handsome young man named Julien (Billy Crudup). Julien starts right off by saying he is a Communist and that after the war they will be at odds, but the level-headed Charlotte advises that they win the war first.

Up to this point Armstrong's painstaking historic authenticity—and some wonderfully telling shots—have primed the audience to expect a substantial and serious wartime drama. Then, after much has been made about Charlotte's ability to speak France, the movie arrives in France and . . . everyone speaks English! The dread of subtitles is so strong that it instantly capsizes the film's verisimilitude. It is clear now that we have a Hollywood-style picture in which everyone in France speaks English with a French accent. Expectations for the effort immediately lower—and for good reason.

Charlotte has been told that this first mission is merely a test, and that she will shortly return. But everything goes wrong. She is supposed to deliver a package to a contact in a cafe; as soon as she does, however, the police arrive, confiscate the package, and arrest the woman, and she goes to her death. Oddly, they don't even bother to ask Charlotte more than one question.

Alarmed, Charlotte returns to Julien, who says she must assume a new identity—that of a servant on his father's country estate. Julien's father, Levade (Michael Gambon), is a grumpy farmer whose home serves as a way station for Resistance efforts. Julien is using the house to hide two Jewish boys whose parents have been taken away by the Nazis.

Eventually, Charlotte meets her English contact, who relays orders to her concerning a new air drop in the field where she recently parachuted in. It turns out to be a Nazi ambush: all the local members of the Resistance, except Julien, go to the field with flashlights to bring in the plane and they are gunned down. Julien blames Charlotte, and Charlotte wonders if she has been set up by a double agent, but the mystery is never resolved.

In fact, nothing is resolved. The Nazis close in on Julien's father and the two Jewish boys, and Charlotte becomes enmeshed in a relationship with a local schoolteacher, who threatens to turn her in unless she has sex with him. She eventually begins an affair with Julien, but it blows hot and cold with the fortunes of war.

The main problem with *Charlotte Gray* is that the plot lacks overall tension. It never becomes clear what Charlotte's purpose or mission is, or even whether she is being unwittingly used by the enemy. Plot twists and turns march along, one after another, in pedestrian fashion, while the overall scheme of things remains murky and unresolved.

Blanchett is mesmerizing, as always, but her character's dilemmas do not add up to any consistent personality crisis or challenge. Charlotte seems to have plenty of courage and she is determined and heartfelt, but she is a woman in a world without markings. Worst of all, it's not clear whether she has succeeded or failed, and if she has failed, whether it was because of her own shortcomings. Blanchett's romances with Peter and Julien are rather short-circuited by Armstrong's unwillingness to make the picture too romantic. Chemistry is lacking, and in the end it is a matter of indifference which of the two men she chooses.

As a novel, *Charlotte Gray* was more of a character study and an invocation of a period in history than an action story. As a film, there is not enough action or character. Scenes seem strung together to no good end, and in the fog of war all bearings are lost. Apparently Armstrong's purpose is to show that even behind the lines, war is a muddle, a confusing and frustrating mess, but such a goal does not a compelling movie make.

—*Michael Betzold*

CREDITS

Charlotte Gray: Cate Blanchett
Julien Levade: Billy Crudup
Levade: Michael Gambon
Peter Gregory: Rupert Penry-Jones
Renech: Anton Lesser
Richard Cannerley: James Fleet
Mirabel: Ron Cook
Pichon: Jack Shepherd
Mr. Jackson: Nicholas Farrell
Francoise: Helen McCrory
Daisy: Abigail Cruttenden
Auguste: Charlie Condou

Jean-Paul: David Birkin

Origin: Great Britain, Australia
Released: 2001
Production: Sarah Curtis, Douglas Rae; FilmFour, Senator Film Entertainment, Ecosse Films, Pod Film; released by Warner Bros.
Directed by: Gillian Armstrong
Written by: Jeremy Brock
Cinematography by: Dion Beebe
Music by: Stephen Warbeck
Sound: Clive Winter
Editing: Nicholas Beauman
Art Direction: Tatiana Lund, Sue Whitaker
Costumes: Janty Yates
Production Design: Joseph Bennett
MPAA rating: PG-13
Running time: 118 minutes

REVIEWS

Boxoffice. March, 2002, p. 62.
Chicago Sun-Times Online. January 11, 2002.
Entertainment Weekly. January 18, 2002, p. 55.
Los Angeles Times Online. December 28, 2001.
New York Times Online. November 4, 2001.
New York Times Online. December 28, 2001.
People. January 21, 2002, p. 29.
Sight and Sound. March, 2002, p. 10.
USA Today Online. December 28, 2001.
Variety. December 17, 2001, p. 37.
Washington Post. January 11, 2002, p. WE38.

QUOTES

Peter (Rupert Penry-Jones): "War makes us into people we didn't know we were."

TRIVIA

Director Gillian Armstrong and actress Cate Blanchett also worked together on 1997's *Oscar and Lucinda*.

The Chateau

Director Jesse Peretz (*First Love, Last Rites*) used to be a bass player in the 1990s band The Lemonheads. The band started out being an "alternative" band, to use the lingo of the day, but the Lemonheads' music was so melodic, accessible and peppy-sounding that the band eventually gained widespread mainstream popularity. It doesn't seem very likely that that fate will be shared by his film, *The Chateau.*

The thing that's most in the way of the film becoming a blockbuster is the way it was shot. Like Gary Winick's *Tadpole* and Steven Soderberg's *Full Frontal, The Chateau* was shot on digital video. When it's blown up to 35 mm and put up on a widescreen, the footage is grainy and has a faded tone that makes it look like an old film from the 1970's. Several reviewers speculated that the look of the film was inspired by the aesthetic principles of Denmark's Dogma 95 filmmaking movement. The artistic movement values what's happening on the screen over how it appears on the screen. It's a low-tech, amateur-looking aesthetic that involves handheld cameras, with no special effects, unenhanced sound, and little attention paid to lighting and set design.

With less attention (and less money) being spent on fancy film techniques and post-production, it seems like it lessened the pressure on everyone involved in the film. Coupled with the fact that the actors were allowed to improvise their roles, *The Chateau,* has a markedly loose, relaxed feel. The off-kilter rhythms don't make for the usual Hollywood screenplay, with its regimented march through story beats to the climatic third act, and it's a nice change of pace. Sometimes scenes last a bit too long or conversations don't flow in an orderly matter and that's what's good about the film. The conversations sound like real conversations between real people.

As Dave Kehr of the *New York Times* pointed out, the "informal approach puts the actors' contributions in the foreground, if only because so little coherent emotion is expressed by the neglected formal elements of framing, cutting and lighting." The actor who makes best use of this forum is Paul Rudd, who also showed some excellent comedic skills in the little-seen *Wet Hot American Summer.* He takes advantage of the offbeat rhythms and shows himself to be a master of the awkward social moment. His character, Graham Granville, is constantly saying too much, saying the wrong thing, or saying the right thing at the wrong time.

When the film opens, Graham and his adopted brother, Allen Granville (Romany Malco, the hip-hop artist turned actor), are riding a train, on their way to France to claim a chateau that they've inherited from a great uncle, the Count Jacques de Granville, who they never knew. Things are supposed to be funny about the Allen character that aren't:

he is an African-American, yet he is a white man's brother; and, for some unknown reason, he insists upon being called Rex.

Graham, a perpetual student from Lawrence, Kansas, is thrilled by the prospect of the adventure. He's the kind of guy who would probably consider himself "a student of life." He's a sweet fellow with a zest for life who's also overly self-conscious. He voraciously reads books like *The Celestine Prophecy* and calls his therapist frequently to rehash his every move. His brother Rex is less excited by the trip, particularly because it means he will have to spend a lot of time with Graham. Rex lives in Los Angeles and makes his living selling sexual enhancement devices over the Internet. Rex is a bit of a chameleon. When he's on the phone with clients, he adopts a formal, "white" voice because he thinks people don't want to be buying sexual products "from a brother." With others, he likes to play up the "brother" act, even though he and Graham shared an uneventful childhood on the not-exactly mean streets of Lawrence.

When the guys get to their chateau, they are excited to see their castle, with its 15 bedrooms and live-in servants. They meet the butler, Jean (Didier Flamand), the cook, Sabine (Maria Verdi), and the groundskeeper, Pierre (Philippe Nahon), but are most interested in the young, attractively sad-eyed maid, Isabelle (Sylvie Testud), who has a young son without an apparent father. The servants are surprised and not particularly happy to see the Granvilles but they take them in anyway.

Rex and Graham soon find out that the chateau is in terrible disrepair and deeply in debt. They decide—Rex happily and Graham so so—that they are going to have to sell the chateau at once. They hire a real estate agent, insisting that she sell it in a week, plus make sure that the buyer keeps all the servants on for the rest of their lives. A few buyers comes through, including a obnoxious new-money young hotshot (Donal Logue), while the servants try to dissuade them. There's some sort of insurance scam involved or something. Meanwhile, Rex and Graham are competing for the attentions of Isabelle, with varying degrees of success.

Not a lot happens, but that's not the point—*The Chateau* is more a study of characters and the cultural differences between the French and Americans. Graham and Rex are continually proving themselves to be boorish Americans. Rex treats the servants poorly, ordering them around and demanding that they rush to his side to attend to his needs. Graham tries to relate to everyone and attempts to speak French but is continually showing his ignorance. At a formal dinner in the chateau, he looks at his plate and announces pleasantly "Je t'aime, potate" or "I love you, potato." (For audience members who don't speak French, there are subtitles so that all of Graham's manglings of the language can be easily understood.)

The highlight of the film is watching Graham navigate the awkward social moments that he constantly finds himself involved in. What's funny about Rudd's performance is that he not only lets himself look stupid and awkward, he seems to relish it, and he somehow shares his sense of fun with the audience. When Graham's talking about all the servants yelling at each other in French, he earnestly says, "It's like one of those Fellini movies." You can tell that Graham is secretly pleased with his knowledge of film and also has no idea that Fellini was not French. It's fun to watch him as he tries to impress Isabelle with his soulfulness and ends up talking too much and trying to impress her with his depth by discussing books he's read like, *All I Need to Know I Learned in Kindergarten.*

Critics were not in agreement over whether the experimental style of *The Chateau* worked or not. Steven Rea of the *Philadelphia Inquirer* called the film "a goofy combination of screwball farce and Dogma-style verite grit and gloom." Kehr of the *New York Times* wrote that that Peretz's approach "succeeds when the performers are particularly vibrant and inventive and their characters are colorful and complex enough to sustain interest on their own. That's not entirely the case with *The Chateau*, which flattens occasionally into drawn-out actors' exercises—blaring demonstrations of drunken rage or doe-eyed expressions of wistful yearning." Merle Bertrand of *Film Threat* called the film "an unlikely but winning farce," and wrote, "Once the viewer accepts the huge leaps of faith required in the film's premise, it's a lot of fun to strap oneself in and enjoy this goofy ride." Kevin Thomas of the *Los Angeles Times* wrote that director Peretz "comes up with enough fresh twists to the ugly American vs. surly French confrontation to sustain this delightfully bittersweet culture-clash comedy."

—Jill Hamilton

CREDITS

Graham: Paul Rudd
Allen/Rex: Romany Malco
Isabelle: Sylvie Testud
Jean: Didier Flamand
Pierre: Philippe Nahon
Sabine: Maria Verdi
Real Estate Agent: Nathalie Jouen
Sonny: Donal Logue

Origin: USA
Language: English, French
Released: 2001
Production: Scott Macaulay, Robin O'Hara; Forensic Films, Crossroads Films; released by IFC Films
Directed by: Jesse Peretz

Written by: Jesse Peretz, Thomas Bidegain
Cinematography by: Tom Richmond
Music by: Nathan Larson, Patrik Bartosch, Nina Persson
Sound: Noah Vivekanand Timan
Editing: James Lyons, Steve Hamilton
Costumes: Nathalie de Roscoat
Production Design: Christian Marti
MPAA rating: R
Running time: 92 minutes

 REVIEWS

Boxoffice. November, 2001, p. 140.
Entertainment Weekly. August 16, 2002, p. 48.
Los Angeles Times Online. August 23, 2002.
New York Times Online. August 9, 2002.
San Francisco Chronicle. September 6, 2002, p. D5.
Seattle Post-Intelligencer Online. September 6, 2002.
Variety. March 26, 2001, p. 49.

Chelsea Walls

a million stories tall
—Movie tagline

Besides being a busy actor in recent years, Ethan Hawke has written novels (1996's *The Hottest State* and 2002's *Ash Wednesday*) and directed a music video, "Stray," for Lisa Loeb, which starred his own cat. Hawke has been a leading member of the artistic and filmmaking community in Austin, Texas, and has appeared in several of director Richard Linklater's films, including *Before Sunrise, Waking Life,* and *Tape.* Besides these roles in Linklater's offbeat movies—often exploring the sensitive side of manhood—Hawke has also taken more standard roles in mainstream movies such as *Training Day, Gattaca,* and *Quiz Show.*

"I think most people are good at more things than the world gives them the opportunity to do," Hawke has said. It's no surprise, given this attitude and his penchant for soul-searching roles, that Hawke wanted to try his hand at directing. And he brought his typically artistic, visionary, and unconventional sensitivities to *Chelsea Walls,* a quirky, free-form drama about the denizens of Manhattan's once-famous Hotel Chelsea.

The film is based on a play of the same name by Nicole Burdette, an actress who has had small roles in a half-dozen or so films, including *A River Runs Through It, Goodfellas,* and *Search and Destroy.* Burdette adapted her own play for the screen, and it's her first screenwriting credit.

The Hotel Chelsea was famous in the past for being a residence and hangout for Bohemian artists, including Sarah Bernhardt, Dylan Thomas, Thomas Wolfe, and O. Henry. Writers, musicians, poets, actors, and hangers-on bequeathed the Chelsea a legacy of ghostly muses. But in recent years the on-the-downgrade hotel has attracted more failures and wanna-bes, more drug addicts and prostitutes, than successful artists.

Chelsea Walls presents a crowded cast of a couple dozen characters, many of whom are struggling with their own muses and trying, by living at the hotel, to tap into the magic of its luminaries of the past. The characters include a middle-age novelist, Bud (Kris Kristofferson); two poets, Audrey (Rosario Dawson) and Grace (Hawke's wife Uma Thurman); a songwriter-singer-guitarist from Minnesota, Terry (Robert Sean Leonard), who may or may not be the next Bob Dylan; and the real-life jazz singer Jimmy Scott. Most of the rest of the characters are either lovers, would-be lovers, or rejected lovers of these artists, and there are several other people who roles are so truncated and undeveloped that their purpose is not clear.

From the beginning of the film it is clear that Hawke intends to proceed in an unconventional manner. Through an extended opening credits sequence, he introduces Terry and his wacky friend Ross (Steve Zahn) as they drive in from Minnesota and gives the hotel's history and reputation through shots of some historical markers and the conversation of a couple of police officers who are searching rooms for drugs. Meanwhile a smattering of traffic noises, background conversations, and a free-form musical score by Jeff Tweedy of the rock band Wilco make up the cacophonic auditory ambience.

Hawke and cinematographers Tom Richmond and Richard Rutowski use grainy digital video, tinted lens, stop-motion framing, and other currently popular "artsy" techniques to move the film along in herky-jerky, somewhat confusing fashion. They rely too much on extreme close-ups of the actors. At one point the camera pans along Kristofferson's arm from hand holding drink to shoulder and face, and the mass of flesh looks like an alien monster has intruded in the film. The movie is also packed with shots of characters at the edges of the frame, or taking off-screen and then moving into frame, and other similar efforts at making the production edgy.

Chelsea Walls is accompanied by a lot of music that sounds improvisational, and the film itself is more like jazz than moviemaking. It has jazz's free-floating structure, eschewing logical connections, juxtaposing discordant sounds and images. Occasionally Hawke makes this work well, with beautifully composed images that set the characters in a hotel window or some other framework that evokes a struggle for identity or a lonely pursuit of artistic integrity. Well composed and executed is a sequence in which Audrey's gritty love poem to her young lover Val (Mark Webber, who looks much too young and bland to be a believable romantic interest for Rosario Dawson) is read by both the poet and the recipient. None of this, however, is anything that hasn't been done in countless music videos or low-budget independent films.

The pursuit of artistic touches for their own sakes, devoid of characterization, doesn't make for much of a movie. Thus *Chelsea Walls* is more a series of tableaux and impressions than a real film. It's a lot of riffing with no dramatic structure at all. For a director to make a free-form film such as this interesting, he has to get the audience to care about its characters—and Hawke never succeeds in doing this. There are no arcs of action or character development, no dramatic tension, and no interesting interplay among the ensemble or characters. Relationships don't develop, characters don't change, and people don't play off each other in interesting ways.

Certainly, it is possible to make a slice-of-life movie that is entertaining and worthwhile, but even in that approach the characters have to be compelling. But in *Chelsea Walls* not only are there no plot and no tension, there is little or nothing to explain who these people are and why we should be interested in them. The dialogue is as offhand and indifferent as the filmmaking itself, or—in the case of Kristofferson's character—it is clumsily obvious. Kristofferson's Bud is an alcoholic with an unusual degree of self-awareness despite his foggy-headed approach to life. "I need unconditional love," he says over the phone to either his wife (Tuesday Weld) or his lover (Natasha Richardson), it's not clear which. Burdette doesn't know how to write dialogue that makes her characters come alive; they are iconic but not real. And absolutely nothing happens in the film to advance our understanding of them or their various artistic or romantic plights.

Like countless movies of the 1960s and like countless other first films by young directors, *Chelsea Walls* is about the struggle to find oneself—as an artist, as a human being, and as a person. Like countless other such movies, in *Chelsea Walls* these struggles are never presented in a straightforward fashion. The whole enterprise is gauzy, opaque, and frustrating. Hawke has enough experience and intelligence that he should know that there is more to making a movie than random scenes and thoughts of a passel of disconnected characters. This is a setting in search of an idea. Hawke doesn't even exploit the possibilities of the hotel's lost ghosts, except to use various voiceover readings of some of their poems.

Even purely philosophical movies like Linklater's *Waking Life* have structure and compelling characters; even all-talk, no action films like *My Dinner with Andre* have coherent plots. In *Chelsea Walls,* the self-indulgent artistic tricks would be tolerable if only there were people in the film with fully developed personalities. Instead, we get snatches and glimpses, and most of the characters are complete puzzles. We have no idea what motivates them, what their problems are, and what they are doing with their lives. The

exception is Kristofferson's Bud—he is looking for real love and meaning in his life—but even his work (writing novels) is unexplained. And Kristofferson reminds us why he had more success as a singer than an actor—he is wooden and flat.

There is plenty of acting talent here, including Thurman, but they have little to do except pose and speak meaningless, inconsequential lines. Some characters, like Vincent D'Onofrio's Frank, barely register at all.

Hawke clearly has some talent and potential as a filmmaker. But his debut is all style and no substance, and so it's hard to evaluate whether the stylistic flourishes might be capable of serving a real movie. If you're going to explore the depths of the soul and the vagaries of the artistic impulse, you'd better have some real souls and real human beings to present, rather than just an indifferent collection of underwritten characters rattling around an old hotel.

—*Michael Betzold*

CREDITS

Bud: Kris Kristofferson
Grace: Uma Thurman
Frank: Vincent D'Onofrio
Mary: Natasha Richardson
Greta: Tuesday Weld
Audrey: Rosario Dawson
Val: Mark Webber
Crutches: Kevin Corrigan
Terry: Robert Sean Leonard
Ross: Steve Zahn
Lynny: Frank Whaley

Origin: USA
Released: 2001
Production: Gary Winick, Alexis Alexanian, Christine Vachon, Pamela Koffler; Independent Film Channel (IFC), Killer Films, InDigEnt; released by Lion's Gate Films
Directed by: Ethan Hawke
Written by: Nicole Burdette
Cinematography by: Tom Richmond
Music by: Jeff Tweedy
Sound: Robert Lauren
Editing: Adriana Pacheco
Art Direction: Emmy Castlen
Costumes: Catherine Thomas
Production Design: Richard Butler
MPAA rating: R
Running time: 108 minutes

REVIEWS

Boxoffice. July, 2001, p. 89.
Entertainment Weekly. April 26, 2002, p. 119.
Los Angeles Times Online. April 19, 2002.
New York Times Online. April 19, 2002.
People. April 29, 2002, p. 38.
Variety. May 21, 2001, p. 20.

Cherish

She'd get out more. If it wasn't a felony.
—Movie tagline

 Box Office: $.2 million

Finn Taylor's *Cherish* is a strange hybrid of a movie. While it is primarily an odd character study of a young woman who lives her life through the old pop songs she listens to on the radio, it also incorporates elements of romance and even, at the end, a race-against-the-clock thriller. The overall result may feel a bit disjointed, as if Taylor were not quite sure what he wanted to do and allowed his screenplay to go off in too many directions. But the film becomes a small treat nonetheless, thanks largely to Robin Tunney's sharp and winning performance as the quirky misfit who learns, in the most improbable way, how to put her life together.

Tunney plays Zoe Adler, a Bay Area computer animator obsessed with the escape that pop songs offer from her solitary life. Her main joy comes from listening to an oldies station (featuring primarily '80s tunes, it seems) and calling in requests for her favorite songs. While she is an independent young woman who has just bought her own condo, she is also socially inept. She babbles uncontrollably to her icy, condescending boss, Brynn (Liz Phair), and, uncomfortable with her own solitude, she finds herself dating many men. As she tells her therapist (Lindsay Crouse), "I don't think I'd go out with so many if any one would call me back." To compound her problems, a mysterious stalker, unbeknownst to her, follows her around, snapping photos and fantasizing about her in sexy poses.

Zoe herself has a rich fantasy life, which currently revolves around a coworker named Andrew (Jason Priestley, gently spoofing his heartthrob persona from TV's *Beverly Hills 90210*). They hit it off at a party after work (to which Zoe was specifically not invited but which she crashes anyway), where they share their devotion to old pop songs. Later that night, however, Zoe's stalker carjacks her and runs her car into a policeman, leaving him dead. The stalker flees, and Zoe, who is legally drunk, is left behind the wheel

to take the rap. Her lawyer, Bell (Nora Dunn), tells her that she could get 25 years to life and decides to stall the trial until the publicity dies down. To avoid jail for Zoe in the meantime, Bell gets her in the bracelet program: Zoe is placed under house arrest in a huge apartment, and an electronic ankle bracelet monitors her movement; if she leaves the apartment, a modem will go off and alert the police.

Zoe does her best to deal with her loneliness. She gives herself a new hairstyle by ironing her hair, roller-skates around her apartment to the Human League's "Don't You Want Me" (which could be her anthem), and calls various acquaintances, none of whom seem interested in visiting her. As time progresses, however, her confinement has an odd effect. Instead of being isolated from others, she starts to form some attachments. Her most important relationship is with Bill (Tim Blake Nelson), the deputy who checks up on her and monitors her bracelet. When he discovers that she has tried to remove it, he places another restraint on her— she will receive 15 phone calls per day, each of which she must answer by the fifth ring. So begins a pattern of Zoe stretching her limits and the mild-mannered Bill constantly putting more restraints on her. And yet, even as Bill, a shy, nerdy, by-the-book kind of guy with a short-sleeved shirt and tie, tries to be a strong disciplinarian, he lets slip that he thinks she is attractive, which brightens her spirits and lets her see herself in a new way. Bill quickly becomes infatuated with her, and soon he is secretly staring at her picture at work, while the Turtles' "Happy Together" plays in the background. Pop standards express the longings and desires for many of the characters in this world—even the creepy stalker, who obsesses over "Private Eyes," the Hall and Oates hit about voyeurism.

Cherish does not have much of a plot; scenes of Zoe exploring the building's secret passageways and then racing to answer the police's calls by the fifth ring, for example, are not very suspenseful and do not advance the story. But the movie succeeds in tracing the way Zoe slowly comes out of her shell and alleviates the loneliness of the people around her. Zoe forms a bond with her neighbor downstairs, a gay, crippled dwarf named Max (Ricardo Gil), who offers to get her things from the store. (She has him get her a cordless phone to aid her mobility.) Yearning for some kind of human connection beyond the male prostitute he hires, Max finds an unlikely confidante in Zoe.

Zoe also draws Bill out of his dull routine, and, from their tense relationship, a tentative love story develops. In one encounter, she skates in circles around him instead of sitting still for bracelet inspection and revels in the way he puts up with her antics. Zoe broadens his taste in music when he goes out to a record store to buy a Noe Venable CD, something he never would have done without Zoe's influence. As time passes, Zoe becomes more attractive—her hair grows longer, and she sheds her awkward, self-conscious demeanor. She also becomes more confident as she jokes with Bill, gets him to rub her ankle in a sensual way when he checks on the bracelet, and even encourages him to take yoga to help him loosen up.

Max gets Zoe some extension cord that enables her to go outside, but she is eventually caught, and Bill is forced to punish her with a bracelet that is impossible to take off. But he does not lose his soft spot for her. Because she was recently robbed—a side plot that is never resolved—he promises to bring her his old radio to replace hers. But since he does not have one, he gets a new one and scuffs it up to make it look old. It is a sweet, tender, yet secretive declaration of love—a lonely man reaching out to the woman he likes but being careful to make the gesture look casual. While the film never really finds a comfortable rhythm as a narrative, it succeeds beautifully in these small, revelatory moments when two people connect in the most unexpected of ways. And of course it is fitting that it is through a radio, Zoe's special connection to the world at large, that Bill finds himself connecting to her. If *Cherish* had continued to develop the theme of the way pop music communicates to people and brings them together, it may have become a great film, but instead it revisits the stalker plot for a more conventional conclusion.

With her trial coming up in a week, Zoe insists yet again on her innocence, and, believing her story, Bill transfers her name to a work release list, which gives her nine hours of freedom to find the bad guy. This whole plot turn is ridiculous since Zoe had so many months to convince Bill or her lawyer that the carjacker is real instead of waiting until the last minute. By investigating old phone records, she easily obtains the bad guy's address, enters his apartment, and finds his ripped jacket from the night of the carjacking (apparently he has not noticed the tear) as well as his little shrine of her photos. When he returns home, she narrowly escapes but not without leaving her purse behind. Then, in a sequence seemingly inspired by *Run Lola Run,* Zoe races across San Francisco to get home in time for the dreaded six o'clock phone call from the police.

Finally, in a random, puzzling plot twist, Zoe is hit with the revelation that her stalker is the radio D.J. (Brad Hunt) to whom she makes all of her song requests. When he arrives at her apartment, he seems to imply that he has had his eye on her since college, but his back story is never spelled out, and we never know how much of a threat he poses to Zoe or what he even wants from her. (Surely an obsessed stalker could have found her all the months she was confined to her apartment.)

While the stalker subplot motivates Zoe's incarceration at the outset of the movie, it finally means very little at the end. She leads him on a chase back to his apartment, where she places the torn jacket in plain view as evidence for the police and takes a hammer to her ankle to remove the bracelet. We never see the gory details of what she has to do

to her leg, but it seems that she severs it. She leaves behind the intact bracelet so that the signal will lead Bill there. He and his partner arrive and catch the D.J., but Zoe is already gone. In the end, she has fled (presumably to start a new life) with a cast on her leg, but she sends Bill an e-mail to let him know that she is all right.

Cherish has its share of faults, to be sure, most notably an almost nonexistent plot for much of the film and then too much plot at the end that ties up, however implausibly, the thriller aspect of the story that was never very exciting to begin with. But the film succeeds, despite is narrative shortcomings, in the relationships between the characters, in the little ways Zoe forms some meaningful bonds with people who are, in many ways, outcasts and geeks like her. Robin Tunney is a delight in a performance that valiantly holds the disparate parts of the film together. Indeed, it is hard to imagine the film without her. Because she is eminently watchable and endearing, she carries the story through its less compelling passages and makes Zoe's transformation believable, even when the screenplay itself is sketchy. Had the story itself been stronger and the film reached a wider audience, it could have been a star-making performance.

—Peter N. Chumo II

CREDITS

Zoe Adler: Robin Tunney
Bill Daly: Tim Blake Nelson
Andrew: Jason Priestley
Bell: Nora Dunn
D.J.: Brad Hunt
Brynn: Liz Phair
Therapist: Lindsay Crouse
Joyce: Stephen Polk
Max: Ricardo Gil
Yung: Kenny Kwong

Origin: USA
Released: 2002
Production: Johnny Wow, Mark Burton; Concrete Pictures, WonderFilms; released by Fine Line Features
Directed by: Finn Taylor
Written by: Finn Taylor
Cinematography by: Barry Stone
Music by: Mark De Gil Antoni
Sound: David Nelson
Music Supervisor: Charles Maggio
Editing: Rick Lecompte
Art Direction: Guy M. Harrington
Costumes: Amy Brownson
Production Design: Don Day
MPAA rating: R

Running time: 99 minutes

REVIEWS

Boxoffice. April, 2002, p. 172.
Chicago Sun-Times Online. June 14, 2002.
Entertainment Weekly. June 21, 2002, p. 53.
Los Angeles Times Online. June 7, 2002.
New York Times Online. June 7, 2002.
Variety. January 21, 2002, p. 39.
Washington Post. June 14, 2002, p. WE42.

The Cherry Orchard

World cinema has become an international affair as is the case with Greek filmmaker Michael Cacoyannis' (*Zorba, the Greek*) cinematic adaptation of Russian author Anton Chekhov's *The Cherry Orchard*. Starring the illustrious English actors Charlotte Rampling and Alan Bates, along with a Russian and English cast, this adaptation shows us our small world. However, this stage to screen adaptation doesn't quite capture Chekhov's intended humor (Chekhov once called *The Cherry Orchard* almost farcical) and the dialogue so eloquently recited on a stage feels out of place in a cinematic medium. It comes across as pretentious at times, despite the Russian playwright's lack of pretension and warm qualities.

The Cherry Orchard begins in cramped quarters in a gray in dingy Paris where the dispossessed aristocrat Lyubov Ranyevskaya (Charlotte Rampling) languishes and worries about her debts. We learn that the matriarch left her family five years earlier after her son drowned and then she became involved with a philanderer who sucked her financially dry. Ranyevskaya's teenage daughter, Anya (Tushka Bergen) fetches her mother and takes her back to the family estate located on an infamous 65-acre cherry orchard.

The beauty of the cherry blossoms, fields of poppies, and the family estate doesn't hide the ugliness of the family's denial or their history as slave owners. The men, both the servants and the aristocrats, prove weak and ineffectual while the women are easily swayed by romantic overtures despite the troubles that stare the family in the face. The family has fallen into debt and their estate will be auctioned off at the end of the summer. A variety of subplots emerge involving a love triangle between boy-crazy servant Dunyasha (Melanie Lynskey), randy and lazy valet Yasha (Gerard Butler), and a clumsy butler. Anya falls in love with her former teacher and idealist Trofimov (Andrew Howard).

Meanwhile, peasant-turned-scheming-merchant, Lopahin (Owen Teale) warns Ranyevskaya and her imma-ture brother Gayev (Alan Bates) to cut down the orchard and build villas for the holiday crowd or their estate will be auctioned off. The siblings refuse to face up to the reality that haunts them and think they can save their estate through wishful thinking. Eventually, the family and their servants are dispossessed as Lopahin purchases the estate to the family's dismay. The former peasant gloats over his victory while alienating the family and destroying the friendship they once shared. Ironically, in hindsight his victory will also be the loss that haunts him.

Chekhov wrote *The Cherry Orchard* while he was suffering from tuberculosis, the illness that eventually took his life. Although Chekhov sympathizes with his characters, he also keeps an objective distance from them and anarchist sentiments are also expressed. The teacher, Trofimov, speaks of how the wealthy will reap their punishment and he refuses the money that the wealthy merchant Lopahin offers him. While Lopahin represents the peasant who manages to acquire wealth even if he lacks sophistication. He tells an admirer that he might have money, but he can't even understand the literature of the time. And in his own way, Lopahin represents the vulgarity of the servants and peasants.

Cacoyannis' screen adaptation fails to rise above Chekhov's subtleties. However, the performances make up for the lack of outward drama. Rampling's Ranyevskaya possesses a childlike wonder and a stubborn will as she clings to her ancestral estate. Bates's Gayev also portrays a boyish quality that finally succumbs to reality after losing his family estate. Katrin Cartlidge plays the forthright and taciturn lovelorn Varya with aplomb, while the supporting cast chips in strong performances.

Rampling described her connection to her character in an interview in *The Times*, "Lyubov really lives each emotion to the full. She doesn't censor herself. That comes absolutely natural to me. I love the way she's able to make a dance of her life . . ." The combination of Rampling's and Bates's performances along with pastoral photography that recalls Swedish director Bo Widerberg's *Elvira Madigan* prevent Cacoyannis' film from falling into mediocrity. As long as we have cinema, the classics will never die.

—*Patty-Lynne Herlevi*

CREDITS

Lyubov Ranevskaya: Charlotte Rampling
Gayev: Alan Bates
Varya: Katrin Cartlidge
Lopahin: Owen Teale
Feers: Michael Gough
Anya: Tushka Bergen
Yepihodov: Xander Berkeley

Yasha: Gerard Butler
Trofimov: Andrew Howard
Dunyasha: Melanie Lynskey
Pishchik: Ian McNeice
Charlotte Ivanovna: Frances De La Tour

Origin: France, Greece
Released: 1999
Production: Michael Cacoyannis; released by Kino International
Directed by: Michael Cacoyannis
Written by: Michael Cacoyannis
Cinematography by: Aris Stavrou
Sound: Alexander Bacharov, Costa Vavibopiotis
Editing: Michael Cacoyannis, Takis Hadzis
Production Design: Dionysis Fotopoulous
MPAA rating: Unrated
Running time: 137 minutes

REVIEWS

Boxoffice. May, 2002, p. 62.
Los Angeles Times Online. April 5, 2002.
New York Times Online. February 17, 2002.
New York Times Online. February 22, 2002.
Variety Online. September 27, 1999.
Village Voice Online. February 20, 2002.

QUOTES

Lopahin (Owen Teale) about the Ranevskaya family: "Never have I met people as irresponsible, impractical, and irrational."

Chicago

If you can't be famous. Be infamous.
—Movie tagline

With the right song and dance, you can get away with murder.
—Movie tagline

Murder, greed, corruption, violence, exploitation, adultery, treachery. And all that jazz.
—Movie tagline

In a city where everyone loves a legend, there's only room for one.
—Movie tagline

Chicago, perhaps the most astonishing movie of 2002, is a throwback to happier, escapist days, the days when Hollywood assured us that "movies were better than ever." Nothing like this has been seen on the movie screen since, well, *Cabaret* (1972), maybe, or *All That Jazz* (1980). In fact, the phrase "all that jazz" echoes throughout the film and recalls the genius director who mounted the stage musical *Chicago* in 1975, Bob Fosse. (*All That Jazz* was his autobiographical salute from a man whose manic energy and talent threatened to kill him. The "Good night, folks" Master of Ceremonies from *Chicago* delivers exactly the same line in *Jazz,* and becomes a harbinger of death.)

OK, point taken, *Chicago* is a throwback to the days when Really Big Musicals were made into movies. Conventional wisdom since that time has decided that Really Big Musicals are prohibitively expensive to make, but are they as expensive as *Titanic* (1997)? Well, *Evita* did not do so well in 1996, even with Madonna singing the lead, but Baz Luhrmann seemed to turn things around with *Moulin Rouge* in 2001. A year later *Chicago* became tremendously popular, and then some, and it is sure to recover its expenses, and then some.

Chicago is also a throwback for theatre and film buffs in other ways. The story, "inspired by the headlines," so to speak, made its theatrical debut in the Maurine Dallas Watkins play, based on a spectacular murder case in 1924, which spawned two films, the first also named *Chicago* (1927), and the second, a fantastic movie adaptation by William Wellman in 1942, named after the eponymous heroine played by Ginger Rogers, *Roxie Hart.* Seeing the 2002 film directed peerlessly by Rob Marshall (an experienced Broadway choreographer and director), with stellar performances by Renée Zellweger as Roxie Hart, Catherine Zeta-Jones as Velma Kelly, and Richard Gere as Billy Flynn the razzle-dazzle lawyer will therefore occasion a deluge of nostalgic memories for "mature" viewers, besides reminding younger viewers of the sort of spectacles movies can create. These are all worthy goals.

For some, the story will be familiar. During the Roaring '20s, two women are arrested on the same night for murder. Velma Kelly (played by Zeta-Jones as a flamboyant flapper chanteuse) has murdered her sister and her husband; would-be singer and dancer Roxie Hart has murdered her lover, Fred Casely (Dominic West), who lured her into bed by pretending to have theatrical contacts, then tried to ditch her. In prison they compete for media attention. They both hire shyster lawyer Billy Flynn to represent them. All through the trial and proceedings they are competing with each other for celebrity attention. By the end, the sensation has passed, and they are no longer in the spotlight. Neither can find work on their own, so they pool their notoriety and combine their talents into a sister act. Roxie protests that they don't really like each other, but the more cynical Velma explains that in show business, that really doesn't matter.

While confronting some damaging evidence against his client, the accused murderess Roxie Hart, defense attorney Billy Flynn does his best to spin the testimony in his client's favor. Periodically during his cross-examination, the scene shifts from the courtroom to a stage setting where Billy taps out a dance routine. Back and forth we go, from legal manipulations to a tap dance, "razzle-dazzling" the folks. Back and forth. The cross-cutting makes its point painfully clear—the manipulation of trial evidence is a highly theatrical affair, and not necessarily a legitimate undertaking (all respects to the honorable profession of tap dancing notwithstanding).

And there you have the new film version of the Kander and Ebb classic Broadway musical, *Chicago* in a nutshell. As we watch the lawyer try to extricate Roxie from the hangman's noose, we continually cross cut to a parallel world of song and dance—a world where the tawdry circumstances of Roxie's crime are transformed into the glitzy fantasy of musical theater. Thus, the film in its entirety rests on one of the medium's central capacities—parallel editing. Rarely will you see such a powerful, consistent, and vigorous exercise of this technique.

Consider the components of the visual and musical spectacle. In addition to the aforementioned scene, there are many other outstanding examples: The "Cellblock Tango," where each of the criminal histories of the gray-clad murderesses are cross-cut with their spangled, high-kicking theatrical incarnations; Billy's "ventriloquist" routine, where his legal machinations are cross-cut with trapeze-acrobatics in a circus ring; the "Mr. Cellophane" soliloquy, where Roxie's husband's plain-spoken lament about anonymity is rendered in terms of a somewhat maudlin, baggy-pants burlesque routine. This gives John C. Reilly, who plays Amos Hart, Roxy's husband, his very own show-stopping number. *New Yorker* critic Anthony Lane complained wickedly that the John Kander-Fred Ebb music and lyrics operate on "the old-fashioned principle that every song should be a showstopper, regardless of whether the show deserves to be stopped." This strategy of fusing the sordid world of greed, corruption, and vicious opportunism with a fantasy world of hot-house musical forms was employed in another Kander-Ebb film adaptation, *Cabaret*—when the petty lives of the characters are compared and contrasted with the more dangerous, highly-charged cabaret performances of a Germany poised on the edge of self-destruction. *Cabaret* was essentially a serious piece of editorializing. *Chicago* is just as unrelentingly cynical as its forebear, but the touch is generally lighter. Which is to say that seldom does mankind's worst instincts come off so entertainingly.

This sort of musical film has been called a "realistic" musical, in that the songs and dances spring naturally out of theatrical settings rather than spontaneously out of the inner fantasies of the characters. It won't do for people to launch into musical numbers in the real world at the drop of a hat;

rather, they must be on a stage, where such demonstrations normally belong. Yet, we would argue that such a categorization of *Chicago* doesn't quite add up. Although Roxie and Velma are stage performers and would logically burst into song while on stage, here, until the final scene, they are on stage only in their imaginations. In other words, this movie partakes of both the "realistic" and the "fantasy" musical categories. It honors both the theatricality of the principal characters while indulging in insights into their private psychologies. Ultimately, one can argue, the two spheres are not separable at all; both partake of each other-but that gets us into muddy aesthetic waters.

Chicago is about a lot of things. It's very much an unabashed dissection of our media-made culture. Roxie and Velma each up the ante on the other to attract newspaper headlines. Roxie even feigns a pregnancy by her dead assailant to gain temporary ascendancy over her rival's publicity grabbing. It's not her neck that is most important to her, but her picture in the papers. But no sooner has she won her case than the fickle media drop her like the proverbial hot potato when a fresh new murder case is announced. The movie is also a quite unabashed editorial on pre-meditated, justifiable homicide—or how society contrives to allow gender considerations and bias into its judgments concerning guilt and innocence.

In the meantime, viewers should just sit back and enjoy the super-charged proceedings, from the amazing solo routine by Zeta-Jones that opens the film to the Byzantine legal machinations of the characters that prevails throughout. It's likely to leave you a bit exhausted, it not a little exhilarated. Fortunately, it's not as chaotic as *Moulin Rouge,* although every bit as virtuosic in its camera work and editing. And credit Zeta-Jones, Zellweger, and even Richard Gere with an admirable essay into song and dance. Yes, that's really Gere tap-dancing his way through the trial scene. One wonders if it's a condition of our time that insists on authenticity in singing and dancing, i.e., that the performers on screen must do their own singing and dancing. If so, it's a paradox in a film relying so heavily on this parallel fantasy world. While we insist on the authenticity of performance, we dote on the fantasy of the dream.

In *Chicago* the fantasy of the filmed musical is reclaimed and restored in a wonderfully entertaining way. The film had its naysayers, such as Stuart Klawans, who complained in *The Nation* that the film was shot "like one of those commercials for Broadway musicals," the purpose being "to TELL you that you're being entertained." Likewise, Anthony Lane of the *New Yorker* was not at all impressed by Richard Gere or Renée Zellweger, claiming that the "only player to conquer" *Chicago* was Zeta-Jones, "who is no [Cyd] Charisse in her motions but who gets by on a full tank of unleaded oomph."

Even so, *Chicago* seemed to be critic-proof because of strong word-of-mouth. Rob Marshall was nominated as Best Director by the Director's Guild of America for his work, as was Martin Walsh for Best Film Editing by the American Cinema Editors. From the Screen Actors Guild it got nominations for Best Actress (Zellweger), Best Actor (Gere), and Best Supporting Actress (both Zeta-Jones and Queen Latifah). By February it had already won Golden Globes for Best Picture, Best Actress (Zellweger) and Best Actor (Gere). With all that attention, multiple Academy Award nominations seemed likely. In New York City by the end of January, people were lined up around the block to get into the Ziegfeld Theatre on 54th Street. Audiences in movie theatres have applauded as the credits begin to run after the spectacle has ended. If ever a movie could be a crowd-pleaser, *Chicago*, with its big score, scores big.

—*James M. Welsh and John C. Tibbetts*

CREDITS

Roxie Hart: Renee Zellweger
Velma Kelly: Catherine Zeta-Jones
Billy Flynn: Richard Gere
Matron "Mama" Morton: Queen Latifah
Amos Hart: John C. Reilly
Mary Sunshine: Christine Baranski
Kitty: Lucy Alexis Liu
Bandleader: Taye Diggs
Martin Harrison: Colm Feore
Fred Casely: Dominic West

Origin: USA
Released: 2002
Production: Martin Richards; Producer Circle Co.; released by Miramax Films
Directed by: Rob Marshall
Written by: Bill Condon
Cinematography by: Dion Beebe
Music by: Danny Elfman, John Kander
Lyrics by: Fred Ebb
Sound: David Lee
Editing: Martin Walsh
Art Direction: Andrew Stearn
Costumes: Colleen Atwood
Production Design: John Myhre
MPAA rating: PG-13
Running time: 113 minutes

REVIEWS

Chicago Sun-Times Online. December 27, 2002.

Entertainment Weekly. January 10, 2003, p. 46.
Los Angeles Times Online. December 27, 2002.
The Nation. January 6, 2003, p. 36.
New York Times Online. December 27, 2002.
New Yorker. January 6, 2003, p. 90.
People. January 13, 2003, p. 38.
Rolling Stone. January 23, 2003, p. 76.
Sight and Sound. February, 2003, p. 41.
USA Today Online. December 26, 2002.
Variety Online. December 10, 2002.
Washington Post. December 27, 2002, p. WE41.

QUOTES

Lawyer Billy Flynn (Richard Gere): "If Jesus Christ lived in Chicago today and if he had 5000 dollars and if he had come to me, things would have turned out differently."

AWARDS AND NOMINATIONS

British Acad. 2002: Sound, Support. Actress (Zeta-Jones)
Directors Guild 2002: Director (Marshall)
Golden Globes 2003: Actor—Mus./Comedy (Gere), Actress—Mus./Comedy (Zellweger), Film—Mus./Comedy
Nomination:
Oscars 2002: Actress (Zellweger), Adapt. Screenplay, Art Dir./Set Dec., Cinematog., Costume Des., Director (Marshall), Film, Film Editing, Song ("I Move On"), Sound, Support. Actor (Reilly), Support. Actress (Queen Latifah, Zeta-Jones)
British Acad. 2002: Actress (Zellweger), Cinematog., Costume Des., Director (Marshall), Film, Film Editing, Makeup, Support. Actress (Queen Latifah), Score
Golden Globes 2003: Actress—Mus./Comedy (Zeta-Jones), Director (Marshall), Screenplay, Support. Actor (Reilly), Support. Actress (Queen Latifah)
Screen Actors Guild 2002: Actor (Gere), Actress (Zellweger), Support. Actress (Queen Latifah, Zeta-Jones), Cast
Writers Guild 2002: Adapt. Screenplay.

Chihwaseon: Painted Fire

K orean master filmmaker Im Kwon-Taek, who has directed over a 100 feature films before his latest, *Chihwaseon*, explained the title of his film from the podium of the New York Film Festival. Nowhere in the film do we come to know that it means "drunk-painter-hermit" even though the film makes clear that its subject, the famous late 19th-century painter, Jang Seung-Ob (Choi Min-Sik), later to be known as the famous Oh-Won, was all three. As if these antinomies weren't enough, Im reveals oppositions between what Oh-Won wanted to express in his paintings and the style he was forced to adopt, as well as between the serenity of mind required for such artistic creation and the politically turbulent times he lived through.

We come to know Oh-Won as Jang, the humble, earnest scholar who has been encouraged to study painting by Master Kim (Ahn Sung-Ki). Jang, an orphan of lowly birth, is indebted to the Master for having saved his life. It is Master Kim who enrolls Jang in the Footbridge Art School to study under Master Lee (Han Myoung-Gu). At the School, Jang excels at copying Chinese paintings of nature-scapes.

It should be borne in mind that the film opens, and repeatedly gravitates, towards the seeming spontaneity necessary for such artistic expression. Over a stark white sheet of paper, a brush dabs on black paint which, in a matter of seconds, can evoke a mountainside or a monkey on the branch of a tree. What is plain to see is that this is art borne not out of the preoccupations of the mind but a plane of consciousness that has gone beyond it. Like the blindfolded Zen archer who gets his arrow to strike at the heart of the target, the painter here depicts the life force in nature by becoming one with it. In effect, the few seconds that might take up the act of creation become the result of years of painful practice and soul-searching. The painting thus becomes the aesthetic correlative of the mystical inner flash.

Jang, however, emerges as too practical-minded a man, and eventually too cynical to boot, to devote himself to the rigors of meditative discipline. Like a born genius, he seems to embody the fruits of labor without really trying. Those jealous of him admit that he paints with a "divine strength," that he "follows the rules yet breaks them at the same time." What puzzles them even more is the fact that Jang does not come from an aristocratic background, but is in fact "a country bumpkin." When a visiting Japanese art expert calls his work "sublime" and wants to know how he learnt the craft, Jang mockingly answers that "genius shows, even in a baby."

The film structures itself around this conflict between Jang's innate drive and the dominant style in painting at the time, which in turn was determined by whether the Conservatives, backed by Japan, or the Reformists, supported by the Chinese Army, were in power in the Seoul of the 1880's. Jang's career appears to get a boost under the Reformists though he himself claims to be above political ideology.

Jang is first told by Master Lee that every painter has to know literature, specifically the Chinese texts that speak of the magical flow of 'Qi' or the life force, and "how it irrigates the five senses." But true artistic creation, the film seems to

say, cannot remain confined to any such lofty ideal. As Jang's fame as a "duplicator" spreads, that is, as one whose paintings cannot be distinguished from the original, all kinds of temptation come his way. A dealer in erotic drawings approaches him, and even brings along a female model. Jang turns down the offer, trembling at the sight of the woman.

As he pursues his serious work under Master Lee, Jang takes on the task of imbuing his technique with feeling. "Don't push the brush. Pull it," he's instructed. He's then told, "The subject's sorrow must show in the painting. The imagination must guide the hand." When Jang proudly shows a work that he has completed, he is admonished, "A painting is never finished."

Jang's romantic instincts are stirred when, at a feast thrown in his honor, he is drawn to the beautiful Mae-Hyang (You Ho-Jeong), a flautist, who spurs him to work even harder. This comes at the expense of the physical relationship that Mae is seeking. As Jang is painting a branch of blossoms, she suggestively intones in his ear, "The plum blossom keeps its scent to itself." The film makes clear that Jang was not to enjoy a sexually satisfying or loving relationship with her, or with any other woman. The women in his life were the *kisaeng*, or concubines, whom he hated sharing with other men.

Jang is soon caught up in the political turmoil resulting from the Japanese invasion. As 8000 Koreans are beheaded, Jang begins to see the pointlessness of his effort. In this, he resembles the 15th-century Russian painter of majestic church frescoes from Andrei Tarkovsky's epic film, *Andrei Rublev* (1966). Rublev saw his work destroyed by the barbaric Tartar hordes no sooner he had completed it. Jang is somewhat more fortunate.

Understandably, we see a disenchanted Jang wandering by himself across a lush countryside, then by a river, then in a forest and finally, by the sea, where he looks up to gaze at cranes in flight, a sight he was to eventually immortalize with his brush. With the help of his longtime benefactor, Master Kim, Jang finds sustenance in exploring the work of his own ancestors. In this, he comes across the dichotomy between the painting itself and the words alongside it, as if it were nothing more than an illustration. "Real painting should be without words!" he rants at Mae. "Without bogus philosophy!"

This aesthetic dialectic also serves to usher in that phase of his life when Jang becomes intolerant, jealous and abusive, traits made worse by his heavy drinking. When Mae tries to make love to him, he is too drunk to respond. As he wanders off, his servant boy follows him, all the way to a stretch of wasteland, where the boy cries out wearily, "Does learning to paint have to be so difficult?" We soon see that it does. As lightning streaks across a night sky, Jang yells out, his cry rivaling the thunder, and allowing himself to feel one with it. This elemental power, which he feels within, and which he cannot express through his work, takes the form of distrust and mounting jealousy. When Mae admits to sleeping with another painter, he leaves her for good.

Jang's self-esteem is redeemed when he's commissioned to paint part of a triptych for the local Governor's birthday celebration. This is a custom in which painting becomes a performance art. The work is meant to be executed in front of the Governor, and to musical accompaniment. Jang is not only allowed the honor of painting alongside Master Lee, but of being the first to start. The natural elements pictured, such as peonies and crabs, are meant to evoke ideals such as longevity and wisdom.

The event turns out to be a turning point in Jang's life. Master Lee soon resigns from teaching. He tells Jang, "Your talent is much greater. Now it is for you to set the example." Master Kim's advice to Jang is that he should create his *own* paintings, whatever that means. Jang admits he is haunted by visions he cannot express. The Master warns, "Art created for instant fame is vanity."

As winter strikes, we learn that Jang has become unproductive, spending his time getting drunk and getting into brawls. Whatever he paints, he quickly tears up. In his studio, he is soon up to his neck in torn paper, with no more available on credit. We then see Jang in his late middle age, sporting a moustache and a thin beard. Now it is he who has become the Master, imparting wisdom. Yet despite the orders he receives, and for all his fame and popularity, he paints very little, and even goes about destroying his work, wherever he can find it. A stint at the Royal Painting Office gets him "the sixth rank," which is worthy of an audience with the King. Meanwhile, the triumph of the Conservatives puts Jang's life in danger. He soon learns that Master Kim has been accused of high treason and has gone into hiding.

Even sex holds no solace. While in the throes of intercourse with a *kisaeng*, his house is set on fire by soldiers who are looking for the Governor. They however release Jang when they learn who he is.

We then see Jang as an old man, "drifting like a cloud," overtaken by political events, such as The Peasant Revolt of 1884. By the sea, at low tide, he is reunited with Master Kim, now wizened with age. "Your paintings remain the heartbeat of Korea," he says, bestowing upon Jang the ultimate praise.

In the final phase of his life, Jang seeks work as a painter of porcelain pots. Through this work, he attains the crowning epiphany of his life. After being unable to paint because of his shaking hand, he sits staring into the fire of the furnace. A worker then philosophizes about the various desires a pot embodies. The painter wants the iron powder to stick, the glazer wants his glaze to hold fast, while the owner wants sturdiness, but eventually, it is the fire that "dictates all." Jang nods to the wisdom.

In closing, a voiceover informs us that in 1897 Jang "vanished without a trace" and that legend has it that "he became an immortal hermit" on Diamond Mountain.

Fittingly, critics have paid tribute to the film's majestic beauty. A. O. Scott in the *New York Times* writes of "the movie's wealth of beautiful, perfectly framed images of nature—shots so full of passion and perception that they could almost be paintings themselves." David Stratton in *Variety* calls the film a "vibrantly told saga . . . (that) uses rich colors and vibrant sound to recreate the world of a man who was a law unto himself in a rigidly controlled and traditional era."

—*Vivek Adarkar*

CREDITS

Seung-Up Jang (Ohwon): Mink-sik Choi
Byung-Moon Kim: Sung-Ki Ahn
Mae-Hyang: Ho-Jeong You
Jin-Hong: Yeo-Jim Kim
So-Woon: Ye-Jin Son
Eung-Heon Lee: Myoung-Gu Han

Origin: Korea
Language: Korean
Released: 2002
Production: Tae-Won Lee; Tae-hung Pictures; released by Kino International
Directed by: Kwon Taek Im
Written by: Kwon Taek Im, Young-Oak Kim
Cinematography by: Il Sung Jung
Sound: Choong-Hwan Lee
Editing: Kwang-Jim Choi
Costumes: Hye-Lan Lee
Production Design: Byoung-Do Ju
MPAA rating: Unrated
Running time: 117 minutes

REVIEWS

Entertainment Weekly. February 21, 2003, p. 129.
New York Times Online. September 28, 2002, p. 22.
Variety. June 3, 2002, p. 22.

QUOTES

Ohwon (Min-Sik Choi) tells a fellow artist: "If you want to paint, first learn how to drink!"

City by the Sea

When you're searching for a killer ... the last suspect you want to see is your son.
—Movie tagline

 Box Office: $22.4 million

In 1993, Michael Caton-Jones directed *This Boy's Life,* a potent and moving drama based upon a true story that dealt with the unhappiness between a stepfather and his stepson, which starred Robert De Niro and a clearly promising young actor named Leonardo DiCaprio. Now in 2002, Caton-Jones brings us *City by the Sea,* also based on actual events, also starring De Niro and an up-and-coming young actor (James Franco, Golden Globe-winner for 2001's cable film *James Dean*), and also focusing on the troubled relationship between a boy and his father (in this case biological). Despite these similarities (not to mention supporting roles in both films by Eliza Dushku), *City by the Sea* is not nearly as memorable, although it has its effective and affecting moments.

The source material here is the 1997 *Esquire* article entitled "Mark of a Murderer" by Pulitzer Prize-winning journalist Mike McAlary, a fascinating look at a 1996 ferocious and premeditated killing by junkie Joey LaMarca, the strung-out son of respected retired cop Vincent LaMarca and the grandson of Angelo LaMarca, who had been executed at Sing Sing after being convicted of kidnapping and murder back in 1956. In McAlary's vivid piece, he noted various eerie similarities—physical and otherwise—between Joey and his grandfather that made some wonder if atavism was at work here, some sort of genetic defect lurking in the LaMarca family tree which made Joey's transgression inevitable. The compelling real-life story has been refashioned significantly here into a muted, moderately absorbing character study of Vince, who is endlessly suffering from the long-ago sins of his father, and whose unhappiness has been transmitted down the line to his own son and possibly played a role in the young man's degeneration into drugs and murder.

The film begins with sun-drenched images of Long Beach, New York in its heyday, back when many were attracted to the bustling boardwalk and beaches of this self-titled "City by the Sea." These nostalgic images fade into shots of what it has become, desolate with bombed-out, crumbling buildings strewn with graffiti. While it was once an ideal vacation destination for the whole family, the phrase "being on a trip" in connection with Long Beach now has an entirely different meaning. Drugs appear to be everywhere,

and one of the addicts is Joey LaMarca, known on the streets as Joey Nova because of the car that he drives. Looking gaunt, haggard and at a loss, he is out to score drugs with his cohort Snake (Brian Tarantina) when a melee ensues and, amidst all the confusion, Joey stabs and kills an extravagantly-tattooed dealer nicknamed Picasso.

Joey backs away slowly from the body, appearing unable to fully take in what has just transpired. Soon a menacing motorcycle-riding dealer named Spyder (William Forsythe), assuming Joey has the money police confiscated off Picasso's body, is after him, also threatening his girlfriend Gina (Dushku) and their baby Angelo. Joey wants to escape to Key West, Florida with a reluctant Gina and his son, sure that everything will finally come together in that oceanside paradise of which he has idealized memories from a family vacation back in much happier times. Joey's mother Maggie (Patti LuPone), clearly at wit's end, refuses to give him money for the trip, his history having taught her that he is more likely to shoot up than shape up and ship out.

Called to the scene of the crime is NYPD's Vince LaMarca (De Niro as yet another cop), who shakes his head sadly as he notes how things in Long Beach have deteriorated since his childhood, saying it looks "like the Serbian Army came through." Caton-Jones takes great pains to capture all the disorder and decay, emblematic of Vince's personal life. His father's conviction when Vince was a boy, followed years later by a bitter divorce that led to his gradually losing touch with Joey, has left him full of gnawing anguish and guilt, and he keeps these feelings and himself to himself, unwilling or unable to open up beyond a certain point with anyone. He now lives alone in an apartment, eating in front of the television. No amount of prodding from his long-time, amiable partner Reg (George Dzundza) can get him to accept an invitation to socialize. He has a girlfriend of sorts named Michelle (Frances McDormand), but even she is kept at arm's length. She lives downstairs from Vince, not so close as to make him uncomfortable but close enough for him to accept late-night invitations to her bed.

As the investigation gets underway, Vince is shaken to learn that everything points to Joey. Can the speed at which a cop, especially a dedicated vet like Vince, pursues a perpetrator not be affected when he realizes that the person he is chasing is his own son? De Niro does a nice job of making it clear that Vince is in conflict, it becoming harder and harder to keep a lid on the angst this situation obviously exacerbates. He wants Joey to turn himself in and take responsibility for his actions, but ponders what responsibility he himself bears for his son's rudderless existence which brought them to the present situation.

When he goes to talk to Maggie, she shrilly hurls old accusations of wife beating and abandonment at him. Also disconcerting is the police department's issuance of a press release dredging up facts surrounding the murder Vince's father committed many years before. Newspaper articles speculate about a "killer gene" lurking in the LaMarca family tree. Then Gina shows up and prods Vince to finally just be a dad to Joey, dropping off old possessions of Joey's that only intensify Vince's quandary about how things could have gone so wrong. In an effective scene between De Niro and McDormand, the normally tight-lipped man becomes uncharacteristically verbose, spewing forth a torrent of details about his family's troubled past and present, like a volcano no longer able to contain the pressures within. McDormand effectively registers her character's shock: she wanted to know all but clearly got more than she bargained for, and ends up losing patience with Vince and exiting long before the credits roll.

The script really ratchets up the pressure on Vince by having Gina show up to ditch the grandson Vince never even knew he had, and on both LaMarcas when Spyder, lying in wait for Joey, kills Reg with a gun Joey had stolen. The police now quicken their steps, determined to nail a cop killer. Joey desperately calls his father and asserts his innocence. Upset that the police are so intent upon nailing Joey that they are failing to look for or at any evidence that might point toward someone else, Vince leaves the case, now free to deal with the situation more as a father than as a cop. Amongst what follows are some fairly familiar elements from countless other police dramas which are hardly arresting, but the film is much more concerned with a man's pursuit of redemption as a father and the expiation of his inner turmoil than with the collaring of any criminals.

A nighttime scene in which father and son meet at ocean's edge where they used to spend time together seems underdeveloped and features some lame dialogue, but the emotions ring true. The film's climactic scene, also at night, in which Joey saves Vince from Spyder, Vince saves Joey from getting himself killed by the police, and the two reconcile just before the officers move in, is especially uneven: tense and emotionally powerful, yet also veering too close to the melodramatic and maudlin. In *City by the Sea*'s final scene, the sun is shining once again both literally and figuratively for Vince, as he dutifully plays with little Angelo on the beach where he played long ago with Joey, the family's chain of unhappiness hopefully broken.

Filmed on a budget of $60 million, *City by the Sea* grossed only $22.4 million. It received mixed reviews. During the adaptation process, significant changes were made to McAlary's piece that end up telling a very different story. Vince was retired at the time of his son's crime and played no part in his apprehension. He is apparently not the unsettled man of the film and has been happily married to his second wife for some time. Here, Joey happens to commit the murder in the midst of a confusing scuffle, making him seem more like merely a troubled youth in the wrong place when things got out of hand as opposed to the truly sick real-life individual responsible for premeditated, grotesque butchery.

Ominous but generic bad guy Spyder and the killing of Reg are also inventions for the film, making the wrongly-accused Joey seem like an even more sympathetic character. Little Angelo was also made up for the film, and, given the name of Joey's grandfather, is apparently supposed to underscore the idea of history repeating itself.)

Another alteration for the film was the use of Asbury Park as a stand-in for Long Beach, which has made too much of a comeback in recent years for Caton-Jones' purposes. Community leaders were so vociferous in their outrage about the portrayal that Warner Brothers agreed to add a disclaimer to the DVD and VHS editions saying that no filming was done in Long Beach. Through *City by the Sea*, which is generally well-acted but in need of a better script, Caton-Jones said he was interested in reminding parents that the choices they make can echo down the generations—for better or for worse. That is all too true, even if the story used to make the point is not.

—*David L. Boxerbaum*

CREDITS

Vincent LaMarca: Robert De Niro
Joey: James Franco
Michelle: Frances McDormand
Gina: Eliza Dushku
Spyder: William Forsythe
Reg Duffy: George Dzundza
Maggie: Patti LuPone
Dave Simon: Anson Mount
Henderson: John Doman
Snake: Brian Tarantina
Rossi: Nestor Serrano
Lt. Katt: Leo Burmester

Origin: USA
Released: 2002
Production: Brad Grey, Elie Samaha, Michael Caton-Jones, Matthew Baer; Franchise Pictures; released by Warner Bros.
Directed by: Michael Caton-Jones
Written by: Ken Hixon
Cinematography by: Karl Walter Lindenlaub
Music by: John Murphy
Sound: Tom Nelson
Music Supervisor: Jason Alexander, Don Fleming
Editing: Jim Clark
Art Direction: Patricia Woodbridge
Costumes: Richard Owings
Production Design: Jane Musky
MPAA rating: R
Running time: 108 minutes

REVIEWS

Chicago Sun-Times Online. September 6, 2002.
Entertainment Weekly. September 13, 2002, p. 125.
Los Angeles Times Online. September 6, 2002.
New York Times Online. September 6, 2002.
People. September 16, 2002, p. 31.
USA Today Online. September 6, 2002.
Variety Online. August 26, 2002.
Washington Post. September 6, 2002, p. WE37.

TRIVIA

Much of the movie was filmed in Asbury Park, New Jersey, rather than in Long Beach, which is undergoing a renaissance.

Clockstoppers

Freeze The Future.
—Movie tagline

What if you had the power to stop time?
—Movie tagline

Box Office: $36.9 million

Want to know how to stop time? Want your life to seem to drag on forever? Go to a dull movie. That's what will happen to most adults who go to see *Clockstoppers.* Unless one is about seven years old, this movie is bound to prove that time can slow down when one isn't having fun.

The premise sounds promising enough. Dr. Earl Dopler (French Stewart) has discovered how to slow down time for anyone who uses his invention. Like a hummingbird living in a world of tortoises, those using Dopler's invention would move about the normal world unnoticed. Dopler envisions the good that can come from his invention such as incredibly fast moving doctors being able to do delicate surgery between the beats of a living heart that exists in normal time. Henry Gates (Michael Biehn), however, the head of Quantum Technologies where Dopler works, has other ideas, say using it as a military weapon. In fact, Gates is keeping Dopler under house arrest until he perfects his mechanism. The problem? It seems that the longer one is under hypertime, as it is called, the more quickly one ages. It's a problem that is not only baffling Dopler, it is aging him quickly because Gates keeps him under hypertime so his research goes more quickly.

Desperate, Dopler sends his mechanism—which looks just like a wrist watch—to his mentor and college professor, Dr. George Gibbs (Robin Thomas), who manages to make inroads with the problem. But before he can return the watch and his findings to Dopler, George runs off to attend a scientific conference and the watch falls into the hands of his teenage son Zak (Jesse Bradford). It is at this point that the movie collapses in on itself and the story devolves from slightly promising science fiction into yet one more story of pointless adolescent nonsense.

What makes *Clockstoppers* especially grating even within that genre, though, is the terrible character of Zak. As written (or as portrayed by Jesse Bradford—who truly is at fault here?) Zak is self-centered, manipulative, inconsiderate, petulant, whiny, and by turns cocky or sullen. He is so busy being cool that he trashes his hard-working friend Meeker's (Garikayi Mutambirwa) $5/hour job. He is so lacking in self-discipline that the only thing he truly works at is trying to find the easy way out of everything. One shudders to think this self-absorbed kid is a typical teenager, or even worse, a character admired by teens. What does *Clockstoppers* teach its young audience? To value fast cars and beautiful girlfriends, to value easy money and little work, to value style over substance. Are we having fun yet?

Even the director initially sounds like a good bet: Jonathan Frakes, Commander Will Riker on *Star Trek: The Next Generation.* But then one remembers how he practically single-handedly destroyed the Star Trek movie franchise when he directed *Star Trek: Insurrection.* About the only cute thing to come out of his helming the project is the attempt at "in" humor when Zak's new girlfriend Francesca (Paula Garces) delivers to Zak the line Captain Picard so often delivered to Will Riker, "Make it so, Number One."

Perhaps this is a case of too many writers spoiling the story. You'd think that between the four names listed as being responsible for the story/screenplay that at least one of them would have noticed the many, many problems with this movie. But then again, check the background. Rob Hedden's only claim to cinema fame is *Friday the 13th Part VIII: Jason Takes Manhattan.* Andy Hedden seems to have no cinematic writing credits but is listed as collaborating with his brother Rob on a few unrecognizable TV movies. J. David Stem and David N. Weiss co-wrote *The Rugrats Movie* and its sequel *Rugrats in Paris* as well as *Jimmy Neutron: Boy Genius* and they can't seem to rise above the cartoon level. All in all, there's not much to recommend this foursome. *Clockstoppers* is not likely to enhance their reputation much.

As if it weren't bad enough that the main character in *Clockstoppers* is unlikable and the story dumb and badly executed, it also suffers from the terminal problem of being a science fiction film based on science faulty enough to invoke an Einsteinian curse. There is absolutely no plausibility or even consistency here. Exactly how far does a watch's to be torn down by evil banker, Reed Thimple (Christopher Walken, taking any gig he can get). Beary gets the idea that the way to save Country Bear Hall is to get the band together and have a big fundraising concert.

The rest of the movie involves Beary going around the country in the Bears' dusty old tour bus and finding the rest of the members. In the meantime, his family has sent a couple of bumbling police officers, Officers Hamm and Cheets—ha, ha—(Daryl "Chill" Mitchell and Bader again) to find Beary. They are there so they can do such hilarious things like accidentally get out of their car while in the car wash and get thrown around by the brushes.

While Beary searches, there are plenty of chances for random people to burst into song and dance numbers. Miss Krystal shows up doing a number, Jennifer Paige sings "Kick It Into Gear" and Brian Setzer does a musical duel with Zeb. The studio tried to make the music credible. The music was written by John Hiatt and the Bears' band includes Tom Petty guitarist Mike Campbell, drummer Pete Thomas from Elvis Costello's Attractions, and session bassist Davy Farringer.

The Bears were created by Jim Henson's Creature Shop and have 30 motors to control facial motions. They still look like guys wearing big bear suits, but in a movie that features talking bears, there has to be a little suspension of disbelief. There is a lot to overlook, as many reviewers were eager to point out. For one thing, Ted sounds a certain way when he talks, but when he sings, suddenly he has the voice of Don Henley (Henley and Bonnie Raitt, who does the singing voice of Trixie, show up in cameos that should pass unappreciated by the wee audience.) Then there's the question of how they're playing those instruments since they don't have thumbs. And Roger Ebert of the *Chicago Sun-Times* wondered about this world in which bears roam freely among humans. "Are there real bears in the woods who would maul and eat their victims, or are all bears benign in this world?" he wrote.

All is not bad in the Bears' universe. The musical numbers are energetic and well-done and there are a few good jokes here and there. The best of these is when the Bears watch a cheesy old Saturday morning cartoon of themselves. The cartoon is a dead-on parody of the slapped together 1970s cartoon of popular bands like The Jackson Five and the Osmond Brothers. As the Bears on-screen, who of course have all the wrong voices, put their hands together and say, "Bear Power!," the Bears shake their heads. "That was bad," says one quietly. For those who like cameos, there are plenty of those. Elton John, Queen Latifah, and Xzibit show up in support of the Country Bears.

Critics didn't seem like they'd be rushing out to by the Bears' reunion record. Lisa Schwarzbaum of *Entertainment Weekly* gave the film a C and wrote "It's sort of an ursine *The Last Waltz* with more costumes and no direction from Martin Scorsese." Gene Seymour of *Newsday* wrote, "After a

while, the only way for a reasonably intelligent person to get through *The Country Bears* is to ponder how a whole segment of pop-music history has been allowed to get wet, fuzzy and sticky." Michael Wilmington of the *Chicago Tribune* wrote, "For every bear triumph, *Country Bears* also features clichés jokes, corny sentiment, ludicrous shtick and the most flabbergasting set of star cameos since Martha Stewart and Michael Jackson wandered into *Men in Black II*."

—*Jill Hamilton*

CREDITS

Reed Thimple: Christopher Walken
Officer Hamm: Darryl (Chill) Mitchell
Officer Cheets/Ted Bedderhead: Diedrich Bader
Rip Holland: Alex Rocco
Norbert Barrington: Stephen Tobolowsky
Roadie: M.C. Gainey
Mrs. Barrington: Meagen Fay
Dex Barrington: Eli Marienthal
Cha-Cha: Queen Latifah
Beary Barrington: Haley Joel Osment (Voice)
Big Al: James Gammon (Voice)
Fred Bedderhead: Brad Garrett (Voice)
Trixie St. Clair: Candy Ford (Voice)
Tennessee O'Neal: Toby Huss (Voice)
Henry Dixon Taylor: Kevin M. Richardson (Voice)
Zeb Zoober: Stephen (Steve) Root (Voice)

Origin: USA
Released: 2002
Production: Jeffrey Chernov, Andrew Gunn; Walt Disney Pictures; released by Buena Vista
Directed by: Peter Hastings
Written by: Mark Perez
Cinematography by: C. Mitchell Anderson
Music by: Christopher Young, John Hiatt
Sound: Steve Nelson
Music Supervisor: Nora Felder
Editing: George Bowers, Seth Flaum
Art Direction: Maria Baker
Costumes: Genevieve Tyrrell
Production Design: Dan Bishop
MPAA rating: G
Running time: 88 minutes

REVIEWS

Chicago Sun-Times Online. July 26, 2002.
Entertainment Weekly. August 2, 2002, p. 49.

Los Angeles Times Online. July 26, 2002.
New York Times Online. July 26, 2002.
USA Today Online. April 11, 2002.
USA Today Online. July 25, 2002.
Variety. July 29, 2002, p. 21.
Washington Post. July 26, 2002, p. WE38.

CQ

Every picture tells a story.
—Movie tagline

Roman Coppola no doubt grew up around movie sets, so it's not surprising that his first feature film as a screenwriter/director is about filmmaking. The son of Francis Ford Coppola previously worked as a sound designer for *The Black Stallion Returns* and as a second-unit director for *The Rainmaker* and *Jack*. Rather than tackling a weighty subject like his father almost always does, Coppola in *CQ* has concocted a whimsical spoof of the movies and attitudes of the late 1960s, a period of time when his father was making New Wave-type films like *The Rain People. CQ* is about a young film editor named Paul Ballard (Jeremy Davies) who is in Paris working on a cheesy sci-fi flick with an scantily clad super-heroine named Dragonfly (Angela Lindvall).

The film-within-a-film, eponymously called *Dragonfly,* is an obvious satire of *Barbarella,* the Jane Fonda vehicle which was so exploitative and ridiculous that by itself it must have pushed her from sex object to feminist. Not only does *Dragonfly* have a blonde, leggy star lolling on plush, shag-carpeted, futuristic sets, it has a volatile French director, Andrezej (a beefy Gerard Depardieu), who, like *Barbarella* director Roger Vadim, has fallen for his leading lady and who believes he is making art instead of schlock. The film's producer is a big-mouthed Italian blowhard, Enzo (Giancarlo Giannini), who is clearly a takeoff on *Barbarella* producer Dino DeLaurentiis. For fans of *Barbarella*—if any remain—there are dozens of other in-jokes.

Paul isn't happy with the film he's working on; it's a job, but he's searching for something deeper and more meaningful. So he spends his off-work hours filming himself and his girlfriend, Marlene (Elodie Bouchez), doing everyday things around their apartment. In the cinema verite fashion of the era, he hopes that this film will reveal to him and to his audience hidden truths about life, dreams, and relationships.

Coppola does dead-on work spoofing both the bloated, empty sci-fi epic and the pretentious low-budget, self-absorbed documentary. The best thing about *CQ* is that it perfectly captures not just the clothes and hairstyles of the era, but the attitudes—using the two films as bookends for the cultural schizophrenia of the time. The sets for *Dragonfly* are white and sterile, filled with now-ridiculous-looking "high tech" devices. In the film's flimsy plot, a group of Che Guevara-style revolutionaries, whose leader is played by Billy Zane, have set up a training camp on the dark side of the moon (living in biodomes), where it's somehow snowing. Dragonfly is sent by the world government to capture their secret weapon before they can foment revolution on Earth. Coppola's team of designers carries off the difficult task of making *Dragonfly*'s B-movie third-rate special effects look goofily authentic.

When Paul is seen shooting his own film, Coppola's take is also on target. As played rather blankly by Davies, Paul is the archetypal Searcher of the era, a young man who is vaguely dissatisfied with life but doesn't know where to find answers. Marlene, a stewardess and a more practical woman, tells Paul to his face and on his film that he won't find life's secrets by filming them, but by opening his eyes and looking around him. But Paul is lost in the fog of his own overly acute self-awareness. He often sits on the toilet seat and looks straight into the camera, asking unanswerable questions.

The best bits in *CQ* are Paul's daydreams, including two sequences where he imagines a group of critics interviewing him about his documentary. In the first, he projects himself as a success, and the reporters and critics are fawning over him, trying to pry out revealing secrets about his extraordinarily innovative techniques. Later on, he imagines the critics roasting him, saying the film is self-indulgent, incoherent, and unfeeling—and warning him he'd better have some better grasp of how to make his audiences feel something.

Unfortunately, by the time that second sequence arrives, the critics' barbs seem too on-target—as if they were talking about *CQ*. Having cleverly and quite stylishly set up the period, the characters, and the plot, Coppola's effort goes limp and seems to lose its way. Paul falls for the actress playing Dragonfly early on, and the outcome of this attraction seems predictable, but the romantic scenes are off-and-on, and any tension is defused by repeated interruptions and detours into subplots. Similarly, the fate of the film *Dragonfly* is an off-again, on-again concern. The producer fires the director, who is replaced by a bubble-brained wunderkind, Felix DeMarco (Jason Schwartzman), with aviator glasses and the attention span of a gnat. Schwartzman's performance is boffo, but much too close to Mike Meyers' Austin Powers character to seem very inventive. DeMarco gets in an auto accident and breaks his leg, which doesn't sufficiently explain why the producer hires Paul to finish the film (it's not as if DeMarco is disabled). The producer complains throughout that *Dragonfly* needs a better ending, and while Paul eventually supplies one, it comes out of nowhere—and Coppola can't supply a sufficiently engaging ending of his own for *CQ*.

Paul—and Coppola—seem to lose interest in the cinema verite project; it all but disappears during the second half of *CQ* and when it reappears at the end, with Paul showing it an at artsy film festival, it seems to have gained a consciousness and a voice that Paul never contributed to it before. There's also a fascinating but puzzling scene with Paul and his visiting father (Dean Stockwell), which suggests some intriguing family material but goes nowhere. Neither does a whirlwind New Year's Eve party in Rome.

Eventually, Coppola seems to be piling scene on scene but losing his bearings and his satirical edge. Like the film Paul is making about himself, *CQ* ends up taking itself too seriously. It fails to maintain the disarming, mocking tone that worked so well at the beginning of the film. In the end, as the critics of Paul's film (which ends up with the title *69/70*) ask, you wonder what's the point?

Coppola does have a nifty knack for precisely crafted shots, and the film's clean, crisp credit sequences, opening scenes, dream sequences, and music—an original score by a group called Mellow, which perfectly mimics the pop music of the era—are well done. Occasionally, Coppola shows real promise. The best shot in the movie comes fleetingly at a party, when Paul sees Marlene across the room. Her face is half-hidden by a doorway, and she withdraws slowly until there is nothing left; it perfectly captures the fading away of the relationship.

Coppola's problem is not the little things, it's the big thing—the story. The film lacks coherence, just like the films-within-a-film that it satirizes. The title *CQ* comes from a throwaway scene about code-breaking (and since it stands for "Seek You," seems an obvious rip-off of today's Internet instant-messaging device, ICQ). The film says nothing about the larger issues of the 1960s, and it really adds nothing new to the many efforts of the past to dissect the art of filmmaking. It becomes ingrown.

The cast of *CQ* is a strange mix. Davies isn't at all engaging, and he seems stiff as a board in his scenes with the effervescent, fetching Bouchez, who is underused. Lindvall, a newcomer to film, is intriguing, lighting up the screen in the few romantic scenes where she is out of character. Stockwell is mesmerizing in his one truncated, useless scene. The rest of the cast is mostly just along for the ride; and it includes two former leading European actors who've seen better days (Depardieu, Giannini). The latter makes Enzo into an absurd piece of work—those listening carefully will notice that the number of films he brags about working on declines by exactly 13 with each telling.

Coppola got production help from his father, and it's not clear whether this film will bring him more acclaim down the road. It's promising, but not exactly a star vehicle, and it got belated, limited release in 2002. He'll have to stake out new ground and give audiences something more to care about if he's going to make it on his own as a director. He certainly seems to know the craft of moviemaking; the challenge for him is to grasp the big picture.

—*Michael Betzold*

CREDITS

Paul Ballard: Jeremy Davies
Marlene: Elodie Bouchez
Valentine/Dragonfly: Angela Lindvall
Andrezej: Gerard Depardieu
Enzo: Giancarlo Giannini
Fabrizio: Massimo Ghini
Felix DeMarco: Jason Schwartzman
Mr. E: Billy Zane
Chairman: John Phillip Law
Dr. Ballard: Dean Stockwell

Origin: USA
Released: 2001
Production: Gary Marcus; United Artists, American Zoetrope, Delux Productions, Film Fund Luxembourg; released by MGM
Directed by: Roman Coppola
Written by: Roman Coppola
Cinematography by: Robert Yeoman
Sound: Carlo Thoss
Music Supervisor: Brian Reitzell
Editing: Leslie Jones
Art Direction: Luc Chalon, Oshin Yeghiazariantz
Costumes: Judy Shrewsbury
Production Design: Dean Tavoularis
MPAA rating: R
Running time: 92 minutes

REVIEWS

Boxoffice. November, 2001, p. 138.
Boxoffice. April, 2002, p. 22.
Los Angeles Times Online. May 24, 2002.
New York Times Online. May 24, 2002.
USA Today Online. May 24, 2002.
Variety. May 21, 2001, p. 23.
Washington Post. May 31, 2002, p. WE41.

QUOTES

Marlene (Elodie Bouchez) wonders about boyfriend Paul's (Jeremy Davies) autobiographical film: "What if it's boring? Did you ever think it might not be interesting for others to watch?"

The Crime of Father Amaro (El Crimen del Padre Amaro)

. . . lead us not into temptation . . .
—Movie tagline

 Box Office: $4.3 million

For his fifth feature, Mexican director Carlos Carrera takes on a serious theme in *The Crime of Father Amaro,* but allows it to degenerate into romantic triteness. However, as with most such ventures, he deserves to be lauded for foregrounding such a timely dilemma in the first place. The film's subtext about the loss and rediscovery of religious faith, against the background of a small town in Mexico rife with socio-political corruption, hovers over its melodramatic goings-on, much like the scriptures that are dutifully spouted by the eponymous Amaro (Gael Garcia Bernal) belong to a world clearly removed from the institution of the Catholic Church as portrayed.

Before the young Father Amaro arrives at the small town of Los Reyas—where he is to serve and where his faith will be tested—it becomes clear from his handsome, intense but compassionate demeanor that he's going to prove as much of a challenge to the Church as the latter will to him. In this, he resembles the neophyte samurai in Nagisa Oshima's *Gohatto* (reviewed in the 2000 volume) who tests the samurai code as much as that code tests him.

On his first night at the parsonage, Amaro witnesses the maid, Sanjuanera (Angelica Aragon), sneaking out of the quarters of the middle-aged Father Benito (Sancho Garcia), whom Amaro has been commissioned to serve. Conveniently covering his own transgressions, Benito draws Amaro's attention to the case against Father Natalio (Damian Alcazar), a pastor in a nearby mountain village, whom he suspects of helping guerillas. Amaro is then taken to see the site of the clinic-cum-orphanage that Benito is building. What Amaro doesn't know is that Benito is receiving funds from a money-laundering scheme set up by the drug lord, Chato Aguilar (Juan Ignacio Aranda).

As if to pollute Amaro's purity further, Sanjuanera's attractive teenage daughter, Amelia (Ana Claudia Talancon), comes to him to confess her sexual misconduct. Having rejected the marriage proposal of Ruben (Andres

Monteil), a local reporter, she finds herself physically drawn to Amaro. "I am very sensual . . . very intense," she confides. "I touch myself in the shower." To which, Amaro replies, "Sensuality is no sin," adding, "The body and soul are one." Amelia then says, "But I think of Jesus when I'm doing it." Amaro ponders over that, then concedes, "That is a sin."

Amaro's faith is further tested when he's introduced to another of nature's cruel tricks. Martin (Gaston Melo), the sacristan, who doubles as the driver of the parsonage truck, takes him to see his bed-ridden, mentally retarded daughter, Getsemani (Blanca Loaria). "Is the Devil inside her?" Martin asks him. Amaro rejects any such possibility, but then as he reaches out to bless her forehead, he is repelled as she refuses to let go of his hand. Martin then slaps her violently into submission, as Amaro looks on, shaken.

The film then takes up the socio-political substratum sustaining Amaro's cloistered world. First, there is a hostile confrontation between Benito and Father Natalio. We then see Benito chauffeur-driven to Chato's estate, where a lavish party is in progress. Benito has been called to baptize Chato's baby. The photographs of the event, after the photographer is stabbed by one of Natalio's men, make their way onto the front page of the local newspaper, as part of a scandal reported by Ruben, under the banner: 'Church Linked to Drugs and Guerillas.'

Amaro is then summoned by the Bishop. As Martin drives him, he remarks, "The Devil built his lair in this town years ago." Amaro looks quite prepared to believe that. The Bishop (Ernesto Gomez Cruz) is apologetic. "Even saints make mistakes," he says. He then tells Amaro to write a rebuttal for the newspaper. He also orders Natalio to be transferred to a convent and gives Amaro the letter to take to him.

It is at this stage that Amaro gets involved in the economic power play the Church has been practicing in the town all along. It becomes clear to us, though the film does not play up its effect on Amaro, that he is now being forced to champion not what he knows to be the truth, but the truth by which the Church wishes to defend itself.

When Amaro finds that the newspaper editor is hesitant about publishing his rebuttal, he plays the trump card. "One phone call from the Bishop can put an end to all your advertising," he says simply. The threat works. The editor succumbs even further, and eventually fires Ruben.

As Amaro's hands get dirtier, he seems to realize the ambivalence of the moral abstractions he has been preaching. When he visits Natalio in the mountains, he finds the local villagers joining in a concerted effort to chop down trees for the church to be built. Natalio, after reading the letter from the Bishop, roars: "My only obedience is to God! And to my people!" Amaro knows what he means, but he also knows he cannot take Natalio's side.

At his sermon, as Amaro speaks of "eternal pain and ruin" for those not obeying the Lord Jesus, and then segues into the slanderous charges made against the Church, the local sorceress, Dionisia (Luisa Huertas) hisses loudly. After the service, she leads the townsfolk to throw stones at Ruben's house, screaming, "Heretics!" No one is injured, but the scandal is a blow to Benito's complacency. That night, in his bedroom, he calls Sanjuanera "a priest's whore" and adds that he will be sent to hell for his sin. She quotes back to him what he said a long time ago: "The only hell is loneliness!" To which, Benito mutters, "I hope God sees it that way." Similarly, we see Amaro racked by guilt for the first time. In a gesture of penance, he holds his hand over a fire until he cannot bear the pain.

Amaro soon gets the chastisement he's seeking when he's attacked by the jobless Ruben in the street. Even so, at the police station, he decides not to press charges. In the next scene, we see Amaro praying in the chapel. Amelia enters and places her hand on his shoulder. This time, presumably owing to the moral vacuum within him, Amaro does not withdraw from her touch, as we have seen do twice before. Instead, he feels the side of her face, then kisses her gently on the lips. There is a brief cut to the sculpture of a bleeding Christ, then we see Amelia and Amaro kissing passionately.

As Amaro tosses in bed that night, it is clear that he has reached a point of no return. When Amelia comes to confess the next day, she claims he knows her sins. With self-assuredness, Amaro intones, "Love is the motor of the world." Amelia then wonders aloud, "*Our* love?" Amaro answers, "It's a gift, a blessing." As an afterthought, he adds that they will have to be careful just the same.

Amaro then starts to behave like a man possessed, but also as one who realizes his romantic passion has to be kept a secret from the world. He tells Martin that he needs a place to coach Amelia in order to prepare her for joining a convent. Martin obliges by allowing the two lovers the use of a room in his shed. To Benito, Amaro explains that Amelia will be teaching the catechism to Getsemani. The stage is thus set for the film's first unabashed love scene. As Amelia undresses, we hear Amaro's voiceover reciting the biblical Song of Songs, here intended to praise her physical charms. Soon they're in bed in the throes of intercourse.

The subplots the film has been developing, having to do with Benito and Natalio, now pale in the light of Amaro's passion, which is both "carnal and spiritual." This is the reason that, when Amelia says she's pregnant, he refuses to give up the priesthood, which he considers his lifelong vocation. Also, when Martin squeals to Benito about the love trysts, Amaro is unrepentant. "You took a vow of chastity!" Benito admonishes him. "Because I was forced to," Amaro retorts. The two men tussle, resulting in Benito collapsing from a heart seizure. Hurriedly, Benito is flown to Mexico City, leaving Amaro in charge.

To avoid disgrace, Amaro suggests to Amelia that she get Ruben to marry her. She tries her seductive best, but

Ruben says he no longer loves her. In his darkest moment, Amaro prays to the Virgin Mary for "a miracle." His wish is granted in a most unexpected way. As the film reaches its climax, Amelia dies in Amaro's arms after an unsuccessful attempt at abortion, performed by a backwoods doctor, has left her bleeding to death.

Again, from its omniscient viewpoint, the film makes clear that the townspeople believe that it was Ruben who got her pregnant, and Amaro who tried to save her. As he delivers his sermon at her wake, Amaro recites the scriptural text of forgiveness, but in no way implicating himself personally. The expression on his face, however, is that of a wounded and lost soul. Benito, who attends the ceremony in a wheelchair, turns away, as if unable to accept the hypocrisy. The camera holds on the hurt on Amaro's face, then starts to pull back down the aisle. We take leave of the film, realizing that Amaro will eventually become as hardened a pragmatist as Benito.

Quite understandably, in its home country, where 88% of the population is Catholic (Martin Scorsese's 1988 iconoclastic salvo *The Last Temptation of Christ* has yet to be released there), Carrera's film provoked such a storm of protest from the Church that it went on to become the highest grossing film in Mexico's history. Here, critics have found its narrative just plain soapy. More interesting has been some of the focus on the ideological thrust. Jack Mathews in the *Daily News* cannot accept the implication that if Amaro "were free to love, he'd be free to do the Lord's work." Similarly, Stephen Holden in the *New York Times* notes that the "film's most blasphemous notion is that spiritual passion is essentially repressed lust."

—*Vivek Adarkar*

CREDITS

Father Amaro: Gael Garcia Bernal
Father Benito: Sancho Gracia
Amelia: Ana Claudia Talancon
Father Natalio: Damian Alcazar
Sanjuanera: Angelica Aragon
Mayor: Pedro Armendariz Jr.
Dionisia: Luisa Huertas
Bishop: Ernesto Gomez Cruz

Origin: Mexico
Language: Spanish
Released: 2002
Production: Alfredo Ripstein, David Birman Ripstein; Alameda, BluFilms, Foprocino; released by Samuel Goldwyn Films
Directed by: Carlos Carrera
Written by: Vicente Lenero

Directed by: Danny DeVito
Written by: Adam Resnick
Cinematography by: Anastas Michos
Music by: David Newman
Sound: David M. Kelson
Editing: Jon Poll
Art Direction: Tamara Deverell
Costumes: Jane Ruhm
Production Design: Howard Cummings
MPAA rating: R
Running time: 109 minutes

REVIEWS

Chicago Sun-Times Online. March 29, 2002.
Entertainment Weekly. April 5, 2002, p. 90.
Los Angeles Times Online. March 29, 2002.
New York Times Online. March 29, 2002.
People. April 8, 2002, p. 41.
USA Today Online. March 28, 2002.
Variety. March 25, 2002, p. 36.
Washington Post. March 29, 2002, p. WE41.

TRIVIA

Smoochy's ice dance was choreographed by Barry Lather and Edward Norton did his own skating as Smoochy. The scene was filmed at Maple Leaf Gardens in Toronto.

Deuces Wild

Before gangs had guns . . . they fought with guts.
—Movie tagline
Some lines should never be crossed.
—Movie tagline

Box Office: $6 million

The gang movie *Deuces Wild* opens with a harrowing scene. On a New York City street in a pelting rainstorm, a young man carries his brother's body to the stoop of his mother's tenement. In the mode of high operatic melodrama, the screaming mother confronts the tragedy, as her son angrily and tearfully offers up the corpse. It turns out that the unlucky brother has succumbed to a drug overdose.

In director Scott Kalvert's homage to 1950s gangs, there is an unsupported romantic notion of the nobility of gangs in the days of innocence. *Deuces Wild* is supposed to be a movie about the end of an era, set in a watershed time. It is 1958 in Brooklyn, the first summer after the beloved Dodgers baseball team has moved to Los Angeles. The borough is full of consternation and a feeling that the old certainties no longer hold true. Two brothers, Bobby (Brad Renfro) and Leon (Stephen Dorff), are the leaders of a gang known as the Deuces. Their brother, Alley Boy, was the victim in the opening scene. The Deuces are strictly small potatoes, but they stand for self-defense—for protecting their families and the businesses on their block from the kind of predators and corruption that led to the death of Alley Boy.

The Deuces fight with their fists, not with guns. They drink booze but they don't do drugs. They are tough, profane, and prone to violence, but they are basically good kids. At least, that's how the plot of *Deuces Wild* sets up the situation. It's more than a little bit of a stretch, for what exactly it is about the Deuces that makes them special is hard to find in this muddled drama.

Kalvert's previous film, *The Basketball Diaries,* also trafficked in romanticized notions of violence and how it plays out in the life of urban communities. As in that movie, *Deuces Wild* has scenes of carefully choreographed melees, making lyrical cinematic beauty out of brutal confrontations. *Deuces Wild* also indulges shamelessly in many gang movie clichés. The Deuces are to determined to protect their turf from a rival gang, the Vipers, who are moving in on their territory with no apologies. Leon is a hothead who chafes under the rule of his more evenhanded, thoughtful older brother. And—as might be expected—Leon falls in love with the sister of one of the leaders of the Vipers, Annie (Fairuza Balk). She keeps asking him to prove his loyalty to her, while his brother thinks their romance is a betrayal of the gang, and so there are lots of scenes about the hapless Leon being pushed and pulled apart emotionally.

For reasons left unexplained, the Vipers are in the grip of a mobster named Fritzy Zennetti (Matt Dillon). Dillon plays him as a laid-back, smooth-talking negotiator who puts a soft-soap, corporate face on the mob's plans to move in on the Deuces' turf and set up their own drug dealing enterprise. Dillon, the former teenage star of gang movies has become a sinister, greasy older presence, a street veteran who has become a petty tyrant in semiretirement. The Vipers, themselves just a minor street gang, are getting set up to be the stooges in a larger criminal empire in which Fritzy is only a lieutenant. An air of dread and unrest hangs over the street. What once were rumbles with fisticuffs have escalated into gunfights, and old codes of honor are eroding.

On paper, these themes might have sounded intriguing. As played out in *Deuces Wild,* however, they fall flat. The film plods along in predictable fashion, with plenty of scenes that are supposed to add to the color of the milieu but do nothing to advance dramatic tension. Renfro's Bobby seems aimless and adrift, and is never a grand enough figure to suggest the dilemma of an old-fashioned street gang leader being forced to compromise his morality in the face of new threats to old ways of life. Dorff's Leon is more intriguing. Dorff has a way of making his character's naiveté and stupidity into something sympathetic as he is pulled in several different directions at once by personalities more forceful than him.

Balk plays Annie as a hard-bitten moll with a heart of gold beneath her veneer of sass and brassiness. The trouble is, Annie is so tough on the surface that it's hard to see why Leon falls for her, other than his sheer inability to connect with others. Balk doesn't make her character into an attractive figure, nor does she ascend beyond a familiar feminine stereotype of the era.

Kalvert takes some pains to make his film authentic with period detail, but it's actually merely conforming to the standard cultural view of what the era was like. He adds nothing new to the picture. This is the 1950s as imagined by revisionists who viewed it as the last days of a more simplistic world.

Some critics called *Deuces Wild* a *West Side Story* without the musical numbers, but even that is a stretch. Take away the songs and the choreography, and *West Side Story* still is a classic saga of doomed love. *Deuces Wild* aspires to similar heights and also has broader ambitions as a snapshot of an era that was disintegrating, but it falls far short on both counts. The plot and the action are not compelling enough to make the film iconic at any level; instead, the story line is pedestrian. Kalvert meanders and doesn't do well at maintaining any consistent dramatic tension. *Deuces Wild* succeeds as a period piece, but it's a period that's been depicted time and time again. It fails as social commentary; the romantic subplot is uninteresting; and as a coming-of-age movie, it's not sufficiently evocative.

Screenwriter Christopher Gambale makes his debut with the film, and while he's ambitious in his aims, he can't quite concoct a story strong enough to support his overarching ideas. And he hasn't written characters that are memorable. Nobody really rises to heroic stature in *Deuces Wild,* but neither do the protagonists seem buffeted in the face of forces larger than them. They are just ordinary young men and women, and none of them are memorable. In the end, it's just another movie about urban gangs of a bygone era, awash in misplaced romanticism.

—Michael Betzold

Leon: Stephen Dorff
Bobby: Brad Renfro
Marco: Norman Reedus
Annie: Fairuza Balk
Freddie: Max Perlich
Fritzy Zennetti: Matt Dillon
Betsy: Drea De Matteo
Scooch: Frankie Muniz
Father Aldo: Vincent Pastore
Jimmy Pockets: Balthazar Getty
Tino: James Franco
Philly Babe: Louis Lombardi
Wendy: Deborah Harry
Vinnie Fish: Johnny Knoxville

Origin: USA
Released: 2002
Production: Willi Baer, Fred Caruso, Paul Kimatian, Michael Cerenzie; Cinerenta-Cinewild, Unity Productions, Presto Productions, Antonia Company; released by United Artists
Directed by: Scott Kalvert
Written by: Paul Kimatian, Christopher Gambale
Cinematography by: John A. Alonzo
Music by: Stewart Copeland
Sound: Stephan Von Hase
Editing: Michael R. Miller
Art Direction: Donna Ekins-Kapner
Costumes: Marianne Astrom-DeFina
Production Design: David L. Snyder
MPAA rating: R
Running time: 97 minutes

REVIEWS

Boxoffice. July, 2001, p. 91.
Boxoffice. March, 2002, p. 26.
Los Angeles Times Online. May 3, 2002.
New York Times Online. May 3, 2002.
People. May 13, 2002, p. 44.
Variety. May 6, 2002, p. 43.
Washington Post. May 3, 2002, p. WE44.

QUOTES

Fritzy Zennetti (Matt Dillon): "Bricks don't fall out of the sky in this neighborhood unless I'm throwing them."

Die Another Day

He's Never Been Cooler.
—Movie tagline

Live for the moment and Die Another Day
—Movie tagline

 Box Office: $150 million

Forty years after Ian Fleming published his first James Bond novel, *Casino Royale,* in Britain, the 20th official James Bond film celebrates its anniversary in customary fashion—guns, girls, stunts, farfetched plot, and 007 himself debonair in tuxedo and double entendres. Pierce Brosnan couldn't be more comfortable in his fourth Bond outing and that's a compliment. And Halle Berry is so far the only Bond girl who took a break from filming to accept a Best Actress Oscar (for her role in *Monster's Ball*). Still, *Die Another Day* is a somewhat schizophrenic effort—harder-edged in its first half and over-the-top in its second, thus highlighting the good and the bad of this long-lived series. Since this effort brought in $47 million at the box-office during its opening weekend—the best debut for the franchise—it seems clear that Bond will be back (with Brosnan since he's expressed interest in continuing the role for a fifth film).

The film starts with its usual pre-credit stunt to set the plot in motion. We see three surfers coming into shore off the Pukch'ong Coast of North Korea who turn out to be Bond and a couple of fellow agents. They divert a helicopter and Bond takes the place of a courier carrying a briefcase filled with African conflict diamonds (diamonds mined illegally); Bond places a bomb in the briefcase. Bond then lands in the DMZ where he is greeted by renegade Colonel Moon (Will Yun Lee), who is selling heavily-armed hovercraft that are able to navigate the minefield set up between the north and the south.

Bond also gets his first contact with Moon's second-in-command, Zao (Rick Yune), who discovers that Bond is MI6. When Bond realizes he's been found out, he detonates the briefcase, sending some of the diamonds into Zao's face. He then goes in pursuit (via hovercraft) of Colonel Moon, seemingly sending him to his watery death over a dam. Bond is then captured by General Moon (Kenneth Tsang), the Colonel's father, and taken to a North Korean prison where he is tortured. [The viewer sees this very effectively in a series of quick edits that make it seem like a nightmare that Bond is reliving over and over.] Then come the credits and Madonna's synth-pop efforts at the title song, which is tolerable.

After 14 months, the General comes to the prison and a hairy, haggard Bond is exchanged for Zao. He's then taken to a British hospital ship docked off the coast of Hong Kong and is soon reunited with M (Judi Dench), who seems none too happy to see him, telling her agent that his freedom "came at too high a price" since Zao has killed several Chinese intelligence agents, apparently with information Bond supplied after he cracked under interrogation. Bond insists he was set-up but M rescinds his double-O status and is preparing to send him to the Falkland Islands for evaluation. Instead, James escapes the ship and persuades an agent with Chinese intelligence to help him get revenge on Zao, who is now in Cuba (Cadiz, Spain substitutes for Havana).

Bond's Cuban contact informs him that Zao is at a clinic on the Isla los Organos where a Dr. Alvarez specializes in gene replacement therapy. While passing himself off as an ornithologist, Bond gets up-close and very personal with the sassy and beautiful Jinx (Halle Berry), who rises out of the ocean in a bikini with a knife strapped around her waist (in homage to Ursula Andress' Honey Ryder in *Dr. No*). The duo exchange sexual banter before winding up in bed together. The next morning Bond realizes that Jinx is also heading for the island. Once there, Jinx kills Dr. Alvarez and sets a bomb to destroy the clinic. Bond finds Zao, who is in the middle of having his DNA replaced in order to make him appear western. He's now milk-white, blue-eyed, and bald, with diamonds still embedded in his face. Zao manages to get away from both Bond and Jinx and Jinx manages to get away before James can get an explanation.

Bond does discover that some diamonds Zao was carrying are marked with the initials of Gustav Graves (Toby Stephens), a publicity-seeking business magnate whose latest stunt is to parasail into London and tease the press with his latest project, the Icarus satellite. Bond learns that Graves is practicing at a fencing club and goes to introduce himself. He also meets Graves's publicist, and champion fencer, the chilly Miranda Frost (Rosamund Pike). After showing Graves the diamonds, he is challenged to a vicious and prolonged match with swords. When he bests Graves, Bond is invited to a launching party for the Icarus project in Iceland (which was also featured scenery in 1983's *A View to a Kill*).

M also contacts Bond, who cynically tells her: "You burn me and now you want my help." She is suspicious of the mysterious Graves who went "from nothing to everything in no time at all" according to Bond. Graves appears to be using his (fake) Icelandic diamond mine as a front for laundering the African-mined diamonds but Bond also re-iterates the fact that he was betrayed and he believes that Graves had something to do with it.

Bond then enters Q's workshop, which is now headed by the irascible gadget-maker-formerly-known-as-R (John Cleese, taking over the role from the late Desmond Llewelyn). There are a number of references to previous Bond movies and Q hands Bond another watch—"this will be your 20th, I believe." But Bond's best new toy is a fully loaded Aston Martin V12 Vanquish that Q calls the Vanish because it can be made invisible. Meanwhile, M is meeting with Miranda Frost, who is an MI6 agent. They discuss

Bond whom Frost disparages as a womanizer, among other things, who "kills first" and "asks questions later."

Bond then arrives in Iceland where Graves has constructed an ice palace for his party. Jinx arrives as well (driving a new Ford Thunderbird) and Zao also shows up to rendezvous with Graves. And just who is Graves really? Well, the not-so-dead Colonel Moon, who successfully (more or less) completed the gene replacement process to make himself appear to be a westerner. The better to set his evil plan in motion. The Icarus satellite he's just made operational works as a "second sun," capable of concentrating the sun's rays on any heat signature (including nuclear weaponry) and destroying it.

Jinx breaks into Graves's headquarters in an effort to destroy the project but is captured by Zao. Frost reveals herself as an agent to James and then beds him to keep up the charade. The next morning, James also breaks into Grave's headquarters and winds up rescuing Jinx from being sliced apart by lasers (shades of *Goldfinger*). Bond finally discovers that Graves is Colonel Moon—"So, you live to die another day, Colonel." Oh, and who betrayed him? None other than Miranda Frost for vague reasons about wanting to be on the winning team with Graves. Bond manages to get away using one of Q's gadgets. Then, things start getting tedious.

First there's a protracted chase across a frozen lake with Bond in a sled-like drag racer being targeted by the Icarus satellite (just where is Bond supposed to be driving *to*?). And Bond manages to escape this by windsurfing on a glacier (don't ask, it's ridiculous and looks very, very fake). Then Bond manages to get back to his invisible car at the ice hotel (where Jinx has been trapped by Miranda). Graves and Miranda get aboard a plane and Zao is sent to kill Bond. There's another very protracted drive across the ice with Bond is his tricked-out car and Zao in his missile-loaded Jaguar XKR. After a lot of spinning wheels and melting ice, Bond kills Zao (anticlimactically) and rescues Jinx (whom Bond has learned works for the NSA).

The scene then switches to South Korea and the U.S. command bunker in the DMZ where M is found with Jinx's boss, Damian Falco (Michael Madsen). Troops are on high alert as they await Graves's next move. Bond and Jinx manage to infiltrate a North Korean air base and get on Graves's cargo plane, which is taking off. Graves turns the Icarus satellite to the minefield between the divided country and uses its power to begin exploding all the mines. Then the North's troops will have a clear highway to invade the South and the country will be reunited—the first step in conquering the world (megalomaniacs always want to conquer the world).

Jinx takes over the plane's controls while Bond goes after Graves. A bullet pierces a window causing it to explode and start depressurizing the plane. While Bond battles Graves (did I mention Graves is wearing some kind of electric weapons cyber-suit thingy? Never mind—it just adds to the excess), Jinx battles a sword-welding Miranda. The heroes beat the bad guys, shut down Icarus, and make their escape from the disintegrating plane (which also looks very, very fake) in a convenient helicopter that happens to be loaded with Graves's diamonds.

And so we end up back in London at MI6 headquarters with the ever-faithful Moneypenny (Samantha Bond) greeting Bond's return—with a kiss, a very lascivious kiss that, well it all turns out to be one of Q's little simulation toys. (And so Moneypenny's longings will remain unrequited.) Meanwhile, the real Bond is plying Jinx with diamonds in some remote Korean coastal hut as they banter and end their adventure with a kiss. Fade out.

As is usual with the recent Bond movies, there is too much going on—much of it making little or no sense, although you (should) get so caught up in the action that this doesn't matter. Except this time so many action sequences are piled on (particularly in the latter half of the movie) that they become a bore. At least it's apparent where the budget of some $130 million went.

Since the character of James Bond is made up of any number of well-worn (and expected) clichés, Brosnan's performance can't be faulted. However, after Bond survives 14 months of torture and comes out wanting revenge, wouldn't you expect *some* residual effects from his ordeal? M may not trust her agent at first (she cruelly dismisses him as being of "no use to anyone") but he's business as usual. I guess no one wants to see an angst-ridden 007.

Berry's Jinx still can't top Michelle Yeoh's Chinese agent from *Tomorrow Never Dies* in the capability department but she's at least much more believable than the Denise Richards "scientist" of *The World Is Not Enough*. Stephens shows a positive viciousness during Graves's fencing match with Bond but it's downhill from there, Pike is as frosty as her character's name, and Yune's Zao at least looks odd, which seems to be a tradition with second-tier bad guys in Bond movies (re: Richard Kiel's "Jaws").

It's not a bad effort from director Lee Tamahori but you wonder how free a hand he was allowed in changing a money-making franchise. And it will certainly make money: *Die Another Day* has lots and lots and lots of merchandising that should offset some of those production costs, although the ubiquity of print and television ads for Bond gear may make you sick of the movie before you actually see it.

—*Christine Tomassini*

CREDITS

James Bond: Pierce Brosnan
Jinx: Halle Berry
Gustav Graves: Toby Stephens

M: Judi Dench
Q: John Cleese
Miranda Frost: Rosmund Pike
Zao: Rick Yune
Damian Falco: Michael Madsen
Colonel Moon: Will Yun Lee
General Moon: Kenneth Tsang
Moneypenny: Samantha Bond
Charles Robinson: Colin Salmon
Raoul: Emilio Echeverria
Vlad: Michael Gorevoy
Mr. Kil: Lawrence Makoare

Origin: USA
Released: 2002
Production: Michael G. Wilson, Barbara Broccoli; Eon Productions; released by MGM
Directed by: Lee Tamahori
Written by: Neal Purvis, Robert Wade
Cinematography by: David Tattersall
Music by: David Arnold
Sound: Chris Munro
Editing: Christian Wagner
Art Direction: Simon Lamont
Costumes: Lindy Hemming
Production Design: Peter Lamont
MPAA rating: PG-13
Running time: 130 minutes

REVIEWS

American Cinematographer. November, 2002, p. 34.
Boston Globe Online. November 22, 2002.
Boxoffice. November, 2002, p. 42.
Chicago Sun-Times Online. November 22, 2002.
Detroit Free Press Online. November 22, 2002.
Detroit News. November 22, 2002, p. E1.
The Globe and Mail. September 7, 2002, p. R3.
The Guardian Online. November 15, 2002.
Los Angeles Times Online. November 22, 2002.
Movieline. November, 2002, p. 40.
New York Times Online. September 8, 2002.
New York Times Online. November 22, 2002.
New York Times Online. November 25, 2002.
People. December 2, 2002, p. 39.
Premiere. November, 2002, p. 74.
Rolling Stone. December 12, 2002, p. 106.
San Francisco Chronicle. November 22, 2002, p. D1.
Sight and Sound. November, 2002, p. 16.
TV Guide. November 9, 2002, p. 22.
USA Today Online. November 22, 2002.
Variety. November 11, 2002, p. A1.
Variety. November 18, 2002, p. 23.
Washington Post. November 22, 2002, p. WE41.

QUOTES

James Bond (Pierce Brosnan): "You know, you're cleverer than you look." Q (John Cleese): "Better than looking cleverer than you are."

TRIVIA

Madonna cameos as fencing instructor Verity besides singing the title song.

AWARDS AND NOMINATIONS

Nomination:
Golden Globes 2003: Song ("Die Another Day").

Dirty Cop No Donut

Dirty Cop No Donut should have been a winner, but this feature-length parody of *Cops* loses its way by never getting beyond its one-joke premise. In the story written and directed by Tim Ritter, Gus Kimball (a.k.a. Officer Friendly) (played by Joel D. Wynkoop) turns his graveyard shift duties into an all-night odyssey of police abuse, despite the fact he is being filmed by a documentarian (never seen by the viewer).

Starting in a deli of an unnamed city, Gus takes food off the shelves without paying, because he feels he is entitled to the perks. After stealing drugs from a drug bust, he molests a prostitute (Gertina Willemse), and demands sexual favors. Later, when he runs into a former convict (Bill Cassinelli, the film's special effects director), he harasses and injures the man. Along the way, Gus tells the audience how he is trying to "set the world's wrongs right," then proceeds to destroy a pawn shop when he doesn't like the owner's attitude.

In the wee hours of the morning, Gus breaks up a party, destroys the car of a woman who is driving drunk, beats the woman (Kathleen Ritter), ties and binds a couple (Andrew Gulbrandsen and Lindsay Horgan) who have been reportedly fighting, and finally stops at a bar for a drink. On the way out of the bar, Gus is stopped and arrested by a real cop (Michael Hoffman, Jr., the film's assistant director) for impersonating an officer. Apparently, Gus was never a cop, but merely a mentally ill man.

Tim Ritter's no-budget item barely got a theatrical release in 2001, and it seems to deserve its longer-term fate on video store shelves. But conceptually, at least, *Dirty Cop No Donut* has quite a bit going for it. Apart from the Fox network's *Cops,* which ought to be exposed for the way the police and the show itself exploits and abuses the crime suspects, the film references several other works. The cinema verite style harkens back to Frederick Wiseman's *Law and Order* (1969), which gave a much more nuanced depiction of the same subject. The "crazed" cop antihero (played with rich vulgarity by Wynkoop) sustains a long tradition from the film noir days of *Naked Alibi*(1954), starring Sterling Hayden, which more recently culminated in *The Bad Lieutenant*(1992), starring Harvey Keitel. One maudlin confession scene to the camera is a particularly effective take on that Abel Ferrera meshugass. Ritter keeps the police car light flashing through the car window as Wynkoop delivers his tearful soliloquy: "All I'm trying to do is set the world's wrongs right . . . sometimes I wonder why I'm even doing this."

Yet other parts of the parody are much more obvious and unfunny, especially all the scenes where Gus abuses the suspected criminals. Of course, the whole point of the film is to show the bad behavior of this "officer," but these prolonged displays become either unpleasant—or merely tiring—to watch. The press material for *Dirty Cop* promises the that the filmmaker shooting Gus will also be morally indicted when he "cruelly lenses the events as they unfold without lending a helping hand to any of the unfortunate victims. . . . In fact, he seems to get off on all this as much as the cop . . ." But in the version viewed for this review, no media complicity lesson ever takes place. In fact, one of the few times the documentarian is even acknowledged is when Gus yells at him, "You keep that camera on me—who do think is the star of this video?"

The lack of budget is not a drawback to *Dirty Cop.* In fact, the style is perfect. But some of the supporting cast and extra players look as though they are barely able to control their laughter. Finally, the denouement might be seen as a clever twist in the narrative, but it could also be viewed as a cheat. Sadly, given the reality of police abuse, this coda is reminiscent of how UFA Studios forced the makers of *The Cabinet of Dr. Caligari*(1919) to change the ending of their story, from indicting a corrupt institutional figure to making the "mad" (i.e. mentally ill) protagonist into the party responsible for all the world's sins.

—*Eric Monder*

Officer Friendly: Joel D. Wynkoop
Tommy: Bill Cassinelli
Arresting officer: Michael Hoffman Jr.
Abusive husband: Andrew Gulbrandsen
Abused wife: Lindsay Horgan
Drunk driver: Kathleen Ritter

Prostitute: Gertina Willemse

Origin: USA
Released: 1999
Production: Twisted Illusions; released by Sub Rosa Studios
Directed by: Tim Ritter
Written by: Tim Ritter
Cinematography by: Tim Ritter
Music by: R.M. Hoopes
Editing: Steve McNaughten
MPAA rating: Unrated
Running time: 80 minutes

New York Times Online. June 15, 2001.

Divine Secrets of the Ya-Ya Sisterhood

Mothers. Daughters. The never-ending story of good vs. evil.
—Movie tagline

 Box Office: $69.6 million

O n a warm Louisiana night in 1937, four young girls on a sleep-over slip out a bedroom window to take part in a ritual that will bind them together for the rest of their lives as the Ya-Ya Sisterhood. Fast forward many years into the future, and now it's New York and preparations for the opening of Sidda Lee Walker's (Sandra Bullock) play "Dark Waters" that is center focus. Sidda is being interviewed by a writer for *Time* magazine. But what Sidda doesn't realize is that when some of her comments are incorporated into the article they will enrage her mother Vivi (Ellen Burstyn) when she reads them. How should a mother react when her daughter states nationally, "I owe all my creativity to [my mother]. If I'd had an easy childhood I'd have had nothing to write about"?

So Vivi picks up the phone and calls her daughter. The phone is answered by Sidda's long-time significant other, Connor (Angus MacFadyen), but when Sidda finally does take the phone, things do not go well. After hanging up, one melodramatic gesture follows another. Vivi takes down all the family photos, cuts Sidda out of them, burns them and sends them to Sidda. Sidda replies by sending her mother torn up opening night tickets for her play. Vivi responds by sending a copy of her last will and testament with Sidda written out. Next Sidda sends her mother an invitation to Angus' and her wedding but the time, date and location are cut out.

In the words of Vivi's three childhood friends, her Ya-Ya sisters, this is a "Bloody Mary" emergency. Consequently, undertaking a Ya-Ya mission of mercy, an intervention if you will, brassy and rich Teensy (Fionnula Flanagan), quiet Necie (Shirley Knight), and acidic Caro (Maggie Smith) set out for New York City. Knowing Sidda won't come to Louisiana of her own volition, the trio drug her and fly her home to confront not only her current turbulent relationship with her mother, but her mother's and her past as well.

When Sidda finally wakes up from the drug's effect she is angry at having been taken away from her life in New York and the work involved in putting on her play. The Ya-Ya sisters, however, are determined to reconcile mother and daughter. To aid this process they have place in a prominent position a scrapbook. "There are some things in there that might change your mind about Vivi," they tell her.

Slowly but surely Sidda begins leafing through the book and Vivi's past slowly unfolds before her. She sees that her grandmother Buggy (Cherry Jones) was overwhelmed by young Vivi's (Ashley Judd) life-force, that she couldn't comprehend her daughter's grand goals (to be a big city newspaper woman), and that she was terribly jealous of the attention her husband paid to their daughter. When her father gives Vivi a diamond ring for her birthday, her mother violently takes it away from her, embarrassing her in front of her "sisters." But when her father drags her mother back into the bedroom to apologize and return the ring, it is her mother's turn to be humiliated.

So is a bad mother Vivi's only excuse for her melodramatic behavior and her own bad mothering? How about a lost first love. Vivi is deeply, deeply in love with Teensy's brother Jack (Matthew Settle) and when he enlists as a pilot in world War II and is killed, she is devastated. There are many more secrets in Vivi's past: thwarted dreams of fame, settling for marriage with Shep Walker (James Garner), ending up with more kids than she can handle, and a drinking problem for starters. But when Sidda learns of them all, will it be enough to reconcile mother and daughter?

In 1991, writer Callie Khouri won an Oscar for *Thelma and Louise,* probably one of the best "chick flicks" ever made. With *Divine Secrets* Khouri shares the writing credit with *As Good As It Gets'* writer Mark Andrus, but even more important, it is also Khouri's directorial debut. This is a big, sprawling film, juggling at least four different time periods and three different casts. It may have been more than Khouri should have tackled her first time out. Constantly flipping

back and forth in time, moving too quickly between comedy and melodrama, and trying to match the character identity to the members of the three different casts becomes confusing and maybe even more work than the story is worth. But is this the fault of Khouri's movie or the original story?

Divine Secrets of the Ya-Ya Sisterhood takes its title from the second book written by Rebecca Wells about these characters. The movie, however, also includes parts of her first book, *Little Alters Everywhere.* This not only increased the sprawl of the story, but it is also odd when one considers that Khouri has indicated that she found it difficult to adapt the screenplay from Wells' 350-page, 1996 second novel. So why involve plot elements from the first?

There is no doubt that Wells' novels have a strong appeal to many women readers, but their transition to the screen may only appeal to die-hard Ya-Ya fans. Without being viewed through the lens of an enthusiast, Wells's plotting seems contrived, full of manufactured confrontations, pop psychology, overblown characters and ostentatious Southern dialogue such as Vivi's "Oh, what a surprise. Look what the backstabbing, traitorous cats dragged in. Look who it is—my old exfriends and the biological fruit of my womb that rotted."

That's the kind of dialogue one expects from writers who idolize—and therefore also contribute to—the character of the stereotyped Southern woman. These characters revel in their eccentricities, the colorfulness of their language, clothing and behavior. Others may find their idiosyncratic flamboyance tiresome. There's too much "amusing" alcohol abuse and too much forced charm to all the self-centered behavior. There's also an insufferable reliance on lives based on temperamental emotional actions instead of reason. It's hard to feel sorry for or empathize with characters who cause a lot of their own problems.

The consequence of this is a great cast wasted on stock characters. Especially undervalued is Sandra Bullock whose character has little to do but react to the antics of her mother and the Ya-Ya Sisters. But at least Bullock is more appreciated than James Garner or Angus MacFadyen who are nothing more than background atmosphere. They are no more important than the Spanish moss in the trees.

One thing that does help create time and place in *Divine Secrets* is a great soundtrack. In the able hands of T-Bone Burnett (*O Brother Where Art Thou?*) and David Mansfield, the film's music often carries the viewer where the plot and the characters can't. The film contains two interesting original songs, Bob Dylan's "Waitin' for You" which plays over the film's ending credits (Burnett and Mansfield toured with Dylan's Rolling Thunder Review) and Lauren Hill's "Selah."

Those who loved Wells' books may love this movie, but others may see it as a lost opportunity. Movies about strong women are rare—which is why *Thelma and Louise* was such a hit—but are these drunk southern drama queens really strong women? We may envy their friendships, but can we really envy their lives?

Divine Secrets of the Ya-Ya Sisterhood premiered at the very first Tribecca Film Festival in New York, which is odd for a film oozing with Southern discomfort. It combines the worst of television's Designing Women and Golden Girls and throws in a bit too much Steel Magnolias and Fried Green Tomatoes. It contains scenes that go nowhere, and children who disappear without a trace. Worst of all its secrets are neither divine nor surprising. By the time the movie is ending—with a groanable over-the-top, New-Orleans-marching-band, feel-good birthday party—most of us are probably thinking, please, God, just don't let them yell "Ya-Ya" again.

—Beverley Bare Buehrer

CREDITS

Younger Vivi: Ashley Judd
Sidda Lee Walker: Sandra Bullock
Vivi Walker: Ellen Burstyn
Caro: Maggie Smith
Shep Walker: James Garner
Teensy: Fionnula Flanagan
Necie: Shirley Knight
Buggy: Cherry Jones
Connor: Angus Macfadyen
Younger Teensy: Jacqueline McKenzie
Younger Caro: Katy Selverstone
Younger Necie: Kiersten Warren
Genevieve: Gina McKee
Jack: Matthew Settle
Taylor Abbott: David Rasche
Pete Abbott: Fred Koehler
Willetta: Leslie Silva
Chaney: Ron Dortoh
Younger Shep Walker: David Lee Smith

Origin: USA
Released: 2002
Production: Bonnie Bruckheimer, Hunt Lowry; All Girl Films, Gaylord Productions; released by Warner Bros.
Directed by: Callie Khouri
Written by: Callie Khouri, Mark Andrus
Cinematography by: John Bailey
Music by: T Bone Burnett
Sound: Petur Hliddal
Editing: Andrew Marcus
Art Direction: John R. Jensen
Costumes: Gary Jones
Production Design: David J. Bomba
MPAA rating: PG-13

Running time: 116 minutes

REVIEWS

Chicago Sun-Times Online. June 7, 2002.
Chicago Tribune Online. June 7, 2002.
Christian Science Monitor Online. June 7, 2002.
Entertainment Weekly. June 14, 2002, p. 70.
Hollywood Reporter Online. May 10, 2002.
Los Angeles Times Online. June 4, 2002.
Los Angeles Times Online. June 7, 2002.
New York Post Online. June 7, 2002.
New York Times Online. June 7, 2002.
People. June 17, 2002, p. 37.
USA Today Online. June 7, 2002.
Variety Online. May 9, 2002.
Washington Post. June 7, 2002, p. WE43.

QUOTES

Sidda Lee's (Sandra Bullock) toast to Vivi (Ellen Burstyn): "Here's to Mama. Long may she rave."

TRIVIA

Taj Mahal plays the bandleader at Vivi's birthday party. It is his rendition of Fats Waller's "Keeping Out of Mischief" that's heard in the scene.

Donnie Darko

Dark. Darker. Darko.
—Movie tagline

Dark doings plague the upper-middle class Darko family and their Middlesex, Virginia community, circa 1988. That's all that's known for certain in writer/director Richard Kelly's darkly engaging debut whose metaphysical plot peculiarities allow for various interpretations. Heavy with a Heathers-like brand of high school angst comedy, Donnie Darko also has the feel of the swirling Paul Thomas Anderson drama, Magnolia, filled with open-ended stories of its various, quirky characters. While probably influences, Darko, however, is uniquely a coming-of-ager cum time travel tale which alternately draws—sometimes poignantly, sometimes wittily—on 1980's culture with its haunting soundtrack and homages to movies of the era, including E.T. and The Evil Dead. Citing influences from The Twilight Zone to Stephen King, Kelly injects the film and its lead character with enough moody weirdness and supernatural surprises to overcome some plot inconsistencies and complex ideas that are not fully explained throughout the twisty narrative. Gyllenhaal, playing the title character Donnie, provides a chilling portrayal of a somewhat dazed and lonely but ultimately determined high-schooler whose nocturnal communications with a large fiendish-looking rabbit grant him with an important task to carry out.

A gorgeous opening scene sets the mood of the plot about to unspool: A boy, alone, waking in the middle of the road overlooking a picturesque vista of mountains. The boy is the film's hero, Donnie Darko, and the scene not only signifies the main character's isolation from society, both literally and figuratively, but sets him over and above the rest of society, as well. After 14-year-old Donnie pedals home, we find out why he has awoken in such a strange place. It seems he has been sleepwalking and forgetting to take his medication—prescribed after an earlier antisocial act. Antisocial behavior that seems to be ever-growing in the normally likable, extremely intelligent teenager and which has not gone unnoticed by his concerned parents Rose and Eddie (Mary McDonnell and Holmes Osborne), typically smarmy teenage sister Elizabeth (Gyllenhaal's real life sister Maggie Gyllenhaal), and precocious little sister Samantha (Daveigh Chase). Donnie, though confused, is not portrayed as a loner or as alienated from his family. Nonetheless, events conspire to remove Donnie emotionally from family and friends, alike.

What sets off the film's chain of catastrophic events is one of Donnie's sleepwalking episodes, seemingly orchestrated by a human-sized, menacing looking rabbit that Donnie sees and hears, compelling him to leave the house at night. The ghoulish bunny-like figure, who calls himself Frank, bears the chilling message that the world will end in 28 days. Continuing to see his psychiatrist, Dr. Thurman (Katharine Ross), who prescribes medication and plenty of hypnotherapy, Donnie nonetheless continues sleepwalking, waking up on a golf course one day, and keeps receiving apocalyptic messages from Frank. It seems his hallucinations have brought him luck, however, as one night when he is sleepwalking, an engine from a 747 jet plane falls from the sky and lands in Donnie's bedroom. The rest of the family, unharmed but clearly shaken, breathes a sigh of relief when Donnie wanders over to the crash scene the next morning where a crew is busy loading the mysterious engine onto a huge flatbed truck. Early news of the FBI investigation of the matter brings the intriguing news that no plane has reported an engine missing.

At the center of a bizarre turn of events in a normally sleepy community, Donnie's confusion about what is actually happening to him only continues to grow. He doesn't seem crazy and indeed doesn't think of himself as the paranoid schizophrenic his psychiatrist say he is, but neither the audience nor himself can be sure that he isn't. At school,

he finds support in an unconventional English teacher, Ms. Pomeroy (Drew Barrymore), who senses Donnie's trouble. Conversely, his uptight, New Age gym teacher, Ms. Kittie Farmer (Beth Grant), only irks Donnie with her inane exercise which forces students to evaluate imaginary life experiences and mark them on a lifeline between Fear and Love. When forced to participate against his better judgement, Donnie crudely suggests what she can do with the lifeline. The ensuing scene between the gym teacher and Donnie's rather unconventional parents proves that, though officially upper-middle class Republicans, they are no stereotypes. While concerned about their son, they can still see the humor in the ridiculous teacher's outrage and defend Donnie. Another source of irritation is Kittie's prodigy, motivational speaker Jim Cunningham (Patrick Swayze), whose hokey self-help videos have become part of the school's curriculum.

School, however, does find Donnie a soulmate in a pretty transfer student, Gretchen (Jena Malone) with a disturbing family history. The two are brought together by Ms. Pomeroy who immediately sensed the attraction between them. Perhaps because of all the chaos in his life, or perhaps merely because he is a teenaged boy, Donnie's occasional escape into sexual fantasies now at least have some chance of occurring in reality. Gretchen finds Donnie's antisocial behavior appealing and even desirable as evidenced after Donnie bristles at her remark that he is weird and she counters frankly, "That was a compliment." After the school is mysteriously flooded and an axe found in the head of the statue of the school's mascot, the two further bond as school is canceled for the day.

Girlfriend not withstanding, Donnie's visions are growing right along with his sense of desperation and doom. Frank's prophetic countdown to the end is getting nearer everyday and bringing with it more bizarre events. While Donnie and Gretchen are out on a date, watching the horror classic, *Evil Dead*, Frank appears in the theater after Gretchen falls asleep and commands Donnie to burn down Jim Cunningham's palatial Tudor mansion. Donnie sneaks out and returns sometime later, where Gretchen is still asleep, while the next days' news reports of the fire at the Cunningham residence where no one was harmed but also notes that fire investigators found a secret room in the house that links Cunningham to a child porn ring.

Donnie has also cultivated an interest in time travel and searches for more answers about the topic from his science teacher, Dr. Monnitoff (Noah Wyle), after he starts seeing fluid, tunnel-like protrusions coming out of his family's midsections that seem to be indications of their future paths. It could be that rather than mere hallucinations, signs point to a parallel universe, a break in the space/time continuum brought about by the jet engine incident. Dr. Monnitoff recommends the book, *The Philosophy of Time Travel*, written by Roberta Sparrow. Sparrow (Patience Cleveland) is the

into some kind of larger trailer-trash vindication is ridiculous. When Rabbit finally decides he's got nothing to be ashamed of, it's something the audience knew all along, which is what makes the ending so easy to swallow and so crowd-pleasing.

Hanson and cohorts have fun with the culture-clash motif in scenes like the one where Rabbit and his buddy lampoon Rabbit's mother's boyfriend's music by singing a rap parody of "Sweet Home Alabama." More of that would have catapulted *8 Mile* into rarified territory. As it is, however, with a fabulous hip-hop soundtrack, including one truly remarkable Eminem song that rolls through the final credits, and with a boffo ending skillfully executed, this film is a surprising breakout for its star. Sometimes cheesy melodrama works—as in the going-it-alone ending, with Rabbit walking down an alley into his not-as-yet-achieved fame (the soundtrack should have had a rap version of Frank Sinatra's "My Way"). As with everything Eminem does, *8 Mile* is, at bottom, a masterful piece of chicanery. He has it both ways, real and pseudo-real, because, though Rabbit's future is uncertain, the audience already knows where his alter ego is headed.

—*Michael Betzold*

CREDITS

Jimmy "Rabbit" Smith Jr.: Eminem
Stephanie: Kim Basinger
Alex: Brittany Murphy
Future: Mekhi Phifer
Cheddar Bob: Evan Jones
Wink: Eugene Byrd
Sol George: Omar Benson Miller
DJ Iz: De'Angelo Wilson
Janeane: Taryn Manning
Greg Buehl: Michael Shannon
Papa Doc: Anthony Mackie
Lily: Chloe Greenfield
Manny: Paul Bates
Paul: Craig Chandler

Origin: USA
Released: 2002
Production: Brian Grazer, Curtis Hanson, Jimmy Iovine; Universal Pictures, Imagine Entertainment; released by Universal Studios
Directed by: Curtis Hanson
Written by: Scott Silver
Cinematography by: Rodrigo Prieto
Music by: Eminem
Sound: Danny Michael
Editing: Jay Rabinowitz, Craig Kitson

Art Direction: Kevin Kavanaugh
Costumes: Mark Bridges
Production Design: Philip Messina
MPAA rating: R
Running time: 118 minutes

REVIEWS

Boxoffice. November, 2002, p. 122.
Chicago Sun-Times Online. November 8, 2002.
Detroit Free Press. November 3, 2002, p. J1.
Detroit Free Press. November 8, 2002, p. 14E.
Detroit News. October 26, 2002, p. D1.
Detroit News. November 8, 2002, p. E1.
Entertainment Weekly. November 15, 2002, p. 103.
Los Angeles Times Online. November 8, 2002.
New York Times Online. September 8, 2002.
New York Times Online. November 8, 2002.
People. November 18, 2002, p. 41.
Rolling Stone. November 28, 2002, p. 97.
USA Today Online. November 8, 2002.
Variety Online. November 3, 2002.
Washington Post. November 8, 2002, p. WE37.

QUOTES

Jimmy Smith Jr. (Eminem): "Do you ever wonder at what point you got to stop living up here and start living down here?"

AWARDS AND NOMINATIONS

Nomination:
Oscars 2002: Song ("Lose Yourself")
Golden Globes 2003: Song ("Lose Yourself").

8 Women
(Huit Femmes)

Living in a house full of women can be murder.
—Movie tagline

 Box Office: $3 million

From the beginnings of the French New Wave in the late 1950's, French filmmakers have been paying homage to American directors. Francois Truffaut, Jean-Luc Godard, and Claude Chabrol were heavily influenced by American genre films, especially film noir. The influence worked the other way in the late 1960's and 1970's when American directors began imitating the styles of Truffaut and Godard, most notably with Arthur Penn's *Bonnie and Clyde* (1967). Such cross-influencing of filmmakers continues, of course, with Francois Ozon's *8 Women* being an especially overt example. Ozon combines elements of the melodramatic soap operas of Douglas Sirk with the Technicolor dollops of such musical directors as Vincente Minnelli (who also knew a thing or two about melodrama) with occasionally engaging if mixed results.

In a country house in the winter somewhere in France in the 1950's live seven women. Gaby (Catherine Deneuve) is married to Marcel (Dominique Lamure). Their daughters are Suzon (Virginie Ledoyen), a university student in Paris, and Catherine (Ludivine Sagnier), a teenager. Also in residence are Gaby's wheelchair-bound mother, Mamy (Danielle Darrieux), and her spinster sister, Augustine (Isabelle Huppert). Madame Chanel (Firmine Richard) is the housekeeper, and Louise (Emmanuelle Beart) is the recently employed maid.

Shortly after Gaby brings Suzon home for a visit, Marcel is discovered dead in his bedroom with a dagger in his back. Soon, the telephone lines are discovered to have been cut, the family car is disabled, and snow cuts the women off from the rest of the world. The killer must still be on the premises, and one of the seven must be the murderer. Make that one of the eight. Marcel's flamboyant sister, Pierrette (Fanny Ardant) arrives. Estranged from Gaby, she has secretly been staying at Chanel's nearby cottage. With her arrival, an already tense situation becomes even worse. Soon, numerous secrets are unveiled. Suzon is pregnant. Louise has been having an affair with Marcel. Mamy is not really crippled. Gaby and Augustine constantly bicker, as do Gaby and Pierrette.

While Ozon's previous films are very realistic, he revels here in the artificial. Each character gets to sing a solo, with every song a French pop tune from the 1960's, 1970's, or 1980's, all apparently well known to Gallic audiences, most pretty banal. While the pop songs sung by the characters in such Dennis Potter television miniseries as *Pennies from Heaven* (1978) and *The Singing Detective* (1986) usually reveal something poignant about the characters, Ozon's songs serve primarily to showcase the limited musical talent of the actresses. (Darrieux comes off the best.) Ozon thinks he is celebrating these women, but there is a strong strain of misogynism running through the film.

As for homage, while Ozon, cinematographer Jeanne Lapoirie, production designer Arnaud de Moleron, and costume designer Pascaline Chavanne attempt an approxima-tion of Technicolor, especially through the use of reds, the film remains merely an approximation. The muted colors actually more closely resemble Sirk's use of color than Minnelli's, despite what Ozon has said in interviews. With musicals such as *An American in Paris* (1951) and, especially, *The Band Wagon* (1953), Minnelli used vibrant colors. Moreover, none of his musicals, nor any of Hollywood's in the 1950's, were on such a small scale as *8 Women*.

Ozon originally wanted to adapt Clare Booth Luce's bitchy play *The Women*, filmed in 1939 by George Cukor, but when he was unable to secure the rights, he resorted to a 1960's play (showing the influence of Agatha Christie) by the French writer Robert Thomas. Ozon does nothing to overcome the staginess of his source, setting most of the action in one room. The film even ends with the characters lined up side by side as if about to take bows. There's something a bit perverse about the staginess of *8 Women* because of the director's stated goal of paying tribute to his masters, not just Minnelli and Sirk but Stanley Donen, Alfred Hitchcock, and Max Ophuls as well. Most of their films are extremely cinematic; even in the rare instance when Hitchcock adapts a play, *Dial M for Murder* (1954), to which *8 Women* has a very slight resemblance, he makes the material fit his style. Minnelli is able to make *The Cobweb* (1955) both claustrophobic and cinematic. Ozon's mostly static approach just makes little sense.

8 Women opens with a tracking shot ending with a deer nibbling in the snow, a direct reference to a shot in Sirk's *All That Heaven Allows* (1956). In his 1950's melodramas, Sirk indulged in the emotional excesses of his characters, but with a strong sense of style and a wonderful eye for color, he managed to override the limitations of his material and of such performers as John Gavin, Rock Hudson, Lana Turner, and Jane Wyman. Sirk's characters suffer but triumph in the end, and not just in ways dictated by the moral code of the time. In his masterpiece, *Written on the Wind* (1957), Dorothy Malone plays a selfish alcoholic, but the final shot indicates she has learned from her excesses and will persevere.

Ozon has been heavily influenced by the films of Rainer Werner Fassbinder, especially their melodramatic explorations of homoeroticism, and even adapted a Fassbinder play, *Water Drops on Burning Rocks* (2000). Fassbinder's idol was also Sirk, but he takes elements from the master and adapts them to his own sensibility and cinematic style. *8 Women* is a personal film only in smug, annoying ways.

For example, Ozon casts two performers, Deneuve and Ardant, both of whom not only worked with Truffaut but had love affairs with him. Ozon makes the two become embroiled in a ridiculous catfight ending in a long, passionate kiss. Since the director has stated that he does not like Truffaut's films, this scene becomes doubly embarrassing. Younger artists often snub their noses at their elders— Truffaut and Godard are, in fact, famous for it—but Ozon's gesture can be seen as being in bad taste. The revelation of the truth behind the mystery of the dead husband might also strike some as a bit jarring to the essentially lighthearted tone of the film.

Ozon was surprised that so many highly regarded performers were eager to work with him on this project. Giving them tapes of his *Under the Sand* (2000) before it was released cinched the deal. *Under the Sand* is one of the best films ever made about a sense of loss, and Charlotte Rampling gives the best performance of her career as a devoted wife whose husband disappears.

Even though Ozon gives nothing so substantial to his eight women, all of them do reasonably well with the material. Richard is excellent as the film's moral consciousness. Her role is also part of the Sirk tribute since her character resembles the loyal black maid played by Juanita Moore in *Imitation of Life* (1959). One slight problem is that the audience is supposed to wonder who killed Marcel, and several characters, most notably Chanel, have no apparent motive.

Ardant throws herself completely into the role of the trashy sister-in-law. Her energy is surprising because of the calm dignity of most the characters she usually plays. Her best moments come with her modified striptease during her song, a tribute to Rita Hayworth in *Gilda* (1946). Likewise, Deneuve has fun mocking her ice-queen image. At times, she almost seems to be winking at the audience.

Huppert, who has come to specialize in sullen, moody characters, shows the most abandon. This usually subtle performer goes over the top in a way not seen since Al Pacino in *Dick Tracy* (1990). The role, the most substantial in the film, is meant to comment on lonely, repressed, slightly crazy women like those played by Judith Anderson in Hitchcock's *Rebecca* (1940) and Agnes Moorehead in Orson Welles' *The Magnificent Ambersons* (1942). With her hair tied in a tight bun and wearing ugly eyeglasses, Huppert resembles Bette Davis before her transformation in *Now, Voyager* (1942). The best moment of *8 Women* comes when Pierrette gives Augustine a quick lesson in hairstyle, makeup, and clothing, and Huppert also is transformed from an almost unrecognizably harridan to her glamorous self. Despite the limitations of the material, Ardant, Devenuve, and Huppert seem to be having a very good time, and their spirits help keep the audience going and apparently helped convince many of the film's reviewers that it is much better than it is.

Darrieux is one of the treasures of the cinema, having made her first film in 1931. Her credits include three Ophuls films, including his masterpiece, *The Earrings of Madame de* (1953). Her presence is another reminder of how limited is *8 Women*, for Ophuls excels, perhaps more than any filmmaker, in camera movement, with using the medium to underscore the connection between the characters, their setting, and theme. Even more than Sirk, Ophuls is a compassionate director, always forgiving of his protagonists' sins

and weaknesses. Ozon, who has the potential to be a major talent, displays similar compassion in his other films, especially *Under the Sand*, making the mostly bitter tone of *8 Women* even more of a puzzlement.

—*Michael Adams*

CREDITS

Gaby: Catherine Deneuve
Augustine: Isabelle Huppert
Louise: Emmanuelle Beart
Pierrette: Fanny Ardant
Suzon: Virginie Ledoyen
Mamy: Danielle Darrieux
Catherine: Ludivine Sagnier
Mme. Chanel: Firmine Richard
Marcel: Dominique Lamure

Origin: France
Language: French
Released: 2002
Production: Olivier Delbosc, Marc Missionier; France 2 Cinema, Mars Films, Fidelite Productions; released by Focus Features
Directed by: Francois Ozon
Written by: Francois Ozon, Marina de Van
Cinematography by: Jeanne Lapoirie
Music by: Krishna Levy
Sound: Pierre Gamet, Jean-Pierre Laforce
Editing: Lawrence Bawedin
Costumes: Pascaline Chavanne
Production Design: Arnaud de Moleron
MPAA rating: R
Running time: 103 minutes

REVIEWS

Boxoffice. September, 2002, p. 140.
Chicago Sun-Times Online. September 27, 2002.
Entertainment Weekly. October 11, 2002, p. 56.
Film Comment. March/April, 2002, p. 23.
Los Angeles Times. September 20, 2002, p. 16.
New York Times. September 20, 2002, p. E1.
New Yorker. September 16, 2002, p. 106.
People. September 30, 2002, p. 39.
Sight and Sound. April, 2002, p. 13.
USA Today. September 27, 2002, p. D16.
Vanity Fair. October, 2002, p. 150.
Variety. February 11, 2002, p. 43.
Washington Post. September 27, 2002, p. WE41.

QUOTES

Louise (Emmanuelle Beart): "Monsieur died in his bed with a knife in his back."

TRIVIA

Danielle Darrieux has also played Catherine Deneuve's mother in *The Young Girls of Rochefort* (1967) and *Scene of the Crime* (1986).

Elling

They're packed and ready for the greatest adventure of their lives. All they have to do is get out of the house.
—Movie tagline

When one imagines Norwegian film many people do not normally think lighthearted, comical cinema. I have to admit I think long drawn out character studies directed with a darker vision, such as an Ingmar Bergman film. After viewing *Elling,* my preconceived notions of Norwegian cinema were shattered.

Elling, directed by Petter Næss, is a heartfelt and insightful look into the inner world of two men living together after being released from a mental hospital. Elling (Per Christian Ellefsen) is put in the hospital initially due to an inability to deal with the death of his mother. He is the epitome of a momma's boy and doesn't hide the fact he is obsessed and unable to cope without her. Elling really finds it near impossible to cope with many small details of life. He is not unaware of his quirkiness however, as he notes in one scene. He comments on his inability to move alone through a restaurant while other "normal" people in the world can travel to exotic locales on their own. He many have some difficulties navigating through life but he is not so challenged he doesn't see these things within himself.

Kjell, Elling's roommate, cannot stop thinking of sex. Sven Nordin, who has been extremely popular in his homeland of Norway since he starred in an extremely popular sitcom, portrays Kjell. Kjell hasn't had sex thus far in his life and so much of his world and daily existence is spent thinking of it.

Elling is returning to the outside world after having spent two years in a psychiatric hospital. He has been lucky enough to receive a council flat and is allowed to live there with his roommate Kjell, a simple man. Elling's naivete leads him to believe the outer world is normal and stable. He has forgotten the general discord in which the world functions.

As we all know, the world is anything but secure and the situations these men find themselves in is both heartwarming and heartfelt.

I very much felt protective of these characters right off the bat. I cannot say I identified with them, as I have never struggled with or known anyone to have struggled with the exact personality disorder of these two. What really kept me watching was their very awkwardness in life and learning to negotiate in the world. This made me feel protective of them and wanted them very much to succeed. To some degree or at least at some point in our lives many of us have felt the kinds of pressures Elling feels. Regular situations are highly charged for him. Take his attempts to buy a train ticket. When he is asked a simple question of, "One way?" he becomes visibly confused and considers the questions for quite some time. His reply of "Is there more than one way" is hilarious! There is clearly numerous ways to interpret simple everyday questions and Elling reminds us of that.

Difficulties with simple tasks are part of the reason for Elling's initial hospital stay so one can only imagine what daily navigation would do to this sensitive soul. With a strong will, increasing courage and a little bit of help (together with the threat of being sent back to the psychiatric ward), Elling and Kjell stumble along this new path of life. Soon numerous situations arise where the two easily terrified men must really give it their best shot out in the world.

I feel it would be easy to write this film off as just another sickly sweet look at the curious behavior of the mentally ill. On the surface this film looks as though it was merely a saccharin rendition of *Rain Man* or *Nuts,* and to be fair it does have some elements of these types of films. But to give it its fair shake, *Elling* is so much more. It is about the struggle for stability in a highly chaotic world. It is the world of the innocent and this is something so very rare in film today. When a director is brave enough to give a very innocent film a life and a voice in this time of over confident, sarcastic characters in film, it makes me want to see more.

In all honesty *Elling* takes a while to get used to. At first you feel as though you should dislike it on principle. The grandstanding and emotional spoon-feeding is a bit hard to handle and seemed too American at first. Once it becomes clear there is more below the surface it is easier to let oneself go and enjoy the unfolding of this character. *Elling* was nominated for an Academy Award in the category of best foreign film. It lost to *Amelie,* another great film about navigating through life. *Elling* found itself a bit luckier with other festivals however, and walked away with six other major wins at various international festivals.

The film is an adaptation from a book by Ingvar Ambjørnsen and was performed earlier as a stage production. Both Ellfinson and Nordin starred in the same roles for the film as they did for the stage, which is why they are so consistently good at working in these character's skins. They clearly understand their characters and move easily and confidently around in them. *Elling* is a joy to watch for a number of reasons. The directing is a nice mix of comedy and drama with competent actors carrying off both aspects of the film. As long as one is able to suspend the sort of cynicism of contemporary urban life this film about two innocents is a pleasure to watch.

—*Laura Abraham*

CREDITS

Elling: Per Christian Ellefsen
Kjell Bjarne: Sven Nordin
Reidun Nordsletten: Marit Pia Jacobsen
Frank Asli: Jorgen Langhelle
Alfons Jorgensen: Per Christensen

Origin: Norway
Language: Norwegian
Released: 2001
Production: Dag Alveberg; released by First Look Pictures
Directed by: Petter Naess
Written by: Axel Hellstenius
Cinematography by: Svein Krovel
Music by: Lars Lillo Stenberg
Sound: Morten Solum
Editing: Inge-Lise Langfeldt
Art Direction: Haralds Egede Nissen
Costumes: Aslaugh Konradsdottir
MPAA rating: R
Running time: 89 minutes

REVIEWS

Boxoffice. June, 2002, p. 63.
Chicago Sun-Times Online. September 13, 2002.
Entertainment Weekly. June 21, 2002, p. 49.
Los Angeles Times Online. September 6, 2002.
New York Times Online. May 29, 2002.
People. June 10, 2002, p. 40.
Variety Online. November 11, 2001.
Washington Post. September 13, 2002, p. WE40.

AWARDS AND NOMINATIONS

Nomination:
Oscars 2002: Foreign Film.

The Emperor's Club

In everyone's life there's that one person who makes all the difference.
—Movie tagline

Box Office: $13.7 million

By now, the prep-school film has become its own genre. The most notable recent version was *Dead Poet's Society*, which stuck to the usual conventions (see also: *Goodbye, Mr. Chips, The Browning Version,* etc.) These types of films feature young men of wealth who are being groomed to be the future leaders of society, gorgeous and stately New England-area school grounds, and lots of blue blazers. Second in importance to the blazers is the presence of an inspirational teacher. Usually said teacher breaks all the rules and alienates the school powers-that-be, but is loved by students and is the best teacher the school has ever seen.

The Emperor's Club follows the formula but with a few twists. It's a classy entrant to the genre, though not particularly outstanding. The story is based on the short story "The Palace Thief," written by Ethan Canin. Neil Tolkin (who has the Pauly Shore film *Jury Duty* to his credit, if that's the right word) adapted the story for the screen. The film was directed by Michael Hoffman who also did *One Fine Day* and *A Midsummer Night's Dream*.

In this film, the requisite inspiring teacher is Mr. Hundert (Kevin Kline). His first name is William, but he is much more of a Mr. Hundert. Mr. Hundert presides over a class of Western Civilization at the fictional St. Benedict's School for Boys where future movers-and-shakers learn the minute points of the history of Roman Civilization. Mr. Hundert is a very proper man, who carries himself with a ramrod straight spine and truly believes that studying the great thinkers of the ancient world are the key to shaping these young mens' characters. He sees himself as the person to mold these young men and teach them proper ethics. He truly preaches following the straight and narrow. When he spies one student cutting across the school yard, he points them back to the path, extolling the boy, "Follow the path where great men have walked."

The story is bookended by Mr. Hundert in the present, attending a special reunion. The now gray-haired teacher is the invited guest of one of his students, Sedgewick Bell (Joel Gretsch). Why, Mr. Hundert can remember when Bell was a teen and one of his students. He can remember it was like it was yesterday.

The film cuts back to a more youthful Mr. Hundert as a teacher in the mid-1970s. He presides over a class of smart, somewhat timid boys who take very seriously the study of ancient civilizations. Their greatest dream is to be selected to participate in the Mr. Julius Caesar contest. The three final contestants are chosen from the students who do the best on a series of written quizzes given in class. The three finalists then compete in a contest in front of their parents and classmates in a quiz show format. The winner is crowned Mr. Julius Caesar.

A few weeks late into the semester, Sedgewick Bell (the young Sedgewick is played by Emile Hirsch of *The Dangerous Lives of Altar Boys*) arrives in class. Mr. Hundert is shocked by Sedgewick insolent attitude. Why, the boy doesn't even seem to care about competing to be Mr. Julius Caesar! (Several critics made the point that it seemed odd that Mr. Hundert appears to have never had a student who was a discipline problem.) Sedgewick's attitude has a lot to do with being the son of a West Virginia Senator (Harris Yulin) who doesn't spare any of his important time for his son.

The other students are afraid of Sedgewick but they are also fascinated by his badness. This kid is so rebellious that he has girlie magazines, cigarettes and communist literature. Sedgewick, with his Leonardo DiCaprio squinty eyes, leads his fellow students in such hijinks as taking a forbidden boat across the lake to the even more forbidden girls' school.

When Mr. Hundert first meets Sedgewick, he attributes the boy's insolence to new student jitters. He then gets angry. But then his true teacher-ness comes through and he realizes that Sedgewick is a boy who is not living up to his true potential. His belief in Sedgewick leads the boy to take his studies seriously. In an inspiring sequence, Sedgewick starts applying himself and soon rises near the top of his class. When Mr. Hundert grades the final entry papers for the Mr. Julius Caesar contest, Sedgewick has done so well that he comes in . . . fourth, just missing the cut by one point. Mr. Hundert doesn't want to ruin his good story of his own inspiring teaching and changes Sedgewick's grade, moving him to the top and bumping out the nerdy, round-headed, nervous boy, Martin Blythe (Paul Dano).

During the contest, Mr. Hundert, the master of ceremonies, is disappointed when he notices that Sedgewick is cheating. He informs Headmaster Woodbridge (Edward Herrmann) while the contest is still going on, but the Headmaster waves for him to continue without disqualifying the boy. Apparently, it would be too risky to offend the Senator who is important and generous to the school. Mr. Hundert then finds himself making another ethical violation. He gives Sedgewick a question that he knows the boy won't know and that his competitor, Deepak Mehta (Rishi Mehta) will know. After the contest, Sedgewick gives up studying and returns to his naughty behavior with renewed vigor.

Years later, Sedgewick is a successful CEO, who plans to be a Senator. Despite his poor showing at school, his father managed to get him into Yale, and the family's money got him a company. He invites all the classmates to a party for a rematch of the Mr. Julius Caesar contest. The older Sedgewick is played by an actor (Gretsch) who has not an iota of the bad-boy charm of Hirsch's younger version. This is coupled with what seem like the overly easy resolutions of Mr. Hundert and Sedgewick's relationship. In a scene between the two, the clean-cut Sedgewick tells Mr. Hundert things like "I had my moments, didn't I?" He returns the teacher's beloved textbook and says, "Now I understand how much it meant to you."

The tone of the scene and the departure from the more subtle ethical questions of the earlier part of the movie are a disappointment. Why tackle difficult issues if they're just going to be wrapped up abruptly, Hollywood-style? But the writers have a few more tricks left. Sedgewick turns out to be not as repentant as he seems and it might be that Mr. Hundert has not been a success in molding at least one man's character.

What makes this movie better are the performances of Kline and Hirsch. Kline, who is always good, gives his character life. His Mr. Hundert is proper, but Kline doesn't take an acting shortcut and make the teacher overly fussy and prudish. He visibly yearns for his colleague's wife, Elizabeth (Embeth Davidtz), and struggles with being the son of a more famous academic. And Hirsch is quite good as Sedgewick. He has the right kind of heavy-lidded, brooding look and the charisma of someone who could inspire these nerds into making trouble. And he shows the little boy part of himself that really does wish he could do well in school.

Critics weren't too inspired by the film. A.O. Scott of the *New York Times* wrote, "*The Emperor's Club* carefully sets itself up as an obvious, transparent morality play, and then just as deliberately refuses the easy payoff. This is both impressive and a little disingenuous: The film is in effect congratulating itself for refusing to offer a neat and tidy view of life without offering much else." Michael Wilmington of the *Chicago Tribune* praised Kline's acting, writing "It's an extraordinary performance in an often brave and intelligent film that, unfortunately, tends to collapse around him in the end." And Kenneth Turan of the *Los Angeles Times* wrote, "Though the message of *The Emperor's Club* is not precisely what you might expect, it's an awfully familiar one nevertheless, a theme that's too comfortable for its own good." 🎥

—*Jill Hamilton*

CREDITS

William Hundert: Kevin Kline
Sedgewick Bell: Emile Hirsch
Elizabeth: Embeth Davidtz
James Ellerby: Rob Morrow

Martin Blythe: Paul Franklin Dano
Headmaster Woodbridge: Edward Herrmann
Senator Bell: Harris Yulin
Mr. Castle: Roger Rees
Louis Masoudi: Jesse Eisenberg
Deepak Mehta: Rishi Mehta
Older Sedgewick: Joel Gretsch
Older Martin: Steven Culp
Older Louis: Patrick Dempsey
Older Deepak: Rahul Khanna

Origin: USA
Released: 2002
Production: Andrew Karsch, Marc Abraham; Beacon
Pictures, Longfellow Pictures, LivePlanet; released by
Universal Pictures
Directed by: Michael Hoffman
Written by: Neil Tolkin
Cinematography by: Lajos Koltai
Music by: James Newton Howard
Sound: William Sarokin
Editing: Harvey Rosenstock
Art Direction: Dennis Bradford
Costumes: Cynthia Flynt
Production Design: Patrizia Von Brandenstein
MPAA rating: PG-13
Running time: 109 minutes

REVIEWS

Boxoffice. November, 2002, p. 126.
Chicago Sun-Times Online. November 22, 2002.
Entertainment Weekly. November 29, 2002, p. 81.
Los Angeles Times Online. November 22, 2002.
New York Times Online. November 22, 2002.
People. December 2, 2002, p. 42.
USA Today Online. November 22, 2002.
Variety Online. September 9, 2002.
Washington Post. November 22, 2002, p. WE41.

QUOTES

William Hundert (Kevin Kline): "All of us at some point are forced
to look at ourselves in the mirror and see who we really are."

The Emperor's New Clothes

*The world's most powerful man is about to fight
his greatest battle . . . between love and glory.*
—Movie tagline

Alan Taylor's *The Emperor's New Clothes* is a bit of an international anomaly in that even though Germany and Great Britain are listed as countries of origin for the film, two of the film's four producers and the production crew sport Italian names. And the French emperor, Napoleon Bonaparte sports a proper English accent instead of a French one. Viewers will either see this international flavoring as charming or as a distraction. The film's press notes claim, English actor "Ian Holm is delightful in the role he was born to play—twice,", but couldn't the actor at least fake a French accent? Other than this minor distraction, Holm does embody the historic French figure with the right blend of pathos and arrogance. After all, the actor plays two versions of Napoleon, the real Napoleon that travels back to France under disguise as a deckhand and the faux Napoleon that refuses to give up his role as the imposter.

Although Taylor has racked up TV writing credits for such popular American series as *Sex and the City* and *The Sopranos,* he takes on the added challenge of directing a what-if farce as his sophomore feature. Based on Simon Leys' novel, *The Death of Napoleon* and adapted by Taylor, Kevin Molony and Herbie Wave, *The Emperor's New Clothes* takes us on a farcical journey back to the island of St. Helena in the year 1828. This tongue-in-cheek film causes us to ponder what would have happened if Napoleon returned to France under a disguise while an imposter died in his place on the island? And what if history actually didn't happen the way we have been told in our history books?

Napoleon is languishing on St. Helena as a British prisoner of war. He writes his memoirs as he awaits the arrival of his imposter, a French deckhand lacking in all the social graces. When the deckhand, Eugene, arrives, Napoleon doesn't think that Eugene will be able to pass himself off as an emperor, but Napoleon leaves the island anyway, posing as Eugene, aboard a French ship. However, Napoleon's plans go awry after the captain of the ship refuses to stop in France and docks in Belgium instead. Napoleon trudges through the forest, takes a slow boat , and eventually arrives in Paris, only to learns that his contact just passed on.

Meanwhile, on St. Helena, Eugene refuses to give up his imposter's role of Napoleon and he continues to live the good life. He rewrites Napoleon's memoirs while adding juicy details of sexual trysts and describes his ex-wife, Josephine, in vulgar terms. No amount of coaxing can convince

Eugene and he eventually dies from overeating—leading all of Europe to believe that Napoleon died on St. Helena in 1828. Back in Paris, the real Napoleon has taken up with commoners and fallen in love with his contact's widow, Pumpkin (Iben Hjelje), a melon hawker. Napoleon, so keen on strategies, maps out a plan for the local vegetable sellers to hawk their vegetables in the perfect neighborhood. Armed with maps and rhetoric, Napoleon as Eugene becomes a local hero despite the fact that he wants to come out of the closet and tell the truth about his identity.

Pumkin's confidante Dr. Lambert (Tim McInnerny) learns the truth of Napoleon's identity when he finds a painting of Napoleon's son among the emperor's possessions, but he refuses to reveal his findings since he wishes to claim Pumpkin for himself. One night, when Napoleon begs Lambert to reveal the truth, Lambert tricks Napoleon and leads him to a facility for the mentally ill where Napoleon watches a group of inmates posing as the infamous French emperor. At this point, Napoleon gives up the game and decides to live the life of a commoner since no one would ever take him seriously. And although the "real" Napoleon most likely lived many years beyond the early 1800s, it is written in history books that Napoleon Bonaparte died in 1828.

The Emperor's New Clothes does provide viewers with laugh-out-loud scenes, but for the most part, the film portrays a sober story about mistaken identity and the yearning to be oneself. Similar to Tom Stoppard's screenplay for *Shakespeare in Love*, *Emperor* reinvents history in an entertaining manner or so we think.

—*Patty-Lynne Herlevi*

CREDITS

Napoleon/Eugene Lenormand: Ian Holm
Pumpkin: Iben Hjejle
Dr. Lambert: Tim (McInnerny) McInnery
Gerard: Tom Watson
Montholon: Nigel Terry
Bertrand: Hugh Bonneville
Antommarchi: Murray Melvin
Marchand: Eddie Marsan
Bommel: Clive Russell

Origin: Great Britain
Released: 2001
Production: Uberto Pasolini; Mikado Films, Senator Film Entertainment, FilmFour, Redware Films; released by Paramount Classics
Directed by: Alan Taylor
Written by: Kevin Molony, Herbie Wave
Cinematography by: Alessio Gelsini Torresi

Music by: Rachel Portman
Sound: Clive Winter
Editing: Masahiro Hirakubo
Art Direction: Carlo Rescigno
Costumes: Sergio Ballo
Production Design: Andrea Crisanti
MPAA rating: PG
Running time: 107 minutes

REVIEWS

Boxoffice. April, 2002, p. 185.
Chicago Sun-Times Online. June 28, 2002.
Entertainment Weekly. June 21, 2002, p. 50.
Los Angeles Times Online. June 28, 2002.
New York Times Online. June 14, 2002.
Variety Online. August 16, 2001.
Washington Post. June 28, 2002, p. WE31.

QUOTES

Napoleon (Ian Holm): "So many have betrayed me. I place my trust in only two things now: My will, and the love of the people of France."

TRIVIA

Ian Holm also played Napoleon in 1981's "Time Bandits" and the 1974 miniseries "Napoleon and Love."

Enigma

Unlock the secrets.
—Movie tagline
Crack the Code.
—Movie tagline

While hackers of the modern computer age are a public nuisance, code breakers in the 1940s helped to end World War II. Similar to the hackers of today, the English code breakers, including the infamous mathematicians Alan Turing, Max Newman, and Tommy Flowers, lived for solving puzzles and are also known as the founding fathers of the computer age. *Enigma*, directed by Michael Apted (*The World is Not Enough*), written by playwright Tom Stoppard (*Shakespeare in Love*), and based on the best-selling novel by Robert Harris, portrays a romantic view of the men that broke Nazi code and the intelligent women that supported them. Although *Enigma* represents a fictional account of the code breakers, it mirrors the life of real code breaker Alan Turing, sans the controversy. Kevin Thomas of the *Los Angeles Times* described the film as "such a grand romantic entertainment that it sweeps the viewer along in swiftly escalating suspense." Although the film proves educational, it's potboiler entertainment.

The film *Breaking the Code* portrayed the controversial life of Alan Turing. Similar to the fictional character of Tom Jericho (Dougray Scott), portrayed in *Enigma,* Turing also lived a turbulent life but, unlike Jericho, Turing did not have a nervous breakdown over a woman because Turing was a homosexual and suffered torment for different reasons. Screenwriter Stoppard merely hints at the multitude of eccentricities and radicalism that existed at Bletchley Park. While Bletchley Park provided a scene for some of the greatest intellectual achievements of the 20th century, many of those intellectuals were iconoclasts similar to most geniuses. According to *The Secrets of Bletchley Park* pamphlet, "Bletchley Park, during the Second World War, seethed with life, intellectual stimulus, individuality, and eccentricity. It was a hotbed of revolutionary thinking." and revolutionaries.

Enigma's story deals mostly with two mysteries. The first involves the disappearance of Claire (Saffron Burrows), the love interest who led Jericho to experience a nervous breakdown. She has been missing for 14 hours and disappeared around the time the Germans mysteriously changed their code system. The second mystery revolves around the German's changing the way they send codes to their U-boats. Stoppard and director Michael Apted create a drama filled with intrigue that resembles the James Bond series (without the glamour and sexual images) and the romantic war time movies of Hollywood's golden age. And *Enigma* proves to be both smart and romantic entertainment even if it is not historically accurate. According to A.O. Scott of the *New York Times,* the discovery of Stalin's prewar massacre of Polish officers found in the Katyn Forest was "an atrocity which came to light much later" than 1943, the time in which *Enigma* takes place.

Robert Harris's novel was first published in the UK in 1995, where the paperback edition remained on the bestseller list for 15 weeks. It has been published in 23 languages and over a million copies of the novel have been sold worldwide. However, *Enigma* the film failed to excite English film critics. *The Guardian* critic Peter Bradshaw delivered his own British wit: "Preposterous Boy's Own Stuff which is light years away from the closeted realities of Bletchley Park, but it gives director Michael Apted a chance to show the form he developed on the recent Bond extravaganza *The World is Not Enough.*" *Observer* critic Jason Solomons compared the film to "a tweed jacket with crackled leather patches on the elbows. It is comfortable and sensible, a sturdy sort of film . . ."

As the film credits roll, we see a disheveled and nervous man on a train. He hallucinates and sees a gorgeous blonde woman visiting him on the train and it becomes obvious that the blonde represents the lover that has led to the man's nervous breakdown. The man, mathematician Tom Jericho, is returning to Bletchley Park after a stay at a mental institution in Cambridge. Only his return to Bletchley isn't welcomed by his superiors and the news that the German's have changed their code, along with the news of his former lover Claire's mysterious disappearance, hardly seems like an antidote for nervous exhaustion. Jericho has leaped from the frying pan into a colossal fire and this reluctant hero will have to save the world with his brains and not his brawn.

Upon his arrival, Jericho runs into Claire's mousy chum, Hester (Kate Winslet), in the company cafeteria. Hester brushes Jericho off and fails to mention Claire's disappearance. That evening, Jericho sneaks into the cottage that Claire and Hester share. He trashes Claire's room and accidentally locates papers revealing cryptograms that Claire has hidden beneath the floorboards. Hester catches Jericho in the act and reluctantly tells Jericho about Claire's disappearance. Jericho pleads with Hester to help him discover Claire's whereabouts, but Hester refuses to play the role of a sleuth. After arriving home, Jericho is greeted by a spy, Wigram (Jeremy Northam), who interrogates Jericho about Claire's disappearance and comes short of accusing Jericho of leaking their code-breaking operations to the Germans. Fortunately, Jericho is able to hide the papers that he found in Claire's cottage.

Jericho divides his time between figuring out the new German code and meeting with Hester as they try to figure out Claire's involvement with the cryptograms. In both situations, Jericho finds that he is racing against time. The Americans have sent a convoy of ships across the Atlantic where German U-boats await. Now the code breakers must decipher the new German code or the convoy will be destroyed. Meanwhile, Hester and Jericho sneak into a military unit where codes are filed and they steal other codes that will assist them in learning Claire's involvement with the cryptograms. But Wigram is hot on their trail and eventually leads them to a site where Claire's clothing had been discovered. But Claire's body still remains missing.

Eventually, the code breakers figure out the crib to decoding the German signals and, true to history, some of the convoy's ships are rescued and the breaking of the code leads to events that end the war. We finally learn about Claire's involvement with a traitor and also her possible involvement with Wigram, yet the mystery of her disappearance remains unsolved. Fast forward to 1946, where we see Jericho waiting for a pregnant Hester at a concert hall. Claire glides past Jericho, but Jericho only smiles when he recognizes Claire and he turns his attention to Hester.

Enigma features an exceptional cast, but critics singled out performances by Winslet, Scott, and Northam. Roger Ebert of the *Chicago Sun-Times* praised Winslet's performance: "Kate Winslet is very good here, wearing sensible shoes, with the wrong haircut—and then, seen in the right light, as a little proletarian sex bomb." Peter Travers from *Rolling Stone* mostly praises musician-turned-film-producer Mick Jagger for bringing us an intriguing film, but he also praises Northam's performance: "Northam is a real smoothie, with looks and style of a younger and nastier Cary Grant." However, critics for the *Village Voice* and the *New York Times* did not succumb to the English film's charms and delivered scathing reviews.

Even though Harris' novel excited book lovers, the feature film came on the tail of a multitude of WWII movies, including *Pearl Harbor, U-571,* the French film *Lucie Aubrac,* and the British film, *Charlotte Gray.* Perhaps the producers' comparison of the world of the code breakers with the contemporary computer age will draw an audience to the film (especially on video). In the meantime, actor Dougray Scott is being primed for stardom, Kate Winslet can add another captivating performance to her belt, and the infamous Bletchley Park awaits your visit, complete with a walk-through tour and fine dining.

—Patty-Lynne Herlevi

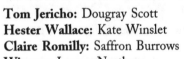
CREDITS

Tom Jericho: Dougray Scott
Hester Wallace: Kate Winslet
Claire Romilly: Saffron Burrows
Wigram: Jeremy Northam
Puck: Nikolaj Waldau
Logie: Tom Hollander
Admiral Trowbridge: Corin Redgrave
Skynner: Robert Pugh
Cave: Matthew MacFadyen
Leveret: Donald (Don) Sumpter

Origin: Great Britain
Released: 2001
Production: Mick Jagger, Lorne Michaels; Broadway Video, Jagged Films; released by Manhattan Pictures International
Directed by: Michael Apted
Written by: Tom Stoppard
Cinematography by: Seamus McGarvey
Music by: John Barry
Sound: John Midgley
Editing: Rick Shaine
Art Direction: Rod McLean, Stuart Rose
Costumes: Shirley Russell

Production Design: John Beard
MPAA rating: R
Running time: 117 minutes

REVIEWS

Boxoffice. April, 2001, p. 217.
Chicago Sun-Times Online. April 19, 2002.
eye Weekly Online. September 6, 2001.
Los Angeles Times Online. April 19, 2002.
New York Times Online. April 19, 2002.
Rolling Stone. May 9, 2002, p. 80.
Sight and Sound. October, 2001, p. 16.
Variety. January 29, 2001, p. 47.
Village Voice Online. April 17, 2002.

TRIVIA

Enigma is the first film from Jagged Films, the production company formed by Mick Jagger and Victoria Pearman.

Enough

Self defense isn't murder.
—Movie tagline
Everyone has a limit.
—Movie tagline

 Box Office: $39.2 million

Mini-mogul Jennifer Lopez hasn't had the best of luck with her acting career since her presence-defining role in 1998's *Out of Sight.* She voiced the minor role of a worker ant in 1998's *Antz;* was overwhelmed by the visuals in 2000's *The Cell;* tried romantic comedy with Matthew McConaughey in the overdone *The Wedding Planner* (2001); played a tough-and-troubled cop in the predictable *Angel Eyes* (2001); and is stuck as the wronged wife out for justice in the equally predictable *Enough.* Let's hope that her second release of 2002—the romance *Maid in Manhattan* with Ralph Fiennes—proves to be more satisfying.

Actually, *Enough* and *Maid* share some story similarities: Jennifer is the working-class woman looking to better herself and finding romance with a wealthy, socially-advantageous man. It's the working girl Cinderella story but J.Lo's character learns that having a Prince Charming isn't the be-all and end-all to a woman's life. Particularly if the Prince turns out to be an abusive, psycho frog in disguise.

Slim (Lopez) is a hard-working L.A. waitress at the Red Car Diner where she's made a substitute family of her co-workers, single mom Ginny (Juliette Lewis), and diner owner, Phil (Christopher Maher). She's not adverse to the flirtations of a handsome customer, Robbie (Noah Wyle), who says he's studying law enforcement. That is until he is "exposed" by the equally handsome Mitch Hiller (Billy Campbell), a wealthy construction company owner, who just happens to be sitting in the next booth. Mitch tells Slim that he previously overheard Robbie bet a buddy that he could have sex with her and forces him to leave. If this smells like a set-up, it is, but the film will take a while to connect the dots.

Before you know it, it's Mitch and Slim's wedding reception. Slim wants to know if Mitch will love her "forever and ever" and not only does he reply in the affirmative but he reassures her that his new bride will be "safe" with him. Also at the reception is an ex-boyfriend of Slim's from college, Joe Carter (Dan Futterman), who still carries a torch for his now-friend. Soon, Slim is pregnant and Mitch's less-than-savory characteristics start to come out. It seems Slim has fallen in love with a house she sees on a drive and Mitch immediately makes an offer to the astonished owner. Mitch refuses to take "no" for an answer, saying "Just think how miserable a crazy person can make you." The next thing you know, the Hiller's are moving in.

Slim gives birth to daughter Gracie and seems content enough being a stay-at-home wife and mother. A few years pass (Gracie [Tessa Allen] is about five) and Slim notices that Mitch is working a lot, seems distracted, and turns down her sexual come-ons. It's no surprise when Slim discovers that Mitch has been unfaithful. He apologizes but Slim comes to realize that it wasn't a one-time thing. Mitch tries to justify his behavior by saying: "I make the money, so I set the rules." When Slim objects, he slaps and punches her. He also warns that "Love is a scary thing." And it's about to get scarier.

Mitch's snooty mother (Janet Carroll) doesn't seem surprised when Slim turns up with a battered face and blames Slim for setting Mitch off, so Slim looks for a more sympathetic ear down at the diner. But she won't take Ginny's advice to file a formal abuse complaint with the cops. Mitch knows all about the meeting and retaliates by picking Gracie up from school and not telling Slim. Slim learns that she can't legally bar Mitch from seeing Gracie if he's no threat to the child even if she has a personal protection order against him. So Slim decides to take Gracie and sneak out of the house with Ginny and Phil's help. Although Mitch catches them leaving and beats Slim, they manage to escape.

But Mitch gets his revenge by canceling Slim's credit cards and freezing her bank account. Depending on the kindness of her friends, Slim hides out at a motel where Mitch tracks them down. She again manages to get away and Phil fronts her and Gracie a ticket to Seattle where Joe agrees to help her (and where Gracie decides that Seattle is like "Emerald City" in the *Wizard of Oz*). But Mitch sends three thugs after them and Slim runs again—this time to San Francisco. She begs aid from her birth father, an insouciant internet multi-millionaire named Jupiter (Fred Ward), who thinks she's running a scam. Again, Phil comes through and Slim takes Gracie to some friends of his who live in northern Michigan (the scenes were filmed in Washington state) where Slim gets herself a new identity. Life gets easier when Jupiter has a change of heart and manages to send Slim a substantial wad of cash so they can rent a house and start a normal life.

But Mitch is hardly done. For some inexplicable reason, Slim maintains (pay) phone contact with Mitch's mother and even agrees to let a pouty Gracie speak with her father. Mitch gets Robbie (who is apparently a police detective) to trace the call and forces him to shadow Mitch's wife and daughter. But first, Robbie wants to know why Slim is any different from all the other girls they once pulled that meeting scam on but Mitch did marry Slim and is obsessed with keeping her and his daughter. Meanwhile, Slim decides it's safe to ask Joe to come visit them and they re-kindle their feelings for one another.

Slim has a nightmare about Mitch finding her and there's a lot of pretentious build-up until he makes an appearance in their home. Mitch warns Slim that "If I can't have you, nobody will." Gracie sees Mitch attacking Slim and tries to defend her mother; Slim has learned something from her trials and has booby-trapped the house, so she and Gracie get away. But Robbie follows their car and tries to run them off the road. This is an unpleasant scene because Gracie is obviously scared and crying when Robbie repeatedly rams their car to get Slim to stop. [You wonder how director Michael Apted and/or the actors managed to explain the brutal situation to the child actress and have her "act" terrified while filming the scene.] Slim gets away after causing Robbie's car to crash and he disappears from the rest of the picture (one of many plot blips).

Slim has planned for such a situation and has another car, clothes, money, and identity waiting for them. She contacts a lawyer (Bill Cobb) about her situation and the fact that she is planning to attend a custody hearing set up by Mitch so that she can get full custody. The lawyer warns her that the hearing is probably just a ploy to get Slim somewhere Mitch can find and kill her. She manages to contact Ginny without Mitch's knowledge and has her best friend take Gracie on an extended vacation with her own children. Slim then returns to San Francisco and begins training with an instructor, recommended by Jupiter, in Krav Maga, a self-defense method. She is told to keep attacking and never stop—even if her larger and stronger opponent appears to have the better of her.

Slim also sets up Mitch by using a decoy and having him believe she is still in San Francisco when she instead travels to Los Angeles and breaks into Mitch's ultra-modern new house to set her final plan in play. Slim re-routes the alarm system, knocks out the phones (even setting up a machine to block cell phone access), and gets rid of Mitch's guns and other potential weapons. She plants forged letters that detail his abuse and that ask her to met him and talk things out. Then she changes into her fighting gear—complete with heavy boots and duct-taped hands. Slim makes a phone call to Ginny for reassurance that Slim is doing the only thing she can—and then she waits.

Mitch is amused to find his wife waiting for him—apparently ready to kick his ass. She has to slap him around to get his attention and taunts him: "Are you such a coward that you can only hit me when I'm not expecting it?" Knowing that Mitch plans to kill her since she won't come back to him, Slim repeatedly tells him during their fight that "Self defense is not murder." But when she does manage to knock Mitch unconscious, she can't go through with killing him as she hysterically tells Ginny when she calls her (never mind that the phone should not be working). Of course, Mitch is not out for long and comes after Slim; she knocks him over a stair railing and he crashes into the glass coffee table below. Mitch is dead. After having disposed of her "tools," Slim waits outside for the cops whom Ginny has called. A patrol officer tells Slim that she is "one of the lucky ones" for having survived her abusive husband.

The film ends with a spiffed-up Slim picking up Gracie from the airport and asking her daughter where she wants to go now. Grace tells her mother "Emerald City" and the closing credits show Gracie and Slim happily together with Joe aboard a Seattle ferry.

The film is workmanlike but hardly compelling. Apted does a lot of strained foreshadowing and characters tend to pop-up and then disappear just as quickly and their actions are frequently inexplicable. How do Mitch and the obviously younger Robbie know each other and what hold does Mitch have over Robbie's career (as a dirty cop?) that he would continue to risk himself for Mitch. There's also the peculiarity that Slim tells Robbie on their first meeting that "Slim" is her waitress name for the customers, not her real name, but no one ever calls her anything else. And why would Slim continue to contact Mitch's obviously unsympathetic mother, even to reassure the woman about her granddaughter's safety, when she's gone to such lengths to make a new identity for herself and it's likely to expose her to Mitch. (Why contact Joe for that matter, knowing that Mitch has threatened him, even if she does miss him? To set-up the "happy" ending?)

Would Slim really return for a custody hearing when she knows Mitch will portray her as an unfit mother and that her refusal to go to the cops about her abuse weakens her custody case? Maybe that's how she gets the idea that the only way to be free of Mitch would be to kill him since the lawyer tells Slim that Mitch will certainly keep coming until he kills her. Also, isn't it remarkable that Slim has this rich (if initially unsympathetic) dad lurking in the background to come to her aid?

Of course, *Enough* isn't the sort of movie that a viewer should hold up to nitpicking. Lopez does a professional job moving from "doormat" to fighter and Campbell probably was ready to show a "darker" side after playing put-upon nice guy Rick Samler for several seasons on TV's *Once and Again.* Lewis is a staunch best friend, Wyle turns out to be an unexpectedly scary character, and Fred Ward doesn't have enough to do—he charms even in his brief screen time. However, *Enough* doesn't add anything new to the "woman-in-peril" genre; *Enough* turns out to be not enough.

—Christine Tomassini

CREDITS

Slim: Jennifer Lopez
Mitch Hiller: Billy Campbell
Ginny: Juliette Lewis
Joe Carter: Dan Futterman
Robbie: Noah Wyle
Gracie: Tessa Allen
Jupiter: Fred Ward
Jim Toller: Bill Cobbs
Phil: Christopher Maher
Mrs. Hiller: Janet Carroll

Origin: USA
Released: 2002
Production: Irwin Winkler, Rob Cowan; released by Columbia Pictures
Directed by: Michael Apted
Written by: Nicholas Kazan
Cinematography by: Rogier Stoffers
Music by: David Arnold
Sound: Robert Jangier
Editing: Rick Shaine
Art Direction: Andrew Menzies
Costumes: Shay Cunliffe
Production Design: Doug Kraner
MPAA rating: PG-13
Running time: 115 minutes

REVIEWS

Chicago Sun-Times Online. May 24, 2002.
Entertainment Weekly. May 31, 2002, p. 76.
Los Angeles Times Online. May 24, 2002.

New York Times Online. May 24, 2002.
People. June 3, 2002, p. 34.
San Francisco Chronicle. May 24, 2002, p. D1.
USA Today Online. May 24, 2002.
Variety Online. May 12, 2002.
Washington Post. May 24, 2002, p. C1.
Washington Post Weekend. May 24, 2002, p. WE44.

Equilibrium

*In a future where freedom is outlawed outlaws
will become heroes.*
—Movie tagline

 Box Office: $1.2 million

Futuristic science fiction films, like science fiction novels, generally can be grouped into two categories in terms of their visions of the future. The first category consists of those futuristic stories that present an optimistic picture of what may conceivably come to pass one day, while the second group imagines a dark future, usually one that is born out of technological, sociological, or economic trends or issues that face the world today. Interestingly enough, the latter category, which tends toward dystopian views of the future, has always dominated the genre, from the stories of H. G. Wells to *The Matrix,* due partially to science fiction's usefulness for taking today's environment and projecting what may happen if society does not "wise up;" thus, such stories function as commentary on current culture just as much as they try to imagine the world to come (optimistic science fiction, of which *Star Trek* is probably the best contemporary example, also provides cultural commentary but puts an optimistic spin on it, imagining how things will get better rather than worse).

When *The Matrix* hit theaters in 1999, it brought with it a nightmarish picture of technology run amuck couched in an intelligent, thought-provoking plot and presented in a dynamic and visually innovative style—a style that has since been imitated (and even parodied) by numerous films. The influence of *The Matrix* on the science fiction thriller *Equilibrium* is obvious (and not surprising), but unfortunately *Equilibrium* fails to provide an engaging and intelligent plot and lacks enough style to make up for its weaknesses. *Equilibrium* has moments and qualities that only serve to heighten the realization that this film, with its dark picture of an oppressive future, may have had the potential to be a thought-provoking drama but wasted that potential with an emphasis on nearly mindless action.

Set in the not-too-distant future some time after a horrific world war, the film introduces us to the nation of Libria, an authoritarian state governed by an individual called "Father." Believing that the last world war came about because people were too driven by their dangerous emotions, the state has outlawed emotion and anything that might encourage it—art, literature, music, etc. The people of Libria are required to take the drug Prozium, which suppresses their feelings, and violators of the law—labeled Sense Offenders—may be punished by death. Enforcement is carried out by a special force of police called the Clerics, who do not hesitate to shoot Sense Offenders in cold blood.

The protagonist of the story is a Cleric named John Preston, played by Christian Bale with a convincing lack of emotion that initially seems right for the character but later seems to clash with the revelatory odyssey Preston takes through the course of the film. Preston appears to be the ideal Cleric, so detached from passion that he is unmoved when his own wife is killed for violating the law. When he discovers that his partner Partridge (Sean Bean) has been reading poetry, Preston shoots him in the head. Predictably, however, Preston begins to dabble in experiencing those "dangerous" emotions. He secretly reads the poetry of W. B. Yeats, and after accidentally forgetting to take his Prozium dosage, he intentionally starts missing it on a regular basis.

Soon he meets and captures a Sense Offender named Mary O'Brien (Emily Watson), a woman linked with a bomb-building rebel movement whose members hide out underground. Already weakening from his exposures to emotion, Preston rapidly finds himself falling in love and feeling a happiness that had previously been foreign to him (evidently his wife was never capable of stirring the kinds of feelings Mary does). Preston's new partner Brandt (Taye Diggs) suspects something is amiss, however, and fiendishly attempts to expose him. Naturally, a series of battles ensues between the newly converted Preston and his old allies.

Battles between Preston and his foes (whether they are Sense Offenders in the beginning or Clerics in the end) are in fact the primary focus of *Equilibrium.* The gun battles are highly stylized, kinetic, and violent, combining martial arts with loud, endless showers of bullets. These vibrant scenes are skillfully constructed and genuinely interesting to watch (though they are also often outlandish in their results, in that Preston never once comes close to being harmed). Unfortunately, however, they become a substitute for a thought-provoking story. Style is emphasized at the expense of content.

In many ways the premise behind *Equilibrium* seems inspired not only by The Matrix but classics of science fiction such as *Fahrenheit 451, Brave New World,* and *1984.* Despite the apparent goals of the filmmakers to craft an important and cautionary tale, the movie simply doesn't measure up to its more lofty predecessors, chiefly because its storyline is really quite thin and short on relevance. First, it is difficult to relate the "emotions are dangerous" philosophy to any truly significant or influential movement in existence today. (Actually, it sounds more like the philosophy of the Vulcans in *Star Trek*—except, of course, Vulcans don't kill dissidents.)

Unlike the classic stories mentioned above, and unlike *The Matrix,* it is difficult to imagine the world of Libria springing from any seeds in the contemporary world. Additionally, Libria's society betrays some inherent self-contradictions that undermine its credibility. The state believes that ridding people of emotions will put an end to war, yet the state itself has essentially declared war on dissenters. And war it certainly is, for the Clerics shed blood—and much of it—without a second thought. Really, then, the state of Libria is a kind of emotionless war machine, engaging in battle for the same reasons many wars have been started throughout history: to enforce conformity and to stifle independence.

Even the premise that emotions are good and should be celebrated is undermined somewhat, simply because the Sense Offenders (and their new champion, Preston) are frequently as violent as the Clerics. In many ways, Preston does not really change much throughout the course of the story. Although he does embrace the experience of emotion and the passions that come with it, he is still just as much of a killer in the end as he was at the beginning. Here the movie fails most significantly, in that the underlying theme of the importance of passion is never truly developed. The filmmakers are content to presume that the audience will automatically accept that the Sense Offenders are right and that emotions should be embraced, celebrated, and explored. The story itself does not try very hard to illustrate or dramatize these truths. Passion—supposedly this is at the core of the story, yet ironically it is conspicuously missing, replaced by energetic stunts and shootouts. *Equilibrium* is a tale about the beauty of the human soul and the power of the human heart, but sadly the film itself lacks both.

—*David Flanagin*

John Preston: Christian Bale
Mary O'Brian: Emily Watson
Brandt: Taye Diggs
Dupont: Angus Macfadyen
Partridge: Sean Bean
Jurgen: William Fichtner
Robbie Preston: Matthew Harbour

Origin: USA
Released: 2002

Production: Jan De Bont, Lucas Foster; Blue Tulip; released by Dimension Films
Directed by: Kurt Wimmer
Written by: Kurt Wimmer
Cinematography by: Dion Beebe
Music by: Klaus Bedelt
Sound: Byron Miller
Editing: Tom Rolfe, William Yeh
Art Direction: Eric Olson
Costumes: Joseph Porro
Production Design: Wolf Kroeger
MPAA rating: R
Running time: 106 minutes

REVIEWS

Boxoffice. January, 2003, p. 57.
Chicago Sun-Times Online. December 6, 2002.
Los Angeles Times Online. December 6, 2002.
New York Times Online. December 6, 2002.
People. December 6, 2002, p. 48.
USA Today Online. December 6, 2002.
Variety Online. December 2, 2002.
Washington Post. December 6, 2002, p. WE43.

Esther Kahn

An homage to the world of floodlights and greasepaint, *Esther Kahn* shines with a surprisingly unpredictable nature, much like the title character herself (winningly played by Summer Phoenix).

Most critics disliked French director Arnaud Desplechin's English-language film debut. It had been a few years since Desplechin's last film, *My Sex Life . . . How I Got Into An Argument* (1995), but many of the same reviewers who liked that quirky, interesting effort were disappointed with this tender study of young woman's life in the 19th-century London theater. Ironically, *Esther Kahn* is the better of the two extended character studies, but (in a typical lambast) Peter Bradshaw, critic for *The Guardian,* called *Esther Kahn,* "a very long, very unsuccessful two hours and 40 minutes in the cinema." (Apparently, the film was cut before the U.S. release.)

Based on a short story by Arthur Symons, but also modeled loosely after Francois Truffaut's *Wild Child*(1970), the screenplay by Desplechin and Michael Sloan takes place in the tenements of London's East End, where the youthful Esther grows up as one of the daughters of the Jewish tailor, Ythzok (Laszlo Szabo). However, unlike her more obedient sisters (Berna Raif, Claudia Solti), the doleful, introverted youngster resists working in the family business, so when Esther is older (as played by Summer Phoenix) her mother, Rivka (Frances Barber), allows her to work in a factory.

Consequently, Esther discovers a much more interesting profession. On a nightly basis, she frequents the local theater to see the latest productions, and eventually she auditions for a bit part herself. Unexpectedly, Esther excels at acting, and she gains an assured air, a new maturity, and a circle of friends (including Ian Holm as an older confidant), along the way.

Esther's life changes even more fundamentally after a dashing French playwright, Philip (Fabrice Desplechin), takes an interest in her—on and off the stage. Esther leaves her parents' home for good and moves in with Philip. Later, with Philip's help, she wins the prestigious role of Hedda Gabler in an upcoming production of the Ibsen play.

Yet, on the night before the opening, Philip leaves Esther for another, more beautiful woman (Emmanuelle Devos). The heartbroken Esther is so upset, her costars express concern she might actually commit suicide during her performance. But Esther comes through in the end, sober and wiser.

Critics compared *Esther Kahn* to such films about turn-of-the-century theater as William Wyler's *Carrie* (1952), John Turturro's *Illuminata* (1999), and Mike Leigh's *Topsy-Turvy* (1999). But Desplechin also references George Cukor's *The Actress* (1953), George Sidney's *Jeanne Eagels* (1957), and John Cassavetes's *Opening Night* (1977). (One of the few defenders of the film, Kevin Thomas of the *Los Angeles Times,* also saw glimmers of Stanley Kwan's *Actress* (1992) and Kon Ichikawa's 1987 film also titled *Actress*.) Through its conjunction of expressionism and impressionism, *Esther Kahn* transforms the old-style Hollywood biopic into a contemporary independent art film of high quality.

Director Desplechin examines the minuscule details of Esther's painful growth with great sensitivity, yet refuses to explain his heroine's inner life—or outward motivations. This method confers intricacy and suspense to an otherwise linear narrative (particularly in such sequences as Esther's haunting childhood dream and her bravura turn—shot without sound—as Hedda Gabler).

Feminists will debate the use of a male voiceover to narrate Esther's story and the fact that a minor scoundrel is the catalyst for Esther's collapse. Yet Desplechin's compassionate direction, Summer Phoenix's glowing performance, and the fastidious production values make *Esther Kahn* into a film worthy of association with Truffaut's best cinematic poems.

—*Eric Monder*

CREDITS

Esther Kahn: Summer Phoenix
Nathan Quellen: Ian Holm
Sylvia: Emmanuelle Devos
Philip Haygard: Fabrice Desplechin
Rivka Kahn: Frances Barber
Ytzhok Kahn: Laszlo Szabo

Origin: France, Great Britain
Released: 2000
Production: Alain Sarde, Gregoire Sorlat, Chris Curling; France 2 Cinema, France 3 Cinema, Zephyr Films, Why Not Productions; released by Empire Pictures
Directed by: Arnaud Desplechin
Written by: Arnaud Desplechin, Emmanuel Bourdieu
Cinematography by: Eric Gautier
Music by: Howard Shore
Sound: Ray Beckett, Malcom Davies
Editing: Herve De Luze
Art Direction: Jon Henson
Costumes: Nathalie Duerinckx
MPAA rating: PG
Running time: 145 minutes

REVIEWS

Boxoffice. June, 2002, p. 67.
The Guardian Online. November 23, 2001.
Los Angeles Times Online. April 12, 2002.
New York Times Online. March 1, 2002.
Sight and Sound. December, 2001, p. 47.
Variety. June 19, 2000, p. 34.

TRIVIA

The film was originally released at 163 minutes.

Evelyn

Pierce Brosnan is best known as the suave and witty James Bond. After racking up a successful run of the films, he has enough clout to get the kind of films made that he wants. To his credit, with *Evelyn,* he's made a nice choice. Although, upon first hearing about *Evelyn,* it doesn't sound like it's going to be very good at all.

The film is based on the true story of Irishman Desmond Doyle, who in the 1950s, successfully battled Irish law and the Catholic Church to regain custody of his kids. His story involves a wronged daddy who just wants his children; scary orphanages and, worse, cute kids who help save the day. It sounds ready made for Hallmark to sponsor. Without even seeing the film, you can almost picture the adorable moppets looking mournfully at their daddy, saying through missing front teeth, "You are going to thave uth, daddy? Aren't you?" as the music swells up to a soaring crescendo.

Luckily, *Evelyn* doesn't go for all the obvious emotional clichés that you'd expect. Part of this has to do with the people that Brosnan was able to recruit for the project. He got director Bruce Beresford (*Breaker Morant* and *Driving Miss Daisy*) to helm the picture and lined up a quality cast, including Stephen Rea, Aidan Quinn, Julianna Margulies, and Alan Bates. The choices of actors promise that this might be a subtler film than expected.

Also, *Evelyn* has many chances to wallow in particularly sad points of the story, but it doesn't. It manages to keep a fairly light tone about it even though losing one's children is not exactly the most upbeat of topics. For example, there are scenes of Evelyn (Sophie Vavasseur) in a Catholic orphanage. Here, we'd expect harrowing scenes of evil nuns and dreary, unlivable conditions. There is indeed a mean nun, but the movie doesn't focus on this. We get the idea that Evelyn doesn't like being there, but the orphanage isn't portrayed as being completely evil and hideous. Evelyn has friends and there are some nice nuns. It's nice that the film doesn't feel the need to force the drama by making the orphanage any worse than it has to be.

In the 1950s, Desmond Doyle's life wasn't so great. He had three children that he adored—Evelyn and sons, Dermot (Niall Beagan) and Maurice (Hugh Mac-Donagh)—but his wife is uninterested in him and his job opportunities are not good as a house painter and decorator. On Christmas, his wife leaves the family and disappears to Australia. Desmond's situation comes to the attention of the authorities, and his case is brought before the judge. Because Desmond is fond of the drink, has no female to care for the kids and doesn't have stable employment, the judge rules that Desmond's kids should be sent to church-run homes until he is able to create a better home situation.

Desmond takes the situation seriously and starts making money by singing in pubs. He doesn't seem as willing to give up drinking; but, hey, the movie seems to say, the guy's Irish. When he tries to get custody of his kids again, he learns of a rule of Irish law that says that he must get the signature of his wife even though she can't be found.

At this, Desmond starts assembling a quality, though ragtag, team of lawyers. With the help of the local comely barmaid, Bernadette Beattie (Margulies), he hires her brother, the local solicitor, Michael Beattie (Rea). They get Irish-American attorney, Nick Barron (Quinn) to plead the case. But their most valuable weapon is Tom Connolly (Bates), a former sports star turned maverick lawyer. There is much talk of the case being impossible and a David-and-Goliath situation. "As I recall, David won that particular battle," replies Desmond. Okay, so the dialogue, penned by screenwriter Paul Pender, can get a bit overwrought, but it's a movie about a man saving his children, and that's bound to happen. The team realizes that to win this case, they are going to have to fight the powerful and seemingly unstoppable Catholic Church and Ireland's Ministry of Education. When people won't help him, Desmond says a lot of stuff like, "If you were trying to get your kids, wouldn't you do everything you could?"

During all this, Desmond develops a relationship with the understanding barmaid, Bernadette. He's a drunk without much apparent future, but even as a Irish schlub on a losing streak, the guy's still Pierce Brosnan, after all. She steers him to the right path, even suggesting such crazy ideas like he should quit drinking. We also see Evelyn at her orphanage. She gets yucky food and a spanking from a mean nun. All along though, she is helped through her tough situation by "angel rays." These are rays of sunshine coming through the window that her late grandfather told her were angels offering a helping hand. Many critics found this part of the film particularly objectionable. Perhaps the people that should have been more offended by these scenes were the boys playing Evelyn's brothers. They are suffering the same fate as Evelyn, but we never see them in their orphanage, and barely ever hear them speak. Even the name of the film contains no reference to them. Perhaps they should have gotten their agents to cut them a better deal on this film.

Still, it's easy to see why the filmmakers focused on Evelyn because Vavasseur does a wonderful job. She is never cloying, and this is despite the angel rays business and having to play somewhat of a holier-than-thou character. Her nose sprinkled with freckles, the girl is cute, but not in a Hollywood child actor way. She expresses her emotions about her situations, but there are never Oscar-contention kinds of scenes with her sobbing about her miserable lot in life. Brosnan is also good. He's kind of a loser, but is charming and shows that he's a good man underneath his sometimes rash and ill-planned actions. It's a step away from Bond, and he's up for the task. The one quibble about his performance is that the man is too well put-together to ever look down-and-out. When his hair is mussed, it looks somehow artfully mussed.

Critics tended to like the film, but they generally blunted their praise by throwing in some kind of line like they knew it was sentimental claptrap, but the film was good anyway. Jonathan Foreman of the *New York Post* wrote, "Despite its treacly sentimentality, predictability and gutless evasiveness about the power of the church in 1950s Ireland, *Evelyn* manages to be an enjoyable piece of family entertainment." Kenneth Turan of the *Los Angeles Times* wrote, "*Evelyn* is awash in sentimentality and doesn't care who knows it. Despite a story predictable enough to make *The Sound of Music* play like a nail-biting thriller, its heart is so much in the right place it is difficult to get really peeved at it." And Elvis Mitchell of the *New York Times* wrote, "Though the film is spongy and drenched in sweetness, Bruce Beresford's direction is steady and well oiled. *Evelyn* has a breeziness of spirit; nothing lingers too long, for Mr. Beresford keeps the modest movie moving."

—*Jill Hamilton*

CREDITS

Desmond Doyle: Pierce Brosnan
Nick Barron: Aidan Quinn
Bernadette Beattie: Julianna Margulies
Evelyn Doyle: Sophie Vavasseur
Michael Beattie: Stephen Rea
Tom Connolly: Alan Bates
Mr. Wolfe: John Lynch
Sister Brigid: Andrea Irvine
Sister Felicity: Karen Ardiff
Dermot Doyle: Niall Beagan
Maurice Doyle: Hugh MacDonagh

Origin: Ireland, Great Britain
Released: 2002
Production: Pierce Brosnan, Beau St. Clair, Michael Ohoven; Irish DreamTime; released by United Artists
Directed by: Bruce Beresford
Written by: Paul Pender
Cinematography by: Andre Fleuren
Music by: Stephen Endelman
Sound: Brendan Deasy
Editing: Humphrey Dixon
Art Direction: Ian Bailie
Costumes: Joan Bergin
Production Design: John Stoddart
MPAA rating: PG
Running time: 94 minutes

REVIEWS

Boxoffice. November, 2002, p. 125.
Chicago Sun-Times Online. December 13, 2002.
Entertainment Weekly. January 10, 2003, p. 50.
Los Angeles Times Online. December 13, 2002.
New York Times Online. December 13, 2002.
Variety. September 24, 2002.
Washington Post. December 20, 2002, p. WE42.

TRIVIA

Bruce Beresford and Pierce Brosnan previously worked together on the 1991 film *Mr. Johnson.*

Extreme Ops

Fear is a trigger.
—Movie tagline

Box Office: $4.7 million

Extreme Ops seems almost as if it was created by drawing plot elements out of a hat. There's stunt snowboarding, bad guy Yugoslavian terrorists, and a couple hot chicks. It could have just as well been motorcyclists, bad guy South American rebels, and three hot chicks. *Extreme Ops* wants to follow the same path of attracting a younger audience set by action/thrill movies like *XXX* and the *The Fast and the Furious.* It's James Bond . . . Junior!

Here, we are introduced to the bad guy, war criminal Slobovan Pavlov (Klaus Lowitsch), in a bit of foreshadowing. The hunted former dictator has supposedly perished in an airplane crash. But he'll come back into play later when the plot needs a little dramatic tension for that third act.

The first order of business is Ian (Rufus Sewell) and Jeffrey (Rupert Graves), who want to film a TV commercial for a video camera called the Avalanche. Yes, we've really come to a point where action heroes are advertising execs. (Director Christian Duguay, who also did *The Art of War* and *Screamers,* has a background in making commercials so maybe that's why he felt that commercial directors would make for fascinating action heroes.) Jeffrey decides that instead of using expensive CGI effects (something the film itself could have used a lot more of) they need to shoot extreme skiers and snowboarders escaping a real avalanche.

They gather their videographer, Will (Devon Sawa) and ask him to round up some of the best extreme sportspeople around. He gets daredevil Silo (Joe Absolom) and Kittie (Jana Pallaske). Kittie is supposed to be wild because she is the lead singer of a band that looks like it would have been wild about 20 years ago. They also have to bring along Chloe (Bridgette Wilson-Sampras) who is marketable since she won a gold medal in skiing at the World Games. One of the poorly written side stories in the film is whether or not Chloe will be brave enough to abandon her well-mannered skiing techniques for the more wild and spontaneous techniques of the extreme skier. (One might argue that her bigger problem is why she wears her gold medal around as a matter of course.)

The crazy crew heads off to mountain top ski resort that's under construction. Despite the fact that the hotel isn't finished and doesn't appear to have any heat, the characters never seem to wear hats, gloves or anything that might mess up their cool hairstyles. Perhaps their braving the cold without proper attire is one of their better extreme feats of the film.

While they are at the hotel, Will accidentally takes some footage of another visitor who turns about to be Pavlov. The war criminal decides that he must kill these meddling kids but not before they are first brought to him alive. When a failed attempt by Pavlov's son to get the kids ends up with him getting killed, the kids are in even bigger trouble. Naturally, their attempts to save their lives will involve lots of extreme skiing stunts.

Whenever the ad folks are not in actually danger, writer Michael Zaidan throws some random stunts into the film to keep the action going. At frequent intervals in the film, music by bands like the Crystal Method pops up and an action sequence ensues. Some of these are interesting, like when Silo and Kittie decides to snowboard by hooking themselves up to a moving train. They leap over roads on ramps and generally seem to defy gravity. Other action sequences are more dutiful. During one slow point, Duguay cranks up the music and the kids get into . . . a snowball fight.

The action sequences generally work. Duguay is good at conveying the idea that these stunt riders will do anything for a thrill. They snowboard in the middle of the night, ride their boards on top of bar counters and don't seem to care about the laws of physics. Like *The Fast and the Furious*, *Extreme Ops* is a really bad movie that's nonetheless interesting to watch. Many of the stunts require a mind that doesn't dwell on the practical. When Will and Kittie decide to make a middle of the night run down the mountain, it's best not to pay attention to the fact that the isolated, unlit mountain is, for some reason quite well-lit. Also, one mustn't consider just how long it would take for them to trudge back up the mountain after taking so long to get down—especially in the dark of night and with Will wearing ski boots.

Some critics found fault with the way the stunt scenes were filmed. Rob Blackwelder of *Spliced Wire* was particularly vehement in his criticisms. He wrote, "As stunt people slice and trick-maneuver down steep snowy slopes on location (daylight, blue skies, depth of field), Duguay cuts back and forth to close-ups of the action-pantomining actors on a laughably obvious soundstage (unnatural lighting, flat mountain-scene backdrop, fake snow blowing form one corner of the screen). Sometimes the continuity is so sloppy that a scene will look like noon from one angle and dusk from another."

The characters are barely there, but that's beside the point. Wilson-Sampras is annoying and wimpy, but that's probably how the character was written. Pallaske's Kittie is a one-note tough girl and Absolom's Silo seems to have no more personality that just being a guy who likes to go fast. Sewell adds a little bit of depth as, ironically, the director without any depth.

Critics didn't like the film too much. Elvis Mitchell of the *New York Times* wrote, "It is hard to say what *Extreme Ops* is a bigger waste of—time or money." Tom Maursaud of the *Dallas Morning News* wrote, "This film is so slick, superficial and trend-happy, that it's easy to imagine that a new software program spit out the screenplay." Mick LaSalle of the *San Francisco Chronicle* wrote, "*Extreme Ops* doesn't have two brain cells to rub together, but it's an extreme sports thrill ride with a certain appeal."

—*Jill Hamilton*

CREDITS

Will: Devon Sawa
Chloe: Bridgette Wilson-Sampras
Jeffrey: Rupert Graves
Ian: Rufus Sewell
Mark: Heino Ferch
Yana: Liliana Komorowska
Pavel: Klaus Lowitsch
Zoran: Jean-Pierre Castaldi
Silo: Joe Absolom
Kittie: Jana Pallaske
Slavko: David Scheller

Origin: Great Britain, Germany
Released: 2002
Production: Moshe Diamant; MDP Worldwide, Apollomedia, Carousel Picture Co.; released by Paramount Pictures
Directed by: Christian Duguay
Written by: Michael Zaidan
Cinematography by: Hannes Hubach
Music by: Normand Corbeil, Stanislas Syrewicz
Sound: Ed Cantu
Editing: Clive Barrett, Sylvain Lebel
Art Direction: Andreas Olshausen
Costumes: Maria Schiker
Production Design: Philip Harrison
MPAA rating: PG-13
Running time: 93 minutes

REVIEWS

Los Angeles Times Online. November 29, 2002.
New York Times Online. November 28, 2002.
San Francisco Chronicle. November 29, 2002, p. D3.
Variety Online. November 27, 2002.

Far from Heaven

Box Office: $10.3 million

What if Douglas Sirk, the master of such 1950s melodramas as *Magnificent Obsession, All That Heaven Allows,* and *Written on the Wind,* had been able to make a movie that dealt openly with issues of homosexuality and interracial love? The Production Code in force during Hollywood's Golden Age would have prevented such a film from being made. But, in *Far from Heaven,* writer-director Todd Haynes has beautifully imagined what such a film might look like, creating a pastiche that pays tribute not only to Sirkian melodrama but to the florid Technicolor look that characterized his most famous work. *Far from Heaven* initially has a coldness to it. The stylized '50s vernacular and heightened visual palette threaten to distance us from the emotions at the heart of the story, but Haynes, aided by three stellar performances, gradually draws us in to a web of repressed desire and painful yearning that is ultimately heartbreaking.

Julianne Moore, who starred in Haynes's *Safe* as a contemporary homemaker falling ill to modern life, plays Cathy Whitaker in *Far from Heaven,* another homemaker whose world gradually falls apart. She is married to a television sales executive named Frank (Dennis Quaid) and is the mother of two small children. The paragon of '50s suburban womanhood, Cathy keeps order over her household while maintaining an active social life in her small town of Hartford, Connecticut. But all is not well behind the façade of normalcy. Frank, we soon learn, is a repressed homosexual who goes out after work cruising the local movie theater and out-of-the-way gay bar, hidden in an alley in the seedy part of town.

Meanwhile, Cathy finds herself with a new gardener, Raymond Deagan (Dennis Haysbert), who has taken over his father's business. Raymond is black, and even the smallest hint of concern she shows him, a touch on the shoulder when she learns that his father recently passed away, registers in her community. A profile in the town's social paper mentions that she is "as devoted to her family as she is kind

to Negroes," publicity that Cathy's friends take with good humor.

When Frank is working late one night, Cathy brings him his dinner and is shocked to discover him kissing another man. She flees the office, and, when he finally meets her at home, she tries to avoid the subject, turning her attention to other business, but of course they cannot pretend that there is no problem. Frank explains that he had such a condition years ago but thought that he had conquered it, and now he vows to seek help. He visits a psychiatrist, who can only promise a small chance of conversion to heterosexuality, but Frank forges ahead with psychotherapy to save his marriage and family.

With the increasing strain in her marriage, Cathy begins to strike up a tentative friendship with Raymond, whom she happens to see at a local art show. A widower, Raymond is attending with his 11-year-old daughter, Sarah (Jordan Puryear), and his appreciation for modern art broadens Cathy's mind as the white townspeople send disapproving looks their way. Cathy seems to be attracted to Raymond, but it is a forbidden attraction, one that she cannot acknowledge even to herself.

Cathy's relationship with Raymond is Haynes's most explicit homage to Sirk. In 1955's *All That Heaven Allows,* a widow (Jane Wyman) falls in love with her gardener (Rock Hudson) to the disapproval of her town and her grown children. The romantic barrier in *All That Heaven Allows* is not race but rather class and age. Wyman's character is wealthy, while Hudson's character has eschewed an interest in material things in favor of a kind of bohemian life revolving around an appreciation of nature. *Far from Heaven* does not mimic this conflict but uses the essential divide between society's expectations and the more unfettered natural life as a jumping-off point for its own concerns.

But capturing Sirk's sense of style, his sumptuous visual palette, is just as important to Haynes as adapting his narrative conventions. When Cathy's lavender chiffon scarf floats away on the wind, later to be returned by Raymond, it suggests their two worlds coming together, if only for a brief moment. Such a detail is as integral to the texture of the film as plot and dialogue. Production designer Mark Friedberg sets up beautiful contrasts between the autumnal landscapes and the richly appointed décor of the Whitakers' home. And Edward Lachman's stunning cinematography mirrors the innermost longings of the characters. There is one gorgeous shot as Cathy waits for Frank in front of the medical center. She sees something across the street, and her face and the background are suddenly imbued with a golden glow. Only then does Haynes cut to what she sees—a young couple kissing on a bench. It is a poignant moment, possibly reminding her of what she once had with Frank and what she hopes to have in the future, the warmth of love shining on her again. Veteran composer Elmer Bernstein's soaring score, complete with clashing cymbals, heightens every emotion while recalling the artificial world of old Hollywood melodrama.

One night, after the Whitakers host a swanky party, Frank, who has had too much to drink, hits Cathy out of frustration when he is unable to perform sexually. Cathy's best friend, Eleanor (Patricia Clarkson), notices the bruise the next day, but Cathy does not open up to her about the problems in her marriage. Eleanor may be a friend, but perhaps she is too close and Cathy cannot feel completely comfortable revealing her innermost troubles.

Raymond, however, is different. In their first few encounters, Cathy displays the prejudice of the day. She is startled to see a strange black man in her backyard and is taken aback to see him at an art show, as if only white people could have an interest in such cultural activities. Raymond has been understanding through it all, probably because, despite her blind spots, Cathy treats him as a human being, which is more than can be said for the rest of white Hartford. When he invites her to take a drive with him, they end up taking a walk in the woods in a beautifully photographed scene that suggests a new world opening up for her. They go to the black part of town and have drinks at a restaurant where Cathy is the only white person. Meeting with disapproving eyes from his people, they even share a slow dance together.

Soon, however, gossip is spreading throughout Cathy's community after a white woman sees them together. Cathy denies to Frank that there is anything between her and Raymond. Ironically, Frank is worried about his reputation, even though he is the one who could cause a scandal with his secret life, and so Cathy tells Raymond that she cannot see him anymore. He believes that they can be friends anyway, but, when he touches her in public and a white man tells him to take his hands off her, it is clear that some obstacles are impossible to overcome.

Cathy and Frank go on vacation to Miami for New Year's Eve, where Frank's homosexual desires resurface when he makes eye contact with a handsome young man vacationing with his family. When the Whitakers return home, Cathy's world quickly begins to crumble. Frank reveals that he has fallen in love with someone else, and, when Cathy confides her woes to Eleanor, she is sympathetic until Cathy divulges her friendship with Raymond, which scandalizes her friend and drives a wedge between them. Eleanor cannot believe that Cathy and Raymond are just friends and thinks that all the vicious gossip she has heard must be true after all. Cathy also learns that little Sarah was injured when some white schoolboys threw rocks at her because her father was friends with a white woman. Even though Sarah will be fine, Raymond has decided to leave town to start a new life in Baltimore. Cathy tells him that she will soon be single and, by implication, available, but Raymond is not deterred from doing what he feels he must for the good of his daughter.

Cathy in essence has lost everything—her husband, her best friend, and the one man she could confide in. Wearing the lavender scarf that once brought her close to Raymond, she goes to the train station to say good-bye and sees him as he is boarding. In a beautiful, melancholy farewell, no words are spoken, and only the looks exchanged between the characters speak of dreams unfulfilled. *Far from Heaven* opens with a crane shot in which the camera swoops down through the bright red and yellow leaves of autumn to the street below, and the film's last shot echoes yet reverses the opening shot with the camera pulling up and back as Cathy drives away. Now it is winter, and the trees, having lost their leaves, are beginning to form white buds. Winter may be the time of death, but perhaps there remains the hope of rebirth for Cathy.

Far from Heaven is fascinating as a film experiment recalling a whole style of filmmaking foreign to many contemporary eyes. The pace is deliberate, and the acting, which is subtle and stylized, may seem strange at first, but it is in sync with the acting style of '50s melodrama. Dennis Quaid reveals genuine depths of anguish as a man torn apart with self-loathing while waging a losing battle with his hidden urges. Dennis Haysbert handles his role with grace; Raymond may fit old Hollywood's notion of the perfect Negro—smart, thoughtful, nonthreatening—and lack the emotional shadings and flaws of the other characters, but even Rock Hudson's rustic character in *All That Heaven Allows* is an idealized, uncomplicated type.

Anchoring the film is Julianne Moore, who gives a wonderfully nuanced, touching performance in a challenging role. Adopting a non-naturalistic style of acting crucial to the character and genre, Moore is still able to express her character's real, heartfelt feelings. While Cathy may have a couple of emotional outbursts, Moore largely has to communicate Cathy's inner life through the subtlest gestures, rigid body posture, and formalized way a society wife speaks. A lesser actress would have been suffocated by the artifice and delivered a mannered performance, but Moore always lets us see the inner turmoil underneath the perfectly coifed hair, bright red lipstick, and stunning satin dresses. Cathy herself may not fully grasp all the tensions within her (until perhaps the end), but Moore reveals them with seeming effortlessness.

The beauty of *Far from Heaven* is that Haynes clearly loves the Sirkian style he is imitating and does not resort to camp or irony. He can still have fun with some corny '50s movie moments—the vocabulary of Cathy's son as he exclaims, "Aw shucks" or calls his dad "Pop," for example, and the self-conscious use of rear projection when Cathy is driving through town. But the gradual unfolding of lives thwarted by rigid social norms is quite devastating, and, as Cathy is left alone at the end to face an uncertain future, we are left to contemplate the full weight of her tragedy.

—*Peter N. Chumo II*

CREDITS

Cathy Whitaker: Julianne Moore
Frank Whitaker: Dennis Quaid
Raymond Deagan: Dennis Haysbert
Eleanor Fine: Patricia Clarkson
Dr. Bowman: James Rebhorn
Mona Lauder: Celia Weston
Sybil: Viola Davis

Origin: USA
Released: 2002
Production: Christine Vachon, Jody Patton; Killer Films, Section Eight, Vulcan Productions; released by Focus Features
Directed by: Todd Haynes
Written by: Todd Haynes
Cinematography by: Edward Lachman
Music by: Elmer Bernstein
Sound: Drew Kunin
Editing: James Lyons
Art Direction: Peter Rogness
Costumes: Sandy Powell
Production Design: Mark Friedberg
MPAA rating: PG-13
Running time: 107 minutes

REVIEWS

Boxoffice. November, 2002, p. 127.
Chicago Sun-Times Online. November 15, 2002.
Entertainment Weekly. November 8, 2002, p. 81.
Los Angeles Times Online. November 8, 2002.
New York Times Online. November 8, 2002.
People. November 18, 2002, p. 42.
Rolling Stone. November 14, 2002, p. 95.
USA Today Online. November 8, 2002.
Variety Online. September 2, 2002.
Washington Post. November 15, 2002, p. WE41.

QUOTES

Cathy (Julianne Moore): "So often we fail in that kind of love, the kind that makes us abandon our lives and plans, all for one brief touch of Venus."

AWARDS AND NOMINATIONS

L.A. Film Critics 2002: Actress (Moore), Cinematog., Score
Natl. Bd. of Review 2002: Actress (Moore)

N.Y. Film Critics 2002: Cinematog., Director (Haynes), Film, Support. Actor (Quaid), Support. Actress (Clarkson)
Natl. Soc. Film Critics 2002: Cinematog., Support. Actress (Clarkson)
Nomination:
Oscars 2002: Actress (Moore), Cinematog., Orig. Screenplay, Score
Golden Globes 2003: Actress—Drama (Moore), Screenplay, Support. Actor (Quaid), Score
Ind. Spirit 2003: Actress (Moore), Cinematog., Director (Haynes), Film, Support. Actor (Quaid)
Screen Actors Guild 2002: Actress (Moore), Support. Actor (Quaid)
Writers Guild 2002: Orig. Screenplay.

Feardotcom (fear dot com)

Want to see a really killer website? It's the last site you'll ever see.
—Movie tagline
Abandon all hope . . . Access all evil . . . Enter Feardotcom.
—Movie tagline

 Box Office: $13.2 million

A man nervously walks into an underground subway station. It is raining and he clutches his coat around him as well as a book. He anxiously looks around, but it is amazing he can see anything for he is bleeding from his eyes. Suddenly a bouncing white ball and a strikingly blonde young girl in a summer dress appear looking very out of place. To the man's alarm the little girl begins playing with her ball on the electrified subway tracks . . . and a train is coming. The man knows what he must do; he must jump onto the tracks and save the little girl. It is a decision that will cost him his life.

Detective Mike Reilly (Stephen Dorff) is assigned to investigate the man's death but the police are very worried about the fact that the victim was bleeding from the eyes before he was killed. Consequently the Department of Health is called in. Fearing Hemorrhagic fever (i.e. Ebola), Terry Huston (Natascha McElhone) soon determines that the man's bleeding was not caused by any virus. Perhaps the book he was clutching is some kind of clue. It's called *The*

Secret Life of the Internet and it was co-authored by the victim, a man named Polidori (Udo Kier).

Back at his office Mike finds another letter from "The Doctor," a man who tortured and killed women while people watched via live broadcasts over the Internet. Because "The Doctor" kept moving his website he was never caught, and even though the case has been turned over the Feds, it still haunts Mike. Mike's partner, Styles (Jeffrey Combs), tells Mike to let it go, but how can he when "The Doctor" keeps sending him taunting letters?

Soon the police have a young German exchange student in custody who is not only acting strangely, he is also bleeding from the eyes. However, instead of sending him to the hospital, the police throw him in a cell and Terry and Mike go off to the student's apartment to investigate. There they find a young girl submerged in a bathtub full of water, dead and displaying the same hemorrhagic symptoms. When they return to question the student in the cell, he, too, is dead, but not before he writes the word murderer on his cell wall in his own blood.

At least Terry and Mike now have a clue, a videocamera is found under the bathtub. Watching what the couple filmed they discover that they logged on to a website that involved a woman screaming and which made them so uncomfortable they turned off the videocamera. The next images are of the German student acting crazy and the camera falling under the bathtub.

When Terry reports back to her office she is surprised to find her boss, Eddie Turnbull (Nigel Terry) preoccupied, bleeding from the nose and his computer missing. It's not long before Turnbull is seeing the same blonde girl with the same bouncing white ball. Chain smoking in his car he drops his cigarette, starts a small fire, and panics as his car races out of control and smashes into a wall, killing him instantly.

While all this is going on, across town (one assumes) "The Doctor" is again open for business and is torturing an unwilling young woman live on the Internet. Is there a connection between "The Doctor," who is really Alistair Pratt (Stephen Rea), and the people who are dying in the most unusual ways?

Perhaps. That's just one of the many, many questions left hanging in *Feardotcom*. We know there is a website by that name that is somehow luring people to their death, but we're not sure it's the Doctor's site. We see the number of viewers logging on to the Doctor's site escalate as he tortures the young woman, but obviously not that many people are dying throughout the city. So why are some dying and not others? Or perhaps fear.com is NOT the Doctor's site. This is implied later in the film, but it is never cleared up, and quite honestly, audiences shouldn't have to work so hard at figuring out a horror film.

The fear.com site is eventually logged on to by Mike's computer expert Denise (Amelia Curtis), who is asked a set of provocative questions such as, "Do you like to watch?" and

"I'm waiting for you, Denise." How did the computer know her name, Denise wonders? Spooked, Denise logs off and turns off the computer, which turns itself back on and reconnects. "Do you want to play with me?" the computer asks her. "Do you want to hurt me?" And now it's Denise's turn to see the little blonde girl and her bouncing white ball . . . and lots and lots of beetles before she, too, dies.

Desperate, Mike and Terry search out the other author of Polidori's book, Frank Bryant (Michael Sarrazin). He claims that if one could connect computers together like one supercomputer then it is conceivable that one could receive, store and send out energy. Polidori claimed that he knew where that site existed; Bryant claims he just wrote the book for the money, he needed a new car. (Is Bryant a metaphor for this film's producers? Now that's scary!)

One just knows what's going to happen next. Either Terry or Mike or, more likely both of them, will log on to the fear.com site. The problem is, when he/she/they do, it's not Alistair "The Doctor" Pratt's site. (See? Is it one site or two?) Instead there are more questions like those asked of Denise. A sexy woman's voice asks "Do you want to play?" and "Find me. You have 48 hours." And what does one win if one does find her, whoever "her" is? One gets her. And if they fail? They die. "What are you afraid of?" the voice asks. Well, duh!!! What follows is a lot of Dutch angles, wobbly and distorted point of view shots, that darned bouncing white ball and our heroes bleeding from various facial orifices.

There are a lot of "duh" moments in *Feardotcom*. Its script is a mess. From inane dialogue like "Let's start over. We've got to be missing something," to obvious flubs—I could swear that at one point Mike says that Terry is from the DOA (dead on arrival) when he means the DOH (Department of Health)—it's amazing to think how many people had to be asleep at the switch to let this one get through. One may be inclined to lay the blame at the doorstep of its author, Josephine Coyle, and shake one's head in wonder at why it ever made it to the screen. But then one notices that it is based on a story idea by Moshe Diamant. Moshe Diamant is one of the film's way-too-many producers. Well at least one mystery is solved. But there are so many others!

Should one even bother mentioning some of the many inconsistencies and lapses of logic in *Feardotcom*? Sure, why not. Why is it that when Terry sees a face in the German student's videotape, she doesn't bother to investigate any further? If one is supposed to die from one's greatest fears, why is that a plot point totally dropped when we get to the heroes? Why is it that when Mike logs on to the forbidden site he is incapacitated quite quickly, but not Terry? In fact, although Mike almost immediately ends up in the psych ward of a hospital after logging on, Terry ends up having plenty of time to solve an old murder case and the only consequence she suffers, besides a few nose bleeds, is that she constantly falls asleep and wakes up just fine. And does anyone believe that Montreal and Luxembourg can pass for New York City??

One can easily imagine the profit motive for the producers making this film, but what on earth were the actors thinking? They may have gotten paid, but this blot on their record is going to be hard to get rid of. Granted, for some of these actors, *Feardotcom* is just one more campy film for them—if only it were campy! In fact, there is a promise of camp when the opening shots feature Udo Kier who not only has appeared in some very good films but is also a veteran of a few by Andy Warhol. (Can anyone who has seen it forget Udo rhapsodizing about "wirgin wampires" in *Andy Warhol's Dracula*?) The camp hope is further fostered when one realizes the hero's partner is none other than *Re-Animator's* Jeffrey Combs. "You suffer from the hero's curse of hope," The Doctor says at one point. It could perfectly describe what happens to *Feardotcom's* audience, too.

Of the three leads, Natascha McElhone sleepwalks through the film looking like the new millennium's Jane Seymour. Stephen Dorff's character is so blank it could have been played by any actor. Only Oscar-nominated Stephen Rea (*The Crying Game*) seems to be trying to have a little fun with the movie by providing The Doctor with a flat Midwestern monotone a la Anthony Hopkins' Hannibal Lechter. And can that really be Michael Sarrazin (*They Shoot Horses, Don't They?*) and Nigel Terry (*Excalibur's* King Arthur) both seedily unrecognizable as Bryant and Turnbull, respectively?

A few critics, most notably Roger Ebert, have raved about the look of *Feardotcom,* especially the end of the film, but it surely isn't enough to save this muddle of a movie. For the record, the film emphasizes monochromatic, washed-out blues, grays and blacks. It is a world where it is always cloudy or rainy, where apartments always look shabby, and where no one turns the lights on when they enter a room. *Feardotcom* looks grainy and dingy, and after a while it doesn't add to the story's atmosphere, it just becomes one more depressing aspect of the film. *Feardotcom* is that most terrible kind of horror film, one that's not scary or even interesting. It's confusing, frustrating, even boring, and with the added aspect of voyeurism, it's just plain unpleasant.

—*Beverley Bare Buehrer*

CREDITS

Mike Reilly: Stephen Dorff
Terry Houston: Natascha (Natasha) McElhone
Alistair Pratt: Stephen Rea
Styles: Jeffrey Combs

Polidori: Udo Kier
Turnbull: Nigel Terry
Frank Bryant: Michael Sarrazin
Denise: Amelia Curtis

Origin: USA, Great Britain, Germany, Luxembourg
Released: 2002
Production: Moshe Diamant, Limor Diamant; MDP Worldwide, Apollomedia, Carousel Films, Film Fund Luxembourg; released by Warner Bros.
Directed by: William Malone
Written by: Josephine Coyle
Cinematography by: Christian Sebaldt
Music by: Nicholas Pike
Sound: Carlo Thoss
Editing: Alan Strachan
Art Direction: Makus Wollersheim, Frank Godt
Production Design: Jerome Latour
MPAA rating: R
Running time: 101 minutes

REVIEWS

Chicago Sun-Times Online. August 30, 2002.
Los Angeles Times Online. August 30, 2002.
New York Times Online. August 30, 2002.
Variety Online. August 30, 2002.
Washington Post. August 30, 2002, p. C5.

QUOTES

Alistair (Stephen Rea): "I'd like to say I feel your pain, but I can't. I can't feel anything."

Femme Fatale

Nothing is more desirable or more deadly than a woman with a secret.
—Movie tagline

Box Office: $6.6 million

The film noirish atmosphere of Brian DePalma's *Femme Fatale* is created right from the first scene: a grainy television broadcast of Billy Wilder's 1944 classic *Double Indemnity.* Eventually the camera backs up and we can begin to see another image reflected on the television screen: a reclined, cool blonde. Laure Ash (Rebecca Romijn-Stamos) is the rapt television viewer. Her enjoyment of Wilder's mystery, however, will soon be interrupted by the arrival of a character just known as "Black Tie" (Eriq Ebouaney), a rather large, black man dressed in a tuxedo. The undressed Laure is totally unperturbed by Black Tie's presence. In fact she is decidedly calm even after he delivers such lines as "Stop dreaming, Bitch. This is not a game tonight. People could die."

Slowly Laure gets dressed and the camera shows us what is outside the room where she is watching old movies—one of the touchstones of new movies, the Cannes Film Festival. As we are shown the red carpet arrivals for that night's screening our attention is focused on director Regis Wargnier (himself) arriving with a sexy model Veronica (Rie Rasmussen) who is wearing a short, hip-hugging skirt, and a Cleopatraesque gold and diamond snaky breastplate . . . worth $10 million. People will be watching more than Wargnier's movie when Veronica enters the theater.

The only problem is, Veronica must make a pit stop before entering the auditorium and, of course, her clothing's male bodyguards are left behind at the restroom door. Inside, Veronica has arranged for a clandestine quickie with Laure, one of the event's photographers. But Laure has more on her mind than sex. As she peels off Veronica's expensive ensemble, it is dropped to the floor and replaced with cheap imitations by Black Tie who is hiding in the next stall.

Meanwhile, in an air shaft, Racine (Edouard Montoute) is drilling through basement walls and attempting to reach a switch that will cut the power to the entire Palais de Festivals. As Racine reaches and Laure lures, Veronica's bodyguards are getting nervous. What's taking so long? Soon one is sticking his head into the restroom and is eventually shot by Black Tie. Interrupted in mid-heist, Black Tie is also shot, and shot by Laure who walks off with the $10 million in breastplates just as the Palais goes dark.

Laure, an American and now wearing a black wig as a disguise, has returned to Paris where she has a girlfriend, but of most importance to her is that Black Tie had been holding her passport and now she needs a new one. As she clandestinely meets her girlfriend outside a Paris church, her photo is taken by Nicolas Bardo (Antonio Banderas). Seeking privacy Laure retreats into the church only to find a funeral going on and two of the people there keep calling to her, but they're calling her Lily.

Confused, Laure runs out and heads for the Sheraton Hotel near the airport, for in room 214 is someone who has a passport for her. In the room, though, is Racine who demands the goods and when Laure refuses the two end up struggling and Laure is thrown from a hotel atrium balcony. Fortunately she lands relatively softly and virtually at the feet of the older couple from the church.

The couple take the groggy Laure to Lily's apartment where she can recuperate. It seems Laure is a dead ringer for Lily whose husband and child have just died and who, in a state of utter despair, must have just disappeared. Pleased to have a safe harbor while being hunted by the police and Racine, Laure will now steal Lily's identity, her passport, and a conveniently left airline ticket for America. As Laure relaxes in the bathtub, though, Lily returns. She is still terribly despondent and soon begins to play Russian roulette with a gun. Will Laure stop her or will she let her die so she can take her identity?

Believe it or not, this is just the tip of the iceberg of DePalma's labyrinthine plot. There will be meetings with rich Americans who become Parisian ambassadors (Peter Coyote), there will be resurrected villains, steamy sex, karmic justice, double crosses, triple crosses, cosmic coincidences, and masterful manipulations. And that last item goes not only for the relationships between the characters in the movie, but also in the relationship between DePalma and the audience. It's a neat trick and DePalma has left us plenty of clues but we're so busy trying to figure out the mystery we may need a second viewing to finally see how we've been maneuvered.

Those who see *Femme Fatale* seem to fall into two groups: those who enjoy the puzzle and the trickery, who can sit back and go along for the ride and enjoy the scenery, and those who feel the mystery is a cheat and that they've been made a fool of by having spent so much time and energy trying to solve a riddle only to be betrayed by the director and/or writer.

In this case both jobs belong to Brian DePalma. When it comes to movies—this is his 24th—DePalma has had is share of misses (*Bonfire of the Vanities, Mission to Mars*) and his share of hits (*Carrie, Snake Eyes, Mission: Impossible*). *Femme Fatale* is his first since 1992's *Raising Caine* where he has done double duty and it has him returning to his roots when he made such classics as *Blow Out* and *Dressed to Kill.*

As the mixed critical response might indicate, *Femme Fatale* could be analyzed as containing everything that is both good and bad about DePalma's movies. What often hurts his films is a muddled or unconvincing script, and for some, that's exactly what is wrong with this effort. There is no doubt that the plot is complex and convoluted, but for some its complexity is a contrivance while for others it is exhilarating. For some the way DePalma plays with our expectations, the way he toys with us, playing with our visual memories and puzzling us with questionable reality is ingenious and clever but for others it's just plain annoying.

There is also no doubt that *Femme Fatale* is visually stunning. From its skillfully filmed, almost dialogue-less, diamond heist opening sequence, DePalma and cinematographer Thierry Arbogast (*The Horseman on the Roof, The Fifth Element, Ridicule*) provide some remarkable tracking shots, a few magnificent long takes, and the occasional split-screen treat. The film almost overflows with dazzling images and cinematic tomfoolery. But again, for some this is amusing and for others it's visual overkill in service of an irritating story.

So, it's not surprising that critics are also divided on DePalma's leading lady, Rebecca Romijn-Stamos. Previously known just for two feature film roles (*X-Men* and *Rollerball*) some feel she is too lightweight to carry the film, that she's all super model and little talent. For others, though, she will be the embodiment of the perfect Hitchcock female lead in what is unquestionably yet another DePalma tribute to that master of mystery. Romijn-Stamos is blond, cool, sexy and duplicitous. She is manipulative, confident, seductive, desirable and out of reach because she is untrustworthy.

And speaking of Hitchcock homage, it's amazing to realize that the soundtrack to the film wasn't composed by Hitchcock's prime composer Bernard Herrmann but by the Japanese Ryuichi Sakamoto. Possibly best known for his soundtrack for *Merry Christmas, Mr. Lawrence* (1987) in which he also appeared, Sakamoto won many awards, including an Oscar, for his soundtrack for *The Last Emperor*. This is the second time Sakamoto has worked for DePalma (he also did *Snake Eyes* for the director), but never has he so perfectly captured the thematic elements that put us subliminally into the Hitchcock/Herrmann mode.

There are dozens of allusions in *Femme Fatale* to other films, both Hitchcock's, DePalma's and others. But that's just another sly wink the director gives to audiences who will give this film half a chance. Like Laure, DePalma visually and mentally seduces us into pursuing the plot while at the same time filling his frames with so many details that it will inevitably take a second viewing to realize the playfulness of many of them. (Notice the time whenever there is a clock is in a scene.) But then again, *Femme Fatale* is a film about vision, about noticing what is going on, about voyeurism and truth.

It's also a film that separates those viewers who can find value and entertainment in a film even if its story is totally unbelievable from those who would prefer their movies have plots that never stretch one's sense of reality. It's for those who believe that movies can create a world where credible characters and plausible plot are not the ultimate goal. Where sometimes being playful with images and expectations can be as interesting and enjoyable as a well-written story.

—*Beverley Bare Buehrer*

CREDITS

Laure/Lily: Rebecca Romijn-Stamos
Nicolas Bardo: Antonio Banderas
Bruce Hewitt Watts: Peter Coyote
Shiff: Gregg Henry
Black Tie: Eriq Ebouaney
Racine: Edouard Montoute
Veronica: Rie Rasmussen
Serra: Thierry Fremont

Origin: France
Released: 2002
Production: Tarak Ben Ammar, Marina Gefter; Quinta Communications; released by Warner Bros.
Directed by: Brian DePalma
Written by: Brian DePalma
Cinematography by: Thierry Arbogast
Music by: Ryuichi Sakamoto
Sound: Jean-Paul Mugel, Francois Groult
Editing: Bill Pankow
Art Direction: Denis Renault
Costumes: Olivier Beriot
Production Design: Anne Pritchard
MPAA rating: R
Running time: 112 minutes

REVIEWS

Boxoffice. July, 2002, p. 77.
Chicago Sun-Times Online. November 6, 2002.
Chicago Tribune Online. November 6, 2002.
Entertainment Weekly. November 15, 2002, p. 107.
Los Angeles Times Online. November 6, 2002.
New York Times Online. November 6, 2002.
People. November 18, 2002, p. 44.
Variety. May 6, 2002, p. 41.
Washington Post. November 8, 2002, p. WE39.

QUOTES

Laure (Rebecca Romijn-Stamos) to Nicolas (Antonio Banderas): "I'm a bad girl, Nicolas."

TRIVIA

The agent who calls Nicolas is an uncredited John Stamos, Rebecca Romijn-Stamos' husband.

Festival at Cannes

The scene behind the scenes.
—Movie tagline

English-born filmmaker Henry Jaglom returns with a film industry farce that both laughs at its own jokes as it extols the pains of Hollywood-style globalization of international cinema. Jaglom focuses on the famous French film festival and succinctly names his farce, *Festival at Cannes*. However, if you remove the story from the French Riviera and unload the characters in the snow-packed Park City or in Toronto, you will find the same producer-sharks, rising ingenues, aging beauties, and naïve screenwriters as they try to conquer the world of cinema. The setting of Cannes, the world's most prestigious film festival that once launched the careers of Federico Fellini and Francois Truffaut, both detracts from the film's scathing themes and lures us in with its nostalgia for another era of cinema, before the cell phone brigade and deal-makers polluted the scene.

Although Jaglom pokes fun at the industry, his characters come across as flat and stereotypical while telling us nothing new. They find romance too easily, sell their souls at the blink of an eye, and draw little empathy from viewers. They are the caricatures one would expect to find in a mockumentary and at times, *Festival at Cannes* resembles a faux documentary with its on-camera interviews and hand-held camera shots. However, *Festival at Cannes* falls flat in its comic intent and delivers instead sentimental sap against a backdrop of sparkling water, sunny décor, and syrupy French music. Jaglom forces his characters into contrived romantic encounters and is equivalent to sharks that decide not to feed on the little fish anymore. The characters, in fact, lose their initial motivations half way through the film when the writer-director decided to turn foes into naïve lovers and the end result is confused actors trying to make the scene in an almost plot-less film.

Jaglom works with multiple narratives, yet his story recalls episodes of *The Love Boat* or Neil Simon plays more so than the work of Robert Altman. In fact, one expects Carol Burnett (a Neil Simon regular) to make a cameo appearance. However, Jaglom hired a talented cast that includes a mix of legendary actors and emerging talent. British actress Greta Scacchi plays middle-aged actress-turned-screenwriter, Alice Palmer. She represents the 40-something actress who knows that her days are numbered and so she decides to fight the feminist cause and direct films about women that matter. After she encounters charlatan deal-maker Zak Naiman (Kaz Norman), she is persuaded to cast the legendary actress Millie Marquand (Anouk Aimèe) in the lead role.

However, producer-shark, Rick Yorkin (Ron Silver) also plans on casting Marquand in his $90 million Tom Hanks' vehicle that will fall through unless Marquand accepts a small role as the mother of Hanks' love interest. Marquand becomes confused while trying to choose between a lucrative small role and the role-of-a-lifetime, which is also a role in a low-budget film. Marquand decides to ask her former husband, director Victor Kovner (Maximilian Schell), for his opinion, but he's distracted by his Italian starlet-lover Gina (Camilla Campanale). Finally, we meet the hot-actress-of-the-moment, Blue (Jenny Gabrielle), who was discovered along with the produced-on-credit-cards film in which she starred. Now that the characters and stories are in place, you would expect a scathing gaze at the Hollywood machine. But Jaglom would rather create unlikely romances between Alice and her foe Rick and Blue and Rick's assistant Barry (Alex Craig Mann), while reuniting Millie with Victor. By the film's end, some of the characters have regained their integrity and broken up with their suitors, yet the gagging reflex is still present.

Festival at Cannes received mixed reviews. Stephen Holden of the *New York Times* praised the film's language: "The screenplay ... cracks with abrasively, authentic dealmaking jargon hurled by fast-talking hustlers." However, Holden also criticized the film's sentimental content, "the abrupt change from bitter to warm-and-fuzzy doesn't compute." *Los Angeles Times* critic Kevin Thomas found *Festival at Cannes* to be a "giddy comic fantasy, full of romance, chicanery and beguiling sophisticated players."

The film does offer us a respite with clever one-liners and a sensual performance by the legendary French actress, Anouk Aimèe, once famous for her roles in Jacques Demy's *Lola* and Federico Fellini's classics, *La Dolce Vita* and *8 ½*. However, similar to the other performers, Aimèe's talents are underused and, at best, she only adds dignity to the overly nostalgic film. Yet, it's refreshing to see an aging actress playing an aging actress.

—*Patty-Lynne Herlevi*

CREDITS

Alice Palmer: Greta Scacchi
Millie Marquand: Anouk Aimee
Rick Yorkin: Ron Silver
Kaz Naiman: Zack Norman
Blue: Jenny Gabrielle
Viktor Kovner: Maximilian Schell
Libby: Kim Kolavich
Nikki: Rachel Bailit
Barry: Alex Craig Mann
Milo: Peter Bogdanovich
Gina: Camilla Campanale

Origin: USA

Released: 2002
Production: John Goldstone; Rainbow Film Company, Revere; released by Paramount Classics
Directed by: Henry Jaglom
Written by: Henry Jaglom
Cinematography by: Hanania Baer
Music by: Gaili Schoen
Sound: Tim White
Editing: Henry Jaglom
Costumes: Jo Kissak
MPAA rating: PG-13
Running time: 99 minutes

REVIEWS

Boxoffice. April, 2002, p. 190.
Los Angeles Times Online. March 8, 2002.
New York Times Online. March 8, 2002.
San Francisco Chronicle. April 12, 2002, p. D3.
Variety Online. November 2, 2001.
Village Voice Online. March 6, 2002.
Washington Post. March 28, 2002, p. WE42.

QUOTES

Director Viktor Kovner (Maximilian Schell): "It's so hard to make a film. Sometimes I think it's enough to dream them."

Formula 51
(The 51st State)

Have a good trip.
—Movie tagline
In a world of shady characters and dirty deals, this is just business as usual.
—Movie tagline

Box Office: $5.2 million

Obviously film critics and general moviegoers often differ in their assessments of what qualifies as a "good movie," a reality of the business that is most evident when a critically-panned film defies the critics by achieving blockbuster success at the boxoffice. Certainly it would be fallacious to superficially equate critical reception or boxoffice performance with quality, for surely there have been more than a few "good" films dismissed by critics and probably many more "poor" films embraced by mass audiences (the reverse is just as true on both counts). Still, one can't help but wonder about the likely quality of a movie that received overwhelmingly negative reviews and that also performed dismally with the general public. Actually, that's a huge understatement with regard to *Formula 51,* which hardly "performed" at all at the boxoffice. What can you say about a film that received some of the worst reviews of the year and that only managed to stay in U.S. theaters a mere four weeks? Made on a budget of $27 million, *Formula 51* made just over $5 million domestically through the course of its short-lived run in wide release. Could the movie be so bad as to merit such all-around failure? In a word, yes. If one were to attempt the impossible task of compiling a list all movies that have been unworthy of committing to celluloid, *Formula 51* would probably not be number one on that list, but it must certainly find its place on that list as quickly as any other release of the year. What's astounding, however, and also quite telling, is that the script for this film actually interested filmmakers and talented actors enough to not only get it made but to launch a new career for its previously unknown writer.

Originally released in the United Kingdom in 2001 under the title *The 51st State,* this film has an unusual history. Screenwriter Stel Pavlou had no previous experience with Hollywood and was in fact a liquor store clerk when he penned the script and managed to get it into the hands of actor Tim Roth. Roth was impressed with the script but ultimately passed on it in favor of another project (apparently a wise move), and the film eventually wound up in the hands of director Ronny Yu and star/executive producer Samuel L. Jackson. As a result of this admittedly ambitious venture (which also involved Pavlou conning his way into Cannes), Pavlou ultimately walked away with a lucrative deal that promised him the opportunity to write future screenplays and publish a few books as well. Upon viewing *Formula 51,* one might easily wonder how so many individuals were "conned" into thinking this was such a great idea for a movie. To be sure, there may be no shortage of Hollywood writers who have churned out one disaster after another, but the amazing part of this story is that the film managed to open the Hollywood door for Pavlou as well as attach itself to several talented individuals. In essence, *Formula 51* is an uninspired, tired, loud, and pointless exercise in bad taste.

The film opens with a pivotal scene from the past that introduces us to the character of Elmo McElroy (Samuel L. Jackson), a brilliant, streetwise American pharmacologist who made the mistake in 1971 of getting busted for smoking pot right after college graduation. Consequently he lost his pharmaceutical license, preventing the realization of his plans for becoming a legitimate, successful pharmacist.

Fast-forward 30 years, where we discover Elmo has been earning a living by inventing illegal drugs for a Los Angeles drug lord called The Lizard (Meat Loaf Aday). Elmo wants out of the business, however—or at least he no longer wants to work for The Lizard—so he cooks up a chemical wonder that he hopes will be his ticket to wealth and happiness. That wonder is a super-drug labeled P.O.S. Formula 51, crafted from simple, legal ingredients. According to Elmo, this blue pill is 51 times as powerful as all other recreational drugs and provides the sensation of a "personal visit from God." It's worth a bundle, of course, and Elmo intends to sell to the highest bidder.

After rigging an explosion that destroys The Lizard's laboratory (and that is supposed to kill The Lizard himself), Elmo heads for Liverpool to make a $20 million deal with a British drug syndicate. Unfortunately for him, The Lizard survived and subsequently sends a hit woman named Dakota Phillips (Emily Mortimer) to track him down. Meanwhile, upon arriving in Liverpool, Elmo meets Felix DeSouza (Robert Carlyle), an aide dispatched by drug lord Leopold Durant (Ricky Tomlinson) to escort the chemist and his brilliant invention to a meeting where the multimillion-dollar deal will be finalized. In one of the plot's many gaps in credibility, Felix just happens to be Dakota's ex-lover, providing the story with what is supposed to be a tension-filled comic/romantic/sexually-charged subplot. From here on, the story is mostly predictable. Elmo and Felix not only deal with Dakota but everyone else who would like to cash in on Elmo's invention—gangsters, skinheads, corrupt cops—and of course mayhem must ensue, complete with plenty of bloody violence, car chases, and vulgar expletives. Everything culminates in what is supposed to be a clever twist-ending that takes place at a Liverpool-Manchester football (i.e., soccer) game.

Many critics observed that *Formula 51* attempts to be a cross between Quentin Tarentino's *Pulp Fiction* (1994) and the kind of British gangster movies made by Guy Ritchie, but it fails as a poor imitation. *Formula 51* tries to infuse its violent, underworld tale with clever humor, but there's very little if anything that is clever about it. Dialogue throughout the movie falls flat (as when the word "bollocks" is discussed), sounds corny, and is filled with meaningless profanity (literally almost every other sentence includes the f-word). Buildings and heads explode, cars fly through the air, skinheads lose control of their bowels courtesy of Elmo's concoctions, and the bad guys are whacked into bloody messes by Elmo and his ever-present golf clubs. Elmo carrying a set of golf clubs around with him is just one of the many inexplicable gimmicks in the film.

The presence of the golf clubs is almost insignificant compared to what is evidently supposed to be one of the funniest and cleverest gags in *Formula 51*—the fact that Elmo wears a kilt throughout the entire movie. An explanation is never provided—in fact, at the end of the movie, we are told that no one ever found out why he wore it. The indication is that no one ever bothered to think through this "clever gag," that it was included simply because someone thought it would be a funny thing to see. And that is actually quite accurate. Stel Pavlou has stated that, when he was writing the script, he had always wanted to see a black man in a kilt and wanted to include that element in a movie simply because he thought it was an outrageous and hilarious image. Essentially, then, the image is there for its own sake, with no context and no meaning; the filmmakers simply assume it is funny.

Elmo's inexplicable kilt illustrates the problem with the entire movie. Rather than a coherent, meaningful plot, *Formula 51* is structured around one gimmick or ploy after another, with no substance to tie it all together. Rather than comedy, the movie gives the audience tired, silly gags. Rather than interesting characters, the movie is populated with unconvincing caricatures that seem to exist simply to service the gimmicks and gags. Even Jackson, who can be a good actor with the right material, cannot instill any believability or likeability in Elmo, a "hero" who seems to view the world with arrogant derision. Had there been a real plot to this story, Elmo's blue pill could have been a classic example of what Hitchcock called a McGuffin—a plot device that propels the story but that is ultimately meaningless. The problem with *Formula 51* is that there is no real story to propel—hence, the entire movie is a McGuffin. Just like Elmo McElroy's kilt, it is ultimately pointless.

—*David Flanagin*

CREDITS

Elmo McElroy: Samuel L. Jackson
Felix DeSouza: Robert Carlyle
Dakota Phillips: Emily Mortimer
The Lizard: Meat Loaf Aday
Det. Virgil Kane: Sean Pertwee
Leopold Durant: Ricky Tomlinson
Iki: Rhys Ifans

Origin: Great Britain, Canada
Released: 2001
Production: Andras Hamori, Seaton McLean, David Pupkewitz, Jonathan Debin, Malcolm Kohll; Alliance Atlantis, Focus Film; released by Screen Gems
Directed by: Ronny Yu, David Wu
Written by: Stel Pavlou
Cinematography by: Poon Hang-Seng
Sound: Bruce Carwardine
Music Supervisor: Abi Leland, Dan Rose
Art Direction: Philip Robinson
Costumes: Kate Carin

Production Design: Alan Macdonald
MPAA rating: R
Running time: 92 minutes

REVIEWS

Boxoffice. October, 2002, p. 58.
Chicago Sun-Times Online. October 18, 2002.
Entertainment Weekly. October 25, 2002, p. 55.
Los Angeles Times Online. October 18, 2002.
New York Times Online. October 18, 2002.
Sight and Sound. January, 2002, p. 41.
Variety. December 10, 2001, p. 33.
Washington Post. October 18, 2002, p. WE37.

QUOTES

The Lizard (Meat Loaf Aday): "I want Elmo McElroy kept alive."
Dakota (Emily Mortimer): "I don't do alive, I do dead."

40 Days and 40 Nights

One man is about to do the unthinkable. No sex. Whatsoever. For . . . 40 Days and 40 Nights.
—Movie tagline

How Long Could You Last?
—Movie tagline

It began as a bet—no sex for 40 days. It's become a phenomenon. Now . . . can one man go the distance?
—Movie tagline

Box Office: $37.9 million

I n *40 Days and 40 Nights,* Josh Hartnett plays Matt, a young dot-commer living the single life in San Francisco. Having been dumped six months ago by his beautiful girlfriend, Nicole (Vinessa Shaw), and unable to recover from the heartbreak, Matt has embarked on a series of meaningless flings. But these encounters have left him feeling empty (symbolized by a black hole he imagines opening in the ceiling whenever he has sex), and he finally hits on the idea that he can put his life back in order by abstaining from all forms of sexual intimacy during Lent, the Catholic Church's period of self-denial.

Coming from director Michael Lehmann, whose smart satire of high school cliques, *Heathers,* has become a cult classic, *40 Days and 40 Nights* could have been a clever send-up of sexual mores among hip twentysomethings. But unfortunately, screenwriter Robert Perez does not do much with his promising idea, and the film devolves into a series of dirty jokes in which Matt is faced with one temptation after another. The press kit calls the film "America's first sex comedy without the sex," but it really has nothing else on its mind but a constant barrage of sex-related jokes that wear thin very quickly.

Shortly after taking his vow of celibacy, Matt meets Erica (Shannyn Sossamon), a sweet, attractive woman who seems to be perfect for him, and he begins a tentative friendship, even though he knows it can only go so far. Meanwhile, the guys at work, who have learned about the vow from Matt's boorish roommate, Ryan (Paulo Costanzo), start an Internet pool where people can bet on what day Matt will give in to his urges. Everyone, it seems, has little faith that Matt can go the distance—Ryan even thinks that the vow "goes against nature"—and the pot eventually grows into the thousands of dollars.

40 Days and 40 Nights is a very raunchy comedy. A scene of pre-celibate Matt faking an orgasm and then searching for semen-like fluid to put in the condom to show the girl that he really did climax sets the tone for what will follow. The Web company where Matt works, which looks like the epitome of cool but now, after the dot-com burnout, feels like a relic of the past, features a bevy of sexy gals all too eager to help Matt break his vow. One sits on the copy machine and spreads her legs to show him her tattoo on her inner thigh, and later a pair of girls French-kiss in hopes of arousing him so that they can win the pool and give the money to Greenpeace. Between the loutish guys and over-sexed girls, all of whom spend an inordinate amount of time worrying about Matt's sex life, one is left to wonder if the dot-com burst happened because no one was really doing any work at these startups.

At the same time, however, the movie exhibits a sweet side that never gels with its raunchiness. (Rare films like the original *American Pie* can combine the two, but it is hard to do.) Matt and Erica develop a rapport, first when he shares fabric softener with her at the local laundry and then when he finally breaks through his reticence and strikes up a conversation with her. He takes her on a cute bus date in which they ride around the streets of San Francisco all day (an excursion that probably looks more fun than it actually is), but she starts to worry that something is wrong when he gives her a high-five instead of a kiss at the end of their first date. Once she learns about his vow through the Internet, she is, naturally enough, mad that he was not honest with her from the beginning. Later, Erica learns the whole story of his obsession with Nicole and encourages him to finish his 40 days before they date each other in earnest. Sossamon is the one bright spot amongst the dreck. She is engaging and fresh and has a spunkiness that could be tapped in better movies. But she is playing opposite a very bland Hartnett, who does not understand the rhythms of romantic comedy and seems to think that simply looking earnest and anxious is an engaging way to play the hapless Matt.

Without much of a script, the movie rambles on from one uncomfortable situation to another. Matt's sexually frustrated boss, Jerry (Griffin Dunne), who is not getting enough sex from his wife, follows Matt's example and takes the vow of celibacy because he thinks that it will have his wife begging him for sex. Such is not the case, and he grows more and more agitated until he unwittingly drinks a Viagra-laced beverage that one of Matt's scheming coworkers intended for him. The low point occurs when Matt finds Jerry masturbating in the men's room. Other episodes attain the same combination of gross and unfunny. A dinner with Matt's parents, for example, turns weird when his father starts talking about what sexual positions he can engage in after his recent hip surgery. When we finally get to a scene featuring Matt coming to work with his erection showing through his pants, it is just one more painfully unfunny gag that may amuse fans of the most pedestrian teen sex comedies, but, in a movie supposedly about adults, is just embarrassing.

40 Days and 40 Nights is Hollywood sex comedy at its most tiresome—easy vulgarity without any wit or creativity. And even when it seems like the film may have a drop of tenderness, as in an offbeat "sex scene" in which Matt uses a flower to pleasure Erica without directly touching her, the moment feels so out of place with the general crassness that it may as well be taken from another movie.

Some jokes strive for an offhanded irreverence that fails miserably. Matt's brother, John (Adam Trese), is a seminarian, and they have several conversations in the confessional about Matt's vow that are not very funny but are probably meant to be naughty simply because the brothers are talking about sex in church. Matt even runs into his brother making out with a nun, a gratuitous scene that must be intended for shock value because it is related to nothing else in the movie, other than to show that even a supposedly dedicated seminarian cannot keep a vow of celibacy. To make it through his last few hours, a feverish Matt even has Ryan tie him to his bed crucifixion-style, yet another religious gag that borders on the blasphemous without exhibiting a shred of cleverness.

But alas, the long-suffering Matt does not quite make it to the very end. Since Matt has spurned Nicole's recent attempt at a reconciliation, she places a wager in the pool and then enters Matt's apartment minutes before midnight at the end of the 40th day and straddles Matt, whose subconscious is plagued by sexual fantasies (including flying over a sea of undulating breasts, an image that perfectly sums up the film). Thinking that she is Erica, Matt has sex with her. Nicole is so evil at the end, one wonders why a nice guy like Matt was involved with her in the first place. She leaves Matt's place in triumph and passes a disheartened Erica, who was arriving for a midnight tryst to cap off Matt's 40 days of denial. When Matt explains to Erica that he was asleep and thought that he was making love to her, not Nicole, Erica storms out in disbelief.

In the end, Matt and Erica do get back together when he explains the big lesson he has learned—that it was a big mistake for him to try to make a part of himself go away. It is not much of a lesson and feels like a flimsy, tacked-on moral to effect a reconciliation that we could hardly care about. There really is no lesson or insight gained, nothing to lift this tired material to a higher level. In the film's last scene, Matt and Erica are secluded in his bedroom, and his obnoxious friends are now placing bets on how long the couple can make love.

Michael Lehmann has demonstrated a dark side in the brilliant *Heathers* as well as a romantic side in the genial *The Truth About Cats and Dogs,* but he cannot juggle the vulgar and the romantic in a movie that wallows in cheap laughs and goes nowhere. The general unpleasantness of *40 Days and 40 Nights* could perhaps have been mitigated somewhat if Josh Hartnett were not such a dull and sullen leading man, huffing and puffing his way through all of the temptations thrown Matt's way. Hartnett was fine as a brooding Iago in last year's teenage version of *Othello, O,* and lent solid support as a soldier in *Black Hawk Down,* but Perez's insipid script needs something else—an actor with a touch of zaniness to help us forget how repetitive the jokes really are. Unfortunately, Hartnett lacks the range for even the most mindless of romantic comedies.

—Peter N. Chumo II

CREDITS

Matt: Josh Hartnett
Erica Sutton: Shannyn Sossamon
Sam: Maggie Gyllenhaal
Nicole: Vinessa Shaw
Ryan: Paulo Costanzo
Chris: Glenn Fitzgerald
Susie: Emmanuelle Vaugier
Bagel Guy: Michael Maronna
Mom: Mary Gross
Father Maher: Stanley Anderson
John: Adam Trese
Dad: Barry Newman
Jerry: Griffin Dunne
Candy: Monet Mazur
David: Dylan Neal
Mikey: Chris Gauthier

Origin: USA
Released: 2002
Production: Tim Bevan, Eric Fellner, Michael London; Working Title Productions; released by Miramax Films
Directed by: Michael Lehmann
Written by: Rob Perez
Cinematography by: Elliot Davis
Music by: Rolfe Kent
Sound: David Husby
Music Supervisor: Bonnie Greenberg-Goldman
Editing: Nicholas C. Smith
Art Direction: Yvonne Hurst
Costumes: Jill Ohanneson
Production Design: Sharon Seymour
MPAA rating: R
Running time: 94 minutes

REVIEWS

Chicago Sun-Times Online. March 1, 2002.
Entertainment Weekly. March 8, 2002, p. 46.
Los Angeles Times Online. March 1, 2002.
New York Times Online. March 1, 2002.
People. March 11, 2002, p. 38.
USA Today Online. March 1, 2002.
Variety. February 25, 2002, p. 70.
Washington Post. March 1, 2002, p. WE46.

QUOTES

Matt Sullivan (Josh Hartnett): "No sex for Lent. Forty days." Ryan (Paulo Constanzo): "You won't last a week."

The Four Feathers

Freedom. Country. Honor. Passion. To save his best friend, one man must risk everything he loves.
—Movie tagline

 Box Office: $18.3 million

This film is the latest in a number of adaptations of the famous novel by A.E.W. Mason. Mason, one of England's most popular and respected storytellers (today, he is revered by mystery buffs for his seminal 1923 detective novel, *The House of the Arrow,* featuring the redoubtable Inspector Hanaud), first published the novel serially in the *Cornhill* magazine from January to November 1901. It came out in a single volume a year later and quickly became his greatest success, selling more than a million copies during its first 40 years.

The story grew largely out of a trip the 36-year-old author made to Egypt in 1901. Among his stops were Khartoum and the ruined city of Omdurman, where Lord Kitchener had broken the Khalifa's power two years earlier. Nearby was the notorious prison called the House of Stone, where Khalifa's captives had been imprisoned like sheep in a pen. There Mason heard legends of a man, disguised as a dervish, who had assisted in the escape of a number of British prisoners. "From all this grew [Mason's] idea of a boy growing to manhood in the belief that he is a coward," writes biographer Roger Lancelyn Green in his book *A.E.W. Mason: The Adventure of a Story-Teller* (Max Parrish, 1952), "forced into the army by tradition and by a father without imagination, losing his honour and with it his fiancée—not by fear, but by the fear of fear—and finding, when it seems too late, that his is that finest bravery of all which can endure danger and pain in spite of the vivid imagination which urges him to run away" (89).

The political and economic contexts behind the events chronicled in Mason's novel are complicated, to say the least. In brief, when Egypt penetrated into the Sudan during the 1820s, it borrowed heavily from European banks; and in an attempt to finance this massive debt, the Circassian bureaucrats taxed excessively the Egyptian and Sudanese people. When engineers finished the Suez Canal in 1869, Egypt became a country of strategic importance, ensuring an alliance with the British, who owned a portion of the canal that linked it to India. Any threat to Egypt also jeopardized the Canal. Meanwhile, mounting unrest led to Colonel Ahmed Bey Urabi's nationalist coup d'etat in September 1881. This in turn unleashed an Islamic revolt in the Sudan, a jihad against the British and their Egyptian allies, led by a Muslin religious leader, Muhammad Ahmed, the Madhi ("The Expected Guide"). When a company of Egyptian infantrymen were slaughtered by the Mahdi in 1881, Col. William Hicks and a British army of 8,000 were dispatched to Obeid, the capital of Kordofan province, where they too were massacred almost to a man. An outraged Prime Minister Gladstone then sent General Charles Gordon to Khartoum to evacuate the European and Egyptian populations against the Mahdi's further incursions. Now it was the turn of Gordon and his troops to fall in bloody defeat. The year was 1885.

Against this historical backdrop, we are introduced to *The Four Feathers*'s hero, Harry Faversham (Heath Ledger), a man with a bright future ahead of him in the military. The story begins in 1869 when young Harry listens with growing alarm to stories by his father of wartime atrocities in the Crimea. His over-active imagination paralyzes him with fear, and he wonders if in times of crisis he might not prove to be a coward: "I saw myself behaving as one," he later tells a friend, "in the crisis of a battle bringing ruin upon my country, certainly dishonouring my father . . ." (46).

Thirteen years later he is a lieutenant in the East Surrey Regiment. While dining with his fellow officers one night he announces that his engagement to Ethne Eustace (Kate Hudson) necessitates his resignation from the regiment. When a telegram arrives moments later alerting his regiment to impending active duty in the Sudan, he feigns ignorance of the news, afraid that his decision to resign will seem to have been inspired by it. But his fellow officers, Trench (Michael Sheen), Castleton (Kris Marshall), and Willoughby (Rupert Penry-Jones), reach their own conclusions and send him a box containing their calling cards and three white feathers, accusations of cowardice. A fourth feather is added by Harry's humiliated fiancée, Ethne. Harry now determines to go to Egypt and return the feathers to his accusers. "They stand in great peril and great need," he says to himself. "To be in readiness for that moment is from now my career" (65). It is obvious that it is not patriotic duty so much as his loyalty to his comrades and his own moral imperative that motivates his decision.

Harry now all but disappears from the main narrative. For more than half the book—spanning five years in time—he flits in and out of the action, briefly glimpsed in a variety of disguises and names, sometimes as an Arab beggar, an itinerant musician, a Greek, and frequently accompanied by a mysterious Arab named Abou Fatma (Djimon Hounsou). Eyewitness accounts, speculations, and hearsay by colleagues and friends Lieutenant Sutch, Jack Durrance (Wes Bentley), and Captain Willoughby track Harry's movements as he penetrates marketplaces and bandit encampments, all the while contriving to return the feathers of cowardice. It is only in the last chapters that Feversham once again resumes stage center as he contrives his and Lieutenant Trench's escape from Khalifa's notorious prison in Omdurman, The House of Stone, a desolate place if there ever was one—"a brown and stony plain burnt by the sun, and, built upon it, a straggling narrow city of hovels crawling with vermin and poisoned with disease" (296).

Meanwhile, back in England, Durrance, Sutch, Willoughby, and Ethne have been incessantly examining and debating the circumstances and the meaning of Harry's withdrawal from his regiment and the nature of his "cowardice." For example, Durrance argues that Harry's resignation from his regiment was not an act of cowardice so much as an act of fear engendered by an over-active imagination concerning the horrors of war. "Don't you see that? It's his opportunity to know himself at last. Up to the moment of disgrace his life has all been sham and illusion the man he believed himself to be, he never was, and now at the last he knows it. Once he knows it, he can set about to retrieve his disgrace. Oh, there are compensations for such a man" (272). Sutch offers a counter view, "that Harry fancied

himself to be a brave man, and was suddenly brought up short by discovering that he was a coward" (272-273).

When Harry reappears, near the end, to return the fourth feather to Ethne, his lined face and scarred body have aged him beyond his years and rendered him almost unrecognizable. He is Ulysses returned home. Only Ethne's collie dog issues a welcome. "The years of probation had left their marks," writes the author. "He had put himself to a long, hard test; and he knew that he had not failed" (354). During his reunion with Ethne, he learns that she has already promised herself to Durrance. It is only Durrance's withdrawal from the engagement that allows Ethne and Harry to reunite.

Mason's novel has proven too complex in its historical contexts and too philosophical in its musings about the issues and contradictions of cowardice, fear, duty, and friendship to survive successfully its numerous translations to the screen. As historian David Levering Lewis observes in the book *Past Imperfect* (1995), "Detailing the connections among finance capital, technology diffusion, and national self-determination was much too tall an order for the filmmakers." Moreover, author Mason's determination to limit the scope of the action and to keep Harry offstage for extended periods of time (effective as it was on the page in transforming him from an individual character to a more universal metaphor) left little room for the rousing spectacle and graphic heroic exploits a commercial cinema audience demanded. Changes obviously had to be made. As is apparent in the various film versions, ethical debates are, for the most part, abandoned and historical contexts are reduced to a scant few references in favor of a handful of sweeping battle scenes. And Harry's near-mythic status in the book's central part is dropped in favor of keeping him in the foreground of the action.

The first film adaptation was directed by J. Searle Dawley in 1915 for the newly-formed Dyreda Art Film Corp., which released through Metro Pictures. Howard Estabrook portrayed Captain Harry Faversham [sic], Arthur Evers was Durrance, and Irene Warfield was Ethne. David Selznick's 1929 version was made for Paramount producer B.P. Shulberg. It had begun as a silent film a year before, but music and sound effects and some dialogue were quickly added as the talkie revolution gained momentum. Selznick reworked Howard Estabrook's script so that several big battle scenes were added to the film's climactic sequences. Richard Arlen was cast as Harry, Clive Brook as Durrance (who here is made to deliver one of the feathers), and Fay Wray as Ethne. Mason himself assisted in adapting his novel for the Alexander Korda Technicolor production in 1939. The cast included John Clements as Harry Faversham [sic], Ralph Richardson as Durrance, and June Duprez as Ethne.

"It's a fascinating story," says screenwriter Hossein Amini regarding the most recent adaptation, directed by Shekhar Kapur. "Imperial England was confronting a world and society about which it knew very little. Those young men went from fantastic country mansions into the middle of the desert, and in the end their overconfidence and belief in their superiority led to mistakes and ultimately disaster. It's a fascinating story," at least so the pressbook proclaims. Canny as Amini had been in his other screen adaptations of literary works—see the admirable job he did on Henry James's *The Wings of the Dove,* for example—he fails miserably here.

Like previous adapters, Amini is determined to sacrifice the complexities of historical contexts, the ethical and psychological issues, and the multiple-viewpoint narrative for the sake of linear storytelling and big battle scenes. Harry is kept at the center of the action. His long-standing fear of war, engendered by the novel's crucial early scene when as a boy he hears the hair-raising accounts of Crimean atrocities, is skipped. All we know is that as a young man he prefers rugby to war, and that he resigns his commission more out of fear than psychological conflict. Moreover, his decision to leave England for the Sudan is spurred by news of his comrade's entrapment by the Sudanese—not, as in the book, by the larger imperatives of his own redemption. He's bent on rescuing his mates, not himself.

Despite the insistence on a linear narrative throughline, there are curious lapses in continuity. One gets the impression that huge chunks of footage have been left on the cutting-room floor. For example, one moment the disguised Harry and Abou are members of a marauding force that overwhelms a British fort; the next, Abou shows up alone in the British camp with warnings of the dangers lying ahead (whatever happened during that split-second gap in continuity will never be known). Later, following the example of the Korda film, Harry rescues Jack after he has been blinded in an attack. Here again, the jump cuts leave the viewer breathless: In one shot Harry is cradling Jack in his arms; and in the next shot Jack is suddenly safely back in England (we ache to know how he negotiated his return).

And when Jack and Trench escape from the House of Stone (with the assistance of the ever-present Abou), they move in the twinkling of yet another jump cut from the desert wastes of the Sudan to the greenwood of Merrie Olde England. It should be noted that an inordinate amount of screen time is expended on detailing with graphic, almost sadomasochistic zeal Harry's sufferings in the House of Stone as he is conked on the head with a rock, whipped by the slave masters, beaten up every few minutes, and finally smashed head down into a sand dune. Ironically, when the film turns at last to the details of the book, the results are listless and boring. Witness the final two sequences, Harry's reunion with Ethne in a chapel and Durrance's withdrawal from his engagement to her.

Reviews were not so enthusiastic. Dismissing the project as a "perilously dated glory-of-England chestnut," Owen Gleiberman of *Entertainment Weekly* was negative in his criticism of Heath Ledger, "who all but disappears as an actor" and who seems to be playing a "19th-century version of the John Walker Lindh Story." Todd McCarthy of *Variety* also complained of the one-dimensional acting in this "dull rendition of the old warhorse about honor lost and redeemed in Africa during Britain's high colonial days." The film is pleasantly atmospheric, however. The impressive location photography includes areas in Morocco, the tall mountains of Fint, and the 600-year-old town of Ait Ben Hobdou, which represents the fortress of Abou Clea; and sites in England, Blenheim Palace and Hyde Claire Castle.

—*James M. Welsh and John C. Tibbetts*

CREDITS

Harry Faversham: Heath Ledger
Jack Durrance: Wes Bentley
Ethne Eustace: Kate Hudson
Abou Fatma: Djimon Hounsou
Trench: Michael Sheen
Castleton: Kris Marshall
Willoughby: Rupert Penry-Jones
General Faversham: Tim Pigott-Smith
Colonel Hamilton: Alex Jennings

Origin: USA
Released: 2002
Production: Stanley Jaffe, Marty Katz, Paul Feldsher, Robert D. Jaffe; Jaffilms; released by Paramount Pictures
Directed by: Shekhar Kapur
Written by: Michael Schiffer, Hossein Amini
Cinematography by: Robert Richardson
Music by: James Horner
Sound: Peter Lindsay
Editing: Steven Rosenblum
Art Direction: Keith Pain
Costumes: Ruth Myers
Production Design: Allan Cameron
MPAA rating: PG-13
Running time: 130 minutes

REVIEWS

Chicago Sun-Times Online. September 20, 2002.
Entertainment Weekly. September 27, 2002, p. 58.
Los Angeles Times Online. September 8, 2002.
Los Angeles Times Online. September 20, 2002.
New York Times Online. September 20, 2002.
People. September 30, 2002, p. 37.
Variety. September 16, 2002, p. 32.
Washington Post. September 20, 2002, p. WE46.

come together to tell the epic story that the subject demands. It is essentially a simple revenge tale dressed up in period garb and shouldering a historical weight that it does not earn on its own. At the same time, the film cannot be easily dismissed—it is an extraordinarily ambitious re-creation of a time and place we hardly ever see in movies. Production designer Dante Ferretti essentially built 19th century New York in Rome, and the meticulous attention to detail is evident from the outset.

The movie begins in 1846 with a bloody street battle between the Nativists and the Irish immigrants, knows as the Dead Rabbits. The Irish are led by "Priest" Vallon (Liam Neeson), whose men face off against Bill's crew for control of the Five Points. It is an amazing sequence of hand-to-hand combat with such weapons as knives and axes; visceral and bloody, even primeval, the fighting climaxes when Bill stabs and kills Vallon. Bill is brutal, but he respects his fallen adversary and insists that no trophies be taken from the body so that he can enter the afterlife whole.

The story picks up 16 years later as Vallon's son, Amsterdam (Leonardo DiCaprio), who witnessed his father's death, is leaving the Hellgate House of Reform. As he makes his way back to New York City to seek vengeance on Bill, we are introduced to the social milieu. The Conscription Act, the first draft in American history, has been passed, while Irish immigrants are arriving in boatloads and being greeted by angry mobs that want them to go away. The infamous political boss of Tammany Hall, William Tweed (Jim Broadbent in a wonderful supporting performance), sees the Irish as a potential political base, while Bill, who is now a powerful crime lord controlling virtually everything in the Five Points, sees them as a foreign horde worthy of death. Amsterdam meets Johnny (Henry Thomas), a boyhood friend who tells him all about the rival gangs jockeying for power. As they are walking through the grimy streets, they exchange a few words with the pretty pickpocket, Jenny (Cameron Diaz). She steals Johnny's timepiece, but, since he is smitten with her, he does not seem to mind.

When a fire breaks out, all the amateur fire brigades converge but spend more time bickering with each other instead of putting out the fire. Amsterdam and Johnny loot the burning building and bring the spoils to their gang, where the crooked cop, Happy Jack (John C. Reilly), collects his share. Happy Jack had fought alongside Amsterdam's father, but now he works for Bill. When Johnny pays Bill a share of the proceeds, Bill sends him to loot a ship. However, Johnny and Amsterdam discover that a rival gang has gotten there first, and Amsterdam gets the idea to sell a corpse they find to medical science. Amsterdam's ingenuity impresses Bill, who makes the quick-thinking young man a trusted part of his inner circle.

In another key plotline, Amsterdam and Jenny begin a love-hate relationship, sparked by her stealing the St. Michael medal his father gave him. He gets it back from her but not before the feisty gal pulls a knife on him. Later, at a dance, she chooses him amongst all the men, but that night, when they are about to make love, Amsterdam discovers that she has also been involved with Bill and rejects her.

The main problem with *Gangs of New York,* especially the lengthy middle section, is that it lacks a strong narrative drive. The screenplay simply gives us scene after scene of gang life as Amsterdam establishes his worth to Bill, and, as a result, we never feel a genuine urgency in what everyone is doing. When boxing is outlawed within the city, for example, Amsterdam comes up with the idea to have the fights take place on the dock, yet one more example of his cleverness that does not carry any significant plot implications.

The movie constantly reminds us of the social history of the time—we see immigrants coming off the boat, becoming citizens, and quickly being sent off to fight in the Civil War, while caskets of Civil War dead are being hauled onto the dock. But the screenplay, credited to Jay Cocks, Steven Zaillian, and Kenneth Lonergan, fails to connect Amsterdam's tedious stint as Bill's protégé and surrogate son with the big historical issues of the day, namely, immigration and the hated draft. The draft could be dodged with a payment of $300, an exorbitant sum that meant only the poor would be forced to fight.

Amsterdam demonstrates his loyalty by trying to save Bill when an assassin takes a shot at him. Bill is wounded, and Jenny nurses him, but then she and Amsterdam end up sleeping together. Their tepid love story is one of the most generic and least consistent aspects of the screenplay. Another puzzlement is Amsterdam's character. DiCaprio's lack of range in the role makes it hard to figure out why Amsterdam is waiting so long to exact his vengeance—perhaps he has grown to like gang life too much, or maybe he has been seduced by Bill's wicked charm.

While DiCaprio's performance may be vague, Day-Lewis's is riveting on every level. Physically, he has hidden his good looks behind a big handlebar mustache and hair as greasy as the character. Fiery and charismatic, with a sly sense of humor and a flair for grand, theatrical displays, Bill is a commanding crime lord, dwarfing everyone around him. Day-Lewis gets all the details just right. Bill really is a professional butcher, and Day-Lewis demonstrates his physical dexterity with knives not only on the battlefield but also on the slabs of meat Bill slices up. For all the ways Bill is a vicious crime lord ruling by fear, Day-Lewis also expertly reveals an inner life that takes us by surprise. On the morning after he is wounded, Bill appears in Amsterdam's room. Unfazed by the fact that Jenny and Amsterdam are in bed together, he proceeds, in one of the film's best and subtlest scenes, to speak eloquently about the last honorable man he killed, Amsterdam's father. He describes Vallon once beating him in a fight and then sparing his life to shame him. Bill could not look his adversary in the eye, so he cut out one of his eyes and sent it to Vallon. It is an odd yet poignant scene showing the way a bloodthirsty mobster lives by a code of honor and looks upon his enemy not with hatred but with respect. And of course the great irony is that he does not realize he is telling the story to the son of Vallon.

At the 16th anniversary commemoration of the battle Bill won against Vallon, Johnny, who is smarting over Jenny's affair with Amsterdam, betrays his old friend by telling Bill Amsterdam's true identity and his plan to kill him. The celebration takes place in a Chinese theater, where Bill is called onstage to do his famous knife-throwing act. Bill summons Jenny to be his assistant and throws knives at her, at one point even nicking her slightly. The tension mounts when Bill raises his glass to toast the memory of Vallon and Amsterdam throws his knife at Bill, who easily deflects it and then throws one back, piercing Amsterdam's stomach. Bill's men hold Amsterdam down, while Bill pummels him. He lets Amsterdam go with a scar burned into his cheek to humiliate him, and Jenny oversees his return to health.

When Amsterdam recovers, he finally feels emboldened to take action and hangs a dead rabbit on a public fence, a provocation since the Dead Rabbits were outlawed when Bill defeated Vallon. But just when it seems that the central conflict is coming to a head, we are treated to more filler on the way to the inevitable showdown. Bill sends Happy Jack after Amsterdam, but Amsterdam strangles him and hangs him crucifixion-style for the whole town to see. Johnny, who regrets betraying Amsterdam, ends up impaled on a fence by Bill's men and begs Amsterdam to put him out of his misery. Meanwhile, more Irish are arriving, and Tweed cuts a deal with Amsterdam by which he will run an Irishman for sheriff in return for the Irish vote. Monk McGinn (Brendan Gleeson), who fought alongside Vallon for a price and has been standing on the sidelines for much of the story, runs and wins the election, but Bill kills him, and, during Monk's lavish funeral procession through the street, Amsterdam finally challenges Bill to a battle.

By the time the gangs agree to terms and weapons and get ready to fight, however, the showdown is overshadowed by mass revolt in the streets against the draft. The army is sent to quell the rioters, and cannons from ships also attack, which breaks up the rival gangs before the fighting begins, leaving everyone in disarray and Bill and Amsterdam stumbling around in a cloud of smoke. Bill is wounded, and Amsterdam finally sticks his knife in for the kill. While Bill's death should feel like a momentous event, the fall of a legendary villain, it instead feels like just one more killing in a prolonged tale of carnage. Moreover, nothing has really been gained other than a son taking vengeance for his father's death. Perhaps it is Scorsese's point that larger historical forces embodied in the Draft Riots of 1863 render gang war trivial, but it is still an anticlimactic ending.

At the end, Bill is buried next to Priest Vallon, and we see the New York City skyline in the background gradually grow and develop into the 20th century. The film seems to suggest that the city sprang from these men, but it is not clear how these turf wars gave birth to a city. Indeed, the message at the end feels very muddled. The last shot features the Twin Towers standing proudly in the city skyline, but, given the emotional weight they now carry, this seems like a sentimental way to conclude a film that supposedly takes an unsentimental view of the thugs who once ruled New York. U2's song, "The Hands That Built America," which plays over the end credits, sounds like a triumphant anthem celebrating the immigrants' contribution to America, but the film itself has chronicled mayhem and destruction. If this is ironic commentary on how America was built, it is ambiguous at best.

From any other director, *Gangs of New York* would probably be considered an ambitious if flawed effort, but, coming from the man many consider America's greatest living director, the film can only disappoint by falling far short of the greatness he was aiming for. While the attention to period detail plunges us into the middle of 19th century New York, ultimately such an epic production needs an epic tale to match, not a choppy story that meanders along to an unsatisfying conclusion. The love story is dull, the political corruption all too familiar, and the revenge tale very predictable. Moreover, these story lines feel like disparate pieces that never work together to create a unified film. Only Day-Lewis's larger-than-life portrayal of Bill gives the film the energy it needs, and, at two hours, 45 minutes long, even a monumental performance such as his cannot carry the entire film.

—Peter N. Chumo II

CREDITS

Amsterdam Vallon: Leonardo DiCaprio
William "Bill the Butcher" Cutting: Daniel Day-Lewis
Jenny Everdeane: Cameron Diaz
Priest Vallon: Liam Neeson
William "Boss" Tweed: Jim Broadbent
Happy Jack: John C. Reilly
Johnny Sirocco: Henry Thomas
Walter "Monk" McGinn: Brendan Gleeson
McGloin: Gary Lewis
Shang: Stephen Graham
Killoran: Eddie Marsan
Reverend Raleigh: Alec McCowen
Mr. Schermerhorn: David Hemmings
Jimmy Spoils: Larry Gilliard Jr.
Hell-Cat Maggie: Cara Seymour
P.T. Barnum: Roger Ashton-Griffiths

Young Amsterdam: Cian McCormack

Origin: USA
Released: 2002
Production: Alberto Grimaldi, Harvey Weinstein; released by Miramax Films
Directed by: Martin Scorsese
Written by: Jay Cocks, Steven Zaillian, Kenneth Lonergan
Cinematography by: Michael Ballhaus
Music by: Howard Shore
Sound: Ivan Sharrock
Editing: Thelma Schoonmaker
Art Direction: Stefano Ortolani
Costumes: Sandy Powell
Production Design: Dante Ferretti
MPAA rating: R
Running time: 168 minutes

 REVIEWS

Boxoffice. December, 2002, p. 25.
Chicago Sun-Times Online. December 20, 2002.
Entertainment Weekly. January 3, 2003, p. 43.
Los Angeles Times Online. December 20, 2002.
New York Times Online. September 8, 2002.
New York Times Online. December 20, 2002.
People. January 13, 2002, p. 39.
Rolling Stone. January 23, 2003, p. 75.
USA Today Online. December 20, 2002.
Variety Online. December 5, 2002.
Washington Post. December 20, 2002, p. WE41.

QUOTES

Bill the Butcher (Daniel Day-Lewis): "Each of the Five Points is a finger, and when I close my hand, it becomes a fist."

AWARDS AND NOMINATIONS

British Acad. 2002: Actor (Day-Lewis)
Golden Globes 2003: Director (Scorsese), Song ("The Hands That Built America")
L.A. Film Critics 2002: Actor (Day-Lewis)
N.Y. Film Critics 2002: Actor (Day-Lewis)
Nomination:
Oscars 2002: Actor (Day-Lewis), Art Dir./Set Dec., Cinematog., Costume Des., Director (Scorsese), Film, Film Editing, Orig. Screenplay, Song ("The Hands That Built America"), Sound

British Acad. 2002: Cinematog., Costume Des., Director (Scorsese), Film, Film Editing, Orig. Screenplay, Sound, Visual FX, Visual FX, Score
Directors Guild 2002: Director (Scorsese)
Golden Globes 2003: Actor—Drama (Day-Lewis), Film—Drama, Support. Actress (Diaz)
Screen Actors Guild 2002: Actor (Day-Lewis)
Writers Guild 2002: Orig. Screenplay.

Gangster No. 1

Being number two wasn't good enough.
—Movie tagline

More than 30 years after Stanley Kubrick's *A Clockwork Orange,* the protagonist-villain of that film remains Malcolm McDowell's most memorable role. McDowell has fashioned a busy, respectable career since then but without any starring roles nearly as fabulous. In the bizarre *Gangster No. 1,* McDowell plays another amoral, violent thug who is somewhat reminiscent of his Alex in *A Clockwork Orange.*

The second feature film for British director Paul McGuigan—the first was *Acid House,* another exploration of the seamy side of British culture—*Gangster No. 1* was adapted by Johnny Ferguson from a play by Louis Mellis and David Scinto. It was released in Great Britain in 2000 but took two years to cross the Atlantic and land in American video stores. Completely unheralded, it is one of the year's most unorthodox and disturbing films. It should come attached with a warning label that says "only for the adventurous moviegoer." The average viewer is likely to find it disgusting, offensive, or tedious.

For fans of the unconventional, though, *Gangster No. 1* is a fascinating piece of semi-experimental filmmaking. McGuigan takes an offbeat mobster character study and makes it into something like cultural anthropology. In the film's view, the criminal mind of McDowell's character is warped and twisted but subject to the same uncontrollable jealousy, envy, rage, and even contrition that affect most people. It's just that gangsters lack the self-control and the social inhibitions that might prevent them from acting out their impulses.

Gangster No. 1 is gruesome, tawdry, fascinating, and perversely fun. We first meet McDowell's title character (who has no known given name) in 1999, as he's drinking and eating in a fancy establishment that is centered around a boxing ring. During the opening credit sequence, McGuigan inventively uses overhead shots of the boxers, overlaid with strips of red, to establish the violence at the heart of his gangster's material success. The boxing match in the fancy restaurant is incongruous in the same way that Gangster No. 1's material success—his expensive suit, his cigar—is incongruously born of blood and guts.

The next indication that this movie is going to break the rules comes when McDowell carries his glass of wine into the bathroom, places it on the floor next to a urinal, lifts it as if to drink it, then turns to the camera and says: "What do you take me for, an [expletive]?" It is the only time in the film when his character talks directly to the audience. But it is far from the last time that the derogatory slang term for female genitalia is used.

McDowell's character then narrates a long flashback that consumes the bulk of the 103-minute film. Most of it takes place in 1968, when he was just breaking into the gangster life; supposedly he is then known as Gangster No. 55 and he is played by Paul Bettany. Bettany is a young, blonde, angular actor with a ferret's eyes and a sickening fake smile. His performance is mesmerizing. The aspiring hoodlum is taken under the wing of a notorious but diffident criminal named Freddie Mays (David Thewlis). Gangster 55 is immediately smitten with Mays—his penthouse apartment with leather sofas surrounding a sunken living room, his Italian designer suits, his cufflinks, watch, and tiepin, with all the things that make him look dapper and successful. He is also taken with his power and authority.

In one key scene, Gangster 55 is riding in a car with Mays and looks longingly at his monogrammed tiepin. Mays takes it off and gives it to his lackey, who puts it on reverentially. Entering a club, Gangster 55 admires himself in a mirror. His image merges with that of Mays, who is behind him with his back facing the mirror. It's a tantalizing little spin on the merging faces of Ingmar Bergman's two female leads in *Persona,* though the style of this movie—fast, rough, offhand, brutal—couldn't be more different from Bergman's work.

Gangster 55 initially gets in hot water with Freddie because he and Freddie's other henchmen are a little too aggressive in collecting debts—they slam a taxi down on one deadbeat, and beat another to a pulp with golf clubs on a miniature golf hole shaped like a dollar sign. In between, they have dance parties on shag carpeting. McGuigan's style sends up the freewheeling, silly moviemaking of the mod 1960s, immersing it with rough language and rougher behavior. It's hard to imagine a more despicable set of young punks than Freddie and his crew, yet at the same time they seem strangely innocent and affectless.

Gangster 55's feelings for Freddie are full of envy at his prowess and style, but whether there's a sexual dimension is impossible to say. In a pivotal scene in a nightclub, Freddie remarks how it might seem to others to be suspicious to see them drinking wine together, implying that someone might think they were gay. A showgirl, Karen (Saffron Burrows) is sent by the club's boss—for reasons not explained—to oc-cupy Freddie. At first she mistakes Gangster 55 for Freddie, and he is insulting to her. But when Freddie returns from the bathroom, he orders his underling to leave, in the middle of eating dinner, to make way for wooing Karen. Karen sings Freddie a song on stage (a sultry version of "Mercy, Mercy, Mercy") and Gangster 55 boils over with jealousy and rage.

This incident seems to be the motivation for Gangster 55's subsequent actions, in which he both betrays and then avenges Freddie, making decisions that lead to disastrous and far-reaching consequences. The events end up giving Gangster 55 control of Freddie's empire, which he expands into a highly successful criminal enterprise. At the end of the film, coming back to 1999, Gangster 55 (now played by McDowell, who terms himself Gangster No. 1) must confront Freddie and his past, and while his former idol has matured, it's obvious his old underling has not.

This fairly simple story is infused throughout with inventive and daring directing, acting, editing, and cinematography. Gangster 55, preparing to go into rage mode, suddenly opens his mouth in a hideous silent scream accompanied by a sound like screeching tires. It's like he's suddenly been taken over by a vampire spirit. Bettany is brilliant with his smarmy, sarcastic demeanor masking a deep well of perverse immorality. The movie's most important scene of violence is shot, disconcertingly, from the point of view of the victim being tortured, adding to its chilling effect. Overall, the film's main impact is to depict characters and a culture where a childish glee in petty things is combined with a hideous view of human expendability. It's all done in a dialogue rife with profane roughneck commentary that merges with a pretense of urbane sophistication. Quentin Tarantino has nothing on McGuigan.

Something is deeply rotten at the core of these people, especially the film's protagonist, and while it may be difficult to watch, *Gangster No. 1* is uniquely perceptive. Watching the title character is like watching a snake coiling, striking, and then turning on itself. He is a hideous character but iconic in a tawdry way, for he represents the dark side of a certain kind of character, the devil-may-care criminal who is so often romanticized in movies. McGuigan strips away all the romanticism and the pretense and reveals a very ugly soul indeed. There is no sugar-coating or glamorizing the type of man who would torture and kill in order to look like a successful businessman. At its best, *Gangster No. 1* smashes the cinematic curtain that masks the depravity of the criminal mind as it exposes the underside of popular culture and standard moviemaking conventions. That it does so with flair, panache, and engaging techniques is a credit to McGuigan.

Gangster No. 1 is not in any way a masterpiece. It is deeply flawed, inconsistent, and occasionally grandiose. But it reveals McGuigan as a potentially powerful if perverse auteur, and it gets many points for originality. Not only that, it's good to see McDowell once again going in for a bit of the old ultraviolence. Stanley Kubrick would probably feel very much at ease with *Gangster No. 1*.

—*Michael Betzold*

CREDITS

Gangster 55: Malcolm McDowell
Young Gangster: Paul Bettany
Freddie Mays: David Thewlis
Karen: Saffron Burrows
Tommy: Kenneth Cranham
Lennie Taylor: Jamie Foreman
Eddie Miller: Eddie Marsan
Maxie King: Andrew Lincoln

Origin: Great Britain, Germany
Released: 2000
Production: Norma Heyman, Jonathan Cavendish; Road Movies, FilmFour, Pagoda Film; released by IFC Films
Directed by: Paul McGuigan
Written by: Johnny Ferguson
Cinematography by: Peter Sova
Music by: John Dankworth
Sound: John Taylor
Editing: Andrew Hulme
Art Direction: Philip Elton
Costumes: Jany Temime
Production Design: Richard Bridgland
MPAA rating: R
Running time: 103 minutes

REVIEWS

Boxoffice. July, 2002, p. 85.
Chicago Sun-Times Online. July 19, 2002.
Entertainment Weekly. June 21, 2002, p. 49.
Los Angeles Times Online. July 12, 2002.
New York Times Online. June 14, 2002.
Sight and Sound. July, 2000, p. 45.
Variety. June 12, 2000, p. 16.

Ghost Ship

Sea Evil.
—Movie tagline

 Box Office: $29.6 million

Ghost Ship is a horror film with a most unusual opening. As sappy, generic music from the fifties wafts over the audience, the credits role by in a perky, hot pink. I guess that could be considered scary to some people, but it seems inconsistent with the dark, ghostly picture one is expecting. Then it becomes obvious that we're being set up with a view of the past, the background to the current story we will soon be experiencing.

The year is 1962 and we're aboard a luxurious, Italian ocean liner, the Antonia Graza. While the wealthy adults dance to that sappy music we were hearing, a little girl on deck is playing with blocks and spelling out "I am so bored." At this point the captain of the ship (Robert Ruggiero) takes her hand and the tall, uniformed man dances with the lonely little girl. As the band plays and the sexy singer Francesca (Francesca Rettondini) croons and the privileged adults dance, a hand suddenly reaches out and pulls a lever. Wires tighten and finally snap, cutting virtually every dancer in half. The only one left standing and alive on the dance floor is Katie (Emily Browning), that bored little girl.

After this jolt the film suddenly flashes forward to the present. We're again on board a ship, but this time it's a tugboat, the Arctic Warrior. The tug's crew is desperately trying to save the derrick they have salvaged. The ship's skipper is Murphy (Gabriel Byrne), his salvage team leader is Epps (Julianna Margulies), and the first mate is Greer (Isaiah Washington). The remainder of the salvage crew consists of Dodge (Ron Eldard), Munder (Karl Urban), and Santos (Alex Dimitriades). Working as a team and taking more than a few risks, Murphy and his crew manage to make it back to port with their trophy derrick.

After this successful salvage, the crew of the Arctic Warrior celebrates at a dockside bar. They are soon approached by a stranger by the name of Ferriman (Desmond Harrington) who claims to fly an airplane for the Canadian Weather patrol. Ferriman has spotted a derelict ship floating in the middle of nowhere and he will tell the salvage crew where it is in exchange for a 20% finder's fee. After a discussion with his crew and a little wrangling with Ferriman, Murphy decides to go after the ship, but Ferriman will come along with them to share in the profits instead of being given a fee.

In the dark of night and the confusion of rain, it's difficult for the crew of the Arctic Warrior to tell if there's a derelict ship out there or not. The radar returns are, well, ghostly at best and sometimes there seems to be something there and sometimes not. Guess there is something there, because the Arctic Warrior slams right into it. The ship, it turns out, is the Antonia Graza, the Italian luxury liner on which doomed Katie was sailing. The liner was reported missing on the 21st of May in 1962 off the coast of Labrador. It sent out no distress signal and was never heard from again . . . until Murphy and his crew stumble onto it in the Bering Straits.

Not waiting for daylight, Murphy and his crew begin exploring the ship, seeing what there is to salvage and trying to figure out what happened to her. While some things they find are expected such as the fact that all the lifeboats are gone, the rudder is stuck, the engine room is flooded and there's a gash in the ship's hull below the water line, there are also a few things they couldn't possibly have expected to find: a digital watch on the bridge, bullet holes in the swimming pool, and wasn't that the Italian Captain's reflection Murphy saw in the mirror?

The next thing you know Epps is seeing a ghostly Katie and sappy dance music is coming in over the crew's walkie talkies. But that's nothing compared to the fact that when the central ventilation shaft in the laundry is opened it is filled with water . . . and bodies. And the bodies aren't that old.

But perhaps the biggest surprise awaiting the crew of the Arctic Warrior awaits them in the ship's cargo hold. There they will find boxes of stolen gold ingots. One can almost see the dollar signs in the eyes of the salvage crew at this discovery, and everyone knows it's finders keepers in international waters. So Murphy and his crew decide to forget salvaging the ship and just take the gold and run. The problem is, after crashing into the Antonia Graza the tugboat is having her own engine problems, and just when they think the tug is ready to sail, it explodes and sinks to the bottom of the ocean taking Santos with it. Now they're all stranded on the Antonia Garza and something tells them their not alone.

It's interesting to note that several horror films this year have used the plot device of a little girl. In *Feardotcom* there is a little girl with a white ball who appears to people who are about to die after logging in to an internet site. In *The Ring* there's a soaking wet little girl who is connected to all the deaths that follow the watching of a certain videotape. And now here's a floating ghost ship in which a well-dressed little girl appears to hold the secrets to the ship's haunted past. When did little girls get scary to anyone but little boys?

Ghost Ship was originally titled *Chimera* and was the first spec script acquired by Dark Castle, Joel Silver and Robert Zemeckis' production company. As the company's name would indicate, the producers have been inspired by the films of William Castle and their goal is to produce mid-budget horror films. The company's first two films, *House on Haunted Hill* and *Thirteen Ghosts* were remakes of William Castle films and were released during the Halloween season of 1999 and 2001 respectively. *Ghost Ship*, Dark Castle's 2002 Halloween release, is their first non-Castle remake. (As an interesting aside, when *Chimera*'s title was changed to *Ghost Ship*, DreamWorks was already at work on its own

haunted ship movie . . . called *Ghost Ship*. DreamWorks eventually changed the title of their film to *Down Deep*, which shouldn't be confused with Dimension's *Below*, about a haunted submarine, which was also released just before Halloween in 2002.)

One of the best things about *Ghost Ship* is the atmospheric cinematography of Gale Tattersall who received an Emmy nomination for his work with Tom Hanks and Ron Howard on their miniseries *From the Earth to the Moon*, and whose theatrical credits include *The Commitments*, *The Addams Family*, and director Steven Beck's first feature film, *Thirteen Ghosts*.

Another is the superior work of production designer Graham "Grace" Walker (*Queen of the Damned*, *Pitch Black*, *Dead Calm*) who is responsible for the incredible set recreating an abandoned ocean liner. Walker has said that Antonia Graza was modeled on the Andrea Doria, one of the greatest Italian luxury liners in the 1950s, and the attention to details like this shows.

Together, Walker and Tattersall have created an environment that is eerie and isolated and are just two facets of a technically well made film. Perhaps two of the most memorable scenes of the film revolve around this ambience and detail. One is the incredibly graphic yet almost poetic telling of the original murders aboard the ship and their later retelling, and the other is when the ship's ballroom reconstructs itself out of the rubble around Greer so Francesca can seduce him. They are both eye-popping scenes, although for slightly different reasons.

Unfortunately, there are also some problems with this story of what is essentially a floating haunted house. For one thing its characters are right from central casting and rely more on stereotyping for details than on writing. They are sketchily drawn, we don't know any of their backgrounds or motives, and in typical style, die in ascending order of their importance and/or stupidity.

Similarly, *Ghost Ship* is rife with the typical horror film cliches: food that looks good enough to eat and is but then is revealed to be crawling with maggots, blood oozing from walls and floors, beautiful women who turn into walking corpses, and "people" who appear and disappear. It also contains a typical twist in its last scene, but one has to admit that it is an interesting twist. One just wishes the whole premise behind why the ship became haunted in the first place had been more completely explained. The script tries to cover the mundane aspects of the horror (the avarice of men) and the mysterious (a ship of captured souls), but in the end neither one is explored or explained very well. In fact some of the story's elements are as much a mystery as is how the Antonia Garza got from the coast of Labrador in the North Atlantic to the Bering Strait off Alaska with out ever being seen. 🎞

—*Beverley Bare Buehrer*

CREDITS

Epps: Julianna Margulies
Dodge: Ron Eldard
Ferriman: Desmond Harrington
Greer: Isaiah Washington IV
Murphy: Gabriel Byrne
Santos: Alex Dimitriades
Munder: Karl Urban
Katie: Emily Browning
Francesca: Francesca Rettondini

Origin: USA
Released: 2002
Production: Joel Silver, Robert Zemeckis, Gilbert Adler; Village Roadshow Pictures, NPV Entertainment, Dark Castle Entertainment; released by Warner Bros.
Directed by: Steve Beck
Written by: John Pogue, Mark Hanlon
Cinematography by: Gale Tattersall
Music by: John (Gianni) Frizzell
Sound: Paul Brincat
Editing: Roger Barton
Art Direction: Richard Hobbs
Costumes: Margot Wilson
Production Design: Graham Walker
MPAA rating: R
Running time: 88 minutes

REVIEWS

Chicago Sun-Times Online. October 25, 2002.
Entertainment Weekly. November 1, 2002, p. 49.
Los Angeles Times Online. October 25, 2002.
New York Times Online. October 25, 2002.
People. November 4, 2002, p. 44.
Variety Online. October 25, 2002.
Washington Post. October 24, 2002, p. WE38.

QUOTES

Epps (Julianna Margulies): "I think I saw something I couldn't possibly have seen."

Girls Can't Swim (Les Filles Ne Savent Pas Nager)

Love is a tidal wave, but friendship runs deep.
—Movie tagline

Coming on the heels of Catherine Briellat's *Fat Girl*, French newcomer Anne-Sophie Birot also offers viewers a shocking coming-of-age film with *Girls Can't Swim.* Similar to Swiss-born director Lea Pool's two adolescent dramas, *Set Me Free* and *Lost and Delirious, Girls Can't Swim* portrays the precarious bond between teenage girls by focusing on sexual power plays, loyalty, and betrayal. These teenagers surrender to their sexual urges and suffer the consequences. They are defining their boundaries in the adult world while still wavering on the edge of childhood. *Girls Can't Swim* follows a tradition of female bonding films by young French women directors that proves both frightening and refreshing. Stephen Holden in the *New York Times* compared the female bonding film to two Spanish-language male bonding films, *Nico and Dani* and *Y Tu Mama Tambien/And Your Mother Too,* and all of the above films set a new standard for international teenage cinema.

Girls Can't Swim gets under viewers' skin and chews away at our collective psyche. These films remind us of the dangerous and explosive adolescent years while at the same time confronting us with the invisible generation that we refuse to take seriously. Earlier films like *Blackboard Jungle* and Luis Buñuel's *Los Olvidados* showed us the result of neglecting children, who might join a gang or became a teenage pregnancy statistic. Today, adolescents partake in unsafe sex, gang violence, and hardcore drug use. Often they are raised by single overworked parents and are ignored by society as a whole. Today's films force us to acknowledge the teens around us.

The structure of Birot's film proves similar to *Y Tu Mama Tambien* in that the film portrays the lives of two 15-year-old girls who are best friends despite their differing backgrounds. Set on the coast of Brittany at the beginning of the summer holidays, Birot shows us the same story from two angles. First we meet the sensual tomboy, Gwen (Isilde Le Besco), who is under threat of her raging hormones, while awaiting the arrival of her best friend, Lise (Karen Alyx). Although Gwen's summer vacation begins on a high note, soon her life begins to crumble around her. She learns that Lise won't be coming to stay for the summer and her fisherman father is unable to earn an income because the motor died on his boat. Her parents, Celine (played by the illustrious Quebecois actress Pascale Bussières) and Alain (Pascal Elso) are forced to rent out their yard to campers for cash and Celine accepts employment at a shoe store.

Gwen tries to extract affection from her unemployed, drunken father and overworked mother, but is constantly brushed off. Couple that with her lusty nature and soon Gwen is engaging in sex with her boyfriend and other men. One day, her father catches her copulating with her boyfriend in the hull of his boat. Enraged, Alain attacks Gwen and later sells the boat.

Birot then switches direction and focuses on Lise, whose estranged father just died in a car crash and whose mother (Marie Rivière) has fallen into a deep depression. Lise escapes from her miserable household and takes a bus to visit Gwen. At first the two girls appear thrilled by their annual reunion. However, subconscious urges take over and the cruelty between the two teenagers takes center stage, leading to betrayal and death.

While it interesting to watch the 36-year-old Brussières portray an overworked mother forced to support a deadbeat husband and troubled daughter, it is young actress Isilde Le Besco who offers a riveting performance. Stephen Holden in the *New York Times* wrote: "Ms. Le Besco ignites the film with a performance of such incandescent spontaneity that the role seems more lived than act." She simply proves unforgettable.

Alyx's Lise also acts as a window into troubled adolescence. The fatherless Lise seeks a father figure in Gwen's father, Alain, but confuses a father image with sexual conquest. Birot also presents an ambiguous sexual bond between Gwen and Lise leading us to wonder if the two had engaged in a sexual relationship with one another in the past. After all, their lusty letters are not the typical of young heterosexual women friends. Birot's debut film acts as both a cautionary tale and provocative international cinema.

—*Patty-Lynne Herlevi*

CREDITS

Gwen: Islid Le Besco
Lise: Karen Alyx
Alain: Pascal Elso
Celine: Pascale Bussieres
Fredo: Julien Cottereau
Anne-Marie: Marie Riviere

Origin: France
Language: French
Released: 1999
Production: Philippe Jacquier; Sepia Production, YMC Productions; released by Wellspring Media
Directed by: Anne-Sophie Birot

Written by: Anne-Sophie Birot, Christophe Honore
Cinematography by: Nathalie Durand
Music by: Ernest Chausson
Sound: Xavier Griette
Editing: Pascale Chavance
Art Direction: Yvon Moreno
Costumes: Brigitte Lauber
MPAA rating: Unrated
Running time: 98 minutes

REVIEWS

Boxoffice. April, 2002, p. 189.
Chicago Sun-Times Online. August 9, 2002.
Los Angeles Times Online. July 19, 2002.
New York Times Online. April 19, 2002.
Variety Online. September 18, 2000.
Village Voice Online. April 17, 2002.

God Is Great, I'm Not (Dieu Est Grand, Je Suis Tout Petite)

French newcomer Audrey Tautou (of *Amelie* fame) recalls the early days of Audrey Hepburn. Both Audreys have doe-eyes that stare out from the screen at us as we watch them endure the comical mishaps of youth. And Tautou, similar to Hepburn, falls into the brunette waif category—often playing the girl next door or an unusual dreamy character. After the release of the hit French film *Amelie,* other films of lesser degree staring the young French star have hit U.S. screens with varying degrees of success. The clever film, *Happenstance,* featuring Tautou as a girl-next-door who loses her job but finds a soulmate, barely made a blip on the radar. Although French director Pascale Bailly's *God is Great, I'm Not* screened to a sold-out crowd at Seattle International Film Festival, the tepid comedy lacks the magic of *Amelie,* despite the lead actress' quirky performance.

Fortunately, Tautou and her co-star Edouard Baer create on-screen chemistry and both exhibit comedic timing and an array of facial expressions and body language that transcend a somewhat dull script. In fact, most of the film's humor derives from close-ups of the actors' faces as every nuance reveals the truth behind the characters' feelings. Although Bailly's film provides us with witty one-liners, bizarre scenes in which Michèle (Tautou) models outlandish clothing for fashion magazines, and pokes fun at people trying out various religions, this screenplay feels too raw. Daydreams crash into real life experiences, leading to a confusing narrative and oftentimes the story wades through dull stretches when nothing of interest takes place.

For the most part, Tautou's clothing appears clownish and her perm recalls Barbra Streisand's hair style in *A Star is Born*, but that's okay because the character Michèle desires to become Jewish. After Michèle breaks up with her boyfriend, Bertrand (Mathieu Demy), she tries to commit suicide in Francois's (Baer) apartment after a night of sex. According to her best friend, Valerie (Julie Depardieu), Michèle's life is a mess. And so Michèle goes on a quest in search of God. She explores Buddhism, but finds staying positive takes too much effort. Then, after becoming further involved with Francois, she decides to study Judaism. She honors the Jewish holidays and wonders why Francois doesn't act like a "real Jew" or take his studies seriously.

However, this doesn't stop Michèle from befriending Francois' parents as she attempts to play the role of the perfect Jewish woman, even though she was raised Catholic. She learns prayers in Hebrew, takes private lessons with a Jewish tutor, and hopes that Francois will marry her despite her religious background. Meanwhile, Michèle's mother is going through a crisis and won't leave her second husband even though he is driving her over the edge. Needless to say, family get-togethers always end in tears. Eventually, Michèle's obsession with Judaism leads to a breakup with Francois, who is actually embarrassed by his religion. Michèle and Francois date other people but, in the end, they find that they can't live without one another. Michèle loses interest in Judaism and the couple reunites.

Bailly's flawed film merely brings up the topics of sexuality and spirituality while diving too deeply into quirky territory. *God is Great* proves too arty for its own good and, unfortunately, Tautou's charm, talent, and beauty are wasted on a cinematic vehicle that stays parked in neutral.

—*Patty-Lynne Herlevi*

Released: 2001
Production: Alain Sarde, Georges Benayoun; Dacia Films, Studio Canal Plus, Centre National de la Cinematographie; released by Mars Films
Directed by: Pascale Bailly
Written by: Pascale Bailly, Alain Tasma
Cinematography by: Antoine Roch
Music by: Stephane Maka
Sound: Gerard Rousseau
Editing: Lise Beaulieu, Jean-Pierre Viguie
Art Direction: Denis Mercier
Costumes: Khadija Zeggai
MPAA rating: Unrated
Running time: 102 minutes

REVIEWS

Boxoffice. October, 2002, p. 56.
New York Times Online. November 8, 2002.
Variety Online. November 16, 2001.

QUOTES

Michele (Audrey Tautou) confides to her diary: "I'm 20 and my life is over."

CREDITS

Michele: Audrey Tautou
Francois: Edouard Baer
Valerie: Julie Depardieu
Bertrand: Mathieu Demy
Evelyn: Catherine Jacob
Jean: Philippe Laudenbach
Florence: Cathy Verney
Regine: Anna Koch

Origin: Fance
Language: French

The Goddess of 1967

Hong Kong émigré Clara Law's latest release, *The Goddess of 1967*, proves to be a gem for those viewers with plenty of patience and a knowledge of cinematic language. The Chinese writer/director, who immigrated to Australia in 1990, covers as much territory as her two protagonists, two strangers on a five-day road trip. While Yoshiyashi (Rikiya Kurokawa) travels to Australia in search of his dream car, a 1967 Citroen, the blind Dierdre (Rose Byrne) desires to return to her home to end a nightmare. And director Law, with the help of her protagonists, embarks on a cinematic quest in which she explores issues revolving around child abuse, rape, theft, love and transcendence. As German director Wim Wenders has proven in the past, road movies create a canvas in which to paint a variety of social or relational issues. Oftentimes, people find their true identity away from the confines of domesticity, as is the case with Law's characters.

Unlike Wim Wenders, Law meanders away from the three-act structure. Her screenplay bounces through time and it doles out exposition in pieces. Viewers take on the role of a detective as they are forced to sniff out clues to the characters' odd behavior. At times, the characters' situations seem completely implausible, adding to frustration. And yet, by the film's transcendental end, we get a clear idea of the characters' personal lives. Despite the painful themes present in the film, Law gazes in a detached, almost matter of fact at her characters' traumas. After all, she seems to tell us, life is life and suffering is part of life.

Law presents us with a stylistic film that recalls Lou Ye's *Suzhou River*. Law's film features over-saturated colors, staccato editing and roaming cameras. Cinematographer Dion Bebee (*Crush, Holy Smoke*) appears to be influenced by Mexican cinematographer Gabriel Figueroa as his lens captures fluffy clouds floating through an electric blue sky. In a sex scene between Yoshiyashi and Deirdre, Bebee pulls into close-ups of the characters' mouths as they kiss, then travels over various body parts while never exploiting the performers. We are left with an intimacy that can only be shared by strangers that just met. Despite scenes of rape and shades of child abuse, this intimate scene is the most excruciating to watch in *The Goddess of 1967*.

The film opens with Yoshiyashi feeding his exotic snakes in his Tokyo apartment. A message appears on a computer screen regarding a 1967 Citroen DS 19 (the Goddess of the title) that is for sale. Yoshiyashi offers to purchase the dream car and he travels to Australia where he hopes to quickly buy the car and return to Tokyo. Only he's harboring a secret and his fate leads him in an alternate direction. Upon arriving at the home of the car's alleged owner, Yoshiyashi learns that the owner and his wife are dead—a murder/suicide in a battle over money. Deirdre entices Yoshiyashi into a road trip in which she will introduce Yoshiyashi to the car's real owner. However, Deirdre brings along her emotional baggage and a secret desire to murder her grandfather (Nicholas Hope), the cause of her misfortunes.

Newcomers Rose Byrne and Rikiya Kurakawa deliver stoic performances and, despite the characters' collective suffering, they never participate in histrionics. Thankfully, Law and her co-writer Eddie Ling-Ching Fong did not write long drawn-out monologues in which the characters relay painful events to each other. Instead, Law and Fong flashback to various scenes from the characters' past in which we meet the individuals that shaped their lives. Some viewers might find this approach too objective, while others will be thankful that their tear ducts didn't get the usual workout.

Richard James Havis of the *Hollywood Reporter* described Law's film as "A bold narrative experiment supported by some striking and surreal photography, *The Goddess of 1967* sees Hong Kong/Australian director Clara Law allowing her imagination to have free reign in the Australian outback." The Vancouver International Film Festival 2001 program described Law's film as "a fine stew of mysteries, fetishes and wolf-in-sheep's clothing gags." And *The Goddess of 1967* carries the ability to shock and charm its viewers at the same time as it gazes at the fringe of humanity and the atrocities humans inflict on one another. Law returns to cultural dislocation as her characters embark on a Zen road trip that leads to transcendence.

—Patty-Lynne Herlevi

CREDITS

Yoshiyashi: Rikiya Kurokawa
Deirdre: Rose Byrne
Dad/Granddad: Nicholas Hope
Marie: Elise McCredie

Origin: Australia
Released: 2000
Production: Eddie Ling-Ching Fong, Peter Sainsbury; Australian Film Finance Corp., New South Wales Film & Television Office
Directed by: Clara Law
Written by: Clara Law, Eddie Ling-Ching Fong
Cinematography by: Dion Beebe
Music by: Jen Andersen
Editing: Kate Williams
Costumes: Annie Marshall, Helen Mather
Production Design: Nicholas McCallum
MPAA rating: Unrated
Running time: 118 minutes

REVIEWS

eye Weekly Online. April 26, 2001.
Jam! Movies Online. April 27, 2001.
Variety. September 11, 2000, p. 28.

The Good Girl

It's her last best chance . . . is she going to take it?
—Movie tagline
Is finding what you could have worth losing what you've got?
—Movie tagline

 Box Office: $14 million

The heroine of Miguel Arteta's *The Good Girl,* Justine Last (Jennifer Aniston), leads a dreary life in her small Texas town where she works the cosmetics counter at the Retail Rodeo, a cheesy discount store staffed by an assortment of oddballs. Justine rarely smiles, her dominant expression being a grimace of clenched teeth. Her husband, Phil (John C. Reilly), is a housepainter and essentially a decent if unambitious fellow who seems to be in a state of arrested adolescence. He spends his free time planted on the sofa, smoking pot with his buddy and coworker, Bubba (Tim Blake Nelson), who does not have the common sense to remove his paint-covered overalls before sitting down, which is just one more frustration gnawing away at the suffering Justine.

"As a girl you see the world like a giant candy store," Justine tells us in her opening voice-over, "but one day you look around and see a prison." At 30 years old, she realizes that her lot in life is not changing for the better, and, while she is not sure exactly what she wants, she knows that she yearns for something different, an escape of some kind.

The Good Girl is a shrewd character study of people living stagnant, soul-deadening lives but is tinged with odd, quirky details and idiosyncratic characters that make it more darkly comic and wryly observant of human foibles than outright depressing. It does not offer neat, tidy solutions to Justine's malaise, nor does it present simplistic characters; rather, the smart screenplay by Mike White paints refreshingly honest portraits of small-town desperation, lives slowly being ground down by the dullness of routine.

Justine's life begins to change when she strikes up a friendship with a coworker called Holden (Jake Gyllenhaal), a misfit and loner who aspires to be a writer. His real name is Tom, which he thinks of as his slave name, but he has named himself after the archetypal disaffected youth from *The Catcher in the Rye.* Like his chosen namesake, Holden is sensitive and disturbed and feels that his parents "don't get" him, words that also apply to Phil's relationship to Justine. Holden and Justine bond over their outsider status—"I saw in your eyes that you hate the world; I hate it too," she tells him—and he shares with her two of his short stories, highly autobiographical, morbidly funny tales of youthful alienation in which a loner confronts the hypocrisies of the world and finally kills himself.

Despite the fact that Holden is troubled and eight years her junior and she is married, Justine embarks on an affair with him. She scurries off to be with Holden right after she drops off a sick coworker, Gwen (Deborah Rush), at the hospital. Gwen dies a few days later, with Justine having neglected to visit her. Sneaking around with Holden in a local motel and even the storeroom of the Retail Rodeo, she is too busy having wild sex to care about others, making her anything but the good girl of the title.

One of the great strengths of White's screenplay is the bleakly funny atmosphere he establishes at the Retail Rodeo, populated by an assortment of slightly weird yet endearing characters. The most entertaining is Cheryl (Zooey Deschanel), who peppers her announcements over the store's PA system with touches of sarcasm and is moved to the cosmetics counter upon Gwen's death. Cheryl survives the boredom at her new post by experimenting with the makeup, even creating a garish look wholly inappropriate for one of the town's elderly shoppers and then claiming it is the latest style in France. Deschanel's offbeat charm makes Cheryl a small gem of a character—she may not figure prominently in the plot, but she is a joy to watch, and her ironic detachment makes her a kind of spiritual cousin to the girls in last year's marvelous *Ghost World.*

White gives the other characters enough nuance to make them more than stereotypes. White himself plays Corny, the store security guard, who invites Justine to Bible study. He may come across as a narrow-minded Bible-thumper, but he has a sense of humor about himself and even jokes with Justine about her spending eternity in Hell. The seemingly uptight boss (John Carroll Lynch), playfully billed in the credits as "Jack Field, Your Store Manager," is actually more patient with his ragtag crew than most bosses would be, and even the sometimes irritating Phil is really a sweet, hapless lug of a guy who simply lacks his wife's intelligence and desire for something better.

Justine is emboldened by her adulterous adventure but pays the price when Bubba spots her and Holden at the motel and launches a blackmail scheme. Because Phil got the beautiful Justine, Bubba has always been jealous of him and has labored under the feeling that his own life could never match up. But now that Phil is a cuckold and has been reduced in his esteem, Bubba has been freed from his hero worship; moreover, if he too can have sex with Justine, he will feel better about himself. But if she refuses him, he will snitch to Phil about her affair. She acquiesces, and their sex scene is a sad yet comic interlude in which he huffs and puffs on top of her while she remains virtually motionless. Unfortunately, Holden is spying on them through a window and is immediately disillusioned. He calls Justine a hooker and never really gets over his feeling of betrayal.

Soon Justine seems to be in a no-win situation. She suspects that she may be pregnant, and Phil, who feared that his pot smoking may have affected his sperm, is ecstatic, thinking that he has proven the doctors wrong. Phil, however, does not know that Holden, or possibly Bubba, is the father of Justine's baby, and, when he finds out that his sperm is indeed no good, the poor guy cannot figure out how she can be pregnant. All Justine can do is convince him that the doctors must be wrong about him. Despite her foolish choices, she never meant to hurt anyone, and yet now so many lives are riding on her decisions.

Growing more desperate, Holden finally steals $15,000 from the Retail Rodeo and disappears. Since Justine and Holden have been seen together so much, Jack questions her, but Justine denies knowing anything about the robbery or Holden's whereabouts. Holden, however, makes contact with Justine and begs her to flee with him, which leaves Justine with the options of running away into some outlaw life with a mixed-up kid or remaining with Phil. Her dilemma is literally framed in terms of choosing between two roads—driving her car through the pouring rain, Justine can either turn right to meet Holden in a motel room or go left to the Retail Rodeo. She finally chooses her regular life and even tells Jack where he can find Holden, thus betraying his trust and leading to his suicide when the police surround him at the motel.

If the movie's title were not already ironic, Jack calls her "a good girl" for helping him. Holden's suicide, while foreshadowed in his fiction, is nonetheless tragic, but the movie barely deals with Justine's reaction to his death. In a film that otherwise takes an honest look at the bad choices people make and their consequences, it is disappointing that Holden's fate is not given more attention.

Phil finally finds out that Justine cheated on him through the motel charges on the credit card bill. He slaps her when she admits the truth, but he quickly regrets what he has done. Justine swears to him that the baby they are expecting is his, and, even if he has doubts, Phil seems willing to suppress them. When he guesses that Corny was the one she was sleeping with, she goes along with the story, and the next day Corny comes to work with a bruised face from a beating he suffered the night before.

Even in the end, then, Justine's actions continue to do harm. We do not know if she has learned any real lessons or just figured out how to get out of a jam any way she can, but, despite her ambiguous sense of morality, we sympathize with her because she seems to be the only character with any measure of self-awareness. She knows that her youth is slipping away, that opportunities are fading fast, and that she must make peace with the life she is leading. With her somber look, subdued expressions, and exhausted cadences, Aniston gives Justine a perpetually beleaguered quality and makes us care about her even when she makes one morally dubious choice after another.

In the last scene, Justine reads a short story that Holden left her. It is essentially their idealized story—a girl and guy whom society does not "get" fall in love with each other and disappear into the wilderness. The story presents the road not taken, the fantasy ending that Justine rejected, and, as she is reading, Phil brings their new baby into the bedroom. This is her bittersweet reality and, if not ideal, at least something that she seems to be able to live with.

The Good Girl is the second collaboration between Arteta and White. Their first project together, *Chuck and Buck*, was the darkly comic portrait of a man-child whose obsession with his boyhood friend was creepy, funny, and oddly touching at the same time. While *The Good Girl* is not as unsettling or perverse as *Chuck and Buck*, it also deals with the fantasies that desperate people create for themselves. Arteta and White here explore a more mundane human problem—trying to break out of a crippling rut—and offer another poignant tale of sad people trying to fashion a world that reflects their rich inner life.

—Peter N. Chumo II

CREDITS

Justine Last: Jennifer Aniston
Holden Worther: Jake Gyllenhaal
Phil Last: John C. Reilly
Bubba: Tim Blake Nelson
Cheryl: Zooey Deschanel
Corny: Mike White
Gwen Jackson: Deborah Rush
Jack Field: John Carroll Lynch

Origin: USA
Released: 2002
Production: Matthew Greenfield; Myriad Pictures, In Motion Productions, Flan de Coco; released by Fox Searchlight
Directed by: Miguel Arteta
Written by: Mike White
Cinematography by: Enrique Chediak
Sound: Yehuda Maayan
Music Supervisor: Margaret Yen
Editing: Jeff Betancourt
Art Direction: Macie Venier
Costumes: Nancy Steiner
Production Design: Daniel Bradford
MPAA rating: R
Running time: 93 minutes

REVIEWS

Boxoffice. April, 2002, p. 176.
Chicago Sun-Times Online. August 16, 2002.
Entertainment Weekly. August 16, 2002, p. 46.
Los Angeles Times Online. August 7, 2002.
New York Times Online. August 7, 2002.
People. August 19, 2002, p. 34.
USA Today Online. August 7, 2002.
Variety. January 21, 2002, p. 37.
Washington Post. August 16, 2002, p. WE44.

Justine (Jennifer Aniston): "I used to lie in bed and imagine other lives, other cities, other jobs. Now I don't even know what to imagine anymore."

AWARDS AND NOMINATIONS

Nomination:
Ind. Spirit 2003: Actress (Aniston), Film, Screenplay, Support. Actor (Reilly).

Gossip

William Shakespeare proclaimed, "All of the world's a stage," but what he didn't predict was the day when actresses would steal the spotlight and both their public and private personas would write the script. Actresses are known for grabbling for public sympathy or adoration, depending on the situation at hand, and the famous Swedish actresses who play actresses in Colin Nutley's *Gossip* provide enough drama to keep viewers occupied for the duration of the film. An ex-patriate of Great Britain, Nutley (Oscar-nominated *Under the Sun*) appears to have the insider's view of the Swedish film industry, not to mention a knack for writing features tinged with Swedish temperament. After all, Nutley has been making films in his adopted home for nearly 20 years and is married to Swedish actress Helena Bergstrom, who plays the role of Stella in this film.

Written, produced and directed by Nutley, *Gossip* stars a who's who of Swedish actresses who share nine Swedish Film Awards and 12 international awards between them, working for such directors as Ingmar Bergman, Bo Widerberg, Jan Troell and Billie August. For starters, Pernilla August, who plays the character Molly in Nutley's film, won Best Actress at Cannes for her role in *Best Intentions;* Helena Bergstrom won Best Actress at the Montreal Film Festival for Nutley's *Last Dance* and Best Actress at the Swedish Film Awards for her role in *Still Crazy*. This time around the ten actresses featured in this multiple-narrative comedy cum soap opera perform roles close to the bone.

Love or hate them, actresses can be exasperating to their relatives, colleagues, directors and to the public. Blend performance anxiety and the fear of aging with infidelity and madness ensues. As the film opens, we see various actresses auditioning for the title role of *Queen Christina* in a remake of the film that starred the famous Swede Greta Garbo. Nutley presents us with a collage of the actresses reciting the line, "I thank almighty God that I was born of royal stock." Next, we see a fateful day beginning for all of the actresses as they go about their business, gossip about one another and wait to hear which actress landed the prestigious role in the Hollywood film.

As the day progresses, pregnant Cecilia (Marie Richardson) gives birth to her married lover Magnus' (Rolf Lassgard) child. Meanwhile, director Magnus's actress wife Karin (Marika Lagercrantz) engages in an affair with her co-star Stella (Bergstrom). Stella is playing a character having an affair with a diplomat played by Ake (Mikael Persbrandt), who is Rebecca's (Lena Endre) husband. Meanwhile, Rebecca celebrates her 40th birthday while she and Ake visit a fertility clinic and later we learn that Ake impregnated his colleague Molly (Pernilla August). Eivor (Stina Ekblad) and her actor husband Tomas (Peter Andersson) argue over Eivor starring in a musical when she can't sing or dance. Git (Gunilla Roor) has an unhealthy obsession with one of her films and insists on playing Joan of Arc even though she's hardly an adolescent virgin. Finally, Alexandra (Suzanne Reuter) has upset her jealous husband by accepting a sexy role in which she plays a lover with her ex. This over-the-top comedy mirrors a gossip rag with its false assumptions, sexual betrayals and juicy secrets.

Nutley offers us a 24-hour glimpse into these 40-plus year veterans of Swedish film and television. We are presented with a collage of the lives of not only the actresses but also their husbands, directors and producers. In one telling scene, Magnus directs the lesbian Stella and the Swedish sex symbol Ake in a scene in which Stella forgets her lines. Conflict arises when Ake storms off the set and Stella tells Magnus that he's a better actor than he is a director. Then just as Magnus witnesses the perfect take in which Stella remembers her lines and the actors bleed emotions, Magnus cell phone rings and blows the take. Cecilia is on the other line and she wants to talk to Magnus about the baby she is carrying because it is his. And if that doesn't prove stressful enough, Magnus wife shows up on the set.

Although a library of films about actresses already exists, Nutley offers a refreshing gaze at aging actresses fighting for their last chance at international stardom while losing their privacy.

—*Patty-Lynne Herlevi*

CREDITS

Eivor Pellas: Stina Ekblad
Cecilia Falck: Marie Richardson
Rebecca Olsson-Frigardh: Lena Endre
Git Jeppson: Gunilla Roor
Stella Lindbergh: Helena Bergstrom
Molly Fischer: Pernilla August

Tomas Berg: Peter Andersson
Magnus Wiktorsson: Rolf Lassgard
Karin Kalters: Marika Lagerkrantz
Georgina Seth: Ewa Froling
Camilla Steen: Harriet Andersson
Ingrid Seth: Margareta Krook
Alexandra Furustig: Suzanne Reuter
Ake Frigardh: Mikael Persbrandt

Origin: Sweden
Language: Swedish
Released: 2000
Production: Colin Nutley; Sweetwater; released by Svensk Filmindustri
Directed by: Colin Nutley
Written by: Colin Nutley
Cinematography by: Jens Fischer
Music by: Per Andreasson
Sound: Bo Persson, Lasse Liljeholm, Bernt Eklund
Editing: Perry Schaeffer
Art Direction: Bengt Froderberg
Costumes: Camilla Thulin
MPAA rating: Unrated
Running time: 126 minutes

 REVIEWS

Variety. January 29, 2001, p. 45.

The Grey Zone

The story you haven't seen.
—Movie tagline
While the world was fighting . . . a secret battle was about to erupt.
—Movie tagline

Well-meaning but deeply flawed, *The Grey Zone* recreates actual events from Auschwitz's Death Camp. Writer-director Tim Blake Nelson tries to infuse his Holocaust drama with noble intentions, but the more his characters confront the issues, the more *The Grey Zone* sounds like a hot-tempered "bull session" in an Ivy League dorm-room.

Based partly on memoirs by Dr. Miklos Nyiszli, a Hungarian Jewish doctor forced to work on Dr. Mengele's ghoulish "experiments," Nelson's screenplay recounts a plot, in the fall of 1944, by a group of prisoners to launch an armed rebellion, the only one ever to take place at an Auschwitz Concentration Camp.

The organizers of the revolt are members of a Sonderkommando, a "Special Squad" of Jewish captives who have been given some additional months to live in exchange for leading oblivious fellow Jews to their doom in the infamous gas chambers.

What confounds the rebellion plan is the unexpected discovery of a teenage girl (Kamelia Grigorova) who inexplicably survives one of the gassings. The members of the Sonderkommando quarrel amongst themselves and with a sympathetic doctor (modeled after Dr. Nyiszli and played by Allan Corduner) about allowing the girl to live and transporting her during their escape. But the escape never occurs. The leader of the Nazi unit, Muhsfeldt (Harvey Keitel), finds the girl and punishes the unit with shotgun executions.

Those fortunate to have seen Claude Lanzmann's recent documentary, *Sobibor, October 14, 1943, 4 p.m.*, will recognize with interest some similarities between *The Grey Zone*'s story and the triumphant revolt of Sobibor (the only recorded successful rebellion and escape amongst Jewish prisoners against their Nazi captors). Also both films reveal how strong, angry, and fearless some Jewish inmates were (in contrast to the conventional victim stereotype in so many Holocaust dramas and documentaries).

But aesthetically the two films are as disparate as possible, not only because one is a so-called documentary and one is a "docudrama," but that Lanzmann uses subtlety and moderation in his storytelling, while Nelson (the director of *O,* the controversial high school *Othello* update), allows his high-minded project to become sensational, even exploitative at times.

The debate about the Sonderkommando complicity in Nazi inhumanity and the dilemma about risking the success of the revolt to save the one girl are both worthy subjects to ponder, but many scenes become overwhelmed by dialogue that sounds suspiciously like something from a stage play (sure enough, Nelson first wrote *The Grey Zone* as an off-Broadway play in 1996).

The casting doesn't help, either, because the lead actors—including Steve Buscemi and David Arquette—are just too distractingly recognizable and speak in modern cadences (frankly, it is insulting even having Arquette cast at all, given the goofy nature of his persona in several films). Moreover, nearly everyone in the cast speaks in modern-day English (sans accents), but Harvey Keitel (one of *The Grey Zone*'s producers) uses a comically heavy German accent as the sinister commander. One half expects Keitel to utter, "Ve hef vays uf making you tuk," during his interrogation scenes, which resemble *Saturday Night Live* sketches. Thus, the best work comes from the lesser-known players—and the less recognizable female stars—including Mira Sorvino and Natasha Lyonne, playing munitions factory inmates who are caught and tortured for supplying gun powder to the men.

Though the gassing and corpse-burning scenes are not graphic, some of the moments leading up to them are disturbing—both for the terror they suggest, but also for their inescapably faulty details—for example, none of the bodies that are burned look very starved (perhaps a less neo-realist and more impressionistic style would have overcome this problem).

Like the overrated *Schindler's List* (1993), *The Grey Zone* attempts to be grandiloquent, but ends up merely pretentious—in a gruesome sort of way. For those curious about Holocaust horrors, *Night and Fog* (1955) still makes the essential cinematic primer, while the TV-film *Playing for Time*(1979) effectively depicts the torturous quandaries of surviving within a Nazi Concentration Camp.

—Eric Monder

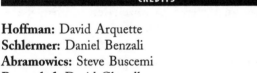

CREDITS

Hoffman: David Arquette
Schlermer: Daniel Benzali
Abramowics: Steve Buscemi
Rosenthal: David Chandler
Dr. Nyiszli: Allan Corduner
Muhsfeldt: Harvey Keitel
Rosa: Natasha Lyonne
Dina: Mira Sorvino

Origin: USA
Released: 2001
Production: Pamela Koffler, Christine Vachon, Avi Lerner, Danny Lerner, Tim Blake Nelson; Millennium Films, Killer Films, Goatsingers; released by Lion's Gate Films
Directed by: Tim Blake Nelson
Written by: Tim Blake Nelson
Cinematography by: Russell Fine
Music by: Jeff Danna
Sound: Petur Hliddal
Editing: Michelle Botticelli
Costumes: Marina Draghici
Production Design: Maria Djurkovic
MPAA rating: R
Running time: 108 minutes

REVIEWS

Boxoffice. November, 2001, p. 133.
Boxoffice. November, 2002, p. 58.
Chicago Sun-Times Online. October 25, 2002.
Entertainment Weekly. November 1, 2002, p. 48.
Los Angeles Times Online. September 8, 2002.
Los Angeles Times Online. October 18, 2002.
New York Times Online. October 18, 2002.
New York Times Online. October 20, 2002.
Variety. October 1, 2001, p. 38.
Washington Post. October 25, 2002, p. WE35.

QUOTES

Jewish Dr. Nyiszli (Allan Corduner) justifies his work with the Nazis: "We're all just trying to make it to the next day."

The Guys

How do you find the words?
—Movie tagline

The Guys was one of the first literary responses to the bombing of the World Trade Center towers on September 11. It began when Jim Simpson, the husband of actress Sigourney Weaver, commissioned the play for his off-off Broadway theater. The theater is located seven blocks from where the tragedy took place. The writer, Anne Nelson, is the director of the international program at the Columbia University School of Journalism. She hadn't written a play before but was inspired to do so by the dramatic events of the day. The play debuted December 4, 2001, and the two main roles have been played by a variety of actors, including Bill Murray, Susan Sarandon, Tim Robbins, Swoosie Kurtz, and Amy Irving.

In adapting the film to the screen, director Simpson, making his film debut here, essentially just moves the action (or lack thereof) to the screen. There are a few scenes of children coming in the room and some news footage of things like slow motion images of paper blowing down the street, but these seem there just to break up the monotony of two people sitting in a room talking. The news footage is far from the horrifying and gritty images that was played over and over on the news, but is abstract and evocative.

In a sense, it's odd that such a restrained, quiet play could come from such a catastrophic event. The play manages to be both deeply emotional and almost boring at the same time. It follows a meeting between a successful freelance journalist from the Upper West Side, Joan (Weaver), and Nick (Anthony LaPaglia), the captain of a firehouse who needs to write eulogies for eight firefighters from his firehouse that were lost that day. While visiting her younger sister in Park Slope, Brooklyn, Joan agrees to help Nick write the eulogies. She is traumatized by the tragedy and

Hart's War

Beyond courage, beyond honor.
—Movie tagline
Heroes Are Measured By What They Do.
—Movie tagline

 Box Office: $19 million

The World War II-set film *Hart's War* doesn't know what it wants to be: a growing to manhood movie, a prisoner of war film, a military courtroom drama, or an escape thriller. In the end, it turns out to be not much of anything at all, which is a shame since at least a couple of the performances are worth watching.

The film opens with a panning shot of a winter landscape and a title informing "Belgium December 16, 1944." Lt. Thomas Hart (Colin Farrell) explains in a voiceover that, because of his senator father's pull, his war has been spent at Army headquarters behind the lines as a military attaché. He's never seen any real action and is a little bored, which may be why he eagerly offers to drive an officer back to his regiment. This is a bad idea since the jeep gets stopped by the Germans, the officer is killed, and Hart is captured.

He's then subjected to interrogation by a Nazi officer who's interested in whether the American military knows about the location of German fuel supplies. Although the viewer doesn't see this at once (Hart experiences a number of flashbacks to his questioning), he eventually gives up the location of one of the supply areas. Hart's then placed aboard a POW train where he meets up with Capt. Peter Ross (Linus Roache). At a stop at a German-held station, the Germans and the train are strafed by American fighter planes. The prisoners manage to escape from the train cars and form a human POW sign to let the fighters know who they are attacking. The train is blown up but most of the soldiers are spared; however they are now forced to march to their destination—Stalag VI A in Augsburg, Germany.

The camp is run by Col. Werner Visser (Marcel Iures), a weary officer who likes to make his priorities clear: escape attempts result in immediate execution by hanging. He demonstrates this to the new detainees when he hangs some Russian prisoners in front of them, casually dismissing the Russians as dogs. Hart learns that the Russian POWs (each of the Allies have their own separate camps) are being used as slave labor in a munitions factory located next to the stalag. Hart and Ross are then taken to the officers' barracks, where they meet the ranking officer among the Americans, Col. William McNamara (a stoic Bruce Willis), a fourth-generation West Point grad who has seen a lot of action.

Ross is permitted to stay in the barracks but McNamara informs Hart that there is no more room and he must bunk with the enlisted men in Barracks 27. Seeing several empty bunks, Hart knows this is a lie but doesn't know why he's being singled out.

In Barracks 27, Hart meets the "fixer" of the group—a redneck staff sergeant named Vic Bedford (Cole Hauser) who seems to have a thriving black market trade going on. Bedford is able to get Hart new boots and socks in exchange for Hart's expensive watch. Hart also discovers that though the barracks are locked at night, Bedford uses an escape hole in the latrine to leave and trade with some of the German guards.

Just after New Year's Day two more American officers arrive at the camp. They are black airmen Lt. Lincoln Scott (Terrence Howard) and Lt. Lamar Archer (Vicellous Shannon). Once again, McNamara refuses to let them bunk in the officers' barracks and assigns them to Barracks 27 where they are immediately harassed by Bedford. Hart tries to come between them and establish some order. One night, the men are rousted by the German guards who discover a metal spike concealed in Archer's bunk. This is regarded as a weapon by Col. Visser and Archer is immediately taken out and shot despite McNamara's protests. Both Hart and Scott know Archer has been set up and both suspect Bedford. When Bedford is murdered and Scott is found over his body, nobody seems surprised, although Scott proclaims his innocence and Hart is sure much more is going on. He's right of course but it will take a long time before what's obvious is explained to the audience.

Although Visser wants to execute Scott immediately, McNamara argues that he is entitled to an American court-martial hearing and he appoints a surprised Hart, who was a law student at Yale, as Scott's counsel. Visser seems amused and agrees as long as the proceedings move swiftly. Visser also seems suspicious of McNamara's attitude towards Hart and informs the young officer that he also studied at Yale (a graduate of the class of 1928) and that he is willing to offer Hart any support the young man needs: "It seems only fair what with your colonel throwing you to the wolves."

It's apparent to everyone involved that the trial is a farce—Col. McNamara himself is the head of the tribunal and he appoints an officer who is an actual lawyer to be the prosecutor. He also isn't afraid to pull rank on Hart when necessary to get the proceedings to go his way. Hart doesn't know if this is simple prejudice because Scott is a black man or if something else is going on. Visser gives Hart a copy of the Army manual of court-martial so that he can contest McNamara's high-handed procedures though this enrages the Colonel and he castigates Hart for accepting any help from Visser. McNamara goes to see a drunken Visser who wonders if the American is somehow planning an escape from the camp.

Although Hart repeatedly tries to reassure Scott, the black man knows that he's not receiving justice. When given a chance to speak, he protests Archer's summary execution and states to McNamara that Archer and himself just wanted to serve their country and that "what you let happen to him—what you *allowed* to happen to him—is appalling and so is this." McNamara goes to visit Scott in his prison hut and, for a moment, you think he is going to reveal what is really going on, but he merely gives Scott his personal copy of the New Testament.

Hart finds something hidden in Bedford's bunk and reveals it the next day at the trial. Bedford was trading with a German guard for identification papers and German marks to use in an escape. In exchange, he let the Germans know about the officers' hidden radio, which they destroyed. Hart calls Visser to the stand and tries to place the blame on the German guard who traded with Bedford. It's just one more strategy that backfires on Hart despite his good intentions.

That night, Hart follows Sgt. Carl Webb (Rory Cochrane) out of the barracks and into the camp theater where he discovers that a select group has been working on an escape tunnel. Hart tells Ross that he realizes that the trial is meant as a distraction and goes to see McNamara whom he knows has been lying about everything. Hart accuses McNamara of killing Bedford because he was trading with the Germans and endangering the escape plan and using both Archer and Scott as convenient scapegoats. McNamara tells Hart that the escapees are going to blow up the munitions factor and he needs the trial deliberations as a diversion since the attempt will happen the next day. Hart tells McNamara that he should cause a distraction during the proceedings by admitting that McNamara himself is the killer. Instead, McNamara and several men come down with a suspiciously convenient case of food poisoning and McNamara excuses himself from the trial.

During a recess, Hart informs Scott of the escape plans and wants him to be part of the attempt. Instead, Scott tells Hart that his duty is to aid the soldiers any way he can, even if it means sacrificing his own life. He wants Hart to let his young son know the truth. When Hart gives his summation to the court he remarks on the sacrifice of the one for the good of the many but he doesn't seem to truly believe his words. Indeed, Hart seems furious that the absent McNamara would callously choose Scott as a sacrificial lamb even if Scott is now willing to do his part. The action switches from the escape being carried out to courtroom scenes. Hart supplies his own distraction to an increasingly suspicious Visser by declaring that he himself murdered Bedford.

A furious Visser demands Hart's immediate execution and tells his guards that all the American POWs must witness it. When the guards discover that some 35 prisoners are missing, Visser begins to search the theater and finds the escape tunnel. He then orders all the men involved in the court martial proceedings to be shot alongside Hart. Just as the executions are about to begin, McNamara shows up at the camp gates wearing a Nazi uniform, which he removes as he approaches Visser. The munitions factory blows up behind them. An enraged Visser supposes that now McNamara wants to trade his own life for the lives of his men. McNamara agrees and Visser obliges by pulling out his pistol and shooting the Colonel himself. The Americans all salute their fallen comrade as Visser walks away and Hart stands looking at the body. A Hart voiceover informs that McNamara was buried by his men and that the stalag was liberated three months later and also that he learned what "honor and courage, duty and sacrifice" really meant.

If only that were the case. In fact, there doesn't seem much that is honorable about any of the proceedings and there are any number of questions to be raised by the plot beginning with the adversarial relationship of Hart and McNamara. McNamara seems to know too much about Hart at their first meeting, suspecting him of breaking under interrogation and being a coward. Since Visser appears to keep McNamara informed when new arrivals are expected into the stalag, had McNamara decided that any of the new guys will provide the needed distraction (the tunnel has obviously taken a long time to construct)? His plan seems quite elaborate to have been worked out at the spur of the moment but how would he have known that all the various elements would fall into place?

Was McNamara always suspicious of Bedford and did he plan on killing him and using a court martial to cover the bigger operation? Was scapegoating a black officer really necessary? It certainly was convenient but it led to the very obvious parallels between the Nazi Visser's contempt for his Russian prisoners and his chiding of McNamara for the way that American whites treat blacks. McNamara is also overly smug and heavy-handed. He continually rails at Hart for his interference but offers no explanation for his obviously prejudicial tactics. Does he suspect that Hart will betray them if McNamara informs him of the escape plan? Is the middle-aged McNamara trying to show a callow Hart what it means to be a man? Is it really necessary to use the only black officer as firing squad fodder? Are there any black enlisted men who fought and were captured? 'Cause this camp is completely white. If a point about racism was to be made, need it be quite so heavy-handed?

Hart's War takes a remarkably long time to get anywhere, particularly with its protracted opening scenes. Which is a shame because Colin Farrell and Terrence Howard do a fine job in their thankless roles, while Willis gets by with a faint smirk and a commanding presence in an equally underwritten role and Iures is stuck with a variation on the cultured (he appreciates American jazz) but ruthless Nazi officer. *Hart's War* tries to tell too many stories and winds up telling none of them very well at all. 🎬

—Christine Tomassini

Harvard Man

CREDITS

Col. William McNamara: Bruce Willis
Lt. Thomas Hart: Colin Farrell
Lt. Lincoln Scott: Terrence DaShon Howard
Staff Sgt. Vic Bedford: Cole Hauser
Col. Werner Visser: Marcel Iures
Capt. Peter Ross: Linus Roache
Sgt. Carl Webb: Rory Cochrane
Pfc. W. Roy Potts: Michael Weston
Lt. Lamar Archer: Vicellous Reon Shannon
Cpl. Joe Cromin: Scott Michael Campbell
Pvt. Daniel Abrams: Adrian Grenier
Pvt. Lewis Wakely: Jonathan Brandis
Col. J.M. Lange: Joe Spano
Cpl. B.J. Guidry: Sam Worthington

Origin: USA
Released: 2002
Production: David Foster, David Ladd, Arnold Rifkin, Gregory Hoblit; Cheyenne Enterprises; released by Metro-Goldwyn-Mayer
Directed by: Gregory Hoblit
Written by: Billy Ray, Terry George
Cinematography by: Alar Kivilo
Music by: Rachel Portman
Sound: David Ronne
Editing: David Rosenbloom
Art Direction: John Warnke
Costumes: Elisabetta Beraldo
Production Design: Lily Kilvert
MPAA rating: R
Running time: 128 minutes

REVIEWS

Chicago Sun-Times Online. February 15, 2002.
Entertainment Weekly. February 15, 2002, p. 42.
Los Angeles Times Online. February 15, 2002.
New York Times Online. February 15, 2002.
People. February 18, 2002, p. 31.
Variety. February 11, 2002, p. 40.
Washington Post. February 15, 2002, p. WE47.

QUOTES

Lt. Lincoln Scott (Terrence Howard): "I came here to kill Nazis; if I wanted to kill crackers, I could've stayed in Georgia."

Sex, Drugs and Heidegger.
—Movie tagline
Some lessons can't be taught in the classroom.
—Movie tagline

James Toback is a director who is known for making movies about his pet obsessions. Previous efforts like *Fingers, The Pick-Up Artist, Black and White* and *Two Girls and a Guy,* were about Toback's favorite fetishes like sex, drugs, talking about life, basketball and sex again, preferably involving three people. In *Harvard Man,* Toback is still passionate about these subjects. This one is about a student, Alan Jensen (Adrian Grenier), who is experiencing all those things as a student at Harvard. Toback himself was a student at Harvard, class of 1966. Reportedly, part of the story is based on an eight-day acid trip that the director took in 1965 when he was a student.

When we first meet Alan, he is having athletic sex with Cindy Bandolini (Sarah Michelle Gellar). Alan is a point guard for the Harvard basketball team and Cindy is a cheerleader for Holy Cross. For Alan, who's the kind of undergrad who's always trying to find ways to experience life more deeply or truthfully, it's more than just sex, it's a kind of experiment. He's also watching TV, listening to two different kinds of music, and smoking some sort of drug. By getting himself into an altered state, Alan's trying to get beyond the self that he presents to the world and find out if there's something there, or if it's going to be the void. If questions like that are a bit too precious and navel-gazing for a viewer, then that viewer is going to hate *Harvard Man.* There are a lot of discussions like that in this film.

There's more of it in one of Alan's philosophy classes, "The Self and Its Loss," taught by instructor, Chesney Cort (the squeaky-voiced Joey Lauren Adams), who tosses out names like Kierkegaard and Heidegger with ease. Alan also happens to be sleeping with the teacher, and the two continue their discussions about the nature of the self during breaks in their bedroom activities.

Alan gets jolted out of his world of the philosophical when he finds out that his parents have lost their house in a Kansas tornado. Despite the fact that his parents are sleeping on the floor of a high school gym and seem to have no hope for getting a loan to rebuild their house, his gruff father (Booth Savage) insists that the best way for Alan to help them is to return to school.

But Alan wants to do more than that. He decides to ask Cindy if she will ask her father, Mr. Bandolini (Gianni Russo), for a loan of $100,000. Cindy says that her father is in "construction," but it seems a lot more likely that he's a mob kingpin. Cindy tells Alan that her father will give him the money, but there's a little something he'd like in return. He'd like Alan to make sure that the team has a favorable point spread in its next game. Alan debates endlessly (but of course) over whether he should do this and decides that it's a good idea. What Cindy doesn't tell him is that she is placing a side bet on the game of $250,000. Cindy secretly places the bet with her father's number two man, Teddy Carter (Eric Stolz) and his girlfriend and helper, Kelly Morgan (Rebecca Gayheart).

Alan does his part in throwing the game, but darned if things don't go as smoothly as he'd planned. It turns out that Teddy and Kelly are actually undercover FBI agents looking to bust Bandolini. By association, Cindy and Alan are in big trouble, too. Bandolini has also sent two of his unintelligent thugs to come and kill Alan. Right when this is all starting to happen, Alan decides that it would be a good time to try some of the LSD that his friend in the chemistry department has given him. Although he's never tried the drug before, he decides it would be smart to take a triple dose.

Alan's subsequent bad trip makes for some of the most interesting footage of the film. When Alan talks to someone, we see how he sees them. Their faces bubble and stretch like the goo in a lava lamp. At first Alan is intrigued and amused by all this, but as it continues, he starts getting scared. In one funny (and scary) sequence, he's running crazed around campus ranting to himself and hearing several layers of voices in his head. He comes across an eager alumni dad (Al Franken) who is trying to get his high school daughter interested in Harvard and decides that she should talk to some of the students. As the dad is trying to have a schmoozing conversation with Alan, Alan can only see his head stretching and distorting. There's another inventive drug sequence in a scene where Chesney is pleading with Alan to get some help with his drug trip. As she's talking, Alan is looking at the Gaugin poster behind her. One of the topless Tahitian women in the picture steps out of the poster and begins to touch Chesney suggestively. It's very bizarre.

The film has some interesting ideas and some good performances but ultimately, the success of the film relies on Grenier's performance as Alan. And Grenier does not pull it off. Even though all the things that he is going through are engaging, the actor is unable to engage the audience enough so that anyone cares what happens to him. "He absorbs the camera's gaze and gives absolutely nothing back," is the way that Stephanie Zacharek put it in *Salon*. Megan Turner of the *New York Post* called Grenier's role a miscasting and wrote that he is "way too short to shoot hoops and appears to have the intelligence of pea soup."

Luckily, Grenier is helped out by the actresses in the film. Adams' character is already pretty interesting on her own—a smart, beautiful professor who talks philosophy and engages in the occasional threesome—but Adams makes the character even more watchable by playing her like she's a real, intriguing person. Also good is Gellar. Gellar showed

that she could play a calculating sexually-charged character in *Cruel Intentions* and here she slides easily back into that mode.

Critics seem to have a love-him-or-hate-him reaction to Toback's films, mostly hate him. Kevin Thomas of the *Los Angeles Times* wrote: "Audacious, imaginatively sustained mayhem ensues right to the finish, but most everyone involved is so craven or calculating or both, starting most crucially with Alan, that it's hard to care much about how everything turns out." Lisa Schwarzbaum of *Entertainment Weekly* called it "a characteristically engorged and sloppy coming-of-age movie from the filmmaker who, in his body of work, indulges his fantasies as fetishistically as other men finger their cigars." Megan Turner of the *New York Post* wrote, "This confused film is hung on a reality-snubbing plot that consistently begs the question: 'Why on earth would that happen?'" And A. O. Scott of the *New York Times* wrote, "*Harvard Man* resembles the term paper that a talented, feckless undergraduate might pull an all-nighter to finish. It has a caffeinated, sloppy brilliance, sparkling with ideas you wish had been developed with more care, but animated by an energy that puts the dutiful efforts of more disciplined grade-grubbers to shame."

—*Jill Hamilton*

CREDITS

Alan Jensen: Adrian Grenier
Cindy Bandolini: Sarah Michelle Gellar
Chesney Cort: Joey Lauren Adams
Teddy Carter: Eric Stoltz
Kelly Morgan: Rebecca Gayheart
Andrew Bandolini: Gianni Russo
Marcus Blake: Ray Allen
Russell: Michael Aparo
Alumni dad: Al Franken

Origin: USA
Released: 2001
Production: Daniel Bigel, Michael Mailer; released by Cowboy Pictures
Directed by: James Toback
Written by: James Toback
Cinematography by: David Ferrara
Music by: Ryan Shore
Editing: Suzy Elmiger
Costumes: Maxyne Baker
Production Design: Rupert Lazarus
MPAA rating: R
Running time: 100 minutes

REVIEWS

Chicago Sun-Times Online. July 12, 2002.
Entertainment Weekly. July 12, 2002, p. 56.
Los Angeles Times Online. July 5, 2002.
New York Times Online. June 28, 2002.
San Francisco Chronicle. April 12, 2002, p. D3.
Variety. June 11, 2001, p. 20.

Heaven

What would you risk for love?
—Movie tagline

Polish director Krzysztof Kieslowski and his writing partner, Krzysztof Piesiewicz—known for their beautifully recognized trilogy *Trois Coleurs: Blanc, Bleu, Rouge*—began writing a new trilogy: *Heaven, Purgatory* and *Hell.* before the director's death in 1996. After what seemed like a long time, *Run Lola Run* director Tom Tykwer picked up the project and began working on it.

While some critics are disappointed at the idea of a script penned by a man known for thoughtful, deliberate pieces being given to the director of the such a hyper kinetic film, I am not so quick to judge. Sure, *Heaven* is more deliberate in its movement than films previously directed by Tykwer. On the other hand, it is a film about chance encounters and a woman taking charge of her destiny and life, which is exactly what *Run Lola Run* was about. It did not, with this in mind, seem odd to me that the direction of such a piece would be given to Tykwer.

Both directors seem to enjoy the idea of love and lovers, Kieslowki just adds morality into the mix a bit heavier than Tykwer. The film is a glowing tribute to the idea of love and the many transparent binders that lovers have. The symbolism of the film, especially in conjunction with the idea of love, was a bit overstated and heavy handed, but tolerable. It was primarily tolerable because the pace of the film was perhaps a bit faster with Tykwer behind the helm, than if Kieslowski had directed his own script.

A teacher of English in Turin, Italy, Philippa, played by Cate Blanchett, is a woman desperate to have her voice heard. She has lost her own husband to drugs and becomes incensed when the police do not listen to her warnings. She places a bomb in the office of the man she knows to be the kingpin of the drug trade of this area. The man escapes without injury due to a series of coincidences. What occurs instead has Philippa reeling in guilt and agony. The bomb accidentally kills a cleaning lady plus three more innocents. She is devastated at the news, but does not lose her resolve to end the supply of drugs to her community.

Philippa is taken into police custody and questioned about her activities and it becomes clear after all her loss, she is about to lose her freedom as well. She is desperate to clear herself so she may finish the work she started. During her painful interrogation she meets Filippo (Giovanni Ribisi).

Filippo is a new cop who, as it turns out, is willing to risk his job and entire career to help her out. He has immediately fallen in love with her. Ribisi is right for some parts, such as Danny McCann in *The Other Sister,* and not so perfect for other roles. In that film he wonderfully played a mentally-challenged character, and while this is also a character of questionable abilities, he is not very convincing. He appears static and almost childlike throughout, which takes away from the plausibility so necessary here.

Many of Kieslowski's films had moral paradoxes, which made his films so fascinating and moving. We can move thorough life making choices and trying to correct wrongs but we can never account for what may happen. Kieslowski penned scripts in a way many people are simply unable to do, and his films are wonderful because of it. This can not be counted as a Kieslowski film alone. He has the moral ambiguity, similar to his earlier work, but it most certainly has the energy evident in Tykwer's films as well. Many people wanted it to be signature Kieslowski, however, if one looks at it as a collaboration, the film becomes much more than palatable to a variety of audiences.

Cate Blanchett's performances have been better at times. As was the case with *Elizabeth,* where she portrayed the queen with such accuracy and conviction it rivaled Glenda Jackson's version. In *Elizabeth* she held the screen for moments at a time with little more than her expression. Here, even with some wonderfully written ideas, she was not at the top of her game. She has a stillness in her performance that worked but I saw her as distant at points and unable to completely appreciate the subtleness combined with the rage Philippa was experiencing.

This is a truly superior film to many completed in the same year because it brings so much to the table but doesn't overwhelm the audience. It calmly lays down the ideas of morality and justice and lets us watch the characters discover themselves at a pace that is perfect for us to swallow.

—*Laura Abraham*

Charlie Kaufman's screenplay, *Human Nature,* turns the wild child myth on its ear while depicting an unusual twist that revolves around a child who wasn't brought up by apes but by a father believing himself to be an ape. Those viewers looking for a rendition of Francois Truffaut's *Wild Child* will be in for a bit of a shock when viewing Kaufman's stylized contemporary tale about nature and civilized society. *Human Nature* also acts as a wild cousin to *The Royal Tenenbaums* with its absurd characters, dry sense of humor, and stylized settings. Even the forest was recreated on a sound stage; one would expect fairies to traipse through its lush greenery. Instead, we are shown an assortment of creatures that fall somewhere between real and mechanical.

Directed by acclaimed French music video director Michel Gondry, *Human Nature* possesses the flow of a well-written screenplay with dense visuals we would expect to find in a commercial or video clip. Gondry successfully blends Kaufman's wry social commentaries and magical characters with astute montages that speak directly to the subconscious mind. Gondry relies on short takes and staccato rhythm while revealing the characters' personalities through what they wear or don't wear and by the characters' props. *Human Nature,* with its odd sets, (the dead scientist Nathan Bronfman tells his story while languishing in a room completely painted in white), again recalls the odd atmosphere in which *The Royal Tenenbaums* find themselves. The characters in both films resemble mythological characters residing in a world that is at the same time familiar and unfamiliar to us.

Human Nature exposes us to several themes such as learning to love ourselves despite our human frailties and connecting with mother earth. The filmmakers also allow us to laugh at our gullibility as they poke fun at people who believe that those who live closer to nature are more liberated and somehow wiser than the rest of us. Nature author Lila Jute (Patricia Arquette) learned how to live close to nature because she felt that only the animals could accept her hairy body. Eventually, however, her need for sexual contact brings her back to urban life. She meets anal-retentive scientist Nathan Bronfman (Tim Robbins), who is still a virgin at 35, and is ashamed of his small penis. The couple's collective inadequacies lead them to fall in love and set up house. That is, until the ugly truth sneaks into the picture.

Meanwhile, we see wild man Puff (Rhys Ifans) telling the story of his life to Congress. We learn that his deranged father raised him in the forest. Nathan and Lila encounter Puff in the wild; Lila acts on her animal impulses, stripping off her clothing and stalking Puff while Nathan weakly watches this call of the wild. Nathan convinces Lila to allow him to transform Puff into a civilized man, but after Puff is placed in a glass laboratory cage and taught proper table manners, we see the beginning of the end. Eventually, the confident Lila's secret reveals itself and Nathan begins an affair with his duplicitous and faux-French assistant Ga-

brielle (Miranda Otto). Gabrielle manipulates Nathan, then Nathan confesses his affair to Lila, who later seeks revenge by abducting Puff and returning him to the forest. Do not expect the usual happy ending or for the characters to act in the usual fairy tale manner. Kaufman presents a few surprises—leaving us to question the premise of his adult bedtime story.

Human Nature boasts an extremely talented cast who delve into their challenging roles. Patricia Arquette plunged into the complex Lila role while enduring six-hour make-up sessions where tuffs of hair were glued to her body. Arquette also had the added discomfort of appearing naked in a majority of her scenes. However, Gondry never exploits his actors, instead giving the impression of a Victorian painting of wood nymphs frolicking in the forest. Arquette's biggest challenge was riding the gamut of Lila's emotions. The character finds empowerment living in the woods, then loses her body hair temporarily so that she can seduce Bronfman. She then becomes weak and vulnerable after Bronfman discovers her hairy secret. Lila sells her soul by assisting her lover in transforming Puff from wild man to civilized man. Then Lila turns on her ex-lover by returning Puff to the forest.

Arquette commented on her role, in which she appeared both hairy and nude: "Obviously that's not easy, but on top of that Lila is a character who starts out strong and confident and is slowly broken into pieces, until she is totally reduced emotionally." Arquette handles her role with aplomb while going where no other actress has gone before.

Arquette's co-star Rhys Ifans also relished the challenge of performing his unusual role. Best-known for his role opposite Hugh Grant in *Notting Hill,* Ifans loses all inhibition in his role of an ape-man-turned-scholar. The biggest challenge that Ifans faced was playing both an ape and a dignified human. In a single scene he would move from vulgar to dignified behavior within the blink of an eye. In a restaurant scene, Puff orders his dinner, then attempts to hump the waitress who simply brushes off Puff's advance by stoically asking, "will that be all?" Ifans accepted the once-in-a-lifetime role because "Puff was an opportunity to really invent something original. He may take steps to be civilized, but from the beginning of the film, he's still a child . . . I wanted to explore Puff's very human feelings of isolation, loneliness and fear . . ."

Director/producer/actor Tim Robbins plays the role of the scientist-villain who extracts Puff's instinctual behavior, then replaces it with anal-retentive and repressed behavior to match his own. His character recalls the weak Victorian male who proved his manhood by conquering the natural world or missionaries who re-educated the "savages" who resided in the wilderness they wished to conquer. Bronfman's character comes as a result of a repressed childhood in which his oppressive parents punished him for using the wrong fork with his salad. Couple that with the fact that his mother (Mary Kay Place) despised anything natural and one can easily see that, similar to Puff, Bronfman also exhibits the damage caused by his childhood. Although Bronfman was raised by overly-civilized parents and Puff was raised by a deranged wild man of the forest, both men lack maturity. Robbins utilizes a deadpan approach while rendering his character both vulnerable and clinical. Similar to the other lead characters, Bronfman also reflects duality between nature and civilization while being torn between two women, his fake French assistant Gabrielle and his subjugated lover Lila.

Screenwriter Charlie Kaufman has lived out a fairy tale of his own by proving that persistence does pay off. In the eighties, Kaufman couldn't even enlist an agent, then in the nineties, according to an article in *RANT,* Kaufman was "Hollywood's favorite un-produced screenwriter." In 1999, Spike Jonze turned Kaufman's script for *Being John Malkovich* into an independent hit, which garnered several Golden Globe and Oscar nominations. Now Kaufman, with his unusual take on contemporary life, has become one of the most sought after scribes in Hollywood.

Director Michel Gondry makes his debut feature with *Human Nature,* but he has already collected awards and kudos in both the commercial and music video industry. His first spot for Levi's won the Lion D'Or at Cannes in 1994. A French art school graduate, Gondry's career took off after he directed a music video for the French group, Oui Oui, for which he also played drums. Since 1993, Gondry has directed music videos for The Rolling Stones, Bjork, Beck, Chemical Brothers, Foo Fighters, Lenny Kravits, and Shery Crow. Gondry demonstrated with *Human Nature* that he also possesses the proper visual tools to deftly handle the long form too.

—*Patty-Lynne Herlevi*

CREDITS

Nathan Bronfman: Tim Robbins
Puff: Rhys Ifans
Lila Jute: Patricia Arquette
Gabrielle: Miranda Otto
Nathan's father: Robert Forster
Nathan's mother: Mary Kay Place
Wendall the therapist: Miguel (Michael) Sandoval
Puff's father: Toby Huss
Frank: Peter Dinklage
Louise: Rosie Perez

Origin: USA, France
Released: 2002

Production: Ted Hope, Anthony Bregman, Spike Jonze, Charlie Kaufman; StudioCanal, Good Machine, Beverly Detroit Studios, Partizan; released by Fine Line Features
Directed by: Michel Gondry
Written by: Charlie Kaufman
Cinematography by: Tim Maurice-Jones
Music by: Graeme Revell
Sound: Drew Kunin
Music Supervisor: Tracy McKnight
Editing: Russell Icke
Art Direction: Peter Andrus
Costumes: Nancy Steiner
Production Design: K.K. Barrett
MPAA rating: R
Running time: 96 minutes

REVIEWS

Boxoffice. September, 2001, p. 142.
Chicago Sun-Times Online. April 12, 2002.
Entertainment Weekly. April 19, 2002, p. 47.
Los Angeles Times Online. April 12, 2002.
New York Times Online. April 12, 2002.
People. April 22, 2002, p. 36.
RANT. March/April, 2002, p. 18.
USA Today Online. April 11, 2002.
Variety. May 28, 2001, p. 19.
Washington Post. April 12, 2002, p. WE39.

QUOTES

Nathan's (Tim Robbins) definition of civilization: "When in doubt, don't ever do what you really want to do."

AWARDS AND NOMINATIONS

Natl. Bd. of Review 2002: Screenplay.

Hush!

From writer-director-editor Ryosuke Hashiguchi, comes *Hush!,* a simply warm, fun film with enough twists to keep it entertaining. While it initially appears to be a love triangle, it quickly transforms into a much deeper film showing the conservative political nature of Japanese culture.

Hashiguchi introduces his characters independently from each other, moving back and forth between the three of them. While they are all living different lives internally and externally, the similarity is that they all are alone and lonely.

Naoya (Kazuya Takahashi) is an openly gay man who is accepted by all around him, except his mother. She seems to live under some very old misconceptions about what it means to be gay, which is often a bit over the top and especially ridiculous to American audiences. Naoya works in an upscale pet store where he encounters very eccentric customers daily, which provides a lot of comedic relief.

Katsuhiro (Seiichi Tanabe) is a researcher who is so closeted he cannot even put the brakes on a coworker who is in love with him. He allows her to continue with her obvious attraction because he is more afraid of coming out.

As the two meet and fall in love, their relationship is sweet and at times very funny. They are truly the example of opposites attracting as Naoya makes it clear he is not interested in having children. He has accepted his life as a man who will grow old alone. Katsuhiro is not so ready to accept this type of life and dreams of being a father.

The third character in this film is a self-destructive young woman, Asako (Reiko Kataoka). She has lived through a string of bad relationships and abortions and quite frankly, is tired of it. She is near 30 and has decided, in her free wheeling liberal way, that single motherhood is the next step in her life. She really doesn't see the need in being married to have a child; however a sperm bank is too impersonal for her. She meets Katsuhiro in a restaurant where he politely offers her his umbrella after hers was stolen and she instantly decides he's the one.

If you are thinking of the fag hag cult film, *The Next Best Thing,* I wouldn't blame you. The similarities are there. The premise is the same. However, American films such as *The Next Best Thing* reek of formulaic marketing while *Hush!* is the type of film that feels real in its conviction to delve into the characters' psyches. It is less concerned with sticking to the formula than it is with fleshing out characters. *Hush!* is subtle in its observations about the lives of three people dealing with their environments.

Although it seems quite lighthearted at times, Hashiguchi creates a film of substance. He clearly wants us to rethink our positions on family, friends and homosexuality. Certainly he is concerned with challenging his audience to open our minds towards gay culture and relationships, but he is really asking us to understand the larger impact on family and society as a whole. All the characters are dealing with issues with their family, which certainly lends a sense of truth and honesty to the characters. Given the problems with their respective families it seems like a logical choice that the three would choose to build their lives together. In a way, *Hush!* is asking us to build happy family lives in any way possible, because they are important parts of our lives as individuals and as a society. It is not a film necessarily requesting people to rebuild their traditional families to fit their politics but telling people to take control of their own circumstances.

This idea alone sets it apart from the more sugar-coated Hollywood equivalents. To say *Hush!* is a gay film and Hashiguchi is a gay director is not giving either of them much credit. As Hashiguchi says himself, "in *Hush!* I didn't stress about gay issues and tried to show the real world where people are different in every way." Yes, the themes are gay and yes, Hashiguchi does not shy away from that, but the general premise of the film is so much grander. *Hush!* is a pleasurable, cute and often demanding comedy/drama with three wonderful actors. The acting demands attention because it is so truthful and real. The story demands attention because it is a mirror into the changing Asian culture. *Hush!* is a film of innumerable ideas and thoughts, so much larger than just another "gay" film.

—*Laura Abraham*

CREDITS

Katsuhiro: Seichi Tanabe
Naoya: Kazuya Takahashi
Asako: Reiko Kataoka

Origin: Japan
Language: Japanese
Released: 2001
Production: Tetsujiro Yamagami; Siglo; released by Strand Releasing
Directed by: Ryosuke Hashiguchi
Written by: Ryosuke Hashiguchi
Cinematography by: Shogo Ueno
Music by: Bobby McFerrin
Sound: Yoshiteru Takahashi
Editing: Ryosuke Hashiguchi
Production Design: Fumio Ogawa
MPAA rating: Unrated
Running time: 135 minutes

REVIEWS

Entertainment Weekly. November 15, 2002, p. 108.
Los Angeles Times Online. November 8, 2002.
New York Times Online. November 8, 2002.
Variety Online. May 15, 2001.

I Spy

Attitude Meets Espionage.
—Movie tagline

Espionage With Attitude.
—Movie tagline

 Box Office: $33.1 million

There seems to be no quicker way to get a movie made in Hollywood than to base it on an old TV series. Good or bad, loved or unloved, movie version TV shows have been showing up on the big screen with alarming consistently. One of these conversions that might have had more promise than some (many) of the others is a movie based on the series *I Spy.* The show, which ran from 1965–68, starred Robert Culp as a tennis player and Bill Cosby posing as his trainer. The two toured the world being spies and cracking jokes. The show had a wry humor and cool casualness that left it well-loved in many viewers' memories. Additionally, it was the first show that had an African-American guy starring as something other than a servant or other stereotypical role. Even better, Cosby's character was the smoother of the two and little was made of the fact of the racial differences. Each year that the show was on the air, the actors scored Emmy nominations.

The casting for the film version sounded promising, too. This time out, the pair is played by Eddie Murphy, who has done great comedic work in films like *The Nutty Professor,* and Owen Wilson whose humor comes from his gabby, over-analytical chatter (see *Shanghai Noon*). The movie was directed by Betty Thomas, the former actress, who did good work in *The Brady Bunch Movie* and worked with Murphy in *Dr. Doolittle.* So far, so good.

But the first sign that something isn't right is the fact that the film used four credited writers. This is rarely good. Secondly, the film makes little reference to the TV show. Yes, there is a multiracial spy team, but that's where the resemblance ends. Where the show's humor was dry and cool, the film's humor is obvious or missing. And Thomas doesn't seem to know what to do with the film. She puts some action in there and some comedy in there, but not enough for fans of either of them to be satisfied. And she doesn't know how to exploit the comedic talent that she has. It seems like watching the two actors eat lunch might yield better laughs than their poorly scripted banter. Right there, that's plenty of problems for one film to deal with and that's without even mentioning the ludicrous and dull plot.

In this *I Spy,* Alex (Wilson) is a spy who's fairly successful, but not quite good enough to outdo his rival, Carlos (Gary Cole). Carlos gets the good assignments, the praise from the bosses and possibly even the coworker that Alex has his eye on, Rachel (Famke Janssen). Alex is thrilled when he gets his big chance to best Carlos—an assignment in Budapest to track down The Switchblade. The Switchblade is a United States-developed plane that is invisible to radar and the human eye. The bad guy of the story, Gundars (Malcolm McDowell) had gotten a hold of the plane and is planning to auction it off to the highest bidder.

Alex is less happy when he finds out that he's going to have a partner on his big job. The president (voiced by a George Bush soundalike) makes a personal phone call to boxer Kelly Robinson (Murphy). Kelly, struck by patriotism agrees to the job. Kelly Robinson is 57-0 and he has a match coming up in Budapest. The idea is that Kelly, with his celebrity, can get invited to a party given by Gundars and that Alex can go posing as one of his entourage. The two will then locate the plane, thus saving the whole world. Or something like that.

Of course, it doesn't all go as planned. For one thing, Alex can't stand Kelly, who is an egomaniac who constantly refers to himself in the third person. And Kelly, while brave in the ring, is kind of skittish when it comes to the heavy-duty spy stuff. So in times of danger, he says stuff like, "We gonna die?" Way to get rid of those scaredy black man stereotypes, guys.

Stuntwise, there is a car chase involving a car trailer, a car that blows up and a crazy plane ride. None of this is going to engage the action freaks. Romance-wise, there is some flirtation going on between Alex and Rachel. Again, this isn't going to please anyone out for romance. As for intrigue, there is some double crossing and double agents, but it becomes so confusing in one scene that it's difficult to even figure out what's going on. In classic Owen Wilson fashion, Alex responds to the confusing plot twists by riffing on about the "murkiness" of the situation and ruminates on who is truly good and who is truly evil.

And, as for comedy, it's there. It's just not there enough. One of the best running gags is how Alex's spy gadgets are always worse than Carlos'. His spy camera is huge and an upset Alex moans to the designer that in spy gadgetry smaller is better. During one crucial scene, he tests out some super spy earphones, but they only give off a horrible muffled buzzing sound. And the "microtracer" that he's to put on the bad guy's car is huge and hardly undetectable. "I can't help but notice that my spy stuff looks like you got it from Radio Shack in 1972," he complains. Murphy's jokes are less successful. He's played the cocky, obnoxious character many times before and the lines he is given with this one just aren't enough to make the character fresh. He gets a few good lines in here and there. When he is threatened with getting a sensitive body part cut off, he yelps, "What ever happened to 'rough the man up'?"

Thomas never gets the hang of how to use the two comedians together except in one scene. Alex is trying to put the moves on Rachel, and Kelly—who is smoother with the ladies—counsels him over a hidden earpiece. It's not exactly the most original of conceits, but it's a reliable standby. Kelly feeds Alex the lines from the Marvin Gaye song "Sexual Healing," and Alex is stuck trying to romance Rachel with lines like "When I get this feeling, I need sexual healing." Alex's awkwardness and lack of any kind of smooth moves is what makes the scene work.

Most critics couldn't seem to get away from the fact that the new *I Spy* was just a pale imitation of the old TV show. Kenneth Turan of the *Los Angeles Times* wrote, "*I Spy*, with more dead spots than a Jerry Lewis Telethon, is content to mark time." Wesley Morris of the *Boston Globe* wrote, "Eager to get the early jump on Thanksgiving, the folks at Columbia Pictures deliver the Eddie Murphy-Owen Wilson gadgetfest, *I Spy*, a bigger, drier turkey than whatever you were planning on having at the end of the month." John Anderson of *Newsday* called the film "lackluster at best" and wrote that "There are a few funny moments in *I Spy*, though it makes the worst use possible of Eddie Murphy's enormous comic gifts." And Roger Ebert of the *Chicago Sun-Times* wrote, "This is a remake by the numbers, linking a halfwit plot to a series of standup routines in which Wilson and Murphy show how funny they could have been in a more ambitious movie. When they riff with each other, there's an energy that makes us smile. When they slog though the plot, we despair."

—*Jill Hamilton*

CREDITS

Kelly Robinson: Eddie Murphy
Alexander Scott: Owen C. Wilson
Rachael: Famke Janssen
Gundars: Malcolm McDowell
Carlos: Gary Cole
Jerry: Phill Lewis
T.J.: Viv Leacock

Origin: USA
Released: 2002
Production: Jenno Topping, Betty Thomas, Mario Kassar, Andrew G. Vajna; Tall Trees, C-2 Pictures, Sheldon Leonard Productions; released by Columbia Pictures
Directed by: Betty Thomas
Written by: Cormac Wibberley, Marianne S. Wibberley, Jay Scherick, David Ronn
Cinematography by: Oliver Wood
Music by: Richard Gibbs
Sound: Rob Young
Music Supervisor: Elliot Lurie
Editing: Peter Teschner
Art Direction: Doug Byggdin, Bo Johnson
Costumes: Ruth Carter
Production Design: Marcia Hinds-Johnson
MPAA rating: PG-13
Running time: 96 minutes

REVIEWS

Chicago Sun-Times Online. November 1, 2002.
Entertainment Weekly. November 15, 2002, p. 106.
Los Angeles Times Online. November 1, 2002.
New York Times Online. November 1, 2002.
People. November 18, 2002, p. 42.
USA Today Online. November 1, 2002.
Variety Online. October 14, 2002.
Washington Post. November 1, 2002, p. WE42.

QUOTES

Alexander Scott (Owen Wilson) to Kelly Robinson (Eddie Murphy): "Are you going to be referring to yourself in the third person the whole time? Cause that can get a little irritating."

Ice Age

The Coolest Event In 16,000 Years.
—Movie tagline
They came, they thawed, they conquered.
—Movie tagline

 Box Office: $176.3 million

One of the most crowd-pleasing parts of *Ice Age* was its trailer. In it, a bug-eyed little squirrelish rat creature, Scrat, is attempting to bury an acorn in the frozen tundra. In one scene, he crams it into the ice, only to create a rift in the ice, which becomes a large crack, which becomes a huge chasm, which leads to a iceberg breaking loose, etc. In another, he overcomes various frustrating obstacles and finally ends up atop a tree, with his beloved nut held aloft, as he readies to hide the nut in the tree's hollow trunk. At the exact moment that he lifts his nut in triumph, he is struck by lightning. The scenes with Scrat—who, in the film, appears as a character in a running side gag—recall the classic

Warner Bros. cartoons. The exaggerated expressions, the futility and the absurdity are all familiar territory—not to mention the never-ending comedy to be found in seeing a creature fall off a cliff and getting hurt.

It's funny that the movie returns to old themes because, technologically, it's far ahead of those old animated cartoons. Like *Shrek* and *Monsters, Inc*, *Ice Age* showcases the latest in computer animation. Even though the technology had been around for awhile in 2002, it was still striking enough that many reviewers felt compelled to mention it. Kenneth Turan of the *Los Angeles Times* wrote that director Chris Wedge (who won an Oscar for the animated short "Bunny") has a style that "is a kind of storybook photo-realism, giving those characters the unusual look of living and breathing plush toys." Liz Braun of the *Toronto Sun* wrote "some details—water drops and animal fur, for example—are realized in a lifelike fashion, while others (like faces) are stylized and a tad surreal. It is very cool." And Owen Gleiberman of *Entertainment Weekly* wrote, "The animation in *Ice Age* has a funky, laws-of-physics tactility that makes your average hand-drawn cartoon look about as textured as Colorforms."

Even though we have seen this sort of animation before, director Wedge does have a unique style. Scenes with water flowing and water droplets are shockingly realistic. Other times the animation serves to further someone's character. The way that Scrat's ribs heave with his exertion and general nervousness say more about him than anything he might say (not that he can talk). In other scenes, the animation just looks cool. In one scene, several characters end up taking a long ride down ice flues that look a lot like water slides at a water park. The ice glows with a cool blue and the characters whoop it up and/or say "Woooooaaah!" as they careen down through the ice tunnels. The scene doesn't do much for furthering the plot, but it's a lot of fun to watch, especially for kids. The animation of the humans in the story is unusual. They're not made to look realistic, but they aren't cartoony either. The stylized look is sort of creepy in a way, like they are statues that have come to life.

It seems like so much attention went to the look of *Ice Age* that there wasn't much creative power left for the story. Even though the timing of the film made it impossible that *Ice Age* could have cribbed its story line from films like *Shrek* and *Monsters, Inc* there were enough overly familiar elements in it to make it seem less fresh when it did come out. The cranky, slow-moving mammoth, Manfred (Ray Romano of *Everybody Loves Raymond*), meets up with the small, hyper and annoying sloth, Sid (John Leguizamo). More than one critic noted that their relationship of annoying and annoyee looked a lot like Michael Myers' and Eddie Murphy's in *Shrek*.

Sid is universally hated—so much so that his family has snuck off to migrate south without him to escape the impending ice age. Sid tries to ingratiate himself with Manfred, even though the mammoth, for no apparent reason, is headed the wrong way. Manfred keeps brushing Sid off until the two find a baby human who's been left alone. This is part of a tragic lost mother story line that seems like it surely must have come from a Disney picture. The baby's mother, who was trying to escape a pack of sabertooths, has used her last bit of strength to float down a river, clutching her boy. After she places the baby safely in the mammoth's arms, she disappears into the rapids. Manfred agrees to stick with Sid until the two can return the baby safely to his father.

They are joined by a sabertooth, Diego (Denis Leary), who pretends like he's going to help them find the human's compound. In reality, he plans to steal the baby and take it to his Mafia don-like boss who wants the baby to avenge the human hunting of sabertooths (saberteeth?). For extra menace, he also plans to set up an ambush by his pack of fellow tigers to eat the supersized Manfred. It seems unlikely that that will ever actually happen since the movie quickly turns into a prehistoric version of *Three Men and a Baby*. The three bond over diaper changing, looking for food and watching the little one take his first wobbly steps. When they're not busy being Mr. Moms, they escape from various dangers like a sudden fire pit of smoking lava.

But the danger is never that menacing since the point of *Ice Age* is to be light and funny. Sid gets chased by some apparently gay rhinos (Cedric the Entertainer and Stephen Root), and the trio comes upon a pack of Dodo birds who show how they became extinct. The film tries to be hip with the parents by having the kind of humor that adults could enjoy, but the humor is never as sharp as that in, say, *A Bug's Life* or *Toy Story*. Some of these are funny just because of the way the actor delivers the line. For that reason, Sid is the most consistently funny character. When Diego tries to get Sid to go through a treacherous pass, Sid blurts, "No thanks! I choose life!" Later, after Diego apologizes to him, Sid says, "Oh you know me, I'm too lazy to carry a grudge." Other times the humor is overly forced. When one character sees an arrangement of rocks ala Stonehenge, they remark "Modern architecture—it'll never last." Da, dum-dum. A mammoth mother remarks to her children, who are playing in a tar pit, "Come on! You can play Extinction later."

Leguizamo does an excellent job as the hapless Sid. He manages to be an annoying character who is not completely annoying to the audience—a rare feat. He's funny and sad and endearing. It's difficult to tell if Romano is doing any acting with Manfred. He sounds exactly like he always does. That's not exactly bad, but it's not any kind of acting tour de force. Leary is good as the conflicted Diego. He keeps his voice low and sounds nothing like his usual chain-smoking comic persona. He gives the right amount of gravity to his threats to Sid like, "You're a little low on the food chain to be mouthing off like that."

Most critics had a fairly good time at *Ice Age.* Gleiberman of *Entertainment Weekly* wrote, "*Ice Age* never matches the brilliance of *Toy Story* or the heartfelt heft of *Shrek,* but it's an antic and sweet-spirited pleasure." Roger Ebert of the *Chicago Sun-Times* wrote, "I confess the premise did not inspire me. But Peter Ackerman's screenplay is sly and literate, and director Chris Wedge's visual style is so distinctive and appealing that the movie seduced me." Braun of the *Toronto Sun* wrote, "What sets *Ice Age* apart from similar family fare are a witty script and the all-digital animation that is so fresh to the eyes." Others weren't so impressed. Elvis Mitchell of the *New York Times* wrote, "The blandly likable computer-animation extravaganza *Ice Age* actually seems like a fossil, a relic from another era." And Kenneth Turan of the *Los Angeles Times* wrote, "This relentless, all-wise-guys-all-the-time approach tries way too hard and gets tiring in no time at all."

—*Jill Hamilton*

CREDITS

Sid: John Leguizamo (Voice)
Diego: Denis Leary (Voice)
Manfred: Ray Romano (Voice)
Soto: Goran Visnjic (Voice)
Zeke: Jack Black (Voice)
Rhino: Cedric the Entertainer (Voice)
Rhino: Stephen (Steve) Root (Voice)
Roshan: Tara Strong (Voice)
Tiger: Diedrich Bader (Voice)
Tiger: Alan Tudyk (Voice)
Female sloth: Lorri Bagley (Voice)
Female sloth: Jane Krakowski (Voice)
Scrat: Chris Wedge (Voice)

Origin: USA
Released: 2002
Production: Lori Forte; Blue Sky Productions; released by 20th Century-Fox
Directed by: Chris Wedge
Written by: Michael Berg, Michael J. Wilson, Peter Ackerman
Music by: David Newman
Sound: Sean Garnhart
Editing: John Carnochan
Production Design: Brian McEntee
MPAA rating: PG
Running time: 81 minutes

REVIEWS

Chicago Sun-Times Online. March 15, 2002.
Entertainment Weekly. March 22, 2002, p. 78.
Los Angeles Times Online. March 15, 2002.
New York Times Online. March 15, 2002.
People. March 25, 2002, p. 40.
USA Today Online. March 15, 2002.
Variety. March 18, 2002, p. 23.

QUOTES

Sid the Sloth (John Leguizamo): "For a second there I thought you were actually going to eat me." Diego the Sabertooth: "I don't eat junk food."

AWARDS AND NOMINATIONS

Nomination:
Oscars 2002: Animated Film.

Igby Goes Down

Insanity Is Relative.
—Movie tagline

Box Office: $4.7 million

Because the protagonist of writer-director Burr Steers's *Igby Goes Down* is a prep-school dropout fed up with the hypocrisies he sees all around him in his old-money world of wealth and privilege, many critics dubbed him a Holden Caulfield like character and the movie a worthy successor to Salinger's *The Catcher in the Rye.* Steers himself cites the influence in the film's press notes, but such a comparison is facile at best. Igby Slocumb (Kieran Culkin), the 17-year-old disaffected youth who wanders New York, is just as shallow and mean-spirited as the adults he despises while lacking the self-awareness, depth, and humor of Salinger's hero. Holden was not a sour misanthrope at heart—indeed, he loved his sister Phoebe and, at his best, envisioned himself a savior of children. Igby, on the other hand, constantly demonstrates the very contempt he sees in everyone else.

The film is meant to be a pointed satire of the rich, the world Steers himself grew up in, but, instead of letting us see this environment in a new way, he simplistically trots out the familiar clichés about the rich being empty, cold, and desperately unhappy. From Igby's shrewish mother, who sits on the maid to vent her frustration, to his schizophrenic father and cold-hearted brother, just about everyone is a walking poster child for upper-class dysfunction.

The movie opens with Igby and his older brother, Oliver (Ryan Phillippe), killing their sick mother, Mimi (Susan Sarandon), in her sleep by suffocating her with a plastic bag. Only later will we learn that this murder has been committed at Mimi's request, but it is hardly a mercy killing, just a callous act borne of selfishness. It is a ghastly opening—Mimi's eyes suddenly pop open after she draws her last breath—followed by short flashbacks depicting the Slocumb patriarch, Jason (Bill Pullman), gradually descending into madness.

The main narrative begins before Mimi's death. Igby is flunking out of prep school, and Mimi, having been called to pick him up, slaps him around for being a bad reflection on her and promptly enrolls him in a Midwest military school, where he is beat up by his classmates. Even a psychiatrist whom Igby toys with cannot resist hitting him. Unlike Oliver, a smug, materialistic Columbia student whom Igby thinks of as a fascist, Igby is an aimless rebel who cannot fit in anyplace and routinely gets beat up.

When Igby's wealthy godfather, D.H. (Jeff Goldblum), wants him to work for him renovating one of his buildings during the summer, it seems that Igby may have found his place. But D.H. turns out to be a pompous jerk who espouses a social Darwinist line about certain people being meant to fail to serve as warnings for everyone else. Igby soon meets Rachel (Amanda Peet), D.H.'s young trophy mistress and a dancer, who lives in D.H.'s building. Later, at a party thrown at D.H.'s home in the Hamptons, Igby marvels at the hypocrisy of D.H. having his mistress and wife together at the same gathering, but his observation seems trite, and his outrage feels like a moralistic pose. At the same party, Igby meets a slightly older girl named Sookie Sapperstein (Claire Danes), a Bennington student who works for the catering company. She seems aimless and emotionally detached like Igby, and they hit it off.

Making his escape from the limousine that is taking him to the airport and hence his next school, Igby dashes to Rachel's loft, which is also occupied by a bohemian friend and sometime artist/drug dealer of ambiguous sexuality named Russel (Jared Harris). Maybe Rachel and Russel are supposed to be cool hipsters, or perhaps they are just self-deluded artists of dubious talent, but Igby has no qualms about worming his way into staying with them, even though it means risking the wrath of D.H. should he find out.

The most infuriating aspect of *Igby Goes Down* is that Igby is essentially a spoiled brat who thinks that he is better than everyone else, yet he is anything but a charmer and actually fits in well with the pretentious people he hates. Unbelievably, both Rachel and Sookie are taken with Igby.

Each sleeps with him, although it is difficult to fathom why two pretty girls who mix with New York's chic set would be seduced by Igby's lost-boy posturing. His self-importance is tiresome, and Culkin generates no sympathy as the rich kid gone bad. Full of adolescent clichés, Igby tells Sookie that he wants to go away to discover the meaning of life. The fact that he is being at least somewhat ironic in his plans does not make him less of a cliché, just more of a poseur trying to seem cool.

The movie's structure is fairly random as we follow Igby on his monotonous journey to nowhere. Along the way, we are treated to a harrowing flashback of Jason in which Igby as a little boy sees him going crazy in the shower, bashing himself against the glass door and bleeding everywhere. But Jason's back story is so sketchy that we hardly care about his illness or understand how his mental breakdown affected his family.

Nothing seems to go right for Igby. Just when it seems that he has a confidante in Sookie, the calculating Oliver starts to seduce her away from him. Meanwhile, Rachel, who is really more of a drug addict than a dancer, suffers from an overdose. While Igby helps save her life by getting her to the hospital in time, D.H. beats him for sleeping with his girl. Then Igby tries to run off with Sookie, only to have her refuse to go with him. In what is supposed to be a powerful moment, Igby screams to her in front of her locked door and warns her that Oliver will use her up and dump her and that their anti-Semitic mother would never accept her. Only moments later, Oliver emerges from her apartment, in essence declaring himself the winner in their rivalry for Sookie. For all of his supposed sophistication, Igby is really nothing more than a whiny little boy when he does not get his way.

But even Sookie's painful betrayal seems to mean little in the long run. Soon Igby is dealing drugs for Russel for no apparent reason than he has nothing else better to do. When he ends up selling to a former teacher of his, it is probably meant to be an ironic touch showing that yet another authority figure is a phony, but it ends up being just another random detail in Igby's pointless travels.

The last major sequence is Mimi's death, which circles back to the beginning of the movie. Stricken with cancer, she is having her sons kill her. As Oliver feeds her the drugs that will knock her out, she casually tells Igby that D.H. is really his father, a seemingly big revelation that means little and feels like the last spiteful act of a selfish woman. It does explain why Jason did not make financial arrangements for Igby as he did for Oliver, but it seems unlikely that the well-connected Igby will ever be poor. When Mimi has finally suffocated to death, Igby climbs on top of her and screams his heart out, wishing that the woman he loathed were still alive. We are probably meant to feel sorry for this boy who hated his ice-cold mother but now feels conflicted about her death, but it is hard to sympathize with him after he has taken part in her murder. Moreover, he is soon back to his sarcastic self, making snide phone calls to old friends and relatives telling them that his mother would love to talk to them but cannot because she is dead. In the end, he watches her funeral from the back of the church, pays a visit to the seemingly comatose Jason staring at the wall in the sanitarium, and heads for California to start a new life.

Given the talent involved, it is surprising that even the acting in *Igby Goes Down* is disappointing. Sarandon gives an uncharacteristically shrill, one-note performance as a stereotypical pill-popping, self-absorbed socialite, and the wooden Phillippe seems to be reprising his *Cruel Intentions* role as a nasty, emotionless cad. Pullman is given little to do but look vacant and pathetic in his few scenes, and Goldblum comes off as a parody of a wealthy jerk, mouthing empty platitudes and ceremoniously flashing big bills to impress people. Danes gives the best performance only because there actually seems to be a hint of humanity in Sookie, who really does seem to care for the unlikable Igby, but Danes cannot make us believe that the bright Sookie would sleep with Igby and then fall for Oliver.

Igby Goes Down is relentlessly sour about the world of New York affluence but offers no fresh insights, just caricatures of one unpleasant rich person after another. Everyone in Igby's family is either cold-blooded or crazy, but, to make matters worse, Igby himself constantly comes across as just one more poor little rich kid too sensitive for all the phonies who populate high society. The setting itself is seductive in the way it conjures up our notions of the New York elite, from fancy restaurants to an extravagant party in the Hamptons. Yet ultimately the film indulges the fantasy of having it both ways—we can vicariously enter the world of the wealthy, and yet, through Igby's jaundiced view, feel superior to it, thankful that we are not as miserable and wretched as the people in his orbit. Steers's screenplay is far more disingenuous than anything Igby himself sees around him.

—*Peter N. Chumo II*

Origin: USA
Released: 2002
Production: Lisa Tornell, Marco Weber; Crossroads Films, Atlantic Streamline; released by United Artists
Directed by: Burr Steers
Written by: Burr Steers
Cinematography by: Wedigo von Schultzendorff
Music by: Uwe Peterson
Sound: Gary J. Coppola, Michael Mullane
Music Supervisor: Nic Harcourt
Editing: William M. Anderson
Art Direction: Roswell Hamrick
Costumes: Sarah Edwards
Production Design: Kevin Thompson
MPAA rating: R
Running time: 98 minutes

REVIEWS

Boxoffice. August, 2002, p. 54.
Entertainment Weekly. September 20, 2002, p. 71.
Los Angeles Times Online. September 13, 2002.
New York Times Online. September 13, 2002.
People. September 23, 2002, p. 53.
Rolling Stone. October 3, 2002, p. 111.
USA Today Online. September 12, 2002.
Variety. June 3, 2002, p. 21.
Washington Post. September 20, 2002, p. WE46.

QUOTES

Sookie (Claire Danes): "You call your mother Mimi?" Igby (Kieran Culkin): "Heinous One is a bit cumbersome, and Medea was already taken."

CREDITS

Igby Slocumb: Kieran Culkin
Oliver Slocumb: Ryan Phillippe
Mimi Slocumb: Susan Sarandon
Sookie Sapperstein: Claire Danes
D.H.: Jeff Goldblum
Jason Slocumb: Bill Pullman
Rachel: Amanda Peet
Russel: Jared Harris
Young Igby: Rory Culkin
Mrs. Piggee: Cynthia Nixon
Mr. Nice Guy: Eric Bogosian

AWARDS AND NOMINATIONS

Nomination:
Golden Globes 2003: Actor—Mus./Comedy (Culkin), Support. Actress (Sarandon).

Skarsgard's character falls to pieces as the film progresses, Pacino, thanks to the pending investigation of Dormer's possible corruption, is a mess from the first shot: haggard, forlorn, truly tormented. What transpires in Nightmute only makes a bad situation worse.

Pacino's Dormer is a contrast of confidence and insecurity. The former is displayed, in one of the best scenes, when Dormer examines the dead girl's body and draws conclusions missed by the local police. Pacino subtly conveys that the detective has both seen the depths of human depravity and identified with these horrors. Even though the film was not shot in sequence, Pacino expresses Dormer's growing exhaustion by making his voice progressively, almost imperceptibly weaker until it reaches a whisper. No one other than Pacino could have captured so well Dormer's dual nature of victim and victimizer. *Insomnia* joins *The Godfather* (1972), *Serpico* (1973), *The Godfather, Part II* (1974), *Dog Day Afternoon* (1975), *Scarface* (1983), *Heat* (1995), and *Donnie Brasco* (1997) in the growing list of a master's greatest performances. No actor has better captured moral ambiguity.

—*Michael Adams*

CREDITS

Will Dormer: Al Pacino
Walter Finch: Robin Williams
Ellie Burr: Hilary Swank
Rachel Clement: Maura Tierney
Hap Eckhart: Martin Donovan
Fred Duggar: Nicky Katt
Chief Nyback: Paul Dooley
Randy Stetz: Jonathan Jackson
Tanya Francke: Katharine Isabelle
Farrell: Larry Holden
Kay Connell: Crystal Lowe
Mrs. Connell: Tasha Simms

Origin: USA
Released: 2002
Production: Paul Junger Witt, Broderick Johnson, Andrew A. Kosove, Edward L. McDonnell; Alcon Entertainment, Section Eight; released by Warner Bros.
Directed by: Christopher Nolan
Written by: Hillary Seitz
Cinematography by: Wally Pfister
Music by: David Julyan
Sound: Larry Sutton
Editing: Dody Dorn
Art Direction: Michael Diner
Costumes: Tish Monaghan
Production Design: Nathan Crowley

MPAA rating: R
Running time: 116 minutes

REVIEWS

Atlanta Journal and Constitution. May 24, 2002, p. 11.
Baltimore Sun. May 24, 2002, p. E1.
Chicago Sun-Times Online. May 24, 2002.
Entertainment Weekly. May 31, 2002, p. 73.
Film Comment. May/June, 2002, p. 26.
Los Angeles Times Online. May 24, 2002.
New York. May 27, 2002, p. 42.
New York Times. May 24, 2002, p. E1.
New Yorker. May 27, 2002, p. 124.
Newsweek. June 3, 2002, p. 56.
People. June 3, 2002, p. 33.
Rolling Stone. May 23, 2002, p. 88.
San Francisco Chronicle. May 24, 2002, p. D1.
Time. May 27, 2002, p. 65.
USA Today. May 24, 2002, p. D9.
Variety Online. May 10, 2002.
Washington Post. May 24, 2002, p. WE43.

QUOTES

Will Dormer (Al Pacino) about the killer: "This guy crossed the line and he didn't even blink. You don't come back from that."

TRIVIA

The logging town of Squamish, British Columbia represents the fictional town of Nightmute, Alaska in the film.

Invincible

One foresaw the future of the Nazi Party. One fought for the destiny of the Jewish people. Two lives bound by one moment in history . . . and one unforgettable legend.
—Movie tagline

Werner Herzog has always been fascinated by freaks of history. His first non-documentary feature film in ten years, *Invincible,* displays that same interest in a quirky, obscure tale, but it is not nearly as bizarre as some of his earlier work. Based on the true story of a Polish Jewish strongman who became a sensation in 1932 at a Berlin night club that was popular with Nazis, *Invincible* is surprisingly gentle for Herzog, a director often given to excesses of emotion. The film is characteristically observant, languid, and contemplative—a moody, engrossing evocation of a time when powerful forces were simmering but had not yet been unleashed. It's a curiosity that has moments of great power amid dull and awkward stretches—just like many of Herzog's earlier films such as *Aguirre, the Wrath of God.*

The film opens in a small, rural village in eastern Poland, where the young adult son of a blacksmith, Zishe Breitbart (Jouko Ahola), endures the anti-Semitic taunts hurled at him by local villagers in a pub until they tease and throttle his precocious young brother, Benjamin (Jacob Wein). Enraged, Zishe pummels his tormentors and overturns tables and a keg of beer. The owner demands compensation and suggests that Zishe can earn it by challenging the strongman at a circus that's in town. Under a rather small Big Top, Zishe humiliates his opponent without breaking a sweat.

A talent agent hears of Zishe's prowess and offers him a chance for fame and fortune in Berlin, under his management. At first Zishe refuses; as the oldest of a large brood of siblings, he wants to remain a blacksmith, working alongside his father and helping to provide for his family. In one of many fuzzy parts to the film, it's unclear why Zishe changes his mind and leaves. But his decision causes Benjamin, who speaks with the syntax and wisdom of an adult, to become heartbroken. As Zishe leaves the village, his father admonishes not to forget who he is and where he comes from.

When Zishe arrives in Berlin, the agent gets him a job at an unusual club. Run by clairvoyant magician impresario Jan-Erik Hanussen (Tim Roth), it's a popular gathering place for Nazi party members. Hanussen, a shrewd and heartless showman, plays to the Nazis by clouding his conjuring tricks and psychic predictions with a heavy veneer of German nationalism. In channeling sessions held in a back room around a circular table, he predicts the rise of Adolf Hitler and the unification of the German people.

Hanussen dresses Zishe as a Teutonic warrior for his stage acts, making him put on a blonde wig. Zishe chafes at this treatment and eventually rebels, revealing himself to be a Jew. He becomes a cause celebre in the Jewish community, whose members then flock to the night club to sit across the aisle from the Nazis. The tension in the club sometimes breaks out into fights.

An underdeveloped subplot has Zishe falling in love with Marta (Anna Gourari), the club's pianist and Hanussen's assistant for some of his acts. She is also Hanussen's mistress, and the showman is abusive towards her. But since she is a Czech national without papers, she is at his mercy. One of *Invincible*'s many incongruities is that Zishe and Marta have several scenes together in and outside the club where they are holding hands and looking like lovers, yet it's not clear how they are able to carry on so openly without Hanussen's finding out. The tension of the love triangle is never carried out; if it had been so more

explicitly, the rivalry between Zishe and Hanussen could have been much more compelling.

Similarly, when Zishe reveals he is Jewish, one might expect more repercussions. Instead, Hanussen revels in the commercial possibilities of Zishe as a Jewish icon, and he has another, secret reason for indulging his new star—one which is not that hard to guess and which is the film's only surprise.

Herzog is brilliant in staging the scenes at the night club, shifting perspective from backstage to onstage to the audience, showing how masterful Hanussen is in controlling the show and manipulating the Nazis at the club. The mixture of Hanussen's probing of the occult, the dark side of the human psyche, and the knowledge of what is about to unfold historically is fascinating. As usual, however, Herzog is almost too worshipful of the historical material, as if the oddity of the story itself is enough to carry the film. Written by Herzog himself, a German transplanted to Hollywood, the English dialogue is often stilted and clumsy, and there are many missed opportunities for smoother plot connections; the film lurches from one haunting scene to the next, like a jumbled nightmare.

Essentially, *Invincible* is an extended meditation on the different forms of human power and strength. Zishe's physical prowess is contrasted with Benjamin's mental acuity, with Hanussen's shrewdness, and with Marta's artistic talent—she dreams of being a great concert pianist. Zishe's straightforward and courageous embrace of his heritage stands opposed to Hanussen's cunning and hypocrisy. The Nazis' insatiable need to be courted and stroked, their hunger for power, is inferior to Ziske's purity of heart, body, and mind.

All this makes for fascinating material, even if Herzog stumbles frequently along the way. His worst mistake is dragging out a tragic ending that occurs after Hanussen has been eliminated from the picture. But even that error provides another level of irony to a story that is loaded with irony: the hero adopted belatedly by the Jewish people becomes a Cassandra whose warnings of imminent doom are ignored, and the legendary "invincible" man himself can be felled by physical weakness and the indifference of his followers.

As he often does, Herzog uses non-actors in key roles, and the film suffers because of it. Gourari, a concert pianist, is wooden and looks confused, and, strangely enough, her least convincing bit of acting comes when she is playing the piano: she looks like she is trying to look like an actress trying to capture the emotion of concert performance. Ahola, who is a Finnish weightlifting champion, is also problematic. Though he has an appealing, boyish, fresh, and honest face, he doesn't have the acting skills to make his character compelling. His reactions and lines are all of a piece, and his performance is a cheery monotone.

Standing out especially strongly against these two co-stars is Roth, a gifted actor whose portrayal of Hanussen is chilling and brilliant. Roth makes Hanussen into a devilish, calculating, and commanding impresario—a brooding, mindful, corrupt character who, despite all these traits, is almost sympathetic. Roth wisely resists the temptations to overact that are almost inherent in Herzog's melodramatic style. He stays focused and low-key, and his lines are delivered with stunning power and precision.

As the club's master of ceremonies, Max Raabe is also fascinating in a small role. He perfectly captures the mannered command of a host of the era, helping spin a wondrous air of authenticity to the club scenes, which are by far the movie's strongest ones. Herzog, to his credit, refuses to lapse into sentimentality or judgmentalism, letting the story speak for itself and indulging himself in one cryptic dream sequence which may leave some viewers scratching their heads and others feeling moved by the subtle invocation of terrors to come.

With the audience fully aware of what is about to be unleashed, and Hanussen's club brimming with the barely held-in-check energy of the young Nazi soldiers, Herzog doesn't need to moralize or comment. The film, like the nightclub, is a stage for spellbinding and storytelling, for necessary and egregious illusions. *Invincible*'s greatest strength is the illuminating light it shines on the human soul and psyche and on the many varieties and possibilities of human power and perversion.

—*Michael Betzold*

CREDITS

Hanussen: Tim Roth
Zishe Breitbart: Jouko Ahola
Marta Farra: Anna Gourari
Master of Ceremonies: Max Raabe
Count Helldorf: Udo Kier
Benjamin: Jacob Wein
Alfred Landwehr: Gustav Peter Wohler

Origin: Great Britain, Germany
Released: 2001
Production: Werner Herzog, Gary Bart, Christine Ruppert; Little Bird, FilmFour, Tatfilm; released by Fine Line Features
Directed by: Werner Herzog
Written by: Werner Herzog
Cinematography by: Peter Zeitlinger
Music by: Hans Zimmer, Klaus Badelt
Sound: Simon Willis
Editing: Joe Bini
Costumes: Jany Temime

Production Design: Ulrich Bergfelder
MPAA rating: PG-13
Running time: 135 minutes

REVIEWS

Chicago Sun-Times Online. October 4, 2002.
Entertainment Weekly. October 11, 2002, p. 55.
Los Angeles Times Online. September 20, 2002.
New York Times Online. September 20, 2002.
Sight and Sound. April, 2002, p. 38.
Variety. September 24, 2001, p. 28.

QUOTES

Hanussen (Tim Roth) to strongman Zishe (Jouka Ahola): "We will Aryanize you. A Jew should never be as strong as you."

TRIVIA

The character of Hanussen was also played by Klaus Maria Brandauer in Istvan Szabo's 1988 film *Hanussen*.

Jason X

Evil Gets An Upgrade!
—Movie tagline

He's been drowned, chainsawed, knifed, axed, hammered, shocked, burned, spiked, nailed, shot and frozen. Now he's back for more.
—Movie tagline

 Box Office: $12.6 million

Few things are as inevitable as the return of Jason Voorhees, the apparently indestructible killing machine from the *Friday the 13th* series of slasher-films. While *Jason X*, the tenth installment in the franchise (and the first since 1993's *Jason Goes to Hell: The Final Friday*), tries to improve on a tired formula with a clever premise and by borrowing from a host of far superior films, it ultimately fails by settling for the same storyline of the nine films before it. In the end, *Jason X* is a supremely squandered opportunity.

While it is a bit more intelligent than the sequels preceding it, it is not clever enough to provide any real spark of life to this long dead franchise.

Finally captured, Jason Voorhees (Kane Hodder, revisiting the role for the fourth time) is being prepped for cryostasis at the Crystal Lake Laboratory. It would seem that the powers that be have finally figured out that there was no way to actually kill Jason, so that he would actually stay that way. Unfortunately, the physician in charge of Jason's incarceration, Rowan (Lexa Doig), is overruled by a colleague, Dr. Wimmer (director David Cronenberg in a very brief appearance), who believes Jason's regenerative abilities are worth studying and that he should be analyzed and not frozen. Predictably, the prisoner transfer goes awry, giving Jason the chance to escape and kill everyone in the lab except, of course, for Rowan, who manages to trap Jason (and herself) in the cryostasis chamber where they are both frozen for over 400 years at which time they are found by a group of students on a "field trip" to the now uninhabitable Earth. The students then take Rowan and Jason to their spaceship, thaw them out and all hell breaks loose.

While the setup of Todd Farmer's script is clever and somewhat amusing, the rest of the story is little more than, as Roger Ebert put it in the *Chicago Sun-Times,* "a low-rent retread of the *Alien* pictures." While plenty of films have successfully "borrowed" from plenty of other films, *Jason X* lifts the entire premise of marines hunting the monster, one woman against the monster, and benevolent android against the monster directly from *Aliens.* While director Jim Isaac does an adequate job of laying out the proceedings, the inevitability of it all is the biggest problem that the movie has to overcome. The non-marine characters are gathered in a central location, the marines are picked off one by one, and then the students are taken down systematically. Then Jason is stopped only to come back as uber-Jason, it's all just a predictable mess.

It's not that it's impossible to watch. It's actually the freshest entry in the *Friday the 13th* series to date (a dubious honor). The problem is that, after the killing begins, as Owen Gleiberman wrote in *Entertainment Weekly,* "it's clear that this is the same old Jason Voorhees, with the same old singed flesh peeking out the back of the same old goalie mask, going on a mad-slasher rampage that's destined to put audiences in the same old stupor." It's as if the filmmakers were beaten down by the ghost of the nine earlier films and opted to merely give the same old stories a new location.

There is one sublime moment, approximately 65 minutes into the film, wherein Jason Voorhees is duped via a virtual reality program into believing he is back at Camp Crystal Lake in the late-20th century and not on a space ship in the year 2455. Jason is then accosted by two teenage girls who wistfully declare their love of drugs, alcohol, and premarital sex. They disrobe and frolic with each other in sleeping bags encouraging Jason to join them. Jason quickly dispatches them in an excruciatingly hilarious manner. The scene is fantastic. It's nostalgic and brilliantly self-satirizing. Unfortunately, it is the only part of the movie that succeeds on this or any level.

Ever since its inception, *Friday the 13th* has been looked at, according to Andrew O'Hehir on *Salon.com,* as "the unloved stepchild of the horror genre." This is due mostly to the lack of original storytelling or character development in any of the entries in the series. The sole purpose of the films is to show how many different ways Jason can dispatch of his victims. While that might be what enables these films to make back the money it takes to make them, it is also what keeps them from gaining a larger audience. The filmmakers responsible for *Jason X* seemed to be aware of this problem and it would appear that they tried to up the stakes a bit by initially trying to make the film appeal to a broader audience. Sadly, they just didn't go far enough. What they made was a film that can only appeal to the most fanatical of *Friday the 13th* fans.

There used to be a sort of gleeful pleasure involved in watching Jason dispatch misbehaving teenagers, a sort of communal cleansing of sorts. More appropriately, the *Friday the 13th* films were, as Owen Gleiberman describes them, "soft-core teensploitation." Similarly, while the "magical simplicity of Jason's character," as Andrew O'Hehir observes, "makes him a little boring, it's still the secret of his longevity: He doesn't want to sing or dance, or take off the mask and cry with Katie Couric. He just wants to punish you for that thing you did with you-know-who out at that place." *Jason X* does away with both of these notions, or perhaps they were gone a long time before *Jason X* ever made it to theatres.

The film is ultimately a wasted opportunity in the sense that it could have re-imagined Jason Voorhees as a viable horror monster instead of merely updating the old formula. Not that the filmmakers had to embrace the already staid formula of the *Scream* films but they might have perhaps gone the self-referential route of say *Wes Craven's New Nightmare* to give Jason some much needed zest.

—Michael J. Tyrkus

CREDITS

Rowan: Lexa Doig
KAY-EM 14: Lisa Ryder
Jason Voorhees: Kane Hodder
Professor Lowe: Jonathan Potts
Tsunaron: Chuck Campbell
Sgt. Brodski: Peter Mensah
Janessa: Melyssa Ade
Kinsa: Melody Johnson
Azrael: Dov Tiefenbach

Dr. Wimmer: David Cronenberg
Waylander: Derwin Jordan

Origin: USA
Released: 2001
Production: Noel J. Cunningham; released by New Line Cinema
Directed by: James Isaac
Written by: Todd Farmer
Cinematography by: Derick Underschultz
Music by: Harry Manfredini
Sound: Bruce Carwardine
Editing: David Handman
Art Direction: James Oswald
Costumes: Maxyne Baker
Production Design: John Dondertman
MPAA rating: R
Running time: 93 minutes

REVIEWS

Chicago Sun-Times Online. April 26, 2002.
Entertainment Weekly. May 3, 2002, p. 61.
New York Times Online. April 26, 2002.
USA Today Online. April 26, 2002.
Variety. April 29, 2002, p. 24.
Washington Post. April 26, 2002, p. WE45.

QUOTES

Janessa (Melyssa Ade) as she is sucked into space: "This sucks on so many levels."

TRIVIA

Lexa Doig and Lisa Ryder are costars on the syndicated sci fi TV series *Gene Rodenberry's Andromeda.*

John Q

Give a father no options and you leave him no choice.
—Movie tagline

Box Office: $71 million

John Q. is a hot-button message movie that wears its heart on its sleeve and is designed to disturb viewers. It is a domestic melodrama starring Denzel Washington as John Quincy Archibald, a factory worker whose son, Mikey (Daniel E. Smith), collapses one afternoon while he is playing baseball and attempting to steal second base. He is taken to the ironically named Hope General Hospital, where Dr. Turner (James Woods), a high-powered cardiologist, diagnoses him as having an enlarged heart. The boy needs a heart transplant that will cost at least $250,000. The father and mother, Denise (Kimberly Elise), believe they are insured and that the insurance will cover their son's operation, but hospital administrator Rebecca Payne (Anne Heche) informs them that they are wrong.

The picture demonizes the managerial class and idealizes the working class, to make this point, as articulated by *USA Today*: "If you're privileged, you'll get the medical help you need, but that's not the case for the common man." The point is surely worth making, but the delivery is rather ham-fisted. One reviewer described it as "feel-bad filmmaking at its best," adding that "despite all its flaws, it is highly effective entertainment." Todd McCarthy's *Variety* review speculated that this New Line "button-presser" had "a chance of becoming a fluke hit if its topical charge happens to strike the public in just the right way."

The company John works for has transferred health care to an H.M.O. that has imposed limits. The economy is not good, and John is only able to work half time, dropping his salary to $18,000 per year. Denise works as a clerk in a supermarket, so her earnings are marginal. Friends at their church take up collections to help pay for the operation, but not enough money can be raised. When they go to state agencies to find additional funding, they are told that they would have a better chance if they were on welfare. The situation is grim. Health care these days is a highly politicized emotional issue, and the film makes a valiant effort to dramatize it effectively. It helps, of course, to have such a likable actor as Denzel Washington on board as the frustrated father.

When the hospital decides that Mikey will be released and sent home to die, Denise tells her husband that he will have to do something to help their son. At his wit's end, John goes to the hospital armed and takes hostages at the emergency ward. This desperate action sets up the drama that drives the plot. One of the hostages is Dr. Turner, who has the skill to save the boy's life, but there is no donor in sight, although the film begins by showing an auto accident that kills a woman who has the right blood type for the transplant. This is the mechanism that could bring about a happy ending for the boy, but there are many complications standing in the way.

The police are summoned and hostage negotiator Lt. Frank Grimes (Robert Duvall) soon arrives at the hospital. His authority is undercut, however, by grandstanding Police

Chief Monroe (Ray Liotta), who attempts to take charge and sends a sniper into the hospital, putting the lives of the hostages at risk. A local television reporter is also on the scene, and his technicians are able to tap into the hospital's television surveillance system, so the public knows the details of the negotiation and witnesses the failed assassination attempt. That the Police Chief is not operating in good faith therefore becomes a matter of public knowledge and outrage.

John Q. has a pistol, but, amazingly, it is not loaded, since he does not really intend to use it against the hostages. His last desperate move is to offer his own life in order to save his son. He intends to shoot himself and wants Dr. Turner to transplant his own heart for his son. Dr. Turner at first does not agree to this on ethical grounds, but finally is persuaded to do the operation. The hostages are on the side of the terrorist, and so are the people waiting outside the hospital. But the cold-hearted administrator, Rebecca Payne, has a change of heart, so to speak, and assigns the donated heart from the accident to the boy. Mikey is rushed to the operating room. One of the hostages, a black man, pretends to be arrested and is spirited away by the police chief, so that the father can stay on the scene until the heart transplant is successfully accomplished.

Finally, actions must have consequences, so John Q. must be brought to trial. A sympathetic jury finds him "not guilty" of all charges, of course, except for taking hostages. Not even this highly contrived screenplay (written by playwright James Kearns in 1993) can dodge that issue, since the father is clearly guilty, but the film ends with the implication that John Q. will only serve minimal time for what he has done. By the time the trial is over, Mikey is on the mend and has been released from the hospital to say goodbye to his father as John Q. is taken away.

The film was directed by Nick Cassavetes, the son of the late, great film director John Cassavetes and his wife, the actress Gena Rowlands. According to Sharon Waxman of the *Washington Post,* the film had personal resonance for Nick Cassavetes, whose 14-year-old daughter has conjunctive heart disease and has undergone four heart operations and is herself in need of a replacement heart. His main motive for making the film was to draw attention to the need for health care reform. In attempting to deal sympathetically with this highly emotional situation, the film is distinguished by an exceptionally gifted cast, but the screenplay, by James Kearns, falls short of being entirely convincing. "Do movies like this ever really raise political consciousness?" the Baltimore Sun critic wondered. Other, earlier hostage movies set an impressively high standard, notably *Dog Day Afternoon* (directed by Sidney Lumet in 1975) and *Mad City* (directed by Constantin Costa-Gavras in 1997), but both of these better films were released before the current paranoia over terrorism that followed the events of September 11, 2001.

If, in Israel, Stephen Hunter wrote in his *Washington Post* review, "a man goes to a busy emergency room, pulls a gun, takes the place over and demands policy changes or he'll start killing hostages," he would be considered a terrorist, but, in the United States, "according to the grotesquely inverted moral compass of *John Q.,* he is considered a hero." Hunter dismissed the film as being "as crass and manipulative as a Stalin-era poster." In the *Baltimore Sun* Michael Sragow criticized the way the movie "shamelessly constructs a worst-case scenario that will trigger rage in anyone who's paid out-of-pocket for a medical catastrophe."

Claudia Puig's more positive *USA Today* review, however, was more forgiving of "the movie's missteps and melodramatic moments in the greater interest of the strong statement it makes about our health care system." Even *New Yorker* reviewer David Denby, who described it as "a trashy, opportunistic piece of pop demagoguery" and hated the way it "justifies hostage-taking," conceded that, "as awful as *John Q.* is, the picture does touch a nerve." Denby, who speculated that both James Kearns and Nick Cassavetes "may be consciously working below their level," going for the gut rather than for the mind, found it "both curious and terrifying that liberal filmmakers would consider intelligence itself a political liability."

The performance by Denzel Washington cannot be faulted, however. As Michael O'Sullivan wrote in his *Washington Post Weekend* review, "Denzel Washington is so good I would pay to watch him think. He's so good I would even sit through a two-hour infomercial, starring him, on the subject of the flaws of the American health care system," for that "is exactly what *John Q.* is." Washington is an American Everyman in this film. The "John Q." of the title surely represents "John Q. Public," a good, loving father and a hard worker screwed over and humiliated by a heartless bureaucracy. His motives are beyond question, but the coincidences of the plot are overly contrived and ultimately unconvincing. In the emergency ward, for example, John Q. easily wins the hostages over to his side, all but one, who happens to abuse women and is made out to be a total jerk.

Ray Liotta's Chief of Police Monroe is a stereotyped sleazy politician, interested only in his own political survival. The television reporter who is ringmaster of the media circus is an even more transparent stereotype. But if viewers can get beyond the absurdity of the propagandistic plot, the performances of Denzel Washington and Robert Duvall's "steely but sympathetic police negotiator" certainly have merit and impact. Even though the film opened to lackluster reviews, by mid-March it had grossed $59 million, outperforming several of the major Oscar nominated films of 2001, notably *Gosford Park* ($33 million), *In the Bedroom* ($30 million), and *Monster's Ball* ($15 million), not bad for a film Owen Gleiberman of *Entertainment Weekly* dismissed as "a shrill, didactic cartoon."

—*James M. Welsh*

John Q. Archibald: Denzel Washington
Lt. Frank Grimes: Robert Duvall
Dr. Turner: James Woods
Rebecca Payne: Anne Heche
Lester: Eddie Griffin
Denise Archibald: Kimberly Elise
Mitch: Shawn Hatosy
Police Chief Monroe: Ray Liotta
Mike Archibald: Daniel E. Smith
Jimmy Palumbo: David Thornton
Max: Ethan Suplee
Steve Maguire: Kevin Connolly
Tuck Lampley: Paul Johansson
Miriam: Troy Beyer
Sgt. Moody: Obba Babatunde
Gina Palumbo: Laura Harring

Origin: USA
Released: 2002
Production: Mark Burg, Oren Koules; released by New Line Cinema
Directed by: Nick Cassavetes
Written by: James Kearns
Cinematography by: Rogier Stoffers
Music by: Aaron Zigman
Sound: David Lee
Editing: Dede Allen
Art Direction: Thomas Carnegie, Elis Lam
Costumes: Beatrix Aruna Pazster
Production Design: Stefania Cella
MPAA rating: PG-13
Running time: 118 minutes

 REVIEWS

Baltimore Sun. February 15, 2002, p. E1.
Chicago Sun-Times Online. February 15, 2002.
Entertainment Weekly. March 1, 2002, p. 42.
Los Angeles Times Online. February 15, 2002.
New York Times Online. February 15, 2002, p. B19.
New Yorker. March 4, 2002, p. 90.
People. March 4, 2002, p. 32.
USA Today. February 15, 2002, p. B13.
Variety. February 11, 2002, p. 41.
Washington Post. February 15, 2002, p. C1.
Washington Post Weekend. February 15, 2002, p. 45.

John Q. Archibald (Denzel Washington): "When people are sick, they deserve a little help."

Just a Kiss

Every kiss has a story.
—Movie tagline
Love and Learn.
—Movie tagline

Just a Kiss is more like *Seinfeld* than the spin-offs from *Seinfeld* alums Julia Louis-Dreyfus, Jason Alexander, and Michael Richards. It has bizarre coincidences, convoluted plotting and over-the-top consequences for minor social infractions. For example, one character in *Just a Kiss* uses a cell phone on a plane. He is warned that it will interfere with the plane's computer equipment, but he uses it anyway. His mistake causes the plane to crash to the ground, killing everyone on board, except for him and the others in first class. It is definitely a George Costanza kind of move.

Just a Kiss is also like the charming Gwyneth Paltrow film, *Sliding Doors.* Both films explore the idea of making a decision, then explore the different realities that the decision would spawn if it were decided differently. And *Just a Kiss* shares something with the inventive Richard Linklater film *Waking Life.* Both films use an animation technique called rotomation. The technique turns live action footage into animation.

Unfortunately, though *Just a Kiss* shares a lot of ideas and inspiration with these other productions, it doesn't have half the wit or cleverness that they do. Where the rotomation in *Waking Life* was groundbreaking and interesting, the animation in *Just a Kiss* is distracting, overly showy and seems sort of pointless. The animation is so bright and colorful that it make the film's regular old straightforward footage look bland and boring. In *Sliding Doors* the alternate realities that the characters explored were surprising and fun. In *Just a Kiss,* they are less involving. The events seem so ridiculous that they don't seem real. For this technique to work, the realities have to be engaging and believable. Here, one reality seems just as fake as another so it's hard to care about either of them.

The crazy coincidences in *Seinfeld* always had a certain Rube Goldberg-esque charm to the way they were constructed. They were usually absurd but somewhere in there, they were held together by a beautiful logic. In *Just a Kiss,* the coincidences don't have that same grace. They seem to be put in the film less for the amusement of the audience than for the convenience of the screenwriter Patrick Breen.

For example, one of the characters has an affair with a woman who just happens to be married to a man who's sleeping with the first guy's girlfriend. The various love (or sex) match-ups between the few characters in *Just a Kiss* would give even the bed-hopping characters in *Melrose Place* pause. With the two different realities in *Just a Kiss* and the various mix 'n' match relationships, the film sounds more confusing than it really is. On paper it sounds like a jumble, but in the film, it's quite easy to follow.

The title refers to the main decision of the film. Dag (Ron Eldard) is a director of commercials and seems to be quite pleased with himself. He lives with his lovely girlfriend, Halley (Kyra Sedgwick), who makes "personal biography" videos of her clients lives. While traveling in Europe, Dag goes to see a dance performance by Rebecca (Marley Shelton). Rebecca is a talented dancer but she's driven ceaselessly by her demanding choreographer mother, Jessica (Zoe Caldwell). Rebecca is a delicate girl who is interested in committing suicide. When she's not walking around in dazed depression, Rebecca tends to sleep around on her boyfriend, Peter (Breen). Peter is a nice guy who acts in commercials. He's a minor celebrity because he appeared as the Peanut Butter Eagle in a series of popular TV ads. He's in love with Rebecca, but she doesn't love him.

On the night that Dag comes to see her performance, the two decide to go to bed together. "This is going to be one of those terrible mistakes that you can't take back," says Dag. "Is there any other kind?" replies Rebecca. The complication is that Peter happens to be Dag's best friend. This leads to a series of events that end badly.

Halley decides that she needs to leave Dag since his dalliance with Rebecca is just one of a string of such indiscretions. She, for dumb plot reasons, ends up staying at Rebecca's apartment, where she meets Andre (Taye Diggs). Andre is a cello teacher, who provides Halley a shoulder to lean on, and later than night, quite a bit more. Andre also happens to be married to Colleen (Sarita Choudhury). The two have an "open" marriage. Colleen meets Peter at the airport and invites him on a plane ride because she only likes to watch films in the air. She can afford such a habit because she works for the airline. This is the point where Peter uses the forbidden cell phone and crashes the plan.

Somewhere in there is Paula (Marisa Tomei), a waitress at a bowling alley. She is obsessed with Peter's peanut butter commercials and is thrilled when she sees him arguing with Dag in the alley. After Peter leaves in a huff, she starts flirting with Dag. Dag, who is as usual unable to pass up a flirting opportunity, ends up in bed with Paula. But Paula ends up being a dominatrix. After having her way with Dag, she ends up putting him in the hospital. Her ultimate plan is to get to Peter, but she has a strange way of going about it. Due to Paula's devious plans and other plot permutations, three main characters end up in the hospital and all three end

up dying. It's supposed to be absurd humor, but mostly it's just absurd.

The film then cuts back to Dag and Rebecca's affair in Europe, but this time, Dag decides to leave at "just a kiss." Will this end in less destruction and less death? At this point, it starts becoming hard to care. When someone is dead, then alive, it's hard to be interested in what's going to happen to them next. If even a consequence as serious as death is just nothing, then why should we worry about anything that happens to them? The movie also switches back to the past and how various characters met. This, like the gimmicky animation technique, just manages to obscure the plot weaknesses and doesn't add much to the mix.

Just a Kiss could have worked. It has some of the right ideas and Breen shows a willingness to put absurd humor in the film. There are some really weird jokes. When Paula is at the funeral of a character she (secretly) killed, she pretends to cross herself, but actually she's murmuring "One potato, two potato, three potato, four." There are some lines that are sort of funny, but not great. When Dag gets a call on his tiny cell phone, Halley and Peter tease him about the size. "It came with my Jet Set Barbie," Dag replies. But most of the jokes are much less clever. There are several jokes involving people mishearing Dag's name as "Dog." (For the record, he was named for former U.N. Secretary-General Dag Hammarskjold.)

Just a Kiss premiered at the Seattle International Film Festival and got a limited release a few months later. The film's not funny or entertaining enough to get that final push to wider release and will probably soon only be found on the shelves of very well-stocked video stores. Critics mostly didn't care for the film. Kenneth Turan of the *Los Angeles Times* wrote, "As a stage and screen veteran, Breen knows how to write the kind of slick, pleased-with-itself dialogue that performers can attack with relish. And Stevens (actor Fisher Stevens) directs in a noticeably actor-friendly way. But though the cast ends up looking good, the film's unwillingness or inability to have things add up hurts everyone's efforts." Stephen Holden of the *New York Times* wrote that the film "only half-succeeds in making its surreal game of mixed doubles transcend soap-opera spoof. After a while the endless complaining begins to wear thin, and the more surreal the story becomes, the more it pulls away from the characters, who seem more and more like pieces in a board game."

—*Jill Hamilton*

CREDITS

Dag: Ron Eldard
Halley: Kyra Sedgwick
Peter: Patrick Breen

Paula: Marisa Tomei
Rebecca: Marley Shelton
Andre: Taye Diggs
Colleen: Sarita Choudhury
Jessica: Zoe Caldwell

Origin: USA
Released: 2002
Production: Matthew Rowland; Greenstreet; released by Paramount Classics
Directed by: Fisher Stevens
Written by: Patrick Breen
Cinematography by: Terry Stacey
Music by: Sean Dinsmore
Sound: Ira Spiegel
Music Supervisor: Dan Lieberstein
Editing: Gary Levy
Art Direction: Mario R. Ventenilla
Costumes: Arjun Bhasin
Production Design: Happy Massee
MPAA rating: R
Running time: 89 minutes

REVIEWS

Boxoffice. September, 2002, p. 150.
Los Angeles Times Online. September 27, 2002.
New York Times Online. September 27, 2002.
Variety Online. June 24, 2002, p. 27.
Washington Post. October 4, 2002, p. WE41.

QUOTES

Dag (Ron Eldard): "This is going to be one of those terrible mistakes you can't take back." Rebecca (Marley Shelton): "Is there any other kind?"

Juwanna Mann

The only way he can stay pro, is to play (like) a girl.
—Movie tagline

As a woman, he got game.
—Movie tagline

Box Office: $13.6 million

I t's hard to believe it, but there have been enough cross-dressing films that there's now a genre, with its own customs and conventions. *Juwanna Mann* takes the rules of the genre too seriously. Instead of working with the usual elements of this kind of film to create a lively new story, writer Bradley Allenstein seems to think that the idea is to trot out the usual plot points and be done with it. *Juwanna Mann* brings nothing new to the screen—it's difficult to see why it was even made. The humor in it is some distant descendent of *Some Like It Hot,* but it's not nearly as sharp as that. It's more directly related to the recent *Sorority Boys,* another tiresome cross-dressing film with rehashed jokes and the same old situations.

Jamal Jeffries (Miguel A. Nunez Jr.) is a cocky basketball player for the fictional Charlotte Beat. He's an outrageous Dennis Rodman type of character who's constantly getting in trouble with the team owner for his disrespectful antics. He cheats on his girlfriend, insults fellow players and signs autographs for young fans using a rubber stamp. His career in the league ends abruptly after one game when he strips down to nothing and does a naked dance for the shocked fans. Even though Jamal is a great player, the powers that be in the league decide that he's not worth the trouble.

Jamal isn't too worried, after all, he's the famous Jamal Jeffries, surely he'll be able to get back in with a little sweet-talking. His agent, Lorne Daniels (Kevin Pollack), arranges a meeting with the league bigwigs, but Jamal doesn't take it seriously and ruins any chance he has of getting his old job back. As Jamal's career prospects dim, his life falls apart. His gold-digging girlfriend (Lil' Kim) leaves him, his house and his things are repossessed and he has to move back in with his stereotypically sassy Aunt Ruby, (Jennifer Lewis). He's even taunted by some neighborhood kids. But one of those kids happens to be a girl basketball player who's really good. It gives Jamal an idea . . .

Jamal decides that he will enter the WUBA, the women's basketball league. He puts on a wig and some lipstick and names himself Juwanna Mann. In a typically lame joke, he decides upon Juwanna after overhearing somebody say "Do ya wanna pizza?" (Note to filmmakers: this joke is officially old. Please write that down.) One of the main problems with this film is that Juwanna and Jamal look an awful lot alike. For this kind of film to work, the character should undergo some sort of transformation. Even Dustin Hoffman and Robin Williams could get it together enough to look like *Tootsie* and *Mrs. Doubtfire.* Surely, Nunez, who already looks somewhat feminine could have been made to look more like a woman. Nunez also adopts a strange sort of Southern accent, ala *Tootsie.* Is it feminine to have a Southern accent?

Once in the women's league, playing for the fictional Charlotte Banshees, Juwanna Mann starts putting his team in contention for the championship. The team's games start getting televised and Juwanna, as one of the starters, gets a lot of screen time. Doesn't it seem like at least one WUBA fan would recognize Juwanna? Doesn't it seem like even one of his fellow teammates would have a passing knowledge of famous men's players? After all, his "disguise" during games consists of the wig, the make-up and some fake cleavage. That's it. And Jamal Jeffries is the most notorious player in basketball. The whole thing becomes even more ridiculous at the end when Juwanna's wig accidentally gets bumped from her head. (Oops, sorry to ruin it for you. And you were just going to run out and rent it, too.) The entire crowd immediately recognizes Juwanna as Jamal. I mean, this wig is okay, but it's certainly not enough to change a person's entire identity.

But before the grand unwigging, there's more hackneyed plot to wade through. Juwanna takes a liking to his feisty teammate, Michelle Langford (Vivica A. Fox, who is a woman who needs a new agent). The two fight and then become best friends. As it must happen in these sorts of films, Michelle unknowingly fuels Jamal's passions by doing things like innocently showering in front of Juwanna. In one scene, she coos to Juwanna, "Oooh, my muscles are soooo sore. Could you massage them?" In films written by men, when female characters are alone, they often spend their time giving each other late night massages. In actuality, when women are alone, they are much more apt to discuss food.

Michelle is dating Romeo (Genuwine), a famous singer who croons while holding a rose. He cheats on Michelle, but she doesn't know it. This makes Jamal mad, but Romeo is messing up Jamal's life another way too. He sets him up with his rapper friend, Puff Smokey Smoke (Tommy Davidson). Puff is an undesirable, gold-toothed pursuer who thinks that Juwanna is the sassy woman of his dreams. Predictably, Jamal becomes a better man by being a woman (see *Tootsie*, again), learns to become more humble and gets the girl. He even gives a big sappy speech. As Rob Blackwelder of *Spliced Wire* put it, Jamal inevitably has to "give the girl a bunch of roses and wait for her to forgive him like all stupid movie women do at the end of men-centric comedies."

There are too many problems in this script that require a lot more than the usual suspension of disbelief. There are big things, like the whole-no-one-recognizes-Juwanna problem, and little ones, like the fact that Jamal, a supersized basketball player happens to wear the same sized clothes as his Aunt Ruby, an average-sized woman. In an early scene, Lorne makes a big point of telling Juwanna that he shouldn't dunk in the woman's league, since dunking is not allowed. But later, Juwanna scores the winning point with a big old, slow-motion dunk. And after Juwanna is exposed as being Jamal, his team goes on to play in the finals. Shouldn't they have suffered some sort of penalty for playing the season with a man on their team?

And it's not like the humor in the film is so good that you can overlook the plot problems. When Lorne tells Jamal that he is going to have to go into Chapter 11 bankruptcy, Jamal says, "Chapter 11? What happened to the first ten chapters?" It's not exactly the sparkling banter of *The Thin Man*. When Jamal forces Lorne to represent him as Juwanna, Lorne protests, "But this is blackmail!" "No," retorts Jamal, "this is black FE-male!" Someone (who shall remain nameless to protect the guilty) got paid to write jokes like that.

Critics weren't fans of the film, though a small percentage did offer it some tepid praise. Jeffrey M. Anderson of the *San Francisco Examiner* wrote, "If it wasn't so tame and boring, *Juwanna Mann* might have been the *Booty Call* of 2002, living on in bad-movie infamy. Instead, it's destined to evaporate from everyone's memory as quickly as it arrived." Jonathan Foreman of the *New York Post* wrote, "It's all so insincere, you can almost imagine the filmmakers rubbing their hands together at the prospect of ripping off the public." David Germain of the *Associated Press* wrote that "the movie is sloppily edited, the gags limply staged, the dialogue and jokes stiff and stale." A.O. Scott of the *New York Times* was one of the kinder critics. Scott wrote that it is "a sloppy, amusing comedy that proceeds from a stunningly unoriginal premise."

—*Jill Hamilton*

CREDITS

Jamal Jeffries/Juwanna Mann: Miguel A. Nunez Jr.
Michelle Langford: Vivica A. Fox
Lorne Daniels: Kevin Pollak
Puff Smokey Smoke: Tommy Davidson
Latisha Jansen: Kim Wayans
Aunt Ruby: Jenifer Lewis
Tina Parker: Kimberly (Lil' Kim) Jones
Coach Rivers: Annie Corley
Romeo: Ginuwine

Origin: USA
Released: 2002
Production: James G. Robinson, Steve Oedekerk; Morgan Creek Productions; released by Warner Bros.
Directed by: Jesse Vaughan
Written by: Bradley Allenstein
Cinematography by: Reynaldo Villalobos
Music by: Wendy Melvoin, Lisa Coleman
Sound: Carl Rudisill
Music Supervisor: Maureen Crowe
Editing: Seth Flaum
Art Direction: Jennifer O'Kelly
Costumes: Peggy Farrell

Production Design: Eve Cauley Turner
MPAA rating: PG-13
Running time: 91 minutes

REVIEWS

Chicago Sun-Times Online. June 21, 2002.
Entertainment Weekly. July 12, 2002, p. 56.
Los Angeles Times Online. June 21, 2002.
New York Times Online. June 21, 2002.
Variety. June 24, 2002, p. 26.
Washington Post Online. June 21, 2002, p. WE45.

QUOTES

Puff Smokey Smoke (Tommy Davidson) to Juwanna Mann (Miguel A. Nunez, Jr.): "Girl, you are one tall glass of water, and I'm tellin' you straight up, I'm thirsty!"

K-19: The Widowmaker

Fate Has Found Its Hero.
—Movie tagline

Box Office: $35.1 million

Director Kathryn Bigelow's *K-19: The Widowmaker* featured Harrison Ford as a Russian submarine commander, but it's not the kind of heroic role one might expect Ford to play in the summer market. Ford played Captain Alexei Vostrikov, commander of the K-19, an ill-fated Soviet nuclear submarine. Purporting to be a "true" story, the film plays upon somewhat clichéd Cold War tensions, fabricating an "incident" that, presumably, might have led to a nuclear exchange between the Soviet Union and the United States. Ford's submarine commander plays the crisis close to the chest and by-the-book, and as a result faces a possible mutiny. Although ultimately "right" in his stance, he is distant and aloof, not exactly loved by his men. "It was critical to me to get the audience to understand this was no typical Harrison Ford summer fodder," the actor told the *Washington Post.* But the picture was a summer release, likely, therefore, to disappoint Ford's fans.

The ship was considered cursed from the start, which explains the "Widowmaker" nickname. Nine shipyard workers died while the vessel was being retrofitted for nuclear power. The ship's doctor was killed in a traffic accident when the launch was being prepared. Even the champagne bottle refused to break the day the ship was launched. Crew members later called the jinxed ship the "Hiroshima," after it sails out of the gloomy harbor at Murmansk. Bigelow had reason to worry about whether that jinx would carry over to her film. The film was both a stretch and a risk for both the director and the principal actor.

The film's backstory is unusual and related to the new image of the time-honored National Geographic Society, which in 2003 released the first swimsuit issue of its magazine to help change the magazine's somewhat stogy and educational image. According to the Society's president John Fahey, past president Alexander Graham Bell "urged the Society to use all popular means to fulfill its mission for the dissemination of knowledge to the widest audience possible." The first move was towards National Geographic television, which reaches an audience of 40 million viewers, a number equivalent to the readership of the magazine. Film production was the next logical step for National Geographic Ventures, the Society's profitmaking subsidiary.

According to Ken Ringle in the *Washington Post,* the feature film was a "dramatization of a true story" originally broadcast on the *National Geographic Explorer* television series. However, "dramatic liberties" were taken in the way the story was dramatized. In reality the submarine was under the command of Captin Nikolai Zateyev when the nuclear accident occurred on June 4, 1961. This was caused by a bursting pipe that flooded part of the ship with radioactive coolant, contaminating the sailors who had to make repairs in the lethal reactor room. "For 30 years," Ringle reported, "the survivors were sworn to secrecy by the Soviet regime." But when the Russians saw the script, they objected to its distortions of the Cold War era as being a "desecration of the memory of the real defenders of our Homeland who died in that tragedy." Irina Zateyev, the daughter of the Captain of the K-19, said in Moscow that the picture is not about her father: "This film is about Harrison Ford."

Of course, history was distorted by the dramatization, but Tim Kelly, chief of the Society's Television and Film division put a cheerful spin on that potential problem: "The way I look at it," he said, confidently, while marginalizing truth and accuracy, "these are all just forms of storytelling." That should have given him pause, since he admitted later that "a great portion of the American public gets its knowledge from feature films," which he positively embraced as "the supercharged Ferarri of storytelling," adding, in a wonderfully mixed metaphor, that the Ferarri was capable of engraving "a story on your brain." Did President Woodrow Wilson really think writing history "with lightning" was a good idea?

As the feature film begins, Mikhail Polenin (Liam Neeson) is in command of the untested submarine, soon to be replaced by Captain Vostrikov (Ford), though Polenin, whom the sailors adore, remains aboard, so that those who distrust Vostrikov can rally around him. Neither officer believes that the ship is seaworthy, but they are both overruled by Marshal Zelentstov (Joss Ackland) and ordered out into the Atlantic. The year must be 1961, since that was when the real K-19 was launched. The submarine has problems from the outset, smaller problems that turn into larger ones, until, finally, the submarine's nuclear reactor threatens to explode after a meltdown is discovered. In that event the 1.4 megaton explosion "most likely" would have provoked an American counterattack (though how this follows as a certainty is dubious), starting World War III.

The day is saved for Western civilization when eight Russian sailors volunteer to go into the radiation chamber and rig a cooling system to avert the disaster at sea. These heroes knew they would die and did die of radiation poisoning. Bigelow traveled to Russia to interview the surviving crew members. She knew she had a significant story. but she was not sure how or where to draw the dividing line between a documentary and feature-film treatment. Her solution was to invent the conflict between Captain Vostrikov and his more genial and likable subordinate, Polenin.

The release of this film was a career defining moment for director Kathryn Bigelow, whose last pictures, *Strange Days* (1995) and *The Weight of Water* (2001), were not boxoffice successes. Bigelow told Jamie Diamond of the *New York Times* she first heard of the 1961 submarine incident on which the script is based in a meeting with National Geographic, which went on to become one of the film's producers. The stakes were high for this offbeat, high-budget picture. Diamond speculated that "Ms Bigelow's future in Hollywood may rest on how well the film is received. It would take $25 million in profits to recover Harrison Ford's reported salary."

Reviews were mixed. Michael Sragow titled his *Baltimore Sun* review "Sub Standard," claiming the "Hollywood clichés dampen a true story of Cold War heroism and sacrifice aboard the Soviet nuclear submarine K-19." He speculated that perhaps the filmmakers did not know or trust "the strength of their own story." *Variety* had speculated that the film would be challenged "by Yank disinterest in Cold War history from the Soviet perspective," but Sragow dismiss this as a "non-issue." Stephen Hunter of the *Washington Post* described it as a "pretty good sub movie with some pretty good performances," but ultimately, he claimed, "*Widowmaker* sinks under its own weight." And in truth it was oppressively heavy for summer fare. Hunter claimed that in the film's last half-hour, the screenplay by Christopher Kyle "goes all nutsy-Hollywood and tries to bring in our old friend, The End of the World."

Hunter also protested that the film had essentially been made before, a notion also cited in the *Variety* review, which opened by mentioning *Das Boot* (1981), *The Bedford Incident* (1965), and *Run Silent, Run Deep* (1958). Stanley Kauffmann added *The Hunt for Red October* (1990) to this list in his *New Republic* review, remembering Sean Connery as the commander of a Soviet nuclear sub who is considering defecting to the United States. At least Connery did not try to speak with a phony Russian accent. Anthony Lane started his cynical and dismissive review by evaluating the film's "ping" potential. There is a certain way that Hollywood thinks a submarine film should sound, and this one didn't "sound" right for Lane. Stanley Kauffmann wondered why the film was made since, "The actual story of K-19, which was grim and almost became a world catastrophe, was kept secret until the collapse of communism in the Soviet Union."

Although Desson Howe claimed the film's "drama fails to surface" (keeping those nautical metaphors potent), the hard-to-please Gary Arnold of the *Washington Times* claimed *K-19* was "red hot after [a] slow start." Arnold, one of the film's strongest supporters, disliked the fumbling introductory episodes, which made it appear that the director might be "way out of her league" in attempting to imitate *Das Boot*. But for him that "ill-founded skepticism" was reversed when the picture "finally concentrates on the crisis that makes it distinctive and heartbreaking. Eventually," Arnold concluded, "it's a submarine saga like no other." Well, there certainly is some truth in that, but is it ethical to mix fact and fiction together in the interest of (profitable) historical entertainment? And is the mission of history to entertain or illuminate? Does any of this matter to the National Geographic Society?

—James M. Welsh

CREDITS

Alexei Vostrikov: Harrison Ford
Mikhail Polenin: Liam Neeson
Vadim Radtchenko: Peter Sarsgaard
Marshal Zelentstov: Joss Ackland
Admiral Bratyeev: John Shrapnel
Dr. Savran: Donald (Don) Sumpter
Partonov: Tim Woodward
Suslov: Ravil Isyanov
Pavel: Christian Camargo
Demichev: Steve Nicholson

Origin: USA
Released: 2002
Production: Joni Sighvatsson, Edward S. Feldman, Kathryn Bigelow, Christine Whitaker; Intermedia Films, Palomar Pictures International; released by Paramount Pictures
Directed by: Kathryn Bigelow
Written by: Christopher Kyle
Cinematography by: Jeff Cronenweth
Music by: Klaus Badelt

Sound: Bruce Carwardine
Editing: Walter Murch
Art Direction: T. Arrinder Grewal
Costumes: Marit Allen
Production Design: Karl Juliusson, Michael Novotny
MPAA rating: PG-13
Running time: 138 minutes

REVIEWS

Baltimore Sun. July 19, 2002, p. E1.
Chicago Sun-Times Online. July 19, 2002.
Detroit News. July 15, 2002, p. E1.
Entertainment Weekly. July 26, 2002, p. 42.
Los Angeles Times Calendar. March 4, 2001, p. 3.
Los Angeles Times Online. July 19, 2002.
New Republic. August 19, 2002, p. 24.
New York Times. May 12, 2002, p. 31.
New York Times. July 19, 2002, p. B15.
New York Times. July 21, 2002, p. 1.
New Yorker. July 29, 2002, p. 92.
People. July 29, 2002, p. 33.
USA Today Online. July 18, 2002.
Variety. July 15, 2002, p. 23.
Washington Post. July 18, 2002, p. C1.
Washington Post. July 19, 2002, p. C1.
Washington Post Weekend. July 19, 2002, p. 33.
Washington Times. July 19, 2002, p. B5.

QUOTES

Vostrikov (Harrison Ford) to Polenin (Liam Neeson) about their mission: "We deliver or we drown."

The Kid Stays in the Picture

Success Scandal Sex Tragedy Infamy. And that's just in the first reel . . .
—Movie tagline

Box Office: $1.4 million

"There are three sides to every story: my side, your side and the truth. And no one is lying. Memories shared serve each one differently," is the quote from Robert Evans that begins the documentary, *The Kid Stays in the Picture.* Filmmakers Brett Morgen and Nanette Burstein, who previously made the boxing documentary *On the Ropes,* are letting it be known up front that their documentary may not exactly be the whole truth and nothing but the truth. The thing is, the film is so entertaining that it's hard to imagine that anyone is really going to care.

The Kid Stays in the Picture is based on producer Evans' biography of the same and the subsequent audiotape version he made of it. The cassette version reportedly became a cult item due to his straight-talking, gruff and colorful narration. Evans is the kind of character who could say to a woman (or would that be a dame?), "Take my number, then I'll always be seven digits away." Other non-PC Evansisms include: "Never plan. Planning is for the poor." Or to the Italian Francis Ford Coppola about *The Godfather*: "You shot a great picture. Where is it? In the kitchen with your spaghetti?" The *New York Times* reported that the tape was a popular Christmas gift in Hollywood and that Evans imitations the order of the day. (Dustin Hoffman's character in *Wag the Dog* is reportedly based on Hoffman's own imitation of Evans. The rumor is pretty much verified in this film since it ends with Hoffman doing a foul-mouthed imitation of Evans.) The film was first conceived as a DVD that was going to be put in issues of *Vanity Fair* magazine, but when that proved too expensive an idea, it released into theaters. Lucky for viewers, though, because *The Kid Stays in the Picture* is a hoot.

What makes the movie so great is that Evans is a fascinating character, with a great story, who tells his story well. He went from New York City clothier to bit actor to bigwig producer and back down again. But what puts this film over the top is the kaleidoscopic direction by Morgen and Burstein. Their lively direction could make an instructional manual seem witty and hip and, when they have a good subject like this one, it's a dream match-up.

Even though Evans never appears in the film being interviewed except in brief shadow, he's all over the film. There are no talking head interviews and the commentary is all provided by Evans's colorful narration. Evans is an enthusiastic storyteller. When he's telling a story about trying to get Mia Farrow to stay on *Rosemary's Baby* even though Frank Sinatra wanted her off the picture, he recreates his conversations with Farrow, even imitating Farrow's voice. Morgen and Burstein combine film footage, news clippings, and photos from Evans's very extensive collection in an onslaught of clever ways. Instead of taking a still photo and panning over it slowly and endlessly, ala Ken Burns, they doctor the photo to make it look super three-dimensional and slide the images around so much they appear to be anxious to be telling part of the story themselves. A black-and-white photo of Frank Sinatra, for example, features colorized bright blue eyes that flash and sparkle. Another photo of someone smoking has a plume of real smoke floating up from the cigarette.

Evans started his Hollywood career while staying at a Beverly Hills hotel while on a business trip for his older brother Charles's clothing firm, Evan Piccone. While hanging out at the pool, he met Norma Shearer, who thought that the young and handsome Evans would be great to play her husband, Irving Thalberg, in the film version of the mogul's life. Evans got the part in the 1957 film *Man of a Thousand Faces.* The story of a regular guy being "discovered" so dramatically made Evans a popular subject for magazine profiles.

Evans wasn't that great of an actor. When he was cast as the bullfighter in *The Sun Also Rises,* Ernest Hemingway, Tyrone Power, Ava Gardner, and Eddie Albert sent producer Darryl F. Zanuck a telegram insisting that Evans be removed from the picture. According to Evans, Zanuck replied, "The kid stays in the picture and anybody who doesn't like it can quit." It was at that moment that Evans realized that he didn't want to be an actor; he wanted to be the guy who said, "The kid stays in the picture." He didn't need to worry about his acting career much longer. There are some clips of him doing some really bad acting in a horror film, *The Fiend Who Stalked the West.* The film effectively ended his acting years.

Throughout Evans's life, there has been a pattern of being in the right place at the right time, having extraordinary luck, and knowing how to take advantage of these lucky breaks. To reach his goal of becoming a Hollywood mogul, Evans decided that owning a story was the way to hold power. He bought the rights to a best-selling book, *The Detective.* Even though it was his first deal, he showed fiery bargaining instincts and ended up with quite a good deal. This attracted the attention of a writer at the *New York Times,* Peter Bart, who wrote a profile on Evans. The profile, in turn, impressed Charles Bluhdorn, the chief of Gulf & Western, who wanted Evans to work for him at the company's newly acquired movie studio, Paramount Pictures. Even though he had little experience, Evan was somewhat miraculously named the head of production.

Evans didn't waste his big chance. He kept his focus on good scripts and became the most successful producer of the 1970s. He pulled Paramount from being a minor studio in ninth place to the number one studio with films like *Love Story, The Godfather, Chinatown, Rosemary's Baby,* and *Harold and Maude.* He gave Roman Polanski and Coppola their big breaks and made loyal friends of Jack Nicholson and Henry Kissinger. In one particularly bizarre anecdote, Evans recalls how he forced Kissinger to come to one of his movie premieres, even though Kissinger was in the middle of dealing with a crisis in Vietnam.

When he wasn't producing pictures, he was romancing the ladies. In his voiceover narration, he claims that he didn't date much and stayed home a lot. Morgen and Burstein tell a different story with an onslaught of photos showing Evans over the years with various women on his arm. Although

Evans was married five times, the film only covers his most famous marriage to Ali MacGraw. He refers to her as "Miss Snotnose," but it seems obvious that she was his great love. He blames himself for the breakup of their marriage and her affair with Steve McQueen, saying that he was working too much and didn't pay proper attention to her.

Evans' later fall from glory is less interesting, possibly because Evans himself is less enamored of these particular years of his life. In the 1980's, he gets hooked on cocaine, produces some bombs like *The Cotton Club* and was associated with a tawdry murder. Even though Evans is never a suspect himself, he loses his job. After hitting bottom and ending up in a mental institution, the man ends up doing pretty well. The movie reports that Stanley Jaffe gave him a producing job, which he still holds today. Even though Evans is still recovering from a stroke he suffered in a pitch session, he continues to make movies.

Critics fell under the spell of these storytellers and gave the film good marks. Owen Gleiberman of *Entertainment Weekly* gave the film an A and called it "a candy story for film buffs." He called the direction "akin to watching a scrapbook of Evans' mind come to life; it's almost tactile in its vibrant nostalgia." Ron Wells of *Film Threat* wrote, "I'm willing to bet . . . that I don't see another picture this year as richly entertaining or as cathartic." Kevin Thomas of the *Los Angeles Times* wrote that it was a "witty, colorful and poignant account of Evans' life" and David Edelstein of *Slate* called it "a breezy hoot."

—*Jill Hamilton*

CREDITS

Narrator: Robert Evans

Origin: USA
Released: 2002
Production: Graydon Carter, Brett Morgen, Nanette Burstein; Highway Films Production, Ministry of Propaganda Films; released by USA Films
Directed by: Brett Morgen, Nanette Burstein
Written by: Brett Morgen
Cinematography by: John Bailey
Music by: Jeff Danna
Sound: Calude Letessier
Editing: Juan Diaz
MPAA rating: R
Running time: 93 minutes

REVIEWS

Boxoffice. April, 2002, p. 179.

Chicago Sun-Times Online. August 9, 2002.
Entertainment Weekly. August 2, 2002, p. 47.
Los Angeles Times Online. July 26, 2002.
New York Times Online. July 26, 2002.
New York Times Online. July 28, 2002.
People. May 5, 2002, p. 34.
USA Today Online. July 25, 2002.
Variety. January 28, 2002, p. 32.
Variety. February 25, 2002, p. 23.
Washington Post. August 9, 2002, p. WE34.

QUOTES

Robert Evans on the film: "It's not a documentary—it's perseverance."

Kissing Jessica Stein

A Funny, Smart, Fresh Look at Sex and the Single Girl.
—Movie tagline

 Box Office: $7 million

Kissing Jessica Stein is a refreshing romantic comedy with a twist—it's a witty and intelligent film that explores the topic of same-sex romance. Actors-screenwriters Jennifer Westfeldt and Heather Juergensen adapted the movie from their 1997 Off Broadway play, *Lipschtick,* which was based on their own disappointing dating experiences.

Jessica (Westfeldt) is a pretty, neurotic, Jewish woman who works as a copy editor in New York City. Disillusioned with a series of blind dates with loser guys, Jessica decides on a whim to respond to a personals ad that quotes the poet Rilke. The only catch is that the ad was placed by a woman, and Jessica is straight. Helen (Juergensen) is an attractive, bisexual, hip art gallery manager who is looking to expand her dating options. The women meet, and much to Jessica's surprise, they discover they have a lot in common. Helen and Jessica awkwardly begin a relationship, although Jessica is very skittish and insecure when it comes to sex. She shows up on their first real date with a bunch of lesbian how-to sex manuals, and proceeds so slowly that it drives Helen crazy. Just as Helen is about to call the whole thing off, Jessica finally eases into the relationship, even though she steadfastly refuses to divulge anything about her new romantic partner to family and friends.

The women's love affair reaches a crisis point when Jessica's brother is about to get married, and Jessica can't bring herself to invite Helen to the wedding. The women eventually manage to work it out, and in one touching scene, Jessica discovers her mother (expertly played by Tovah Feldshuh) is much more perceptive than she thinks.

Westfeldt and Juergensen, who are good friends (and for the record, straight) in real life, deliver credible, natural performances as the would-be lovers. They know their characters well and there's no mistaking their onscreen chemistry. In addition to the leading ladies, the supporting cast is first-rate. Besides Feldshuh as the overprotective Jewish mother, Jackie Hoffman plays Jessica's meddling, pregnant co-worker, Joan, and Scott Cohen stars as Josh, Jessica's boss and former boyfriend. Although the entire cast does a commendable job, Feldshuh easily steals the show as Jessica's doting mother, Judy.

Shot on a low budget, the film makes the most of its Manhattan locations, and it also features a good jazz score. A few critics made references to Woody Allen's *Annie Hall,* which the movie occasionally imitates, but the two comedies offer very different cinematic experiences. *Kissing Jessica Stein*'s smart script and likable characters makes for a charming and tame (sex is only hinted at verbally) girl-girl romantic comedy. However, it does have one noticeable flaw—the ending, in which the women decide to take different paths, seems incredibly abrupt. Overall though, open-minded audiences will find this alternative indie film to be worthwhile.

Although *Kissing Jessica Stein* won several awards at various film festivals around the country, critical reaction was mixed. Its detractors include Elvis Mitchell of the *New York Times,* who called the film "amusing but extremely derivative. The movie shamelessly takes the neuroses of Annie Hall and her tormented beau, Alvy Singer, melts them down and pours the secondhand brew into the troubled Jessica Stein." Lisa Schwarzbaum, writing for *Entertainment Weekly,* cited the film as being "all too content to be a comedy of surfaces and stereotypes."

On the other hand, several critics had high praise for the film. Lael Loewenstein gave the movie high marks in his review for *Variety,* "A fresh take on sex and the single girl, this buoyant, well-crafted romantic comedy blends pitch-perfect performances with deliciously smart writing." Desson Howe, of the *Washington Post,* commented on the film's witty dialogue, "This is the endearing stuff of any good romantic comedy. And that their sexual preferences aren't the usual heterosexual fare matters not a whit." *Los Angeles Times* critic Kevin Thomas wrote that the picture "has the look and feel of a smart, stylish New York romantic comedy in which the principals are articulate and forthright about their intelligence and sophistication. Yet for an American film it is a groundbreaker in exploring the realm of sexual fluidity, and it does so with wit, wisdom, and in a completely entertaining fashion."

—*Beth Fhaner*

CREDITS

Jessica Stein: Jennifer Westfeldt
Helen Cooper: Heather Juergensen
Judy Stein: Tovah Feldshuh
Josh Meyers: Scott Cohen
Joan: Jackie Hoffman
Martin: Michael Mastro
Sebastian: Carson Elrod
Dan Stein: David Aaron Baker

Origin: USA
Released: 2002
Production: Eden H. Wurmfeld, Brad Zions; Cineric Inc., Michael Alden Productions; released by Fox Searchlight
Directed by: Charles Herman-Wurmfeld
Written by: Jennifer Westfeldt, Heather Juergensen
Cinematography by: Lawrence Sher
Music by: Marcelo Zarvos
Sound: Theresa Radka
Editing: Kristy Jacobs Maslin, Gregory Tillman
Art Direction: Tema Levine
Costumes: Melissa Bruning
Production Design: Charlotte Bourke
MPAA rating: R
Running time: 96 minutes

REVIEWS

Boxoffice. November 1, 2002, p. 129.
Chicago Sun-Times Online. March 13, 2002.
Entertainment Weekly. March 15, 2002, p. 21.
Entertainment Weekly. March 22, 2002, p. 75.
Los Angeles Times Online. March 13, 2002.
New York Times Online. March 13, 2002.
People. March 18, 2002, p. 34.
San Diego Union Tribune. March 22, 2002, p. E3.
San Francisco Chronicle. March 13, 2002, p. D3.
US Weekly. March 25, 2002, p. 59.
Variety. March 7, 2001, p. 62.
Washington Post. March 22, 2002, p. WE39.

QUOTES

Jessica (Jennifer Westfeldt) to Helen (Heather Jurgensen) on their first date: "I didn't know lesbians accessorized!"

TRIVIA

The original title of the film was *Seeking Same.*

Knockaround Guys

If they don't finish the job, their fathers will finish them.
—Movie tagline
How many friends can you trust with your life?
—Movie tagline

 Box Office: $11.6 million

Pity today's poor young mobster. He's living in the shadows of his father's reputation, hemmed in on all sides by authorities hassling him, unable to make it big in the underworld or to get a straight job without questions being asked, jealous of the good old days when mob bosses ruled the roost. He has to settle for being a pathetic mob wannabe or, worse yet, an ordinary citizen.

Like most people, it never occurred to me that young men in Brooklyn who are the sons of organized crime figures are victims of societal prejudices. Now that I have seen *Knockaround Guys,* I understand their sad plight. Hollywood has been woefully negligent in not exposing their tragic circumstances until now. *Knockaround Guys* takes care of that deficiency.

What? You don't care about how terrible life is for the sons of the now-diminished capos? You have no sympathy for spoiled little grown-up mobster children commiserating about how society has conspired to prevent them from measuring up to their daddies' phallic powers? Then I'm afraid you'll be left cold by the film. Unless, of course, you have a thing for the latest grunting, gutter-voiced, tattooed, muscle-bound superstar: Vin Diesel.

Actually, Diesel's the only reason *Knockaround Guys* saw the light of day late in 2002. New Line Cinema buried this turkey, originally slated for release in January 2001, for reasons that are obvious upon viewing, but revived it when Diesel suddenly rocketed to action-movie stardom with the disarmingly named *XXX* (which, despite its title, is not pornography—unless you think random, senseless violence is pornographic). Diesel originally got fourth billing in *Knockaround Guys,* which was on life support because it had to depend on the flickering star power of Barry Pepper (briefly, in 1999, one of Hollywood's Next Big Things), John Malkovich (being John Malkovich being cinema's most well-enunciated heartless mobster), and a diminished Dennis Hopper (shackled to a script that doesn't allow him to be crazed and therefore leaves him beached).

To have to depend on some barely articulate hulk named after a truck fuel to rescue your movie might be ignominious, unless your movie is co-written, co-directed, and co-produced by Brian Koppelman and David Levein (whose only previous credits were as the co-screenwriters for the John Dahl flop *Rounders*), in which case, Vin Diesel is a godsend.

The movie opens with a prologue in which Malkovich's Teddy Deserve is being a good mob uncle to his 12-year-old nephew Matty Demaret, taking him to see the man who squealed on Matty's father and got him sent off to prison. It turns out the guy (played by Josh Mostel), tied to a chair, is someone Matty felt close to, and, after being handed the gun to kill him, Matty can't pull the trigger. Uncle Teddy tells him that's alright, that now Matty knows he doesn't have it in him, and he doesn't have to pursue "the life"—and he sends Matty outside while he dispatches the victim.

Cut to a grown-up Matty (Pepper) trying to get a job as a sports agent, and being spurned by a boss when he finds out Matty's the son of notorious crime figure Benny "Chains" Demaret (Hopper). Matty complains that "I get coldcocked whenever my father's name is mentioned" and says all he wants is a fair shake and a chance to get a decent job despite his father's reputation. But, a few minutes later, we find out he's been lying. He goes to the handball court where his father reigns supreme, and talks with Teddy and his dad. It turns out Matty is a low-level errand boy for his father, "running crap games, collecting taxes, overseeing the odd union meeting," in his words.

Matty is chafing at his father's lack of trust in him, and at his relative unimportance in the family business. He shares his displeasure with his friend Chris Scarpa (Andrew Davoli), and Chris, who runs a small restaurant for *his* dad, has his own list of complaints about being a modern mob son: "I get all the hassles of his old life—bad press, federal surveillance, and frequent liquor board inspections." And neither of them, Matty and Chris agree, ever get to experience the power trip of being mob kingpins like their fathers did in the gangsters' heyday. There is one perk, though, says Chris, who is a ladies' man: "The name gets me laid at least once a week."

For some time, Matty has been pleading with his father to get an assignment that involves some real responsibility, and now, at the urging of Uncle Teddy, who helps present Matty's case that he is "ready," Benny Chains reluctantly doles out a job for Matty. First, though, his father wants to understand why Matty is so interested in the work. "Most guys go in for it because they got no other way to survive," he notes. Matty replies: "Well, neither do I." This is the script's way of letting us know that it's tearing Matty's heart out that he can't wield as big a gun as his father.

The job involves picking up a big bag of cash from someone in Seattle. Matty unwisely entrusts the task to his friend Johnny Marbles (Seth Green), a supposedly reformed cokehead with his own small plane. But Johnny can't resist snorting a line on his way back from Seattle, and, when he stops in a backwater airport at Wibaux, Montana, to refuel,

he gets spooked when he sees a sheriff and his deputy inside the terminal. So he dumps his bag in with a bunch of other luggage that is on the runway ready to be loaded on a plane to Billings. But the stash doesn't go to Billings—it's discovered by the airport's two baggage handlers, a couple of young dope-smoking, skateboard-crazy teenage burnouts.

As a test of Matty's readiness to be a dependable adult mobster, this job is hardly the right one. If Johnny had brought the bag home and Matty had delivered it to his dad, what perils would Matty have faced? It's only because of Matty's lack of initiative and his poor choice in friends that he gets to prove his mettle after all. It's a strange plot, made every stranger by the clumsy device of having Johnny panic and drop his bag at the airport. It really proves little more than that Matty has a bunch of irresponsible friends. No wonder they whine so much.

When Johnny can't figure out how to begin to find the money, Matty flies in from New York with the other members of their junior mob foursome—Chris and Taylor Reese (Diesel), a genuine bad-ass. They decide to flush out the money by announcing their presence, and Taylor says the thing to do is to find the toughest guy in town and lay waste to him. This he does in a barroom fight notable for its one-sidedness, for a long preparatory speech by Taylor about how he has trained to be a tough guy, and for the strangely cheery pop-country music that accompanies Taylor's head-butting, punching, and kicking.

Co-directors Koppelman and Levein can't settle on a style for their film, or maybe they don't have a style, so they keep shooting scenes in random fashion and cueing up the sound track. *Knockaround Guys* is more a series of music videos than a film, though the tunes keep getting interrupted with the kind of dialogue that explains the character's thoughts and motives in easily digestible, pedestrian fashion. And the talk keeps returning to how awful it is for the characters to be living in the declining days of mob influence. "It isn't the way it was 30 years ago," Diesel's Taylor, in a rare contemplative mood, complains to Matty. "Now it's either a bullet in the back of your head or jail for life."

The plot is a simple one in strange surroundings. The four New York hoods wear black leather jackets and look like Hollywood-standard-issue mobsters as they throw their weight around the tiny rural town. They run up against a taciturn sheriff (Tom Noonan, who looks like he's doing a Billy Bob Thornton imitation) who throws a few unanticipated obstacles in their way. When Matty inexplicably calls his father to tell him there's a glitch, Uncle Teddy comes to town with his seasoned gangster henchmen, and there are some more incongruous scenes with the local inhabitants confronting the New Yorkers. It's sort of like *Sweet Home Alabama* without the yucks, and with the big-city guys always winning the fights.

If you ventured a guess that the movie would end with Matty earning the respect of his father and then deciding he doesn't want "the life" anyway, you've been paying way too much attention to mob movies, which seem always to be wrapped up in father-son rivalry. But *Knockaround Guys* is one of the first to posit that a whole generation of mob sons are getting the short end of the stick, and it does so in a singularly graceless, unappealing way.

Vin Diesel fans aren't going to find enough Vin Diesel action to keep this movie on its feet, and for the rest of us, there's nothing to hold our interest. Pepper looks and behaves just like every young actor of the last 20 years trying to look like a mobster; that is to say, he tries to imitate James Dean and Marlon Brando and be tight-lipped and cool, but there is nothing new here. Hopper is totally wasted in a role that could have been played by anybody—the legendary crazy onetime hippie seems merely tired and beaten down.

The oddest bit of casting is the Shakespearean Malkovich as a lisping, cruel mob madman. He keeps going in and out of a Brooklyn street accent and lapsing into his high-toned pronunciation. At the end, he lectures Matty about his own sorrow at the passing of the good old days: "It used to be no room for whining, no room for mistakes, now everybody's feelings are involved," he says, doing his best to look menacing but coming off for the most part looking goofy. Malkovich manages to be chilling and convincing and at the same time hilarious, as if he has stumbled onto the wrong set. What is he doing in this movie anyway? It is safe to say it's the only time he'll ever be eclipsed by Vin Diesel.

Knockaround Guys at least got a decent burial in October 2002—quickly released and forgotten before Halloween.

—*Michael Betzold*

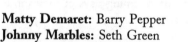

CREDITS

Matty Demaret: Barry Pepper
Johnny Marbles: Seth Green
Benny "Chains" Demaret: Dennis Hopper
Taylor Reese: Vin Diesel
Chris Scarpa: Andrew Davoli
Teddy Deserve: John Malkovich
Sheriff: Tom Noonan

Origin: USA
Released: 2001
Production: Lawrence Bender, Brian Koppelman, David Levien; released by New Line Cinema
Directed by: Brian Koppelman, David Levien
Written by: Brian Koppelman, David Levien
Cinematography by: Tom Richmond
Music by: Clint Mansell
Sound: Douglas Ganton
Editing: David Moritz

Art Direction: Kei Ng
Costumes: Beth Pasternak
Production Design: Lester Cohen
MPAA rating: R
Running time: 93 minutes

REVIEWS

Boxoffice. October, 2002, p. 59.
Chicago Sun-Times Online. October 11, 2002.
Entertainment Weekly. October 18, 2002, p. 90.
New York Times Online. October 11, 2002.
Newsday Online. October 11, 2002.
Variety. December 3, 2001, p. 33.
Washington Post. October 11, 2002, p. WE48.

QUOTES

Teddy Deserve (John Malkovich): "Used to be there was a way to do things. Now, everybody's *feelings* are involved."

The Lady and the Duke (L'Anglaise et le Duc)

ormer French New Wave auteur Eric Rohmer's historical drama, *The Lady and the Duke* comes as a bit of departure for the director who is known for his romantic comedy cycles. However, Rohmer had tried his hand at historical dramas in the past with such French classics as *The Marquis of O* (1975), which was shot on location, and *Perceval le Gallois* (1978), shot on a soundstage while employing the tenets of mise-en-scène. Rohmer devised a new approach to staging and shooting *The Lady and the Duke* by inserting real-life characters into scenic backgrounds (paintings by Jean-Baptiste Marot) representing 18th-century Paris. According to Rohmer in an interview with Aurèlien Ferenczi, "Inserting characters into sets is one of the oldest tricks in the filmmaker's book. Mèliès (pioneer of French filmmaking), was probably the first to do it." Couple that with digital technology and Rohmer created yet another cinematic achievement with a youthful appeal.

Based on Lady Grace Elliott's memoir, *Journal of My Life During the French Revolution*, *The Lady and the Duke* focuses on a refreshing portrayal of revolutionary France and the reign of King Louis XVI. Unlike Victor Hugo's *Les Miserables*, which made the French revolution fashionable in contemporary times, *The Lady and the Duke* revolves around the views of members of the aristocracy instead of the cries of the masses. And in fact, the masses are shown as crass ruffians crying "string up all the aristocrats" or patriots all-too-willing to surrender their aristocratic employers in the name of duty. Enter the English Lady and self-proclaimed Royalist Grace Elliott (Lucy Russell) and her former lover/revolutionary the Duc d' Orleans (Jean-Claude Dreyfus) and what entails is a juicy plot based on a volatile historic era.

Rohmer avoids voice-over narration and instead divides the film into chapters based on dates from Lady Elliott's journal. Although Lady Elliott was born in Scotland in 1760, married, then divorced, from Sir John Elliott, a mistress to the future George IV of England, and then a lover to the Duke of Orleans, her journal begins in 1789. The story here begins on July 14, 1790 or the anniversary of the fall of the Bastille. The Duke of Orleans returns to Paris and warns Lady Elliott to return to England to avoid a breakout of another revolution, but Lady Elliott declines to leave her adopted king and country. The gentlewoman is adamant about siding with the aristocracy, even though we see her involved with charity work. The Duke (a cousin of Louis XVI) joined the revolutionaries against Elliott's best wishes.

The former lovers test each other's loyalty. Upon the fall of King Louis XVI, Lady Elliott escapes on foot to her house in Meudon. A month later, she returns to perilous Paris on behalf of a favor for a friend. She hides a sworn enemy of the Duke and of the anti-Royalists and is nearly caught by the patrol that raids her home. Later, against his best interests, the Duke assists the fugitive who eventually escapes to England. Later, the Duke would vote to execute King Louis against Lady Elliott's pleas—leading to an estrangement of their friendship. King Louis XVI's execution took place on January 21, 1793, and Lady Elliott wrote in her journal that the king's execution led to her saddest day ever. Later, the lady would be carted off to jail twice and released after Robespierre's death. Her royal friends, including the Duke would all lose their heads at the guillotine. Lady Elliott returned to England under the Empire and again to France during the Restoration until her death in 1823.

Once again, Rohmer collected kudos from the press. A.O. Scott, in the *New York Times,* found the historical drama to be "Astonishingly and reassuringly a Rohmer film!" Lisa Schwarzbaum from *Entertainment Weekly* wrote, "exquisitely composed . . . surprisingly suspenseful!," and Glenn Kenny in *Premiere* repeated Schwarzbaum's praise: "an exquisite work!" Fans of Rohmer's romantic comedies will also find much to love in Rohmer's cinematic achievement and will find many of Rohmer's regular performers playing bit roles, including Marie Riviere and Alain Libolt (*Autumn Tale*) and Charlotte Very (*A Tale of Winter*). And in fact, it is a pleasure to see the comedic actors appearing in this serious costume drama.

This epic showcases luminous performances by its two leads, Russell and Dreyfus, and blends the authenticity of 18th-century France with the current digital revolution. The octogenarian Rohmer shows no signs of slowing down.

—*Patty-Lynne Herlevi*

CREDITS

Grace Elliott: Lucy Russell
Philippe, Duke d'Orleans: Jean-Claude Dreyfus
Dumourier: Francois Marthouret
Champcenetz: Leonard Cobiant
Nanon: Caroline Morin
Duke de Biron: Alain Libolt
Madame Laurent: Marie Riviere
Madame Meyler: Helena Dubeil

Origin: France
Language: French
Released: 2001
Production: Francoise Etchegaray; Pathe; released by Sony Pictures Classics
Directed by: Eric Rohmer
Written by: Eric Rohmer
Cinematography by: Diane Baratier
Sound: Pascal Ribier
Editing: Mary Stephen
Costumes: Pierre-Jean Larrogque
Production Design: Antoine Fontaine
MPAA rating: PG-13
Running time: 129 minutes

REVIEWS

Boxoffice. November, 2001, p. 132.
Chicago Sun-Times Online. June 7, 2002.
Entertainment Weekly. June 7, 2002, p. 46.
Hollywood Reporter. October 2, 2001, p. 22.
Los Angeles Times Online. May 10, 2002.
New York Times Online. October 5, 2001.
New York Times Online. May 5, 2002.
People. May 20, 2002, p. 40.
Sight and Sound. February, 2002, p. 36.
USA Today Online. May 10, 2002.
Variety. September 10, 2001, p. 57.
Washington Post. May 31, 2002, p. WE42.

such force might have the opposite effect, resulting in losing Zaza for good.

Yasha himself becomes powerless as Lily's anger boils over. "No divorcee is going to live under my roof!" she vows. The two families thus traipse into Judith's apartment, hoping to catch Zaza and her "in action." As it happens, Zaza is playing with Madona in the living room. As his relatives, including his grandmother, look on, Yasha tries to make Judith see how important age is in a marriage. "I'm 56," he begins, "my wife is 51. My sister is 47, her husband is 55." Lily intrudes by demanding Zaza hand over his father's credit card. He does so at once. Judith the replies by stating flat out that she loves Zaza, and no one else. This is more than Simon can bear. He unsheathes a sword, which he finds hanging, then pins Judith against the wall, and threatens to behead her. Zaza then takes the sword from him, and hands it to Yasha, offering his own head instead. The scene veers back to the serious, as Yasha pleads with Zaza, "Don't break your mother's heart!" Zaza can only walk out after that. The others follow. Interestingly, the grandmother is amongst the last to leave. She actually smiles at Judith, and feels her arms, as if admiring her fortitude.

For all its haphazardness, the scene does accomplish its desired effect. The next we see of Judith, she is returning jewelry and other mementos to Zaza, and saying she doesn't want to see him again. She adds that he is worse than her ex-husband, though she doesn't say just how.

At home, Zaza's clash with his father reaches its climax. "Your woman is better," Zaza tells him, "in her having raised only your children!" After which, Yasha spits in his face. Though the scene takes place in a bathroom, Zaza does not clean his face in defiance, but treats the saliva as his just due. As if sensing Zaza's change of heart, Lily enters and gives him the phone number of one Lea, the daughter of a goldsmith. "I promised her mother you'd call," Lily says, then adds, "Don't shame me!"

The film then goes out of its way to bring the generations together. Lily visits Judith with a present for her daughter. Judith sets Lily's mind at rest by telling her that she has broken off with Zaza. She then explains, "The way he acted that night, I realized he loves you more than he loves me." Lily responds by saying, "You're a good woman!"

After that, all Yasha and Lily can do is wait to see if their son gets over the affair. The film cuts to Zaza's wedding day, as he embraces Yasha in, of all places, an urinal. Yasha then expresses his wish, "Next year, I want a grandson!" At his zaniest peak, Zaza kneels down and tries to kiss his father's testicles, saying, "That's where I come from! You made me with those!" When he's alone in the washroom, Zaza slaps himself repeatedly, as if trying to shake himself out of more than a mere drunken state. There is a trace of misgiving on his face, to which he doesn't give in. Instead, he winks and says out loud, "Good luck, suckers!" It remains

ambiguous whether he is preparing to join their lot, or vowing to get the better of them.

At the reception, we see that Lea (Maria Ovanov) is a voluptuous embodiment of fecundity. The drunken revelry with which the film ends asserts its conservative stance as being the best for the happiness of all concerned.

Stephen Holden in the *New York Times,* writing at the time of the film's showcasing at the Museum of Modern Art's New Directors/New Films series, finds that the film raises issues of arranged matrimony in relation to customs that have long since eroded in the west, but are alive and healthy elsewhere. What is "ugly and shocking to western sensibilities," he writes, "is only to be expected" in Zaza's case. For Holden, this is what makes *Late Marriage* a "powerful and very bitter comedy."

—*Vivek Adarkar*

CREDITS

Zaza: Lior Loui Ashkenazi
Judith: Ronit Elkabetz
Yasha: Moni Moshonov
Lili: Lili Kosashvili
Madona: Sapir Kugman
Ilana: Aya Steinovits Laor

Origin: Israel, France
Language: Hebrew
Released: 2001
Production: Marek Rozenbaum, Edgard Tenembaum; Transfax Production, Morgane Production; released by Magnolia Pictures
Directed by: Dover Kosashvili
Written by: Dover Kosashvili
Cinematography by: Dani Schneor
Music by: Joseph Bardanashvili
Sound: Oleg Kaiserman, Nathalie Vidal
Editing: Yani Perlov
Art Direction: Avi Fahima
Costumes: Maya Barsky
MPAA rating: Unrated
Running time: 100 minutes

REVIEWS

Boxoffice. March, 2002, p. 58.
Chicago Sun-Times Online. May 31, 2002.
Entertainment Weekly. May 24, 2002, p. 67.
Los Angeles Times Online. May 22, 2002.
New York Times Online. May 19, 2002.
Sight and Sound. March, 2002, p. 48.
Variety Online. June 1, 2001.

Leela

Somnath Sen's debut feature, *Leela*, like its eponymous heroine, tries to be up-to-date and bold and, at the same time, not offend East Indian sensibilities. If there is one trend that can be discerned in the recent subgenre of films about expatriate Indians living the cushy life in the U.S. (*American Desi* (2000), *ABCD* (2000) and *American Chai* (2001) to name just three), it is an attachment to the world of tradition left behind in the Old Country. This results in these films falling between two stools, or two driveways, to be more precise. They are neither American in spirit nor Indian in their unabashed vulgarity. One thing that can be said in *Leela*'s favor is that it doesn't fall. It just remains suspended, like a mystic whose destination is the place he started from. Unfortunately, the film's quasi-mystical stance cannot generate the dramatic quotient needed to sustain our interest. Thanks to spot-on casting, which is chock full of glamor, it does make for pleasant viewing, for audiences prepared to accept just that.

The film opens with a lofty invocation to the purifying aspect of fire, as the beautiful Leela (Dimple Kapadia) stands weeping beside the funeral pyre of her mother on a beach. Her voiceover tells us that she will now have "a lot to think about." With the quickness of a tabla beat, she is saying farewell to Nashaad (Vinod Khanna), her husband, a famous Urdu poet, and leaving Bombay to serve as a Visiting Professor at an American university. With the same rapidity, we're introduced to the film's other protagonist, Krishna (Amol Mhatre), or Kris as he's called, an 18-year-old American-born East Indian, in the middle of shooting hoops with his gang, which consists of two white boys, JC (Kelly Gunning) and Chip (Garrett Devereux), and a black, Jamal (Kyle Erby).

Leela's beauty, and the stately way she carries herself in a sari, throws everyone for a loop. Her class in 'Studies of World Culture' shows her pointing to an universality of spiritual heritage transcending national boundaries. The film shows us the irony involved in Leela's academic agenda by briefly cutting to a group of Asian students protesting nuclear proliferation in South Asia. A lot of this is lost on Krishna. He's so taken up by Leela's looks that, despite the considerable difference in age and intellect, he makes a bet with his pals that he will sleep with Leela within a month.

By this time, the film has already sketched out Leela's devotion to Nashaad, to whom she's writing letters in every spare moment, and Krishna's dysfunctional home life. His mother, Chaitali (Deepti Naval), who is also a professor, ensconced in a plush suburban home, has separated from her husband, Jai (Gulshan Grover, a Joe Mantegna lookalike), a decision that Krishna approves. When Krishna learns she has found an American lover, Summer (Brendan Hughes), it is too much modernity for him to accept.

The film hobbles along on this skimpy narrative track, taking time to include slice-of-life digressions. There's a scene where Leela even gets her class to meditate. "The sound you hear," she intones, "is the link between the material and the spiritual world." Then, there's a Discussion Forum organized by Chaitali at her house, at which members of the East Indian community, including Leela, debate about the extent of morality to be absorbed from America. In a tete-a-tete, Chaitali describes herself to Leela as "a postmodern woman" who proved "too independent" for her husband. On her part, Leela admits that she and Nashaad share "an open marriage." Meanwhile, Krishna teaches Leela how to play basketball and eat a hot dog, both of which she does without changing from her ornate sari.

Despite their contemporary sensibilities, the intimacy between Leela and Krishna is slow to develop. When they do eventually make the leap into bed, the film etherealizes the event by superimposing an iconic blazing fire, behind which the two appear as a play of shadows.

Their union results in the foreseeable melodramatic consequences. Chaitali turns against Leela who, on her part, decides to keep Krishna at a distance. Meanwhile, Nashaad arrives to clear up a misunderstanding with his wife. Krishna, who has been seriously entertaining hopes of marrying Leela, is eventually disappointed to find her rejecting both Nashaad and him, in favor of wanting to discover herself by herself. In the film's final scene, Krishna prepares to travel with his mother to India to see his ailing grandfather, a prospect he had earlier found abhorrent.

The film's innocuous charm has elicited a kind reaction from critics. Dave Kehr in the *New York Times* describes it as "an unusual combination of Bollywood and Hollywood sensibilities" that "veers between the light naturalism of American television and the pulsing melodrama of Bollywood entertainment." Lisa Sweetingham in *Time Out New York* even calls it a "sparkling ... gem" that "aptly reflects the challenge facing many immigrants whose Americanized children favor MTV culture over their ancestral heritage."

—Vivek Adarkar

CREDITS

Leela: Dimple Kapadia
Kris: Amol Mhatre
Chaitali: Deepti Naval
Nashaad: Vinod Khanna
Jai: Gulshan Grover

Origin: USA

Released: 2002
Production: Kavita Munjal, Anjalika Mathur; Lemon Tree Films; released by Cinebella Entertainment
Directed by: Somnath Sen
Written by: Somnath Sen
Cinematography by: Steven Douglas Smith
Music by: Jagjit Singh
Sound: Brian Linder
Editing: Suresh Pai
Art Direction: Joshua Erlich
Costumes: Celeste Hines
Production Design: Aradhana Seth
MPAA rating: Unrated
Running time: 97 minutes

REVIEWS

Los Angeles Times Online. November 8, 2002.
New York Times Online. November 8, 2002.
Time Out New York Online. November 7, 2002.
Variety Online. August 6, 2002.

QUOTES

Chaitali (Deepti Naval) to her son Kris (Amol Mhatre): "I'm a postmodern woman, and I do what I please."

Life or Something Like It

Destiny is what you make of it.
—Movie tagline
What if you got a chance to discover who you really are?
—Movie tagline

 Box Office: $14.4 million

I f you had less that one week to live, what would you do? Given two hours to entertain, this *Life,* marketed as a comedy, instead incorporates some lighter moments within the syrupy, melodramatic framework about a quest for the meaning of life. The quest, in turn, is as glibly portrayed as the film's heroine stepping back from career aspirations for a family trip to the amusement park that symbolizes a return to what really matters. That, and almost all the other turn of events in the film, can easily be gleaned

before the first reel has unspooled, leaving only the uninspired writing, direction and performances with a cast and crew from which we have certainly seen far better. Although the movie's message of live each day as if it were your last is certainly timely in this post-September 11th world, the formulaic, trite presentation leaves little to inspire such lofty sentiments. A more apt title for the film might be *Suddenly Soulful.*

Her perfect world shattered in an instant with the prediction of a homeless psychic, Seattle TV newswoman Lanie Kerrigan (Angelina Jolie) begins to seriously reevaluate a life that, up until that point, she was not only content with, but prized as the quintessence of success. Of course, the moment she actually has the nerve to utter the words, "My life is perfect," one can practically hear the groaning and creaking of the rafters and rest assured that the roof is about to collapse. Looking like a cross between Marilyn Monroe and Steven Tyler, the bleach blond broadcaster seems to have it all—the perfect job (local star reporter), the perfect boyfriend (Seattle Mariners star) and the perfect apartment (elegant and spotless). Having it all and loving it to pieces, Lanie has not meticulously groomed herself for success only for it to be spoiled by an untimely death—but that is exactly what threatens to happen, when, on a routine assignment, she meets up with Prophet Jack (Tony Shalhoub).

Lanie interviews the street seer for a fluff piece about the score of the upcoming football game. He not only tells her the game's outcome but adds that it will hail the following day and finally that she, Lanie, will die in less than one week. When both of his other predictions come to pass, Lanie is peeved to the max by the now growing possibility that she will die—at a most inopportune time, too, as she is being considered for a network job on *AM USA,* in New York, no less. Helping her prepare for her big step up in journalism is seasoned news cameraman Pete (Edward Burns), forced to work together despite their obvious dislike of one another.

With loads of sexual tension underlying their tritely written banter, no psychic is necessary to predict the outcome of the relationship of these two attractive coworkers. Making digs about each other's personal appearance, the equivalent of playground hair pulling, Pete mocks her bubble-headed bleach blonde mane. Lanie comes back with the completely serious statement that her hair is her trademark just as his, she wryly observes, is the, "I don't like to shower look." Pete and Lanie also enjoy playfully critiquing every other aspect of each other's psychological make-up in depth. As scrubbed, made-up, and tightly-pulled together in Dolce & Gabbana as Lanie is, Pete is her polar opposite— an unshaven schlub with a life as equally as messy. Pete, it seems, did not have the perfect marriage and now divorced, is raising his son from the failed union. This low-key, low maintenance family guy is hardly Lanie's idea of the perfect mate but one wonders what's with the hostility.

Other than their obvious differences, there is another reason for all their animosity—it is revealed much later that the two had previously had a relationship that, surprise, didn't work out. However, now convinced that her life may be over, Lanie does some serious soul-searching about what is really important in life. Scratching all the surfaces in her exceedingly superficial life, Lanie begins to see that Cal (Christian Kane) isn't very deep and is actually self-involved and one-dimensional. Quickly deep-sixing her jock, Lanie now has only a few days to reconnect with things and people that really matter which will also reconnect her with her real self. This leads her to the remainder of her family—her competitive sister and blue-collar dad. Her begrudging sister (Lisa Thornhill) seems to be living out her own vision of suburban motherhood perfection and just seems put-out by the reappearance of Lanie quizzing her on the meaning of it all. Via flashbacks segs, one sees that Lanie's ambition and quest for perfection is rooted in her early childhood weight problem resulting in unpopularity and her sister's ridicule, nicknaming her "Pudge."

Pete is more amenable, naturally, to come to Lanie's aid, advising her that by changing her life, she might also change her destiny. He helps her tap into her more earthy side, apparent in montages of trips to the amusement parks, where the former obsessive work-out queen happily snacks on drippy ice-cream. All is not sno-cones and roses for the fulsome twosome for long however, and a half-hearted break-up is penned just to add more drama to the last reel and so that they can happily reunite once more.

Apparently, director Stephen Herek (*Mr. Holland's Opus*), who recently directed the flop *Rock Star*, couldn't resist inserting one of rock's most famous anthems in this film, resulting in the distasteful, "(I Can't Get No) Satisfaction" segment. Yes, the famous Rolling Stones song becomes a pivotal plot point when the new Lanie, sans skin-tight Italian skirt suits and teased hair, does a story involving a bunch of striking workers and most publicly sympathizes with their plight by launching into an unfortunate, "impromptu" chorus of the famous song. Now, as her transformation to regular gal is nearly complete, this on-screen, unprofessional, embarrassment has, of course, brought her more positive recognition resulting in a final test of her newfound values. Of course, Pete factors into all of this as Lanie is probably incapable of making any decisions on her own.

The film's lone highlight occurs when Stockard Channing shows up playing a Barbara Walters-esque colleague, Deborah Connors, whom Lanie is interviewing. Although only onscreen for a short time in her few scenes, Channing runs away with the picture and reminding us what a superb performance is necessary to pull off this material. The painful scene, however, requires Lanie to go for her idol Deborah's jugular, seeking to humiliate the TV veteran by

underscoring the personal sacrifices she made in order to achieve such professional success—success that Lanie herself is doubting that she actually wants anymore.

Performances are uninspired, to say the least. The Oscar-winning Jolie seems ill-suited to play the glamour queen turned soul machine, perhaps confused by what genre of film this actually is. A late scene with Pete has her emoting and hysterical, perhaps venting her frustration of playing such an ill-defined character. Burns has played the glib, good-guy character before and there is nothing in his down-to-earth portrayal that demands viewing. Support Errico serves as a foil to the glam Jolie and vets Shalhoub and Channing could do with more air time.

Much of the writing is cringe-worthy and derivative. Pete constantly asking for the definitions of words: "Define happiness." Lanie: "Your death." Similarly, when talking to Pete about the prophet with the power to see the future, the half-asleep Pete lamely replies, "Like ESPN?" Some of the dialogue does make you think, however. As in the break-up exchange between Cal and Lanie when he asks, "Is this you breaking up with me? Well, will you think about it for a minute?" to which she replies, "A minute just seems like a really long time to waste." Amen—two hours wasted on this film is a really long time for someone with two lifetimes to live.

Without subtlety of direction, Herek, nonetheless, manages to keep things rolling and production values are typically high Hollywood caliber. The characters, especially the main characters, are crudely drawn and unbelievable much of the time. Injecting a dose of reality, the KOMO-TV studios in Seattle were used as sets (changing the logo to KQMO-TV) and several on-air personalities KOMO make cameo appearances, including Margo Myers, Dan Lewis, and Steve Pool.

—*Hilary White*

CREDITS

Lanie Kerrigan: Angelina Jolie
Pete: Edward Burns
Prophet Jack: Tony Shalhoub
Cal: Christian Kane
Andrea: Melissa Errico
Deborah Connors: Stockard Channing
Lanie's father: James Gammon
Dennis: Gregory Itzin

Origin: USA
Released: 2002
Production: Arnon Milchan, John Davis, Toby Jaffe, Chi-Li Wong; New Regency Pictures, Epsilon Motion Pictures; released by 20th Century-Fox

Directed by: Stephen Herek
Written by: John Scott Shepherd, Dana Stevens
Cinematography by: Stephen Burum
Music by: David Newman
Sound: Tim Chau
Editing: Trudy Ship
Art Direction: Helen Jarvis
Costumes: Aggie Guerard Rodgers
Production Design: Bill Groom
MPAA rating: PG-13
Running time: 104 minutes

REVIEWS

Chicago Sun-Times Online. April 26, 2002.
Entertainment Weekly. May 3, 2002, p. 59.
Los Angeles Times Online. April 26, 2002.
New York Times Online. April 26, 2002.
People. May 6, 2002, p. 39.
USA Today Online. April 26, 2002.
Variety. April 29, 2002, p. 23.
Washington Post. April 26, 2002, p. WE45.

QUOTES

Lanie Kerigan (Angelina Jolie): "If you had a week to live, what would you do?" Pete (Edward Burns): "I would—ya know—I'd have sex with you."

Like Mike

Box Office: $51.4 million

L*ike Mike* won over audiences by being a whole lot better than it looked like it was going to be. Trailers for the film showed a kid putting on magic sneaker and becoming a great basketball player. It didn't seem very promising. The trailers didn't lie—that is the story of the film—but they also didn't convey just how well star Lil' Bow Wow (who now prefers to be called the more adult-sounding Bow Wow), director John Schultz and screenwriter Michael Elliot and Jordan Moffet would handle this pretty lame premise.

Calvin Cambridge (Bow Wow) is a cute kid who is living in a semi-run-down orphanage near downtown Los Angeles. He and his friends are hopeful that they'll get adopted but are beginning to think that it might not happen.

At the resident bully Ox (Jesse Plemons) says, "We're like dogs. Parents only want the puppies." The place is run by Stan Bittleman (Crispin Glover), whose fake sincerity hides his true profiteering self. One night when Bittleman has the kids hawking candy outside the stadium of the fictional basketball team the Los Angeles Knights, huge fan Calvin runs into Coach Wagner (Robert Forster). Wagner is impressed by Calvin's knowledge of the game and he gives him some free tickets.

Calvin gets another stroke of luck when his tutor, Sister Teresa (Anne Meara), gives him a pair of used basketball sneakers. She mentions that they're from "some famous basketball player." Calvin is thrilled when he sees the initials "M.J." inside. They must have been Michael Jordan's! Ox, who is an embittered bully, won't stand for someone being happy and he quickly takes the sneakers from Calvin, tossing them up onto a power line. That night, during a lightning storm, Calvin climbs up the pole to retrieve the sneakers. As he's up there, lightning hits and Calvin, the wire, and the sneakers are struck. He's okay, miraculously, and mumbles to the sneakers, "Let me be like Mike." Folks at the utility companies raised a ruckus over this particular scene, complaining that kids would be climbing up utility poles and getting into dangerous situations.

When Calvin and his pals get to the Knights game, the announcer Frank Bernard (Eugene Levy), picks a random ticket to come onto the court to play a game of one-on-one with star player Tracey Reynolds (Morris Chestnut). Calvin, wearing his lucky sneakers, surprises himself, Tracey and the entire crowd by beating the star, including sinking an incredible three-point shot. Bernard and the team owners sign the four-foot, eight-inch boy to a one game contract as a gimmick.

At Calvin's first game, the coach decides to put him in and Calvin starts making points. The kid is obviously the best player on the field and the Knights quickly sign him to a longer contract. Tracey is put in charge of being Calvin's mentor, an assignment that Tracey isn't pleased with. Tracey is a ladies' man who thinks that Calvin is cramping his style. Calvin orders too much food from room service, snores and ruins Tracey's dates with his various groupies.

Along the way, Calvin gets to interact with his idols, including real life NBA players Jason Richardson, David Robinson, Allen Iverson, and Chris Webber, plus several announcers. He also gets to experience living out his dream, being famous, rich and playing the NBA. As Calvin gets more famous, he starts getting offers of adoption. In one montage, he reviews potential parent, including a bizarre musical theater couple and a couple that looks just like the family on the *Fresh Prince of Bel-Air.* There's also an unnecessary car chase at the end, but at this point, that must be some sort of requirement of kids' films. Kids in the audience were yukking it up over the gentle humor of things like the sound of Calvin's snoring.

The stakes in the film are high—Will Calvin find parents? Will Tracey ever love him? Will Ox take away his magic sneakers?—but the movie doesn't make these things overly important and stressful. The director is more content to let the human relationships develop. It's a smart move because the best thing about *Like Mike* is the acting, particularly in the film's main relationship between Tracey and Calvin. Bow Wow, in particular, makes the movie. The kid, who first became famous as a rap star, is making his screen debut, but he looks like a professional. He's loose, charismatic and completely charming. Bow Wow plays his role with a conviction that helps the audience believe in the fantasy, too. Jeffrey M. Anderson of the *San Francisco Examiner* noted that, "Even when uttering groan-worthy lines that Shirley Temple might have said 70 years ago, like 'I'm an orphan' and 'All I really want is a family,' he comes across as perfectly sincere."

Also well-cast is Chestnut as Tracey. Chestnut is a reserved actor and that quality serves this part well. He's closed off from Calvin at the beginning and slowly, we get to see him start succumbing to Calvin's charms. Their developing relationship is a lot more believable—and handled more realistically—that what passes for character development in many non-kid movies. The casting in the minor roles works well, too. It's always nice to see Meara, Levy and Forster on-screen. Glover takes another turn at playing an offbeat character. His villainous orphanage manager is interesting to watch because his villain is a cardigan-sweater-wearing type who seems harmless and meek.

The film also does a good job of promoting multiculturalism. It's nice that the main character is black and his sidekick, Murph (Jonathan Lipnicki), is a vaguely nondescript white guy instead of the usual opposite. And Calvin's third friend, played by Brenda Song is Asian. When Calvin begs her for some help with his math homework, it looks like it's going to be yet another smart Asian on the screen. But Song says, "I'm not going to help you with your geometry because I don't understand it any better than you." (Poor Song doesn't score as well on screen time. She seems to be a victim of some last minute cutting. At the end of the film when Calvin finally gets adopted, he asks that Murph be adopted, too. And what about Song? Her story is wrapped up abruptly when we see a picture of her smiling with what must be her new family. So long.) Some of this pro-multiculturalism was lost in a boorish marketing campaign that appeared after the film came out. In what seemed to be an obvious bid to appeal to white moviegoers, 20th Century Fox released a new ad featuring a huge picture of the white Lipnicki, with Bow Wow standing behind him. It's pretty strange since Bow Wow is in every scene and is the obvious star of the movie and Lipnicki is only peripheral. It's like if posters for the *Wizard of Oz* featured a big photo of Auntie Em with Dorothy standing behind.

Generally, critics liked the film, and especially Bow Wow. Kevin Thomas of the *Los Angeles Times* wrote, "*Like Mike* is a surefire heart-warmer: lively, funny yet emotion-charged and uplifting." Sean Axmaker of the *Seattle Post-Intelligencer* wrote, "The surprisingly shaded performances of Plemons and Jonathan Lipnicki, the warm turns by fatherly coach Robert Forster, and the charisma of L'il (sic) Bow Wow's spirited screen presence turn a contemporary Cinderella gimmick and a by-the-numbers script into a better film that anyone would have expected." And Anderson of the *Examiner* wrote, "You might expect *Like Mike* to be one of those 'it wasn't the shoes, it was really you all along'-type stories. But instead it's a warm, bright, jerk-redeemed-by-the-love-of-a-child movie—similar in many ways to *About a Boy*."

—*Jill Hamilton*

CREDITS

Calvin: Lil' Bow Wow
Murph: Jonathan Lipnicki
Tracey Reynolds: Morris Chestnut
Frank Bernard: Eugene Levy
Stan Bittleman: Crispin Glover
Coach Wagner: Robert Forster
Reg: Brenda Song
Ox: Jesse Plemons
Marlon: Julius Charles Ritter
Sister Theresa: Anne Meara

Origin: USA
Released: 2002
Production: Barry Josephson, Peter Heller; NBA Entertainment; released by 20th Century-Fox
Directed by: John Schultz
Written by: Jordan Moffet, Mike Elliot
Cinematography by: Shawn Maurer
Music by: Richard Gibbs
Sound: David MacMillan
Music Supervisor: Billy Gotlieb
Editing: Peter E. Berger, John Pace
Art Direction: John R. Zachary
Costumes: Mary Jane Fort
Production Design: Arlan Jay Vetter
MPAA rating: PG
Running time: 100 minutes

REVIEWS

Chicago Sun-Times Online. July 3, 2002.
Entertainment Weekly. July 12, 2002, p. 55.

Los Angeles Times Online. July 3, 2002.
New York Times Online. July 3, 2002.
People. July 15, 2002, p. 31.
USA Today Online. July 3, 2002.
Variety. July 15, 2002, p. 25.
Washington Post. July 5, 2002, p. WE31.

Lilo and Stitch

There's one in every family.
—Movie tagline

 Box Office: $145.7 million

Lilo and Stitch may be the oddest animated feature to hail from Disney in quite some time. In an age dominated by computer-generated animation, *Lilo and Stitch* is a refreshing throwback to the studio's classic work, featuring hand-drawn figures and, for the first time since the 1940s, gorgeous watercolor backgrounds. It also offers familiar thematic elements—a traditional lesson about the importance of family and a spunky little girl overcoming her loneliness with the help of an unlikely friend. Yet the film also contains one of the most anarchic characters to appear in a Disney cartoon—an initially hideous little creature from outer space with crooked teeth and a built-in penchant for mass destruction. To top off the weirdness, the screenplay by directors Chris Sanders and Dean DeBlois blends science-fiction action, an Hawaiian setting, offbeat humor, and even a tribute to Elvis Presley. Such a mix of disparate elements might seem like a recipe for disaster, but the happiest surprise of *Lilo and Stitch* is that they somehow come together to form a cheerful, energetic comic adventure and one of the best animated features of the last few years.

The story begins at Galactic Federation Headquarters on a faraway planet called Turo, where a mad scientist named Jumba (David Ogden Stiers), an imposing four-eyed creature with a Russian accent, is being tried for the crime of "illegal genetic experimentation," that is, creating a monster. Voiced by co-director Sanders and called Experiment 626, the little monster is a maniacal blue creature whose natural impulse is to destroy everything in its path. It is slated to be sent into exile on a distant asteroid when it escapes in a police cruiser with the authorities following behind. When the creature eludes his pursuers and is heading toward Earth, the Grand Councilwoman (Zoe Caldwell) of Turo is determined to annihilate him but is not allowed to destroy the planet because it is considered (in a funny aside) a protected wildlife preserve whose sole purpose is to rebuild the mosquito population. So she releases Jumba from prison to go to

Earth along with Pleakley (Kevin McDonald), a sidekick with one giant eye, to retrieve the creature.

The film then introduces us to Lilo (Daveigh Chase), a little Hawaiian girl who is essentially good-hearted but, like a lot of bright, lonely kids, cannot seem to find her place and seems to get in trouble despite herself. She is tardy for her hula class, starts a fight with one of the other girls, and is shunned by her peers because her doll is a grotesque creature. In short, Lilo is the classic outcast the other kids avoid. To make her life more difficult, she is an orphan being cared for by her older sister, Nani (Tia Carrere), and a well-meaning but intimidating social worker with the improbable name of Cobra Bubbles is threatening to separate them. Voiced by Ving Rhames and seemingly modeled after his character in *Pulp Fiction,* Mr. Bubbles looks more like a crime lord than a social worker, with his fancy suit and tie, matching gold earrings, and name tattooed on his knuckles.

A precocious child looking for someone who will understand her, Lilo has enough delightful quirks to make her a memorable Disney character. She is darling when she is dancing in the hula line but then turns pensive at home, lying on the floor and lip-syncing to Elvis Presley's "Heartbreak Hotel" after the other girls have rejected her. She also has a mischievous streak—when Mr. Bubbles catches her using a book called *Practical Voodoo,* she deadpans, "My friends need to be punished."

As Experiment 626 is hurtling toward Earth, Lilo mistakes his ship for a falling star and makes a wish for a friend, pleading that an angel will come to her. Experiment 626, however, emerges from the wrecked craft more like a devil than an angel and eventually ends up in the dog shelter. Lilo picks him out as a pet and names him Stitch, while Jumba and Pleakley, who have landed on Earth, shadow Stitch in the hope of capturing him.

No ordinary house pet, Stitch wreaks havoc everywhere, including the restaurant where Nani works—he nearly swallows Pleakley's head when he tries to catch him. As a result, Nani loses her job and is on the verge of throwing Stitch out when Lilo reminds her of the principle of "ohana," or family, which means that "nobody gets left behind or forgotten."

The plot of *Lilo and Stitch* may be familiar (think of a strange cross between *E.T. The Extra-Terrestrial* and *Gremlins*), but it works beautifully nonetheless. The animation is vivid, the characters are quite endearing, and the themes of friendship and family are heartwarming without being heavy-handed. The film, in short, embraces the best of the Disney tradition while still feeling fresh, especially in the warm rapport that Lilo develops with Stitch through some clever comic episodes. Trying to temper his violent impulses, Lilo encourages Stitch to create rather than destroy, and he quickly builds an elaborate model of San Francisco before smashing it like Godzilla run amok. In another cute moment, Lilo discovers that she can play a phonograph record through Stitch; when she places his fingernail on the spinning record, Elvis Presley's "Suspicious Minds" plays out of his mouth.

But the heart of their relationship lies in the way Lilo tries to civilize Stitch. Mr. Bubbles's insistence that Nani find a job and that Stitch be made into a model citizen if they want to remain a family sets up a whimsical montage in which Lilo tries to turn Stitch into a good citizen via a crash course in all things Elvis (her idol) while Stitch's destructive tendencies continually foil Nani's efforts everywhere she looks for work. The climax of the sequence is Stitch in an Elvis jumpsuit playing guitar on the beach while "You're the Devil in Disguise" is heard on the soundtrack. When everyone around him snaps his picture, Stitch's violent reaction prevents Nani from getting a lifeguard job, which seems like her last chance.

But the fun continues anyway when Lilo, Stitch, and Nani go surfing with David (Jason Scott Lee), the local hunk who has his eye on Nani. While they are surfing, Jumba pulls Stitch underwater, and Lilo almost drowns when she too is pulled down. They survive and escape capture, but Mr. Bubbles witnesses this brush with danger and decides that he is going to have to take Lilo away for her own good.

Lilo and Stitch has a predominantly cheery, playful mood, complemented by its colorful palette, but the story does not shy away from somber moments that speak to the serious undercurrents of the story. In a heartbreaking scene, Nani sings to Lilo when she cannot bring herself to talk about their being separated, and a little later Lilo explains the loss of her parents to Stitch when he sees the family photo she keeps under her pillow. For his part, Stitch starts to show a tender side when he becomes fascinated by the classic story of the ugly duckling and identifies with the outcast who did not know where he belonged until he found his true family.

At the end, everything comes together in a frenetic, action-packed climax more in the style of a Looney Tunes short than a Disney feature. Fed up with Jumba and Pleakley's incompetence, the Grand Councilwoman fires them and sends the fierce Captain Gantu (Kevin Michael Richardson) to bring Stitch home. Now acting as a free agent, Jumba chases Stitch all over Lilo's house, which leaves it a wreck and culminates in an explosion. Just when Nani finds a job with David's help, she discovers her house has been destroyed. Moments later, Captain Gantu captures both Lilo and Stitch, but Stitch escapes, leaving Lilo flying to Stitch's home planet. To rescue Lilo, Stitch wins over Jumba to his side. The action grows wilder when a midair rescue fails and Stitch is knocked back to Earth, where he commandeers a gasoline truck, drives it into a sea of lava, and then releases the gasoline as Captain Gantu fires at him. This sets off a big explosion that shoots Stitch back up to Captain Gantu's craft, where Stitch proceeds to overpower him.

When everyone finally lands on the beach, the Grand Councilwoman is already there with her troops. She is set to take Stitch away when he makes a poignant appeal to stay based on family—"It's little and broken," he tells her, "but still good"—that shows how civilized he has become. The Grand Councilwoman, however, is unbending until Lilo, at Mr. Bubbles's urging, shows her the deed to Stitch, which proves that she is entitled to keep her new friend, who is formally exiled to Earth.

Lilo and Nani's home is rebuilt, both literally and figuratively (Mr. Bubbles and the exiled Jumba and Pleakley also become part of Lilo and Nani's extended family), and the film joyfully concludes with a series of darling photos chronicling everything from a Christmas celebration to a trip to Graceland. The final shot is of Lilo's original family photo but with Stitch taped into the corner—a possible metaphor for the movie itself, which magically interweaves Stitch's rambunctious personality and even some wild action into a touching portrait of family endurance.

—Peter N. Chumo II

CREDITS

Lilo: Daveigh Chase (Voice)
Nani: Tia Carrere (Voice)
David Kawena: Jason Scott Lee (Voice)
Jumba: David Ogden Stiers (Voice)
Stitch: Christopher Sanders (Voice)
Pleakley: Kevin McDonald (Voice)
Cobra Bubbles: Ving Rhames (Voice)
Grand Councilwoman: Zoe Caldwell (Voice)
Captain Gantu: Kevin M. Richardson (Voice)
Mrs. Hasagawa: Amy Hill (Voice)
Rescue Lady: Susan Hegarty (Voice)

Origin: USA
Released: 2002
Production: Clark Spencer; Walt Disney Pictures; released by Buena Vista
Directed by: Dean DeBlois, Christopher Sanders
Written by: Dean DeBlois, Christopher Sanders
Music by: Alan Silvestri
Editing: Darren T. Holmes
Art Direction: Ric Sluiter
Production Design: Paul Felix
MPAA rating: PG
Running time: 85 minutes

REVIEWS

Chicago Sun-Times Online. June 21, 2002.

Paula Burns: Frances Conroy
John Bextrum: Christopher Eigeman
Veronica Ventura: Priscilla Lopez
Rachel Hoffberg: Amy Sedaris

Origin: USA
Released: 2002
Production: Deborah Schindler, Paul Schiff, Elaine Goldsmith-Thomas; Revolution Studios, Red Om Films; released by Columbia Pictures
Directed by: Wayne Wang
Written by: Kevin Wade
Cinematography by: Karl Walter Lindenlaub
Music by: Alan Silvestri
Sound: Allan Byer
Music Supervisor: Randall Poster
Editing: Craig McKay
Art Direction: Patricia Woodbridge
Costumes: Albert Wolsky
Production Design: Jane Musky
MPAA rating: PG-13
Running time: 105 minutes

 REVIEWS

Boxoffice. December, 2002, p. 29.
Chicago Sun-Times Online. December 13, 2002.
Detroit Free Press Online. December 13, 2002.
Detroit News. December 13, 2002, p. 3E.
Los Angeles Times Online. December 13, 2002.
Movieline. December/January, 2003, p. 48.
New York Times Online. December 13, 2002.
People. December 23, 2002, p. 35.
Premiere. December, 2002, p. 16.
Premiere. January, 2003, p. 37.
San Francisco Chronicle. December 13, 2002, p. D1.
Variety Online. December 1, 2002.

QUOTES

Chris (Ralph Fiennes) to political manager Jerry (Stanley Tucci): "Do I look as stupid as you think I am?"

The Man from Elysian Fields

Your pleasure is his business.
—Movie tagline

Pleasure is his business . . . call him old-fashioned.
—Movie tagline
Wealth affords the ultimate extravagance.
—Movie tagline

 Box Office: $1.3 million

In some ways, *The Man from Elysian Fields* is like an old-time movie. It's presumably set in the present, but it also has a certain timeless quality. It could just as well be set 100 years ago. It's the kind of story that seems more literary, somehow, than most movies. Perhaps it has something to do with the fact that its about authors and books, but there's something else. Watching *The Man from Elysian Fields* gives the same kind of feeling as reading a good story. The director, George Hickenlooper (who also made *Hearts of Darkness: A Filmmaker's Apocalypse* which covered Francis Ford Coppola's making of *Apocalypse Now*), enjoys the process of telling a story. He lets the events unfold in a leisurely, skillful rhythm.

The big fault of the film is also something it shares with older films. It has a contrived, corny and moralistic ending. The events that lead up to the ending suggest that a man can lie, prostitute himself, and break up his family and still be rewarded by success and fame. It's too bad that screenwriter Philip Jayson Lasker backed down from the more interesting turns his story could have taken.

But until the letdown of an ending, *The Man from Elysian Fields* is full of interesting twists and turns. It follows the usual three-act structure of a screenplay, but somehow, Lasker manages to disguise the fact that he's following the formula. There's a noticeable feeling while watching the movie of having absolutely no idea what's going to happen next. In a release schedule dominated by screenplays full of predictable heroes saving the world, romances conquering despite obstacles, and people overcoming adversity, unpredictability is a quality that really stands out.

The film is about Byron Tiller (Andy Garcia, who was also one of the co-producers of the film). Byron is an author who lives in a charming, albeit small and not-so-fixed-up, bungalow in Pasadena, California. His first book, *Hitler's Child,* imagined a child of Hitler and Eva Braun. The book got several rave critical reviews but has ended up in the remainder bins. He's pinning his hopes on his next book that's something about King Arthur's sword Excalibur and migrant farm workers. Byron and his wife, Dena (Julianna Margulies) desperately need a new cash infusion to help in raising their young son.

When Byron brings his story to his agent, his agent turns him away. Desperate, Byron begs the agent for a loan. "Are you really that desperate?" asks the agent. "Yes," replies Byron. "Good," answers the agent jovially. "The best books come from desperate writers." Things continue to get worse for Byron. He tries to get a job back at his old ad agency but is turned down. He eventually resorts to asking his rich, unfriendly father-in-law for a loan, but is just mocked. All the while, Byron is lying to his wife, telling her that his book was indeed sold and he is busy meeting with people from his literary agency.

When Byron is completely down on his luck, he has a chance meeting with a mysterious figure, Luther Fox (Mick Jagger). Luther gives him a business card and offers Byron a job if nothing else pans out. Byron is so worried about money that he soon finds himself at Luther's office, offering his services. When Byron finds out that Luther runs a male escort service, he refuses the job, but eventually decides that being an escort is the only way he's going to be able to support his family. He tells his wife that his book is under consideration for the Book of the Month club so that he'll need to be attending many night meetings.

Byron's first client is the beautiful Andrea Alcott (Olivia Williams). Andrea is the much younger wife of a famous Hemingway-esque writer, Tobias Alcott (James Coburn). At first Andrea just hires Byron to escort her to social functions, but Byron soon finds himself in the bedroom of the Alcott's Pasadena mansion (played by the Los Angeles home of silent movie star Antonio Moreno). While in an indiscreet act in the bedroom, Andrea's husband walks into the room. He greets his wife cheerfully and introduces himself to Byron. It seems that Tobias, who was once a robust and virile man, encourages his wife to take in gentlemen, since he can no longer please her in that manner.

Things continue to get stranger. Tobias, who in his later years has been suffering from a low writing output, has been working for years on his latest novel. When he finds that Byron, too, is a writer, he asks for a critique. Byron reads it, then tells Tobias that it's not good. Tobias punches him in the nose, then asks him to collaborate on a new book. The deal is that both of them will share writing credit and Byron will collect 30% of the book's earnings. Byron pretty much moves into the Alcott's mansion. He writes with Tobias and services Andrea. In the meantime, his marriage is breaking up. Byron is too thrilled with the chance to work with such a respected figure and doesn't much notice when his wife leaves him. At this point, the story has gotten so strange that it's difficult to guess what possible course it is going to take from there.

Besides the interesting story, one of the highlights of the film is the acting. Especially good is Coburn. The veteran actor's hands are rendered gnarled and nearly useless by arthritis and he's playing a man who is dying, but is still the Alpha Male of the story. Even though he's contained in a body that's failing, he is full of vitality and masculinity. It's a great turn for Coburn. Also really good, perhaps surprisingly so, is Jagger. On the surface, Jagger is the perfect guy to play the slightly devilish, aging gigolo, but Jagger brings more to the role than his appearance and reputation. He gives his character a lot of depth and soul. There is a side story between Jagger's Luther and one of his longtime clients, wealthy Jennifer Adler (Anjelica Huston). Luther no longer services any of his clients except Jennifer. It turns out that suave and jaded old Luther has fallen in love with her. On one of their dates, he takes her out to dinner and asks her to marry him. Jennifer laughs and sputters out, "Why would I do that?" Luther smiles back gamely, but at the same time, Jagger also conveys his great hurt. It's a great scene. Also good is another now-craggy rock star, Michael Des Barres, as one of Byron's fellow escorts who shares horror tales like having to kiss a client's toes.

Critics gave the film mixed reviews. Kevin Thomas of the Los Angeles Times wrote, "With its poetic, moody camera work by Kramer Morgenthau, a frequent Hickenlooper collaborator, this is an elegant film with often surprising twists and an intermingling of naiveté and sophistication." A.O. Scott of the New York Times wrote, "At times, especially when Mr. Coburn is in full billy-goat bluster or Mr. Jagger is purring in his snug designer suits, The Man from Elysian Fields has a raffish, unpredictable charm. These two old-timers grasp the absurdity of the film's premise and appear to enjoy themselves mightily. The filmmakers and the younger cast members are less sure of themselves, lurching from tongue-in-cheek tartness to moist sincerity without finding the right balance of humor and melancholy." Megan Turner of the New York Post wrote, "Stylishly shot by Kramer Morgenthau, Elysian Fields suffers from an air of frosty detachment and a disappointingly stiff performance from Jagger, who also provides an unnecessary voice-over narration."

—Jill Hamilton

CREDITS

Byron Tiller: Andy Garcia
Luther Fox: Mick Jagger
Dena Tiller: Julianna Margulies
Andrea Allcott: Olivia Williams
Tobias Allcott: James Coburn
Jennifer Adler: Anjelica Huston
Greg: Michael Des Barres
Edward Rodgers: Richard Bradford

Origin: USA
Released: 2001
Production: Andrew D.T. Pfeffer, Donald Zuckerman, Andy Garcia; Cineson; released by Samuel Goldwyn Films, Fireworks Pictures
Directed by: George Hickenlooper
Written by: Jayson Philip Lasker

Cinematography by: Kramer Morgenthau
Music by: Anthony Marinelli
Sound: Steuart Pearce, Peter V. Meiselmann
Music Supervisor: Randy Gerston
Editing: Michael Brown
Art Direction: Jay Spratt
Costumes: Matthew Jacobsen
Production Design: Franckie Diago
MPAA rating: R
Running time: 106 minutes

REVIEWS

Boxoffice. December, 2001, p. 54.
Boxoffice. November, 2002, p. 58.
Chicago Sun-Times Online. November 1, 2002.
Los Angeles Times Online. September 27, 2002.
New York Times Online. October 2, 2002.
People. October 14, 2002, p. 44.
Variety. October 29, 2001, p. 30.
Washington Post. October 18, 2002, p. WE37.

QUOTES

Byron (Andy Garcia): "This business you're in. Does it ever make you ashamed?" Luther (Mick Jagger): "No. Poverty does that."

TRIVIA

Title is inspired by Virgil's *Aeneid* where the Elysian Fields is an oasis in Hell for the virtuous.

The Man Without a Past (Mies Vailla Menneisyytta)

Finnish filmmaker Aki Kaurismaki, in his sprightly comedy-drama, *The Man Without a Past*, rejects all artistic flourishes with a deceptive simplicity. His protagonist, referred to in the end credits as M (Markku Peltola), is a man who has forgotten his name and identity. His "past" thus becomes a displacement for the art film culture Kaurasmaki would like his audience to forget, or at least to leave behind at the door.

The setting of his story is an industrial backwater near Helsinki. Yet it is only the surface touches that localize it. In the Third World of today, under tin roofs, the have-nots enjoy *Who Wants to Be a Millionaire?* The homeless that M encounters can be seen as a kind of affirmation of this recent economic development. Like Vittorio De Sica's shanty dwellers in the neorealist classic, *Miracle in Milan* (1950), these outcasts have built their own world, improvising conveniences where none exist, and out of what a supermaterialistic culture has discarded.

Kaurasmaki doesn't need to cut to the affluence and waste of his time to make his point. By showing the contentment and momentary joys of homelessness, his antithesis becomes an assault upon the viewer's conscience which, in the context of elitist art cinema, has become adjusted to the thesis of materialism and accumulation. Kaurasmaki's film thus emerges as a parable for our economically unsettling times.

His own protest that accompanied its screening at the New York Film Festival served to extend his argument. Kaurasmaki, who had planned to attend the event, decided at the last minute to boycott it. His letter to the audience chided the U.S. government for depriving Iran's master filmmaker, Abbas Kiarostami, of a visa so that he could attend the Festival. Submerged within Kaurasmaki's missive was his rage that prevented him from being a party to such bureaucratic outrage.

The Man Without a Past shows up the retrogressive aspect of Finnish bureaucracies as they come up against M's unique plight. The film opens with M on a train, rolling a cigarette and lighting up in a passageway between carriages. Dark-haired and middle-aged, with a physique strengthened by manual labor, there is a kindness beneath his machismo. He appears preoccupied as he returns to his seat. At the station, he alights with his suitcase. It is night as he sits on a park bench, then falls asleep. With one strike to the back of his head, he's knocked out cold by a gang of young hoods. They riffle through his wallet, remove the money, open his suitcase but find nothing of interest except the helmet of a foundry worker. In frustration, they hit and kick him repeatedly, then bury his wallet at the bottom of a trash can, leaving him lifeless and deprived of any vestige of identity.

M is soon placed in intensive care, but to no avail. The life support is quickly turned off and his head covered by a bedsheet. When he's alone, he sits up and tears off the fetters of the operating table. We then see him the following morning, his head completely bandaged, lying motionless on the banks of an inlet. Soon, he is adopted by a homeless family comprised of Nieminen (Juhani Niemela), a night watchman, his wife, Kaisa (Kaija Pakarinen), and their two little boys. Kaisa feeds him soup through his bandage, and is very open in her hospitality, while Nieminen fears that he may have run away from a prison mental hospital.

It soon becomes clear that M has suffered a loss of memory. While availing of the kindness showered on him, he admits, "I don't remember who I am." No matter. The man we see now seems to have benefited from that hard knock. He is no longer the depressed individual we saw at the start of the film, but someone with a purpose. Soon, we see that the character he is pretending to be could be the character his earlier life never allowed him to be. Kaurasmaki doesn't offer us any medical basis for M's plight. Instead, the film chooses to locate M's psychopathological disability within its own brand of "magic realism."

Amongst these homeless, M is accepted for his new self. Whatever may have been the life that he is unable to recall, M emerges as a Finnish "John Doe," not far removed from Frank Capra's eponymous protagonist in the classic *Meet John Doe* (1941). Kaurasmaki's "John Doe," like the Capra model, is perfectly at home living amongst the bottom rung of society. We see Nieminen's two boys pouring water down a chute for a makeshift shower. An obese accordionist sits amongst junk happily playing. As Kaisa waters her plants near where her washing is hung to dry, she is photographed in low-angle against a blue sky, making her look part of an idyllic moment. More important, the Scandinavian cool that pervades the film makes Kaurasmaki's tale appear that much more organic and lifelike.

Even customary rituals are followed by these folk. On Friday night, Nieminen takes M for a drink at a nearby café. While attempting to jog his memory, Nieminen remarks that it's to M's advantage that "life goes forward," implying that if life went backwards, M would really be in trouble. Despite his sincere effort, all M can recall is that he was on a train, and nothing more. Nieminen notices from M's hands that he has been a workman.

We soon see that the scene is not without its do-gooders. For entertainment, there's the Salvation Army choir, listening to whom is a small price to pay for the free food. In fact, it's in their soup line that M meets his love interest, the attractive blond worker, Irma (Kati Outinen). The film momentarily follows Irma to show the lonely life she leads in her one-room dwelling. Though expounding on Christian values to the homeless, when Irma is by herself she finds release in listening to "sinful" rock music.

With the help of Antilla (Sakari Kuosmanen), a ruthless and corrupt security guard, M finds a place of his own, constructed out of shipping containers, near the water's edge. It is a ramshackle dwelling which Antilla rents for "a 100 a week with a sea view." M washes the place, and even manages to get an electricity connection. "What do I owe you?" he says to the lineman who obliges him. Back comes the reply, "If you see me lying face down in the gutter, turn me over." Soon, with his help, M gets a discarded fridge, stove, and even a jukebox to work. To wash his clothes he uses a neighbor's wringer.

Ironically, the obstacles M encounters in his new life come from the state-run institutions designed to help those like him. At the employment office, the lady worker can do

nothing since M can provide no name or social security number. When she calls her boss, M tells him, "I was hit on the head." Her superior, thinking M is making fun of them, barks, "There's a drama school round the corner."

It is at a bar that M gets a free cup of hot water, into which he inserts a tea bag of his own, and is even served a plate of leftover food. Similarly, at the Salvation Army thrift shop, Irma finds him a suit, a shirt and tie, wearing which he begins to look respectable. She even gets him a temporary job at the Army.

As their relationship develops, we can see that Irma is shy of physical intimacy when she allows M to walk her home. When she tries to draw him out, all M can say of his past is "I remember a factory hall . . . a bright flame." He then adds, "But it could be a dream." After a picnic, she speaks of the joy of life that is now visible on his face. He says it is from the strength she has inspired in him. She merely calls it "Mercy."

What the film now makes clear is that M doesn't just take, but gives as well, and that his giving makes a difference to those around him. He advises the gospel choir to sing rock and roll melodies so as to reach a larger audience, and even offers them his jukebox to scavenge for ideas. The lady manager at the Army, who has always wanted to be a singer, decides to sing lead, and sing about the "futility of life without Christ." Soon, instead of sitting morosely, the homeless are dancing to pop arrangements, as lyrics speak of how "pain can be found in the smallest of hearts" and how one can be "haunted by the Devil."

In the film's scheme of things, the quirkiest twists of fate can spring out of the everyday in the most unexpected manner. When M sees a group of iron workers near the Army building, something draws him to them. He shows his expertise, and is soon hired. When he goes to the bank to cash his first paycheck, he has to open an account. Just then, a gunman, who turns out to be an employer who wants to meet his payroll, storms in with a rifle. The bank has only one employee, a female teller. After procuring his loot, the gunman locks the teller and M inside the vault. The event brings M tabloid popularity as the victim who cannot remember his name. This in turn leads to his ex-wife contacting the police.

It is then that we come to know that M's name is Jacko. When he visits his ex-wife, he, and we, learn that after their divorce, he decided to head south to look for a job. "We fought a lot," she tells him. "You gambled and our marriage broke down." He is grateful but unrepentant, as he returns to Irma's arms and the new life he has found.

The film can elicit no higher praise than that bestowed on it by A. O. Scott in the *New York Times*. He compares it to the "great films of the 1930's and early 40's" and finds that "it is at once artful and unpretentious, sophisticated and completely accessible, sure of its own authority and generous toward characters and audience alike—a movie whose intended public is the human race."

—*Vivek Adarkar*

CREDITS

M: Markku Peltola
Irma: Kati Outinen
Nieminen: Juhani Nielmela
Kaisa Nieminen: Kaija Pakarinen
Anttila: Sakari Kuosmanen

Origin: Finland, Germany, France
Language: Finnish
Released: 2002
Production: Aki Kaurismaki; Pandora Film, Pyramide Productions, Sputnik; released by Sony Pictures Classics
Directed by: Aki Kaurismaki
Written by: Aki Kaurismaki
Cinematography by: Timo Salminen
Sound: Jouke Lumme, Tero Malmberg
Editing: Timo Linnasalo
Costumes: Outi Harjupatana
Production Design: Markku Patila, Jukka Salmi
MPAA rating: Unrated
Running time: 97 minutes

REVIEWS

New York Times Online. October 2, 2002.
Variety. May 27, 2002, p. 24.

AWARDS AND NOMINATIONS

Nomination:
Oscars 2002: Foreign Film.

Margarita Happy Hour

Hipsters, single moms, and the cycles of life.
—Movie tagline

Margarita Happy Hour proves conclusively that the most influential director on the contemporary independent cinema scene is the late John Cassavetes (1929-1989). First-time director Ilya Chaiken uses Cassavetes fly-on-the-wall, naturalistic style to tell her story of several working-class women friends who meet regularly to unwind over drinks. The results are only partly successful.

Margarita Happy Hour concentrates mainly on the plight of Zelda (Eleanor Hutchins), a struggling freelance illustrator who lives in Brooklyn and takes a job writing for a porn magazine in order to help raise her daughter, Little Z (Jonah Leland). Zelda is given little assistance from Little Z's father, Max (Larry Fessenden), an alcoholic struggling writer who lives with Zelda.

Zelda's one weekly respite is a "Margarita Happy Hour" with her single-mother friends (played by Holly Ramos, Barbara Sicuranza, Amanda Vogel, Macha Ross, and Kristin Dispaltro). But trouble begins in Zelda's routine when Max develops a romantic interest in one of the friends, Natali (Ramos), a drug addict who has moved in with Zelda, Max and Little Z, following a near-fatal overdose. In the end, the relationships are sorted out after Zelda realizes she has outgrown aspects of her friendships with her "happy hour" drinking buddies.

Critic Megan Turner, in her *New York Post* review, amusingly compared *Margarita Happy Hour* to *Sex and the City*, but of course this indie film is far less slick in its (low-budget) presentation and focuses admirably on a more economically challenged group of women (their warts and all). In fact, sex isn't always the topic of the ironically-named "happy hours." Rather, the garrulous women discuss child-rearing, problems at work, even Medicaid. The free-flowing discussions form the heart of the film, since the plot is minimal.

What hurts this slice-of-life portrait are the performances by the supporting cast: somehow the fast-paced over-lapping dialogue ends up sounding like prepackaged diatribes about working-class concerns. Perhaps the actors needed to improvise more or perhaps they were improvising too much! In either case, the most important scenes come off unconvincingly, despite Chaiken's use of cinema verité camerawork (lensed by Gordon Chou). At least the lead, Eleanor Hutchins, is more than adequate in her other scenes. (Megan Turner calls her "a bright new talent . . . who looks remarkably like Courtney Cox.") Larry Fessenden, the indie horror film director (see *Wendigo*, reviewed in this edition), playing the role of Max, doesn't make his character particularly touching or even memorable, but he lends competent support.

At least Chaiken's debut contains interesting touches, even if these touches aren't part of the key dialogue scenes; they indicate this director's nascent talent. In one shot, the women, following a "happy hour" session, walk along the street as they vocally imitate an annoying nearby car alarm. The drunken demeanor and false giddiness is neatly summed up in the tableaux long-take, made all the more poignant by the presence of the women's toddlers walking alongside their mothers in the frame. Another, more stylistic moment features a hallucinogenic box-light effect during a loft party with Zelda's friends.

Margarita Happy Hour tries hard to portray the type of characters who are rarely given a voice, single mothers trying to lead better lives, though the film is most eloquent when the characters aren't saying anything at all.

—*Eric Monder*

CREDITS

Zelda: Eleanor Hutchins
Max: Larry Fessenden
Natali: Holly Ramos
Graziella: Barbara Sicuranza
Raquel: Amanda Vogel
Sofia: Macha Ross
Marie: Kristen Dispaltro
Will: Will Keenan

Origin: USA
Released: 2001
Production: Michael Ellenbogen, Susan Leber; Susie Q Productions; released by Passport Pictures
Directed by: Ilya Chaiken
Written by: Ilya Chaiken
Cinematography by: Gordon Chou
Music by: Max Lichtenstein
Sound: Stephen Altobello
Editing: Meg Reticker, Ilya Chaiken
Production Design: Bridget Evans
MPAA rating: Unrated
Running time: 98 minutes

REVIEWS

Los Angeles Times Online. July 5, 2002.
New York Times Online. March 22, 2002.
Variety. February 12, 2001, p. 38.
Washington Post. May 17, 2002, p. WE43.

QUOTES

Zelda (Eleanor Hutchins) to her girlfriends: "It was my decision to keep the baby, so it's my responsibility."

Mariages
(Marriages)

Quebecois director Catherine Martin creates a stunner debut feature with *Mariages,* set in Victorian-era Quebec. Martin successfully blends elements of magic realism (a ghost, a corpse that transformed into a salt woman) and an erotic love story that recalls the Mexican sensation *Like Water for Chocolate.* And in fact, if we forget that Martin's story takes place in rural Quebec we find that the film's narrative, with its forbidden love, unquenchable erotic desire, and the supernatural elements comes dangerously close to *Like Water for Chocolate*'s story sans the Mexican cuisine. Replace Mexican cookery with the magical qualities of the deep and lush forest and we still feel like we have dove into an enticing literary experience.

Martin, however, proves that she has an eye for detail and a talent for directing her actors. Martin joins the ranks of other Quebecois women directors such as Guylaine Dionne (*The 3 Madeleines*) and Swiss-born Lea Pool in offering provocative, feminine stories. Martin's protagonist, Yvonne (Marie-Ève Bertrand) recalls the titular character from Roman Polanski's *Tess* or perhaps the character Catherine from *Wuthering Heights* in that, despite the confines of her Victorian upbringing, wildness flows in her blood. Yvonne is most happy tramping through the forest with her skirt hitch up or swimming nude beneath a waterfall. And one day, while prancing about like a wood nymph, Yvonne spies on a young man swimming nude, which arouses her latent desires.

Set in 1890, Yvonne has been raised by her elder sister Hélène (Guylaine Tremblay)—their mother died young—to enter a convent. However, the rebellious Yvonne has fallen in love with nature and sneaks out to the forest or to swim in a pool under a waterfall, two forbidden acts. Yvonne feels the call of the wild and is entranced by the spirits of the natural world. She often visits a sick friend whose caretaker is a witch who lives in a cabin. After Charles (David Boutin), a man promised in marriage to Yvonne's niece, arouses her desires, Yvonne begs the witch to arrange a secret marriage ceremony between her and Charles. Charles is forced to leave Yvonne soon after their secret tryst and Yvonne finds that she is pregnant. Yvonne undergoes an herbal abortion and nearly dies. After she recovers, Hélène threatens to take Yvonne to the convent, but Yvonne has other plans and escapes to live alone in the woods until her lover returns to her. The final scene marries supernatural elements with the natural world and eroticism as the two lovers are reunited during a windstorm. They lie on the ground spooning each other while braving the elements.

Based on the story of a distant relative, Martin chose to give the story a happy ending while fictionalizing real events. The distant relative had left her village after an arranged marriage and was forced to give up her baby for adoption, then she spent the rest of her life in a deep depression. Martin portrays the dynamics between a domineering matriarch, Hélène, her 15-year-old daughter whose hand has been promised in an arranged marriage to Charles, and Yvonne who has been promised to the convent. Martin then carefully arranged a set of subplots revolving around a dying friend, a witch, and her father's decision to display his deceased wife's body to the public where she is honored as a saint.

Although the film didn't attract Quebecois audiences, it did open in Toronto to critical acclaim. Liz Braun of the *Toronto Sun* called *Mariages* "... an auspicious debut." And Martin found that male viewers saw the erotic tale as a doorway into a woman's soul.

—*Patty-Lynne Herlevi*

CREDITS

Helene: Guylaine Tremblay
Yvonne: Marie-Eve Bertrand
Charles: David Boutin
Maria: Helene Loiselle
Noemie: Markita Boies

Origin: Canada
Language: French
Released: 2001
Production: Lorraine Dufour; Coop Video de Montreal, Productions 23; released by Film Tonic
Directed by: Catherine Martin
Written by: Catherine Martin
Cinematography by: Jean-Claude Labrecque
Music by: Robert Lepage
Editing: Lorraine Dufour
Production Design: Real Chabat
MPAA rating: Unrated
Running time: 95 minutes

REVIEWS

eye Weekly Online. March 7, 2002.
Toronto Sun Online. March 8, 2002.
Variety Online. September 9, 2001.

Master of Disguise

Disguise the limit.
—Movie tagline
1,000 faces . . . and not a single clue.
—Movie tagline

 Box Office: $40 million

In a way, all you really need to know about *The Master of Disguise* is that the main character is named Pistachio Disguisey. If that seems like the kind of gut-busting name that's right up your alley, then, hey, *The Master of Disguise* is for you. If, on the other hand, the name makes you groan silently and gives you a tiny sinking feeling, then maybe you have a little something called sophistication. The whole dumb name thing is a great test joke for the film because, amazingly, the humor level of the movie stays exactly at the same level throughout the movie. It never goes up, which is not good. But, on the other, it never goes down, which is not bad, since it means we're spared a bunch of bathroom jokes.

Well, actually, the humor level does go down a couple of times. There is a segment in the film in which Dana Carvey is dressed as a pile of animal poo. And it's a big pile, too, so, consider yourself forewarned. Also, there is a villain, Bowman (Brent Spiner), who, as villains are wont to do, laughs maniacally whenever he's being evil. Whenever Bowman does his evil laugh, he ends up farting, then looking abashed. This was a big hit with the younger folks in the audience at a screening in Los Angeles.

But anyone who's seeing the movie gets fair warning of what they are going to be in for. For one thing, the ads for the film read, "Disguise the Limit." Trailers for the movie showed star Dana Carvey in a variety of unfunny roles, including being dressed as a turtle and saying, "Turtle, turtle." Even folks who were unawares and were waiting for the movie to begin would soon see the words, "A Happy Madison Production." Those words mean Adam Sandler's production company and promise another quality film along the lines of *Mr. Deeds, Deuce Bigalow: Male Gigolo,* and *Joe Dirt.* Just to keep in mind, theaters will refund your money if you leave within 15 minutes of the movie's start.

The Master of Disguise was to be Carvey's comeback of sorts. The comedian made his name on *Saturday Night Live* for his characters like the Church Lady, Johnny Carson, George Bush, and Garth, Wayne's goofy sidekick in the *Wayne's World* films. He tried a half-hour show on TV but it was very edgy and came off the air as quickly as it went on. In 1998, Carvey had heart surgery, but his doctor accidentally worked on the wrong aorta. (Carvey subsequently sued the doctor for millions of dollars and gave his settlement to charity.)

Carvey didn't exactly have momentum coming in to this film, but he did have a degree of audience sympathy due to his health problems and he had a high degree of creative control. Carvey and Harris Goldberg wrote the film. Add to those the fact that the premise—Carvey wears a bunch of disguises—plays up perfectly to Carvey's particular set of talents, and the film had a pretty good chance to be a nice comeback. Reportedly, Carvey wanted to make a film that his kids could enjoy. Unfortunately, Carvey seems to associate being kid-friendly with being only vaguely funny. His characters are all different, and he jumps into them with great zest, but they don't go anywhere. They are just sort of there.

Pistachio (Carvey) is that great Sandler archetype, the idiot man-child. He works in his father's restaurant, spilling plates of pasta on the guests (ha-ha!) and involuntarily imitating them. Unbeknownst to Pistachio, his imitations are a family trait. His family comes from a long line of people who disguise themselves and help save the world. His father, Frabbrizio (poor James Brolin), was once a master of disguise who was always busy saving the world. Once, while imitating Bo Derek (Derek is played by Derek herself), he gets into too close of a call and decides that he will quit the business and never tell his son about it.

One night, Frabbrizio and his wife (Edie McClurg) are kidnapped by Bowman. Bowman has an evil plan to steal the world's greatest treasures (i.e. the lunar module, the constitution, the liberty bell, etc.) and auction them off at a black market ebay. Bowman makes Frabbrizio disguise himself as a variety of celebrities like Michael Johnson, Jessica Simpson, and Jesse Ventura (who all play themselves) so that he can charm his way past security guards to steal the goods. It's amazing that celebrities, except the collection of b-listers that do appear, seemed to know that they should stay far away from this film.

Pistachio needs to rescue his parents but doesn't have a clue how to do it until his grandfather (Harold Gould) shows up and tells him about his heritage. He shows Pistachio his father's secret "nest" or laboratory in the attic and shares the secret of "energico" which is a lot like The Force. Here, there are some tiresome segments where Pistachio learns how to do things like fight by slapping a dummy and saying "Who's your daddy?" He also gets a comely assistant, Jennifer (Jennifer Esposito), to help him find his parents. She ends up being a love interest, which is completely fantastical, since Pistachio is so immature that it seems like their love is more like cradle-robbing than anything else.

While tracking down his parents, Pistachio dons his various disguises. Besides the turtle and the poo, he's also a Belgian tax collector, a British detective, George W. Bush, and a schoolgirl. The most promising character is an old lady who seems to think that everyone is hitting on her, but it doesn't get into any good humor territory. This is typical for the film. Carvey dresses up as a character, he speaks in a funny voice and that's it. He doesn't give his characters anything funny to do or say—they simply appear. It's too bad, because Carvey certainly seems to have energy when he's portraying the character. The problem is that he needed to hire a new writer who could give his characters something funny to say.

Carvey has a good screen presence, but it's not enough to overcome the dismal script. Gould is over-the-top as the Disguisey grandfather, but that's appropriate in this role. Esposito has to do some fancy acting to not only appear to think that Carvey's antics are funny, but that she finds his character appealing. Brolin is fine, but did he really need to be in a film like this? (Can you imagine him and wife Barbra Streisand at home discussing their respective days? Barbra: "I was writing and directing an original film today, and you?" James: "We did the fart scene.")

Critics hated the movie immensely. On Rotten Tomatoes.com, a web site that collects movie reviews, a mere 2% of reviewers gave the film a positive review. Lisa Schwarzbaum of *Entertainment Weekly* gave the film a D— and wrote, "Watching this awful, stillborn comedy assembled out of rusty spare parts from secret agent movies and run-of-the-mill *Saturday Night Live* skits . . . children who never knew Dana Carvey in his glory years on SNL will be nonplussed by the overwound, elfin doofus trying so hard to entertain." Jonathan Foreman of the *New York Post* wrote, "No one but a convict guilty of some truly heinous crime should have to sit through *The Master of Disguise,* an unbearably tedious and unfunny comedy." And Elvis Mitchell of the *New York Times* wrote that the film is "so family-safe it feels sheathed in plastic Bubble Wrap. Unfortunately, it's not even as much fun as popping the bubbles."

—*Jill Hamilton*

CREDITS

Pistachio Disguisey: Dana Carvey
Jennifer: Jennifer Esposito
David Bowman: Brent Spiner
Frabbrizio Disguisey: James Brolin
Mother: Edie McClurg
Grandfather: Harold Gould
Sophia: Maria Canals
Barney: Austin Wolff

Origin: USA
Released: 2002
Production: Barry Bernardi, Todd Garner, Sid Ganis, Alex Siskin; Revolution Studios, Happy Madison

Productions, Out of the Blue Entertainment; released by Columbia Pictures
Directed by: Perry Andelin Blake
Written by: Dana Carvey, Harris Goldberg
Cinematography by: Peter Collister
Music by: Marc Ellis
Music Supervisor: Michael Dilbeck
Editing: Peck Prior, Sandy Solowitz
Art Direction: Domenic Silvestri
Costumes: Mona May
Production Design: Alan Au
MPAA rating: PG
Running time: 80 minutes

REVIEWS

Boxoffice. July, 2002, p. 30.
Chicago Sun-Times Online. August 2, 2002.
Entertainment Weekly. August 18, 2002, p. 48.
Los Angeles Times Online. August 2, 2002.
New York Times Online. August 2, 2002.
TV Guide. July 27, 2002, p. 22.
USA Today Online. August 2, 2002.
Variety Online. August 5, 2002, p. 20.

Max

Art + Politics = Power
—Movie tagline

Anyone vaguely familiar with the history of the twentieth century knows that Adolf Hitler was an aspiring artist before becoming the century's greatest symbol of evil. Fictional treatments of the German dictator always focus on the monster Hitler became rather than his earlier life. Looking at the young Hitler might be a way of better understanding the horrors he created. *Max,* writer-director Menno Meyjes' treatment of this material, unfortunately doesn't find much interesting to portray. Meyjes creates Max Rothman (John Cusack), a composite of real-life art dealers with whom Hitler associated, as a means of achieving the easy—some might say uneasy—irony of a Jew trying to help the Jews' greatest enemy.

The upper-middle-class Rothman, who lost an arm in the Great War, owns a Munich gallery converted from a factory, complete with bare walls, hanging chains, train tracks, dripping water, and echoes, all meant not-so-subtly to suggest the Holocaust. Rothman specializes in the work of contemporary German artists like George Grosz (Kevin McKidd), whose paintings, inspired by the war, find the horrors lurking in everyday life. A chance meeting with

Hitler (Noah Taylor) spurs Rothman to encourage the artist. Interestingly, the work Rothman initially sees is not shown to the viewer, though later sketches are. By this omission, is Meyjes suggesting that Hitler's paintings are so mediocre that the audience would not understand Rothman's sympathetic interest? The drawings eventually displayed resemble Albert Speer's Third Reich architecture.

Thereafter, *Max* shifts between Hitler's efforts to find a distinctive subject and style, his growing involvement with an as-yet-unnamed group of disaffected soldiers and ex-soldiers, and Rothman's relations with his wife, Nina (Molly Parker), parents (David Horovitch and Janet Suzman), and mistress, Liselore (Leelee Sobieski). While Grosz finds an outlet for trying to make sense of the chaos of the twentieth century, the average German has trouble coping with the humiliation of losing the war. Bunking with his former garrison because of his poverty, Hitler finds himself surrounded by growing feelings of nationalism and anti-Semitic resentment. Though he initially resists the latter, he slowly finds himself caught up in his fellows' emotional turmoil.

In comparison, Rothman's life is rather dull. He has devoted himself to art as a way of finding meaning. Neither art, however, nor the women in his life are enough to soothe his restlessness. The film is built around a contrast between the different ways Rothman and Hitler deal with their ennui. The two aren't friends and don't truly understand each other, but they recognize a similar vague yearning in each other, in part because both were in the deadly battle at Ypres. While some might praise Meyjes for the subtlety with which all this is conveyed, others might think it's all too low key to have much of an impact.

For a film about the passions swirling around art and politics, *Max* is strangely remote. It's as if Meyjes' sole idea was wondering would happen if a Jewish art dealer tried to help the young Hitler without ever deciding exactly what the result would be. The characters and situations need fleshing out for the film to have the desired effect. Rothman is more an outline than a fully realized character. His obliviousness to the growing evidence of the threat to Jews may bother some viewers, and the presentation of Hitler is likewise simplistic.

Meyjes' Hitler, though far from sympathetic, is offered as a rather pathetic figure who falls into what he will see as his true calling by accident. The young Hitler seems almost annoyed by how easily he can sway crowds, and since they become mesmerized by the rambling shouting of an overly excited neurotic, it is not at all clear why they are so easily swayed. To present Hitler as a compelling orator, regardless of his sick message, might suggest he is a sympathetic character, and Meyjes definitely does not want that. The dilemma for the filmmaker is his desire to explain Hitler while keeping his subject at some distance, not to mention his trying to deal with a highly complex subject with a few brushstrokes.

While this Hitler seems too ordinary to become a powerful dictator who spins the entire world out of control, that may be Meyjes' point: that great evil can grow out of pettiness. On the other hand, Meyjes also seems to suggest that if only Rothman had given Hitler, who clearly prefers art to politics, a one-man show, history might have been different. Rothman's belief in the healing power of art, while commendable, seems naïve in these circumstances. If only Meyjes had explored what drew Hitler to art, what he hoped to express, and how his aesthetic ambitions influenced what he was to become. As it is, Hitler's artistic yearnings are vague and inconsequential.

The most interesting and successful segment of *Max* involves a bit of performance art performed by the frustrated artist Rothman. The art dealer strips and enters a gigantic meat grinder to suggest how German society destroys individuality. Hitler, of course, also becomes a performance artist, yet his screaming diatribes have the desired effect, while Rothman's effort is seen as an embarrassing failure. The numerous parallels between the characters give the film some impetus, but most are too obvious, almost banal. Much more could have made of Hitler's accidental discovery of propaganda as art. Making his directorial debut, Meyjes is a veteran screenwriter best known for *The Color Purple* (1985), which also suffers from underdeveloped characters and situations, with conflicts occasionally popping up out of nowhere.

Taylor, a fine actor, receives little help from his director, portraying Hitler as a greasy bundle of tics and self-pity. Taylor's Hitler is a more extreme variation on his young David Helfgott in *Shine* (1996), in which he offers more insight into the schizophrenic's complexity than Geoffrey Rush's one-note performance as the older Helfgott. His Hitler, however, is either moping or outraged, with no layers in between.

A greater deficit is Cusack. When given a well-written part in a good film, such as *The Grifters* (1990) and *Being John Malkovich* (1999), Cusack can be effective. Yet he doesn't bring much to his roles, and when a part is underwritten, as with Rothman, he's at a loss. Compare his work here with what Liam Neeson does with a similar role in *Schindler's List* (1993). Cusack is a modern throwback to such stars of the past as Glenn Ford and Van Johnson—likable but bland.

The rest of the cast has too little to do. Parker looks elegant as Rothman's wife, but her role consists mostly of thoughtful poses. Sobieski seems too young for her part, and why Rothman is drawn to Liselore is never clear, other than a man of his class is entitled to a mistress. Suzman can be excellent, as with *The Draughtman's Contract* (1982), *The Singing Detective* (1986), and, especially, in a 1972 television production of *Hedda Gabler*, but Meyjes gives her only a couple of lines, reducing her to standing around in the background while others chatter on. McKidd has some pres-

ence as the drunken Grosz, and it would have been interesting to see some parallels between this successful artist and Hitler the failure.

In an interview with the *New York Daily News*, Cusack said that *Max* "tries to understand evil in a more sophisticated way, so we might stop it from happening again." There's a big difference between aiming for sophistication and achieving it, between hinting at understanding and truly grasping a complex subject. The film's heavily ironic ending, with an overhead shot suggesting the great divide between the fates of the two protagonists, elicits not insight but a shrug.

—Michael Adams

CREDITS

Max Rothman: John Cusack
Adolf Hitler: Noah Taylor
Liselore Von Peltz: Leelee Sobieski
Nina Rothman: Molly Parker
Max's father: David Horovitch
Max's mother: Janet Suzman
David Cohn: Peter Capaldi
George Grosz: Kevin McKidd
Nina's father: John Grillo
Captain Mayr: Ulrich Thomsen

Origin: Hungary, Canada, Great Britain
Released: 2002
Production: Andras Hamori; Pathe, Aconit Pictures, H2O Motion Pictures; released by Lion's Gate Films
Directed by: Menno Meyjes
Written by: Menno Meyjes
Cinematography by: Lajos Koltai
Music by: Daniel Jones
Sound: Istvan Sipos, Fred Brennan
Editing: Chris Wyatt
Art Direction: Tibor Lazar
Costumes: Dien van Straalen
Production Design: Ben van Os
MPAA rating: R
Running time: 106 minutes

REVIEWS

Boxoffice. November, 2002, p. 124.
Chicago Sun-Times Online. January 24, 2003.
Entertainment Weekly. January 17, 2003, p. 57.
Los Angeles Times Online. December 17, 2002.
Los Angeles Times Online. December 27, 2002.
[New York] Daily News. December 27, 2002, p. 52.
New York Times. December 27, 2002, p. E19.

People. January 13, 2003, p. 39.
Premiere. January, 2003, p. 22.
USA Today. January 3, 2003, p. D12.
Variety Online. September 11, 2002.

QUOTES

Hitler (Noah Taylor) to Rothman (John Cusack): "I am the new avant garde and politics is the new art."

Me Without You

In *Me Without You*, which screened at the 2002 London Film Festival, we meet the main characters, Holly (Ella Jones) and Marina (Anna Popplewell), when they are teenage girls laughing together on a sunny day in 1973. The two girls, who live next door to each other in a London suburb, have been friends forever. They decide they need to make the friendship more official so they create a special ceremony. With great seriousness, they write "Holly and Marina = Harina. Now we two are one" on a piece of paper, seal it up in a Charlie perfume bottle and bury it in the yard. Meanwhile, Marina's soulful older brother, Nat (Cameron Powie), strums his guitar and looks on from a far corner of the yard. The scene is, in a sense, a microcosm of how the whole movie will play out. There's the intense relationship between Marina and Holly, the possible intrusion of a third party (Nat) and the great attention to period detail (the Charlie bottle.)

The film is the project of Sandra Goldbacher, who was the force behind *The Governess*. Goldbacher directed the film and co-wrote it with Laurence Coriat, who wrote 1999's *Wonderland*. According to the *Los Angeles Times*, Goldbacher used her own experience of being in a best friendship from the ages 11 to 17 when writing the film.

It's typical that young girls would want to have such a close friendship, so close that it becomes an entity of its own, but for Holly and Marina, it's obvious why they need each other. They each have in their lives what the other lacks. Marina has grown up in a wreck of a home. Her father, Ray (Nicky Henson), has left the family and only returns periodically. When he comes back, he doesn't seem to realize how his absence has affected the family and he has the unrealistic expectation that the family should treat him with love and respect. Marina's mother, Linda (Trudie Styler, who is the wife of Sting), is somewhat of a mess. She's an ex-croupier and a former wild child who doesn't want to give up her youthful party girl ways. She wears loud, sexy clothing, piles on the make-up and wouldn't be at all out of place in an

episode of *Absolutely Fabulous*. Linda is a loving mother though and instills Marina with confidence.

Confidence is just what Holly needs. She comes from a solid Jewish family that values education and solid citizenship. Where Marina's house is all tacky fur rugs and gaudy 1970s colors, Holly's house is decorated in somber, dark hues. Her father, Max (Allan Corduner), is a gentle loving man but not particularly charismatic. Every time Marina comes over to visit Holly, he always greets her with the same lame joke. Holly's mother, Judith (Deborah Findlay), is a button-downed woman who expects the same kind of restraint from her daughter that she's used all her life. She tells Holly things like she shouldn't expect too much from life so that she won't be disappointed. She also makes sure that Holly knows that she is smart, not pretty, so she might as well not even try to enhance her looks. At the same time, Judith is fascinated by Marina's wild ways and appearance. Whenever Marina comes over to their house, Judith fawns over her like a groupie, making sure that Holly realizes that she shouldn't even bother trying to be as glamorous as Marina.

As they grow older, they slip more deeply into their designated roles. Marina (now played by Anna Friel) is a daring party girl who wears all the latest fashions, listens to all the latest music and smokes cigarettes that she holds between her fishnet stockinged toes. Holly (Michelle Williams of TV's *Dawson's Creek* sporting a fine English accent) reads Sylvia Plath, feels depressed and secretly pines for Marina's older brother Nat (Oliver Milburn).

When Marina finds out about a party that is rumored to be attended by the Clash, she knows that they have to go. The two girls get dressed up in their finest new wave gear. Marina looks smashing, Holly looks like she is wearing some kind of black garbage bag. When they get to the party, it's just a few guys sitting around drinking and doing drugs. Marina, not wanting to appear unsophisticated, agrees to try heroin. She ends up retching in the restroom the whole night, but declares the experience fabulous. Meanwhile Holly ends up having sex with Nat, even though he has a girlfriend.

Before leaving town, Nat writes Holly a loving note explaining that while the night they shared had been "beautiful," it was poorly timed and he was sorry that things couldn't work out for them—at least not right then. Nat gives the note to his sister to pass on to Holly, but Marina reads the note then throws it away. It's the first sign that, although Marina seems to be the stronger of the two girls, she actually feels very threatened by Holly.

As the two move to Brighton to study at Sussex University, their friendship becomes more complex. Marina is an indifferent student, while budding writer Holly is thrilled by school. She is especially interested in one of her professors, Daniel (Kyle MacLachlan), a youngish Literature professor who encourages his students to study both Adam Ant and

Baudelaire. Daniel meets with some of his students at a local pub, and he and Holly start up a spirited intellectual discussion on Bergman films.

Marina, feeling left out, senses that she could gain some sort of superiority over Holly if she could seduce Daniel. Holly and Daniel begin a slow courtship, while unbeknownst to her, Marina has been scoring drugs for the professor and has been a frequent visitor to his bed. Their relationships with Daniel are not especially satisfying—he is condescending to Marina about her lack of intellect and openly annoyed by Holly's constant chatter—but that's not the point. When Holly finds out what has been going on, she has a realization of just how far her friend will go to undermine her.

Their friendship doesn't immediately end, it's too big and binding for that. Holly knows that Marina is bad for her, but they've been friends for so long. Plus, Holly doesn't have the confidence to realize that she can strike out on her own. It's a gradual process for Holly to start coming into herself and what makes her powerful. Marina fights Holly's emerging sense of self with every tool in her arsenal. Holly doesn't know the extent of what's going on, but she knows that their friendship has become more of a pain than a joy. "When I'm with you, I feel ugly and 11 and depressed and jealous and stuck!" shouts Holly as Marina becomes progressively clingier.

Years pass, Marina marries and is horrified to find herself pregnant. It's all so pedestrian and boring. Meanwhile, Holly does a courtship dance with Nat, coming together with him, only to be separated by some circumstance of timing or events. She is crazy for him, but he's married to a beautiful French actress. The obstacles that keep them apart might be a little soap opera-ish, but they seem far more believable than those in a typical Meg Ryan lite romance.

One of the better aspects of the story is the acting. Particularly good is Friel. She's perfect as the train wreck of a girl who's both exciting but big trouble. It's fun to watch her ever changing wardrobe and parade of hair colors. Williams underplays her role as the girl coming into her own power. As Stephanie Zacharek of *Salon* put it, "Williams, an extraordinary and underrated actress, plays Holly's evolution from awkward, timid kid, to poised, self-aware grownup without banging any pots and pans." Milburn is energetic and appealing as Nat and plays the role with appropriate passionate longing. Styler is fun as the aging party girl and Findlay does a nice job showing how repressed emotions come back to the surface in such a toxic and harmful manner.

The other strong suit of the film is the attention to detail. The period music is right on, from just the right songs from the 1980s, coupled with songs by troubadours like Nick Drake and Tim Buckley. Marina's house is perfect in all its 1970's glory and Marina and Holly's poster-decorated college flat is exactly as it should be. Also accurate (and fun to watch) is Marina's wardrobe. For people who grew up during that era, it's fun to see forgotten fashions (i.e. wearing 1950's party dresses) again.

Critics liked the film. Zacharek called the film "alert and beautifully crafted." Kevin Thomas of the *Los Angeles Times* wrote, "Goldbacher gives us a sense of a real friendship, strained by the need of both women to mature, and embraces the emotional messiness of growing up." Maitland McDonagh of *TV Guide* wrote, "Anchored by Friel and Williams's exceptional performances, the film's power lies in its complexity." Some critics didn't agree. Merle Bertrand of *Film Threat* wrote, "This might just be an example of one of those films that women relate to better than us guys."

—Jill Hamilton

CREDITS

Marina: Anna Friel
Holly: Michelle Williams
Nat: Oliver Milburn
Daniel: Kyle MacLachlan
Linda: Trudie Styler
Ray: Nicky Henson
Max: Allan Corduner
Judith: Deborah Findlay
Isabel: Marianne (Cuau) Denicourt
Carl: Steve John Shepherd

Origin: Great Britain
Released: 2001
Production: Finola Dwyer; Dakota Films; released by Samuel Goldwyn Films, Fireworks Pictures
Directed by: Sandra Goldbacher
Written by: Sandra Goldbacher, Laurence Coriat
Cinematography by: Denis Crossan
Music by: Adrian Johnston
Sound: Alan O'Duffy
Music Supervisor: Kle Boutis
Editing: Michael Ellis
Art Direction: Stephen Carter
Costumes: Rosie Hackett
Production Design: Michael Carlin
MPAA rating: R
Running time: 107 minutes

REVIEWS

Boxoffice. February, 2002, p. 55.
Chicago Sun-Times Online. August 16, 2002.
Entertainment Weekly. July 26, 2002, p. 46.

Los Angeles Times Online. July 12, 2002.
New York Times Online. July 5, 2002.
Sight and Sound. December, 2001, p. 54.
Variety. September 17, 2001, p. 25.
Washington Post. September 13, 2002, p. WE37.

QUOTES

Judith (Deborah Findlay) to daughter Holly (Michelle Williams): "Some people are pretty people and some people are clever people."

Men in Black II

Same planet. New scum.
—Movie tagline

Back In Black.
—Movie tagline

 Box Office: $190.4 million

T he plot of *Men in Black II* is minimal at best, but then the reason one would go to a *Men in Black* movie is not necessarily for the great storyline. However, just so one has the proper bearings, here it is. In 1978 aliens called Zarthans came to Earth to escape an evil Kylothian alien called Serleena (Lara Flynn Boyle). Serleena wants the "Light of Zartha" with which she will conquer the Zarthans (or something like that). The Zarthans, led by Ambassador Lauranna (Linda Kim) work with Earth Agent Kay (Tommy Lee Jones) to convince Serleena that the Light has just left in a rocket. So, for the last 24 years Serleena also has been rocketing through the universe, destroying an assortment of planets and looking for the Light. What Serleena has just discovered, though, is that the Light of Zartha never left the Earth and now, in 2002, Serleena is back. Oh, and by the way, if the Light is still on the Earth at Midnight tomorrow, the Earth will be destroyed.

Unfortunately, the only person who might know where the Light of Zartha is is Agent Kay who, if one remembers from 1997, was "neuralized" (had his memory wiped out) at the end of the previous movie which means he can't possibly be of much help to either the secret government organization he used to work for or to Serleena. Unless, of course, he can be "de-neuralized." Agent Kay, now known as Kevin Brown, is the postmaster in Truro, Massachusetts and Agent Jay (Will Smith) is sent to bring him in so he can be de-neuralized, find the light, defeat Serleena and save the Earth.

A lot of the original talent behind the original 1997 film have returned in this 2002 sequel, but one who is missing may be the one critics have noticed the most, the original writer, Ed Solomon. Most reviews for *Men in Black II* have criticized the fact that little is new in the movie and that the plot is unexceptional. The blame for this, therefore, would seem to fall at the word processors of replacement writers Robert Gordon (*Galaxy Quest*) and Barry Fanaro (*The Crew*).

Of course there are new elements in the film. For example, there's Lara Flynn Boyle as the tentacle-spouting primary villain Serleena—which was to be played originally by *X-Men*'s Famke Janssen who had to drop out when a family member became ill a few days into shooting. Boyle plays her role with a high level of world-weary boredom and a Victoria's Secret wardrobe but is not as much fun as Vincent D'Onofrio's buggy performance in the first film. Also new is Johnny Knoxville from MTV's *Jackass* playing Serleena's henchman, or should I say henchmen? With two heads and only a half a brain between the two of them, his double-named character, Charlie and Scrad, seems to have the sole purpose of being stupid and pointing Serleena in the direction of the Light.

This will lead both Serleena and Agent Jay to another new element, Rosario Dawson's Laura Vasquez. As a witness to Serleena's first attempt to find the light, Dawson's pizza parlor waitress will not only prove to be a pivotal plot point she will also provide a love interest for Agent Jay. (The disappearance of Linda Fiorentino's character who becomes agent L at the end of the last film is explained for those who care.)

While the all-conspiracy video store that provides Agent Kay with information to jog his memory is amusing, perhaps the best new thing about the sequel, providing one of its few highly laughable surprises—which abounded in the first film—is the sudden appearance of an entire civilization living in a locker in Grand Central Station. It seems whoever opens their locker becomes their god, but then they also seem to be quite drunk! Wish the script had done more with them.

There are also a few entertaining cameos. Peter Graves is the host of a cheesy Ed-Wood-type television show called *Mysteries in History* which, in episode 27 we are given most of the 1978 background for the story. Watch for master make-up effects man Rick Baker (or at least his ponytail) as a passport control officer and director Barry Sonnenfeld as the stunned father of the family that now lives in Agent Kay's apartment where he has quite a stash of weapons hidden away. (And by the way, that is Tommy Lee Jones' real daughter playing Sonnenfeld's daughter in that scene.) Perhaps the most anticipated cameo, though, belongs to Michael Jackson who refused to be listed as one the aliens passing as human while living on Earth from the first program. Now he appears as Agent M, part of the alien affirmative action program who is desperate to get a better assignment.

However, as indicated earlier, it is not necessarily the new things that attract moviegoers to this *Men in Black* movie. Maybe it is the familiar that appeals to them. The unlikely pairing of odd couple 55-year-old Jones and 33-year-old Smith with their unflappable manner and deadpan dialogue for example. Their easygoing partnership with Jones as the stoic brains and Smith as the hip energy is always entertaining to watch.

Also back is Tony Shalhoub as Jeebs, the pawn-shop owning alien whose lop-sided head can be blown off then grow back. This time he is the source of a black market de-neuralizer which consists of the beaters from an electric mixer, a bowling ball and an Evinrude outboard motor. Similarly, the worms return but they no longer work at headquarters because they have been suspended for stealing from the duty free shop. They don't seem to be suffering much though in their low-ceilinged, shag-carpeted bachelor pad where Laura takes refuge.

Best of all, though, is the expanded role for Frank the Pug (Mushu). Several critics have groaned over the scene of Frank barking along to "Who Let the Dogs Out" on the car radio, but less jaded audiences found it to be hilarious. And one has to admit Frank makes quite a dashing figure in his Men in Black suit.

One thing that's not so funny are the annoying corporate tie-ins which should soften the fact that Columbia has to share 50% of the film's gross (up to a certain point) with the film's major players, Smith, Jones, Sonnenfeld, and executive producer Steven Spielberg to name a few. Consequently we are bombarded with references to Burger King, Mercedes-Benz, Mountain Dew, Spring PCS, Hamilton Watches . . . and who can forget the agents' trademark Ray-Bans?

This *Men in Black* sequel took five years to reach the screen. It had a number of false starts and a lot of behind-the-scenes problems, especially concerning salaries and profit percentages. Also, like *Spider-Man, Men in Black II* was one of the many movies delayed because changes had to be made after the attack on the World Trade Center on September 11. In the original finale the space ship was supposed to launch from the roof of one of the twin towers but in the wake of the tragedy it was converted to just a generic New York City rooftop. In fact, any shots that included the WTC resulted in their being digitally erased.

The original *Men in Black* was a monster 4th of July hit back in 1997, grossing $587.2 million worldwide and giving Will Smith, who proceeded this with another 4th blockbuster, *Independence Day,* the honor of basically owning that weekend for movie releases. *Men in Black II* has already made more money its opening weekend than did the original. Even though most reviews have not been kind, with this kind of money at stake, you can rest assured there will be a *Men in Black III.* If *III* is as lightweight as *II,* it will still attract audiences. The franchise is funny and it's comfortable and familiar like a favorite pair of jeans. The special effects are good and this time we even ended with 4th of July fireworks over the Statue of Liberty. What more do we need from a laid-back summer film?

—*Beverley Bare Buehrer*

CREDITS

Kay: Tommy Lee Jones
Jay: Will Smith
Serleena: Lara Flynn Boyle
Scrad/Charlie: Johnny Knoxville
Laura Vasquez: Rosario Dawson
Zed: Rip Torn
Jeebs: Tony Shalhoub
Agent Tee: Patrick Warburton
Ben: Jack Kehler
Newton: David Cross
Hailey: Colombe Jacobsen
Motorman: Peter Spellos
New York guy: Lenny Venito
Agent M: Michael Jackson
Frank the Pug: Tim Blaney (Voice)

Origin: USA
Released: 2002
Production: Walter F. Parkes, Laurie MacDonald, Steven Spielberg; Amblin Entertainment; released by Columbia Pictures
Directed by: Barry Sonnenfeld
Written by: Robert Gordon, Barry Fanaro
Cinematography by: Greg Gardiner
Music by: Danny Elfman
Sound: Peter Kurland
Editing: Steven Weisberg, Richard Pearson
Art Direction: Sean Haworth, Alexander Hammond
Costumes: Mary Vogt
Production Design: Bo Welch
MPAA rating: PG-13
Running time: 88 minutes

REVIEWS

Chicago Sun-Times Online. July 3, 2002.
Chicago Tribune Online. July 6, 2002.
Christian Science Monitor Online. July 5, 2002.
Entertainment Weekly. July 6, 2002.
Hollywood Reporter Online. June 25, 2002.
Los Angeles Times Online. July 3, 2002.
New York Post Online. July 3, 2002.

New York Times Online. July 3, 2002.
People. July 15, 2002, p. 31.
USA Today Online. July 3, 2002.
Variety. July 1, 2002, p. 25.
Washington Post. July 5, 2002, p. WE30.

QUOTES

Jay (Will Smith): "I'm about to attack one of the most feared aliens of the universe with four worms and a mailman."

Men with Brooms

There's more than one way to sweep a woman off her feet.
—Movie tagline
A comedy that will sweep you off your feet!
—Movie tagline

Box Office: $4.2 million

Coming from the country that brought us *Jesus of Montreal, The Black Robe,* and *Mon Oncle Antoine* and sweeping across Canadian boxoffice is the new Canadian hit *Men with Brooms*. All the right ingredients present themselves in actor-writer-director Paul Gross's release and yet this film came out half-baked. The debut feature boasts an all-star Canadian cast featuring Gross, Molly Parker, Leslie Nielsen, and Peter Outerbridge that attracted public response. With a budget of $7.5 million Canadian, *Men with Brooms* played on 213 screens across Canada and earned $1,040,000 during its first week. However, while *Men with Brooms* portrays a few laughable moments, the actors wade through trite dialogue and melodramatic scenes through a great deal of the film.

Men with Brooms at times comes across as a farce, at other times as a spoof on the underdog wins theme, and yet, this curling film fails to achieve success in either genre. As a farce, it fails at the absurdity factor and as a spoof, the filmmakers assume that their viewers will catch on to all of the analogies. The film proved to be the most popular film at the Seattle International Film Festival and a third screening was added to meet audience demands. However, the Canadian film industry is in danger if its most popular film of the year is represented by cliched Canadian humor and a badly-written script while other deserving films remain in the shadows.

Although Canadian filmgoers flocked to see *Men with Brooms,* Canadian film critics panned Paul Gross's debut effort calling it "bland" (Jason Alexander, *eye Weekly*) and an "an example of promise unfulfilled despite many charming moments" (Bruce Kirkland, *Toronto Sun*). Alexander not only criticized the film, but also attacked the Canadian film industry: ". . . since our film industry craves the validation only a hit movie can create, I hereby pledge $50 towards the marketing of *Atanarjuat* (*The Fast Runner*), a forthcoming Canadian film that deserves support and boasts a superior array of bare asses." Alexander also compares *Men with Brooms* to the Farrelly Brothers, known for appealing to the lowest common denominator.

As the film opens we see old man Foley and his daughter Amy (Molly Parker) retrieving a championship curling stone from the bottom of the lake. The old man dies of a heart attack, but leaves his one wish—that his curling team, estranged for the past 10 years would reunite and win the championship. After the funeral, the four players, who include slick Chris Cutter (Paul Gross), who threw the previous championship by cheating, Eddie Strombeck (Jed Rees), the sleazy James Lennox (Peter Outerbridge), and a yes-man Neil Bucyk (James Allodi), reluctantly agree to follow the old man's wishes.

However, it soon becomes apparent that the men (and the women in their lives) have the sort of problems that can't be solved by the film's duration. Chris, with his chiseled good looks, is haunted by his past, including jilting his fiancée Julie Foley (Michelle Nolden) and let his teammates down. One might add, that his father (Leslie Nielson), a former curling champion, has disowned Chris—leading to more dramatic complications. A thug is in hot pursuit of Lennox, who turned drug dealer after leaving his curling teammates. And Neil's ice princess wife (Kari Matchett) threatens to divorce Neil if he has any plans to participate in the curling championship.

Meanwhile, Amy, a struggling alcoholic, pursues a relationship with Chris even as he tries to patch things up with Julie. But Julie, now an astronaut, is more interested in going off into space as her name moves up a list of alternates. Amy catches Julie and Chris engaging in steamy sex in an automobile and she goes off the wagon. And while it seems that we have a soap opera instead of a comedy, Gross and his writing team will solve all of the characters insurmountable problems by the film's end even if that means pushing a comedy into farce territory.

Men with Brooms, although clever at times, is an example of the Canadian film industry's attempt to compete at the Hollywood boxoffice. However, the industry has lost sight of what they do best, idiosyncratic art films.

—*Patty-Lynne Herlevi*

Chris Cutter: Paul Gross
Amy Foley: Molly Parker
James Lennox: Peter Outerbridge
Gordon Cutter: Leslie Nielsen
Neil Bucyk: James Allodi
Donald Foley: James B. Douglas
Joanne: Polly Shannon
Eddie Strombeck: Jed Rees
Julie Foley: Michelle Nolden
Eva Foley: Barbara Gordon
Linda Bucyk: Kari Matchett
Lilly Strombeck: Jane Spidell

Origin: Canada
Released: 2002
Production: Robert Lantos; Serendipity Point Films;
released by Alliance Atlantis
Directed by: Paul Gross
Written by: Paul Gross, John Krizanc
Cinematography by: Thom Best
Music by: Paul Gross, Jack Lenz
Sound: Sylvain Arsenault
Editing: Susan Maggi
Art Direction: Nigel Churcher
Costumes: Noreen Landry
Production Design: Paul Denham Austerberry
MPAA rating: Unrated
Running time: 102 minutes

REVIEWS

Boxoffice. June, 2002, p. 70.
eye Weekly Online. March 7, 2002.
Variety. March 3, 2002, p. 39.

AWARDS AND NOMINATIONS

Nomination:
Genie 2002: Actress (Parker), Orig. Screenplay.

Merci pour le Chocolat (Nightcap)

Although there is no blood in sight and this psychological thriller reflects on a possible murder that took place in the distant past, Claude Chabrol's 53rd feature, *Merci pour le Chocolat,* proves unsettling to say the least. Viewers familiar with the "French Hitchcock"'s filmography, who are waiting for a violent climax will be rewarded instead with a tricky puzzle revolving around identity and psychosis. The Swiss haute bourgeoisie setting appears glacial on the surface and the protagonists seem to be swimming their way through a drug-induced stupor for a good part of the film. And yet, violent tendencies at least for the character Mika (Isabelle Huppert) curdle below her placid exterior, threatening to erupt at any time. Most of the film's tension revolves around Mika's mysterious behavior, which is spider-like as she spins psychological webs. We would expect her to kill and eat her husband, virtuoso pianist Andrè Polonski (Jacques Dutronc), at any moment.

We witness a wedding between Polonski and Mika at the beginning of the film that resembles a claustrophobic victory for Mika (who set her sights on Polonski a long time ago). We learn that the couple had married, then divorced, and are now reunited once again. The childless Mika runs her family's chocolate factory, but like everything else in her life, this seems like a passionless venture based on her bourgeois status and filled with self importance. She lives in a mansion with her famous husband and stepson, Guillaume (Rodolphe Pauly), who acts as a constant reminder of Polonski's deceased wife.

Young piano virtuoso Jeanne Pollet (Anna Mouglalis) learns that she was almost switched at birth with Guillaume Polonski. She begins to question her true parentage and decides to visit Polonski at his home, against her concerned mother's wishes. Although Polonski denies that Jeanne is his daughter, Mika takes a fancy to the young pianist. And her undeniable talent causes all to question her blood connection to Polonski. But this mysterious connection is one of many of Chabrol's red herrings and the director plays with our usual expectations, even as he plans on leading us to another conclusion. Jeanne grows suspicious of Mika after she spills hot chocolate meant for her stepson onto Jeanne's sweater. Jeanne, the daughter and girlfriend of pathologists, decides to have the chocolate analyzed and learns that the chocolate contained Rohypnol, also known as the date rape drug.

When Jeanne pushes her possible relationship to Polonski onto her mother, Louise (Brigitte Catillon), the mother confesses that Jeanne was a result of artificial insemination since her father was unable to impregnate Louise.

However, this doesn't stop Jeanne from spending a weekend at Mika and Andrè's home. One night, Mika spikes Guillaume and Jeanne's drinks, then sends them out to renew Andrè's Rohypnol prescription. Jeanne falls asleep at the wheel and the car hits a wall, but the driver and passenger avoid injury. Meanwhile, Mika confesses her original crime, (she drugged Polonski's wife then sent her out to pick up a prescription), to a sympathetic Polonski and awaits justice.

The British press celebrated Chabrol's film. George Perry (*BBC-Films*) praised the actresses' performances: "Isabelle Huppert excels as the enigmatic Mika and Anna Mouglalis is a stunning new young talent in one of Chabrol's most intense psychological mysteries." *Sight and Sound* critic Keith Reader made several comparisons between English psychological thriller master Alfred Hitchcock and Chabrol. He found many similarities between Isabelle Huppert's Mika and Ingrid Bergman's performance in *Notorious* and Judith Anderson's Mrs. Danvers in *Rebecca,* while also taking note of Chabrol's use of mirrors, stairways, and the audience's sense of vertigo and claustrophobia. And *Evening Standard* critic Neil Norman cited, "Regarded by many as the French Hitchcock, Chabrol's intricate and assured exercise in mood shifts is here more akin to the rigorous tonal authority of Stanley Kubrick."

Chabrol not only deftly handles various cinematic devices, but his film recalls the work of other directors besides Hitchcock. The use of close-ups of the actresses' faces echoes Ingmar Bergman's psychological dramas. Similar to Bergman's *Persona,* Chabrol's camera also zooms into the actresses faces in which very little emotion is expressed. We do not see any stock emotions such as the obligatory fear or relief exhibited here. The character Jeanne comes across as self-assured and we don't get the feeling that she fears for her life. And Mika seems enraptured by grief rather than the need for vengeance. After all, Mika is a victim suffering from a need to kill those that she loves, acting out her spider-like tendencies if only as a reflex. She in fact, is more likely to harm herself rather than the innocent bystanders that surround her.

Huppert, who won Best Actress at Cannes (2001) for her portrayal of a sadomasochistic piano instructor in Michael Haneke's *Piano Teacher,* is an actress infamous for risk-taking. Many fans of Huppert will find her synonymous with Chabrol's films and recall her performances in *La Cèrèmonie* (1995), in which she did take part in a blood bath, *The Story of Women* (1988), and *Violette* (1978). Isabelle Huppert was also The Golden Space Needle audience award for Best Actress at the Seattle International Film Festival for her performance in *The Piano Teacher* and she received a runner-up mention for her performance in *Merci pour le Chocolat.* And many viewers who had seen both films would have found similar themes, sans sadomasochistic eroticism between the two films.

Similar to Hitchcock, Chabrol's films often feature elegant icy blondes as both victim and predator. While Hitchcock often portrayed male surrogates of himself (often men with neurotic tendencies and a multitude of fears), Chabrol focuses more on women protagonists. Hitchcock was also accused of misogynist tendencies, whereas Chabrol tends to sympathize with his female protagonists and antagonists even when they protect a murderer (Stefane Audran's character in *Le Boucher*) or slay an entire family (Isabelle Huppert and Sandrine Bonnaire's characters in *La Ceremonie*). Chabrol once again empathizes with a murderess in *Merci* as the director shoots Huppert's Mika breaking down under the weight of her past deed. As the film's end credits roll, we watch Huppert languish on a couch and her facial expressions reveal her suffering and anguish. The spider has trapped herself in a web of her own making. Chabrol makes certain that we, the audience, also sympathize with Mika even though we might have liked her to reap her karmic reward earlier in the film.

Chabrol proves that with time and practice a filmmaker can become a true virtuoso. Serving up his usual dark and bittersweet noir, *Merci pour le Chocolat* has been spiked with audience-pleasing poison du jour, which we happily drink.

—Patty-Lynne Herlevi

CREDITS

Mika Muller: Isabelle Huppert
Andre Polonski: Jacques Dutronc
Jeanne Pollet: Anna Mouglalis
Guillaume Polonski: Rodolphe Pauly
Dufreigne: Michel Robin
Louise Pollet: Brigitte Catillon
Axel: Mathieu Simonet

Origin: France, Switzerland
Language: French
Released: 2000
Production: Marin Karmitz; MK2, France 2 Cinema, YMC Productions; released by First Run Features, Empire Pictures
Directed by: Claude Chabrol
Written by: Claude Chabrol, Caroline Eliacheff
Cinematography by: Renato Berta
Music by: Matthieu Chabrol
Sound: Jean-Pierre Duret
Editing: Monique Fardoulis
Art Direction: Yvan Niclass
Costumes: Elisabeth Tavernier
MPAA rating: Unrated
Running time: 99 minutes

REVIEWS

BBC Films Online. June 6, 2001.
Boxoffice. December, 2000, p. 53.
Chicago Sun-Times Online. August 23, 2002.
Evening Standard Online. June 7, 2001.
Los Angeles Times Online. August 16, 2002.
New York Times. July 28, 2002, p. AR11.
New York Times Online. July 31, 2001.
Sight and Sound. June, 2001, p. 49.
Variety. September 18, 2000, p. 39.

TRIVIA

The film is based on Charlotte Armstrong's (the pen name of Jo Valentine) 1948 novel *The Chocolate Cobweb.*

Millennium Mambo (Qianxi Mambo)

Taiwanese director Hou Hsiao-hsien is considered a cinematic master by film critics and has been directing films in Taiwan since 1985. Although the director had created a solid filmography in his own country, his films finally made it to the U.S. in 2000 with the release of *Flowers of Shanghai,* the director's only period drama. *Flowers of Shanghai,* along with a retrospective on the director's work toured arthouses and the films were later distributed on video. Make no mistake, Hsiao-hsien's work would never be shown outside the arthouse circuit or international film festivals and even then the films received mix reviews from the audience. Viewers of *Millennium Mambo* walked out of screenings at the Vancouver International Film Festival and the Seattle International Film Festival. The two most common complaints about the film were that it moved too slow and viewers had a difficult time relating to the characters.

James Luscombe, a reviewer for the Canadian online publication *Exclaim!,* panned *Millennium Mambo* by calling the film an "... oddly infuriating work." Then the critic went on to say, "stunningly shot (every image glows and hums like neon) ... for a film with such a character-driven focus, it consistently resists any audience identification with its protagonist." Written by Tien-wen Chu, this film focuses on restless and rebellious Taiwanese youth who spend all their time nightclubbing and drugging. However, besides a thin plot in which the character Vicky (Qi Shu) lives with an abusive and possessive boyfriend that she can't seem to leave, this film lacks an actual story.

Perhaps, the writer wanted to draw in young viewers who would be intrigued by the rave culture, pulsating house music and beautiful lead actress. However, combined with Hsiao-hsien's contemplative style of filmmaking, the filmmakers miscalculated the film's audience reaction. Hsiao-hsien works in a style similar to the French director Robert Bresson in that he prefers long takes, a static camera and low-key performances in which the actors internalize their emotions. The film audience that would appreciate this approach to filmmaking tends to be of an older generation not raised on MTV-style images and probably not interested in the rave culture. And yet, *Millennium Mambo* awkwardly combines rave culture with a non-linear structure, long takes and uninteresting characters. One is left to wonder if the Taiwanese filmmakers had felt the pressure of the dominant film market that includes 18- to 25-year-old males.

As the film opens, we see Vicky running in a subway as she narrates her story from ten years into the future. In 2001, she's a barmaid and dancer who's finally left her abusive boyfriend and who experiences an epiphany while on a trip to Japan where she saw snow for the first time. Taiwanese actress Shu's (*Beijing Rocks*) talent is under-utilized in this film. She throws tantrums, drinks herself into a stupor, vomits and lights up cigarettes in every scene. The character Shu plays never moves past one-dimensional airhead and we never experience any epiphanies as we stare at our watches hoping that one, the film will end soon, or two, the character would undergo a less subtle transformation. Even more infuriating is the film's non-linear approach in which Vicky's story reveals itself from various angles while hopping back and forth through time.

Perhaps it is best to place *Millennium Mambo* in context with the director's other films. For instance, the provocative *The Flowers of Shanghai* revolved around various escorts or flowers that took care of middle-class Taiwanese men's sexual needs. Similar to *Millennium Mambo,* the flowers entrenched themselves in the drug culture of their time, which revolved around the use of opium. However, due to the fact that the director was moving back through time to a distant era, slow takes, static camera shots and careful framing of the scenes embellished *The Flowers of Shanghai* and the same approach acted as a hindrance to *Millennium Mambo.* And quite possibly filmgoers have grown tired of watching characters throw their lives away on drugs.

According to film scholar Geoff Andrew in his book, *The Director's Vision,* "His style is at times reminiscent of Ozu, with its generally static camera and simple compositions ..." and his "quiet, impressionistic narratives build steadily to an emotional pay-off that is often devastating when it finally comes." *Millenneum Mambo* offers us a small pay-off when we see Vicky playing with snow in Japan. However, viewers lose two hours wading through contemplative moments for five minutes of transcendence.

—*Patty-Lynne Herlevi*

CREDITS

Vicky: Shu Qi
Jack: Jack Kao
Hao-Hao: Chun-hao Tuan
Xuan: Yi-Hsuan Chen
Jun: Jun Takeuchi

Origin: Taiwan, France
Language: Chinese
Released: 2001
Production: Eric Heumann, Tien-wen Chu; Paradis Film, 3H Productions, Orly Films, Sinomovie; released by Ocean Films
Directed by: Hou Hsiao-Hsien
Written by: Tien-wen Chu
Cinematography by: Pin Bing Lee
Music by: Yoshihiro Hanno, Giong Lim
Editing: Ching-Song Liao
Production Design: Wen-Ying Huang
MPAA rating: Unrated
Running time: 106 minutes

REVIEWS

Variety Online. May 22, 2001.

Minority Report

Everybody Runs
—Movie tagline
Crime can be predicted, the guilty arrested before the law is broken, the system was never wrong . . . until it came after him.

Box Office: $132 million

When Stephen Spielberg first became widely known to the movie-going public, it was for a film about a huge great white shark which endangered people swimming off the Atlantic Coast. For more than a quarter of a century since directing *Jaws* (1975), he has been responsible for numerous other thrilling cinematic spectacles, including popcorn films featuring the heroic adventures of an intrepid archeologist (the Indiana Jones films of the 1980's), fearsome dinosaurs run amok (1993's *Jurassic Park* and its sequel), and two stirring encounters of a most memorable

kind with aliens (1977's *Close Encounters of the Third Kind* and 1982's *E.T.: The Extraterrestrial*). In recent years, his output has increasingly grown more serious and thoughtful, the threat to survival in these films coming not from sharks, snakes, dinosaurs, or unfamiliar creatures from outer space, but from ourselves. In *Schindler's List* (1993), *Amistad* (1997), *Saving Private Ryan* (1998), and *A.I.: Artificial Intelligence* (2001), characters struggle arduously in situations set in motion by mankind's own dark, destructive, and senseless impulses.

Now, in his admirable sci-fi mystery *Minority Report*, a man finds himself imperiled in a society where pervasive advances in technology allow businesses to anticipate your desires and target you based upon your past purchases, and the police to anticipate your intentions and target you for permanent imprisonment based upon what they claim will be your future actions. Spielberg chose to set *Minority Report* in 2054, futuristic but not so far ahead of today as to lose its relevance to our current lives. He has noted in interviews how new technologies we have embraced are already stripping us of our privacy. Spielberg has also pointed out that the film may have even greater relevance due to government actions in the wake of the September 11th attacks which have caused concerns not only about privacy but also about civil liberties and due process. Are we being foolhardy, and will we someday look back and feel we allowed things to go too far? Such serious, thought-provoking questions come to mind while watching *Minority Report*, which raises them amidst some thrilling action, suspense, and amazing special effects.

The film takes place in Washington, D.C., and accompanying its instantly-recognizable government buildings, monuments and memorials are structures featuring decidedly newfangled architecture and magnetic highways upon which traffic can hurry along both horizontally and vertically. Also relatively new is the government's Department of Pre-Crime, which in the previous six years has been able to eliminate murder and mayhem by detecting, arresting, and imprisoning transgressors before they have a chance to transgress. This beneficial pilot program, seemingly infallible and incorruptible, relies on the extraordinary psychic abilities of three Pre-cogs, a trio of mutant human beings who have been drugged and forced to lie suspended in a pool of special solution with wires leading from their brains relaying their visions of people's evil intentions to a sophisticated computer system. The department's elite police unit then gets a jump on criminals using the Pre-cogs' foresight, and act to prevent the crimes from ever actually occurring.

Pre-Crime's highly-capable chief is John Anderton (suitably-determined Tom Cruise), brought in by his superior and "the father of Pre-Crime" Lamar Burgess (always welcome vet Max von Sydow). Anderton believes vehemently in this setup, which has effectively prevented others from going through the agony he has endured since the kidnapping and apparent murder of his young son. That event, which filled him with a gnawing guilt since it happened while he was supervising the boy at a crowded public pool, blew apart Anderton's life, leading to the dissolution of his marriage to Lara (Kathryn Morris. Anderton not only attempts to assuage his grief through his work but also through the use of drugs scored during late-night jogs through the seedier sections of town, as well as repetitive viewing of holographic images of his son and wife in happier times.

We are first introduced to Anderton and his specialized unit when the Pre-cogs pick up on a man's intention to murder his philandering wife and her lover. This information is forwarded to Anderton, who stands before a large screen and sees what the Pre-cogs saw, expertly manipulating the images before him with vigorous gesticulations of his laser-lit gloves reminiscent of an orchestra conductor (or, perhaps, a film director piecing together shots for his latest work). His fascinating "scrubbing" of the images allows him to pinpoint and extract the all-important clues about who, where, and when. That done, Anderton and the other officers don jet packs to fly to the scene of the impending offense, swooping down in exhilarating fashion to apprehend the would-be assailant. The man is then sent off to the eerie and amazing Hall of Containment, where prisoners are sealed in coffin-like tubes and forced to view the images of what they had intended to do on an endless loop.

There is no investigation, no chance to defend oneself with legal representation in a court of law, just swift, sure interception and permanent incarceration. Constitutional rights are subjugated in the name of public safety. Before the system goes national, cocky and questioning detective Danny Witwer (Colin Farrell, so good in 2000's *Tigerland*) arrives to scour the operation for flaws on behalf of the Department of Justice, much to the annoyance of firm-believer Anderton. This firm belief is shaken to the core when the Pre-cogs foresee Anderton murdering someone he has never even heard of named Leo Crow within 36 hours, something which he has no intention of doing. Aghast, he angrily accuses Witwer of somehow rigging the setup to frame him and makes a speedy getaway, the department's top pursuer now the focus of a vigorous pursuit.

In preparation for *Minority Report,* Spielberg assembled a think tank of scientists, urban planners, architects, writers, and others for a three-day brainstorming session about what is just around the corner for our society. One thing all agreed upon is that we are currently enjoying the last vestiges of privacy. As 2054 is depicted in Spielberg's film, it is virtually impossible to be inconspicuous in a society filled with technology like retinal scanners to identify you and your location, holographic store greeters who address you by name and inquire about your satisfaction with recent purchases, and billboards like the one for Guinness which calls out to

Anderton as he dashes by that it sure looks like he could use a cold one.

There are a number of highly-effective and exciting scenes as hunted Anderton tries to "stay below the radar" as best he can while struggling to make sense of his situation. He leaps from car to car on a high-speed vertical freeway. He narrowly escapes Witwer and other jet pack-propelled officers in dramatic fashion in a dark alleyway and inside an automobile factory. Anderton seeks advice from creepy Iris Hineman (highly-effective Lois Smith), whose pioneering research into precognition led to the unit's founding. Surrounded by rather viscous vegetation, she informs him that while the three Pre-cogs are never wrong, they sometimes disagree. The differing or dissenting viewpoint, called the minority report, most often comes from the most gifted and reliable one named Agatha (an impressive Samantha Morton). If Anderton could extract a minority report from her, its alternate view of the future would surely point to his innocence.

Of the many striking shots in *Minority Report,* probably the most remarkable comes when the police and an army of tiny robotic spiders are closing in on Anderton, holed up in a rundown tenement after having a ghoulish surgeon (memorable Peter Stormare) replace his eyeballs to escape detection. One continuous overhead shot follows the spiders as they spread out through the building and identify its inhabitants in the midst of various activities until finally focusing on Anderton submerged in a tubful of water. He almost escapes detection until a spider doubles-back and scans his still-raw new eyes, scurrying away without knowing that it had encountered the wanted man. Anderton keeps his old eyes for the retinal scanners he must pass to get into the restricted home of the Pre-cogs, where he abducts a shivering, dazed, and distressed Agatha. A well-constructed and even comical scene take place in a mall as Agatha's abilities allow Anderton to escape one step ahead of his pursuers. When the two are able to locate Crow, they find out that he is part of a plot to frame Anderton, pretending to be the killer of his son. Even though all three Pre-cogs predicted murder, Anderton asserts his free will and chooses to take the man into custody. However, a struggle ensues, and Crow ends up dead.

Witwer's investigation into the Pre-Crime system convinced him that both Anderton and the man sent away for murdering a woman named Anne Lively were innocent, but when he reports this to Burgess the senior official promptly silences him with a well-placed bullet. Soon Anderton is taken into custody and shipped off to the Hall of Containment. A talk Lara happens to have shortly thereafter with Burgess makes her realize that he is behind all this sinister activity, afraid that Anderton would find out that he had killed Lively, Agatha's mother, to seize her unusually-skilled daughter. At gunpoint, Lara frees Anderton and the two publicly confront Burgess in a tense scene that ends in the elder man's suicide. With faith shattered in the Pre-Crime system, it ceases operation, and in a final peaking through of Spielbergian sentiment, the three liberated Pre-cogs live happily ever after as do Anderton and Lara, who is revealed to be pregnant.

Minority Report is based upon a 1956 short story by the late science fiction writer Philip K. Dick, whose works have been previously adapted in such films as *Total Recall* (1990) and *Blade Runner* (1997). Spielberg signed onto the project after Cruise sent him an early script, later revised by Scott Frank (1998's crime drama *Out of Sight*). Dick's story was only used as a starting point, an intriguing means by which he could raise questions about the advisability of the path our choices are taking us down, especially with regard to the loss of our privacy. Spielberg has said that, as he gets older, he finds himself contemplating matters of greater import that are bound to be reflected in his films. This exciting and intelligent cautionary tale is both easier to follow and swallow than *A.I.,* being accompanied by both seamlessly-integrated, amazing special effects and a simple core premise of a hero we can root for who struggles to unravel a mystery amidst a hostile environment, his life and the truth at stake.

To tell such a tale, Spielberg wanted the look and feel of classic film noir, accounting for its grittier images and the use of low key and high contrast lighting techniques by his cinematographer and frequent collaborator Janusz Kaminski. An effective score is provided by another frequent Spielberg collaborator, John Williams. Their efforts, along with the laudatory work of production designer Alex McDowell, special effects magic by at least six companies, and, of course, the star power of Cruise, combined to make *Minority Report* a hit with a majority of critics. It also went over well with audiences: filmed on a budget of $102 million, it grossed just over $132 million in domestic boxoffice before also doing good business overseas.

—*David L. Boxerbaum*

CREDITS

Chief John Anderton: Tom Cruise
Agatha: Samantha Morton
Danny Witwer: Colin Farrell
Director Lamar Burgess: Max von Sydow
Fletcher: Neal McDonough
Dr. Iris Hineman: Lois Smith
Dr. Solomon Eddie: Peter Stormare
Gideon: Tim Blake Nelson
Jad: Steve Harris
Lara Clarke: Kathryn Morris
Leo Crow: Mike Binder
Wally the Caretaker: Daniel London
Sean: Spencer (Treat) Clark

Evanna: Jessica Capshaw
Knott: Patrick Kilpatrick
Anne Lively: Jessica Harper
Sarah Marks: Ashley Crow
Howard Marks: Arye Gross

Origin: USA
Released: 2002
Production: Gerald R. Molen, Bonnie Curtis, Walter F. Parkes, Jan De Bont; 20th Century-Fox, Dreamworks Pictures, Cruise-Wagner Productions, Blue Tulip; released by 20th Century-Fox
Directed by: Steven Spielberg
Written by: Scott Frank, Jon Cohen
Cinematography by: Janusz Kaminski
Music by: John Williams
Sound: Ronald Judkins
Editing: Michael Kahn
Art Direction: Chris Gorak
Costumes: Deborah L. Scott
Production Design: Alex McDowell
MPAA rating: PG-13
Running time: 145 minutes

REVIEWS

Chicago Sun-Times Online. June 21, 2002.
Entertainment Weekly. June 28, 2002, p. 115.
Los Angeles Times Online. June 21, 2002.
Nation. July 22, 2002, p. 34.
New Republic. July 22, 2002, p. 30.
New York. July 8, 2002, p. 44.
New York Times. June 21, 2002, p. E1.
Newsweek. July 1, 2002, p. 57.
People. July 1, 2002, p. 33.
Time. June 24, 2002, p. 60.
USA Today Online. June 23, 2002.
Variety. June 24, 2002, p. 25.
Wall Street Journal. June 21, 2002, p. W1.
Washington Post. June 21, 2002, p. WE45.

QUOTES

John Anderton (Tom Cruise): "I have to find out what happened to my life."

TRIVIA

Cruise's character John Anderton drives a 2054 Lexus concept car.

AWARDS AND NOMINATIONS

Nomination:
British Acad. 2002: Visual FX.

Mr. Deeds

Don't let the fancy clothes fool you.
—Movie tagline

Box Office: $126.2 million

M r. *Deeds* is not the first movie a comedic actor would put out. It's the kind of movie an actor would put out after they had done some early first movies that they cared about, become famous as a result, then needed to release some more movies to keep the cash flowing. This movie is sort of a placeholder, a sort of "I'm still here. Don't forget to keep buying tickets to my movies." It's not as bad so much as it is not good. It's like no one really cared enough to put any passion into the film.

Part of the problem might be that Sandler made the film with several of his longtime collaborators. Tim Herlihy, who wrote the screenplay, has written or co-written six of Sandler's other films. Jack Giarraputo, the producer, has produced all of Sandler's films. Those two were college pals of Sandler's. Also on the Sandler gravy train, er, payroll are director Steven Brill (who was responsible for *Little Nicky* as well as two *Mighty Ducks* sequels), associate producer Allen Covert and production designer Perry Andelin Blake. These guys have stated in several interviews that they love working together and have a great time of it (and who wouldn't love to hang out with their college buddies and be paid big bucks for it?), but they need to let some new people in their clique. Everyone is too comfortable and lacks the raw edges and passion that comedy needs to be sharp.

The film is a remake of the Frank Capra 1936 classic *Mr. Deeds Goes to Town*. That film, which starred Gary Cooper, was well-noticed at Oscar time, with nominations for Best Picture, Best Screenplay (for Robert Riskin) and Best Actor (for Cooper). It won for Best Director (Capra). It's safe to say that Sandler and Co. needn't be placing early orders at the tux rental place this year.

Longfellow Deeds (Sandler) is a popular guy in the small New England town of Mandrake Falls, New Hampshire. He owns a pizza parlor and spends his days penning sappy greeting cards in hopes that one day Hallmark will buy one. He's the kind of super-nice guy who delivers pizzas just because he likes seeing the people and he gives hugs instead of shaking hands. He even lifts a feeble local across the street so that the man doesn't have to exert himself. It's interesting to see how Sandler loves to portray himself as such a hero in his films. Women, dogs, kids—all end up falling under the spell of his charms.

Deeds' life changes when his 82-year-old uncle, Preston Blake (Harve Presnell), dies while trying to scale Mt. Everest during a snow storm. Blake, who Deeds never knew, was the head of a giant conglomerate, Blake Media. Blake's sleazy number two man, Chuck Cedar (Peter Gallagher), flies to Mandrake Falls, along with his sidekick (Erick Avari), to tell Deeds that he's inherited all of Blake's stock. Cedar's plan is that he will buy out Deeds' shares in exchange for $40 billion (in the original film, it was $20 million). Cedar figures that Deeds is too much of a rube to take the stocks instead of the quick cash.

The odd thing about this film is that Cedar's plan is to gain control of the company, then break it up, selling off the various parts. The big moral climax of the film involves Sandler giving an impassioned speech to stock holders, asking them to keep the company together. It is decidedly un-Capraesque to have the lone hero fighting to keep a huge, powerful media conglomerate together. It's a strange thing to be placing as the moral centerpiece of a film.

But then *Mr. Deeds* is pro-corporation in a lot of ways. There is product placement galore. Some of the placements are kind of weird, too. In one scene, a woman's house is on fire and there is box of a certain kind of cereal that's noticeably on fire. Cereal is big in another scene where Sandler is talking to his valet, Emilio Lopez (John Turturro, veteran of many much better Coen brothers' films). The box is placed with its front pointed to the camera and Sandler mentions it by name two times. After offering it to Lopez, Sandler carefully places the box on the table exactly how it was, with its face pointing to the camera. In another scene, characters fly the Blake company helicopter to a particular fast food joint because Deeds just has to have the stuff. They eat the food, oohing and aaahing over just how good that food is. In another scene they again discuss the virtues of the food and Avari's character wistfully says of the restaurant's shakes, "I tried to make one at home, but it just wasn't the same."

But before all that, there's some plot to contend with. Deeds needs to fly to New York City while Cedar finishes the paperwork that will allow him to buy Deeds out. This is where the story turns into ye olde fish out of water tale. Deeds shakes up the hoity-toity world of high society by doing things like having his various servants stand in the grand hallway of Blake's apartment and yelling out to hear their voices echoing. This is sticking it to the rich guy world? Moe, Larry and Curly riled up the rich guys better than this in every episode of *The Three Stooges*. In another scene, a famous opera singer and his fans make fun of Deeds' sappy greeting cards. Deeds punches them all out in the middle of a crowded restaurant. While the opera singer is going down, he lets out an operatic wail. Sorry, but it's just so dumb.

A lot about *Mr. Deeds* is just willfully dumb. Sandler seems to have a problem with anything that he doesn't perceive as being what a "normal," regular guy would like. There's a big speech in the film deriding those that have "ironic detachment." You see, Sandler and the small town folk are real and good. The city folk, with their intelligence and all, are unhappy and bad.

While Deeds is in New York, he meets a girl, Babe Bennett (Winona Ryder). Bennett is really a tabloid reporter for a sleazy tabloid show called, "Inside Access." She pretends to be a small town girl who's a school nurse. In the meantime, she's really videotaping their dates, which end up making it into segments on the show. Sandler starts falling in love with her and Bennett, charmed by his simple ways, falls in love with him, too. Will their relationship survive this big obstacle? Yawn, maybe.

Along the way, the film is spiced up by Turturro's frequent appearances, as well as spots by Kathy Bates, Steve Buscemi, John McEnroe and (!) the Reverend Al Sharpton. But it's not enough to give *Mr. Deeds* the fire it needed. And, in a way, seeing a great actor like Buscemi reduced to playing a character called Crazy Eyes, whose main characteristic is that he has eyes pointing in different directions, is just plain painful.

Critics, who tend to fancy themselves big city intellectuals, didn't particularly care for Sandler's down-home brand of humor. Kenneth Turan of the *Los Angeles Times* wrote, "What's most interesting about this new film is how lacking it is in any of the things, from humor to emotion to halfway decent acting, we might go to a movie for. There's not even enough here to get mad at." Elvis Mitchell of the *New York Times* called the movie "scandalously lazy" and wrote that it "Is most terrible, a shambles of a comedy that looks as if it was shot by a tabloid news crew." And Owen Gleiberman of *Entertainment Weekly* gave the film a C, and wrote "it feels sort of like the dumbest corporate comedy of 1987." William Arnold of the *Seattle Post-Intelligencer* felt more kindly toward the movie and wrote, "If your expectations are very low, there are some decent laughs and the film makes for a guilty pleasure."

—*Jill Hamilton*

CREDITS

Longfellow Deeds: Adam Sandler
Babe Bennett: Winona Ryder
Emilio Lopez: John Turturro
Chuck Cedar: Peter Gallagher
Crazy Eyes: Steve Buscemi
Mac McGrath: Jared Harris
Marty: Allen Covert
Cecil Anderson: Erik Avari
Murph: Peter Dante
Jan: Conchata Ferrell
Preston Blake: Harve Presnell
Buddy Ward: Blake Clark
Reuben: JB Smoove

Origin: USA
Released: 2002
Production: Sid Ganis, Jack Giarraputo; New Line Cinema, Happy Madison Productions, Out of the Blue Entertainment; released by Columbia Pictures
Directed by: Steven Brill
Written by: Tim Herlihy
Cinematography by: Peter Collister
Music by: Teddy Castellucci
Sound: Felipe Borrero
Music Supervisor: Michael Dilbeck
Editing: Jeff Gourson, Stephen McCabe, Stephen H. Carter
Costumes: Ellen Lutter
Production Design: Perry Andelin Blake
MPAA rating: PG-13
Running time: 97 minutes

REVIEWS

Chicago Sun-Times Online. June 28, 2002.
Entertainment Weekly. June 28, 2002, p. 117.
Los Angeles Times Online. June 28, 2002.
New York Times Online. June 28, 2002.
People. July 8, 2002, p. 27.
USA Today Online. June 27, 2002.
Variety Online. June 16, 2002.
Washington Post. June 28, 2002, p. WE31.

Monsoon Wedding

Box Office: $13.8 million

Shot in 40 locations in 30 days, Mira Nair's latest release, *Monsoon Wedding,* successfully captures contemporary India. One of Nair's former film-directing students, Sabrina Dhawan, penned the multiple narrative-screenplay that features 68 characters, sweet comic moments, and social commentaries about middle-class Indian life. Described as "henna and cell phones" by the British film magazine *Sight* and Sound, Monsoon Wedding offers its viewers plenty of eye candy in the form of elaborate saris and banquets of traditional Indian cuisine. And music composer Mychael Danna provided the film with a tasty fusion of traditional Indian (Punjabi) wedding music with modern techno and pop. However, Monsoon Wedding proves more than a feast for the eyes and ears since it also resonates in our hearts.

Nair began her directorial career back in the 1980's with a series of controversial and non-flinching documentaries reflecting on Indian culture. Nair's Salaam Bombay! garnered a Camera d'or prize at Cannes in 1988 and the director has gone on to collect other awards and recognition for her work without ever compromising her ethics or integrity. Although Nair did not write Monsoon Wedding, she opted for a documentary approach when shooting the script. Cinematographer Declan Quinn's lens travels across crowded and polluted Bombay streets while capturing bits of humanity in between shots of middle-class Indians celebrating an impending arranged marriage. It is as if Nair could not resist showing us the other India without the dotcoms and wealth. And along with writer Dhawan, Nair zooms in on other social issues surrounding arranged marriages, child abuse, and the effects of globalization on Indian life.

Despite the social issues, Monsoon Wedding offers us romance and comic relief by inviting us to an elaborate traditional wedding. The film itself chronicles events leading up to an arranged marriage over a four-day period. The bride-to-be, Aditi (Vasundhara Das), struggles with getting over a breakup with her married boss. Later she confesses her transgression to her fiancée with surprising results. Meanwhile, family maid Alice (Tilotama Shome) falls in love with the slacker event organizer, P.K. Dubey (Vijay Raaz). Another story involves Aditi's cousin Aliya (Kemaya Kidwai) and an uncle who molested her as a child. And the final story revolves around a teenage crush the young and vivacious Ayesha (Neha Dubey) has with a suitor who has forgotten his Indian roots now that he has relocated to Melbourne. We see the hip and high tech New Delhi clashing with traditional India. Arranged marriages and e-commerce might be uttered in the same breath and this adds to Monsoon Wedding's unusual charm.

The film opens with the bride's father, Lalit Verma (Naseeruddin Shah), stressing out over his hired help. The engagement party is moments away, the family members haven't dressed yet for the occasion, and a traditional marigold archway has fallen asunder. Meanwhile, the bride-to-be has involved herself with her married boss days before her wedding. Estranged family members arrive from all corners of the globe to celebrate a traditional Punjabi wedding. Soon the household fills up with wedding guests and singing, dancing, and eating color the atmosphere. The camera zooms across many gorgeous faces and bodies as each of the main characters reveal their stories.

We are filled with sadness for the parents as they prepare to lose their only daughter to marriage. But our hearts gladden as we see love blossom between the sweet-natured maid and the overzealous-turned-lovelorn event organizer. The scenes prove to be touching without appearing sentimental. In the love scenes between Alice and Dubey, both characters appear shy and awkward. Alice drops a tray of glasses while trying to attract Dubey's attention; later Dubey finds himself in a situation that resembles puppy love. Dubey eventually wins Alice's heart after a sincere display of affection involving gifting Alice with a large heart constructed of marigolds. Alice and Dubey tie the knot—finally satisfying Dubey's aging mother and her dying wish for her son to marry and give her a grandchild.

The budding romance between Hemant Rai (Parvin Dabas) and Aditi proves more complicated. Although Aditi wishes to marry Hemant, she feels that she must choose between passion with her former lover and the security that her husband will provide. Aditi would also be leaving her close-knit family and culture behind to live in Houston with Hemant. As Aditi and Hemant grow closer, she feels that she must confess her sexual transgressions. She believes that as soon as she tells Hemant the truth, he will abandon her and she is floored when Hemant thanks her for her honesty. Hemant believes that the couple can put their past behind them and create a solid marriage based on honesty.

Nair now makes her home in New York where she teaches directing classes at Columbia University. She recently returned to her documentary roots and shot a digital video about a laughing society in India called The Laughing Club of India and has completed a U.S.-made film for cable, Hysterical Blindness, starring Uma Thurman. Monsoon Wedding collected awards from various film festivals and film societies, including a Golden Lion Award from the Venice Film Festival and a Golden Globes nomination for Best Foreign Language Film. After two decades of hard work, Nair has proven to be a strong contender on an international scale. The director should also be applauded for bringing issues that effect Indian women to the forefront. After all, if a middle-class Indian professional woman doesn't tackle those issues who will?

Similar to the Indian director Deepa Mehta, who emigrated to Canada, Nair tends to make films about her Indian roots and the society in which she spent her formative years. Nair and Mehta both make films with powerful feminine allure and maternal instincts. The women characters in the directors' films tend to be both sensual and motherly—likened to any number of Hindu goddesses ironically worshipped by a culture in which women are still degraded on a daily basis. While Mehta's Fire (featuring lesbian sex) was banned in India, Nair fought the censors when releasing Kama Sutra and was able to portray bits of nudity in her film. However, both women have displayed formidable courage when facing up to Indian society. Nair and Mehta have proven themselves as uncompromising and have pushed the feminist agenda despite opposition.

In an interview that appeared in *RANT,* Nair stated: "I don't really believe that I am the best person to make Sunday afternoon, pleasant movies that you go to and then forget about. I still look at film as a way to get under your skin, to make you question and hold a mirror to your world." And while *Monsoon Wedding* comes laced in pleasantries, the issue of child abuse still comes crashing down on the film's viewers. And yet, *Monsoon Wedding* strikes a balance between a romantic comedy and a tragedy-of-the-week. Although set in India, the film's familial themes prove universal. It is true that many of us living in the west do not experience the turmoil or joys found in arranged marriages, but we do know what it feels like to lose a child to marriage.

The production and distribution of *Monsoon Wedding* proved as chaotic as the film's implied wedding. Young, screaming girls stormed the set in search of their idol, Parvin Dabas. And later, X-rays destroyed much of the film's key footage on its way to New York. However, none of the chaos hindered the completion of the film. Perhaps this is a testament to the director's strong will and talent or luminous performances from her Bollywood actors.

The press sang praises for *Monsoon Wedding.* Peter Travers of *Rolling Stone* wrote "(Nair) aims for pure joy and achieves it." Jason Anderson of the Toronto-based *eye Weekly* commented, "Mira Nair's distinctive, wholly engaging approach is somewhere between DOGME-style immediacy and Bollywood-caliber excess." Philip French from the London-based *The Observer* praised the performances, "the acting and interacting of the ensemble cast is exemplary." And finally, Peter Bradshaw of *The Guardian* described Nair's film as a "richly detailed, funny and gutsy family comedy."

Nair demonstrates with this feature that a director's job is to facilitate strong performances from her actors and to bring out the talents of her crew. The director rehearsed the actors for two weeks before shooting, thus creating a sense of family on the set. And three of her crew members from *Kama Sutra,* cinematographer Declan Quinn, producer Caroline Baron, and production designer Stephanie Carroll returned to work with Nair on *Monsoon Wedding.* Although Nair has achieved varying degrees of success with past films, *Monsoon Wedding* marks her first feature with popular appeal. We won't turn down this invitation to a Punjabi wedding.

—*Patty-Lynne Herlevi*

CREDITS

Lalit Verma: Naseeruddin Shah
Pimmi Verma: Lillete Dubey
Ria Verma: Shefali Shetty
Aditi Verma: Vasundhara Das
Hermant Rai: Parvin Dabas
P.K. Dubey: Vijay Raaz
Alice: Tilotama Shome
Tej Puri: Rajat Kapoor

Origin: India, USA
Released: 2001
Production: Caroline Baron, Mira Nair; Mirabai Films, Pandora Film, Paradis Film; released by USA Films
Directed by: Mira Nair
Written by: Sabrina Dhawan
Cinematography by: Declan Quinn
Music by: Mychael Danna
Sound: Magdaline Volaitis
Editing: Allyson C. Johnson
Costumes: Arjun Bhasin
Production Design: Stephanie Carroll
MPAA rating: R
Running time: 113 minutes

REVIEWS

Boxoffice. November, 2001, p. 130.
Chicago Sun-Times Online. March 8, 2002.
Entertainment Weekly. March 1, 2002, p. 50.
eye Weekly Online. September 6, 2001.
Los Angeles Times. February 10, 2002, p. 3.
Los Angeles Times Online. March 1, 2002.
New York Times Online. February 17, 2002.
New York Times Online. February 22, 2002.
People. March 4, 2002, p. 31.
RANT. January/February, 2002, p. 28.
Sight and Sound. January, 2002, p. 18.
USA Today Online. March 8, 2002.
Vanity Fair. March, 2002, p. 112.
Variety. September 10, 2001, p. 63.
Washington Post. March 8, 2002, p. WE37.

QUOTES

Hermant (Parvin Dabas) to Aditi (Vasundhara Das): "I know it's a risk, but what marriage isn't? If our parents introduced us or we met in a club, what difference does it make?"

AWARDS AND NOMINATIONS

Nomination:
British Acad. 2001: Foreign Film
Golden Globes 2002: Foreign Film.

Moonlight Mile

In life and love, expect the unexpected.
—Movie tagline

 Box Office: $6.7 million

Grief and mourning are tough subjects to depict honestly in motion pictures. The emotions attending the loss of a loved one can be so raw and punishing that a dramatic portrayal risks sentimentalizing the feelings and failing to capture the truth of the experience. A rare masterpiece such as Atom Egoyan's *The Sweet Hereafter* can offer wrenching insights into this complex subject, and occasionally more mainstream fare deals honestly with the profound sadness of a person coping with loss. Rosie Perez's character in *Fearless* trying to come to terms with the airplane crash that took her child from her and Robin Williams's character in *Good Will Hunting* eloquently speaking about his late wife are two moving examples.

Brad Silberling's *Moonlight Mile,* set during the Vietnam War (although the period detail is almost nonexistent save for the music), may not bring anything new to the subject. But it is an often observant, heartfelt look at loss, poignantly depicting how the violent death of a young woman affects her parents and the man who had been her fiancé. Unfortunately, Silberling succumbs to the temptation of simplifying a complex subject and ultimately takes a fairly safe, predictable route in laying out the all-too-familiar healing process.

The film opens on the morning of Diana Floss's funeral. She was accidentally killed in a diner by a madman trying to kill his wife, who, incidentally, took two bullets in the head and is in a coma. Diana's parents, Ben (Dustin Hoffman) and JoJo (Susan Sarandon), are accompanied by Joe Nast (Jake Gyllenhaal), Diana's fiancé, who has taken up residence in their home. Silberling begins with a subtle passage gently reminding us how cruel everyday life can look to people who are in mourning. On the drive to the cemetery, the procession of cars passes such happy activities as a wedding, kids playing in the park, a couple kissing—little reminders of how, even in death and sorrow, life continues on for everyone else, oblivious to the loss felt by those who are about to bury a loved one.

Silberling establishes fairly early the family's character traits. JoJo, a writer who has been blocked since Diana's death, has a sardonic edge, eager to gossip about all the guests at the funeral and their annoying behavior at the reception. She casually throws into the fireplace the self-help books on coping with loss that well-meaning friends have

given them. Ben, on the other hand, fusses over details like making sure the car doors are locked before the funeral procession begins and cleaning the house after the guests have left. He is willing to look at the good intentions of their friends offering condolences and give everyone the benefit of the doubt. Determined to pull his family together and get on with life, he goes so far as to make Joe a partner in his commercial real estate business. He obviously has an idealized picture of how things were going to be and does not want to lose that ideal. Joe is stuck in the middle, a confidant and friend to JoJo and a surrogate son to Ben.

When Joe goes to the local post office to retrieve the sent wedding invitations (Ben does not want people to receive them and feel uncomfortable), he meets Bertie Knox (Ellen Pompeo), a cute girl who, we eventually learn, is harboring her own sense of loss. Her boyfriend is missing in Vietnam and is most likely not coming back, even if she cannot admit this to herself. There is an immediate attraction or at least interest between her and Joe, but Joe's residence in the home of his almost in-laws makes it impossible for him to proceed at anything more than a cautious pace.

Complicating Joe's dilemma is the fact that he had broken up with Diana three days before she was killed and thus feels like a phony playing the good son in the Floss household. Moreover, when Diana was in the diner, she was waiting to meet her father to tell him about the breakup. Joe has no ambition or direction in life and can therefore be the malleable young man willingly molded by other people's desires and expectations. One is reminded of Dustin Hoffman's character in *The Graduate* (the fact that Hoffman's name in *Moonlight Mile* is Ben just strengthens the allusion), and even Joe's whirl of confusion at the funeral reception is shot in a similar way to Ben's graduation reception in *The Graduate.* Of course, the allusion does not go very deep since *The Graduate* uses its aimless protagonist for larger social satire, which is not Silberling's concern.

Ben embraces Joe not only as a son but also as a business partner as he embarks on a plan to acquire a whole block of property and turn it into a mall. The key building is a bar where Bertie works for her absent boyfriend. Unfortunately, the subplot involving the proposed business deal goes nowhere and seems to be a convenient device that allows Joe to get to know Bertie better.

The acting in *Moonlight Mile* is uniformly fine, with Sarandon standing out in a strong cast. Her sarcastic JoJo, always unafraid to speak her mind, is the breath of fresh air in the house. Sarandon is so genuine that even a potentially schmaltzy speech explaining how she and Ben have stayed together for so many years and extolling the importance of finding one's home feels convincing coming out of her mouth. Hoffman plays Ben as the go-getter who seems not to have become the success he hoped to be but is trying his best to act like one. His character seems a bit one-dimensional, and, while the performance is believable, Hoffman does not transcend his character type the way Sarandon does hers. Gyllenhaal generally acquits himself well opposite these Oscar winners, but his mopey, troubled kid feels like a variation on the characters he played in this year's *Lovely and Amazing* and *The Good Girl*. Pompeo is quite appealing as his love interest, and their burgeoning romance has some beautiful moments, like a spontaneous dance in the bar, but it also feels like a forced requirement of the script that they get together simply because each has to cope with losing someone they love.

As the story progresses, it becomes harder and harder for Joe to continue to fit in with his makeshift family. He misses a crucial business dinner, thus disappointing Ben and triggering a fight between JoJo and Ben that touches upon the distance between him and his late daughter. Later, when JoJo discovers that Joe has been sneaking out to see Bertie, this normally strong woman has a minor breakdown. She cannot deal with the realization that Joe and her daughter had broken up and he is now seeing another girl, but, more important, she is coming face-to-face with the void left by her daughter's death. For his part, Ben is in such denial that he cannot bear facing the truth that Joe and Diana were not a couple when she died and breaks down in tears.

Interwoven into the family drama is the pending trial of the man who killed Diana. In a sharp supporting turn, Holly Hunter plays the prosecuting attorney, Mona Camp, who consults the family periodically. When it seems that the case has taken a turn for the worse—the injured wife is going to stand by her husband and testify on his behalf—the prosecution enlists Joe's help to make Diana come alive on the stand, to make the judge see her as a real person whose loss has devastated him. Instead, Joe practically has his own breakdown on the witness stand and uses the trial as a way to exorcise his own demons. He reveals publicly that he and Diana were no longer a couple, that she saw he did not have the courage to go through with the wedding, and that he cannot lie anymore because Diana brought out honesty in people. This is meant to be the emotional climax that heals the family, but it comes across as self-indulgent and even selfish. Joe is essentially using the justice system and jeopardizing the case to make everyone confront the truth about his relationship with Diana. Gyllenhaal effectively brings out the anguish that envelops Joe, but the scene itself feels contrived to bring about a tidy resolution.

Indeed, everything that follows also feels too neat. JoJo suddenly conquers her writer's block and begins writing about her daughter. The broken window in the diner—a stark, everyday reminder of Diana's murder—torments Ben throughout the film, and, at the end, he gives the owner the money to fix it, thus signaling closure for Ben. Failing to acquire the town property, he also gets out of the real estate business. He admits that he never had a chance against the big-time developers, thus making this subplot even less im-portant that it already was. The film concludes with Joe and Bertie driving off together, presumably to get a fresh start. Of course, life rarely presents such neat closure for a whole family at once. Everyone mourns in a different way and at a different pace, and some people may need more time than others, but Silberling's screenplay suggests that all the principal characters are healing their wounds at the same time. Given the serious subject, the pat ending feels like a copout.

Silberling loosely based his script for *Moonlight Mile* on the 1989 murder of his own girlfriend, actress Rebecca Schaeffer, and his subsequent relationship with her family. He knows the subject matter and has fashioned an often moving portrait of a family doing the best to cope with the unimaginable, but he also has the unfortunate tendency to take the easy way out. It is hard to feel that these characters have grown or changed dramatically, only that the screenplay calls for everyone to get on with their lives at the end. *Moonlight Mile* has some powerful moments, but it would have been better if it did not try to clean up the messy subject of grief, especially the grief that accompanies a tragic death.

—Peter N. Chumo II

CREDITS

Joe Nast: Jake Gyllenhaal
Ben Floss: Dustin Hoffman
JoJo Floss: Susan Sarandon
Mona Camp: Holly Hunter
Bertie Knox: Ellen Pompeo
Ty: Richard T. Jones
Stan Michaels: Allan Corduner
Mike Mulcahey: Dabney Coleman
Cheryl: Akelsia Landeau

Origin: USA
Released: 2002
Production: Mark Johnson, Brad Silberling; Hyde Park Entertainment, Gran Via; released by Touchstone Pictures
Directed by: Brad Silberling
Written by: Brad Silberling
Cinematography by: Phedon Papamichael
Music by: Mark Isham
Sound: Pud Cusack
Music Supervisor: Dawn Soler
Editing: Lisa Zeno Churgin
Art Direction: Mark Worthington
Costumes: Mary Zophres
Production Design: Missy Stewart
MPAA rating: PG-13
Running time: 112 minutes

Italian quality threatened to challenge Hollywood, but the main focus here is on the postwar period, presenting extended examples from the work of Rossellini and DeSica, then Visconti, Fellini, and Antonioni, a very impressive line-up.

My Voyage to Italy premiered at the 2001 New York Film Festival, appropriately enough, at the Walter Reade Theater. Scorsese's title echoes that of Roberto Rossellini's *Voyage to Italy* (1953), a generally "forgotten" film that the *Cahiers* critics in France considered "revolutionary." Scorsese examines this film in detail, said to be the "flipside" of Fellini's *La Dolce Vita* (1960) and one of the very best Rossellini-Ingrid Bergman collaborations. Because he intends to make his points visually, Scorsese takes his time. This exercise in artistic autobiography is in two parts and runs to 246 minutes total. Scorsese is very generous in his coverage of this treasure-trove. Some of the chosen clips run up to 15 minutes, so as to encourage viewers to seek the films out in their entirety. Despite the length of some of the clips, however, there is nothing dull about them. Post-war "classics" are discussed in the historical context and in the Scorsese context. Scorsese explains, for example, that Federico Fellini's *I Vitelloni* (1953) was "the main inspiration" for Scorsese's breakthrough film made 20 years later, *Mean Streets* (1973), which has similar, drifting young characters, and a similar message: "The realization that you can either grow up or remain a child."

Noting that the Italian neo-realists tended to blur the line between fiction and documentary, *New York Times* reviewer Stephen Holden saw the documentary as containing a history lesson: "Especially in the excerpts from Roberto Rossellini's *Open City* and Vittorio De Sica's *Bicycle Thief* and *Umberto D.* [the director's tribute to his father, Umberto De Sica], you feel you are watching life as it was lived in the most desperate of times." Edward Guthmann was impressed by Scorsese's "intimate and unguarded" sincerity: "Scorsese isn't lecturing or simply dispensing shrewd commentary. He opens himself to us—describing the seeds of his inspiration, sharing family memories, showing the points where art. mythology, and personal experience intersect."

"The more films I made," Scorsese explains in his introduction to the documentary, "The more I realized what an indelible mark Italian cinema had made on me. . . . If I'd never seen the films I'm going to talk about here, I'd be a very different person and, of course, a very different filmmaker." The *San Francisco Chronicle* described the film as a "deeply personal love letter to Italian cinema—to his family, to the power of film to illuminate our lives." One is tempted to say, of course, it helps to be Italian, if not Sicilian, like Scorsese, but that is utterly false. There is a universal humanity and both illuminates and is demonstrated by such films as *Paisan* (1946), *Shoeshine* (1946), and *La Dolce Vita* (1960)

In his enthusiasm for cinema in general and Italian cinema in particular, Scorsese resembles the most gifted directors of the French New Wave and the "New" German Cinema (Wim Wenders and Werner Herzog in particular). Scorsese's discourse is authoritative but never dull, and his enthusiasm is infectious. As the pioneering French director Abel Gance once said, "Enthusiasm is essential in the cinema. It must be communicated to people like a flame. The cinema is a flame in the shadows fed by enthusiasm. It can dispel them. This is why enthusiasm is everything to me. It is impossible to make a great film without it." No doubt Scorsese would fully agree with Gance.

—*James M. Welsh*

CREDITS

Narrator: Martin Scorsese

Origin: Italy
Released: 2001
Production: Barbara De Fina, Giuliana Del Punta, Bruno Restuccia; Cappa Films, Paso Doble, Mediatrade; released by Miramax Films
Directed by: Martin Scorsese
Written by: Martin Scorsese, Suso Cecchi D'Amico, Raffaele Donato, Kent Jones
Editing: Thelma Schoonmaker
MPAA rating: PG-13
Running time: 243 minutes

REVIEWS

Boxoffice. September, 2001, p. 146.
Film Journal International. July 16, 2002.
Hollywood Reporter. July 16, 2002.
Los Angeles Times Online. October 24, 2001.
New York Times Online. October 12, 2001.
San Francisco Chronicle. June 7, 2002, p. D2.
Variety. May 28, 2001, p. 17.

My Wife Is an Actress (Ma Femme Est une Actrice)

he loves her. she loves acting.
—Movie tagline

 Box Office: $1 million

Yvan Attal's unassuming light marital comedy from France, *My Wife Is an Actress,* cleverly juxtaposes the concepts of "acting" in the sense of playing a role and "acting" as performing a meaningful action, until the two merge in the end in the most ordinary, yet unexpected, manner. In fact, the film seems to revel in its ordinariness, to the point of seeming trite at times.

Yvan, played by Attal himself (looking a dead ringer for Griffin Dunne), is a 35-year-old sports reporter who is forced to come to terms with his beautiful and successful actress-wife, Charlotte (Charlotte Gainsborough) having become a sex goddess of sorts, owing to her films. Yvan's dilemma is that Charlotte is off to London to play opposite John (Terence Stamp), a gray-haired, middle-aged smoothie who is still a hottie to adoring young women.

Attal, as writer-director, bolsters this basic situation built around Yvan's jealousy, with three subplots. In one, Nathalie (Noemie Lvovsky), Yvan's pregnant sister, is obsessed with her Jewishness, and what she perceives as its concomitant social stigma. She and Vincent (Laurent Bateau), her accommodating gentile husband, keep arguing endlessly about whether to circumcise their unborn baby. In the second, John, it so happens, has rediscovered himself as a painter, and sees Charlotte, with her French background, as the only one on the set who can understand his aspirations. In the third, Charlotte has a tiff with David (Keith Allen), her brazen director, over her nude scenes. She is for suggestion; he for artistic frankness. In a fit of rage, Charlotte insists that everyone on the set be made to strip down as well. Sure enough, they do; allowing the film to introduce frontal nudity in a setting where one would least expect it.

Charlotte, on her part, is more than ready to answer Yvan's accusations. She admits, "When I kiss in a movie, I give it all I have!" As for her own enjoyment, she cites instances of her co-stars having "garbage breath" at eight A.M. Yvan, however, remains unconvinced. He abandons his professional work and remains in London. When he stumbles onto the set, carrying a bouquet, only to find every-one in the buff, he recoils and becomes physically sick, before taking the next train back to Paris.

From here on, the film boldly goes where more sophisticated recent French film comedies about marital discord—such as Agnes Jaoui's *The Taste of Others* (2001)—have feared to tread: down to the level of a mindless sitcom.

Yvan, in order to understand the "acting trip," decides to take drama lessons. As an initial exercise, he has to act out the birth of a flower. His improvisational skills impress Geraldine (Ludivine Sagnier), a congenial neophyte. However, when Yvan finds her and her girlfriends mentioning John as a "major babe," his jealous streak has him racing back to London. Not that that brings him any closer to Charlotte. In fact, it has the opposite effect. When she denies any entanglement with John, he refuses to believe her. She then turns the tables on Yvan. "You put it into my head!" she screams, then adds, "With your questions and your paranoia. It's as if you wanted it!" Yvan's only answer is to storm back to Paris.

We then see Yvan dating a sexpot from his office, and Charlotte leaving John's hotel bedroom at dawn. On a day off, Charlotte takes the train to Paris, and reaches her apartment building in time to catch Yvan, unbeknownst to him, kissing Geraldine passionately on the sidewalk. She promptly gets back into her cab and heads for a night spot. When Yvan catches up with her that night, he refuses to believe that she hasn't slept with John. "You're a great actress!" he declares at her repeated denials.

After the birth of Nathalie's baby, Yvan opposes Charlotte's wish to have one. But it's too late. In the next scene, Charlotte announces she's pregnant, joyously mimicking an abdominal protuberance. A startled Yvan looks on, unsmiling, as if realizing for once the real scope of Charlotte's acting prowess, now that it has got her what she wanted out of him all along.

If Elvis Mitchell's review in the *New York Times* is any indication, critics should be warming up to Attal's modest soufflé. Writing at the time of the film's screening at the Museum of Modern Art's New Directors/New Films showcase, Mitchell finds the film is "organized to find its comedy simply and quickly." He also points out that since Attal is married to his co-star in real life, the film could be "a nightmare version of his own experience."

—*Vivek Adarkar*

CREDITS

Yvan: Yvan Attal
Charlotte: Charlotte Gainsbourg
John: Terence Stamp
Nathalie: Noemie Lvovsky
Geraldine: Ludivine Sagnier

David: Keith Allen
Georges: Lionel Abelanski
Vincent: Laurent Bateau
Assistant director: Jo McInnes

Origin: France
Language: French
Released: 2001
Production: Claude Berri; Renn Productions, TF-1
Films; released by Sony Pictures Classics
Directed by: Yvan Attal
Written by: Yvan Attal
Cinematography by: Remy Chevrin
Sound: Didier Sain
Editing: Jennifer Auger
Costumes: Jacqueline Bouchard
Production Design: Katia Wyszkop
MPAA rating: R
Running time: 93 minutes

REVIEWS

Boxoffice. July, 2002, p. 85.
Chicago Sun-Times Online. August 2, 2002.
Entertainment Weekly. July 19, 2002, p. 46.
Los Angeles Times Online. July 12, 2002.
Los Angeles Times Calendar. July 14, 2002, p. 21.
New York Times Online. March 29, 2002.
Variety Online. September 28, 2001.
Washington Post. August 16, 2002, p. WE46.

QUOTES

Yvan (Yvan Attal) about the acting profession: "My wife's in a cult."

The Mystic Masseur

A time and place of magic and miracles.
—Movie tagline

Ismail Merchant's fifth feature, *The Mystic Masseur,* based on the first novel by Nobel prize winning author V.S. Naipaul, focuses on the sensibility of "underdevelopment" within a colonial setting. Rather than a meeting of minds, however, the film emerges more of a confused hodgepodge.

Naipaul's narrative is straightforward, linear and unassuming. Merchant and his scenarist, Caryl Phillips, have chosen to go one better by exploiting their literary source for their own art-house ends. Banished from the film are the mosquito larvae breeding in backyards, as well as the street life of Port of Spain, or the "slavery" of the workers in the sugarcane fields. In their place, the film provides picture postcard views of Trinidad. Also, the fancy narrative pattern the film chooses to adopt does away with the "progress" of Ganesh (Aasif Mandvi), the central character, as reflecting the equally ambivalent "progress" of the island of Trinidad under British rule.

In Naipaul's vision, Ganesh is someone who allows Fate to dictate the course of his life. When he succeeds, he does so without being dishonest. This is what makes him endearing. At the very end of the novel, he has found his identity as a "wog," the British acronym for "westernised Oriental gentleman." The film, however, turns Ganesh into a crafty, ambitious and mercenary native while, at the same time, remaining faithful to the novel's picaresque narrative. The result is a film that can neither put across satisfactorily the irony in Ganesh's story nor the dramatic conflict inherent in his ambition conflicting with the backlash of colonial rule.

The film's most crippling departure from Naipaul's text is its first one. After quitting his job as a schoolteacher in Port of Spain, Ganesh calculates that his decision must have coincided with the precise moment of his father's death, and so is meant to augur a new phase in his life, though he cannot foresee as what. He thus becomes a drifter, in the tradition of the "wanderer after Truth." The film omits this nodal point, thereby depriving its narrative of the antinomy underlying the events to follow.

When Ganesh attends his father's funeral in the village of Fourways, he soon learns that the rites have been paid for by a neighbor, Ramlogan (Om Puri), a shopkeeper who would like Ganesh to marry his pretty, half-educated daughter, Leela (Ayesha Dharker). Ramlogan also provides Ganesh with a set of paperback books, classics of literature printed in England. Ganesh promptly finds his calling in life, inspired by a chance meeting with a British renunciate, known as Mr. Stewart (James Fox in a cameo appearance), who sets Ganesh thinking along religious lines.

At this point, Ganesh has Ramlogan bearing down on him to follow his father's calling as a masseur, a profession within the local setting that encompasses everything from bonesetting to internal medicine. Ganesh gives it a shot, but fails, then vows that he will write books as worthy as any that Ramlogan has presented to him. He also marries Leela and moves into one of Ramlogan's houses in the very boonies of the island, a village bordering sugarcane fields known as Fuente Grove.

Ganesh's married life gets off to a shaky start when he finds that Leela cannot have any children. "The books I go write, they go be my children," he tells her one night in bed, as she nestles her head against his shoulder. He then adds, "I go make sons and daughters of literature." It is a romantic sense of purpose wholly absent in the novel. It neither jells with the kind of writing Ganesh does produce, nor does it inspire Leela to stick with him. Finding she has married a man who is not bringing in any income, she runs back into the protective fold of her father.

In his single-minded devotion to writing, Ganesh is encouraged by Beharry (Sanjeev Bhaskar), a soft-spoken shopkeeper at Fuente Grove who is nagged by his attractive wife, Suraj (Sakina Jaffrey), about the dangers of reading. Beharry presents Ganesh with the scriptures of the world's great religions. After all the buildup and personal sacrifice, Ganesh's long awaited first "book" turns out to be more of a pamphlet. Entitled, *101 Questions about Hinduism*, it embodies the spirit of literature as a cottage industry. Ganesh has the book printed by his friend, Basdeo, then decides to market it himself. All to no avail. The locals fear that Ganesh might be out to convert them with his own brand of catechism. The pamphlet does however serve one purpose: it brings Leela back to him. She is now ready to stand by her husband-author in his endeavors.

As it happens, Ganesh's life is destined to take another twist. On Beharry's advice, he sets himself up as a "mystic masseur," even adopting the turban and robes of the profession. One morning, his former landlady in Port of Spain drives up seeking his help in curing her mentally afflicted son, Partap, who feels he is being tormented by a cloud. The situation provides the film with a set piece of occult quackery. The scene is amusing as Ganesh tries to get the most mileage out of a standard Hindu chant, repeating it over and over, thereby frightening the stricken boy into submission, and thereby back to his senses. Even Leela joins in the fake ritual. In the novel, Ganesh spends long hours consulting "his uncle's books," so that when the séance works, it marks a triumph of traditional wisdom, converting Ganesh as much as the boy. In the film's scheme of things, Ganesh emerges a mountebank, who happens to strike pay dirt.

The film's satiric thrust now gathers full steam. Partap (Jimi Mistry), now a young man, whom the film has been using for its ongoing narration, tells us in a voiceover of how news spread of Ganesh's "mystic" prowess. A montage of scenes shows Ganesh "curing" a woman who refuses to eat, a man who thinks he can fly, and even a bicycle racer who cannot stop making love to his bicycle. As people from all over the island come to Fuente Grove in droves, Ganesh uses the opportunity to sell them copies of his pamphlet. Soon the complexion of the backwoods community changes as Ganesh's prosperity translates into more customers for Beharry, who sells the "patients" the accoutrements needed for their consultation. The village receives its first standpipe, an event intercut with Ganesh furiously at work on his next book. Soon a small Hindu temple is built in his front yard.

Ganesh's popularity sets into motion two subplots. One, a scandal ensues from the exorbitant rates being charged by the taxi drivers for plying customers all the way to Fuente Grove. When Ganesh learns from Beharry that it is Ramlogan who owns the taxis, he erupts in rage, first against his wife and then against his father-in-law. Ganesh resolves the matter by offering to buy the fleet of cabs; Ramlogan humbly acquiesces. The second subplot proves stickier. As the movement for local government spreads through Trinidad, Narayan, the editor of the local newspaper, who has been maligning Ganesh through gossip columns, decides to run for office. Ganesh responds by changing his public relations strategy. He visits various villages, where he sets himself up as the voice of wisdom and reason, settling minor disputes. The ploy is intended to precede his own run for office.

The film uses Partap's voiceover to gloss over any conflict within Ganesh borne out of his having to make the switch from "mystic" to politician. Soon Ganesh is declaiming to a gathering of unanimous supporters, "It's Narayan we're fighting, but it's Hindu unity we're fighting for!" Cleverly manipulating the election process of the Hindu Association, Ganesh gets himself elected its president. The next step is for him to run for local office. Ganesh campaigns tirelessly, even though there is no one running against him. "I'm just staying close to the people!" he explains to Beharry. Even so, as Member of the Legislative Council, he decides to move into a lavish bungalow in Port of Spain. It is a strike by dock workers that jolts him into realizing his distance from his earlier base of support. As irate workers at a rally crowd around him, Ganesh is hustled away to safety.

The Governor now comes to his rescue. Soon Ganesh is climbing the ladder of elitism as a Member of the British Empire, and of the Executive Council where, as an appointee of the Governor, he won't have to run for election.

Through Partap's voiceover, the film provides its own epilogue, reversing the satiric impact of the novel. We take leave of Ganesh on a porch swing with Leela, back in the boonies of Trinidad. Unlike the novel, which shows him having sacrificed his West Indian identity to become a wog, the film transforms Ganesh into someone who has found himself as a native, and as a respected man of letters loved by his people.

Critics unable to resist the film's exotic charm have remarked on its detached view of its amoral protagonist. Stephen Holden in the *New York Times* finds the film "a subtle, humorous, illuminating study of politics, power and social mobility . . . (whose) quirks ultimately transcend period and location." Similarly, Jan Stuart in *Newsday* writes how the film "refuses to pass judgment on its protagonist's ever-expanding ego and self-absorption." Critics who have found the film falling far short of its ambitions have come down hard on Merchant and his scenarist. For Jami Bernard in the *Daily News,* the film "pleases and lulls where it could have pricked the intellect." Jonathan Foreman in the *New York Post* calls the script "loose" and "plodding" with a plot that "sometimes lacks purpose." He goes on to argue that "you never get a sense of whether Ganesh can truly write." Even Stuart finds the screenplay "makes narrative leaps in Ganesh's metamorphosis that pose more questions than they answer."

—Vivek Adarkar

CREDITS

Ganesh Ransumair: Aasif Mandvi
Ramlogan: Om Puri
Leela: Ayesha Dharker
Partap: Jimi Mistry
Auntie: Zohra Segal
Mr. Stewart: James Fox

Origin: Great Britain, India
Released: 2001
Production: Nayeem Hafizka, Richard Hawley; Merchant-Ivory Productions; released by ThinkFilm
Directed by: Ismail Merchant
Written by: Caryl Phillips
Cinematography by: Ernest Vincze
Music by: Richard Robbins, Zakir Hussain
Sound: Peter Schneider
Editing: Roberto Silvi
Costumes: Michael O'Connor
Production Design: Lucy Richardson
MPAA rating: PG
Running time: 117 minutes

REVIEWS

Boxoffice. March, 2002, p. 57.
Chicago Sun-Times Online. May 17, 2002.
Los Angeles Times Online. May 17, 2002.
New York Daily News Online. May 3, 2002.
New York Post Online. May 3, 2002.
New York Times Online. May 3, 2002.
Newsday Online. May 3, 2002.
Sight and Sound. April, 2002, p. 50.
Variety. October 15, 2001, p. 36.
Washington Post. May 17, 2002, p. WE43.

QUOTES

Ganesh (Aasif Mandvi): "The books I write gonna be my children. I'm gonna make sons and daughters out of literature."

Narc

Moral ambiguity drenches the characters in *Narc,* making its standard undercover-drug-cop plot into an excruciating and challenging exercise in ethics and values. A brilliant, career-defining performance by Ray Liotta and a fine accompanying turn by Jason Patric elevate the high-powered, sometimes over-the-top *Narc* and take it beyond its genre and its formulaic conventions. Joe Carnahan's movie is both emotionally powerful and thought-provoking, and it is a deeply sensitive exploration of the impact of brutal violence on human lives. But it is also full of tense, believable action scenes.

Patric plays Nick Tellis, an undercover cop looking for redemption after several difficult years as a narc. While running with the street players of inner-city Detroit, Tellis not only got hooked on drugs, he blew his cover and got into a fight in which he gunned down a fleeing drug dealer and his bullets killed a baby. Haunted by his actions, he was fired by the department, but he reluctantly agrees to return to help investigate the unsolved murder of a fellow undercover officer, Michael Calvess (Alan Van Sprang). If he can score a conviction, he is promised he will get his cushy desk job.

The man who knows the most about the investigation is Calvess's ex-partner and close friend, Detective Henry Oak (Liotta). Oak is a volatile, bitter cop who often loses his temper and brutalizes the people he arrests; he is so dangerous he's been put in cold storage by the department. Tellis joins forces with Oak, after Oak tells him in no uncertain terms he will break any departmental rules if that's what it takes to collar the men who killed Calvess.

Tellis, however, has trouble explaining to Oak—or to his wife Jeanine (Lina Felice)—exactly why he has taken on this assignment when he has gotten clean and settled down with a young child. (Oak is suspicious that Tellis has been put on the case by police internal affairs.) Tellis, looking through the case files, is haunted by images of the dead cop, his wife, and two daughters. He clearly identifies with the slain narc. At home, however, he and his wife argue vociferously because she can't abide his decision to go back on the streets, even temporarily. She saw how it nearly destroyed him the last time, and she is afraid of him getting hooked again on drugs or getting killed. But the deeper Tellis gets into the case, the more he is willing to risk to find out what really happened.

Oak is a man of principle and rage, a dedicated cop who can't deal coolly with the tragedies he finds on the streets. He has a big, broken heart and a bellyful of resentment. In a beautifully shot and haunting scene, the two men, waiting outside a suspect's house in their car, with the car's windows reflecting bare branches of trees blowing in the wind, share their personal stories. Oak tells how his wife used to soothe conceal his duplicity. As a portrait of a petty thief, always getting deeper in trouble but wiggling his way out, Darin's performance is convincing; his Marco is the kind of overly confident but almost transparent con artist often encountered not only on the streets, but in corporate suites. Pauls is wonderful as the innocent babe in the woods, a soft-faced man who specializes in charming his victims and who seems to have a warm heart that's been warped by a lifetime of trying to emulate his con-artist father. The pair of them look like a snake and a lamb, and Bielinsky and his principal actors do such a good job of swindling their audience that it's easy to fall for their story hook, line, and sinker.

There's nothing in *Nine Queens* that approaches the intricacies of Mamet's con-game films, but that just might make this film all the more believable—until the rather fantastic ending when the actors are unmasked. These guys aren't such smooth talkers as the glib hustlers in Mamet films. Bielinsky is wonderful at revealing the haunted, one-step-away-from-being-caught look that lurks beneath Marco's facade of being completely in control of every situation. The movie subtly pokes fun not just at the hubris of the crooks and the cupidity and stupidity of their victims, but also at the desperately ridiculous way that deals are played and poses are struck.

Though this is a portrait of a world within a world—of the special moral dilemmas of the con artist—in a larger sense it's a film that pokes fun at the foibles of all human dealings. The way these guys do business isn't that much different from the way "aboveboard" characters do business. In *Nine Queens*, the civilized world is about transactions—and the mistakes made when our instinctual ability to trust gets in the way of our sophisticated worldly judgment.

The dialogue, at least as it is translated into English subtitles, is lively, fresh, and profane. Some of it is rapid-fire, so be prepared to speed-read the text on screen. Though *Nine Queens* doesn't break any new ground in terms of script or technique, it is near flawlessly executed and always closely observant of its keenly delineated characters. In the end, there is a too-neat connection to audience sympathy, but Bielinsky isn't maudlin. His film is clever without being cutesy, dense without being overbearing, and comic without being ludicrous. You might call it Mamet Lite—but that's hardly an insignificant achievement.

—*Michael Betzold*

CREDITS

Marcos: Ricardo Darin
Juan: Gaston Pauls
Valeria: Leticia Bredice
Gandolfo: Ignasi Abadal
Federico: Tomas Fonzi

Origin: Argentina
Language: Spanish
Released: 2000
Production: Pablo Bossi; Patagonik Film Group; released by Sony Pictures Classics
Directed by: Fabian Bielinsky
Written by: Fabian Bielinsky
Cinematography by: Marcelo Camorino
Music by: Cesar Lerner
Sound: Osvaldo Vacca
Editing: Sergio Zottola
Costumes: Monica Toschi
Production Design: Marcelo Salvioli
MPAA rating: R
Running time: 115 minutes

REVIEWS

Boxoffice. November, 2001, p. 130.
Chicago Sun-Times Online. May 10, 2002.
Entertainment Weekly. April 26, 2002, p. 119.
Los Angeles Times Online. April 19, 2002.
New York Times Online. April 7, 2002.
Sight and Sound. August, 2002, p. 46.
Variety. September 17, 2001, p. 27.
Washington Post. May 10, 2002, p. WE42.

No News from God (Sin Noticias de Dios) (Don't Tempt Me!)

The portrayal of heaven and hell often leads to entertaining movies since our visions of the celestial realm and the subterranean inferno ignite our imaginations with possibilities. Spanish director Agustin Diaz-Yanes explores these possibilities while presenting us with an international cast made in heaven with his second feature film, *No News from God.* Starring Victoria Abril in the sexy role of the heavenly nightclub chanteuse/angel Lola Nevado and Penèlope Cruz as a brow-sweating waitress/devil from down under (not Australia) in this soul-saving romp guarantees laughter. However, *No News from God* isn't without its narrative flaws and a light mood turns black three quarters of the way through the film when the women engage in a *Thelma and Louise*-style desperate act in order to save the soul of a retired boxer.

No News From God proved to be a crowd pleaser when it screened at the Seattle International Film Festival and to an audience that obviously adored Abril's performance. After all, the sexy actress has been pleasing arthouse enthusiasts since the ripe age of 15 when she starred in her first role in 1976. Since that time, Abril has appeared in Pedro Almodovar's classics, *Tie Me Up, Tie Me Down, High Heels,* and *Kika* as well as in films by Jean-Jacques Beineix, Nagisa Oshima, Vicente Arada and Josiane Balasko, just to name a few. Abril starred in Icelandic director Baltasar Kormàkur's *101 Reykjavik* in which she played a lesbian dancer called Lola. And again, with *No News From God,* Abril delivers another solid performance playing a character perceived as less sexy than her costar Penèlope Cruz's Carmen Ramos. Except of course when she performs her nightclub act and steams up the screen with a hot number about wanting to be "bad."

Cruz returns to Spanish cinema after appearing in several American films, including *Vanilla Sky, All the Pretty Horses,* and *Woman on Top.* She plays against her usual type by portraying a gum-smacking, lesbian waitress who was a mob boss in a former life. Although the onscreen chemistry between Cruz and Abril offers viewers much entertainment for their hard-earned dollar, Cruz's most memorable scene is a solo act in which the actress dresses in men's clothing and dances to "Kung Fu Fighting."

The film revolves around a political battle between heaven and hell as angels and devils vie for the soul of retired boxer Many (Damian Bechir). Lola's heavenly boss Marina D' Angelo (Fanny Ardant) hires Lola to play the role of Many's estranged wife and to save the boxer's soul by having him ask his mother for forgiveness. The scenes in heaven (which resembles Paris) are shot in black and white while the remainder of the film is shot in color, reminding us that earth is more hell than heaven. Meanwhile, Davenport (Gael Garcia Bernal) and his hellacious employers search for a dark angel to steal Many's soul for their own. Davenport spots Carmen working a horrendous waitress' shift in which she has too many tables and too many orders of fries to contend with and is practically raped by her customers! Davenport saves Carmen, then offers her the job of stealing Many's soul. In exchange for her deed she will be relocated to "circle 22," a more user-friendly spot in hell. She accepts the role as Many's long-lost cousin, but her plans soon go awry after Davenport reveals the ugly politics involved with sending the boxer to hell.

When Carmen and Lola first meet, they meet as adversaries since both are vying for the same soul. But halfway through the film, they team up and raise hell at the supermarket where they work, which results in violence and later imprisonment. However, Many's soul goes to heaven after a battle in court between officials from heaven and hell. Lola returns to heaven and Carmen transforms into a man (who resembles Javier Bardem).

Featuring a "who's who" of French, Spanish and Mexican cinema, *No News from God* draws fans of Cruz, Abril, Fanny Ardant and Mexican newcomer Gael Garcia Bernal (*Y Tu Mama Tambien* and *Amores Perros*). Spotting the various actors almost proves more entertaining than the film itself. *No News from God* proves to be a mix of hot performances and uneven narrative that bends darkness with light.

—*Patty-Lynne Herlevi*

CREDITS

Lola Nevado: Victoria Abril
Carmen Ramos: Penelope Cruz
Many: Damian Bechir
Marina D'Angelo: Fanny Ardant
Davenport: Gael Garcia Bernal

Origin: Spain, France, Italy, Mexico
Language: Spanish
Released: 2001
Production: Gerardo Herrero, Eduardo Campoy, Edmundo Gil Casas; Tornasol Films SA; released by First Look Pictures
Directed by: Agustin Diaz Yanes
Written by: Agustin Diaz Yanes
Cinematography by: Paco Femenia
Music by: Bernardo Bonezzi
Sound: Antonio Rodriguez Marmol
Editing: Jose Salcedo
Costumes: Sonia Grande
Production Design: Javier Fernandez
MPAA rating: R
Running time: 115 minutes

REVIEWS

Variety. January 21, 2002, p. 32.

No Such Thing

A myth. A monster. A world gone media mad.
—Movie tagline
a modern day fable
—Movie tagline

Hal Hartley has always marched to a different drummer, but with *No Such Thing* he has taken his sardonic humor down an unproductive if occasionally intriguing path. A twist on the classic fable of Beauty and the Beast, the film starts promisingly enough with a soliloquy delivered by a monster with scaly hands, horns, and scraggly hair. He looks like a Viking crossed with Swamp Thing, and he speaks like a profane, bored, burned-out hippie.

"I'm not the monster I used to be, I admit it," he says, speaking into a microphone in his corrugated shack on the rocky cliffs of Iceland. "I'm tired, I'm weak, I'm losing my memory, and I can't sleep." The Monster (Robert John Burke, a regular in Hartley films) is making an audiotape to send to a New York television station to verify that he has killed its cameraman and two reporters, who were trying to track down tales of bizarre occurrences near the site of a former U.S. missile silo. The audience doesn't know that all this until a bit later, so you're left to puzzle out what the Monster is talking about.

"The time it takes to kill these idiots is depressing," the Monster complains, pausing occasionally to belch flames that replenish his torch. He goes on to bewail how horrible it is to watch human beings messing up the world and "killing the air itself with your unending pointless noise" while he is doomed to be immortal and indestructible. "I can't go on like this," he says, but adds: "If you won't come to kill me, I'll have to kill you—every last one of you."

His tape is received by Beatrice (Sarah Polley), a mousy, unglamorous secretary at the New York TV station, whose news team is commanded by a hard-bitten, cynical boss (Helen Mirren). She hectors her crew of shamelessly exploitive TV journalists to find something new that will capture jaded audiences' attention. The cigarette-chewing harridan is not interested in the fact that the U.S. government has gone on strike unless the president follows through on his threats to commit suicide. She doesn't think minor terrorist attacks that leave only dozens of people dead are sexy enough. All this is rather over-the-top satire. But the boss is intrigued when Beatrice comes to her with the tape and tells her about the Iceland monster legend. Beatrice, who reminds her boss that she went to journalism school, begs to go on the assignment because the cameraman was her fiancé and she hopes to find him alive.

It's a promising start, and Hartley bravely bites off some controversial satire as he sends Beatrice on his way to the airport dodging terrorist attacks and religious cults exploding gases in the subway B she rides in a pickup truck with two demolitions experts and tells the audience in voice-over that it's the safest way to go in a bewildering world. Her flight to Iceland is rerouted through Brussels and Lisbon, and it crashes before it reaches Europe. Some fishermen spot and rescue her, but she has sustained life-threatening injuries. When she refuses to tell her story of surviving the crash for her boss's TV cameras, she is abandoned by Mirren's

unnamed character, but then she is taken under the wing of kindly Dr. Anna (Julie Christie). The doctor and colleagues then administer some real tough love to Beatrice, subjecting her to a painful experimental surgery that reawakens her paralyzed body parts. The purpose of this entire plot detour is unclear—it adds nothing to the movie except to make Beatrice seem more like a brave victim.

Eventually, Beatrice recovers and, with the help of Dr. Anna, finds her way to the remote village that is closest to the Monster's lair. There, the locals get her drunk, she passes out, and they leave her on the Monster's doorstep as a sort of tribute or sacrifice. The Monster and Beatrice then have a talk. The Monster blusters and threatens, and proves he has killed her fiancé and the others, but Beatrice is not cowed. "There's no such thing" as monsters, she maintains to his face—presumably, her caring heart can solve his problem. But as he continues to provoke her, she shoots him, and he shoots himself in the head, but he cannot die. Only one man, he says—a Dr. Artaud, who used to do experiments at the missile site—knows how to kill him. Beatrice promises to find Dr. Artaud. She takes the Monster back to New York after getting him to promise he won't harm anyone.

Up to this point, there is a chance that Hartley can meld his sardonic humor and offbeat world view to give us a new twist on this rather familiar story. (After all, a plot that involves a beautiful young woman bringing a monster to the big city has been done many times before, though usually the monster is a gorilla.) From Hartley's previous, consistently clever and outrageous body of work (including *The Unbelievable Truth* and *Flirt*), there is hope he's going to turn this story into something special. But his plot falls flat on its face and the movie runs out of steam. Scenes and dialogue begin to be so severely truncated that it becomes obvious that the writer-director himself has lost interest in his story.

The New York station that Beatrice works for gets exclusive rights to the Monster interview, but first there is a whirlwind party. This is when everything in the film starts falling apart. Beatrice, who's been angelic and kind-hearted throughout the film, suddenly shows up in an erotic black outfit (featuring on the cover of the video, of course) and spends the night having sex with a groupie, while the Monster, who is an alcoholic, spends the night on the couch. The next day is the big press conference; its's funny enough, but Hartley races through it as if it's a hot potato. Then the government gets hold of the Monster for more experiments, the TV station loses control and interest in the story, the boss sabotages Beatrice's plan to hook up the Monster with Dr. Artaud (Baltasar Kormakur), and finally she spirits both off to the Monster's lair for a final encounter. Nothing unexpected happens, and the movie ends with a shrug and a whimper.

Hartley movies are an acquired taste, but even Hartley aficionados may wince at how heavyhanded and preachy he seems to have become with this film, which takes clumsy potshots at rather obvious targets (such as television journalism). A sharper piece of writing might have made more out of Hartley's occasional suggestions that civilization has become so jaded and commercialized that it no longer has rooms for monsters or legends. The Monster turns into rather a tame and lifeless creature, but it's hard to work up much sympathy for him. And though Beauty and the Beast was a love story, this version of it has no romance. The closest it gets is when the Beast complains that he doesn't scare anyone any more, and Beatrice insists (contrary to her earlier protestations) that he still scares her, and she rests her head on his shoulder.

Burke gives a fine, deadpan comic performance in his monster's garb, but the character is rendered so limp and lifeless by the end of the film that he can't do much to revive interest. The same goes for Polley, a wonderful actress who deserves better roles. She gives some life and heart to the Beatrice character, who seems, along with Christie's Anna, to be among the only human beings left on earth with compassion and kindness. But as written, Beatrice is too bland and angelic, and there is no tension between her and the Monster, and no spark either.

The characters don't connect, the satire fizzles, the story goes nowhere, and the audience is left to wonder what Hartley had in mind with a concept and a project that seems half-baked and listless. There might be something to be said for contrasting the pre-civilized beliefs of remote Iceland with the cynicism of modern civilization, but if this is such an effort, it stumbles badly and collapses of its own inertia and weightlessness. No Such Thing fails to maintain a consistent tone, shifting wildly from black comedy to maudlin scenes, and it's not even outrageous enough to arouse more than a shrug. Even by Hartley's established standards of blank verse, this film lacks poetry and pizazz.

—*Michael Betzold*

CREDITS

Beatrice: Sarah Polley
Monster: Robert John Burke
The Boss: Helen Mirren
Dr. Anna: Julie Christie
Dr. Artaud: Baltasar Kormakur

Origin: USA
Released: 2001
Production: Hal Hartley, Fridrik Thor Fridriksson, Cecelia Kate Roque; True Fiction Pictures, American Zoetrope, Icelandic Film Corp.; released by United Artists
Directed by: Hal Hartley
Written by: Hal Hartley

Cinematography by: Michael Spiller
Music by: Hal Hartley
Sound: Kjartan Kjartansson
Editing: Steve Hamilton
Costumes: Helga I. Stefansdottir
Production Design: Arni Pall Johannsson
MPAA rating: R
Running time: 103 minutes

REVIEWS

Boxoffice. July, 2001, p. 89.
Chicago Sun-Times Online. March 29, 2002.
Entertainment Weekly. April 5, 2002, p. 89.
Los Angeles Times Online. March 29, 2002.
New York Times Online. March 29, 2002.
Variety. May 21, 2001, p. 22.
Washington Post. March 28, 2002, p. WE42.

TRIVIA

Robert John Burke also worked with Hal Hartley on *The Unbelievable Truth* (1989), *Simple Men* (1992), and *Flirt* (1995).

One Hour Photo

 Box Office: $31.5 million

Although Robin Williams appears to be a natural clown, liable to ham up any serious role, he has also provided evidence that he deserves to be taken seriously as an actor, but never so convincingly as in *One Hour Photo*. Don't expect the Robin Williams of *Patch Adams* or *Death to Smoochy* here. Williams doesn't wear a clown face this time, only the sad, ordinary features of a lonely Everyman who desperately needs human contact. Though a natural clown and gifted stand-up comedian, Williams studied acting with the great John Houseman at Julliard. His character this time, Seymour "Sy" Parrish, looks like part of the furniture at the drug chain SavMart, where Sy works behind the one-hour photo counter. He likes his work, and he treats his customers like family. That's the creepy part. All the audience knows about Sy is that he lives for his job, and, off the job, he lives quite alone in a grim, sterile apartment. He is desperately driven by a need to belong. But Sy is a cipher with the rim rubbed out, a nothing, an anonymous presence. "To know him is to ignore him," one critic wrote.

At first sight, then, it is difficult to "read" Sy's character. Williams looks older than he is, with thinning bleached hair and a winning smile; he also looks tired, exhausted, and frayed. For all one knows, he could be a psychopath, a serial killer. He certainly takes voyeuristic pleasure in examining the photos of his "favorite" customers. He duplicates prints to take home and place on his wall of honor. He is especially obsessed with a picture-perfect model family whose photos he develops. The trophy wife, Nina Yorkin (Connie Nielsen), who brings him the film knows his name, but has no clue about his peculiar motivation, or interest, as when Sy wants to give a present to her son, Jake (Dylan Smith). As he confides to one of his colleagues at the store, he would like to be "Uncle Sy" to his clients. Sy is a very eccentric, mysterious, and unpredictable character. As one critic noticed, the director was "stingy about depicting Sy's rather empty life beyond the workplace." In short, Sy needs to get a life, as they say, but one wonders if he is capable of taking one, especially when he starts stalking the Yorkin family.

Sy certainly understands that people do not photograph their "real" lives but only capture fleeting moments or remembered happiness, real or pretended. As a stalker, Sy learns more than he needs to know about the Yorkins. Nina's husband, Will (Michael Vartan), turns out to be a philandering architect. Things are certainly not as happy on the home front as the photogenic family photos seem to suggest. Under pressure at work when his boss (Gary Cole) begins to complain about Sy's performance, Sy's life really begins to crumble when he decides to teach Will Yorkin a lesson. Sy presumes to correct the problem, so as, perhaps, to restore his fantasy illusions. This complication explains why Sy narrates the story in flashback from a police interrogation room, framed as a madman's confession.

Writer-director Mark Romanek told the *Washington Post* that he had written the role with someone else in mind but was pleasantly surprised when Williams showed interest. "Robin's made 40, 60 movies, so at that point you're running out of challenges," Romanek explained. "I was going for an archetypal character, an intensely bland threat. He had to be an invisible man. And I cast one of the most charismatic people around." That increased the challenge for both the actor and the director, but Williams was up to the challenge. Stephen Hunter nailed the film's "most astonishing achievement: It begins by scaring you to death by evoking a monster, and by the end it has seduced you into caring for him."

Recalling the star's cameo as a hateful nihilist in the 1996 adaptation of Joseph Conrad's *The Secret Agent,* Gary Arnold of the *Washington Times* wrote that Williams is "often at his most persuasive when simulating predatory personalities." Romenek's direction excels "at a form of ominous miniaturization that blends exceptional atmospheric precision with a methodical heightening of apprehension," Arnold claimed, but the director's "control is sometimes conspicuous to a fault," as if he were "emphasizing design at the expense of genuine misgiving and pity for a victim of character disintegration."

Writing in the *New Republic,* Stanley Kauffmann, always dependable in his evaluation of screen acting, suggested that the performance could best be appreciated "by those who have seen the actor in his talk-show appearances," when he is at his most manic and hyperactive and unpredictable. Kauffmann was reminded "of the German Expressionist drama that flowered in the early 1920s" and of Georg Kaiser's *From Morn to Midnight* in particular, concerning "a bank clerk whose temperament is much like Sy's and whose hunger for some flavor in his life leads to catastrophe." Romanek directed the film "with as consistent a vacant, echoing tone as his screenplay permitted," but the "plot reduces the film to a performance and a problem— Williams's good work and the author's quandary about what to do with it."

Lisa Schwarzbaum's *Entertainment Weekly* review, entitled "The Grim Peeper," was more cute and less thoughtful than Kauffmann's. Noting that Romanek had been influenced by such "trip-wire loners" of such films as Scorsese's *Taxi Driver* (1976), Polanski's *The Tenant* (1976), and Coppola's *The Conversation* (1974), she criticized Romanek for becoming too "enthralled by his own portrait-of-alienation camera shots at the expense of laying a believable foundation for that estrangement in the script." True enough, though Sy Parrish is far less convincingly dangerous than Travis Bickel, the De Niro character in *Taxi Driver.* Perhaps because he is less disturbed.

In the *Baltimore Sun,* Chris Kaltenbach complained about "a certain disconnectedness" in the film that creates the sense, "even after its all over, that we haven't been let in on everything." But he was fully appreciative of Williams, so effectively cast against type: "With a posture that's a bit too ramrod-straight, and a manner suspiciously self-effacing, Sy is a cloudburst waiting to happen." Kaltenbach also notes that Connie Nielsen, "famous for having seduced Keanu Reeves in *The Devil's Advocate* (1997)," is also cast against type here as an all-American supermom.

There is a disturbing emptiness that makes the character and the film so effectively creepy. Romanek told David Hochman of the *New York Times* that he first imagined the film when he visited an all-night pharmacy near his West Hollywood apartment. Romanek wondered how the one-hour photo manager felt, "being inundated by images of people's lives that on the surface probably seemed much richer and happier than his own." Romanek made a low-budget independent feature called *Static* in 1985, but then rose to prominence as a director of music videos for MTV, like David Fincher, Spike Jonze, Roman Coppola, and Jonathan Glazer. His first mainstream feature, *One Hour Photo* was made on a budget of $13 million. By contrast, the five-minute "Scream" video he made for Michael and Janet Jackson was made on a budget of $7 million.

Sy Parrish is too bland to be very menacing as a psychopath. In fact, some reviewers went astray by thinking of the film as a thriller rather than a disturbing and pathetic character study. It's about photography and images, and Sy's fascination may seem menacing if one thinks of another film-processing psychopath, Francis Dolarhyde, the serial killer from *Red Dragon* who used processed film to find and study his eventual victims, but he was really whacked, and Sy simply is not that disturbed, though disturbed enough to keep the film edgy. In both pictures film processing becomes a consistent visual metaphor, all the way from beginning to end in *One Hour Photo*.

"I've always been interested in how images communicate ideas," Romanek a gifted photographer, told David Hochman of the *New York Times*. "Strong images have a dreamlike quality that lets the message seep in, right brain first." *One Hour Photo* is an extended study of how images can distort reality and stir emotions. The film is light-sensitive. As Gary Arnold noticed, for example, the "eerie neatness and fluorescent sheen within the SavMart may tell us more about Sy's state of mind than the place where he's employed." Arnold was reminded of Stanley Kubrick's visual design for *2001: A Space Odyssey* (1968). Like Kubrick, Romanek is a talented photographer as well as a filmmaker, and certainly, the subject of his latest film is, first and foremost, photography. This is as good a debut picture as can be found.

—*James M. Welsh*

Orange County

It's not just a place. It's a state of mind.
—Movie tagline

 Box Office: $41 million

If nothing else, *Orange County* has a lot of talented people involved with it. High on that list is Jack Black, the ferociously energetic character actor who lit up the screen in *High Fidelity*. Director Jake Kasdan, whose debut film was *Zero Effect* has directed the acclaimed television series *Undeclared* and *Freaks and Geeks*. Kasdan worked on the series with screenwriter Mike White, who also wrote and starred in the severely offbeat *Chuck and Buck,* a film the *Los Angeles Times* described as "dazzlingly uncompromising." The supporting cast includes SCTV alum Catherine O'Hara, *Third Rock From the Sun*'s John Lithgow, Harold Ramis, and Lily Tomlin.

One of the interesting things about *Orange County*—and, unfortunately, the only real interesting thing about the film—is that it is populated by Hollywood offspring. Kasdan is the son of Lawrence Kasdan, writer and director of films such as *The Big Chill* and *Body Heat*. *Orange County* star Colin Hanks is the son of Tom Hanks and Schuyler Fisk, who plays his love interest, is the daughter of actress Sissy Spacek.

With all this talent and Hollywood lineage, it seems like *Orange County* would be a whole lot better. But, surprisingly, the film never hits its stride. It's a hard film to get a handle on because it's difficult to tell what the film is trying to be. It's a teen comedy, but lacks the subversive wit of even *Josie and the Pussycats*. To its credit, the film is not filled with raunchy jokes, but the jokes it does have are barely there. It's supposed to be sort of funny, plus have kind of a message, but the humor is way too unfocused and the message ends up playing like sentimentality. Comedy and meaning don't have to be mutually exclusive. A film like *The Wonder Boys* handled the two just fine. An approach like that could have worked well on *Orange County*. But like the county itself, the film looks good on the surface but there's not much beyond that surface.

Shaun Brumder (Hanks) is a surf dude in a wealthy Orange County coastal town. He's happy with his life until one of his fellow surfer's dies while trying to ride a really big wave. Shaun is overwrought until his finds a book buried in the beach. The book is a *Catcher in the Rye* type of book that Shaun ends up reading 52 times. He's so affected by the book that he decides that instead of becoming a professional surfer, he's going to become a writer. The only way to do this is to attend Stanford and study under the book's author Marcus Skinner (the senior Kasdan's crony Kevin Kline). Shaun gives up surfing and applies himself to school, ending up with the kind of transcript that Stanford would be drooling over, if indeed a school could drool.

Shaun is shocked, then, when he gets a rejection letter from Stanford. He rushes into the guidance counselor's (Lily Tomlin) office and discovers that there has been a terrible mistake. The counselor switches his transcript with one of the other students, a dim stoner. (Amusingly, we see a cutaway of the shocked boy reading his acceptance letter to his equally dim friends. "Hey, cool," they murmur, not seeming to realize just how unqualified the boy is.) In real life, this kind of mix-up could probably be easily solved by a call from the guidance counselor to the admission's office at Stanford, but—as bright as Shaun seems to be—this kind of non-movie logic doesn't dawn on him.

Shaun decides to make it his personal quest to get into Stanford. In stead of making that reasonable phone call, he instead cooks up plans like having his drug-taking, TV-watching slug of a brother, Lance (Black), drive him up to Stanford in a wild ride trip in Lance's dilapidated old van. (Why Shaun, who, unlike his brother, is not a crazy drug addict and who happens to have a perfectly nice, newer car doesn't drive himself is one of the movie's mysteries.)

In yet more evidence indicating that Shaun is not as bright as his grades would indicate is the fact that he decides that the best course of action is to head to the private house of Don Durkett (Harold Ramis), the dean of admissions, and demand that Durkett look at his transcript, even though it's 10 at night. Of course, if Shaun hadn't decided that, then we wouldn't have the scene in which the dean accidentally pops a few of Lance's psychedelic drugs, thinking they're Excedrin.

In other inane plot news, Shaun's girlfriend, Ashley (Fisk), who also thinks the pills are Excedrin, urges the dean to take several extra pills. Apparently she thinks those dosage instructions are just there to make the bottle look more official or something. The visit also gives Lance a chance to have a sexual encounter with a worker in the admissions office that ends up with the whole building being burned to the ground. (Ben Stiller shows up in a quick cameo as one of the firemen.)

Even though Ashley doesn't want Shaun to go to Stanford because that would mean he'd be leaving her, she is game for helping him get into the school. She blackmails her promiscuous friend into having her grandfather (Garry Marshall), who is on Stanford's board, come and visit Shaun's house so that Shaun can make his case. Here, writer White assumes that the wackiness of Shaun's family will be enough to equal comedy fun. Shaun's mother (O'Hara), a divorcee who remarried an old man to keep her financial status intact, gets drunk and starts regaling the grandfather with tales of how Shaun's father (Lithgow) dumped her for a young blonde from the gym. Meanwhile, Lance makes an appearance in his underwear and Shaun's surfer friends show up at the door and refuse to leave.

All the wackiness eventually turns into sappiness when Shaun decides that he doesn't need to go to Stanford to be a writer and that he can be a great writer by just staying put. And that maybe, just maybe, the things he hates about his family are really the things he loves about them. Or something like that.

Orange County relies way too heavily on the craziness of its characters, but there are a few moments of stronger humor. When Shaun goes in to see his guidance counselor, she asks, "Are you a student here?" even though Shaun is class president and probably the most prominent kid in his class. A large chunk of the best humor comes from Lithgow as Shaun's Type-A father, Budd Brumder, who spends most of his time on the phone, making deals. When Budd goes to his old house and his disheveled ex-wife answers the door, he offhandedly tosses off the line, "Got a beer, coyote ugly?" that makes the line seem much funnier that it is written down. When Shaun argues that he can make a living as a writer, Budd yells that all writers are poor. Shaun counters with Tom Clancey, Anne Rice and Steven King. "Three people in the history of literature!!" spews Budd peevishly.

Critics couldn't seem to agree on whether the film was good or bad. Stephanie Zacharek of *Salon* wrote, "*Orange County* is a feebly pleasant surprise: It's not as cheap, loud and sleazy as it might have been, but it's also too eagerly well-meaning and indistinct to really stick. It's a piece of mildly entertaining, inoffensive fluff that drifts aimlessly for 90 minutes before lodging in the cracks of that ever-growing category: unembarrassing but unmemorable little pictures that, had their directors and writers fought to take a few extra chances, might have been something close to wonderful." Lisa Schwarzbaum of *Entertainment Weekly* gave the film a B + and called it "a generous little story about the sons and daughters of incarcerating privilege." And Kevin Thomas of the *Los Angeles Times* wrote that "*Orange County* starts out deliriously funny but allows sentimentality to squeeze it to a pulp by the time it's over."

—*Jill Hamilton*

CREDITS

Shaun Brumder: Colin Hanks
Lance: Jack Black
Ashley: Schuyler Fisk
Cindy Beugler: Catherine O'Hara
Bud Brumder: John Lithgow
Don Durkett: Harold Ramis
Mona: Jane Adams
Arthur Gantner: Garry Marshall
Vera Gantner: Dana Ivey
Principal Harbert: Chevy Chase
Charlotte Cobb: Lily Tomlin
Bob Buegler: George Murdock
Krista: Leslie Mann
Arlo: Kyle Howard
Marcus Skinner: Kevin Kline

Origin: USA
Released: 2002
Production: Scott Rudin, Van Toffler, David Gale, Scott Aversano; MTV Films; released by Paramount Pictures
Directed by: Jake Kasdan
Written by: Mike White
Cinematography by: Greg Gardiner
Music by: Michael Andrews
Sound: Keith Wester
Music Supervisor: Manish Raval, Tom Wolfe
Editing: Tara Timpone
Costumes: Debra McGuire
Production Design: Gary Frutkoff
MPAA rating: PG-13
Running time: 81 minutes

REVIEWS

Boxoffice. March, 2002, p. 61.
Chicago Sun-Times Online. January 11, 2002.
Entertainment Weekly. January 18, 2002, p. 55.
Los Angeles Times Online. January 11, 2002.
New York Times Online. January 11, 2002.
People. January 21, 2002, p. 30.
USA Today Online. January 11, 2002.
Variety. January 14, 2002, p. 49.
Washington Post. January 11, 2002, p. WE39.

TRIVIA

Screenwriter Mike White has a cameo as an English teacher.

The Other Side of Heaven

An ordinary boy and his journey among extraordinary people who would change his life forever.
—Movie tagline

 Box Office: $4.1 million

The Other Side of Heaven is a picture based on the book *In the Eye of the Storm*, a memoir by John H. Groberg, a Mormon elder, who went to the Kingdom of Tonga in the 1950s as a missionary. The film was directed by first-timer Mitch Davis, who graduated from Brigham Young University. Despite the story being by Mormons and about Mormons, Mormons aren't mentioned specifically in the film. Besides audience clues like the fact that Groberg (Christopher Gorham) is first seen at his school, Brigham Young, the religion in the film is portrayed as being a vague sort of Christianity.

Groberg is the oldest son from a big, wholesome family, headed by a wholesome dad who's one of the few Democrats in his Idaho hometown. Groberg is a regular teen who plays horn in a band and tries to keep his girl, Jean Sabin (Anne Hathaway) away from his rival, Edward. All that changes when he gets a letter giving him his missionary assignment. He and his family are delighted that he'll be going to Tonga, although it doesn't seem like anyone is too sure where exactly that is. (It's in the South Seas.)

Groberg has quite an assignment. His instructions from higher-ups in the church are to go to the island and "build a kingdom." No matter that he doesn't speak the language.

But armed with a supply of white shirts and ties, a midwestern can-do attitude, and the firm idea that his religion = good, other religions = bad, he sets off on his adventure. He will eventually be gone for two and a half years.

From the outset, he is beset with a little more adventure than he is looking for. He has to take boats to various islands where he contends with circumstances like people who are supposed to meet him but aren't there and being thrown in a prison for not being on the list of permitted visitors. When he gets to his tiny island, he gets translation help from a local Christian, Feki (Joe Folau). Feki immediately buys into everything Groberg tells him. "I believe you because you travel so far," says Feki, in explanation. The islanders, who already have a local priest (Nathaniel Lees), a Christian one in fact, aren't particularly happy to see Groberg, although they aren't unkind to him. He doesn't endear himself to them when he gives his first speech to the Tongans, making a language mistake that causes him to make repeated mistaken references to outhouses.

Groberg being the all around swell guy that the movie constantly insists that he is, takes to a sandbar to learn the language. He refuses food and sits, comparing the Tongan Bible to his own English one. He emerges a few days later, perfectly versed in the Tongan language. (At this point, oddly, all the actors in the movie start speaking English.) Because this incredible feat doesn't impress the islanders much, Groberg has to come up with something else. When a local boy falls from a mango tree and is apparently dead, the desperate father appeal to Groberg to use his "powers" to resurrect the kid. Groberg spends a feverish night, pushing on the boy's back and saying "out with the bad air, in with the good." In the morning, the boy . . . is . . . alive! Groberg's magic healing powers do a lot towards increasing his popularity among the local people. He still has somewhat of a feud with the local priest, but other than that, he's pretty much won over his public.

That leaves Groberg left fighting other battles, generally health and weather disasters. Through the rest of the movie, these happen with a tiresome regularity. Groberg's feet get bitten by rats in the night, someone dies of lockjaw, and Groberg faces a storm at sea with waves the size of those in *A Perfect Storm*. When that's not happening, there's other fun stuff like a guy accidentally chopping off his foot, a girl lost in a storm, and a giant hurricane on the island that leaves everyone without food for weeks and nearly dead. It gets to the point that whenever a scene starts with the islanders engaging in regular, everyday activity, you think, "Oh, no" and wait for the inevitable disaster.

Interspersed with the mayhem and Groberg's repeated upstandingness, are scenes in which he corresponds with his girlfriend, Jean. We see her in a virginal white dress, doing things like swinging on a swing in a garden. She looks like she is straight from an ad for some sort of feminine product. It is this image of Jean that helps Groberg stay chaste when he's approached by beautiful island woman, Lavania (Miriama Smith). He rejects her with talk of a more eternal love with God. Her mother is mad about this because she wants Groberg's white man's "seed" for her daughter. Groberg calms the hysterical woman down with a speech that sounds prudish or highly moral, depending on your point of view about the promise that he's made to his lady and his God. Groberg gets out a picture of his girl and the woman, struck by Jean's pure smiling face, burst into tears of shame. There will be no seed for her daughter.

A later scene makes Groberg's views even more clear. Some of the native young women have headed out with some questionable white sailors for some activities of a salacious nature, despite their parents anguished cries that they remain on the island. The scene cuts between one woman on the boat being led by an unpleasant-looking old sailor into what's probably his bedroom, contrasted with shots of the lovely Lavania, wearing white, being baptized in the ocean by a white-clad Groberg. To make the contrast greater, the women who make the "wrong" decision are stocky and plain, not like beautiful Lavania.

It's heavy-handedness like this that are the downfall of the film. Groberg insists that the Tongan people change their entire ways of thinking but never once does he consider the possibility that he might change his views. When one of the islanders is dying, Groberg insists on performing a blessing. No matter that this blessing wasn't asked for and, in fact, is unwanted. "It can only help!" insists Groberg, plowing ahead anyway. And there's the problem of whether coming to an island and enforcing your religion on a group that's perfectly happy without it is the great idea that the movie unthinkingly accepts it to be. As Kirk Honeycutt of the *Hollywood Reporter* put it, "The religious imperialism at the heart of such an experience is accepted at face value without any critical examination of the notion of a young man from Idaho going to such a far-flung land to help the natives not by bringing better food or medicine or education but simply a 'better' God." Stephen Holden of the *New York Times* wrote that "The Tongan natives resemble a 1950's *National Geographic* cliché of childlike pagans being taken in hand by wiser, smarter Westerners."

The one non-debatable point in the film is that it looks great. The film was made on a small, indie budget of $7-8 million and the film makers got a lot of bang for their buck. It was filmed on Rarotonga in the Cook Islands and Auckland, New Zealand, and watching the numerous multicolored sunsets in it is like taking a vacation (albeit an unpleasant one with the hurricanes and such.) But the lush scenery wasn't enough to win over critics. Jan Stuart wrote in the *Los Angeles Times* that the film "is an unabashed Mormon propaganda piece disguised as an adventure film" and called it "a howler." Al Brumley of the *Dallas Morning News* wrote "Apart from the movie's in-your-face, artless directing, there's a disturbing 'Great White Hope' undertone to

The Other Side of Heaven that subtly undermines its message of Christian love and compassion." Even Jeff Vice of the *Deseret News* in Salt Lake City called the film "good-looking but rather superficial."

—*Jill Hamilton*

CREDITS

John Groberg: Christopher Gorham
Jean Sabin: Anne Hathaway
Feki: Joe Folau
Lavinia: Miriama Smith
Kelepi: Nathaniel Lees
Asi: Whetu Fala

Origin: USA
Released: 2002
Production: Gerald R. Molen, John Garbett; 3Mark Entertainment; released by Excel Entertainment Group
Directed by: Mitch Davis
Written by: Mitch Davis
Cinematography by: Brian J. Breheny
Music by: Kevin Kiner
Editing: Steve Ramirez
Production Design: Rick Kofoed
MPAA rating: PG
Running time: 113 minutes

REVIEWS

Los Angeles Times Online. April 12, 2002.
New York Times Online. April 12, 2002.
San Francisco Chronicle. April 12, 2002, p. D3.
Variety. January 28, 2002, p. 29.
Washington Post Online. April 12, 2002, p. W40.

Panic Room

It was supposed to be the safest room in the house.
—Movie tagline

 Box Office: $95.3 million

Having three determined burglars break in and terrorize you the first night in your new home is especially bad luck. That is what happens to the principal character and her teenage daughter in *Panic Room,* an above-average thriller that encountered its own share of misfortune during production. The first bad break was an actual one, a fracture in the leg of its initial leading lady, Nicole Kidman. An injury she had suffered while making *Moulin Rouge,* which later caused a delay during *The Others,* was exacerbated about three weeks into filming, forcing her to bow out. There must have been panic in more than one room at Sony Pictures, as a scramble ensued to find a suitable (and available) replacement of similar stature, or else the plug would have to be pulled on the production.

Director David Fincher was relieved to be able to snag Jodie Foster, who was unexpectedly at liberty after an injury to Russell Crowe shut down her production of *Flora Plum.* Shortly thereafter, however, Fincher was chagrined to learn that Foster was pregnant, forcing a reworking of the shooting schedule to deal with the slim actress's impending expansion. There was also a change made in the young actress playing the lead's daughter, and a more significant replacement of the director of photography due to "creative differences" after filming had already begun. *Panic Room*'s release date had to be pushed back at least five times. Still, despite being so plagued by unexpected obstacles, the film, like its heroine, triumphed in the end.

Meg Altman (Foster) is hardly in need of any more unpleasantness in her life, still thrown off balance from a painful divorce caused by her millionaire husband Stephen's (Patrick Bauchau) dalliance with a younger woman. She has left the cozy Connecticut countryside and spent a good chunk of her settlement on a spacious 1879 townhouse on Manhattan's Upper West Side, where she will raise her spirited daughter Sarah (Kristen Stewart) while heading back to school to begin anew. As Meg and Sarah get a tour of their new digs, they learn that it features a panic room, a hidden safe haven installed by the wealthy and paranoid financier who previously lived there. In the event that someone or something threatens the house's occupants, they can hole up in this impenetrable room and call for help on a special secure phone line to the police. The panic room also has its own ventilation system, and a bank of surveillance monitors would enable those inside to safely observe what is transpiring in various parts of the home.

Meg clearly gets claustrophobic just thinking about being shut up in the room, and she makes a reference to Edgar Allen Poe's short story "The Cask of Amontillado" in which someone meets their death entombed within a wall. The recent upheaval in Meg's life has clearly made her on edge, and she keeps running her fingers distractedly through her hair. Meg releases her tears in private, crouching in the bathtub with a bottle of wine. A scene later on in which Meg tucks Sarah into bed tells us three things: Meg is a fiercely protective and loving mother, Sarah is a spunky young lady, and the two share both a strong bond and a bitterness toward Stephen. Clearly, this newly-single mother and her only child make a great team, which will soon come in handy.

Once the lights are turned off for the night in the house and a thunderstorm begins, the stage is suitably set for trouble to arrive. The complicated security system beeps when the house is entered, but Meg does not hear. Three men enter who know about a hidden stash of money from the previous owner, but are unaware (and none too happy to learn) that the new tenants have already moved in. Junior (Jared Leto), the ultra-hyper, clearly off-kilter grandson of the previous owner, is hell-bent on getting his hands on the loot. A late edition to the plan is gun-toting Raoul (Dwight Yoakam), a menacing, ski-masked presence. Unhappy with Raoul's unexpected inclusion in the plan is Burnham (Forest Whitaker), who knows a thing or two about panic rooms because he installs them for a living. Unable to resist the lure of a big take, Burnham clearly hungers for the money but has no stomach for any bloodshed or loss of life that might ensue since people are in the house. "I don't hurt people," he stipulates.

The three proceed despite Burnham's reservations about doing so in an occupied house, and soon a terrified Meg is scooping up Sarah and making a frenzied dash for the panic room. Once sealed, it is impossible for the bad guys to get in, but since Meg had not hooked up the room's phone line as of yet, it is also impossible to summon help. Meg tries some false bravado over the speaker system to try to scare the intruders away, but they respond by holding up a series of handwritten notes for her to see on the monitors that make their intentions chillingly clear: the men are not leaving until they get what they came for, and what they came for is locked in the panic room with Meg and Sarah.

What follows is an increasingly dangerous game of chess between the two sides. The men first use sledgehammers and then introduce gas into the panic room's ventilation system. Meg counters by covering the vents with duct tape, instructing Sarah to get under a fire blanket, and igniting a blaze, which explodes back through the pipes at the burglars. Sarah finds a small hole to the outside and tries to send an SOS with a flashlight to a neighbor across the way (played by Andrew Kevin Walker, who wrote Fincher's gripping 1995 film Se7en). While Burnham, Junior and Raoul are otherwise occupied downstairs, Meg dares to sprint out briefly to retrieve her cell phone, but it will not work in the panic room. So she starts splicing together wires and gets an abbreviated call out to Stephen, who eventually arrives and is beaten to a bloody pulp. (If remarkably resourceful Meg is ever looking to remarry, an ideal match would seem to be the title character from the 1980's TV show MacGyver.)

As if Meg did not have enough to contend with already, Sarah is apparently a diabetic and her blood sugar is sinking fast. This increased challenge draws them closer together, while the men are being blown apart, literally in the case of Junior, who is slain by Raoul. Burnham is aghast, and is even more disconcerted when Raoul threatens him, as well. When Meg returns from another mad dash, this time to get a vital syringe for Sarah, she is horrified to find that she and the enemy have switched encampments, the men now locked in the room with her fading daughter. While Raoul voices a desire to kill Sarah, Burnham cannot image hurting a child and kindheartedly gives the poor girl her shot. An especially suspenseful scene is when Meg deals with the police at the front door, thinking quickly on her feet to get them to leave so that Raoul will not kill Sarah then and there. When the two men finally exit the room with the money they came for and Sarah, they encounter one extremely enraged mother, and much violence ensues. Burnham heroically shoots Raoul after he punches Sarah and is about to kill Meg, and is then apprehended by the police as he flees with the money. When the film ends, everything is sunny and serene, with Meg and Sarah now amidst chirping birds in the park, perusing the real estate ads.

Filmed on a budget of $48 million, *Panic Room* grossed $95.3 million. The screenplay was written by David Koepp, who had an even bigger hit this year with *Spider-Man*. Director Fincher stated that he was interested in the challenge of holding an audience's interest while telling a story restricted almost completely to a single set and taking place during a single night. He cited such classics as John Huston's *Key Largo* (1948) and Alfred Hitchcock's *Rear Window* (1954) as influences. Although not nearly as absorbing or satisfying as those films, *Panic Room* is genuinely intriguing if not always gripping, and enjoyable throughout if never quite extraordinary.

One of its most interesting elements is Fincher's camera work, inventive, intricate shots exhaustively planned out before production commenced. As the burglars first try to get in, his camera pulls back from Meg in bed, glides down the stairs and across the room to the front door, goes into the keyhole and back out again, and then rises up through the various floors to the skylight where Burnham is successfully entering. When they are trying to gas Meg and Sarah out of the panic room, we travel through the hose along with the hissing gas. These roaming, observational shots are quite impressive without being flashy or distracting. Also noteworthy is the atmosphere Fincher creates with the low-key lighting used throughout most of the film, which he had once amazingly pondered shooting in totally darkness. Anyone watching can relate to feeling uneasy and insecure in the dead of night, especially in new, unfamiliar surroundings when the weather outside is as unsettled as you are. Kudos go to cinematographer Darius Khondji and his successor Conrad W. Hall, production designer Arthur Max, and Howard Shore's score in helping create the creepy mood Fincher wanted.

Cinematography by: Christian Berger
Sound: Jean-Pierre Laforce, Guillaume Sciama
Editing: Monika Willi, Nadine Muse
Costumes: Annette Beaufays
Production Design: Christoph Kanter
MPAA rating: Unrated
Running time: 130 minutes

REVIEWS

Boxoffice. September, 2001, p. 146.
Chicago Sun-Times Online. April 26, 2002.
Entertainment Weekly. April 5, 2002, p. 92.
Hollywood Reporter. May 15, 2001, p. 17.
Los Angeles Times Online. April 12, 2002.
New York Times Online. March 24, 2002.
New York Times Online. March 29, 2002.
Rolling Stone. April 11, 2002, p. 138.
Sight and Sound. November, 2001, p. 54.
Time Online. April 1, 2001.
Variety. May 28, 2001, p. 18.
Village Voice Online. April 2, 2002.
Washington Post. May 24, 2002, p. WE44.

AWARDS AND NOMINATIONS

Cannes 2001: Actor (Magimel), Actress (Huppert),
Grand Jury Prize
Nomination:
Ind. Spirit 2003: Foreign Film.

Pinocchio

Box Office: $2.6 million

How much one likes Roberto Benigni's *Pinocchio* depends, to a large extent, on how much one likes the actor-director himself. Playing the part of the mischievous puppet who yearns to be a real boy, Benigni throws himself into the role with the unbridled enthusiasm we would expect from the comedian who bounced up the stage when he won an Oscar for his moving performance in *Life Is Beautiful.* Many critics found it disconcerting to see a grown man playing a classic child's part, but Pinocchio is more than a child; he is an Italian icon, and Benigni is a favorite son whose childlike exuberance fits the role perfectly.

Indeed, if one can suspend disbelief and enjoy Benigni's clowning, this version of the classic tale actually offers some-thing most American audiences have not seen before, namely, a very faithful rendering of the Carlo Collodi story, first published in serial form from 1881–83. Collodi's tale differs markedly from the 1940 Disney animated classic, which is probably the way most audiences know Pinocchio today. The original story is very episodic and casts a darker shadow on what has since become a beloved children's tale, and Benigni tries to be true to that spirit, which sometimes means hasty transitions in tone. Much harder to deal with, however, is the dubbing of the voices into English, which is so bad that the film's visual splendor is constantly at war with the laughable vocal delivery.

In Benigni's *Pinocchio,* a log enchanted by the Blue Fairy (played by Nicoletta Braschi, Benigni's real-life wife and producer of the film, and voiced by Glenn Close) makes its way to the workshop of Geppetto (Carlo Giuffré, voiced by David Suchet), the lonely carpenter who carves a wooden puppet to compensate for the son he never had. Following Collodi's lead, the log itself is alive and feels the pain of the carving as Geppetto whittles away. Once Geppetto's work is done, Pinocchio emerges in the form of Benigni, who plays the part of the naughty boy to the hilt. He swipes Geppetto's hairpiece and is soon jumping around and climbing on everything. He even runs wild in the streets and is chased by police. From the outset, then, Benigni plays up the untamed aspect of the puppet, which of course fits well with his own wild-man persona.

The talking Cricket (Peppe Barra, voiced by John Cleese) tries to warn the rascally Pinocchio to change his ways, but Pinocchio heeds no advice and even hits Cricket with a hammer, a violent moment taken from Collodi. Pinocchio ventures out into the world and sells the school-book Geppetto bought him so that he can go to the puppet theater, where the puppets immediately recognize him and welcome him onstage. To win the sympathy of the fierce giant who runs the theater and wants to eat him, Pinocchio spins a yarn of his sad home life, which moves the giant to give him five gold coins.

When Pinocchio brags about his money to the unscrupulous Fox (Max Cavallari, voiced by Cheech Marin) and the Cat (Bruno Arena, voiced by Eddie Griffin) he encounters, they tell him about a field where he can turn his five coins into millions. Despite Cricket's warning that get-rich-quick schemes do not work, Pinocchio goes along with his new friends, who later abandon him and then reappear disguised as assassins to take his money from him. In a stark, nightmarish image that may be too disturbing for some children but which follows Collodi's tale, they hang him from a tree, and his body dangles against the moonlight.

Feeling sympathy for Pinocchio's plight, the Blue Fairy has her servant, the dog Medoro (Mino Bellei, voiced by Eric Idle), take him down from the tree and bring him to her. Even after all he has been through, Pinocchio refuses to drink the medicine she gives him until he is confronted with a harrowing image of rabbits carrying a coffin, a portent of Pinocchio's future if he does not learn to obey. It is difficult to balance whimsy with a sense of dark foreboding—something Benigni achieved in *Life Is Beautiful*. The shifts in tone in *Pinocchio* are not as smooth, but at least Benigni does not shy away from trying to embrace the many moods, even the darkest, of the original tale.

When Pinocchio lies to the Blue Fairy about losing the gold coins, his nose starts to grow. And with each successive lie, his nose grows even longer until he finally tells the truth and the Blue Fairy reaffirms her love for him. Meeting up with the Fox and the Cat again, he does not realize that they were the ones who attacked him, and he naively follows them to a field to bury his coins and let them grow. They of course steal them, and when Cricket tells him what happened and Pinocchio appeals to a judge, he sends Pinocchio to jail for being a dimwit.

In jail, Pinocchio meets another mischievous lad named Leonardo (Kim Rossi Stuart, voiced by Topher Grace), and they strike up a friendship just as Leonardo is about to be released. But Pinocchio himself is released along with all of the jail's criminals, and he faces more heartache when he stumbles upon the grave of the Blue Fairy, who apparently died of grief over Pinocchio. A dove leads him to Geppetto, who has been searching the world for him, but no sooner does Pinocchio see his father out at sea in a little boat than the boat goes underwater. Pinocchio, thinking that he has lost both the Blue Fairy and his father, is overcome with sorrow, but he is redeemed once again when he helps an old lady who turns out to be the Blue Fairy in disguise. He cries at her feet and is forgiven because of the sincerity of his grief.

While Pinocchio wants to turn over a new leaf and go to school, more misadventures befall him. He is arrested when another kid is injured in some roughhousing (although Pinocchio himself was not responsible). He escapes only to get his foot caught in a metal trap and is forced to work as a watchdog until Leonardo, who just happens to be passing by to steal some chickens, frees him. Pinocchio lies to the Blue Fairy about going to school, but she forgives him yet again when he admits the truth, and she grants him his wish to be a real boy. Braschi is not only beautiful but has a kind of iridescent quality as the Blue Fairy. She can be both regal and warm, and, like a good mother, she is the stable center of Pinocchio's world, which is constantly spinning out of control.

When she throws a party for Pinocchio, he invites Leonardo, who is going to a place called Funforeverland, a children's paradise where there is no school and kids just play all year round. Pinocchio vacillates on what to do, but once again temptation gets the better of him, and soon he is joining Leonardo. Following Collodi's story, however, the dark secret of Funforeverland is that the kids, indulging their lazy ways, are transformed into donkeys and are then sold. Pinocchio becomes part of a circus, but, when he falls down

and becomes useless, he is thrown into the ocean. He miraculously bobs to the surface back in puppet form, only to be swallowed by a shark. In the belly of the shark, he encounters Geppetto, and, after a tearful reunion, they make their way through the shark and are finally spit out.

In the last major sequence, Pinocchio redeems himself. To earn some milk for his weak father, he finds employment turning a waterwheel and becomes a hard worker. He also encounters his old friend Leonardo, still in donkey form, as he is dying. In the end, Pinocchio bids farewell to the Blue Fairy, and he becomes a real boy, finally setting off for school, although the naughty puppet self remains in shadow form, a hint that perhaps Pinocchio has not completely abandoned his mischievous side altogether.

Benigni's film is essentially composed of a series of vignettes that closely follow the serialized original, which means that we get a true sense of Collodi's classic work. At the same time, it may have been better if Benigni and his co-screenwriter, Vincenzo Cerami, had found a way to streamline a rambling tale that follows a predictable pattern of continuous disobedience and unconditional forgiveness. Still, the fanciful visuals, courtesy of cinematographer Dante Spinotti, are often stunning, as are the sets and costumes by the late Danilo Donati. The first shot of the Blue Fairy's carriage drawn by a team of mice is magical, the nighttime scenes are beautiful yet always hint at the dangers lurking for a lost little boy, and Funforeverland is a nonstop carnival brimming with Felliniesque excess.

The dubbing of the voices, however, seriously compromises *Pinocchio*. Since children are the film's target audience, it makes a certain kind of sense that the producers would not want to release a subtitled version of it in America, but the dubbing is so bad that it constantly jerks the audience out of what should be an enchanted world. The worst of all, unfortunately, is Breckin Meyer's delivery as Pinocchio. His voice is flat and grating and has absolutely none of the lyrical quality that one might imagine in Benigni's original Italian. Glenn Close is better as the voice of the Blue Fairy, and John Cleese lends an imperious quality to Cricket. Nonetheless, the disjunction between the actors' mouths and the voices coming from them is a major distraction and even an insult in a film that should wear its Italian heritage proudly.

In *Pinocchio*, Benigni has created a beautiful, extravagant world and does not shy away from the true brattiness of this iconic character and the dark, scary elements of the original story. The film may have a cobbled-together feel to it, and ultimately it may be for hardcore Benigni fans, that is, people who appreciate his manic energy and playfulness. But despite its flaws, Benigni gives us a taste of the authentic *Pinocchio* of his childhood. It is a shame we could not have heard it in the original language.

—*Peter N. Chumo II*

Pinocchio: Roberto Benigni
Blue Fairy: Nicoletta Braschi
Medoro: Mino Bellei
Geppetto: Carlo Guiffre
The Cricket: Peppe Barra
Fox: Max Cavallari
Cat: Bruno Arena
Leonardo/Donkey: Kim Rossi-Stuart
Pinocchio: Breckin Meyer (Voice)
Blue Fairy: Glenn Close (Voice)
Medoro: Eric Idle (Voice)
Geppetto: David Suchet (Voice)
The Cricket: John Cleese (Voice)
Fox: Richard "Cheech" Marin (Voice)
Cat: Eddie Griffin (Voice)
Leonardo/Donkey: Topher Grace (Voice)

Origin: Italy
Released: 2002
Production: Gianluigi Braschi, Elda Ferri, Nicoletta Braschi; Melampo Cinematografica; released by Miramax Films
Directed by: Roberto Benigni
Written by: Roberto Benigni, Vincenzo Cerami
Cinematography by: Dante Spinotti
Music by: Nicola Piovani
Sound: Tullio Morganti
Editing: Simona Paggi
Costumes: Danilo Donati, Jane Law
Production Design: Danilo Donati
MPAA rating: G
Running time: 108 minutes

REVIEWS

Boxoffice. January, 2003, p. 28.
Entertainment Weekly. January 10, 2003, p. 53.
Los Angeles Times Online. December 27, 2002.
New York Times Online. December 26, 2002.
USA Today Online. December 22, 2002.
Variety Online. October 7, 2002.

TRIVIA

Miramax also released the film in its original Italian-language form.

Pipe Dream

It's not who you are, it's who they think you are.
—Movie tagline

John C. Walsh (*Ed's Next Move*) creates a ruse in which a lowly plumber poses as a film director to attract women with *Pipe Dream* and one might call the film a *Wag the Dog* of the Hollywood film industry. *Pipe Dream* reflects on artificial worlds that we create out of self-importance and, by creating the right aura and image, we can fool even the experts whochoose to go along with illusions. We might even believe that a film shot in Manhattan in the autumn actually takes place in Hollywood during the hot summer months. Thanks to the delusions that the film industry has pumped out, we are likely to believe anything so it should come as no surprise that the characters in Walsh's story fall for the ruse and desire to be a part of a hot film production that in actuality doesn't exist.

Pipe Dream proves more than a simple romantic comedy since the film brings up issues about class distinction and how we perceive various occupations. While Walsh and his co-writer Cynthia Kaplan wrote their script, Walsh came across a story about the composer Philip Glass who was a plumber before his breakout opera. Glass shocked a music critic at a major national magazine when he showed up and made a repair in the critic's apartment. Yet, instead of seeing Glass as a Renaissance man, the critic could only distinguish between an upper class composer and a lower class plumber. However, we are aware that many celebrities worked lowly day jobs at some time in their career. Actor Martin Donovan (David Kulovic) worked as a drapery installer at one point and Mary-Louise Parker (Toni Edelman) worked as an office worker before her big break.

Pipe Dream recalls Hollywood classics by George Cukor and Preston Surges. Walsh claims that he was influenced heavily by the movies *Pillow Talk* and *Bedtime Story* in which the men characters posed as another person in order to attract a woman's affection. *Pipe Dream* does have a sophisticated aura that recalls such Hollywood classics and even the sex scenes are subtle yet comical. You would almost expect Tracy and Hepburn to walk on to the set. Parker's Toni, a New York cynic, recalls Katharine Hepburn, while Donovan's sly and vulnerable performance recalls Cary Grant in Stanley Donen's *Charade*.

Plumber David Kulovic has become frustrated with his invisible status. One day he returns home after another condescending gig and he witnesses Toni Edelman breaking up with her boyfriend on the stairs. David and Toni hit it off and after a night of lovemaking, David overhears a phone conversation that Toni has with a friend in which she utters

"I don't know where my brain was. I can't ... he's a plumber."

Later that day, David fixes his friend RJ Martling's (Kevin Carroll) shower and learns from RJ, a commercial casting director, that film directors are chick magnets. Over lunch, David convinces RJ to set up a fake casting session. David steals a section from Toni's screenplay, changes the title to *Pipe Dream* and is surprised when the industry takes him seriously. Soon actors beg their agents to get them auditions for the hot new film even if the plumber-turned-director doesn't know the difference between a grip and a gaffer.

But Toni gets wind of David's ruse and chastises him until she realizes that her screenplay could become a hit movie if only they could pull off the scam. Toni takes the role as a script consultant, but is really a behind-the-scenes director and David's eyes and ears. However, just when it seems like smooth sailing, rough waters lie ahead. David hits on the lead actress, Marliss Funt (Rebecca Gayheart), causing Toni to feel pangs of jealousy and for Marliss to blow her takes. After all, she was hired for her hot looks and not her talent. David also appears on an undercover TV show in which he's not only shown working as a plumber, but as a dishonest one gouging wealthy clients. The investor/producer fires David, RJ, and Toni from the film. However, Toni is hired back on as a director and David is hired to run the craft service. Despite his lowly job, Toni and David end the film as a couple.

Pipe Dream reminds us that we are more than our professions and that affection knows no boundaries in this world filled with illusions.

—*Patty-Lynne Herlevi*

CREDITS

David Kulovic: Martin Donovan
Toni Edelman: Mary-Louise Parker
R.J. Martling: Kevin Carroll
Marliss Funt: Rebecca Gayheart
Arnie Hufflitz: Peter Jacobson
Charlotte: Cynthia Kaplan
Mitch Farkas: Tim Hopper
Diane Beltrami: Guinevere Turner
Lorna Hufflitz: Marla Sucharetza

Origin: USA
Released: 2002
Production: Mike Curb, Carole Curb Nemoy, Sally Roy; Curb Entertainment; released by Castle Hill Productions
Directed by: John C. Walsh
Written by: Cynthia Kaplan, John C. Walsh
Cinematography by: Peter Nelson

Music by: Alexander Lasarenko
Sound: William Tzouris
Editing: Malcolm Jamieson
Costumes: Elizabeth Shelton
Production Design: Paul Avery
MPAA rating: R
Running time: 94 minutes

REVIEWS

Entertainment Weekly. October 11, 2002, p. 55.
Los Angeles Times Online. October 18, 2002.
New York Times Online. October 4, 2002.
Variety. May 6, 2002, p. 45.

QUOTES

Agent's assistant Charlotte (Cynthia Kaplan): "This little nothing movie has inspired the most pathetic actor frenzy I've ever seen."

Possession

The past will connect them. The passion will possess them.
—Movie tagline

 Box Office: $10.1 million

*P*ossession seems an odd choice for writer-director Neil LaBute. Such LaBute films as *In the Company of Men* (1997) and *Your Friends & Neighbors* (1998) are very American and very male-oriented, so much so that he has been labeled misogynistic. However, while his adaptation of A. S. Byatt's romantic novel about literary secrets did not receive especially enthusiastic responses from reviewers, it is a surprisingly effective look at the contrast in sexual tensions in two centuries. It also offers Gwyneth Paltrow's best performance since winning an Academy Award for *Shakespeare in Love* (1998).

Roland Michell (Aaron Eckhart), a scruffy American working as a research assistant for Professor Blackadder (Tom Hickey) at London's British Museum, is an expert on Victorian poet Randolph Henry Ashe (Jeremy Northam), reportedly devoted to his wife, Ellen (Holly Aird). Roland becomes intrigued when he stumbles across a letter from Ashe to poet Christabel LaMotte (Jennifer Ehle). LaMotte, a beloved figure for feminist literary critics and historians, is a lesbian living with her lover, Blanche Glover (Lena Headey), a painter. At the suggestion of colleague Fergus Wolfe (Toby Stephens), Roland looks up LaMotte authority Maud Bailey (Gwyneth Paltrow) to find out more about any possible Ashe-LaMotte connection.

Maud at first does not take Roland seriously because of his unkempt American maleness, but he soon convinces her of his sincere, if unorthodox, interest in literary scholarship. Maud, a distant relative of Christabel, takes Roland to the Bailey family estate in Yorkshire presided over by the eccentric Sir George (Graham Crowden) and the frail Lady Bailey (Anna Massey). There, against Maud's best instincts, they poke around the attic until they find more evidence linking the two poets.

They hope to keep their discoveries secret for the time being lest the acquisitive American collector Morton Cropper (Trevor Eve) convinces Sir George to sell him the discovered papers. Cropper is aided in his pursuits by the duplicitous Fergus, a spurned would-be lover of Maud. Cropper and Fergus are capable of grave robbing to achieve their ends.

The Ashe-Christabel affair is revealed piece by piece in flashbacks as the scholars make their discoveries. The blossoming love of the poets is paralleled by the attraction between the literary detectives. Just as Maud and Roland find themselves in bed together despite the uncertainty of each about the other, Ashe and Christabel begin their affair. Ashe feels guilty for betraying his wife, just as Christabel does for Blanche, who does her best to make her friend feel remorse. Christabel finds herself pregnant and flees to France to have her baby in secret, while the despairing Blanche commits suicide.

Byatt's 1990 novel was a critical and commercial success, but it has taken 12 years for it to reach the big screen. Playwright David Henry Hwang, best known for *M. Butterfly* (1993), adapted the novel and revised his screenplay three times while four directors, including Gillian Armstrong and Sydney Pollack, dropped out of the project. When LaBute became the director, he rewrote Hwang's screenplay with Laura Jones, whose adaptations include *The Portrait of a Lady* (1996) and *Angela's Ashes* (1999). The difficulties of adapting Byatt's work include making a highly literary and allusive tale palatable for a larger audience.

The major change by LaBute and Jones—and one which he told the *New York Times* that Byatt has endorsed—is enlivening the sexual tensions between Maud and Roland by transforming the latter from a mild-mannered Brit to a hunky, slangy Yank. Many reviewers did not feel LaBute makes Byatt's story work as cinema, and the main complaint was the drastic change in Roland, a move some saw as pandering to American audiences.

Byatt's rather timid Roland is immediately Maud's inferior and has to earn, first, her professional respect and, then,

her love. She is always the dominant figure in the relationship. LaBute's Roland keeps Maud off-balance through not only his sexiness but his professional aggressiveness. He thinks nothing about stealing the necessary documents to prove their case and even converts Maud to theft by the time they go to France seeking evidence of Christabel's baby. Having Roland speak in a semi-inarticulate, sarcastic manner also allows LaBute to put his personal stamp on the film since Roland sounds like a benign version of the cynical males from the director's other films and plays. LaBute, however, sometimes strays over into the cutesy-poo, as when Roland quotes Sigmund Freud to Maud, pauses, and asks, "Or was that Calvin Klein?"

Other complaints against *Possession* include Eric Brace of the *Washington Post* calling it "another shallow film about how repressed the British are." Brace also considers Maud and Roland's detective work on the level of Nancy Drew and the Hardy Boys. Several reviewers said that the modern-day characters pale in comparison to the Victorians. *Newsweek*'s Jeff Giles said that while Christabel and Ashe come to life, they "get so little screen time that their strand of the movie plays like a trailer for a Merchant-Ivory picture." Richard Corliss of *Time* complained that Gabriel Yared's music is forced to do Eckhart and Paltrow's acting for them. In *Entertainment Weekly*, Owen Gleiberman called the film "intelligent yet lifeless; it's all wisps and abstractions." Gleiberman found the ironic contrasts between the present-day and 1859 characters "tame and old hat" compared to the same situation in Karel Reisz and Harold Pinter's 1981 adaptation of John Fowles' very similar *The French Lieutenant's Woman*.

The latter is also a film project that seemed to resist adaptation for years until Pinter came up with an approach that works reasonably well. Like *Possession*, *The French Lieutenant's Woman* was found wanting by most reviewers, but the film's reputation has improved over the years because of the enduring strength of Fowles' story, the elegance of Reisz's direction, the beauty of the great Freddie Francis' cinematography, and, most of all, the lovely performances by Meryl Streep and Jeremy Irons.

While the performances in LaBute's film do not quite reach the same level, the film's weaknesses are overshadowed by its general intelligence and stylishness. It is very watchable and engaging and succeeds on many levels. The literary detective work is engrossing, as is watching the pair of romantic relationships develop. The Maud-Roland romance is rather predictable but works because Paltrow and Eckhart are charming. LaBute makes Maud into a bit of a cliché by having her hair tied in a bun to underscore the uptight feminism that the feisty Roland will try to loosen. The joke on the director is that Paltrow has never been as sexy as she is here and actually loses a bit of pizzazz when the hair finally comes down. As Stanley Kauffmann observed in the *New Republic*, Paltrow does her best work when

Rain

Christine Jeffs' celebrated debut feature from New Zealand, *Rain,* draws its inspiration from a virtually unfilmable first novel by Kirsty Gunn. The novel is structured more like a poem than a linear narrative. Revolving around an adolescent trauma suffered by its narrator, it does away with the chain of cause and effect, making the singular tragic event at its core appear as natural as its seaside setting. Jeffs, on the other hand, chooses a linear structure for her film, and an omniscient viewpoint for the most part, which requires her to fabricate incidents, and build towards a tragic climax, while at the same time making her narrative events seem part of the everyday. The film's dramatic thrust thus falls between two lagoons.

Through abbreviated scenes, Jeffs isolates precious details of speech and action in the day-to-day life of the middle-aged Ed (Alistair Browning), his still attractive wife, Kate (Sarah Pierse), their plain-looking teenage daughter, Janey (Alicia Fulford-Wierzbicki) and her irrepressible kid brother, Jim (Aaron Murphy), as they spend a summer in a house by the sea. The atmospheric detail is captivating, but as the everydayness of the characters' lives unfolds, we are led into expecting a complex subtext, an emotional counterpart to the precipitation evoked by the film's title. Our wait is in vain.

Janey is as precocious and guarded in her sexual encounters with her boyfriend, Sam (David Taylor), as her mother is impulsive and promiscuous in her extra-marital fling with Cady (Marton Csokas), a handsome landscape photographer, who owns a deluxe yacht, and lives down the beach. The film thus uses Janey as a narrator, her voiceover introducing and closing the film. This proves a letdown, since Kate's passion is far more interesting, but remains unresolved. So is Ed's seemingly helpless despondency upon coming to know of his wife's affair.

Jeffs thus pins all her hopes of impacting us on our being able to sympathize with the traumatic event that overtakes Janey in the closing moments of the film. There is nothing terribly original to grab us about Janey's existence before that. Her sporadic flirtation with Sam, or her Lolita-like cavorting before Cady, so as to get him to photograph her, or her precocious encounters with her mother, in which she foresees the impending divorce, are all part of aspects of western adolescence that we have become all too familiar with. Even Janey's lacklustre scenes with Jim appear special only owing to their beach setting and the loving cinematography.

The climactic event transpires when Janey goes on a photo shoot with Cady. She instructs Jim not to follow her. The shoot becomes a love tryst, as Cady at last gives in. The film resorts to poetic visuals to show Janey's sexual liberation, though we are not shown any sex between her and Cady. As Janey is walking back from the shoot, she discovers Jim's lifeless body on the beach. Overcome with guilt, she becomes hysterical that she cannot resuscitate him back to life.

The fact that Jim's drowning comes out of nowhere, and is used as an emotional lever to climax the film, can be perceived as part of a trend in contemporary art-house filmic realism, akin to the violence that erupts out of the dark at the end of Catherine Breillat's adolescent saga, the equally non-dramatic *Fat Girl* (2001). As a narrative ploy, such an event cannot be foreseeable, yet must seem part of the commonplace. While realistically valid, owing to the violent times we live in, the question remains whether its shock value can make up for the dullness wrought by the series of non-events that must necessarily precede it. In the case of *Rain,* the filmmaker's adeptness at rendering the flow of the quotidian in the earlier sections of the film, coupled with a soundtrack of tuneful original songs, cannot sustain viewer interest once the film has crossed the two-third mark.

It can be said in the film's favor, however, that it is easy viewing, infused with the spirit of a beach samba. Moreover, for those willing to accept it on its own terms, *Rain* for all its adolescent focus, does impart a timely truth on a macrocosmic level: a sudden tragic event can shatter the flow of life as we live it, so that the time preceding it becomes tinged with as much of a sense of loss as the time that follows it.

Critics seem to be smitten by *Rain*'s lack of contrivance. In a rave in the *New York Times,* A.O. Scott writes that "an intimation of overwhelming dread is palpable in every scene." Stephanie Zacharek in *Salon* compares Jeffs' effort to Ang Lee's *The Ice Storm* (1977) and finds it superior. As she sees it, Jeffs doesn't rub "our noses in these rather textbook family troubles," as Lee does, with the result that what emerges is a "glum, depressing portrait but with glimmers of a fragile, fleeting intimacy."

—Vivek Adarkar

CREDITS

Janey: Alicia Fulford-Wierzbicki
Kate: Sarah Peirse
Cady: Marton Csokas
Ed: Alistair Browning
Jim: Aaron Murphy

Origin: Australia
Released: 2001
Production: Philippa Campbell; New Zealand Film Commission, Rose Road; released by Fireworks Pictures
Directed by: Christine Jeffs
Written by: Christine Jeffs

Cinematography by: John Toon
Music by: Neil Finn, Edmund McWilliams
Sound: David Madigan
Editing: Paul Maxwell
Art Direction: Kirsty Clayton
Costumes: Kristy Cameron
MPAA rating: Unrated
Running time: 90 minutes

REVIEWS

Boxoffice. April, 2002, p. 189.
Entertainment Weekly. May 24, 2002, p. 68.
Los Angeles Times Online. May 3, 2002.
New York Times Online. April 26, 2002.
People. May 6, 2002, p. 42.
Variety Online. May 15, 2001.
Vogue Online. April, 2002.
Washington Post. June 14, 2002, p. WE43.

Read My Lips
(Sur Mes Levres)

Don't believe everything you hear.
—Movie tagline

She teaches him good manners. He teaches her bad ones.
—Movie tagline

Box Office: $1.3 million

One of the peculiarities of the silent cinema was the way it used the act of speaking as a gesture. The actors who moved their lips on the silent screen often spoke a language of their own, one of gestures, not words. Jacques Audriard's clever thriller from France, *Read My Lips,* brings back the filmic use of lip movement for dramatic effect. By using this ploy to structure its narrative, Audriard lifts his tale above its generic plot.

As a thriller, his film harks back to the subgenre developed, virtually singlehandedly, by the master filmmaker Claude Chabrol, known as the French Hitchcock. Where Audriard differs from his illustrious predecessor is in his take on crime. Chabrol repeatedly demonstrated in masterworks such as *La Femme Infidele* (1968) and *Wedding in Blood* (1973) how genteel souls could be driven by romantic passion to commit murderous acts.

Audriard, while showing the converse, that is, how complicity in crime can lead to passion, goes one step further. His tale introduces into this subgenre the experience of a handicapped individual. We get to see how a particular disability can isolate while, at the same time, allow that person to function normally within society. Thus, Audriard's effort needs to be described more through its poignant scenes of "exclusion" than by its generic thriller quotient. Arguably, the former dilutes the tension of the latter, but it also makes his film that much more original.

Carla (Emmanuelle Devos), the central character, is an attractive secretary for a construction firm outside Paris, in the throes of a busy workday. She is answering calls, making photocopies, as a half-empty cup of coffee on her desk is promptly tipped over by someone rushing past. The sound-track is intentionally muted. Only later do we learn why.

To add to the air of mystery, we see Carla next in the office cafeteria, flipping through a fashion magazine, as this most mundane of settings becomes transformed by cutaways of extreme close-ups of the lips of a couple talking at a nearby table, underscored by silence. The feeling of honing in on Carla's subjective experience becomes accentuated by a quick cut to another extreme close-up, of a man unbuttoning a woman's blouse, a flash of Carla's erotic imagining.

The story then gets under way. In a private meeting with Morel (Bernard Alane), her boss, Carla assumes the worst when he suggests she take a few days off. When he speaks of hiring new blood, Carla fears she is being replaced. He however puts her at ease when he clarifies that what he meant was an assistant for her.

In the next scene, Carla encounters the pressures of political correctness, as she sits with the company's person-nel officer to draft a request to an employment agency. When she says she would like a male, she is told that that would constitute a gender bias. Even so, she specifies that he should be between 25 and 30, friendly and "well-groomed," and hopes for the best.

We soon see the parameters of Carla's social life outside the office. She sits in a bar, drinking by herself, until she is joined by her girlfriend Annie (Olivia Bonamy) with her baby in tow. Annie is too busy for a conversation, but only wants to use Carla as a babysitter, while she rushes off to meet her boyfriend. As an index of her drab, lonely exis-tence, we see Carla in her kitchen with the bawling baby. Here she gets the better of the infant by removing her hearing aid.

Now that the routine of her everyday isolation has been established, Audriard is ready to overturn it by introducing Paul (Vincent Cassel), a scruffy but sharp parolee, who has been sent by the agency. He claims to have no hands-on experience with hi-tech chores, but Carla is taken up by his desire to learn. We can see that it is her liberal conscience that makes her approve him on the spot. It is only later that she gets him to admit that he was serving a jail term, and that he hasn't worked for two years. What becomes clear, on a silent level, is Carla's attraction to the raw machismo he embodies. It is a desire that would ordinarily be considered the most natural in the world, but which Carla seems to repress because of her handicap.

Paul's scenes with Masson (Olivier Perrier), his congenial parole officer, shows he knows even less about the kind of work he has taken on than Carla would have suspected. "You can't even type!" Masson reminds him. Even so, we find that what Paul lacks in experience, he makes up for in manual efficiency, excelling at retrieving faxes and delivering mail.

Carla's curiosity about Paul allows her to probe while keeping the distance of a superior. Across a cafeteria table, the two exchange secrets. He has been in prison for "aggravated robbery . . . banks, stick-ups" and suchlike, he explains. "I read people's lips," Carla confesses, then adding, "I'm kind of deaf."

At this stage, the film introduces the first of the subplots that will test their relationship. At a construction site, we learn that the mayor's son is on the take, which results in his obstructing a project being handled by Carla's firm. Much later in the film, Paul will prove his usefulness by beating up the corrupt official and getting him to acquiesce.

Similarly, the film flits to Carla's second meeting with Annie in a café, in which Annie confides about her "mindless" sex life. This has the effect of arousing a sexual urge in Carla. We see her alone by herself, putting on a red dress and high heel shoes, then stripping down and touching her nude body. The brevity of the scene conveys repression rather than gratification. It is one of the many interior monologues that will take us into the depths of Carla's unconscious, leaving us to fathom the psychopathological condition it represents.

Within the claustrophobic space of the copy room, Carla's sexual attraction for Paul becomes displaced by a sense of being responsible for his behavior in the office. He on his part cannot explain why he has been spending nights in the closet. She therefore finds him an apartment in a building that is still to be occupied. It is here that Paul makes a play for intimacy as he reaches for her breast. She responds by slapping him and rushing into the bathroom. He misinterprets this as a rejection stemming from his economic status, and says as much. Without answering, Carla merely exits the apartment.

At this stage, another brief subplot takes shape. At a high level meeting, Carla is taken off a project she has been slaving over for three years, and her work allowed to be usurped by Keller (Pierre Diot), a ruthless superior. Livid with rage, she approaches Paul about using his expertise to somehow steal the file from Keller. When Paul hesitates, clearly not wanting his past to jeopardize his new life, Carla knows which button to press. She reminds him that he owes her.

The ploy works. For Paul, it turns out to be child's play. He breaks into Keller's car in the office parking lot, stops the alarm and removes the file. Carla is then told to take the original file to the meeting of the municipal council. After the meeting, Keller, suspecting what has happened, is about to strike Carla when Paul intercedes. When Keller then says that he will report the matter to Morel, Carla retorts by threatening to disclose the commissions he has been receiving on the sly. Morel soon announces at an office meeting that Keller has quit.

Carla's success also reveals the underbelly of her character, that despite her exclusion from, and exploitation by, the world of men, she finds through Paul, as Audriard explains in the pressbook of the film, "the possibility of rebalancing things: what she couldn't obtain in a normal way—through competence, dedication—she'll obtain in other ways, through violence, blackmail."

The ground is thus prepared for the generic plot that follows. When a friend pays Paul a visit, Carla eavesdrops as the two men come to blows. Paul then admits to his having to repay a longstanding debt to Marchand (Olivier Gourmet), an underworld boss, who owns a club in which Paul has now to serve as a bartender. More, Paul has to keep this a secret from Masson.

Carla gets drawn in further when she offers to help Paul recover a sack of loot from Marchand. When Paul cannot find it, Carla, using the skeleton key Paul has prepared, locates the stash. Marchand then grabs Paul, tortures him to no avail, then ties him to a radiator near a window. While the two thugs in league with Marchand turn against him, Carla, stationed on an opposite rooftop, armed with binoculars, follows Paul's instructions, rendered through lip movement. As she brings Marchand's unsuspecting wife into the picture, jealousy combines with deceit. Paul, using his expertise, ends up freeing Marchand from the handcuffs the thugs have put on him, which allows Marchand to stab the two thugs to death, leaving Carla and Paul to make off with the loot.

The film's final scene shows the newborn romance between them in extreme close-ups, much as it did the lips of strangers, which Carla had been reading as a means of vicarious escape.

Critics have found the film original in the manner it evokes Carla's near-deafness. Also, both Richard Schickel in *Time* and A.O. Scott in the *New York Times* have found that the film can be divided into two parts, with the second half offering the melodramatic and suspense quotient. For Schickel, it "doesn't achieve a seamless connection," whereas for Scott, it "mutates almost casually from a workplace comedy into a violent, clammy caper film . . . the psychological nuance gives way to the more conventional machinery of suspense." Scott goes on to add that, like other recent imports from Europe, it "seems destined to be remade in Hollywood ..."

—*Vivek Adarkar*

CREDITS

Carla Behm: Emmanuelle Devos
Paul Angeli: Vincent Cassel
Marchand: Olivier Gourmet
Masson: Olivier Perrier
Annie: Olivia Bonamy
Keller: Pierre Diot

Origin: French
Language: French
Released: 2001
Production: Jean-Louis Livi, Philippe Carcassonne; Pathe, France 2 Cinema, Sedif, Cine B; released by Magnolia Pictures
Directed by: Jacques Audiard
Written by: Jacques Audiard, Tonino Beranacquista
Cinematography by: Mathieu Vadepied
Music by: Alexandre Desplat
Sound: Cyril Holtz, Marc-Antoine Beldent
Editing: Juliette Welfing
Costumes: Virginie Montel
Production Design: Michel Barthelemy
MPAA rating: Unrated
Running time: 115 minutes

REVIEWS

Boxoffice. August, 2002, p. 58.
Chicago Sun-Times Online. July 19, 2002.
Entertainment Weekly. July 19, 2002, p. 50.
Los Angeles Times Online. July 19, 2002.
New York Times Online. July 5, 2002.
Sight and Sound. June, 2002, p. 34.
Time Online. April 1, 2002.
Variety Online. October 8, 2001.
Village Voice Online. April 2, 2002.
Washington Post. July 26, 2002, p. WE39.

QUOTES

Carla (Emmanuelle Devos) to Paul (Vincent Cassell) after rejecting his sexual advances: "You think you owe me, and you pay me with what you have. But it's true. You do owe me."

Cesar 2001: Actress (Devos), Screenplay.

Real Women Have Curves

Real women take chances, have flaws, embrace life . . .
—Movie tagline

 Box Office: $5.1 million

What distinguishes Patricia Cardoso's refreshing debut feature, *Real Women Have Curves,* is that unlike recent films by, and about, neo-immigrants, such as *Chutney Popcorn* (1999) and *American Desi* (2000), she doesn't cultivate an artificial identity for her characters intended as a bulwark against the mainstream of American life. On the contrary, the film, like its heroine, boldly embraces what America has to offer the neo-immigrant. Her film is first and foremost about interaction, rather than exclusion.

Also, the issue of identity is never verbalized but lived out, and even embodied, by the central character. Ana (America Ferrera), an 18-year-old Mexican-American at the crossroads between high school and college, is the antithesis of the teenage Hollywood heroine. She is plain-looking, overweight and bestowed with breasts too large to be thought fashionable. Carmen (Lupe Ontiveros), her overbearing mother, is constantly chiding her for being too fat for the stylish dresses she and her other daughter produce at her sweatshop, which masquerades as a garment factory.

The rest of Ana's family embody worthy traits that Ana draws upon for all kinds of support. Some of these are innately part of the Old Country, while others can plainly be seen to have been inspired by the American Dream. Estela (Ingrid Ohu), Ana's fat, spectacled elder sister, designs the dresses; she is domineering when she has to be, but she can also be kind. Raul (Jorge Cervera Jr.), Ana's loving, still handsome father, is a manual worker who cleans yards and public spaces with the help of his two boys. But the one Ana is understandably closest to is her Grandfather (Felipe De Alba), a relic of rustic gallantry, steeped in the myths of a bygone age.

The film opens on Ana's last day of high school. Carmen, in one of her hypochondriacal fits, lies in bed, and orders Ana to prepare breakfast "for the men." When Ana says she has to rush off to school, Carmen promptly erupts in maternal rage, cursing Ana's birth. Ana shouts back that she didn't ask to be born. On the street, as Ana hurries on her way, we see the kind of low income suburban neighborhood, the contemporary form of a community ghetto, that Ana's fate has been tied to. Far behind in the mist, can be seen the skyscrapers of tomorrow's Los Angeles.

In class, Ana lies to her teacher, Mr. Guzman (George Lopez), about her plans after leaving school. "I'll think I'll backpack across Europe," she says. Mr. Guzman, however, sees through to Ana's feelings of economic insecurity. Speaking to her in private, he offers her hope of a scholarship that will cover her tuition and living, even at a college like Columbia. For Ana, it is just so much graduation pep talk that she dismisses it.

Even so, Ana realizes that she has reached a watershed in her life. In a flash of a scene, she grabs her severance pay from a burger joint and vows never to work there again. When she gets home, she finds a surprise party thrown in her honor in her backyard. It is also the moment when Ana, and we, become aware of the force of tradition that underlies the domestic cheer. Carmen wants Ana to come to work in the factory, since Estela could use the help. Ana rebels at the prospect. But the real surprise of the evening is when Mr. Guzman shows up to plead with Ana to reconsider college. This time, it is Raul who tells him very simply, "We need her to work." That night, however, in the privacy of the bedroom, Raul voices his second thoughts to Carmen, who promptly shoots them down. The education that Ana will now receive, if Carmen has anything to do with it, will be to learn "how to sew . . .and raise children." Thus, as this historic day in Ana's life comes to a close, the basic conflict that will shape the events in the days to come is clearly established.

The next morning, to the lilt of a Spanish folk song on the soundtrack, Raul, in his pickup truck, drops Ana and Carmen at the factory. The mannequins and the rows of dresses comprise some kind of an alien world of drudgery for Ana. We soon get to know some of the women who have sacrificed their lives to it. There's the very old Dona Carlota (Sandie Torres), cheerfully at one with her sewing machine, the fat and jovial Pancha (Soledad St. Hilaire), the slim and fair Norma (Lina Acosta), and the darkly attractive Rosali (Lourdes Perez). As if it were a ceremonial gesture, Carmen presents Ana with her own pair of scissors, and assigns her the task of ironing the dresses. What makes it unbearable for Ana is the heat, since breeze from a fan will blow dust on the dresses.

Worse, Ana's conscience revolts at the economic injustice of it all. They are paid $18 per dress, which is sold to the customer for $600. "Does this seem right?" she screams at her co-workers, but receives only silence as a reply. When she burns a dress, she storms out in frustration. Carmen draws away and curses, "Leave! You're ashamed of us! This is

what I get for so much sacrifice!" Ana silently helps her to her feet and back into the factory.

Her stint at the sweatshop causes Ana to change her mind about college. She fills out an application and hands it to Mr. Guzman. He then tells her that Columbia also needs her to write an essay about herself. Outside, she bumps into Jimmy (Brian Sites), a non-Hispanic classmate who has a crush on her. He really believes Ana is going to backpack across Europe, and would like to join her. "Europe is different," he says. "Here you're handed everything." He gives Ana his phone number which she writes on her palm.

At home, as we can see Raul massaging Carmen's back in the living room, we can feel the woman's accumulated tiredness "after 35 years of sewing." Nearby, the boys are practicing with guitars, hoping to strike it big in the world of Spanish pop. In the middle of it all, Ana works on the essay about herself. In bed, she rings Jimmy, but has to hang up in a hurry when Carmen comes screaming at her for not doing the dishes.

At the factory, Carmen is thrown into a tizzy when Norma, her "fastest employee," says she's leaving to get married in Mexico, and worse, is taking her mother and sisters with her, who are also working for Carmen. Estela then walks in with more bad news. She needs four seamstresses to complete an order in time, without which she will not be paid, and so will not be able to meet her payroll. As her co-workers curse, Ana again assails their conscience. "You're all cheap labor for Bloomingdale's!" she jeers, but out of pity for Estela, she agrees to work until she's paid.

Three subplots then take shape: one comic, one romantic, and the other growing out of economic injustice. Carmen wakes Ana up to tell her a secret. "I'm pregnant!" she whispers. Ana disbelievingly remarks that it's probably "just gas." Carmen of course is convinced that isn't because she has been missing her periods.

Then, when Ana sees Estela writing a letter to seek an advance from the company that has placed an order for the dresses, she urges Estela to go in person, and to even accompany her. In the reception area of the swanky office, Estela and Carmen are met by the icy demeanor of Mrs. Glass (Marlene Forte), the chief executive. When Estela is cowed into submission, it is Ana who speaks her mind. "We need an advance," she says flat out, "so we can pay our bills." Mrs. Glass shoots back: "No advances!" and reminds them of their deadline 10 days away.

With Grandpa's help, Ana manages to sneak out and meet Jimmy on a date. Here too she is very forthright. "Are you staring at my boobs?" is the first thing she asks him. "No," he answers, taken aback, then adds, "Yes." This frankness endears him to her, though he will be going away to school shortly. Eventually, when they do tumble into bed on their third date, she wants him to first turn the lights on, so he can see her as she is.

Ana's affirmation of her looks results in a hilarious scene at the factory. After secretly obtaining a loan from Raul to pay Estela's bills, Ana inspires her co-workers to work at peak efficiency. In the process, she removes her blouse because of the heat. This prompts the others to strip down as well, each one proudly exposing their cellulite and stretch marks, hoping to outdo the other. To a shocked Carmen, Ana proclaims, "That's what we are! Real women!"

Keeping to its ideal of espousing the American Dream, the film ends on a happy note. Carmen's anxiety is diagnosed as menopause. The company deadline is met and Ana gets admitted to Columbia with a full scholarship. Carmen remains in her bedroom while Raul and Grandpa see Ana off at the airport. The film's final shot shows Ana proudly striding down a sidewalk in Times Square, alone but self-assured.

Critics have found the film's feminist stance endearing. Elvis Mitchell in the *New York Times* calls the film "effervescent and satisfying, a crowd pleaser that does not condescend." John Anderson in *Newsday* finds that it raises a profound issue about neo-immigrant life, "that people brave enough to leave one country for another can't always shake the fear of what a better life might cost." Jami Bernard in the *Daily News* feels the film "stands out from the crowd of mother-daughter reconciliation movies," since it "doesn't offer any pat resolutions." On a lighter note, she anticipates that it is sure to boost the self-esteem of any "woman who wears more than a size 12 . . ."

—*Vivek Adarkar*

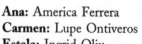

CREDITS

Ana: America Ferrera
Carmen: Lupe Ontiveros
Estela: Ingrid Oliu
Mr. Guzman: George Lopez
Pancha: Soledad St. Hilaire
Jimmy: Brian Sites
Raul: Jorge Cerera Jr.

Origin: USA
Released: 2002
Production: George LaVoo, Effie T. Brown; released by HBO Films, Newmarket
Directed by: Patricia Cardoso
Written by: George LaVoo, Josefina Lopez
Cinematography by: Jim Denault
Music by: Heitor Pereira
Sound: John Taylor
Editing: Sloane Klevin
Art Direction: Deb Riley, Amy Strong
Costumes: Elaine Montalvo

Production Design: Brigitte Broch
MPAA rating: PG-13
Running time: 93 minutes

REVIEWS

Boxoffice. April, 2002, p. 178.
Chicago Sun-Times Online. October 25, 2002.
Entertainment Weekly. November 1, 2002, p. 51.
Los Angeles Times Online. October 18, 2002.
New York Times Online. March 22, 2002.
People. October 28, 2002, p. 34.
USA Today Online. October 25, 2002.
Variety. January 21, 2002, p. 35.

QUOTES

Ana's (America Ferrera) boyfriend Jimmy (Brian Sites) tells her: "You're not fat. You're beautiful."

AWARDS AND NOMINATIONS

Nomination:
Ind. Spirit 2003: Debut Perf. (Ferrera).

Red Dragon

To understand the origin of evil, you must go back to the beginning.
—Movie tagline
Before the Silence, there was the Dragon.
—Movie tagline

 Box Office: $92.9 million

The latest Hannibal Lecter scare machine is not only an adaptation of the novel Thomas Harris used to introduce his psychotic character with a taste for murder and mayhem but also a remake, since Michael Mann had already adapted *Red Dragon* in his film *Manhunter* (1986), which did not do so well at the boxoffice but went on to become a cult classic, believed by some to be better than *The Silence of the Lambs* (1991), which introduced Anthony Hopkins as Hannibal Lecter in an effectively chilling Oscar-winning performance. In point of fact, just as *Silence* is superior to

Red Dragon as a novel, so, certainly, is Jonathan Demme's film superior to *Manhunter*. It is better acted and, thanks to screenwriter Ted Tally, better scripted. The rationale for remaking the film was that *Manhunter* was not widely seen at the time of its release and that as an adaptation of the novel, it was not as faithful as it might have been. (Considering Mann's film a boxoffice flop, Sheila Benson of the *Los Angeles Times* concluded that "style [had] overrun content, leaving behind a vast, chic, well-cast wasteland.") The novel concluded with a double twist that was not taken into consideration by *Manhunter,* when the serial killer known mainly as the "Tooth Fairy" (Tom Noonan) is shot down by investigator Will Graham (William Petersen, who went on to become the star of the CBS television police procedural series, *CSI*). There was no ambiguous ending here at all, since not all of the story was told.

The formula behind the story is essentially the same as *The Silence of the Lambs:* study the monster, consult with another monster (Dr. Lecter), find the monster, and then kill the monster. Harris writes scary, adult fairy tales dominated of unspeakably repulsive characters. In each story, the FBI investigator, Clarice Starling (Jodie Foster) in *Silence* and Will Graham (Edward Norton) in *Red Dragon,* has to seek help from Dr. Lecter (Anthony Hopkins in the remake, Brian Cox in *Manhunter*), Evil personified, who is able to enter the minds of the agents in subtle, seductive, and dangerous ways. In the case of *Red Dragon,* Lecter has a payback agenda with Graham, who was responsible for putting him away. So traumatic was Graham's initial encounter with Lecter that the investigator was hospitalized. He has since retired to the Florida Keys with his wife Molly (Mary-Louise Parker), who does not want him to go back to work for Jack Crawford (played by Harvey Keitel in the remake).

But, as Dr. Lecter tells him, Graham has a "taste" for such work and is lured into the investigation of the serial killer who has wiped out two middle-class families, in Atlanta, Georgia, and Birmingham, Alabama. The killer, Francis Dolarhyde (Ralph Fiennes), is known as the "Tooth Fairy," because he bites his victims, but Dolarhyde prefers to be known as the "Red Dragon," an identity he has lifted from the artwork of the visionary poet and artist William Blake. He believes that he is in the process of "becoming" the Red Dragon. Since the character, who suffered an abusive childhood and a cleft palate, is utterly crazy, his problems need to be contextualized, as was not the case in the earlier film *Manhunter*. The character has worked hard at body-building and is exceptionally strong. He has unexpectedly had a romantic affair with a blind woman named Reba McClane (Emily Watson) that has threatened to "normalize" Dolarhyde, but the alter ego of his split personality, the Dragon, finally proves to be dominant. His very name suggests the Jekyll-and-Hyde nature of his sickness. So like a mad dog, Dolarhyde needs to be destroyed.

Dolarhyde works at a film processing plant in St. Louis, and it is by scrutinizing and copying home movies that he has managed to find his victims, a major clue that Graham eventually discovers, helping to lead him to St. Louis and Dolarhyde's home in the country, where Reba is being held captive. In the process of detection, Graham has fed misinformation to a sleazy yellow journalist named Freddy Lounds (Philip Seymour Hoffman), suggesting homosexual tendencies calculated to infuriate the Tooth Fairy, and marking sleazy Freddy as the Dragon's next victim. Dolarhyde has also become a pen pal with Hannibal Lecter, who communicates in coded language through the personals in Freddy's tabloid, disclosing the Florida address of Graham and his family. Since things become so personal, Graham has to resolve the problem with the Dragon, but the Dragon almost outsmarts him in a surprise conclusion that comes from the book but is not represented in the earlier film.

Perhaps having had enough of Hannibal the Cannibal, reviewers lined up to take their journalistic pot-shots at *Red Dragon,* because, after all, it is in the nature of "critics" to be "critical." But they were not at all fair to the film. An anonymous reviewer for the the *Washington Post* (probably Desson Howe, since the review appeared in the *Weekend* section of the paper), dismissed the film as "Reheated 'Lamb.'" How clever. The reason *Red Dragon* cannot quite compete with *The Silence of the Lambs* is that Edward Norton cannot be as vulnerable playing Will Graham as Jodie Foster had been as Clarice Starling. Her vulnerability transformed *Silence* into a modern-day variant of the Beauty and the Beast legend.

Lawrence Toppman, the *Charlotte Observer*'s critic confessed that he could not tell if *Red Dragon* is more faithful to Harris's book than *Manhunter,* which he had not seen in 16 years, but, then, the film is available on video, and reading the novel should not be a chore, since it is, in the jargon of journalists, a "page-turner," repulsive, of course, in typical Harris fashion, but still fascinating. This "critic" claimed that the film was "less artful and atmospheric" than *Manhunter,* a "straight-ahead thriller that never rises above superficiality." But it does, it does. The film follows the design of *Silence,* and anyone who has seen *Manhunter* recently can tell you that the hospital setting for Brian Cox's Hannibal in that film cannot measure up to the far more atmospheric design of Jonathan Demme's gothic cannibal cage for *The Silence of the Lambs,* which is carried forward into Brett Ratner's *Red Dragon.* Demme knew how to build a proper cannibal cage, incarcerating the Monster and constructing a transparent barrier between the Beast and his "little Starling."

The Hopkins monster is the Beast in the dungeon. What could be more "atmospheric" than that? The difference between Brian Cox and Anthony Hopkins, moreover, as Hannibal Lecter, is the difference between a competent actor and a genius, who made the role his own years ago and is now in danger of hamming it up. But watching him perform is in itself a guilty pleasure. Two points need to be scored and underscored here. No one tops Hopkins in the personification of Evil, and no one tops Demme in the conceptualization and contextualization of Evil.

Writing for *USA Today*, Scott Bowles argued the merits and demerits in contrasting *Manhunter* and *Red Dragon*. In *Manhunter* the first glimpse of Lecktor (the name was changed, but not to protect the innocent) is in the antiseptic and not-so-scary, well-lighted cell. *Red Dragon* introduces Lecter in an establishing flashback, rehearsing the story of an unfortunate musician who hits a wrong note on his flute while performing with the Baltimore Symphony Orchestra and ends up at the cannibal's table, presumably at the wrong end of the fork. The scene also establishes Graham's history with Lecter as the scare doctor attacks Graham with a knife. Bravo. The more famous Hopkins Lecter gets far more screen time; the less famous Cox Lecktor is an almost forgettable minor character.

In *Manhunter* Tom Noonan was a tall Tooth Fairy (6-foot-6), whereas *Red Dragon* uses the shorter (5-foot-11) but far more flamboyant and more "normal" appearing Ralph Fiennes as Francis Dolarhyde. The earlier film does not bother much to explain the Tooth Fairy's motives, taking for granted that he is simply crazy. The remake attempts to confront his inner demons and abusive childhood. Fiennes can transform himself into the Creep Fairy simply by taking his shirt off to display the massive dragon tattoo that covers every inch of his back. The remake also covers his obsession with William Blake and his mission to the Brooklyn Museum of Art to steal and "consume" the original Blake Red Dragon print.

To track Dolarhyde, Graham puts his wife in jeopardy in the novel, and this complication is restored to the film. Graham teaches his wife how to use a pistol, with good reason. *Variety* reviewer Todd McCarthy predicted, rightly, that Ratner's "faithful, immaculately appointed new retelling of the inescapably creepy tale will be an intensely unnerving restraint." Rattner was also particularly praised for his "intelligent restraint," in comparison to Ridley Scott's *Hannibal* (2001).

It should be clear that *Red Dragon* is the better adaptation of the Robert Harris novel. It is also arguable that Brett Ratner's adaptation is the better film, despite the protests of reviewers who regard it as a cult favorite. Ralph Fiennes is the better Dragon than Tom Noonan's Tooth Fairy. Edward Norton is arguably more convincing than William Petersen as the world-weary Graham. Emily Watson was up against stiffer competition in duplicating the role of Reba, originally introduced by Joan Allen. But Rattner serves up sleazier characters in Harris's Freddy (Philip Seymour Hoffman) and Anthony Heald's Dr. Chilton, who eventually will be served up to Dr. Lecter. In his two scenes in *Manhunter*

Brian Cox was all right as Lecter, but, after all, Anthony Hopkins now owns the Lecter franchise, and seems to enjoy taking the bad doctor over the top. On its opening weekend, *Red Dragon* set an October record by grossing $37.5 million, suggesting that the Lecter franchise is as potent as ever.

—*James M. Welsh*

CREDITS

Hannibal Lecter: Anthony Hopkins
Will Graham: Edward Norton
Francis Dolarhyde: Ralph Fiennes
Jack Crawford: Harvey Keitel
Reba McClane: Emily Watson
Molly Graham: Mary-Louise Parker
Freddy Lounds: Philip Seymour Hoffman
Dr. Chilton: Anthony Heald
Police Chief: Bill Duke
Jimmy: Stanley Anderson
Lloyd Bowman: Ken Leung
Bookseller: Azura Skye
Barney: Frankie Faison
Josh Graham: Tyler Patrick Jones
Charles Leeds: Tom Verica
Mr. Jacobi: Dwier Brown
Deputy: Conrad Palmisano
Museum curator: Mary Beth Hurt
Ralph Mandy: Frank Whaley
Grandmother: Ellen Burstyn (Voice)
Young Dolarhyde: Alex D. Linz (Voice)

Origin: USA
Released: 2002
Production: Dino De Laurentiis, Martha De Laurentiis; Metro-Goldwyn-Mayer, Universal Pictures; released by Universal Pictures
Directed by: Brett Ratner
Written by: Ted Tally
Cinematography by: Dante Spinotti
Music by: Danny Elfman
Sound: Kim Harris Ornitz
Editing: Mark Helfrich
Art Direction: Steve Saklad, Tim Glavin
Costumes: Betsy Heimann
Production Design: Kristi Zea
MPAA rating: R
Running time: 124 minutes

REVIEWS

Baltimore Sun. October 4, 2002, p. E1.
Charlotte NC Observer. October 4, 2002, p. 3.
Chicago Sun-Times Online. October 4, 2002.
Entertainment Weekly. October 11, 2002, p. 51.
Los Angeles Times Online. October 4, 2002.
New York Times Online. October 4, 2002.
People. October 14, 2002, p. 41.
USA Today. October 7, 2002, p. D4.
Variety. September 30, 2002, p. 24.
Washington Post. October 4, 2002, p. C1.
Washington Post Weekend. October 4, 2002, p. 39.

Reign of Fire

Only one species will survive.
—Movie tagline
Fight fire with fire.
—Movie tagline

Box Office: $43 million

Hibernating deep under the city of London is evidence that will give credence to the ancient English legend of the dragon. Unfortunately for humanity, this evidence isn't in the form of archeological artifacts, it is the dragons themselves. They evidently have slept there for hundreds of years, waiting for the Earth to replenish itself after their last reign of terror. Now their sleep is interrupted by humans tunneling through their lair to create another underground railway line.

The first to witness the reawakening of the dragons is 12-year-old Quinn (Ben Thornton). He is visiting his mother, Karen (Alice Krige), the project engineer, and because of his small size, he climbs into the void the drilling equipment has discovered to see what's in there. Quickly realizing that there is something alive in the cavern, Quinn races out. As the dragon releases its first lethal, fiery breath, Quinn and his mother race for the tunnel elevator. But before they can reach the top, the dragon passes them and kills Quinn's mother before emerging on an unwary London.

The dragons are now driven on by one purpose, to feed. They eat ash, which is why they set everything on fire, plant, animal and human. In a feeble attempt to stop the quickly multiplying dragons humans have actually waged war against them using weapons that create even more ash, helping rather than hindering the dragons' conquest of Earth.

By the year 2020, things are looking bleak for humans. The Earth has been laid waste and there is less and less food to eat and fewer and fewer humans to eat it. This, however, also means there is less ash so the dragons, too, are getting hungry.

The grown Quinn (Christian Bale) has taken refuge along with what surviving humans he can find in a highly-fortified medieval castle in Northumberland in England. There this makeshift family of several dozen men, women and children live a basically underground existence, passing their days by entertaining themselves re-enacting the plot of *Star Wars,* brewing moonshine, and practicing dragon drills. But because their food is grown outside the castle's walls, Quinn's group is always susceptible to dragon attack when they harvest it.

Then one day it's not dragons that seem to threaten Quinn's castle, it's a band of American soldiers. They are led by Van Zan (Matthew McConaughey), who declares that he is not there to take them over but to enlist their help. Van Zan, with his shaved head, tattooed body and gravelly voice, claims to be a dragonslayer. He knows the secret to killing them—they don't see well at dusk and dawn. The failing light is their Achilles heel. He also says that he knows how to get rid of the dragons once and for all. There is, he says, only one male. All other dragons are female. Therefore if the male can be killed there will be no way to fertilize the females' eggs and they will die out. Since he believes the male must be the one released during the original tunnel dig he must therefore live in London and that's why this band of American soldiers has made its way to the shores of England.

At first Quinn is reluctant to believe anything Van Zan tells him, especially when he makes the incredible assertion that he and his army have flown to England in a rebuilt C5A transport plane. Nothing has flown in the Earth's skies but dragons for years. But then he hears the sound of something mechanical flying overhead. It is a helicopter and its pilot is the beautiful Alex (Izabella Scorupco).

Quinn is still skeptical about Van Zan's crew but when they attack and kill a dragon that is attacking the castle, he is willing to give them shelter. But when it comes to enlisting in Van Zan's army, Quinn is a definite no, and he doesn't want any of his "family" to enlist either. While Van Zan firmly believes that mankind's only hope is to go to London and kill the male, Quinn, who met the male up close and personal when he was 12, realizes that if they fail in their mission, the male will undoubtedly follow them back to the castle and destroy it. What to do? What to do?

It's said that the origin of this story occurred to Wisconsin natives and *Reign of Fire* screenwriters Gregg Chabot and Kevin Peterka when the two took a backpacking trip across England, Scotland and Ireland. One can just imagine them as they crossed moors and dales with visions of St. George dancing in their heads, and one has to admit that fusing ancient dragons and modern weaponry is a new twist, but was it worth it? Well, it depends on what you're looking for.

Some might expect an intellectually challenging, post-apocalyptic message movie about man's own destruction of the Earth, but this isn't it. Some might expect a campy, witty, high-spirited film that will be added to the camp classics list, but this isn't it either. What it is is a flat out, fairly entertaining monster film, and that's it. Don't go looking for anything more.

Don't expect great acting or complex characters. Matthew McConaughey is virtually unrecognizable as the stereotypical Ramboesque leader of the American troops come to rescue the Brits and the rest of the world (haven't we seen this before?). It is rather odd, though, that this hard-bitten, cigar-chomping, Vin Diesel clone also seems perpetually on the verge of tears in all his close-ups. Christian Bale plays the reserved but strong Brit, the reluctant leader who values defensive tactics to McConaughey's character's offensive ones. It's Patton vs. Churchill.

The acting is heavy-handed, and the dialogue corny and we just know these two opposites will end up in an obligatory mano a mano showdown where they both end up bloodied and bruised but also realizing that although their tactics might be different their goals are the same and that success will only come when they unite against their common enemy.

It's that common enemy, the dragons, not the actors that one will want to see in *Reign of Fire*. With their 150-foot wingspan (although their wings often look rather moth-eaten), they flap and swoop and dive in the air and crawl menacingly along the ground and can shoot fire from either location. They look properly menacing and the special effects serve the movie well. (Although I have to admit that during the dragon's close ups I kept wondering—If they were given lines, would they speak in Sean Connery's voice a la *Dragonheart*?)

Similarly the film is appropriately filmed in post-apocalyptic grays and blues which helps set the film's defeated and depressing mood, but won't do much to lift one's spirits. Director Rob Bowman (best known for doing episodes of television's *X-Files* and the 1998 *X-Files* movie), has kept the film on target as strictly a monster movie. For example, although the film has an obligatory pretty blond, there is no real love story here, thank goodness. *Reing of Fire* is *Mad Max Beyond Thunderdome* combined with *Jurassic Park* and there's no room here for love—humor, either, for that matter. It doesn't pretend or try to be anything else than a monster action film.

This is not to say that the movie doesn't have a few problems. The music is a bit heavy-handed, especially at the end, but even worse is the fact that too often the sound is muddy—making the dialogue indecipherable. Add thick cockney accents and it gets worse for American audiences.

And since the entire plot is set up via a long voice over it may take some people a while to catch on to some of the plot points.

On the whole, though, *Reign of Fire* is a well-done production that knows what it wants to be and does it well. While it may take itself a bit too seriously and not have the proper sense of irony to become a classic camp film its special effects and high energy make for an entertaining summer film that will probably do well on video.

—*Beverley Bare Buehrer*

CREDITS

Denton Van Zan: Matthew McConaughey
Quinn: Christian Bale
Alex: Izabela Scorupco
Creedy: Gerard Butler
Jared Wilke: Scott James Moutter
Ajay: Alexander Siddig
Eddie Stax: David Kennedy
Karen Abercrombie: Alice Krige
Barlow: Ned Dennehy
Devon: Rory Kennan
Gideon: Terence Maynard
Young Quinn: Ben Thornton

Origin: USA
Released: 2002
Production: Lili Fini Zanuck, Richard D. Zanuck, Gary Barber, Roger Birnbaum; Touchstone Pictures, Spyglass Entertainment; released by Buena Vista
Directed by: Rob Bowman
Written by: Matt Greenberg, Gregg Chabot, Kevin Peterka
Cinematography by: Adrian Biddle
Music by: Ed Shearmur
Sound: Kieran Horgan
Editing: Thom Noble
Art Direction: Ian Bailie, Justin Brown, Alan Tomkins
Costumes: Joan Bergin
Production Design: Wolf Kroeger
Visual Effects: Richard Hoover
MPAA rating: PG-13
Running time: 101 minutes

 ## REVIEWS

Chicago Sun-Times Online. July 12, 2002.
Entertainment Weekly. July 26, 2002, p. 45.
Los Angeles Times Online. July 12, 2002.
New York Times Online. July 12, 2002.

USA Today Online. July 12, 2002.
Variety. July 15, 2002, p. 23.
Washington Post. July 12, 2002, p. WE32.

QUOTES

Van Zan (Matthew McConaughey): "We kill the male, we kill the species."

Resident Evil

Survive the Horror.
—Movie tagline
A secret experiment. A deadly virus. A fatal mistake.
—Movie tagline
No one is immune.
—Movie tagline

Box Office: $39.5 million

*R*esident Evil has been called a poorly executed retread of earlier, slicker zombie films—particularly those of George Romero, master of the genre. Yet, while the film owes a great debt to Romero, it is far from the rip-off that some have labeled it. Owen Gleiberman, in particular, lamented in *Entertainment Weekly* that "there must now be an entire generation that has never experienced . . . Romero's *Living Dead* films, with their flesh-munching ghouls and frenzied atmosphere of rabid, hyped-up paranoia. *Resident Evil* is a blatant recycling of those queasy pulp classics, notably *Dawn of the Dead* . . . with its claustrophobic setting, its comic-book sociology, and its SWAT-team-on-the-defense ballistics."

On the contrary, the filmmakers have embraced this heritage and have combined it with the post-*Matrix* pacing that is a necessity for today's action films. That is not to say that every action film needs to be modeled this way, or that it should be. Indeed, there are a few shots in the film that are lifted directly from *The Matrix* (Alice's bullet-time fight with the zombie dogs is an excellent example of this already overdone technique), but rather that the tempo of the Romero films was necessary for their time. Similarly, in the age of computer games designed for the quick fix, short attention span generation, *Resident Evil*'s tempo is more kinetic and hyper than Romero had to be. So, while the specter of Romero's legacy looms over the film, it's not so much ripped off as borrowed than energized and given a 21st century re-imagining.

A half-mile below Raccoon City is a research facility called the Hive. This lab is owned by the Umbrella Corporation and is itself the size of a small city. When the experimental "T-Virus" is released in the Hive, the all-powerful computer—the Red Queen—that oversees the facility's functions, shuts down the base and kills the workers trapped inside to prevent contamination above ground. Shortly thereafter a military unit is sent by the Corporation to ascertain what went wrong and bring the Hive back online. The soldiers are joined by Alice (Milla Jovovich), an amnesiac found near the entrance to the Hive. However, unbeknownst to the team is the fact that the T-Virus has transformed all of the Hive's inhabitants into walking dead with an appetite for human flesh. Further complications arise when the team learns that the Red Queen has no intention of letting them escape and has released a mutated killing animal known as the Licker to dispatch them. A cat-and-mouse game ensues as the soldiers and Alice attempt to escape while slaughtering zombies around every corner.

While this formulaic plot has its limitations, namely in being pretty predictable, it does echo more simplistic science fiction themes which succeed in making it far more effective and enjoyable than if it had been meant as a profound intellectual comment on the evils of corporate America or the possible misuse of science. While these concepts are present, they are far from the central themes or concerns of the film. The film is simply put, pulp entertainment. After all, it is based on a video game and its sensibilities are such. With it's dropped-in-the-middle of the action plot and refusal to let up for excessive exposition, the film adequately replicates the thrill of playing a video game. Although the merits of that are questionable, it serves this film well. Director, Paul W.S. Anderson (a veteran of the video-game-to-movie genre having directed the successful *Mortal Kombat*) uses stylized editing (though in some instances, a bit too aware of being such) and frenetic pacing to recreate the gaming experience. Although this does work on a action-film level, some of the imagery is so disturbing that one might agree with Jan Stuart, who wrote in *Newsday* that the film's graphic violence "may make the older members of the audience faintly nostalgic for the primitive innocence of Pac-Man." But, horror films such as this are never intended for the so-called "older" audience.

The film's most intriguing aspect is that the story is told from Alice's point of view as she regains her memory. Nothing is revealed to the audience that Alice doesn't learn firsthand. This communal "awakening" experience has an otherworldly effect on the plot. Which consequently makes the simplistic, comic-book stock characters of the film forgivable since they're the products of a main character with a slightly hazy point of view. As played by Jovovich, Alice is understandably the most effective character in the film. The only other characters that are afforded any substantial depth are Matt (Eric Mabius) and Rain (Michelle Rodriguez). But, even they are seen through Alice's eyes and are essentially players meant to further along the plot. While the use of Alice as a quasi narrator succeeds in giving the film a dreamlike motif, it does lead to a certain amount of apathy for the characters in the film. As David Hunter wrote in *The Hollywood Reporter*, "While one is expected to feel nothing and in fact does feel nothing for the hordes of hungry, reanimated corpses . . . it's also easy to have zero concern for the protagonists." That, unfortunately, is the biggest fault with the otherwise effective, fast-paced, video game style of the film. Although there is almost no character identification with the audience beyond that of Alice, it isn't detrimental since the film is experienced exclusively with/as Alice.

The only serious problem the film has is the too-loud soundtrack that is, at times, very disruptive and jarring. It's not that it's an awful score or the heavy metal music is inappropriate, it's just that it is too loud. There's nothing in the rule book that says having the soundtrack be so loud that little bits of brain matter shoot from the viewer's ears makes the film any scarier or more thrilling.

While it may not be the epitome of the "classic" zombie film, *Resident Evil* does succeed as a respectable action film. Although the characters might be slightly less than developed, the novel way in which the plot is communicated and the frenzied video game like pace of the film overcomes a predictable story to make the film a bit better than one might assume.

—Michael J. Tyrkus

CREDITS

Alice: Milla Jovovich
Rain: Michelle Rodriguez
One: Colin Salmon
Matt: Eric Mabius
Spence: James Purefoy
Mr. White: Stephen Billington

Origin: Germany, Great Britain
Released: 2002
Production: Bernd Eichinger, Samuel Hadida, Jeremy Bolt, Paul W.S. Anderson; Davis Films, Constantin Film, New Legacy Films; released by Screen Gems
Directed by: Paul Anderson
Written by: Paul Anderson
Cinematography by: David Johnson
Music by: Marco Beltrami
Sound: Roland Winke
Music Supervisor: Liz Gallacher
Editing: Alexander Berner

Art Direction: Jorg Baumbarten
Costumes: Richard Bridgland
Production Design: Richard Bridgland
MPAA rating: R
Running time: 100 minutes

REVIEWS

Boxoffice. May, 2002, p. 60.
Entertainment Weekly Online. March 15, 2002.
Hollywood Reporter Online. March 12, 2002.
Newsday Online. March 15, 2002.
Variety. March 18, 2002, p. 24.

Return to Never Land

Box Office: $48.4 million

In a decision based entirely on reasons that had nothing to do with artistic inspiration, Disney Studios decided to start releasing sequels to their kids' film. Most viewers probably thought happily ever after tied up most of these movies quite nicely, but for the powers that be at Disney, that wasn't enough. This means that there are sequels to films that already seemed to have quite satisfactory endings, like *Cinderella*. (One can only imagine what *Cinderella 2* is about. The Prince and Cinderella get married, purchase homeowner's insurance, select tile for their bathroom, then get into a powerful and dramatic fight over whose turn it is to wash the dishes.) Usually these films, like *The Lion King II: Simba's Pride* and *The Little Mermaid II: Return to the Sea* went straight to video, but in 2002 the studio decided to start releasing some of the sequels into theaters. There will be a new release every February and *Return to Never Land* is the first of these.

Return to Never Land is a sequel to 1953's animated classic *Peter Pan*. (Perhaps some credit should be given to the studio for holding out almost 50 years to make the sequel.) The film was based on J.M. Barrie's turn of the century story.

Wendy from the first movie is in this one, too, but this time she's all grown up (The adult Wendy is voiced by Kath Soucie, the young Wendy is voiced by Harriet Owen). She has a 12-year-old daughter, Jane (Owen again), and a cuddly young son, Danny (Andrew McDonough). Jane is the kind of girl that's old beyond her years. Her mother loves entertaining little Danny with wild tales of Peter Pan, Tinker Bell, and Captain Hook, but Jane thinks it's all nonsense. It's easy to see how Jane became such a serious child. She lives in London, England, during the blitz of World War II. Every night they are subjected to air raids, where the citizens climb into bomb shelters, if they're lucky, or door frames, if they're not. Her handsome father, Edward (Roger Rees), is off fighting the war and he's asked Jane to take care of the family. Of course, Jane takes his request quite seriously, so she's even more upset than she would be when she learns that all the children in her area are going to be shipped off to the countryside to avoid the bombing. (Hey, that's some happy subject matter for the kiddies.) If she's sent away, how will she be able to care for her family?

That night, after having a bit of a tantrum, she's paid a visit by Captain Hook (Corey Burton), who flies through London's night sky in his pirate ship. (One critic noted that Hook neatly managed to avoid all the warplanes in the sky.) Hook kidnaps Jane, thinking that he's kidnapped Wendy, and takes her back to Never Land. His plan is to hold her in order to force Peter Pan (Blayne Weaver) to show him where he keeps his hidden treasure. Once in Never Land, it's easy to see how Hook could have mistaken Jane for her mother because in Never Land nothing changes. This could be taken as sort of a charming notion, but it's also kind of tedious. It seems that Hook and Peter have continued battling all these years over the same old issues. Hook tries some sort of scheme to trick Peter into giving him the treasure. Peter outwits him. Repeat scenario again and again. Ho hum. When they're doing the same thing over and over for decades, it seems less like exciting adventures and more like some sort of job.

Once Peter (yawn) rescues Jane, he quickly discovers that she's not Wendy, but seems okay with that. Jane, on the other hand, is miffed to be in Never Land and only wishes to get back home. She considers herself to be very competent and the fact that she's in a situation that she can't control is very bothersome to her. Despite the overtures of Peter and his Lost Boys, a group of (again) cuddly youngsters, Wendy is not interested in being friends. She even declares that she doesn't believe in Tinker Bell, which causes the little sprite to start slowly losing her magic power.

When Captain Hook proposes a deal in which Wendy finds Peter's treasure in return for a ride back home, Wendy eagerly accepts. She does this, Peter loses his treasure, and Captain Hook wins. Oh wait, that's not what happens at all. She does find the treasure, but of course Captain Hook is foiled, she discovers the good magic of Peter's ways, and she even decides to believe in Tinker Bell.

Along the way, we hear some songs (among the contributing artists are such non-Disney types as They Might Be Giants with "So to Be One of Us" and Jonathan Brooke's "I'll Try"), Jane learns to fly, and the audience gets to see some stereotypes. In this film, Tinker Bell is reduced to a caricature of womanhood. She's either hanging faithfully by Peter (Tinker Bell would be wise to give it up because Peter,

the sexually ambiguous man-child, doesn't seem to interested in her as more than a friend, despite her revealing wisp of a dress) or pouting because she is jealous of Peter's friendship with Jane.

The film does at least strike a small blow for feminism. Jane is a fully competent human being, manages to rescue Peter and even becomes the first Lost Girl. Captain Hook is dark and swarthy because, in this film, white British people are good, but all dark people are mean pirates. One of the pirates who is white, Smee (Jeff Bennett, who voices all the rest of the pirates as well), bares an eerie resemblance to Doc from *Snow White*. It's strange to see good old Doc being among the bad guys.

Children probably won't find the film to be too scary. Captain Hook's evil is toned down quite a bit and he's more of a cartoonish failure than an ominous presence. He never gets much of an upper hand in the film and is often being chased by a hungry octopus to supposedly comic effect. Adults looking for any hip, in-jokes, or indeed any funny jokes at all will be left wanting. If you don't think, say, someone falling down is funny, you will be out of luck.

The voices in the film are good, proving that studios could save themselves some money by not using big actors to voice animated characters. The actors stuck to a traditional interpretation and didn't try to make the characters sound modern. In the *Los Angeles Times,* Gene Seymour wrote that "Burton's Hook (is) so redolent of the late, irreplaceable Hans Conreid that you'd swear he'd been thawed for the occasion."

Critics had a mixed response to the film. Stephen Holden of the *New York Times* wrote, "If *Return to Never Land,* directed by Robin Budd, from a screenplay by Temple Matthews, doesn't have a story to match the original's in breadth and imagination, it does a smooth job of recycling its characters and themes." Daphne Gordon of the *Toronto Star* offered this faint praise: "There's none of the intoxicating magic of an original Disney animated feature here. The voices lack sparkling individuality, and the songs lack the infectious melodies that stick in your head for weeks to come. Still, pretty solid for a sequel." Roger Ebert of the *Chicago Sun-Times* wrote, "*Return to Never Land* is a bright and energetic animated comedy, with all the slick polish we expect from Disney, but it's not much more. This movie is more of a Saturday afternoon stop for the kiddies— harmless, skillful and aimed at gradeschoolers." And Owen Gleiberman of *Entertainment Weekly* gave the film a C+ and wrote, "Though the characters may connect as nostalgia for boomer parents, their kiddies will wonder what all the fuss was about."

—*Jill Hamilton*

CREDITS

Peter Pan: Blayne Weaver (Voice)
Jane/Young Wendy: Harriet Owen (Voice)
Captain Hook: Corey Burton (Voice)
Smee/Pirates: Jeff Bennett (Voice)
Wendy: Kath Soucie (Voice)
Edward: Roger Rees (Voice)
Cubby: Spencer Breslin (Voice)
Danny: Andrew McDonough (Voice)

Origin: USA
Released: 2002
Production: Dan Rounds, Christopher Chase, Michelle Robinson; Walt Disney Pictures; released by Buena Vista
Directed by: Robin Budd
Written by: Temple Mathews
Music by: Joel McNeely
Sound: Judy Nord, Jeanette Cremarosa
Editing: Anthony F. Rocco
Art Direction: Wendy Luebbe
MPAA rating: G
Running time: 72 minutes

REVIEWS

Chicago Sun-Times Online. February 15, 2002.
Los Angeles Times Online. February 15, 2002.
New York Times Online. February 15, 2002.
People. February 25, 2002, p. 32.
USA Today Online. February 15, 2002.
Variety. February 18, 2002, p. 34.
Washington Post. February 15, 2002, p. WE46.

The Ring

Before you die, you see the ring.
—Movie tagline

 Box Office: $135 million

Earlier this year the movie *Feardotcom* was based on the premise that not long after logging on to a certain internet site one would inevitably die. Now we have *The Ring,* which is based on the premise that seven days after watching a certain videotape one will die. Hmmmmm. But

there's more. *The Ring* is based on a wildly successful series of Japanese books and movies, and one could get dizzy trying to figure out who is imitating whom.

There are other similarities between the two films. For example, both mix a cinematographic stylishness and a blue-gray, constantly gloomy-rainy environment. Unfortunately, they both also share a minimum of scariness and a maximum of illogicalness. The plots of both could have used a few rewrites by someone who had actually thought through the subtleties of the story.

Obviously the basics of the plot of *The Ring* begins with the above mentioned videotape. As the movie opens, two teenage girls, Katie (Amber Tamblyn) and Becca (Rachael Bella), are alone in the house (naturally) and sitting around in Katie's room during a dark and stormy night (of course) when Becca brings up the latest urban legend going around. It seems there is this tape which when viewed is immediately followed by a phone call and exactly seven days later the viewer dies. Katie is unusually silent in the face of this story. Why? Because exactly seven days earlier, she and her boyfriend Josh and two other friends popped a videotape into the VCR expecting a football game only to see "that tape" and receive "that phone call."

Eventually Katie and Becca become separated in the house and Katie finds that her television has a mind of its own. It turns itself on; Katie turns it off. It turns itself on again, and Katie unplugs it. Soon water is streaming through hallways and dripping from doorknobs, the television is on again, Katie is screaming . . . and director Gore Verbinski quick cuts to a young boy drawing a picture in a classroom.

The boy is Aidan (David Dorfman), the son of newspaper reporter Rachel Keller (Naomi Watts) and cousin to the now deceased Katie. Aidan's teacher is worried that he might be suppressing his grief about Katie's death and his emotions are coming out in his drawings. The only problem is, Katie died three nights ago, but Aidan was drawing these pictures of death last week.

Rachel takes Aidan to Katie's wake where odd bits of information make her think that the 16-year-old's death just wasn't an act of God. For example, Katie's best friend Becca is now in a mental hospital. "Something scared the shit out of her," a friend of the girls tells Rachel. Then she learns that Katie's secret boyfriend, Josh, is also dead. He supposedly killed himself the same night that Katie died. So when Rachel's sister asks her to investigate Katie's death she's already curious.

Her first clue is a one-hour photo receipt Rachel finds in Katie's room. After picking up the film, Rachel sees Katie, her boyfriend Josh, and another couple spending the weekend at Shelter Mountain Retreat. The foursome look as if they're enjoying themselves except that, oddly, one photo shows all their faces distorted.

Rachel now starts scouring newspapers for information on Josh's death and stumbles on another article about the other couple in the photographs. They, too, are dead. And according to the articles, all three died on exactly the same day and at exactly the same hour as each other . . . and Katie.

The next step in the investigation is obvious, a trip to Shelter Mountain Retreat. (A trip that immediately brings to mind Jack Nicholson's first trip to the Overlook in *The Shining*.) There Rachel finds out that the four had complained about the poor television reception and had left without paying. She checks into the same cabin as they were in, but not before she sneaks an unlabeled videotape from the retreat's small library. In her cabin Rachel pops the tape into the VCR and we get to watch it along with her. It is a surreal, grainy, black and white production of seemingly random images: a woman reflected in a mirror, dead horses in the surf, centipedes, and a circle of light that is eclipsed by a circular body leaving just a ring a light. No sooner is the tape over then the phone rings in Rachel's room and the investigative reporter now has seven days left to live, unless she can unravel the mystery of the videotape.

Although Rachel tends not to believe the urban myth, she nonetheless calls in her ex, Noah (Martin Henderson), to help speed up her investigation. Noah, Aidan's father, is some kind of video expert and in order to tell Rachel anything about the tape he has to watch it too. And then his phone rings and the clock starts counting down for him, too.

Eventually several clues come to light. Noah discovers that the videotape has no control track—it's like being born without fingerprints—and if one forces the tracking to the far edge, other images appear, like a lighthouse. Also, when Rachel copies the tape the counter numbers inexplicably go wild. But when Rachel takes digital photos of herself and sees her face is distorted, she starts to believe the legend.

Checking out a book on lighthouses, Rachel discovers the location of the one on the edge of the videotape frame. She also discovers a picture of the lighthouse's restoration group that includes the woman whose face is reflected in the mirror in the fatal tape. Her name was Anna Morgan and when Rachel researches her she discovers that Anna owned a ranch on which all the horses were dying from a mysterious illness. Anna also committed suicide by jumping to her death—another image from the videotape. Interestingly, once Anna was dead, the horses recovered.

The next step obviously is for Rachel to go to the island with the lighthouse where Anna Morgan lived. Before she can leave, however, something terrible happens and her mission is given even more urgency: Her son, Aidan, has watched the forbidden videotape, the phone has rung, and Aidan's days are numbered.

What Rachel finds on the island and whether she, Noah and/or Aidan live or die is not something that should be given out here to ruin the solution to what is a potentially good mystery. Viewers are constantly kept guessing as the story unfolds and they really will be curious about what's going on. The only problem is, the mystery is going to be sabotaged in the end by a lot of over-explaining of things that don't need explaining and the lack of an explanation for a lot of loose ends and logical questions.

Those whose deaths we witness die in connection with a television, so how did those two kids who died in a car crash die? Although there is an implied explanation for how the tape got made, who's making those phone calls? What is the connection between Aidan and "the killer?" Why is the tape killing people in the first place? (Or if you prefer, why is "the killer" using the videotape to kill people?) And why on earth does the one loophole that is found work?

The Ring has its good points. As mentioned, it is a good mystery—although its solution is disappointing—and it is stylistically presented. It has the proper look for a scary movie and even incorporates some interesting psychological ploys on its audience. For example, since we have seen the videotape, theoretically we now have only seven days to live. And although no phones ring in the theater there are subtle almost imperceptible plays on this fear as when a very quick glimpse of the ring appears for no reason just as the reels are about to change. It was unsettling—did I see that or not—and could have been used even more to increase viewer tension.

There is also an homage to Alfred Hitchcock that plays on our, the audiences, voyeurism of watching Rachel watching the videotape. When she's finished, she walks onto her apartment balcony and begins looking into the widows of her neighbors a la *rear Window*. In each apartment televisions are on and she sees people watching or not watching their televisions, including one neighbor with a cast on his leg and in a wheelchair looking eerily like James Stewart.

One scene, however, which is utterly memorable may also be one of the hardest for many people to watch. It involves a horse on a ferry and although the film's end credits give the usual claim of "no animals were hurt in the making of this movie," it is very hard to believe because it is so disturbing.

As mentioned, *The Ring* is an adaptation of the first of three highly successful Japanese movies (*Rungu*) directed by Hideo Nakata and based on the writings of famed horror/suspense author Koji Suzuki (sometimes called the Japanese Stephen King). It is said that Suzuki, in turn, based his series of books on a real psychic named Chizuko Mifune who poisoned herself in 1911 at the age of 25 after being labeled a quack and humiliated. *Rungu* was Japan's top grossing film of 1998 and it didn't take long for the Japanese to release *Rungu 2*, a sequel and *Rungu 0*, a prequel. (It has also given birth to two television series and a series of manga or comic books.) Unfortunately, after viewing *The Ring*, some people might rush to their video store to rent the Japanese original, but at the time of this remake's release it is not available in the U.S.

The Ring is a more intelligent horror film than is often released. It isn't all that gory and fake shocks are minimal. Except for the ending, it is effective and suspenseful, but also oddly cold and distancing. It's not so much that we're worried about if the lead characters will die or not, we're just more curious about solving the mystery. Unfortunately, all that interest in the story doesn't have a payoff in the end. *The Ring* doesn't hold up well to post-viewing analysis, but the ride is a good one until then.

—*Beverley Bare Buehrer*

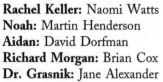

CREDITS

Rachel Keller: Naomi Watts
Noah: Martin Henderson
Aidan: David Dorfman
Richard Morgan: Brian Cox
Dr. Grasnik: Jane Alexander
Ruth: Lindsay Frost
Katie: Amber Tamblyn
Becca: Rachael Bella
Samara Morgan: Daveigh Chase
Beth: Pauley Perrette
Babysitter: Sara Rue
Anna Morgan: Shannon Cochran

Origin: USA
Released: 2002
Production: Walter F. Parkes, Laurie MacDonald; released by Dreamworks Pictures
Directed by: Gore Verbinski
Written by: Ehren Kruger
Cinematography by: Bojan Bazelli
Music by: Hans Zimmer
Sound: Lee Orloff
Editing: Craig Wood
Art Direction: Patrick M. Sullivan Jr.
Costumes: Julie Weiss
Production Design: Tom Duffield
MPAA rating: R
Running time: 115 minutes

REVIEWS

Boxoffice. November, 2002, p. 9.
Chicago Sun-Times Online. October 18, 2002.
Entertainment Weekly. October 25, 2002, p. 54.
Los Angeles Times Online. October 18, 2002.
New York Times Online. October 18, 2002.
USA Today Online. October 18, 2002.
Variety Online. October 3, 2002.
Washington Post. October 18, 2002, p. WE37.

QUOTES

Becca (Rachael Bella): "Have you heard about this tape that kills you when you watch it? When it's over, the phone rings and someone says, 'You will die in seven days.'"

Road to Perdition

Pray for Michael Sullivan.
—Movie tagline

Box Office: $105 million

This is a story about fathers and sons. About family, loyalty and an occupation that would seem to rage in the face of both. The first set of fathers and sons consists of John Rooney (Paul Newman) and his adult son Connor (Daniel Craig). John runs things for the Chicago mob in 1931 Rock Island, which is in western Illinois on the Mississippi. Connor, who is expected to take over the business from the aging John, seems perpetually amused by the world he lives in, but that doesn't stop him from stealing from his own father. Connor is not his father's most loyal employee nor his most loving "son." In fact, Connor is seething inside because he feels someone else has replaced him in his father's affection and trust: Michael Sullivan (Tom Hanks).

John Rooney and Michael Sullivan form the second father and son pair even though they are not biologically related. Michael has been raised by Rooney and is now his trusted enforcer. Michael undoubtedly loves and is loyal to the man who, in Michael's words, "When we had nothing, he gave us a home." Unfortunately for Michael, he will soon discover that blood is thicker than loyalty or even love.

The third set of fathers and sons is Michael himself and his own son, Michael Jr. (Tyler Hoechlin). Michael Jr. is 12-years-old and has a typical youngster's love/hate relationship with his father. He is in awe of this reserved, distant, almost cold man who obviously loves him, his younger brother Peter (Liam Aiken), and his mother Annie (Jennifer Jason Leigh). Michael Jr. knows that his father works for Mr. Rooney, but the closest he's ever given as an explanation as to what he actually does is that he performs "dangerous missions" for him.

Eventually curiosity gets the better of the younger Michael and he decides he will find out the specifics of his father's job. One cold, wintery night he hides underneath the back seat of his father's car when he is sent out on one of Mr. Rooney's assignments. It proves to be more dangerous than either of the Michaels could have envisioned.

What Michael Jr. sees is Connor Rooney shooting Finn McGovern (Ciran Hinds), which forces Michael Sr. to shoot Finn's henchmen. And then Connor Rooney sees the boy. Witnesses to mob killings are not allowed to live, but Michael Sr. vouches for his son. Unfortunately, this event gives Connor the perfect excuse to rid himself of the man he hates and envies, his rival for his father's affection.

Later, Connor gives Michael Sr. a note allegedly from his father telling him to check in with one of their employees. At the last minute, however, Michael realizes that it is a set up so he shoots first. While both Michaels are out of the house, though, Connor sneaks in and shoots Annie and Peter, thinking Peter is Michael Jr. Michael's grief over the duplicity of Connor's acts and the seeming disloyalty of his father-figure John, immediately sends him on a new mission. He must get permission from the Chicago mob to do what he must do, murder the man who murdered his family.

Travelling all night both Michael Sullivans arrive in Chicago but only Sr. goes to see Capone's right hand man, Frank Nitti (Stanley Tucci). Nitti, realizing the importance of John Rooney to their business in Rock Island, cannot agree to let Michael kill Rooney's son. And it's worse, Connor and John are in a room next to Nitti's office and they overhear the entire conversation. Rooney now feels he now has no alternative but to have Nitti kill the man who was more of a son to him than his own son, but then blood is thicker, right?

To do the job, Nitti hires a hitman, a psychopath by the name of Maguire (Jude Law) whose job and hobby is taking photos of corpses at the scene of their murder . . . maybe even providing a few of the subjects himself. Maguire sets out after Sullivan, but Sullivan has plans of his own. He is going to force Nitti and Capone to give up Connor. Since Capone loves his money, Sullivan will go from bank to bank in the Chicago area, robbing them only of Capone's money. "I want dirty money only," he tells the bankers and then gives them a generous tip so no one knows but Capone that there has been a bank robbery.

It becomes a battle of wills and time. Will Capone relent before Maguire finds Sullivan? Will Sullivan figure out who Maguire is before he can kill him? And will the road to perdition lead Michael Sr. to sanctuary in the small Michigan town by that name where his sister-in-law lives, or will it lead to hell? For the actions in his life seem inevitably doomed to send Michael Sr. to his death.

The Road to Perdition is only the second film from director Sam Mendes, who won Oscars for Best Picture and Best Director in 1999 for his first film, *American Beauty.* Here he continues to show characters who are morally complicated and conflicted. Michael Sullivan, like Lester Burnham in *American Beauty,* are men who skirt around moral absolutes and provide Mendes and the film's audience with characters whose ambivalence provide complexity to the story. There are no cardboard characters here, no black and white, just infinite shades of gray and the challenging depth that comes with it.

Mendes' taste for murky subjects and characters causes the "road" in the *Road to Perdition* to be a story of an emotional as well as a physical journey. The physical journey is that of the two Michael's crisscrossing Illinois, asking favors of the Chicago mob, robbing banks, facing John Rooney, and finally finding what they hope is an end to their quest in Michigan. The emotional story, however, centers on men fatalistically caught up in lives that, on the one hand, are dominated by a profession that will damn their souls to hell, and, on the other, are dominated by the Irish Catholic Church that is one of the mainstays of their Irish immigrant's life. Are these lives redeemable? But more than that, it is also the emotional journey of one father, Michael Sr., trying desperately to save his son from succumbing to his own morally compromised fate and in the process it also becomes a journey connecting the hearts of the initially distant father and son.

Amazingly, this captivating and sophisticated story comes from a 1998 graphic novel (a term used to describe a long comic book printed on quality paper) written by Max Allan Collins and illustrated by Richard Piers Rayner. Of course, it has also been revised by screenwriter David Self, who has emphasized the relationships between Michael Sr. and Rooney as well as adding a more troubled one between the two Michaels. Thankfully, Self also reduced the bloodshed from that in the original graphic novel, but he also added a major character, Maguire.

Many critics have compared this Irish gangster film to classics about the Italian mob such as *The Godfather* or *Goodfellows,* but, especially in the hands of Mendes and his expert cinematographer, Conrad L. Hall, perhaps *The Road to Perdition* would be better served if compared to later classic Kurosawa films like *Kagemusha* or *Ran.*

Conrad L. Hall makes *The Road to Perdition* into a work of art, balancing the dark illustrations from the original graphic novel with depression-era paintings. Hall's elegant use of light and dark adds an almost unnoticeable, subtle depth to an already beautifully complex story. He begins by emphasizing the darkness and bleakness of a Midwestern winter and an enforcer's soul. These are scenes shot in shadow, at night, in rain and blue snow. Faces are only half seen behind fedoras. These souls are lost and we are chilled watching them. Hall, a two-time Oscar winner (*American Beauty* and *Butch Cassidy and the Sundance Kid*) and nine-time Oscar nominee, only lets the light into this movie as the relationship between the two Michaels begins to develop and Michael Sr. breaks his relationship with the mob. By the time they reach Perdition, Michigan, it is a sun-drenched beach house radiant against golden sand dunes.

Lake Michigan is implied at this beach house, and it is indicative of Mendes' overwhelming use of water in the film. It begins with a funeral where a coffin is resting on blocks of

World party. Here we meet Lauren Hynde (Shannyn Sossamon of *A Knight's Tale*.) Lauren, feeling depressed about love and wanting to lose her virginity, starts flirting with a film student who she doesn't really like that much. As she gets drunker and drunker, the two end up in a room in the upstairs of the fraternity house. In her stupor, Lauren realizes that she is having sex and it is not with the film student—it's with a townie. The film student is filming the whole thing. This seems like a true low, but it gets even worse when the townie vomits on her.

From here, writer and director Roger Avary, who co-wrote Quentin Tarentino's *Pulp Fiction* and directed the Tarentino-like *Killing Zoe*, rewinds the action to see how this character got to this point. But instead of just jump cutting to a flashback, Avary literally runs the film backwards so we see Lauren get de-vomited on, leaving the room, getting less drunk, etc. As an effect, it's a little showy, but is fun to watch.

At the party, we also meet Paul Denton (Ian Somerhalder), who has picked up a football jock who seems interested. When Paul makes his move, the jock is shocked and tosses Paul into the hallway. In the accompanying voiceover, we learn that the jock comes out of the closet sometime later. We also see Sean (Van Der Beek) picking up a woman and having sex with her. In his voiceover, he's watching the act with detachment and feeling bored by the whole thing. He realizes it's the first time he's has sex sober in some time.

As the tale unfolds, we learn that Lauren is pining away for Victor (Kip Pardue), who's been off in Europe for a semester. Much to the disgust of her roommate, Lara (Jessica Biel of *7th Heaven*), she's not much interested in anyone else. That is, until she meets Sean, when they both show up for a class that's been canceled. Sean has been getting mysterious love notes in his mailbox and assumes that Lauren is the one who's been sending them. For the first time in his life, he's starting to feel smitten. Meanwhile, Paul is feeling smitten himself—with Sean. He invites Sean out to dinner and Sean casually accepts. Sean thinks it's a free dinner; Paul thinks it's a date.

Sean has other problems than love problems. The coked-out drug dealer (Clifton Collins Jr.) he works for wants the substantial sum of money that Sean owes him. Besides the drug dealer, there are a few other characters who drift in and out of the film. Lance Lawson (Eric Stoltz) is a youngish teacher who likes to think that he can still hang out with the students. In one excruciating scene, he has Lauren perform a sex act on him in his office while he smiles down at her smugly. Swoosie Kurtz and Faye Dunaway show up for a few moments for a scene in a restaurant. Dunaway plays Paul's mother and Kurtz the mother of his wild gay friend Dick Jared, played by Russell Sams. Channeling Jim Carrey, Sams is loud and boorish, mortifying his hard-drinking society-type mother. It's nice to see these actresses on the screen, but difficult to see why this scene is even in the film since it doesn't have much to do with the rest of the story.

Avary has a lot of fun telling the story with different usual film techniques. To show Sean and Lauren meeting, Avary plays the Donovan song "Colours" and follows the two characters through their morning routines, waking up and getting ready for class. It's certainly not the usual meet-cute sequence, as Avary goes for the more realistic approach. He shows Sean on the toilet, picking his nose and casually scratching his crotch. When the two finally meet in front of the class, Avary swings the screens together so that the characters share one.

In another scene, Victor tells a friend about his entire trip to Europe in a fast minute or so. As the film speeds through shots of his adventures, Victor rapidly tells of bedding women, scoring drugs, seeing the sights and doing it all over again in a different country. Despite the rapid-fire pace of the telling, Victor's rootlessness and boredom with committing the same old vices around the world comes through. (Reportedly, Pardue improvised his riff in the scene.)

Besides the clever visuals, the other highlight of the film is Van Der Beek's acting. Avary often films him looking into the camera, glowering out from under the eyebrows of his bowed head. Maybe it's a homage to the classic Stanley Kubrick shot, but it's a good way of erasing memories of *Dawson's Creek*. Sean is crude, selfish and the kind of guy who says, "Rock and roll" instead of "yes" or "okay," but he's still kind of charming. It was a big acting stretch for Van Der Beek to tackle such a dark character and he does a great job with it. Also good is Sossamon. She has the same kind of frail, vital energy that Audrey Hepburn had and it's fun to watch her on the screen.

Many critics didn't like the film and one of their major complaints was that none of the characters were likable. Roger Ebert of the *Chicago Sun-Times* wrote, "There is no entry portal in *The Rules of Attraction,* and I spent most of the movie feeling depressed by the shallow, selfish, greedy characters. I wanted to be at another party." Mark Caro of the *Chicago Tribune* wrote, "*The Rules of Attraction* is a bravura exercise in emptiness. Its flashy camera moves, backwards sequences, jumbled chronology and energetic soundtrack make you feel, at least for a while, like you're having fun watching characters who generally aren't." Stephen Holden of the *New York Times* wrote, "The harder the movie tries to shock, the shriller it rings. Too much of the time, its tone suggests the harangue of a spoiled brat trying to fluster Mommy and Daddy by waving snapshots from the orgy room." Stephen Hunter of the *Washington Post* wrote, "Say this for Avary: He's a crude dramatist but an able anthropologist. He seems to have gotten into the tribal rituals of the young and learned their secret code word."

—*Jill Hamilton*

CREDITS

Sean Bateman: James Van Der Beek
Paul Denton: Ian Somerhalder
Lauren Hynde: Shannyn Sossamon
Lara: Jessica Biel
Victor: Kip Pardue
Mitchell: Thomas Ian Nicholas
Kelly: Kate (Catherine) Bosworth
Marc: Fred Savage
Lance Lawson: Eric Stoltz
Rupert: Clifton (Gonzalez) Collins Jr.
Mrs. Denton: Faye Dunaway
Mrs. Jared: Swoosie Kurtz
Richard Jared: Russell Sams
Getch: Matthew Lang

Origin: USA
Released: 2002
Production: Greg Shapiro; Kingsgate Films; released by Lion's Gate Films
Directed by: Roger Roberts Avary
Written by: Roger Roberts Avary
Cinematography by: Robert Brinkmann
Music by: Tomandandy
Sound: Felipe Borrero
Editing: Sharon Rutter
Art Direction: Christopher Tanden
Costumes: Louise Frogley
Production Design: Sharon Seymour
MPAA rating: R
Running time: 104 minutes

REVIEWS

Boxoffice. September, 2002, p. 20.
Chicago Sun-Times Online. October 11, 2002.
Entertainment Weekly. October 25, 2002, p. 52.
Los Angeles Times Online. September 8, 2002.
Los Angeles Times Online. October 11, 2002.
New York Times Online. October 11, 2002.
People. October 21, 2002, p. 44.
Variety Online. October 3, 2002.
Washington Post. October 11, 2002, p. WE46.

Safe Conduct (Laissez-Passer)

Nazi occupied Paris, 1942: Love and art are acts of resistance.
—Movie tagline

In what must surely be the consummate work of a long and prolific career in French cinema *Safe Conduct* by Bertrand Tavernier, explores the ambivalent relationship that existed between the Nazis and the filmmakers under their thumb in Paris. By crosscutting between the real life stories of Jean Devaivre (Jacques Gamblin), a directorial assistant, who becomes a Resistance hero much against his will, and Jean Aurenche (Denis Podalydes), a scriptwriter-cum-compulsive womanizer, Tavernier spins his narratively dense fabric at a frenetic pace, so that despite the film's inordinate, nearly three hour length, it never drags.

Continental Films, the outfit that *Safe Conduct* is intended as a tribute to, was run by the Germans, but attracted courageous French filmmakers, like Henri-Georges Clouzot, Andre Cayatte, and Maurice Tourneur amongst others. Under the guise of horror and period pieces, their films would criticize totalitarian rule.

The film opens on the night of March 3, 1942 as Aurenche is frantically preparing to receive his mistress, the ravishing actress, Suzanne Raymond (Charlotte Kady). He cuts a comic figure as he rushes about ordering the lowly denizens of the small hotel he's staying in to keep out of sight. When Suzanne does arrive, she is in a depressed mood, having lost a part to the famous Danielle Darrieux in the Cayatte film, *The False Mistress.* Just then, air raid sirens send everyone rushing into shelters. It is the British looking for the automobile factory at Boulogne. Suzanne of course insists on having her tumble in bed.

The film then cuts to Devaivre out in the street as bombs drop around him. He rushes into a hospital to retrieve his baby. There, his wife, Simone (Marie Desgranges), tells him to leave the baby there, along with the other wailing infants. "It's 60 degrees here," she explains. "It's 34 degrees at home." In the aftermath of the bombing, through the fires in the street, Devaivre makes his way to the film studio where he works. On the way, he shouts at two technicians from his unit to get a move on. They are fishing because the bombs have got the fish to scurry to the surface.

This opening serves to establish the diverse personalities of Tavernier's two protagonists, and the polar opposites they represent in the French response to Nazi oppression. On the set, Devaivre is accosted by the scriptwriter, Jean-Paul Le Chanois (Ged Marlon), an active member of the Resistance. Le Chanois gives Devaivre a political tract to transcribe for distribution. Devaivre at first hesitates, but relents when he's told that "too many of our accomplices are being nabbed." The film Devaivre is working on is innocuously titled *8 Men in a Chateau.* Le Chanois also convinces Devaivre of the need to move to Continental even though it is run by the Germans. "When you're in the lion's jaw," Le Chanois reasons, "he cannot bite you."

While Devaivre is taken on as an assistant by the famous Tourneur (Philippe Morier-Genoud) at Continental, Aurenche tries to get himself a three-picture contract from a French producer so as to avoid having to work for the German-run outfit. Fearing that the German staying in his hotel will do away with him, thinking him to be a Jew, Aurenche moves into a room in a brothel occupied by Olga (Marie Gillain). To appease the madam, he brings along a cauliflower. To Olga, he confesses that he cannot get himself to say no to "producers, hucksters and women," which is why he now finds himself "juggling four scripts and three women," she being one of them.

For Devaivre, the stakes in the game, as far as his work at Continental is concerned, are very clear. When he pleads with the German supervisor, Greven (Christian Berkel), for an extra day to work on the sets, he is not only turned down but told of the alternative: a stint at the German studios in Babelsberg to study direction. Then, suddenly, in keeping with his commitment to the Resistance, Devaivre receives a cryptic call. He promptly packs two grenades from a hidden wall compartment in his house and meets an agent at the entrance of a metro. The two then head for a railway yard where the agent plants a device that leads to a huge explosion. When Devaivre returns to work immediately after, we can see from his euphoria that he's a changed man: the subversive act seems to have increased his sense of self-worth. As the film progresses, it is his commitment to the Resistance that will be tested, as it begins to affect his family and closest associates.

It is also at this stage in the film that Aurenche's story, while more entertaining and colorful, begins to pale in comparison. As he reads out a scene to Olga, the film cuts to a black-and-white excerpt of that very scene as it was later filmed. Aurenche then admits to Olga that his ambition is to dazzle Pierre Bost, the famous director. Meanwhile, he would like Olga to attend a private party he is organizing for one Pierre Nord, a dealer in antiques. The event turns out to be a comedy of manners as Aurenche has to prevent Suzanne from discovering his relationship with Reine Sorignal (Maria Pirrares), her seamstress, and introduce Olga to the other two women in his life as someone who has been like a sister to him.

Devaivre at work finds that he has to take over the direction of the film from Tourneur who, though present, says that he is too distracted to direct since his wife, an American, has come under suspicion. For the scene from a horror film, Devaivre executes his master's trademark of composing with long shadows, and is so adept at it that Tourneur admits to him that he himself could not have done better.

In sharp contrast, Aurenche tries to wriggle out of writing for Greven by suggesting that the German hire Charles Spaak, the scenarist of the Jean Renoir classic, *Grand Illusion* (1937). Greven argues that Aurenche has just "the light touch" required for a farce starring the famous comedian Fernandel. When Aurenche remains noncommittal, Greven plays his trump card. He says he knows one of his friends at Continental who is a Communist as well as a Jew, and threatens to expose him. Thus pressured, Aurenche finds a way to allay his conscience by introducing Greven to an unemployed scenarist named Rene Wheeler, and agreeing to share credit with him for the proposed screenplay.

The film soon skips to March '43 when Devaivre's life is hit with two crises. First, his wife Simone's brother, Jacques, whom Devaivre has been employing as an extra, is arrested when two political tracts are found on him. Then, Simone herself is taken away for questioning. Devaivre then locates Le Chanois and throws back at him what he had said. "Working for Continental is no protection!" he screams. Le Chanois reminds him of their mission: "Our job is infiltration!" Fortunately, Simone is released soon after, whereupon Devaivre gets her to move to his godmother's house in the country, even if it means bicycling 250 miles to see her. Tavernier provides a beautiful prolonged lyrical interlude that shows Devaivre furiously pedaling through a bucolic countryside, captured in the film's anamorphic format, in total contrast to the time he has just spent within the claustrophobic space of the studio floor.

Devoted as he is to family values, Devaivre's next goal is to use his influence to free Jacques. He thus gets lured into an undercover operation for the Resistance. After making copies of a secret document, which he hopes will have information about Jacques, he finds that it is a military brief and not a police one. He is then told he'll have to get on a plane in order to get that document to the British. When he hesitates, he is admonished, "You have to go all the way!" On the plane, Devaivre thinks aloud to himself, "What the hell am I doing here?"

Despite his crisis of confidence, he completes the mission. The Brits, after obtaining the information they were after about a secret arms cache, test Devaivre's bona fide in a hilarious set piece that develops into a spoof of all such interrogation scenes, which are a staple of the war film genre. Eventually, Devaivre is thanked with a box of tea, a luxury in the France of that time, and made to parachute onto French soil. He is dutifully back at work on Monday morning, after having pretended to be sick for the weekend. Whatever suspicion he has aroused amongst the German authorities, owing to a subplot having to do with a script written by Spaak, is soon put to rest owing to luck being on his side.

The film leaves Aurenche in the arms of Olga, after he has achieved his wish of writing for Bost.

As for Devaivre, it is only when he learns that Le Chanois has been taken away for being a Communist that he decides to leave Continental for good and join the fighters of the Resistance. A voiceover, that of Tavernier, informs us that Devaivre was to make his first film in 1947 and that Aurenche was to become Bost's longtime collaborator. As a footnote, Tavernier adds that when he met Devaivre in 2000, he said that if given a chance, he would do what he did all over again.

Surprisingly, the film's length seems to have elicited a varied critical response. Elvis Mitchell in the *New York Times,* while writing about "the pace and scale of the drama" at hand, believes that the "movie is full of juices that give it a healthy, pungent flow," but that because it has "the reach of an epic . . . it has the sprawl of an epic, too." On the other hand, Mike D'Angelo in *Time Out New York,* finds that "its extreme length doesn't suit its anecdotal structure (or vice versa)." The finest tribute to Tavernier's effort comes from Jan Stuart in *Newsday:* "For devotees of French cinema, *Safe Conduct* is so rich with period minutiae it's like dying and going to celluloid heaven."

—*Vivek Adarkar*

CREDITS

Jean Devaivre: Jacques Gamblin
Jean Aurenche: Denis Podalydes
Olga: Marie Gillain
Dr. Greven: Christian Berkel
Suzanne Raymond: Charlotte Kady
Simone Devaivre: Marie Desgranges
Reine Sorignal: Maria Pitarresi
Paul Maillebuau: Thierry Gibault
Maurice Tourneur: Philippe Morier-Genoud
Pierre Bost: Christophe Odent
Jean-Paul Le Chanois: Ged Marlon
Charles Spaak: Laurent Schilling

Origin: France, Germany, Spain
Language: French
Released: 2001
Production: Alain Sarde, Frederic Bourboulon; France 2 Cinema, France 3 Cinema, Little Bear, KC Medien, Vertigo; released by Empire Pictures
Directed by: Bertrand Tavernier
Written by: Bertrand Tavernier, Jean Cosmos
Cinematography by: Alain Choquart
Music by: Antoine Duhamel
Sound: Michel Desrois, Gerard Lamps, Elisabeth Paquette
Editing: Sophie Brunet
Costumes: Valerie Pozzo Di Borgo
Production Design: Emile Ghigo
MPAA rating: Unrated
Running time: 170 minutes

REVIEWS

Boxoffice. September, 2002, p. 142.
Los Angeles Times Online. October 18, 2002.
New York Times Online. October 8, 2002.
New York Times Online. October 13, 2002.
Sight and Sound. November, 2002, p. 49.
Variety. January 14, 2002, p. 52.

The Safety of Objects

Multiple narrative films have become the norm as opposed to the exception with the arthouse genre. It's as if an entire generation of filmmakers cut their teeth watching Robert Altman's *Nashville.* Where once, the multiple narrative proved intriguing with such films as Don McKellar's *Last Night,* Jeremy Podeswa's *The Five Senses,* and Michael Winterbottom's *Wonderland,* the narrative style's multiple threads have begun to fray. Not only do viewers of the films have to work hard to keep up with the multiple characters, but the filmmakers need to successfully tie all the loose ends together in a satisfying climax. Newer films, such as *Lantana* managed to succeed where Rose Troche's latest release, *The Safety of Objects,* only solidifies our distaste for suburban dwelling.

However, Troche didn't merely use the multiple narrative approach as a trendy device. The writer/director took on the added challenge of adapting A.M. Homes' collection of short stories and created a seamless screenplay. Alison Maclean's team of screenwriters pulled off the same fete with *Jesus' Son* as did Altman with *Short Cuts,* which was based on a collection of short stories by Raymond Carver. According to a brief article that appeared in *Filmmaker,* writer Peter Bowen interviewed Troche about her fusion of seven short stories: "It is a film about four families who share a close geography over four days in their lives. There's a sort of falling apart and philosophical grouping."

Astute viewers might recall such films as *American Beauty* and Todd Solondz's depressing indie classic, *Happiness.* While Troche shies away from biting sarcasm and gazes compassionately on her characters' lives it still becomes increasingly difficult to remove us from a common disdain for suburbanites and their disturbing compulsions. *The Safety of Objects* introduces us to a young boy in love with his sister's Barbie doll, a comatose young man, a lawyer who quits his job after being passed up for a partnership, and other characters. And as the film's title implies all the characters identify with objects that allow them to feel safe among the chaos that surrounds them.

Multiple narrative films often revolve around a single event or character. *The Safety of Objects* centers on a comatose musician, Paul Gold (Joshua Jackson), from the point of view of his sister, parents, friends, lover, and neighbors. Troche doesn't hammer the tragedy into our heads, instead showing us the various ways the characters deal with the loss they feel even as a variety of perversions emerge. Paul's friend Randy (Timothy Olyphant) kidnaps neighbor Annette's (Patricia Clarkson) daughter, Samantha (Kristen Stewart), in order to process his grief. Paul's sister, Julie (Jessica Campbell), enlists her optimistic mother Esther's (Glenn Close) help in winning a car, while his father Howard (Robert Klein) seems resigned to his son's condition.

Neighbor Helen (Mary Kay Place) battles with her aging body while trying to seek solace with young men. She has become a boring housewife and joke to her daughter who laughs at her mother's wise advice. The daughter has discovered boys and cigarettes while she and her friends share their intrigue about the comatose musician. Meanwhile, lawyer Jim Train (Dermot Mulroney) gives up his stagnant career to coach Esther in how to win a car in a stressful and competitive contest in his quest for meaning in his life.

While we can feel compassion for the characters, none of them tell us anything new and they seem rather boring. We never fully feel their tragedies due to Troche's laid back approach to telling their stories. Characters engage in tearful embraces that refuse to moisten our eyes. Perhaps part of the problem is that we have seen these stock characters before. The lawyer who regresses back to his adolescence recalls Kevin Spacey's character in *American Beauty* and we've seen divorced mothers struggle in a variety of movies of the week. And Troche's film has so many characters that it becomes increasingly hard to follow their individual stories and not think of a soap opera. *The Safety of Objects* could be transformed into a television soap revolving around various neighbors toughing it out in the mundane suburbs.

As suburban sprawl takes over America, many stories of perversion will surface. Directors will claim that the stories represent reality even though living in the suburbs is usually far from melodramatic. After all, movies fabricate reality.

—*Patty-Lynne Herlevi*

CREDITS

Esther Gold: Glenn Close

Jim Train: Dermot Mulroney
Julie Gold: Jessica Campbell
Annette Jennings: Patricia Clarkson
Paul Gold: Joshua Jackson
Susan Train: Moira Kelly
Howard Gold: Robert Klein
Randy: Timothy Olyphant
Helen Christianson: Mary Kay Place
Sam Jennings: Kristen Stewart
Jake Train: Alex House

Origin: USA
Released: 2001
Production: Dorothy Berwin, Christine Vachon; Killer Films, Clear Blue Sky Productions, Renaissance Films, Infilm; released by IFC Films
Directed by: Rose Troche
Written by: Rose Troche
Cinematography by: Enrique Chediak
Sound: Kelly Wright
Editing: Geraldine Peroni
Costumes: Laura Jean Shannon
Production Design: Andrea Stanley
MPAA rating: R
Running time: 121 minutes

REVIEWS

Boxoffice. December, 2001, p. 52.
Filmmaker. Winter, 2001, p. 30.
Variety. September 17, 2001, p. 21.

QUOTES

Esther Gold (Glenn Close) to her comatose son Paul (Joshua Jackson): "You know how people are. They think misfortune is contagious."

The Salton Sea

If you're looking for the truth, you've come to the wrong place.
—Movie tagline

While *The Salton Sea* features a character named Pooh-Bear, no one will confuse him with the cute, cuddly, gentle soul created by A.A. Milne. This Pooh-Bear (Vincent D'Onofrio) is a thoroughly unhinged drug dealer it's not irreverent enough. It's not consistently anything—it's a thematic and directorial mess. Morrisette doesn't know how to sustain a plot, or even how to cut from one subplot and character to another, without tripping all over himself. His film is graceless and plodding, with moments of would-be wackiness falling flat and growing grating. It never gets anywhere near where it seems to be heading without stopping to catch up with the story it's trying to reinvent. The result is a film with a few laughs—but not nearly enough—and an insufficient number of clever ideas.

Perhaps there should be a licensing requirement to adapt Shakespeare to film. Morrisette doesn't show he understands what *MacBeth* was about, and he clearly doesn't understand the 1960s. His film moves along with an equally uninspired and all-over-the-place soundtrack. He spends a lot of time fishing around in a murky white-trash cultural milieu, searching for his story's bearings and never finding them. It's not inspired, but merely a trifle, neither comic nor weighty enough to stand the test of time.

—*Michael Betzold*

CREDITS

Pat McBeth: Maura Tierney
Joe "Mac" McBeth: James LeGros
Lt. Ernie McDuff: Christopher Walken
Anthony "Banko" Banconi: Kevin Corrigan
Norm Duncan: James Rebhorn
Malcolm: Tom Guiry
Stacy: Amy Smart
Jesse: Andy Dick
Doug McKenna: Josh Pais
Donald: Geoff Dunsworth

Origin: USA
Released: 2002
Production: Richard Shepard, Jonathan Stern; Veto Chip Productions, Paddy Wagon Productions; released by Lot 47 Films
Directed by: Billy Morrissette
Written by: Billy Morrissette
Cinematography by: Wally Pfister
Music by: Anton Sanko
Sound: Doug Johnston
Editing: Adam Lichtenstein
Art Direction: Shelley Nieder
Costumes: David C. Robinson
Production Design: Jennifer Stewart
MPAA rating: R
Running time: 102 minutes

REVIEWS

Boxoffice. April, 2001, p. 223.
Chicago Sun-Times Online. February 15, 2002.
Los Angeles Times Online. February 8, 2002.
New York Times Online. February 3, 2002.
New York Times Online. February 8, 2002.
Variety. February 12, 2001, p. 40.
Washington Post. March 22, 2002, p. WE38.

QUOTES

Pat (Maura Tierney) to husband Mac (James LeGros): "We're not bad people Mac—we're just underachievers that have have to make up for lost time."

The Season of Men (La Saison des Hommes)

In some parts of the world virgins are sacrificed when forced into ruthless marriages or in misogynistic societies. In any case, these women find themselves powerless in a world still owned and ruled by men. Similar to Amos Gitai's *Kadosh,* in which two Hassidic Jewish sisters find themselves at odds with fundamentalist marriages, and Jafar Panahi's *The Circle,* where Iranian women seek validation, Tunisian director Moufida Tlatli also portrays the plight of entrapped females in *The Season of Men.* However, *The Season of Men* not only reflects on the suffering Arab women endure but also damage that wrecks families within that culture.

To further complicate matters, Tlatli builds her film narrative by creating a parallel between the past, with matriarch Aicha's (Rabiaa Ben Abdallah) painful marriage, and the present, with the lives of her two daughters, Meriem (Ghalia Ben Ali) and Emna (Hand Sabri). As noticed by *Village Voice* film critic, Amy Taubin, in a review of the film that appeared in *Film Comment,* Tlatli refused to rely on the usual narrative devices when flashing back to the past. She doesn't fade away from a close-up of someone's face, but simply shows the past as it's happening today. Taubin cites, "In terms of form, the most radical aspect of the film is Tlatli's refusal to delineate the flashbacks with any of the usual devices such as dissolves, titles, or lingering close-ups of the characters whose memories we're about to enter."

Tlatli, a former film editor, made the right choice when viewing the film in a psychological fashion because, as the director noted in her press kit, the past never leaves us and lives with us in the present moment. While this artistic choice might confuse viewers of the film it also acts as a device to reach the viewers' subconscious minds.

The Season of Men opens in a mysterious fashion. We see two women struggling with a screaming child who refuses to take a bath; then the film cuts to a young woman violinist rehearsing with an orchestra. The conductor's glances at the woman reveal a sexual connection between them. The violinist, Emna, is called away to assist her mother Aicha with the autistic child, Aziz (Adel Hergal), who has become a burden to the family. Aicha has made a decision to return to the island of Djerba where she believes she can heal her son. However, this decision comes as a shock to her two daughters, who like Aicha, couldn't wait to escape the oppressive environment of Djerba. A mystery also surfaces involving Meriem because she has remained a virgin despite her marriage to a supportive husband for the past six months. She appears to be traumatized by sex but why?

As the women return to Djerba, the past catches up with them and solves the above mysterious circumstances for the film's viewers. We learn that Aicha married her husband Said (Ezzedine Gennoun) at the age of 18 and, similar to Said's brothers' wives, Aicha complied with living under the same roof as Said's mother, who is the ruling matriarch. Meanwhile, Said and his brothers reside in Tunis for 11 months where they work while the women languish in a matriarchal prison—constantly reminded of the few liberties allowed to them. Aicha argues with the matriarch and pleads with her husband to take her to Tunis. Said agrees to take Aicha to Tunis if she bears him a son. Eventually she does bear a son, but other complications arise, leading to more misery, but also to the healing of past wounds.

We also learn that Meriem was raped at the age of 13. And the oppression in which the sisters endured led them to painful adult choices. Meriem marries, but refuses to engage in sexual intercourse while Emna falls in love with a married man with whom she has a secret affair. Meanwhile, the autistic Aziz (abandoned by his father) becomes a weaver of rugs just like his mother.

Women are barely tolerated in Tunisian society. Tlatli reveals this observation in a birth scene where Aicha gives birth to a girl and the look of disappointment that crosses her mother-in-law's pained face recalls a similar scene from Panahi's *The Circle* in which the birth of a daughter leads to an impending divorce. Men have forgotten that women birthed them.

The Season of Men reminds us that women suffer everywhere on the planet due to outworn traditions and ignorance. But among us exists sisterhood, laughter, song, and mutual affection. ◉

—*Patty-Lynne Herlevi*

CREDITS

Aicha: Rabiaa Ben Abdallah
Zeineb: Sabah Bouzouita
Meriem: Ghalia Ben Ali
Emna: Hend Sabri
Said: Ezzedine Gennoun
Ommi: Mouna Noureddine

Origin: France, Tunisia
Language: Arabic
Released: 1999
Production: Margaret Menegoz, Mohamed Tlatli; Les Films du Losange, Arte France Cinema, Maghrebfilms Carthage; released by Cowboy Booking International
Directed by: Moufida Tlatli
Written by: Moufida Tlatli
Cinematography by: Youssef Ben Youssef
Music by: Anouar Brahem
Sound: Faouzi Thibet
Editing: Isabelle Devinck
Costumes: Nadia Anane, Naama Mejri
Production Design: Khaled Joulak
MPAA rating: Unrated
Running time: 124 minutes

REVIEWS

Film Comment. March/April, 2001, p. 18.
New York Times Online. September 28, 2001.
Sight and Sound. July, 2001, p. 38.
Variety Online. May 15, 2000.
Village Voice Online. September 26, 2001.

Second Skin (Segunda Piel)

A different triangle.
—Movie tagline

The other woman isn't a woman . . .
—Movie tagline

Spanish director Gerardo Vera's debut, *Second Skin* begins with a graphic sequence that recalls introductory credit sequences for the James Bond series or a daytime soap. Jungian symbolism explodes upon the screen as a lily blossoms, naked men engage in steamy sex and a motorcycle races out of the frame. By watching this credit sequence we are shown the film's transparent plot and the weepy string arrangement that accompanies this sequence sets the dreary tone of the film. In the actual film, a devastating love triangle plays out between a married man with an identity problem, his loving wife and his gay lover who also adores him. However, due to stunted dialogue and lead actor Jordi Mollà's strained performance and nervous tick (he constantly caresses his heavily-gelled hair), *Second Skin* comes across as a second rate Spanish soap opera.

Almodòvar favorites Javier Bardem (who receives top billing here) and Cecilia Roth also star in Vera's drama. Bardem, best-known for his Oscar-nominated performance in *Before Night Falls* in which he played a gay poet, transcends over his trite dialogue and clichèd role while delivering a heart-felt performance in *Second Skin*. Mick La Salle for the *San Francisco Chronicle* praised the leading man's performance: "Mr. Bardem is a great emotional actor, with a face that can seem at once handsome, clown-like, delicate and primitive." In contrast, Jeffrey M. Anderson of the *San Francisco Examiner* gave the film a scathing review and wondered if Bardem should have fought against the release of the Spanish film. In any case, Bardem's performance only proves that he has exceptional talent. After all, it's easy for an actor to shine in a well-written role and a challenge to transform a mediocre role into a mesmerizing portrayal.

Cecilia Roth (*All About My Mother*) also rises above her supporting role in which she plays a doctor colleague of Diego (Bardem). Although she spends little time on screen, we get a sense that the actress delved into her character's back-story and we can sense her attraction to her gay colleague, Diego. Again, she plays a maternal character who sets out to fix her colleague's problems while stoically forgetting her own pain. Along with Bardem and lead actress Ariadna Gil, Roth's performance acts as one of the film's saving graces. After all, there's little one can do when a film suffers from a predictable plot, swelling string arrangements, and psychological jargon. Vera adds steamy gay sex to attract a gay audience, pulls in star appeal, and cribs from Almodòvar's catalogue and yet, *Second Skin* falls short of its mark.

The story focuses on Alberto Garcia (Mollà), a married aeronautical engineer and father of a son. Alberto appears to be psychologically confused so he lies to everyone, including his adoring wife and his lover. He lied to his father by engaging in a career he despises, he married to please Elena (Gil), and he appears to love both his wife and Diego. However, because Alberto is psychologically confused, he throws caution to the wind while leaving clues of his destructive behavior. Elena locates a receipt for an expensive hotel and later she finds Diego's messages on the cell phone that Alberto accidentally left at home. Eventually, Diego learns that Alberto has a wife and child. However, even after the secret is out, Diego and Elena forgive Alberto. That is until

Elena divorces Alberto. Afterwards, Alberto and Diego engage in a conversation that resembles a therapist and client, and Alberto races his motorbike into ongoing traffic—culminating in his death.

Second Skin received mixed reviews from American film critics. A. O. Scott in the *New York Times* praised Bardem's performance—"Bardem's shape-shifting charisma—at one moment he seems as stolid as a bull, the next as sly as a jungle cat"—but criticized the film itself by calling it, "a Lifetime movie about men." Kevin Thomas, *Los Angeles Times,* stated: "*Second Skin* features stellar performances from Javier Bardem . . . Jordi Mollà . . . and Ariadna Gil." Jeffrey M. Anderson, *San Francisco Examiner,* found the film to be "dreadful." But Mick La Salle, *San Francisco Chronicle,* praised Vera's talent, "The director explores all three sides of his story with a sensitivity and inquisitiveness reminiscent of Truffaut."

Vera does add a new spin to the menage a trois so popular among European filmmakers. However, love triangles and psychological dramas have already been played out and are old school. Vera and writer Àngeles Gonzàlez Sinde might have done better in creating an Almodòvar-style comedy instead of melodrama.

—*Patty-Lynne Herlevi*

CREDITS

Diego: Javier Bardem
Alberto: Jordi Molla
Elena: Ariadna Gil
Eva: Cecilia (Celia) Roth
Rafael: Javier Albala
Maria Elena: Mercedes Sampietro
Manuel: Adrian Sac

Origin: Spain
Language: Spanish
Released: 1999
Production: Andres Vicente Gomez; Lola Films; released by Menemsha Films
Directed by: Gerardo Vera
Written by: Angeles Gonzalez-Sinde
Cinematography by: Julio Madurga
Music by: Roque Banos
Sound: Antonio Rodriguez
Editing: Nick Wentworth
Art Direction: Ana Alvargonzalez
Costumes: Macarena Soto
MPAA rating: Unrated
Running time: 104 minutes

REVIEWS

Boxoffice. November, 2000, p. 170.
Los Angeles Times Online. December 7, 2001.
New York Times Online. December 14, 2001.
Sight and Sound. March, 2001, p. 58.
Variety Online. February 21, 2000.

Secretary

Assume the position.
—Movie tagline

The story of a demanding boss and the woman who loves his demands.
—Movie tagline

 Box Office: $3.9 million

In Steven Shainberg's *Secretary,* Maggie Gyllenhaal gives a breakthrough performance as Lee Holloway, a troubled, young woman who takes pleasure in pain and, as a result, paradoxically takes control of her romantic destiny. It is a risky role that could have gone horribly wrong if played as an S&M caricature, but Gyllenhaal balances Lee's endearing girlishness with the basic need to discover her own womanhood, albeit on her own nontraditional terms.

The film's origin is a short story of the same name from Mary Gaitskill's collection called "Bad Behavior." The story is about a secretary who is spanked by her boss and her ambiguous reaction to the experience. Screenwriter Erin Cressida Wilson has taken the central idea but turned it upside down. Instead of becoming an emotionally confused victim of a sadistic boss, as in the short story, the film's protagonist loves the punishment her boss doles out and turns it into a life-changing (perhaps life-saving) experience. Wilson gives the protagonist a back story—Lee had been institutionalized for cutting herself with a collection of sharp instruments she keeps stashed under her mattress. She also has a romantic longing that ultimately is more poignant than kinky, turning the story into a twisted fairytale in which true love is realized in an unexpected way.

After being released from the mental institution, Lee takes a typing class at the local community college and gets her first job, working as a secretary at the law office of E. Edward Grey (James Spader), a buttoned-up type who probably sees in her a kindred spirit. Dressed in an oversized blue raincoat, she looks like Little Red Riding Hood meeting the Big Bad Wolf.

From the outset, their relationship is not that of a traditional boss and employee. One day when Mr. Grey tells Lee that he accidentally threw away some important notes, she volunteers to retrieve them and does not hesitate to step right into the dumpster and rummage through the trash to find them. Mr. Grey is stunned but obviously fascinated by a girl who would do something so degrading for him. One night he happens to see her in a Laundromat-café with Peter (Jeremy Davies), an old friend who likes her but is socially inept and unable to express himself very well. Seeing Lee with another man stirs feelings of jealousy in Mr. Grey, and he immediately begins playing the part of the tough disciplinarian at work. He fumes at her for the typing errors she has made and even criticizes the little things about her that irritate him—the way she dresses, taps her toes, plays with her hair, and sniffles. While the typical employee would be offended or angered by such remarks, Lee likes taking direction from her boss.

Under Mr. Grey's tutelage, Lee begins to improve herself. He gets her to develop a deeper, stronger telephone voice and then has a tender conversation in which he admits that he was once shy, but he overcame his shyness, and, by implication, so can she. He also tells her never to cut herself again (he has seen the Band-Aids on her legs) and to walk home on her own instead of having her mother pick her up. After all, she is not a little girl.

Of course, in many ways, Lee initially seems like a little girl in a state of suspended adolescence. Gyllenhaal walks with an awkward gait and has a winsome quality about her. Lee is embarrassed by Mr. Grey's attention yet flattered by it since she receives no such help anywhere else, certainly not from her overprotective mother (Lesley Ann Warren) or her alcoholic father (Stephen McHattie). Peter, despite his sweetness, is a weakling with nothing to offer her. Lee obviously needs someone to help shape her life, indeed to put her in her place, so to speak, and Grey is just the man to do it, with a firm yet loving hand.

The firm hand soon comes out at work when Mr. Grey, incensed at the latest in a series of spelling errors, has Lee bend over his desk and read aloud the letter she typed as he spanks her. Her behind is red afterward, but she enjoys the experience and, as a result, feels well enough to tell her mother to take the lock off the cabinet containing the knives. In a delightful montage scored to Leonard Cohen's "I'm Your Man," Lee is pictured in various submissive roles—she is particularly sexy crawling on her hands and knees with an envelope in her mouth—and even takes orders from Mr. Grey over the phone regarding what she is allowed to have for dinner.

Lee revels in the games they play and even enjoys richly imagined sexual fantasies in which she is in one of Mr. Grey's exotic flowers. Being submissive to him perfectly fits her personality, but he grows hesitant to continue playing along. He is not used to a secretary enjoying his mild sadism and begins to withdraw emotionally. She leans over his desk for a spanking but gets nothing in return and, in voiceover, laments that he is treating her like a regular secretary. Hitting herself on the rear with a bathroom brush fails to satisfy her, and, when she is making out with Peter and tries to get him to spank her, he simply does not understand her desires.

Lee finally gets Mr. Grey's attention when she sends him an earthworm. He calls her into his office and once again has her bend over, but this time he has her roll up her skirt and take down her pantyhose and underwear before he masturbates behind her. When she goes to the bathroom to clean up, she masturbates as well. This is the most shocking and disturbing scene in the movie. It appears in the short story as well, where it traumatizes the secretary, who never returns to work. But the film challenges us to see this act as one more test of her devotion to him, one more game in the constant power shifts between them.

Later, he summons her to his office, and they reenact her job interview in words that echo their first meeting. The dialogue in Secretary has a formalized, non-naturalistic quality to it that heightens the ritualistic nature of the games the characters play, and this is the most artificial exchange. But instead of distancing us from Lee and Mr. Grey, the formal speech has the wonderful effect of drawing us in and accenting the sexual tension by containing it. In this mock interview, he tells her that her behavior is bad and ends up firing her. Apparently, he is scared of the love he has sparked in her, and he tries to resolve his conflict by sending her away.

Despite all of its kinkiness, Secretary at heart bears some resemblance to a sweet romantic comedy in which two people are clearly meant for each other but cannot overcome their obstacles to love until the end. Peter functions as the genre's wrong man—the essentially good-hearted suitor who is simply too bland for the spunky heroine—and she even accepts a marriage proposal from him, only to become the runaway bride when she flees in her wedding dress to seek out Mr. Grey. Arriving at his office, she declares her love for him and receives a terrified look in return. Then she sits in his chair, and he tells her to place her hands on his desk and feet on the floor until he tells her to move. Mr. Grey leaves, calls Peter to tell him where he can find Lee, and then watches secretly as Peter tries to force her home, only to see her knock Peter down and return to the chair.

In a bizarre, nonsensical turn, the media cover her marathon sit-in for love. This is the least successful aspect of the film since it is not clear why the world at large should care about Lee's fixation to win Mr. Grey. Moreover, this turn takes an essentially tight, two-person story and gives it a broader scope than it can accommodate effectively. Lee's father supports her cause, which is probably meant to be a triumph since he has been battling for sobriety throughout the film. But since his subplot is not very compelling to begin with, her father's show of support means little.

Indeed, this last section feels like a prolonged way for Lee to prove her love and commitment to Mr. Grey. After reading her statement of devotion to him in the newspaper, Grey finally reacts, and when he comes like Prince Charming to carry her away, it is a sweet victory for her. He washes her, kisses her all over her body, and essentially pampers her. Their relationship is not simply about inflicting and receiving pain—it is about being attuned to each other's specific needs. At the end, they are living a happily married life, and, in the last scene, he drives off to work, while she watches him leave and then looks to the camera with an expression of sly satisfaction on her face. The movie suggests that, by being the submissive, Lee has also assumed a measure of control. Indeed, perhaps such traditional categories have little meaning in a complex relationship. Submission, after all, is a way for this woman to grow up, to escape her parents' dysfunctional household and find happiness with a man who understands her better than anyone.

In movies such as sex, lies, and videotape and Crash, James Spader has played sexually deviant yuppies, and he is a perfect fit for the tightly wound lawyer. But Mr. Grey's back story, including a pending divorce with an icy blonde and a lengthy roster of failed secretaries, is touched on only briefly, and overall he is not nearly as well developed a character as Lee.

Maggie Gyllenhaal, in one of the most complex, surprising performances of the year, is fearless, playing Lee not as a sexually twisted woman turned on by pain but as a woman-child looking to grow up and needing to channel her masochistic desires into some kind of healthy relationship. She starts out very girlish, scared, and unsure of herself, but she gradually develops into a driven, confident woman who knows exactly what she wants and will do anything to get it. She even grows more beautiful as the story progresses.

For all its flirtation with the dark side, Secretary is a cheerful treat, maintaining a light, humorous touch while gently challenging our preconceptions of what constitutes true love, an idea that may be more radical than the spankings Lee enjoys so much. The story may offend certain audiences, particularly those feminists who cannot imagine a woman finding her self-worth and a husband by submitting to domination, but Gyllenhaal's persuasive performance makes this politically incorrect proposition not only believable but also something to root for. 🎬

—*Peter N. Chumo II*

CREDITS

E. Edward Grey: James Spader
Lee Holloway: Maggie Gyllenhaal
Joan Holloway: Lesley Ann Warren
Peter: Jeremy Davies

Dr. Twardon: Patrick Bauchau
Burt Holloway: Stephen McHattie
Jonathan: Oz (Osgood) Perkins II
Tricia O'Connor: Jessica Tuck
Lee's sister: Amy Locane
Stewart: Michael Mantell

Origin: USA
Released: 2002
Production: Amy Hobby, Steven Shainberg, Andrew Fierberg; Double A Films, TwoPoundBag; released by Lion's Gate Films
Directed by: Steven Shainberg
Written by: Erin Cressida Wilson
Cinematography by: Steven Fierberg
Music by: Angelo Badalamenti
Sound: Thomas Gregory Varga
Music Supervisor: Beth Amy Rosenblatt
Editing: Pam Wise
Art Direction: Nick Ralbovsky
Costumes: Marjorie Bowers
Production Design: Amy Danger
MPAA rating: R
Running time: 104 minutes

 REVIEWS

Boxoffice. April, 2002, p. 174.
Boxoffice. August, 2002, p. 22.
Chicago Sun-Times Online. September 27, 2002.
Entertainment Weekly. September 27, 2002, p. 57.
Los Angeles Times Online. September 20, 2002.
New York Times Online. September 20, 2002.
USA Today Online. September 20, 2002.
Variety. February 4, 2002, p. 36.
Washington Post. October 11, 2002, p. WE48.

QUOTES

E. Edward Grey (James Spader): "Look, we can't do this 24 hours a day, seven days a week." Lee (Maggie Gyllenhaal): "Why not?"

AWARDS AND NOMINATIONS

Nomination:
Golden Globes 2003: Actress—Mus./Comedy (Gyllenhaal)
Ind. Spirit 2003: Actress (Gyllenhaal), Film.

Serving Sara

The one thing that could bring them together is revenge.
—Movie tagline

 Box Office: $16.8 million

Reviewers seemed shell-shocked after seeing *Serving Sara.* Not content to just share the news that they did not find the film to be a pleasant movie-watching experience, they broke out their thesauri in search of new words that would be adequate to describe the full breadth of their hatred for the film. The scene that was most often cited by reviewers who wanted to show the sheer loathsomeness of the film was one in which a character has to put his (gloved, thankfully) arm up the rectum of a impotent bull. More than one reviewer noted that the gag, while being gross and not funny, also had the problem of being a patent rip-off of a similarly unsuccessful gag in the failed Farrelly brothers film, *Say It Isn't So.*

The spate of horrible reviews was just another problem in the unhappy life of *Serving Sara.* Before becoming known as one of the worst movies of the year, its previous claim to fame was being the film that Matthew Perry (Chandler Bing on TV's *Friends*) had to leave to attend rehab. The ravages that Perry must have been experiencing during the filming aren't readily apparent, but his performance does lack a certain zest. In his regular TV gig, Perry has shown himself to be a quick, witty performer. In his other movies, like *Three to Tango,* Perry's characters have never been nearly as interesting as Chandler, and here it's the same. There are a lot more, and better jokes, in 10 minutes of *Friends* than there are in this whole film. Like his fellow male cast members, Perry can't seem to find a good movie role. (Don't worry too much about their bad movie careers, they'll probably be able to suffer through on the $1 million per episode they makes from their day jobs.)

Perry is Joe, a process server who works for Ray (Cedric the Entertainer). (There is some undeveloped backstory about Joe once being an attorney who becomes fed up with the lack of ethics, but it's never explained why he goes from that to being a poorly paid process server in a sleazy office. Is there no middle ground?) Ray likes to keep a rivalry going between Joe and Tony (Vincent Pastore). Ray gives Joe a plum assignment: serving divorce papers to Sara (Elizabeth Hurley). Her husband, rich Texan rancher Gordon (Bruce Campbell), is cheating on her and wants to divorce her to keep her from getting his money.

Sara and Joe figure out that if they serve Gordon first, then Sara stands to make a lot more money in the divorce. Sara gets Joe to agree that he will serve Gordon instead of her and, if successful, she will give him a million dollars. (The fact that Joe plans to use his million dollars to buy a vineyard—where is it that vineyards cost only a million dollars?—is but one of the plot problems in the film. We don't even need to go into the fact that there's an airport so unsecure that passengers can freely go into the luggage areas or that Sara and Joe find each other on a cross-country bus even though a rich woman like Sara would hardly be taking a Greyhound.)

Their quest is complicated by the problem that while Sara and Joe are trying to serve Gordon, Tony is trying to serve Sara first. Also, Gordon has been tipped off to Sara's scheme and is trying to hide from them. Gordon has also sent one of his mean security guards after the duo.

But all of this is setup for the not-so witty banter and comedy set pieces. The most interesting thing, for example, about the aforementioned hand-up-the-bull's-nether-regions scene is that it was filmed on a ranch owned by Ross Perot. There is a recurring joke that while the boss Ray is a yelling, type A kind of guy, he tries (unsuccessfully) to relax by doing things like raking his desktop Zen garden. Maybe that seemed funny on paper, but Cedric's ham-fisted overacting doesn't help the joke along at all. Furthering the trend of almost-jokes, Joe adopts several accents in the film for no apparent reason. For example, when he and Sara pose as a married couple at Gordon's health club, Joe speaks in a British accent. Could he not just be an American married to the English Sara?

Director Reginald Hudlin (*The Ladies Man* and *Boomerang*) and writers Jay Scherick and David Ronn from *Spin City* don't seem to be able to master witty dialogue, though they certainly do try. The dumbest bantering is between Joe and Tony. "Kiss my ass," says Tony. "My mouth's not big enough," counters Joe. You might want to save that one to use next time a fifth grader taunts you. Other sample dialogue: "Eat me." "Eat you? I've never been so hungry in my life." Or this: "You must have grown up in a house with a lot of lead paint." But the bad banter isn't limited to those two characters. "I need a favor," says Joe to his policeman buddy played by Jerry Stiller. "And I need a smaller prostate," says Stiller, an actor whose every role contains a line of dialogue mentioning prostates.

The banter also isn't so hot between Joe and Sara. When he puts his big moves on her, he says, "If Gordon can't tell how beautiful, sexy and wonderful you are, then he's an idiot." Many reviewers commented upon the lack of chemistry they saw been Hurley and Perry. Stephanie Zacharek of *Salon* wrote, "Their scenes together feel so stiffly scripted and awkward that when they finally kiss, you can't believe their lips fit together right." Rob Blackwelder of *Spliced Wire* also focused on that kiss: "Perry and Hurley

have so little chemistry together that when they first kiss . . . they each look as if they're trying not to use their lips while sucking on a lemon."

As noted, reviewers weren't exactly yukking it up over *Serving Sara*. Blackwelder wrote, "Seeing several hundred movies a year as I do, every once in a while I'll come across one so insufferably inept from beginning to end that it's actually hard to review, simply because I don't know where to begin." Stephen Holden of the *New York Times* wrote, "Mr. Perry and Ms. Hurley have so little chemistry that they barely seem to notice each other even when they're half-heartedly sparring." And Manohla Dargis of the *Los Angeles Times* wrote, "The crushingly unfunny new comedy *Serving Sara* raises the question: Can you kill something that's already dead?" Dargis called the film "one of the more cynical and insulting Hollywood offerings in recent memory" and said that the director and writers "show either guts or foolishness in keeping their names on this odoriferous mess."

—*Jill Hamilton*

CREDITS

Joe Tyler: Matthew Perry
Sara Moore: Elizabeth Hurley
Gordon Moore: Bruce Campbell
Tony: Vincent Pastore
Ray Harris: Cedric the Entertainer
Kate: Amy Adams
Vernon: Terry Crews
Milton the cop: Jerry Stiller
Fat Charlie: Joe (Johnny) Viterelli

Origin: USA
Released: 2002
Production: Dan Halstead; Mandalay Pictures; released by Paramount Pictures
Directed by: Reginald (Reggie) Hudlin
Written by: Jay Scherick, David Ronn
Cinematography by: Robert Brinkmann
Music by: Marcus Miller
Sound: Stacy Brownrigg
Music Supervisor: Mathew Walden, Byron Phillips
Editing: Jim Miller
Art Direction: J. Grey Smith, Drew Broughton
Costumes: Francine Jamison-Tanchuck
Production Design: Rusty Smith
MPAA rating: PG-13
Running time: 99 minutes

REVIEWS

Los Angeles Times Online. August 23, 2002.
New York Times Online. August 23, 2002.
People. September 2, 2002, p. 31.
USA Today Online. August 23, 2002.
Variety Online. August 23, 2002.
Washington Post. August 23, 2002, p. WE45.

TRIVIA

Director Reginald Hudlin has a cameo as a airport baggage handler.

Sex and Lucia (Lucia y el Sexo)

Box Office: $1.5 million

It's hard to believe that Spain was once a conservative country ruled by the Catholic church and the Franco regime. Today Spanish cinema could compete with French cinema with its borderline porn. Julio Medem (*Lovers of the Arctic Circle*) asks his actors to bare all in his release, *Sex and Lucia* and his erotic film runs the gamut from poetic sex between two lovers that have just found each other to raunchy loveless sex. It seems that after 40 or so years of sexual repression, the Spanish are making up for lost time at least in the bedroom if not on the big screen. In time, this eroticism will shock fewer viewers and please more. After all, we were all born naked and sex is a natural human impulse.

The Seattle International Film Festival featured Medem with its Emerging Masters series (2002) in which they honored the honored the director by screening *Sex and Lucia* along with *The Red Squirrel.* And judging from Medem's filmography, the director's work proves versatile and provocative, two important traits found in art film directors. *Sex and Lucia* falls into the art film category since the director writes in an unusual structure that allows viewers to fall through a looking glass and where fantasy collides with reality in a disorienting fashion. Medem's film tugs at heartstrings, works the libido, and acts as a mind bender. Although Medem's work is original it can be compared to Jean-Jacques Beineix's films with its complex characters, unusual plot, and unabashed sexuality. Imagine *Betty Blue*

with a strong woman lead and you come close to describing *Sex and Lucia.*

Two strangers engage in underwater sex off a Spanish island. A full moon shines down on their bodies as they perform under water. The strangers refuse to exchange names, but the man Lorenzo (Tristan Ulloa) tells the woman that it is his birthday. Cut to Lorenzo's apartment where we see him writing a novel on his computer. Later, Lorenzo and his best buddy meet at a café where Lorenzo is approached by Lucia (Paz Vega), a beautiful waitress who makes a confession to him. She brazenly confides that she knows where Lorenzo lives because she has been following him. She tells Lorenzo that she loves him and would like to move in with him. Deeply touched and turned on by Lucia's confession, Lorenzo engages in steamy sex with her.

Medem shows us the couple's erotic desires and love for one another in a sequence that involves the couple taking Polaroids of each other's body parts while engaging in sex. Later, at a café, Lucia shows the photographs to Lorenzo and their bodies tremble with anticipation. Lorenzo dares Lucia to strip while seated at the café. She does, then back at the apartment, Lorenzo and Lucia take turns performing a strip tease act that is both playful and titillating. However, the sex doesn't last forever and soon Lorenzo is back to work on his novel, while Lucia waits tables at a posh restaurant. As Lorenzo writes about a fictitious couple, Lucia reads Lorenzo's saga while Lorenzo sleeps. But Lucia fails to realize that the couple in the novel is based on Lorenzo's real life experiences involving the woman he had sex with on his birthday.

Lorenzo begins to suffer from depression and exhaustion as he tries to live a double life. Only he can no longer decipher between fiction and reality. Lucia becomes fed up with Lorenzo's depression and decides to storm out of his life. However, later that night, she receives a phone call from the police in regards to Lorenzo. Thinking the worse, Lucia leaves her life and returns to the island to seek solace, but instead is thrown into the same world that appears in Lorenzo's novel. Soon all the pieces of the puzzle come together in an unforgettable climatic moment.

Paz Vega, who resembles Caroline Bouquet in *Lucie Aubrac* with her cat-like gaze, delivers a steely yet vulnerable performance as a waitress caught up in her lover's fantasies. Tristan Ulloa (*Open Your Eyes*) blends stoicism with bemusement as he tries to make sense of his double reality and Najwa Nimri's Elena exudes loneliness and sex appeal while she hides a secret from her past. *Sex and Lucia* will most likely be remembered for its bold eroticism as the suspenseful story fades from viewers' minds. 🎬

—Patty-Lynne Herlevi

Lucia: Paz Vega
Lorenzo: Tristan Ulloa
Elena: Najwa Nimri
Carlos/Antonio: Daniel Freire
Belen: Elena Anaya
Luna: Silvia Llanos
Pepe: Javier Camara

Origin: Spain
Language: Spanish
Released: 2001
Production: Fernando Bovaira, Enrique Lopez Lavigne; Sogecine, Alicia Produce; released by Palm Pictures
Directed by: Julio Medem
Written by: Julio Medem
Cinematography by: Kiko de la Rica
Music by: Alberto Iglesias
Sound: Agustin Peinado
Editing: Ivan Aledo
Art Direction: Montse Sanz
MPAA rating: Unrated
Running time: 128 minutes

Boxoffice. April, 2002, p. 186.
Chicago Sun-Times Online. July 26, 2002.
Entertainment Weekly. July 19, 2002, p. 48.
Los Angeles Times Online. July 12, 2002.
New York Times Online. July 12, 2002.
Sight and Sound. May, 2002, p. 52.
Variety. September 10, 2001, p. 61.
Washington Post. July 26, 2002, p. WE39.

Showtime

Lights. Camera. Aggravation.
—Movie tagline

Box Office: $37.9 million

A t the end of *Showtime,* there's a series of bloopers. Even compared to usual bloopers, they're not that good—Robert De Niro flubs a few lines, Eddie Murphy laughs during a scene—Dick Clark has hosted shows containing bloopers that are funnier than these. That the bloopers are tacked on to the end of the film anyway says a lot about *Showtime.* The bloopers aren't there because the director got this great new idea to show flubs at the end of the movie. No, like most of *Showtime,* it's an idea ripped off from earlier films. The goof-ups aren't there because they were too hilarious not to pass on to the audience. They're there for the sole reason that they should be. It's become a cliché to show bloopers at the end of a film, so of course this movie has to do it, too. And, despite the fact that this film purports to skewer movie clichés, it's not done in an ironic way.

The problem with *Showtime* is that it tries to make fun of buddy cop action movies, but ends up being one itself. It's strange because the film's writers seem to be aware of what the usual clichés are. Writer Keith Sharon, who's a news reporter for a Southern California newspaper, wrote the film with the team of Alfred Gough and Miles Millar, who created the TV show *Smallville* and wrote the Jackie Chan/Owen Wilson vehicle *Shanghai Noon.* In the opening scenes, we see that they know their action movie clichés. Detective Mitch Preston (De Niro) is speaking about his job and saying how it's quite unlike police work as seen on TV. "I never jump from one rooftop to another," he says gruffly. "I've never had to choose between the red wire and the green wire. I've never seen a car roll over causing a chain reaction of cars to burst into flames." The joke is furthered when the camera pulls back and we see that Mitch is giving his speech to a group of elementary school age kids. "Don't you have any fun days at the police force?" asks the nervous teacher.

The scene is one of the funniest in the film, which means that after the first few minutes you may as well go home because it never again will reach that peak. Anyone who did leave at that point would also be spared seeing how *Showtime* starts wallowing in the same action movie clichés. As a matter of fact, there is a scene where a car rolls over and causes a chain reaction of cars to burst into flames. Just because a film makes fun of a cliché, doesn't negate that it's lame of the film makers to use the same cliché.

One of the biggest clichés that the movie embraces is the mismatched cops being forced to work together as a team. Mitch is a serious, by the book kind of guy who is trying to get over a divorce. Despite a poorly executed try at making pottery, he has nothing going on in his life besides police work. Trey Sellers (Murphy) is a police officer who is just doing his job until he can get a big break at his real passion—acting. He doesn't seem to be deterred by the fact that he is a bad actor whose only jobs have been in "semi-independent" films or one liners in straight-to-video soft porn He's taken his detective exam but failed it two times. The two first meet when Trey accidentally ruins an important undercover drug bust that Mitch is working on. (It's the same kind of serious-guy-teamed-with-screw-up relationship that caused Sgt. Carter on *Gomer Pyle* to yell "Go-MER!" week after week.) Mitch, who's—of course—a live wire cop, is so angry that he shoots out the lens of a TV person's camera.

Chase Renzi (Rene Russo), who is a new producer, sees the footage and gets the idea for a reality show that would focus on the hard-boiled Mitch. Mitch wants nothing to do with it, but is forced to cooperate after Chase's network threatens to sue the Los Angeles Police Department over the camera shooting incident. When Trey hears about the show, he knows that it's his dream gig. He stages a fake purse snatching in front of Chase so that he can showcase his acting talent. Chase loves it and, when she finds out how much Mitch hates Trey, knows that she has found her team.

The joke of the film is that Trey, who is not a great cop, knows how to work the camera, and thus comes across well on the show, while Mitch, who actually knows what he is doing, is a blah figure on camera. The writers also try to highlight some of the ridiculousness of reality TV, but they're not exactly tackling fresh subject matter. It's mildly amusing to see how the driven Chase tries to format reality to make it more TV-friendly. When she sees the police station, she declares it drab and sets off to bring in high-tech ultramodern offices for her police team. She also overhauls Mitch's boring apartment and fills it with state-of-the-art modern design because her "research" shows that cops live in unique environments. She buys Mitch a dog to make him seem more likable and gives the guys a sports car and a Hummer to make them seem more interesting. (Credit to the movie that driving a gas-guzzling Hummer is seen as being pretentious and dorky.) William Shatner is on hand, playing himself, as the director of the show. The joke of this is that Shatner, who is somewhat well known for being a bad actor himself, is in charge of handing out acting advice to Chase and Trey.

Along the way the two policemen get involved with a case that's just like one that would be in a movie. They have to get a bad guy (Pedro Damian) who's been shooting things up with a giant gun that no one's ever seen before. Solving the case will require numerous chases, shoot-outs and someone falling out of a building. At some point in there, *Showtime* has ceased to become a parody of action movies and becomes an action movie itself.

The best part of the film is watching De Niro and Murphy play off each other De Niro is amusingly exasperated by Murphy's antics and Murphy is a high-energy ham. Trey is never unaware that the cameras are on him, so when Mitch gives him a speech about being there for each other on the job, Trey counters with a tearful speech of his own to make sure that he gets his fair share of screen time. De Niro is reduced to rolling his eyes countless times, but somehow he makes it seem fresh each time. The two are good at what they do, but that's part of the problem. They've done this stuff so many times before that they're just treading familiar ground. Murphy in particular seems to be channeling a character that he would have played in the 1980s.

Most critics didn't think that the film worked. It should be a warning to filmgoers that ads for the film contained blurbs from such non-renowned media sources as EntertainmentStudios.com and KATU-TV. Not that everyone hated it. Kevin Thomas at the *Los Angeles Times* liked the film quite a bit, writing that De Niro and Murphy "hooked up with exactly the right people to give a fresh and funny satirical twist to an old formula." Steven Rea of the *Philadelphia Inquirer* called it "a flat-out attempt to launch a new *Lethal Weapon*-like franchise." A.O. Scott of the *New York Times* wrote, "A small fortune in salaries and stunt cars might have been saved if the director, Tom Dey, had spliced together bits and pieces of *Midnight Run* and *48 Hours* (and, for that matter, *Shrek*)." Roger Ebert of the *Chicago Sun-Times* noted director Dey's illustrious background, including stints at Brown University, the American Film Institute and the Centre des Etudes Critiques in Paris. "He probably knows what's wrong with this movie more than I do," wrote Ebert. And Owen Gleiberman of *Entertainment Weekly* gave the film a D, calling it "a lead-balloon caper."

—*Jill Hamilton*

CREDITS

Mitch Preston: Robert De Niro
Trey Sellars: Eddie Murphy
Chase Renzi: Rene Russo
Captain Winship: Frankie Faison
Lazy Boy: Dante "Mos Def" Beze
Himself: William Shatner
Vargas: Pedro Damian
Ray: Nestor Serrano
Annie: Drena De Niro
Kyle: Kadeem Hardison
ReRun: TJ Cross
Julio: Judah Friedlander

Origin: USA
Released: 2002
Production: Jorge Saralegui, Jane Rosenthal; Village Roadshow Pictures, NPV Entertainment, Tribeca Productions; released by Warner Bros.
Directed by: Tom Dey
Written by: Alfred Gough, Keith Sharon, Miles Millard
Cinematography by: Thomas Kloss
Music by: Alan Silvestri
Sound: J. Paul Huntsman, Christopher Aud
Music Supervisor: Michael McQuarn, Joel Sill
Editing: Billy Weber
Art Direction: Geoff Hubbard
Costumes: Christopher Lawrence
Production Design: Jeff Mann

MPAA rating: PG-13
Running time: 95 minutes

Chicago Sun-Times Online. March 15, 2002.
Entertainment Weekly. March 22, 2002, p. 77.
Los Angeles Times Online. March 15, 2002.
New York Times Online. March 15, 2002.
Rolling Stone. April 11, 2002, p. 138.
USA Today Online. March 15, 2002.
Vanity Fair. March, 2002, p. 112.
Variety. March, 18, 2002, p. 24.
Washington Post. March 15, 2002, p. WE41.

QUOTES

Trey (Eddie Murphy): "Got any tips for me?" Mitch (Robert De Niro): "Stay out of my way and I won't shoot you."

Signs

It's Happening.
—Movie tagline
Don't see it alone.
—Movie tagline
The first sign you can't explain. The second sign you can't ignore. The third sign you won't believe.
—Movie tagline

 Box Office: $227.6 million

Six months ago Father Graham Hess (Mel Gibson) dropped out of his church. It seemed like a drastic move, and it was. But it also had a drastic cause; his beloved wife (Patricia Kalember) was killed in a freak accident and it shook Graham's faith to the foundation. Since then he has been living quietly on his Bucks County, Pennsylvania farm with his two children 10-year-old Morgan (Rory Culkin) and 5-year-old Bo (Abigail Breslin) and his younger brother Merrill (Joaquin Phoenix).

But it would seem his faith is to be tested even more, for one morning he wakes up and finds crop circles tamped down in his corn fields. Like any of us, at first Graham assumes this is an elaborate hoax and calls in his friend, Officer Caroline Paski (Cherry Jones). While investigating the circles, Officer Paski comments about how the animals in the area are acting very strangely, and as if on cue one of Graham's dogs attacks Bo but falls on Morgan who skewers the German Shepherd with a BBQ fork. Could things get any stranger?

Sure, after all, this is an M. Night Shyamalan movie. Next thing one knows there are reports of crop circles appearing all over the globe and coverage of the eerie goings on are covered 24-7 on the all-crop-circles, all-the-time television programming.

Meanwhile, Morgan, the ever-so-serious young man with an asthma problem, has been doing his research and has decided it is aliens who are here either as explorers or aggressors and the crop circles are their mapping guides. In an attempt to listen in on their communications, he uses Bo's old baby monitor and to everyone's surprise he sometimes connects to an odd assortment of hums, buzzes, pops and hisses.

Now as anyone who has experienced it will tell you, cornfields on a breezy night are intrinsically scary. The corn stalks talk to each other in the wind, and the talk sounds very conspiratorial. And, just as we tell ourselves that it is just our imagination, Graham, who undoubtedly is under a lot of stress, has to be wondering if it was just his imagination, too, when he saw a skinny, green, reptilian leg disappear between the corn stalks. Taking no chances, Graham decides to stifle everyone's imaginations and turns off all televisions and radios.

This, essentially, is also what Graham, the ex-Episcopal minister, has done with God: turned Him off. Within the Hess house, though, there are many "hidden" religious references. There are the patterns in the kitchen wallpaper and drapes, and the "cross and bible" style doors. Graham may have lost his faith (on one wall is the dust and dirt outline that is all that remains of a cross that once hung there) but he is surrounded by it. This is not a coincidence.

And that is a theme for *Signs*: there are no coincidences. At one point Graham tells his brother that there are two kinds of people in the world. The kind who believe everything happens for a reason. That we are not alone and that we are all a part of a cosmic master plan. These are the people who see signs of God and His plan everywhere. These are the people with hope. This is the kind of man Father Graham used to be. The other kind of person, however, believes that there is no plan. That everything is nothing more than a random occurrence. This is the kind of man he has become since his wife's senseless death. "There's no one watching out for us," Graham says. "We're on our own."

In the world of M. Night Shyamalan, however, there are no coincidences. Nothing in this film—no detail is too small—is an accident. From his wife's last words to Morgan's asthma to Merrill's home run records to Bo's habit of never finishing a glass of water, they all have a purpose that will eventually be made as clear as St. Aquinas' teleological argument.

Writer/producer/director M. Night Shyamalan, however, takes his time to make his argument. (And one does have to wonder if aliens invading the Earth isn't an over-the-top cosmic plan just to get one man's faith back!) The 31-year-old auteur of the mega-hit *The Sixth Sense* is certainly developing a very distinctive style to his psychological thrillers. Restrained, calculated, suspenseful, atmospheric and beautifully filmed, his films also have a heart which is communicated through the story's layered meanings, excavated emotions, and a general sense of universal humanity. His main characters are everymen with whom we can easily identify, perhaps outwardly confident but inwardly being nibbled or completely consumed by personal demons. Shyamalan has been compared to Orson Welles, Steven Spielberg, and most often to the classic filmmaker, Alfred Hitchcock, but in reality he can stand quite well on his own merits.

Shyamalan likes to prey on our imaginations, to mesmerize us by NOT showing us things, to obsesses us with what we THINK we're hearing. And in the end, all that supernatural stuff is nothing more than a metaphor for our lives. All these occult happenings are nothing more than Hitchcockian McGuffins that are actually Rorschach tests for our humanity. *Signs'* crop circles aren't just a sign of a potential alien invasion, they are a sign that Graham must face the demons in his own soul as well as those that might be lurking in his corn fields.

As played by Mel Gibson, Graham is a strong yet vulnerable character. He is a man who is emotionally shut down but is at the same time emotionally committed to his motherless children. These contradictory qualities are convincingly portrayed by Gibson who also easily conveys Shyamalan's "everyman" quality with which audiences can identify and therefore increasing their personal anxiety as the story develops.

There are other strong performances in *Signs,* from the assured Morgan of Rory Culkin to the innocent Bo of newcomer Abigail Breslin. Even Joaquin Phoenix, who may be best known for his Oscar-nominated role as Emperor Commodus in *Gladiator,* turns in an self-possessed performance as the slightly lost younger brother who holds both the minor league home run record, and the minor league strike out record. It's an intense character who, thankfully, isn't over the edge. Whose sincerity can be nicely summed up by his defense of his batting records by saying, "It just felt wrong not to swing."

As an aside, one thing that might reinforce Shyamalan's connection to Hitchcock is that just like the master of suspense who went before him, Shyamalan also plays small roles in his films. In *Signs* it's much more substantial than just a Hitchcockian cameo, and is in fact quite a pivotal role.

He plays Ray Reddy, the man whose driving cost Graham his wife's life.

The strong performances of *Signs* is just one of the elements that make it a good movie. While the plot may sometimes leaves us scratching our heads at a few points, it is undoubtedly a masterful piece of filmmaking. With artful cinematography, solid editing and relying heavily on the "less is more" school of storytelling, *Signs* is beautifully made.

Some may be disappointed that this latest outing from M. Night Shyamalan doesn't have the surprise ending of *The Sixth Sense* or the twist of *Unbreakable.* And some may feel that in fact there may be no real pay off to the crop circle element of the story. But this is a film that gleefully and effectively defies that convention, recognizing the McGuffin quality of what appears to be the primary story, and instead asks its audience to see the pay off of what appears to be the secondary story. For in reality, Shyamalan has been sending the audience signs all along that it was the true story.

—*Beverley Bare Buehrer*

CREDITS

Graham Hess: Mel Gibson
Merrill Hess: Joaquin Rafael (Leaf) Phoenix
Morgan Hess: Rory Culkin
Bo Hess: Abigail Breslin
Officer Caroline Paski: Cherry Jones
Colleen Hess: Patricia Kalember
Ray Reddy: M. Night Shyamalan

Origin: USA
Released: 2002
Production: Frank Marshall, Sam Mercer, M. Night Shyamalan; Touchstone Pictures, Blinding Edge Pictures; released by Buena Vista
Directed by: M. Night Shyamalan
Written by: M. Night Shyamalan
Cinematography by: Tak Fujimoto
Music by: James Newton Howard
Sound: Tod A. Maitland
Editing: Barbara Tulliver
Art Direction: Keith Cunningham
Costumes: Ann Roth
Production Design: Larry Fulton
MPAA rating: PG-13
Running time: 120 minutes

 ## REVIEWS

Chicago Sun-Times Online. August 2, 2002.

Chicago Tribune Online. August 2, 2002.
Entertainment Weekly. August 9, 2002, p. 43.
Los Angeles Times Online. August 2, 2002.
New York Times Online. August 2, 2002.
People. August 12, 2002, p. 37.
USA Today Online. August 2, 2002.
Variety Online. July 29, 2002.
Washington Post. August 2, 2002, p. WE28.

QUOTES

Bo (Abigail Breslin) to her father (Mel Gibson): "The monster is outside my room—can I have a drink of water?"

TRIVIA

Corn was planted and crop circles actually created at the Delaware Valley College in Bucks County.

Simone

A star is . . . created.
—Movie tagline

Box Office: $9.7 million

Simone is a bizarre and somewhat incoherent satire of Hollywood's star-making machine, a strange and not entirely original story about the creation of an artificial actress. It's an unforgiving role for Al Pacino, who's on camera for almost the entire picture as Viktor Taransky, an idealistic film director who finds himself increasingly unhappy about having to kowtow to pampered and pompous young stars.

Andrew Niccol, the New Zealander who directed and wrote the underappreciated *Gattaca* and was the screenwriter for *The Truman Show,* served as director, writer, and producer for *Simone.* As a sort of flipside to *The Truman Show,* which focused on how "reality" television might create an artificial life for a real person, *Simone* is about how an artificial person becomes "real" through achieving fame.

With cinematographer Edward Lachman, Niccol mounts this film on a Felliniesque canvas, confining almost all the action to a studio lot, a sound stage, and Taransky's beach house. Some of the scenes of real characters in the studio are photographed against a backdrop of movie scenery. The overall impression conveyed is that Taransky and the others are living an enclosed, highly artificial existence in the rarefied, claustrophobic world of Hollywood. In fact, Taransky's family life is completely enmeshed with his job. His ex-wife, Elaine Christian (Catherine Keener), is the studio boss, and their teenage daughter, Lainey (Evan Rachel Wood), hangs around the lot, doing her homework and feeling perfectly at home in her divorced parents' workplace.

As *Simone* opens, Taransky is having a hard time appeasing the ridiculous demands of his lead actress, supermodel Nicola Anders (Winona Ryder), who insists that her trailer be the biggest on the lot and that no red licorice be among her candies. She eventually walks off the set, leaving Taransky with a nearly complete film that he cannot finish. This quandary prompts a showdown with Elaine, who says she has been keeping him on board only for sentimental reasons, and pointing out that he hasn't had a hit movie in years. She fires him right after he gives a speech about how much power directors have lost and she reminds him that he's talking about "good old days" that existed long before his time, if then. In fact, as long as there have been movies, directors have complained about the difficulty of dealing with their star actors, so Taransky's complaint is hardly original.

Luckily, along comes a fan of Taransky named Hank (Elias Koteas), who is dying of an eye tumor supposedly caused by doing nothing but sitting in front of a computer for the last decade. There, he has been creating a program that can simulate a movie actress, and though Taransky initially spurns him, the executor of Hank's estate gives him the program, carrying out Hank's final request. Taransky professes to be incompetent with computers, but it doesn't take him long to learn how to master Simulation One, Hank's program that creates an actress by mixing and matching images, gestures, and attributes of all the great actresses who ever lived. Simone, naturally, is short for Simulation One.

Though he is fired, and though the studio execs have told him he can't finish the movie with a replacement actress without a lawsuit from Nicola Anders, Taransky continues to work on a heavily guarded sound stage, using the computer program to create his new masterwork and subbing Simone for Nicola. Niccol glides by the discrepancies—if Taransky is fired, how is he still working at the studio? And what happens to the threat of legal action? As the movie grows more and more preposterous, such questions of logic seem increasingly irrelevant. The movie is supposed to be a spoof, so it's not supposed to make sense, but is it too much to ask that it at least have some internal logical consistency?

Of course, Taransky's film is an immediate success, thanks to Simone, who is a perfectly appealing star— blonde, gorgeous, with puffy, glistening lips (she is played by newcomer Rachel Roberts). Simone becomes an overnight sensation, and Taransky decides he will make another film with her before he reveals that she is not a real woman but a computer program. The next film, titled "Eternity Forever," is also a hit, and it seems Taransky has triumphed. He has found a way to mold his star completely to his whims, and to make his artsy movies that explore deep universal human questions into boxoffice bonanzas.

But of course, it's not that simple. Simone's fame far eclipses Taransky's, and he finds he has created a modern-day monster. Taransky's energies are expended playing an elaborate game of trying to maintain a public persona for Simone—she even does a few talk shows from remote locations, with Taransky supplying her responses, and eventually she gives a worldwide concert as a hologram (though the concern appears to consist of one song, which is, of course, Aretha Franklin's "A Natural Woman"). The other part of the game is hiding the fact that Simone does not exist.

Long stretches of the middle of the movie try to convince us that Taransky can actually manipulate a major star who does not have a physical presence. Simone is a recluse, he tells the press, she is agoraphobic, she is a computer geek, she has no desire for fame, she lives only to work. Instead of being caught in logical inconsistencies, Taransky floats along unscathed, and he eventually even starts to convey the impression that he and Simone are lovers.

Though its observations on the fame machine are often trenchant, Simone stumbles along from one ridiculous situation to another, including an elaborate ploy where Taransky pretends to spend the night in a hotel room with his star. Then it succumbs to the temptation of a plot twist where Keener falls back in love with her once-again-potent director-husband. Lurching from one idea to the next, it becomes a family drama, then a crime drama, and all its energy oozes away in these machinations.

And Simone doesn't have all that much energy to begin with. It's a cool, even cold movie, and nothing Pacino can do is able to fire up the plot. Taransky is not one of his most endearing roles. Pacino tries to milk some laughs, sending up a haggard, megalomaniacal director who never seems quite on top of the situation, but it's hard working up much sympathy for his character. Throughout the film, Pacino seems as tired and strung-out as his character in Insomnia, (reviewed in this edition) who is supposed to be that way.

For a film about the possibilities of computer simulation, Simone is markedly disinterested in the technology of its fantasy. The keyboard is equipped with buttons marked with words like "MIMIC," even though what Hank left Taransky was only a disc. Taransky instantly turns from a computer-phobe to a geek, and the niceties of points like the holographic concert and how exactly Simone is inserted into live movie scenes is left unexplained. This is a fantasy, after all, but it is not really fantastic enough. Niccol doesn't have the imagination to follow the satire to its most outrageous conclusions. He comes closest in the scenes in which

Taransky tries to disgrace Simone. She directs her own disgusting film called "I Am Pig" and speaks out for arming elementary school children and smoking cigarettes, but her popularity only increases.

Keener, always a remarkable actress, is badly miscast. Her performance lacks the weight necessary to give credence to her character's power as a businesswoman. She bobs her head and speaks her lines in a sing-song manner like a flighty princess, not a studio executive. Minor characters, such as Jay Mohr's actor and a couple of journalists on the trail of Simone, are underdeveloped and inconsequential. Some of the movie is wasted on Hollywood in-jokes.

Most importantly, the target of Simone—the celebrity culture and the Hollywood fame machine—is too easy. Lampooning these things is like shooting fish in a barrel, and it's been done better many times. Unlike films like The Player or even Adaptation (reviewed in this edition), Niccol's fantasy doesn't get to the guts of the problems with the movie industry itself, the deeper perversions caused by its business side dictating to the artistic side. Indeed, Taransky himself is a caricature of an artsy director, and his films with Simone look like Ingmar Bergman has mated with Fellini to produce a hideous existentialist-romantic love child. The antics provide some easy laughs, but nobody needs to take Simone as the serious indictment of Hollywood it aspires to be. Nobody needs to take it seriously at all.

—*Michael Betzold*

CREDITS

Viktor Taransky: Al Pacino
Elaine Christian: Catherine Keener
Hal Sinclair: Jay Mohr
Milton: Jason Schwartzman
Max Sayer: Pruitt Taylor Vince
Frank Brand: Stanley Anderson
Lainey Christian: Evan Rachel Wood
Chief Detective: Daniel von Bargen
Simone: Rachel Roberts
Hank Aleno: Elias Koteas
Faith: Rebecca Romijn-Stamos
Nicola Anders: Winona Ryder (Cameo)

Origin: USA
Released: 2002
Production: Andrew Niccol; released by New Line Cinema
Directed by: Andrew Niccol
Written by: Andrew Niccol
Cinematography by: Edward Lachman
Music by: Carter Burwell
Sound: John Pritchett

Editing: Paul Rubell
Art Direction: Sarah Knowles
Costumes: Elisabetta Beraldo
Production Design: Jan Roelfs
MPAA rating: PG-13
Running time: 117 minutes

REVIEWS

Boxoffice. July, 2002, p. 24.
Chicago Sun-Times Online. August 23, 2002.
Los Angeles Times Online. August 23, 2002.
New York Times Online. May 12, 2002.
New York Times Online. August 23, 2002.
People. September 2, 2002, p. 31.
USA Today Online. August 18, 2002.
USA Today Online. August 22, 2002.
Variety Online. August 16, 2002.
Washington Post. August 23, 2002, p. WE44.

QUOTES

Viktor (Al Pacino): "You know, it's easier to fool a hundred thousand people than just one."

Skins

The Other American Heroes.
—Movie tagline

A new trend of First Nation cinema appears to be emerging in North America. Thanks to Robert Redford and the Sundance Institute, Seattle-based author-turned filmmaker Sherman Alexie and director Chris Eyre released *Smoke Signals* in 1998. Since that time, several First Nation or Native American films have been released with varying degrees of success. Most remarkable though has been the array of Native acting, musical and cinematic talent appearing in the films. And Native Americans could finally portray themselves in films that reflect their culture to the rest of the world. Finally, after many years of oppressed silence, the red man speaks to a captivated audience and perhaps wounds of this nation can finally come to the surface to be healed. At least that seems to be the case with Sherman Alexie's *The Business of Fancy Dancing* and Chris Eyre's 2002 release, *Skins,* two films that deal with alcoholism and Native Americans.

We are informed of the history of the Sioux Indians who were massacred by General Custer and his brigade, then later locked on to the Pine Ridge Indian Reservation where alcoholism and poverty (the worse in the nation) complete their decimation. Mixed with documentary footage of life on the "rez,", writer Jennifer D. Lyne and Eyre blend real life with the fictional characters from Native American author Adrian C. Louis's novel.

Not only are viewers pulled into an intense drama revolving around a Sioux reservation cop, Rudy Yellow Lodge (Eric Schweig) and his alcoholic brother Mogie Yellow Lodge (Graham Greene), but we are given the hard facts about Indian life. Unemployment is up to 75% and death from alcoholism is at a rate nine times higher than the rest of the country on the Pine Ridge reservation. The filmmakers also address the issue of white people operating liquor stores near the reservation and making a huge profit in the process while leading to domestic violence, disease, depression and divorce among the Sioux Indians. That is why Rudy decides to become a vigilante and work his own brand of justice, only this leads to dire consequences.

Similar to Alexie's films, the filmmakers of *Skin* plop viewers in the middle of the reservation. We see the characters shop for groceries at a convenience store called "Ding Bats" and we see the men blowing their VA checks on alcohol while their bodies slowly rot along with their will to live. We see paranoid men beating their wives and we witness a murder of a young man because two hoodlums believe the man is gay. Viewers are not let off the hook as they are thrown into the most miserable of lives. Yet, a glimmer of hope surfaces in Mogie's son who, despite his father's alcoholism, might achieve success through his intelligence and athletic abilities. And we are also shown healing ceremonies practiced by the Sioux such as the sweat lodge ceremony and other rituals to rid of evil influences.

Skins isn't without humor. Mogie, the character played by Greene, with his deadpan expressions offers much comical relief even though he is a tragic figure. He always offers jokes during tense situations and even steals a football from Rudy in the middle of a football game when Rudy shows off. One might even call Mogie a trickster character similar to the trickster spider of Sioux folklore. And the spider itself becomes a minor character in the film that shows up when Rudy attacks the hoodlum killers and also when Rudy throws paint on George Washington's head on Mount Rushmore, certainly another patriotic insult to the First Nation people.

The question arises is First Nation cinema created for entertainment or as statements about societal injustice? Will films such as *Smoke Signals* and *Skins* bring old wounds to the surface to be healed and will the white man offer a long-awaited apology to Native Americans? Only time will tell.

—*Patty-Lynne Herlevi*

CREDITS

Rudy Yellow Lodge: Eric Schweig
Mogie: Graham Greene
Verdell Weasel Tail: Gary Farmer
Herbie: Noah Watts
Aunt Helen: Lois Red Elk
Stella: Michelle Thrush
Teen Mogie: Nathaniel Arcand
Teen Rudy: Chaske Spencer

Origin: USA
Released: 2002
Production: Jon Kilik; Grandview Pictures; released by First Look Pictures
Directed by: Chris Eyre
Written by: Jennifer D. Lyne
Cinematography by: Stephen Kazmierski
Music by: B.C. Smith
Sound: Thomas Gregory Varga
Editing: Paul Trejo
Art Direction: Gonzalo Cordoba
Costumes: Ronald Leamon
Production Design: Debbie DeVilla
MPAA rating: R
Running time: 90 minutes

REVIEWS

Boxoffice. April, 2002, p. 143.
Entertainment Weekly. October 11, 2002, p. 58.
New York Times Online. September 27, 2002.
San Francisco Chronicle Online. September 27, 2002.
USA Today Online. August 21, 2002.
Variety. January 28, 2002, p. 34.
Washington Post. September 27, 2002, p. C5.

TRIVIA

The film was shot on the Pine Ridge Indian Reservation where it is set.

AWARDS AND NOMINATIONS

Nomination:
Ind. Spirit 2003: Actor (Greene).

Slackers

Higher education just hit a new low.
—Movie tagline
When all else fails . . . cheat.
—Movie tagline

Box Office: $5.2 million

O n RottenTomatoes.com—a website that compiles movie reviews from newspapers, magazines and web sites—a mere 7% of critics thought that *Slackers* was "fresh," i.e. good. Movie critics are a notoriously, er, critical lot, but getting a 7% approval rating from them is especially bad.

By virtue of its almost identical title, *Slackers* was held up to the standard of the Richard Linklater film, *Slacker* (1991). A teen comedy coming out among the glut of other lowbrow teen comedies in 2002 had enough problems from the outset. The filmmakers certainly didn't need the extra problem of being unfavorably compared to one of the more acclaimed films of the last decade.

Actually, it's strange that the film, written by David H. Steinberg (*American Pie 2*), is even called *Slackers,* since every character in the film is notably torqued with energy. The "slackers" that the title seems to be referring to are a trio of friends, Dave (Devon Sawa), Sam (Jason Segel) and Jeff (Michael C. Maronna), who are college students getting set to graduate. Jeff is the cool handsome one who thinks that the way to win a woman's heart is to talk meanly to her, Sam is the strange techno geek who likes to break into people's computers and rail against "the man" and Dave is, well, the most normal one.

During their school years, the three have dedicated all of their energy to cheating their way through every class, paper and exam. At the outset of the film, the three are working on a typically complex scheme for cheating. It involves Dave attending a class he's not registered for to get a copy of the exam, Sam and Jeff rerouting a girls' track meet, Sam stealing a blue book and Jeff faking being hit by a delivery truck. It's a complex plan but sort of enjoyable to watch to see how all the pieces fit together.

All their cheating success is threatened, however, when the non-aptly named Cool Ethan (Jason Schwartzman) finds out about their scheme. Ethan blackmails the three. He will tell school authorities about them unless they agree to get the beautiful Angela (model-turned-actress James King) to like him. This is actually a nearly impossible feat since Ethan is a mighty bizarre fellow. Unlike in normal teen movies where Ethan would be a nice, yet too shy, guy with a sweet crush, here he is more like a stalker. In his dorm room, he has a shrine set up to Angela that includes photos of her, video that he's secretly taken of her and, his personal favorite, a doll he's shaped out of hair that he's collected from her chair. He worships at his shrine by intoning things like "We're going to get married. And have 23 kids."

Dave is recruited to be the one to interact with Angela and darned if he doesn't start falling for her himself. She volunteers at a hospital, serves food at a soup kitchen and, well, looks like model-turned-actress James King. Dave tries a little to get Angela to fall for Ethan, but Ethan screws up what chances he has. When he shows up at the hospital where Angela volunteers, he ends up getting caught fondling the bust of an elderly sexpot patient (1950s blonde bombshell Mamie Van Doren either being really game or just making a bad, bad career decision). The whole scene with the patient and Ethan is more creepy than funny and it makes the viewer feel kind of tainted by watching it. It's moments like that that turned critics off en masse.

The questions of the film are: Will the guys graduate? Will Dave get Angela? Will (God forbid) Ethan get Angela? Will Angela ditch the whole lot of them and find someone decent? The movie answers these questions, but they're not the point of the movie, the journey through the plot is.

Although the film was spectacularly unsuccessful with the critics, there are a lot of hints in the film that Steinberg and director Dewey Nicks (a former—and after this, possibly permanent—director of commercials) were going for something a little less ordinary. The film has an interesting off-kilter feel to it. Although there are the obligatory gross-out sex jokes, there are some jokes that are odd, and thus interesting. Director Nicks is especially good with dream sequences. For example, when the three friends talk about how they'll celebrate passing an exam, they decide that they'll do "the usual." The film then launches into a weird montage showing the guys doing unlikely things like riding a three-seated bike together, dressing up like superheroes and tying each other up in a bondage scene. In another montage, Dave imagines Ethan actually being cool and getting a bunch of women. We see Ethan kissing various women including Angela, Cameron Diaz and an older woman. "Hey, that's my mom!" yells out Dave in disgust.

Careful viewers will notice throwaway lines that are fairly clever. When one of the guys is eating macaroni and cheese, he muses, "This IS cheesier." Or when the trio is trying to talk Ethan out of his blackmail scheme, one says, "What do you want? Money? Free dry cleaning? A free Europass?" Ethan briefly considers the Europass. In another scene, Dave dreams that he will be punished by having to take a class that meets at 8 a.m. in a building on the other side of campus. And any college student knows just how truly horrifying that would be.

The music is all just a little bit off. Some viewers might notice that the orchestra music playing at the beginning of the film is actually the Who's "Baba O'Riley" as performed by the London Philharmonic. Later, there is a choral version of the Ace of Base hit, "The Sign."

One of the things that the film hinges upon is the acting of Schwartzman as Ethan. Like in *Rushmore,* Schwartzman gives a unique performance, but this film is no *Rushmore.* Schwartzman doesn't try to parlay his minor *Rushmore* fame into becoming a cute teen actor. Instead, he is utterly fearless at appearing completely unappealing. He races around, rat-like, hunched over from the weight of his ever-present backpack and carrying around that gross hair doll. If critics tended to like anything about the film, it was Schwartzman's performance. "Schwartzman once again proves his expertise at plumbing dicey psychological cesspools as fully and fearlessly as possible," wrote Bob Strauss of the *Long Beach Press-Telegram.* "It's not a pretty sight, but it's the one thing that makes *Slackers* worth seeing."

Segel is good as the oddball Sam. The actor is not the typical pretty boy that shows up in teen movies and that in itself is refreshing. Segel makes his character seem like a real person, albeit a strange person. With his series of crazy wardrobe items, he's good at conveying how people in college are so fascinated with their own created personas. Maronna has a certain charisma as the leader Jeff. It would have been nice to see more of his character. Sawa is relatively bland as Dave, but this role doesn't ask much more of him than he show up and be handsome. In that respect, he really is a good match for King's Angela, since her main characteristic is being shyly pretty.

As noted, the critics weren't big on *Slackers.* Owen Gleiberman of *Entertainment Weekly* gave the film a D + and wrote, "If Jason Schwartzman had forced his agent at knifepoint to come up with a role that would squander the precocious, chewing-gum-on-the-wall, junior-Dustin Hoffman cache that the actor built up in *Rushmore,* the agent couldn't have done much better than to get him cast in *Slackers.*" Rob Blackwelder of *Spliced Wire* wrote, "Trying to disguise the fact that *Slackers* is really just a paint-by-numbers, boys-will-be-boys college comedy, first-time director Dewey Nicks slathers the flick in Tom Green-style bad taste outrageousness." Steven Rea of the *Philadelphia Inquirer* was more succinct. "Ugh," he wrote.

—*Jill Hamilton*

CREDITS

Dave: Devon Sawa
Ethan: Jason Schwartzman
Angela: James King
Sam: Jason Segel
Jeff: Michael Maronna
Reanna: Laura Prepon

Mrs. Van Graaf: Mamie Van Doren
Mr. Leonard: Joe Flaherty
Valerie Patton: Leigh Taylor-Young
Charles Patton: Sam Anderson
Movie star: Cameron Diaz

Origin: USA
Released: 2002
Production: Neal H. Moritz, Erik Feig; Alliance Atlantis; released by Screen Gems
Directed by: Dewey Nicks
Written by: David H. Steinberg
Cinematography by: James R. Bagdonas
Music by: Joseph (Joey) Altruda
Sound: Cameron Hamza
Music Supervisor: Amanda Scheer-Demme
Editing: Tara Timpone
Costumes: Jennifer Levy
Production Design: William Arnold
MPAA rating: R
Running time: 86 minutes

REVIEWS

Boxoffice. February, 2002, p. 57.
Chicago Sun-Times Online. February 1, 2002.
Entertainment Weekly. February 8, 2002, p. 52.
Los Angeles Times Online. February 1, 2002.
New York Times Online. February 1, 2002.
USA Today Online. January 31, 2002.
Variety. January 28, 2002, p. 28.
Washington Post. February 1, 2002, p. WE39.

QUOTES

Dave (Devon Sawa) on himself and his buddies: "When you only see two of us, the other one is probably rifling through your stuff."

Snow Dogs

Get ready for mush hour!
—Movie tagline

Box Office: $81.1 million

More than one film reviewer noted that Oscar winner Cuba Gooding Jr. probably wasn't making the best career move when he signed up for *Snow Dogs.* (Many of these reviewers also thought it was clever to make some mention of Gooding's career "going to the dogs.") After all, when any actor appears with an animal, it generally does not signal that an actor's career is on the upswing. The ads for *Snow Dogs* made Gooding's choice look even worse. Not only was he co-starring with the pack of dogs, but these dogs talked, winked and mugged for the camera. Luckily for the viewer, the dogs only talk during a brief dream sequence. The winking and mugging, unfortunately are real. Director Brian Levant (*The Flintstones* and *Jingle All The Way*) doesn't seem to think that the real dogs are interesting enough on their own so through the magic (or sorcery) of computer animation he anthropomorphizes them up with cutesy facial expressions. Yuck.

Snow Dogs is typical live-action Disney fare. The studio's animated releases are usually pretty prestigious, but for some reason, they often seem to skimp on their live action films. *Snow Dogs* keeps up the tradition. It's not the kind of movie that's going to be the next *Snow White and the Seven Dwarfs* but then it's not meant to be. It's much more along the line of *The Apple Dumpling Gang* than *Mary Poppins.*

It's pretty obvious that the film isn't going to be that creative when the first establishing shots hit the screen. To give the idea of beach life, director Levant shows some people on inline skates. Are these people the regular people wearing normal workout clothes that one would expect to be skating? No, they are busty women wearing bikinis. He then cuts to a shot of more busty young, bikini-clad women. These women are slathering on suntan lotion. Yes, sex sells, but in a kid's movie? How this is supposed to be interesting to the under-nine audience of boys and girls that the movie is aiming for is a mystery. It's never too early to start giving kids unrealistic models of women, I guess.

When the film begins, Ted (Gooding) is the son of a prominent dentist in Miami. Cut to 20 or so years later. Ted's father has passed on and Gooding is the successful owner of a chain of dental clinics. He has a fancy car, modern apartment and is pretty happy with life. One day, Ted is served with some legal papers that say that his mother has died and left him some things. This is a surprise to Ted since his mother, Amelia (Nichelle Nichols, *Star Trek*'s Lt. Uhura), is standing right there. Amelia admits to her son that he was adopted, and Ted decides to head up to the tiny town of Tolketna, Alaska, to claim his inheritance and find out about his heritage.

Tolketna is like a less interesting version of the town in *Northern Exposure.* There's the eccentric airplane pilot/lawyer, George (M. Emmet Walsh); the eccentric old guy who likes to snow golf and has yucky teeth, Ernie (Brian Doyle-Murray, in a role that's barely there); and the guy with no discernible personality but he looks like he could be a Native American, Peter Yellowbear (Graham Greene). Filling out the roster are Thunder Jack (James Coburn, also slumming), a guy who scares most everyone in town, and Barb (Joanna Bacalso), the local tavern owner who looks like she could be a model. (Actually she could. The actress who plays her is indeed a former model.)

Ted is none too impressed when he sees his mother's former digs, a tiny log cabin, and he's just plain frightened when he finds out what comes with the house—a team of sled dogs. The dogs take an instant dislike to Ted and attack him. One dog, the lead dog Demon, is especially vicious. You can be sure that when the movie ends cute, Demon is going to be the one that has turned the nicest and sired—awwww!—a cuddly pile of puppies.

Ted is set to sell off the dogs to Thunder Jack, but for reasons unclear except for plot advancement, he decides to stay. When Ted learns who his birth father is, he thinks that he needs to stay and learn how to race the dogs himself in sort of an "I'll show him" move. This paves the way for numerous instances for Ted to slip on the ice (ha ha!), get dragged over the snow by the dog team (chortle!) and get mauled by his dogs (yuk, yuk). It also allows for many scary, but quick, scenes like Ted almost falling off a cliff and Ted breaking through ice and falling into a lake.

Although the film probably wasn't that good for Gooding, he's good for the film. As anyone who saw him accept his Oscar for *Jerry Maguire* can attest, the man is energetic. That energy is a good fit for this film because he's pretty much a live action cartoon character. His mugging works well for all the slapstick and he's good at making that "Whooa--oooo!" expression that one should make while slipping—again—on the slippery ice. His scenes with love interest, Barb, couldn't be more tepid. Whether it's a Disney rule or just an utter lack of chemistry with his co-star, the romance is barely there. The two share a few hugs and maybe a chaste, quick kiss, then are seen later getting married. (After that chaste kiss, it was really the only right thing for them to do.)

Coburn shows what a professional he is by giving his role his all. It makes one wish that there were a lot more roles for veteran actors in Hollywood movies. Rapper Sisqo is only briefly in the film as Ted's fellow dentist in Miami, Dr. Rupert Brooks. It seems like his character could have been more funny, but the role isn't big enough for anything good to come of it. The dogs are fine, but it would have been nice if they had been allowed to have their natural expressions rather than their hepped up computer generated ones. There's something unnerving about seeing a dog wink conspiratorially at a fellow dog. Singer Michael Bolton shows up in a weird cameo as himself, and unfortunately, the film ends with a Bolton songs blaring over all the happiness and wrapped up loose ends.

Before the film came out, there was some controversy from animal rights groups about the movie's glorification of dog sledding and the movie tries to make it right by showing that the dogs are treated well and are allowed to eat before the humans. (How first shift eating negates the dog's being forced to pull a sled for hours is unclear.) The film missteps on animal rights anyway later when Ted pours water on a barking poodle and bites a dog on the ear.

Reviews for the film were mixed, with a majority of critics coming down against *Snow Dogs*. "Given that this is one of those screenplays with five writers (and who knows how many uncredited others), one supposes that *Snow Dogs* could have been an even bigger mess than it is," wrote Gene Seymour in the *Los Angeles Times*. Lisa Schwarzbaum of *Entertainment Weekly*, who gave the film a D grade, also noted the many writers. "This alleged family comedy, directed by Brian Levant from a screenplay with five writers' names attached, is distressed as a comedy can be without qualifying as a snow emergency." And Even Henerson of the *Long Beach Press-Telegram* wrote, "There's no greater proof that bad things can happen to good actors than Disney's *Snow Dogs*, a movie that makes *Turner and Hooch* (whose ending *Snow Dogs* virtually pirates) look like Fellini."

—Jill Hamilton

CREDITS

Ted Brooks: Cuba Gooding Jr.
Thunder Jack: James Coburn
Dr. Rupert Brooks: Sisqo
Amelia Brooks: Nichelle Nichols
George: M. Emmet Walsh
Peter Yellowbear: Graham Greene
Ernie: Brian Doyle-Murray
Barb: Joanna Bascalso

Origin: USA
Released: 2002
Production: Jordan Kerner; Galapagos Productions; released by Walt Disney Pictures
Directed by: Brian Levant
Written by: Jim Kouf, Tommy Swerdlow, Michael Goldberg, Mark Gibson, Philip Halprin
Cinematography by: Thomas Ackerman
Music by: John Debney
Sound: Rob Young
Editing: Roger Bondelli
Art Direction: Doug Byggdin
Costumes: Monique Prudhomme
Production Design: Steven Lineweaver
MPAA rating: PG
Running time: 99 minutes

REVIEWS

Boxoffice. March, 2002, p. 60.
Entertainment Weekly. January 25, 2002, p. 77.
Los Angeles Times Online. January 18, 2002.
New York Times Online. January 18, 2002.
People. Janaury 28, 2002, p. 35.
USA Today Online. January 18, 2002.
Variety. January 14, 2002, p. 52.
Washington Post. January 18, 2002, p. WE37.

QUOTES

Dentist Ted (Cuba Gooding Jr.) to Thunder Jack (James Coburn): "I need to learn to mush, and you need to learn to floss."

Soft Shell Man (Un Crabe Dans la Tete)

Quebec cinema for the most part has been a well-kept secret outside of the province. Occasionally, a film such as Denys Arcand's *Jesus of Montreal* or Lea Pool's *Emporte-Moi* find their way to an international audience, but when we consider the multitude of films produced in Quebec, only a small percentage reach the States. In Canada, the distribution system proves even more dismal because Canadians still battle with the language issue and poor distribution in general. If film audiences desire to watch Quebec cinema they can either buy a plane ticket to Quebec or hang out at a Canadian film festival. However, even if a Quebecois film wins awards at the Toronto International Film Festival, it still might only receive limited distribution across Canada, only to end up as a video release.

Doom and gloom aside, Quebec is hopping with cinematic talent and a group of 30-something filmmakers, including Denis Villenueve, Manon Briand, Andre Turpin, and Guylaine Dionne have infused Quebec cinema with new ingredients. Andre Turpin's second feature, *Un Crabe Dans La Tete*, which literally translates to "crab in the head" with the English title, *Soft Shell Man*, dazzles as much as it entertains. The film features another sexy performance by the Quebecois Don Juan David La Haye as Alex, a frogman suffering from a foggy brain, and stylishly surreal photography by cinematographer-turned director, Turpin. And in fact, Turpin's film acts as a companion to Denis Villenueve's *August 32nd on Earth* and *Maelstrom*, both shot by Turpin.

The offbeat characters battle unusual situations involving infidelity, the loss of memory and their inevitable transformation. They are 30-somethings trying to stretch into the realm of adulthood while shying away from hints of marriage or child rearing. In an interview with journalist Carlo Mandolini, Turpin discusses the Nouvelle Vague kind of angst which his generation faces. "As I see it, the sense of disquiet arises from certain questions we ask ourselves between the ages of 25 and 35. What do I do with my life? What are we here for? ... And because we don't really believe in God, we don't even have recourse to any spiritual motivations." Turpin states, "On the other hand, we've stopped having children, who constitute a reason to live and tend to put our troubles and fear in perspective and teach us responsibility."

However, Turpin's character Alex does learn how to take responsibility for his life after responding to a catastrophe caused by his actions and the charming Lothario must also confront his fears and endure a painful transformation. Alex finds himself in a holding pattern after a diving accident in which he suffers from amnesia. He doesn't recall taking photographs of a dead child underwater until those images come back to haunt him and alter his life. And a crab that has lodged in his brain only further complicates matters.

When Alex returns to Montreal after the accident, he lives off of his charm while lying to others as a way of pleasing them. He moves into his best friend Samuel's (Emmanuel Bilodeau) flat, seduces savvy journalist Marie (Isabelle Blais), begins delivering drugs for his paranoid drug dealer Audrey (Pascale Desrochers), and eventually seduces Samuel's deaf lover Sara (Chantal Giroux). Meanwhile, Alex's gay agent/gallery owner Pierre (Vincent Bilodeau) has decided to launch Alex's career by exhibiting photographs of the dead child that Alex photographed before his diving accident. His life is a time bomb waiting to blow and this time Alex can't escape taking responsibility for his actions. The film ends with Alex literally removing a crab from his head as he transcends over his troubles.

Soft Shell Man collected praise from Canadian critics. Adam Nayman of *eye Weekly* described the film as "stylish and funny" and James Luscombe of *Exclaim!* praised Turpin's "ingenious script." Playing to full houses since November 2001 and garnering several Genie nominations, we hope this stunner breaks through to U.S. audiences.

—*Patty-Lynne Herlevi*

CREDITS

Alex: David La Haye
Marie: Isabelle Blais
Samuel: Emmanuel Bilodeau
Sara: Chantel Giroux
Audrey: Pascale Desrochers

Pierre: Vincent Bilodeau

Origin: Canada
Language: French
Released: 2001
Production: Luc Dery, Joseph Hillel; Qu4tre par Quatre; released by Film Tonic
Directed by: Andre Turpin
Written by: Andre Turpin
Cinematography by: Andre Turpin
Music by: Jean le Loup
Sound: Sylvain Bellemare
Editing: Sophie Leblond
Production Design: Pierre Allard
MPAA rating: Unrated
Running time: 102 minutes

REVIEWS

eye Weekly Online. February 4, 2002.
Variety. January 14, 2002, p. 54.

QUOTES

Alex's (David La Haye) pickup line to the deaf Sara (Chantal Giroux): "I am fascinated with silence."

AWARDS AND NOMINATIONS

Nomination:
Genie 2002: Actor (La Haye), Cinematog., Film, Screenplay.

Solaris

There are some places man is not ready to go.
—Movie tagline

How far will you go for a second chance?
—Movie tagline

Box Office: $14.8 million

It's a cold, silent world that envelopes Chris Kelvin (George Clooney). He seems to sleepwalk his way through the gloomy, dizzily days of his life. He lethargicly makes his meals and listlessly helms his psychotherapy group.

Then one day two men arrive with a classified video message from a friend of his, Gibarian (Ulrich Takur), who is currently assigned to the space station Prometheus. The station was sold by NASA to a private enterprise that is studying the economic potential of the planet it orbits, a watery giant by the name of Solaris. However, something is wrong on the station but what exactly that is, Gibarian isn't saying. Or maybe he's just not sure because no one seems able to agree on what's going on. One thing he does seem sure of, though, is that if anyone can figure it out it's Kelvin. So the psychologist leaves his empty world on Earth to travel through the emptier void of space to solve the Prometheus' mystery.

Nothing could have prepared Kelvin for what he finds upon docking at the space station. Its pristine metal interior is splattered with blood. He follows the red trail into what appears to be the station's lab and then into its morgue. There he finds two body bags and in one of them is his friend Gibarian. What he doesn't notice is a blood stain on the morgue ceiling.

Kelvin continues to wander about the station looking for any signs of life and eventually hears music. He follows it to the cabin of Snow (Jeremy Davies) whom he finds to be distracted, even nonchalant, about what has happened to his fellow crewmen. When asked about the blood, the best he can respond is, "Yeah, blood, how about that." He does however manage to finally communicate that Gibarian committed suicide, crewman Reese has disappeared, and Dr. Gordon (Viola Davis) is in her room and won't let anyone in. Kelvin makes one last attempt to pry from Snow what has happened, but the only response he can get is the cryptic "I could tell you what's happening, but I can't tell you what's happening."

Perplexed by Snow's odd behavior, Kelvin now searches out Dr. Gordon. Unfortunately, she is basically no more helpful than Snow. When asked what is going on she just replies, "until it starts happening to you, there's really no point in discussing it." Until what starts happening? Could this get any weirder? Yep. On his way to his quarters Kelvin spies a little boy. A little boy who's NOT supposed to be on the station. Where did he come from? Kelvin chases after him but loses him in the station's maze of corridors. Exhausted, Kelvin retires to his room and falls asleep.

Restless dreams await Kelvin. He dreams of his wife Rheya (Natascha McElhone), of seeing her on a train with a doorknob in her lap, of talking to her at a party, of sharing the poems of Dylan Thomas with her. She seems so real . . . and when he wakes up, he is astonished to find her actually lying next to him. How can this be? She didn't come with

Peter that he must be careful of what kind of man he will become and that "with great power comes great responsibility." Peter isn't actually going to the library—he ducks out and heads to the wrestling arena.

The champ, Bone Saw McGraw (Randy Savage), is easily flattening all the competition when Peter becomes next on the list as "The Human Spider" (in a really cheesy homemade outfit). The unctuous wrestling announcer (Bruce Campbell) thinks his chosen pseudonym is lame and proclaims him "the amazing Spider-Man!" Peter finds himself in a cage match but manages to defeat his opponent with his spider skills. But the wrestling promoter (Larry Joshua) welshes on the agreement and gives Peter a measly $100, since he defeated his opponent in two minutes rather than three.

No sooner does an angry Peter leave the office, than the place is robbed. Instead of stopping the fleeing thief, Peter allows him to escape. Out on the street, a crowd is gathered around a dying man. Oh no, it's Uncle Ben who was carjacked while waiting to pick up Peter at the library. Peter hears from the police which way the felon is headed and goes after the killer in his spider disguise. Will it come as a surprise to anyone that the carjacker is also the thief that Peter didn't stop? The thief is killed in a fall after a fight with Peter, who decides he must use his unique abilities to do good.

Then our villain finally makes an appearance—a green fright figure on a glider who bombs and destroys Oscorp's competition for military contracts. This doesn't help Norman though, since the board of directors decide to force him out and sell the company after they all make an appearance at the World Unity Festival. He doesn't take this well and begins hearing an evil voice in his head.

After graduation, Peter, Harry, and Mary Jane are all off to New York City to have their dreams come true. Mary Jane is making do as a waitress while she tries to find acting work and inadvertently tells the unknowing Peter that she and Harry are dating. Peter is busy saving the citizens of the city—"courtesy of your friendly neighborhood spider-man." Blowhard Daily Bugle editor J. Jonah Jameson (J.K. Simmons) is suspicious of the web-swinger and offers a reward for a decent picture to put on page one. Peter, who wants to be a photographer, naturally manages to snap some good shots with a timer and gets a job as a freelancer.

Harry and Mary Jane are with Osborn's board of directors at the festival (and Peter is taking photos below in the crowd) when the Green Goblin appears and blasts the building apart. Peter promptly runs into an alley and rips open his shirt (ala Superman), displaying his costume underneath. (It's improved by this time into the familiar red-and-blue uniform but who on earth made it for him? Maybe he developed super-seamstress skills as well.)

Spider-Man rescues MJ and temporarily defeats the Green Goblin. Norman Osborn is hearing that voice again:

"Who are you?" The voice replies: "Follow the cold shiver running down your spine." Norman looks in the mirror and, well, he doesn't actually see the Green Goblin but he certainly realizes that he hasn't been himself lately. The green meanie tells Norman that his purpose is to "say what you won't, to do what you can't, to remove those in your way." He breaks into Jonah's office to force him to find Spider-Man, who shows up to rescue the newspaper editor. But Spidey's temporarily paralyzed by the Goblin's nerve gas and carried away. The Goblin wants Spider-Man to join forces with him and warns him that though he's chosen the way of the hero, the public want to "see a hero fail, fall, die trying." Jonah promptly decides the two are in cahoots and begins a Spider-Man smear campaign.

Spider-Man also comes to MJ's rescue once again when she's chased by a group of creeps making lewd suggestions. It begins to rain while MJ thanks her hero (even though she refers to him as her "superhero stalker") and while he's hanging upside down, she removes the bottom part of his Spider-Man mask so they can kiss. Spidey also has another fight with the Green Goblin and gets cut on the arm; the fight makes him late for Thanksgiving dinner at the apartment he shares with Harry. Also there are Aunt May, Mary Jane, Harry, and his father who becomes suspicious when he sees Peter's cut. Norman rushes out and rudely tells Harry to dump MJ, who's obviously a girl from the wrong side of the tracks.

Norman/Goblin figures out that while Spider-Man may be invincible, Peter is not and the Goblin bombs Aunt May's home, landing her in the hospital. Peter figures out that Norman/Goblin knows he's Spider-Man. While Mary Jane is visiting Aunt May, she admits to Peter that she's in love with Spider-Man even though she's never seen his face. Harry tells his crazy father that Mary Jane is the love of Peter's life and the Green Goblin promptly kidnaps her and leaves her on top of the Queensboro Bridge, which also has the Roosevelt Island tram filled with kids traveling on its span.

Goblin snaps the cable on the tram and holds it suspended in one hand with MJ held in the other. Spider-Man must make a choice: rescue his one true love or a car filled with kiddies. Of course, he manages to do both—with a little help from some irate New Yorkers who pelt the Goblin with refuse for picking on their hero. The two are forced into a final battle in an abandoned building and the fight is very vicious, with Spider-Man on the losing end until the Goblin makes some nasty remarks about what he plans to do to MJ. This makes Spidey very mad and he turns the tables on the villain who eventually is defeated by his own glider weapons. As he dies, Goblin becomes Norman long enough to ask that Peter doesn't tell Harry what his father had become.

Spider-Man carries the body back to the Osborn mansion and is caught by Harry, who thinks the web-spinner murdered his father. By his father's grave, Harry vows to

Peter that one day Spider-Man will pay. Peter also realizes that "no matter what I do, no matter how hard I try, the ones I love will always be the ones who pay." Of course, Mary Jane picks just this moment to confess that she realizes that it's Peter she truly loves because he's the "only man who's always been there for me." She tells Peter she loves him, but Peter can't say the words back because it will put her in danger. He says they can only be friends. But after kissing Peter, Mary Jane realizes there's something familiar about those lips. As Peter walks away, he knows that his powers are both a gift and a curse: "Who am I? I'm Spider-Man."

Raimi plays it as straight as is possible in his adaptation of Stan Lee and Steve Ditko's Marvel comic book when his hero has weird abilities and dresses in a costume. The director knows that at this stage his character is a teenager struggling to become an adult and having to deal with not only what that encompasses but also with all the responsibilities his powers bring. Peter Parker has already lost his parents, loses his uncle, is betrayed by both his one friend and his new father figure, and is forced to give up the woman he's loved forever because of the danger his secret identity places her in. Peter also learns that his alter-ago will be a hero to some and a menace to others and that public acceptance is a fickle thing.

Tobey Maguire gets all this, which is why he's such a terrific choice to play the leading role. And could he ask for a better villain to play opposite than Willem Dafoe, who deftly shows what happens when obsession slides into madness. Dafoe might even have the tougher role since his armored-plated Green Goblin costume is much more rigid than that of Spider-Man. Maguire at least can use body language to express himself but Dafoe looks much more limited, particularly in his fright mask. (Although the Goblin costume does have eye openings so Dafoe can express some visual emotion, especially during the climatic hero/villain fight to the death.) Kirsten Dunst also strikes just the right note as the popular high school girl who is used to being wanted because she's a babe but, thanks to a lousy home life, is a girl who doesn't have much confidence in her dreams. Or doesn't until she realizes that her "Tiger" will always believe in her.

Spider-Man has nearly 500 CGI shots, many of which could easily translate to a videogame. They can look at little cheesy—some of the Green Goblin's swooping about look particularly Saturday morning cartoon time—but they're not noticeably distracting. And what happens to all that webbing that Spider-Man is covering New York City with? That boy does a lot of web-swinging during his adventures. No matter, *Spider-Man* manages to be a competent combo of heart and action and, if you make if past the typically bombastic rock song over the initial closing credits, you will be treated to the catchy "Theme from Spider-Man" that accompanied the late sixties ABC cartoon show.

—*Christine Tomassini*

CREDITS

Spider-Man/Peter Parker: Tobey Maguire
Green Goblin/Norman Osborn: Willem Dafoe
Mary Jane Watson: Kirsten Dunst
Harry Osborn: James Franco
Ben Parker: Cliff Robertson
May Parker: Rosemary Harris
J. Jonah Jameson: J.K. Simmons
Maximilian Fargas: Gerry Becker
Joseph "Robbie" Robertson: Bill Nunn
Henry Balkan: Jack Betts
Flash Thompson: Joe Manganiello
General Slocum: Stanley Anderson
Dr. Mendel Stromm: Ron Perkins
Hoffman: Theodore (Ted) Raimi
Wrestling promoter: Larry Joshua
The Burglar: Michael (Mike) Papajohn
Opinionated cop: Joseph (Joe) D'Onofrio
Wrestling announcer: Bruce Campbell

Origin: USA
Released: 2002
Production: Laura Ziskin, Ian Bryce; Marvel Enterprises; released by Columbia Pictures
Directed by: Sam Raimi
Written by: David Koepp
Cinematography by: Don Burgess
Music by: Danny Elfman
Sound: Edward Novick
Editing: Bob Murawski, Arthur Coburn
Art Direction: Tony Fanning, Stella Vaccaro
Costumes: James Acheson
Production Design: Neil Spisak
MPAA rating: PG-13
Running time: 121 minutes

REVIEWS

Boston Globe Online. May 3, 2002.
Boxoffice. April, 2002, p. 30.
Chicago Sun-Times Online. May 3, 2002.
Globe and Mail. April 27, 2002, p. R5.
Los Angeles Times Online. May 3, 2002.
New York Times Online. May 3, 2002.
Newsweek. May 6, 2002, p. 54.
People. May 13, 2002, p. 41.
San Francisco Chronicle. May 3, 2002, p. D1.
USA Today Online. May 3, 2002.
Variety. April 22, 2002, p. 27.
Washington Post. May 3, 2002, p. WE43.

QUOTES

Peter tells Mary Jane they can only be friends. MJ (Kirsten Dunst): "Only a friend, Peter Parker?" Peter (Tobey Maguire): "That's all I have to give."

TRIVIA

The film was released in conjunction with the 40th anniversary of Spider-Man's first appearance in the last issue of the "Amazing Fantasy" comic book (Issue 15, August, 1962).

AWARDS AND NOMINATIONS

Nomination:
Oscars 2002: Sound, Visual FX
British Acad. 2002: Visual FX.

Spirit: Stallion of the Cimarron

Some legends can never be tamed.
—Movie tagline
Leader. Hero. Legend.
—Movie tagline

 Box Office: $73.2 million

Spirit: Stallion of the Cimarron goes against all the current trends in children's animated features. Sure, it has something that DreamWorks' honcho Jeffrey Katzenberg awkwardly coined as "tradigital," which is a combination of traditional two-dimensional animation and computer-generated three-dimensional animation, but this is no *Shrek*. There are no in-jokes for the parents, no smart alecky talking critter sidekicks and nary a pop culture reference. The star of *Spirit*, a horse of that name, can't even talk, for goodness' sake's. Even Mr. Ed could talk.

In this day and age, such a movie is a radical concept, but directors Kelly Asbury and Lorna Cook and writer John Fusco are not prepared to take that big a risk. Even though Spirit doesn't talk, no one in the audience is going to wonder what the horse is thinking. His inner horse thoughts are occasionally spoken in voiceover by Matt Damon (who, with

this and *Titan A.E.* seems to be finding a subspecialty in non-crowd-pleasing animated features) and when the voice-overs don't do the trick, an overly literal Bryan Adams song bursts onto the soundtrack. When Spirit is born, for example, we hear Adams singing, "Here I am. This is me. I come to the world. So wild and free."

Furthermore, Spirit and his fellow horses also have exceedingly expressive faces and a seeming command of many human facial gestures. Despite all this amping up, *Spirit* still retains the feeling of being a simple, graceful story. Lou Lumenick of the *New York Post* disparaged this quality of the story as being a "hopelessly old-fashioned, un-hip and simple-minded story that might have worked as an episode of *Wonderful World of Disney,* circa 1959." The old-school feeling that Lumenick disparaged is exactly the thing that will appeal to other viewers.

In a few early scenes, the audience follows Spirit's life from birth through childhood and playing around with other horses in his herd to young adulthood. As his father did before him, Spirit becomes the leader of his herd. During all of this, there are many expansive shots depicting the free lives of wild horses before the west was "won." We see Spirit racing the eagle, horses swimming in ponds and horses galloping across the wide spaces of the old west. Part of the appeal of the film is thinking about an America that was not covered with Targets and Home Depots and could support herds of wild horses.

Spirit's fairly idyllic life is upset when he sees a campfire glowing on a distant mountain. As the responsible leader of his herd, Spirit goes to investigate it. There, he sees the disturbing sight of horses tied up and kept with some men. Spirit has never seen such a sight and can't comprehend what must be happening. Spirit's interaction with the humans ends up getting him captured and sent to a United States military post. But Spirit isn't interested in becoming a tame military horse. He kicks anyone who comes near him and bucks off anyone who tries to ride him. The mean military leader, The Colonel (James Cromwell), is certain that he can break this horse. He orders Spirit tied to a post without water or food for three days.

The utter evil of the white humans is perhaps a bit over the top but one thing that the movie is really good at is reframing the idea that it's perfectly acceptable for people to ride and control horses. The movie shows horse accouterments like saddles, bits and spurs from the horse's point of view. Instead of seeing the usual human interpretation of a saddle as a place for a person to sit, *Spirit* shows saddles as a big, heavy piece of leather that weighs heavily on a horse's back. Reins are a form of bondage. When horses are as humanized as they are in this movie, it's difficult to see their capture by the humans and being put into service as being anything other than a kind of slavery.

While Spirit is being starved by The Colonel, the military men bring a young Lakota captive, Little Creek (Daniel

Studi), to the base. Like Spirit, he is tied up and left without food. The two share an unspoken bond over their common situation and the equally clever and agile Spirit and Little Creek make a break for it together. Spirit is shocked when Little Creek takes him back to his compound to make him a domesticated horse. Spirit will have nothing of the sort and bucks Little Creek and kicks him at every opportunity. But Spirit might have a weakness. An attractive female horse, Rain, (note to the film makers: was it really necessary to give the attractive horse blonde hair?) seems happy with her life as a domesticated horse of the Native Americans. Will she convince him to stick around?

The rest of the film is filled with various scenarios of Rain, Spirit and or Little Creek being in danger and the others saving them. Throughout their adventures, Rain and Spirit fall in horse love and Spirit and Little Creek form a friendship based on mutual respect.

What acting there is in the film is fine (although Spirit sometimes overdoes the facial expressions). Damon's voice-overs are unobtrusive and free of scene-stealing hamminess. Cromwell is appropriately evil as the hard-edged Colonel and Studi's Little Creek is gentle and full of humor.

But the real star of the movie is the look of it. The animation is painterly and graceful. In an opening scene, we see the horses running free over the plains, soaring over obstacles and galloping through streams. The film is filled with such sweeping shots that paint the picture of a lovely unspoiled West. The only obvious point of computer-enhancement is in a scene in which Spirit manages to get a steam engine rolling end over end down a hill and destroying everything in its path. The final fiery crash into a station house is worthy of a Bruce Willis film and seems out of place here.

In the film, the white cavalry men do all the wrong things with respect to nature and animals, while the Native Americans are portrayed as living in harmony with their surroundings. This was a sticking point for some critics who thought this aspect of the story was heavy-handed. Dave Kehr of the *New York Times* wrote, "*Spirit* is strangled by ideological preconceptions that require the Indian characters to be as insufferably saintly as the white invaders are unspeakably evil."

Critics were divided on how the rest of the film worked. Owen Gleiberman of *Entertainment Weekly* gave the film a B + and wrote, "In its very square way, it brings back some of the primal storybook innocence that has been squeezed out of the form in recent years by the attention-deficit vaudeville showiness of cartoons like *Tarzan* and *The Prince of Egypt*." Joe Leydon of the *San Francisco Examiner* wrote, "Even though this big-ticket animated feature offers an adroitly seamless mix of hand-drawn artistry and computer-generated imagery, the pretty pictures aren't enough to enliven a slow-pokey horse opera that plays like blandly generic kid stuff." And Kenneth Turan of the *Los Angeles Times*

wrote, "Despite its good intentions, *Spirit* is more self-conscious and uninspiring from a dramatic point of view than one might have wished. Still, whenever it threatens to get bogged down in earnest dramaturgy, a stirring visual sequence like a surge through swirling rapids or a leap from pinnacle to pinnacle stirs us."

—*Jill Hamilton*

CREDITS

Spirit: Matt Damon (Voice)
The Colonel: James Cromwell (Voice)
Little Creek: Daniel Studi (Voice)

Origin: USA
Released: 2002
Production: Mireille Soria, Jeffrey Katzenberg; released by Dreamworks Pictures
Directed by: Kelly Asbury, Lorna Cook
Written by: John Fusco
Music by: Hans Zimmer
Lyrics by: Bryan Adams
Editing: Nick Fletcher
MPAA rating: G
Running time: 85 minutes

REVIEWS

Boxoffice. June, 2002, p. 63.
Chicago Sun-Times Online. May 24, 2002.
Entertainment Weekly. May 31, 2002, p. 79.
Los Angeles Times Online. May 24, 2002.
New York Times Online. May 24, 2002.
People. June 3, 2002, p. 35.
USA Today Online. May 24, 2002.
USA Weekend. May 17, 2002, p. 22.
Variety. May 20, 2002, p. 25.
Washington Post. May 24, 2002, p. WE43.

AWARDS AND NOMINATIONS

Nomination:
Oscars 2002: Animated Film
Golden Globes 2003: Song ("Here I Am").

Spy Kids 2: The Island of Lost Dreams

Huge new adventure—slightly larger spies.
—Movie tagline

 Box Office: $85.5 million

Richard Rodriguez has over a dozen credits on *Spy Kids 2: The Island of Lost Dreams.* He had the big jobs, like director, writer, editor, director of digital photography and production designer, as well as some lesser known jobs like sound designer, visual effects supervisor and rerecording mixer. He also produced the film with his wife, Elizabeth Avellan, and even composed three songs for the film. While such micromanaging may (or may not) have been difficult to work with, the results are worth it. For all the careful attention to detail that Rodriguez must have put into the film, *Spy Kids 2* has a surprisingly light and carefree feel. Rodriguez has the ability to do things well and carefully, but without the usual attendant overproduction or lack of life.

In this sequel to the generally well-liked *Spy Kids*, the fun starts early. Juni Cortez (Daryl Sabara) and his big sister and fellow child spy, Carmen (Alexa Vega) are called to the amusement park, Troublemaker Theme Park, (Troublemaker is also the name of Rodriguez's production company) run by a brash Bill Paxton. It seems the president's daughter, Alexandra (Taylor Momsen of *How the Grinch Stole Christmas*), has stolen her father's tremendously important spy device, the Transmooker, and installed herself at the top of a ride called the juggler.

The main fun of the scene is not the plot but seeing all the crazy rides that Troublemaker has. The juggler, for example, is a ride where a giant metal clown figure juggles balls with riders inside. There is also the Whipper Snapper, which has riders on the end of a snapping whip, and the Vomiter, which is pretty much a ride that tosses kids around like they're being shaken in a aerosol can.

While Juni is busy using quiet charm to talk the president's daughter down, a team of rival spy kids, Gary Giggles (Matt O'Leary) and his younger sister, Gerti (Emily Osment, sister of Haley Joel Osment), swoops in and gets the Transmooker, and thus all the glory. There is also a rivalry between the Giggles' father, Donnagon (Mike Judge), and the Cortez dad, Gregorio (Antonio Banderas). Both are up for the job of head of the OSS, a national spy agency.

When, under suspicious circumstances, the senior Giggles scores the top job, then gives his kids a plum assignment; Carmen feels justified in hacking into the computer system to give herself and Juni the good assignment and to send the Giggles to the desert. They go to the Island of Lost Dreams to locate the Transmooker, which has disappeared. The device has the capability of making all electronic things unworkable and could thus . . . destroy the world! Traveling in a craft shaped like a giant dragon fly, Juni and Carmen arrive at the island and are chagrined to find out that none of their cool spy gadgets work. They are going to have to do things, ugh, manually.

While exploring the island, they find Romero (Steve Buscemi), the requisite mad scientist with white lab coat and broken glasses. Romero had been working on an idea for a kids' toy. It was a miniature zoo with real animals like a spider monkey (a spider and a monkey combined), a cat fish (a cat and fish combined) and a spork (a flying pig). But something went amok, as mad scientists' projects are wont to do, and the creatures developed super-sized companions which are roaming the island. The animals' movements are digital (of course, since it might be a little difficult to locate real such animals, let alone ones that are trained), but they have a jerky, fake look that makes them look more bizarre. Many reviewers compared the motions to those in an old Ray Harryhausen film. The fake-looking special effects are mixed in with special effects that look quite real and somehow it all works. It just makes the *Spy Kids* universe look like a place that's somehow brighter and more fun than our own.

Juni has to find the Transmooker, as well as deal with interference from the Giggles, plus dad and mom, Ingrid (Carla Gugino), who have come to the island looking for the kids. A further complication is that Ingrid's suave parents (Holland Taylor and Ricardo Montalban, riding a flying wheelchair) who are also spies, want to help their daughter and Gregorio find the kids. The interplay between Gregorio and his in-laws is a treat. The older generation tolerates Gregorio but don't think he's quite good enough for their beloved daughter. Gregorio is less than thrilled to have his in-laws literally looking over his shoulder and making disparaging remarks about his driving and spying ability.

Actually, the interplay between all the characters is good. Gregorio and Carla, despite being about a thousand times sexier than most parents, still come across as being an old married couple. Juni and Carmen have a brother and sister relationship that rings true. Both of them are half disgusted by each other, but are there for each other when it counts. Juni thinks it's gross that his sister has a crush on the bad boy rival, Gary, but his feelings are partially motivated by the very real worry that Gary is not a good choice for his sister. Juni is kind of young to be having a love relationship with the president's daughter, Alexandra, but the two do have a sweet "like" relationship.

The film is populated by actors that are better than you'd expect from a kiddie flick. Besides Buscemi, who does a nice job as the meek 'n' mad scientist, there are returnees from the first film like Floop (Alan Cumming) and his

John calls around to relatives, trying to get a loan but is turned down. His kindly grandmother tells him, "Who do you think I am? Donald (Bleeping) Trump?" Again, these are the jokes, folks. Instead of trying to arrange for further financial aid or trying to arrange a loan through a bank, John goes for the most unreasonable solution. He turns to his friend Duff (Green), a gardener who is really stupid and weird and just not the kind of guy who you'd turn to for major advice. Duff's big idea is that they should steal the money somehow. John, who is apparently much dumber than he seems, agrees that this is an okay idea.

Herein is the bulk of the movie: guys try a crime, they bumble it. In one sequence, John breaks into the house of one of Duff's wealthy clients. The guy is home and, at gunpoint, forces John to dress as his late wife and "spoon" with the guy in bed. Unfortunately, this is the highlight of their various capers. In another, they mess with a bad guy (Chris Penn) and end up inadvertently driving the getaway car for a bank robbery. In another, they try to rob a convenience store, but end up getting shot at by a gun-toting youth behind the counter.

These shenanigans are spiced up with further non-hilarity such as a dog who likes crotches and a police officer who likes to put his toothbrush where the sun doesn't shine. Unfortunately for *Stealing Harvard,* it doesn't have enough of these lame gross-out jokes to attract even the undemanding crowd that would go for such things. It also doesn't make a whole lot of sense. Besides John's unrealistic willingness to jump into a life a crime, it's also a mystery why he's so anxious to please his girlfriend. The two obviously don't get along sexually, he doesn't like her father, and they don't seem to have similar goals at all. At the end of the film, Elaine suddenly decides that she also doesn't like her father so much, which is an utter reversal of anything we'd known about her earlier.

The actors seem to be trying, but they don't have anything to work with. Maybe they were thinking that once the movie hit the editing room and post-production, the film would somehow turn much funnier. Green's part is especially bad. Perhaps the day has come when comedy screenwriters will finally give up the character of the moronic, childlike guy.

It won't come as much of a surprise that critics weren't laughing at *Stealing Harvard.* Bruce Fretts of *Entertainment Weekly* gave the film a D and wrote, "Tom Green has officially become the 21st century Pauly Shore." Kevin Thomas of the *Los Angeles Times* wrote, "It's so bad that you have to wonder whether Tom Green was looking for a project to match last year's *Freddy Got Fingered,* which he directed and which ended up on many worst of 2001 lists. Green didn't direct this turkey, but it surely is a contender for the bottom of the barrel award for 2002." Roger Ebert of the *Chicago Sun-Times* wrote, "*Stealing Harvard . . .* is a singularly unambitious project, content to paddle lazily in

the shallows of sitcom formula. It has no edge, no hunger to be better than it is. It ambles pleasantly through its inanity, like a guest happy to be at a boring party."

—*Jill Hamilton*

CREDITS

Duff: Tom Green
John: Jason Lee
Elaine: Leslie Mann
Patty: Megan Mullally
Mr. Warner: Dennis Farina
Mr. Cook: Richard Jenkins
Detective Charles: John C. McGinley
David Loach: Christopher Penn
Noreen: Tammy Blanchard
Uncle Jack: Seymour Cassel
Fidio the lawyer: Bruce McCulloch

Origin: USA
Released: 2002
Production: Susan Cavan; Revolution Studios, Imagine Entertainment; released by Columbia Pictures
Directed by: Bruce McCulloch
Written by: Peter Tolan
Cinematography by: Ueli Steiger
Music by: Christophe Beck
Sound: Jeff Wexler
Music Supervisor: Manish Raval, Tom Wolfe
Editing: Malcolm Campbell
Art Direction: James E. Tocci
Costumes: Betsy Heimann
Production Design: Gregory Keen
MPAA rating: PG-13
Running time: 83 minutes

REVIEWS

Chicago Sun-Times Online. September 13, 2002.
Los Angeles Times Online. September 13, 2002.
New York Times Online. September 13, 2002.
USA Today Online. September 12, 2002.
Variety Online. September 13, 2002.
Washington Post. September 13, 2002, p. WE39.

QUOTES

John (Jason Lee) describes Duff (Tom Green) as: "A man whose ideas were sometimes so dumb they were brilliant."

Stolen Summer (Project Greenlight's Stolen Summer)

Millions saw the HBO series. Now see the full-length final cut.
—Movie tagline

Project Greenlight winner Pete Jones' film, *Stolen Summer* offers us a good lesson about charity and ulterior motives in the film industry. The cautionary message is be careful what you wish for also plays a hand here. After filmmakers Ben Affleck and Matt Damon won an Oscar for Best Original Screenplay for *Good Will Hunting,* they decided to give back to the filmmaking community by hosting an online screenwriting contest. They received thousands of entries from aspiring filmmakers hoping to find an open door into Hollywood's movie factory. Pete Jones' plaintive screenplay was chosen and surprising released by Miramax, a distributor known for shelving deserving films. However, similar to the numerous bitter tales of lottery winners that surfaced over the years, Mr. Jones learned a harsh lesson about the egos that run the film industry and that, yes, directing a film is hard work. Anyone can win a contest, but it does take a tremendous amount of talent to write and direct a provocative feature film.

Roger Ebert, in the *Chicago Sun-Times,* praised Jones' period piece which is set in Chicago during the summer of 1976. While Ebert cited that "Movies are collisions between egos and compromises,", he called *Stolen Summer,* "charming. . .moving. . .funny . . ." Other critics found the HBO 12-part documentary, *Project Greenlight,* to be of more interest. Peter Travers, in *Rolling Stone,* sang praises for the documentary, "*Project Greenlight* is the smartest, scariest, bitchiest and most informative piece of reality TV ever." And, similar to other critics, Travers skimmed over *Stolen Summer* in his review. Kenneth Turan, of the *Los Angeles Times,* pointed out that the film's title appeared in small letters on the film's poster while *Project Greenlight* and the film's tagline, "You saw the back-stabbing" appeared in larger letters. The film's press kit also buries Pete Jones' name at the bottom of the film credits. Could it be that Mr. Affleck and Mr. Damon's good deed had ulterior motives attached to it? The answer points to yes.

Stolen Summer revolves around eight-year-old Pete O'Malley (Adi Stein, the son of a rabbi) and his quest to get to heaven. The Irish-Catholic Pete has been told by the sisters at his school that he will go to hell if he does not clean up his act and Pete has also been told that one needs to accept Christ in order to get to heaven. So the misguided Pete decides to convert Jews to Catholicism as he embarks on a quixotic quest. Pete sets up a lemon aid stand in front of a Jewish temple hoping to attract a Jewish person willing to convert to Christianity. Rabbi Jacobsen (Kevin Pollak) befriends Pete and believes that Pete's controversial stand will cause members of his congregation to think about their own religion.

One day, the rabbi's house catches on fire and Pete's fireman father, Joe (Aidan Quinn), saves the rabbi's son Danny (Mike Weinberg), but fails to save the church's secretary who was babysitting Danny. This event ties the two families together for better or worse. The scenes that follow involving funerals, familial conflicts and religious tensions between the families feel melodramatic and could easily pass as a made-for-tv special. Whereas, the story revolving around Pete converting Danny to Christianity via a decathlon could easily pass off as an 1970's afternoon school special. In other words, why pay the big bucks to see this small drama on the big screen?

Surprisingly this small film drew at talented cast, including Aidan Quinn, Kevin Pollak, Brian Dennehy (in a small role), and Bonnie Hunt. Comedian Pollack's performance as the open-minded and generous Rabbi Jacobsen plays well with Adi Stein's wide-eyed Pete O'Malley, especially in a scene in which the rabbi gives Pete a tour of the synagogue and Pete asks about the missing crucifix in the temple. However, the talented cast and the small moments do not save Jones' film from falling into the sleeper category.

Project Greenlight might have had good intentions during the conception phase, however, similar to any charity, one can become entangled in the strings attached. After all, if filmmakers wish to reward talent then they could produce the film without all the media hoopla and publicity stunts. If aspiring screenwriters desire to make it in the movie business then they might learn to spot a shark in sheep's clothing and watch Robert Altman's *The Player* for pointers. 🎞

—*Patty-Lynne Herlevi*

CREDITS

Pete O'Malley: Adi Stein
Danny Jacobson: Mike Weinberg
Joe O'Malley: Aidan Quinn
Rabbi Jacobson: Kevin Pollak
Margaret O'Malley: Bonnie Hunt
Patrick O'Malley: Eddie Kaye Thomas
Father Kelly: Brian Dennehy

Origin: USA
Released: 2002

Production: Chris Moore, Matt Damon, Ben Affleck; Live Planet; released by Miramax Films
Directed by: Pete Jones
Written by: Pete Jones
Cinematography by: Pete Biagi
Music by: Danny Lux
Sound: F. Alexander Riordan
Editing: Greg Featherman
Costumes: Stacy Ellen Rich
Production Design: Devorah Herbert
MPAA rating: PG
Running time: 95 minutes

 REVIEWS

Boxoffice. April, 2002, p. 190.
Chicago Sun-Times Online. March 22, 2002.
Entertainment Weekly. March 29, 2002, p. 46.
Los Angeles Times Online. March 22, 2002.
New York Times Online. March 22, 2002.
Rolling Stone Online. March 14, 2002.
Variety. January 28, 2002, p. 38.
Washington Post. May 9, 2002, p. WE44.

QUOTES

Joe O'Malley (Aidan Quinn) about his son Pete's (Adi Stein) interest in religion: "Baseball should be the only thing on an eight-year-old boy's mind."

Storytelling

Todd Solondz's films make many people uncomfortable, and no wonder. They're filled with characters that are too real and way too emotionally flawed—and he doesn't flinch from showing behavior that other filmmakers consider taboo. His characters aren't pretty or glamorous, and often they do things that are disgusting, perverted, and even immoral. *Welcome to the Dollhouse* featured a persecuted adolescent geek who runs away from home and is mistreated. *Happiness* had a whole array of relationship-challenged people with various sexual and emotional problems, including a pedophile and a phone-sex masturbator. But Solondz doesn't usually depict these people to ridicule them—they are not buffoons, but achingly real and desperate misfits.

Entertainment has certain rules, and filmmakers with unique visions defy those rules at their own risk. It's increasingly been acceptable in mainstream movies to explore situa-

tions and characters that are at the edge of civilized behavior. But usually such situations and characters are hyped or glamorized or made violent, seductive, or scary. The intent may be to ridicule, shock, or exploit, but there's always a "hook"—a method to get the audience going, to connect to viewers' easy emotions or ready-made judgments and ideas.

In contrast to most other filmmakers, Solondz's movies can seem flat because they lack such hooks. They even lack the post-modern irony hooks of similar quirky films like *Magnolia* or *American Beauty*. And of his three films, *Storytelling* may be the hardest to get a grip on. As entertainment, it's not compelling—but then Solondz isn't out to entertain. And it is more complex than his other films, for Solondz is working on several levels at once. It's almost as if he's trying to puzzle out what it means to do his kind of filmmaking.

To understand *Storytelling,* two basic assumptions are helpful. First, unlike Solondoz's previous films, this is a comedy. It may not always present itself as such, but the situations and characters are hilarious, though often in a bleak, black way. And at times it appears to be a gentle self-satire. Secondly, it's a film about storytelling, as the title announces—an exploration of what is truth and what is fiction, but, even more to the point, how there are different ways of telling stories, including life stories, and for different purposes, and how entertainment—and giving the audience the pleasure of being entertained—is only one such option.

Storytelling contains two separate pieces. The first, titled "Fiction," is a roughly half-hour film about the participants in a college creative writing class. The second, "Non-fiction," concerns a screwed-up upper-middle-class suburban New Jersey family and an underachieving young college graduate who wants to be a documentary filmmaker and ends up using the family and its aimless oldest son, Scooby, as the core of his film about high schools in America. What connects the two stories? Many things, including the various forms that storytelling can take; meditations on various types of rape and manipulation; and several views on the vagaries of getting an education and growing up in America.

"Fiction" is the simpler, tighter, and less confusing of the two parts. Vi (Selma Blair), a white, suburban college graduate student trying to test her limits of tolerance, is involved with an undergraduate student, Marcus (Leo Fitzpatrick), who has cerebral palsy and is trying to gain acceptance. They are both enrolled in a creative writing class taught by a taciturn, ruthless Pulitzer Prize-winning black novelist, Gary Scott (Robert Wisdom). The sketch skewers the prevailing collegiate atmosphere of hyper-political correctness and students' attempts to navigate the treacherous waters of acceptable discussion and behavior.

When Marcus reads a piece of fiction writing that thinly covers how his sexual affair with Vi makes him feel less like a freak and more like a "cerebral person," the other students in class fawn over it, except for teacher's pet Catherine (Aleksa

Palladino), who calls it trite and banal. The teacher, who everyone in class believes is having an affair with Catherine, agrees that it's a "piece of shit." Marcus leaves the class in tears, then accuses Vi, who didn't comment on the writing, of having patronized him, and angrily tells her that she just wants to have sex with Scott like every other white girl on campus. When Marcus breaks up with Vi, Vi tearfully decides to go out and get some reassuring sex, and then fulfills Marcus's prophecy after meeting her teacher in a bar.

It turns out, however, that Scott is a cold and brutal sexual conqueror, but Vi is so intent on overcoming her upbringing that she goes along with his games. "Don't be a racist," she whispers over and over to herself while looking in the mirror before submitting to sex with Scott (and after learning he keeps kinky nude photos of his other conquests). When Vi comes to the class with a story that relates her degradation at the hands of Scott, again thinly disguised as fiction, she is widely berated as purveying sexism, racism, and trash by her fellow students, until she screams: "But it really happened!" The teacher reminds her that anything written down has already become a story, and must be judged as such, but it's an improvement over her other work.

While "Fiction" concerns denying the validity of things that really happen, "Non-Fiction" is a more complicated exploration of the ways in which people manipulate reality. Toby Oxman (Paul Giamatti) is a uninspired loser with a string of career failures and a new idea: to make a documentary film about how high school has changed since he left it. After encountering Scooby Livingston (Mark Webber) smoking dope in the school bathroom, Toby makes Scooby and his family the center of his film, because Scooby and his father (John Goodman) insist on it. Scooby is desperately trying to resist the demands of his parents that he prepare for college, for he has no ambitions other than to become a TV talk show host.

Less than a minute into a dinner table scene with the Livingstons, Solondz has nailed the uneasily familiar dissonance of a highly dysfunctional modern suburban family. Goodman's father is a mass of boiling, repressed rage and disdain, a heart attack waiting to happen. His wife (Julie Haggerty) is his mousy but manipulative sidekick; son Brady (Noah Fleiss) is a cool athlete and chick magnet, a year younger than Scooby; fifth-grader Mike (Mike Schank) is the prototypical grating brainy smart-ass child prodigy. Scooby doesn't care about much except his CD collection and his TV idols; he is otherwise formless and submits to advances from a gay classmate without seeming to care about his sexual identity.

There are hilarious dinner conversations and preposterous developments. The family has a Salvadoran maid, Consuelo (Lupe Ontiveros), who seems always on the verge of collapsing from her work. She is tormented by Mike, who thinks she is lazy and doesn't understand why she can't overcome her poverty by smiling more. Filmmaker Oxman

seems to ignore the pathos and drama of a family tragedy that occurs, focusing more on whether his film's going to be amusing.

Certainly, these are shallow people, not a sympathetic character in the bunch. They are more broadly drawn than most Solondz characters, and thus easier targets for disdain. Goodman's character pushes his son into college, then pulls strings with alumni donors to get Scooby into Princeton (even though he filled out the SAT scoresheet by punching selectively to spell out an expletive). Scooby is a dolt; when Oxman tells him he's making a documentary film, Scooby replies: "Like *The Blair Witch Project?*" Mike is so annoying that you don't blame the rest of the family for trying to ignore him.

Solondz anticipates the objection that he's taking potshots at easy and familiar targets (all his films are set in suburban New Jersey; Solondz hails from Newark). Oxman's producer points out that his documentary seems rather glib and mean-spirited, and Oxman replies: "What do you mean? I love these people." Along the way, Solondz also finds time to satirize the self-importance of *American Beauty* and to skewer the Hollywood hit machine. The film's final comment, from Scooby to Oxman, in the midst of a family tragedy, is: "You're movie's a hit." This in-your-face ending strikes a bull's-eye in targeting the entertaining industry, for which the bottom line is the only reality.

With solid acting performances from Giamatti, Goodman, Blair, Webber, and the rest of his cast, Solondz continues to take risks in expanding the bounds of what is acceptable dialogue on the big screen. In *Welcome to the Dollhouse,* he broke through the boundaries by which conventional storytelling for the masses treats adolescents in general and those girls not blessed with good looks in particular. In *Happiness,* he viewed sexual dysfunctions—even those most reviled by society—with non-judgmental candor. And in *Storytelling,* he cleverly explores issues of perception and identity.

Running through both segments, for instance, is an expansive and metaphorical dialogue about rape. At one point, Mike asks Consuelo what rape is, and she replies: "It's when you love someone and they don't love you back and you do something about it"—certainly a bizarre definition. Mike later uses his hypnotism tricks to do something about what he perceives as his parents' lack of love for him—he instructs his dad to make him his favorite, get him whatever he wants, and fire Consuelo for being "lazy." In the first segment, when Vi reads her final work, there's a classroom discussion of what constitutes rape. It's another example of how unafraid Solondz is to tackle taboo topics.

Storytelling isn't an easy movie, because it doesn't set out to be entertaining. Viewed as a penetrating black comedy, it's more successful, but it's really an experiment. "Non-fiction," with its series of tragic developments near the end, doesn't hold together nearly as well as "Fiction"—the focus of Solondz's satire keeps shifting, and his points aren't always clearly made. But Solondz makes movies on his own terms—and he demands a suspension of the usual expectations. Not that his films are entirely bleak—they are filled with both pathos and humor. But this time, his characters seem even less sympathetic and more ridiculous than ever, and he does veer dangerously close to getting easy laughs at their expense, while hedging his bets by making such exploitation itself the target of his ridicule.

It's dark, uncertain work, but Solondz is relentless at exposing the charades behind everyday American life and accepted movie-industry storytelling. The song that rolls over the final credits both reveals the ultimate intent of and pokes fun at Solondz's enterprise: "If you're a storyteller, you're without responsibility, and you can let your characters do whatever you want them to do," is a paraphrase of what the song says. And that is the difference between life and a movie, or maybe not—because projecting a personality in society often means adopting a character and telling a story. There are many forms of storytelling, and Solondz wants us to look beyond the usual techniques.

—*Michael Betzold*

CREDITS

Vi: Selma Blair
Marcus: Leo Fitzpatrick
Catherine: Aleksa Palladino
Mr. Scott: Robert Wisdom
Brady Livingston: Noah Fleiss
Toby Oxman: Paul Giamatti
Marty Livingston: John Goodman
Fern Livingston: Julie Hagerty
Consuelo: Lupe Ontiveros
Toby's editor: Franka Potente
Mike: Mike Schank
Scooby Livingston: Mark Webber
Mikey Livingston: Jonathan Osser

Origin: USA
Released: 2001
Production: Ted Hope, Christine Vachon; Killer Films, Good Machine; released by Fine Line Features
Directed by: Todd Solondz
Written by: Todd Solondz
Music by: Belle & Sebastian, Nathan Larson
Sound: Drew Kunin
Music Supervisor: Sue Jacobs
Editing: Alan Oxman
Costumes: John Dunn
Production Design: James Chinlund
MPAA rating: R

Running time: 87 minutes

REVIEWS

Boxoffice. September, 2001, p. 143.
Chicago Sun-Times Online. February 8, 2002.
Entertainment Weekly. February 15, 2002, p. 45.
Los Angeles Times Online. January 25, 2002.
New York Times Online. September 29, 2001.
Sight and Sound. December, 2001, p. 22.
Variety. May 21, 2001, p. 19.
Washington Post. February 8, 2002, p. WE38.

Stuart Little 2

A Little Goes A Long Way.
—Movie tagline

Box Office: $64.7 million

Most mothers have a little trouble cutting the proverbial apron strings and allowing their children the room to begin growing up. They want to keep their offspring from harm, but can sometimes end up smothering the child's burgeoning and desirable sense of independence. All this fretting is understandable, especially if your son is much smaller than most boys, and particularly if he a mouse of only a few inches in height who can only be weighed successfully on a postage meter.

This is the predicament at the heart of *Stuart Little 2,* the sequel to the 1999 hit ($300 million worldwide) which was based upon the 1945 E.B. White classic. The film begins cheerfully with the Little family waking to a new day in their New York City brownstone overlooking Central Park. As "Put a Little Love in Your Heart" is heard on the soundtrack, exceedingly chipper Mr. And Mrs. Little (Hugh Laurie and Geena Davis, reprising their roles) kiss each other and tend to their baby Martha (twins Anna and Ashley Hoelck). Mrs. Little, already bedecked with earrings and a pearl necklace, flings open the window to let some fresh air into the kitchen, and beams as some birds fly off into a sunny sky.

Snug in their upstairs bedroom, Stuart (voiced endearingly once again by Michael J. Fox) and his brother George (Jonathan Lipnicki, also from the original) awaken and prepare for their first soccer game of the season. Stuart sullenly rides the bench, but is then called into the game, much to the chagrin of Mrs. Little. She can barely stifle a strong urge to snatch him off the field, while Mr. Little is and Christina seem to have zero chemistry. It seems impossible to believe that such a dull guy would be so fascinating to Christina. A lot more interesting of a match-up would have been between Christina and Peter's witty brother, Roger (Jason Bateman, in a winning performance).

Once Christina and Courtney get to the wedding they discover that, oh no, the wedding is Peter's own wedding. Don't worry. It all works out in the end. Peter and would-be wife, Judy (Parker Posey, making the most of a wee bit of screen time) decide, on the altar, that marriage isn't right for them, leaving Peter free to pursue Christina. Yawn.

Much more interesting are the comedy bits interspersed with the story. In one scene, Jane has finally found a new man. She has some intimate contact with him and ends up with a dress that has the same problem that a certain blue dress of Monica Lewinsky's had. When she drops in off at her family's dry cleaners, the proprietor asks about her family and asks innocent questions about the nature of the stain. While Jane is stammering out answers, a field trip of kids comes in the store, led by her second grade teacher. Her priest also shows up. It's over-the-top, but it works.

Better are the scenes between Christina and Courtney. When the two are in the bad dress store trying on outfits, one asks, "Do we have time for a movie montage?" The other agrees and they come out dressed in various get-ups including a Madonna outfit and Olivia Newton John's outfit from *Grease*. Courtney, dressed as Julia Roberts in *Pretty Woman*, mocks the scene in that film where Robert's character laughs uproariously when a jewelry box is snapped over her fingers. As John Anderson in *Newsday* put it, it's "so catty you can smell the litter box."

What is unusual about the film is that the actors really do seem to be friends and really do seem to be having a good time. When Christina and Courtney are trying on clothes, they push their stomachs out and giggle, mocking their supposed fatness. Courtney wags her arm, letting the flesh of her upper arm wobble as she asks "What is THIS?" It's fun to see a women's friendship in the movies that seems real. Usually whenever a film about women's friendships makes it to the screen, it seems like it always has to be some big, serious drama where someone ends up dying of a hideous disease.

It's strange, then, that the movie often seems so anti-women. In one scene, Christina and Courtney stand by the side of the road, gyrating in their underwear to "Escape (The Pina Colada Song)." In another scene, women in a bathroom gather around to marvel at Courtney's surgically-enhanced bust line. As they touch the surgeon's handiwork, the restroom door opens and a guy standing outside leers, "Now I know why they always go to the bathroom together." Besides being tasteless and unrealistic, it commits the perhaps worse sin of being a lame joke.

Critics mostly detested the film, with a few exemptions here and there. One such exemption was John Anderson of *Newsday*. "There's a willingness to take chances and a frankness about the emotional and other byproducts of sex that's refreshing, as well as a smartly vulgar script by Nancy Pimental," he wrote. Elvis Mitchell of the *New York Times* felt differently. "For those who thing that movies by the Farrelly brothers or Todd Solondz are the Mount Kilimanjaro of bad taste, it's time to grab your parka and goggles—there's a new peak to climb." Owen Gleiberman of *Entertainment Weekly* gave the film a C + and wrote, "*The Sweetest Thing*, a girls-rule! gross-out comedy pretending to be a romantic comedy, is a movie in which laughter and self-exploitation merge into jolly soft-porn 'empowerment.'"

—*Jill Hamilton*

CREDITS

Christina Walters: Cameron Diaz
Courtney: Christina Applegate
Peter: Thomas Jane
Jane: Selma Blair
Roger: Jason Bateman
Judy: Parker Posey

Origin: USA
Released: 2002
Production: Cathy Konrad; Konrad Pictures; released by Columbia Pictures
Directed by: Roger Kumble
Written by: Nancy M. Pimenthal
Cinematography by: Anthony B. Richmond
Music by: Ed Shearmur
Sound: James Steube
Music Supervisor: John Houlihan
Editing: Wendy Greene Bricmont, David Rennie
Costumes: Denise Wingate
Production Design: Jon Gary Steele
MPAA rating: R
Running time: 84 minutes

REVIEWS

Chicago Sun-Times Online. April 12, 2002.
Entertainment Weekly. April 19, 2002, p. 46.
Los Angeles Times Online. April 12, 2002.
New York Times Online. April 12, 2002.
People. April 22, 2002, p. 35.
USA Today Online. April 11, 2002.
Variety. April 8, 2002, p. 30.
Washington Post. April 12, 2002, p. WE37.

Swept Away

When one sees a remake of a film, it is near impossible not to compare it to the original. Understanding this pitfall, I tried not to compare Guy Ritchie's *Swept Away* with the controversial 1974 original. It was absolutely impossible to do. The director of the 1974 version, Lena Wurtmuller, discussed political issues such as Marxism and capitalism, using the backdrop of relationships to further her dialogue. In 1974, the themes expressed in *Swept Away* were daunting and ahead of their time—placing the film in a category all its own. The current *Swept Away* did not have this particular benefit of naivety in its audience. We are jaded, plain and simple. I am no different than anyone else, however, and I could not stop myself from comparing the two films and, to put it mildly, Ritchie's version did not sweep me away, rather I wanted it to be swept away, like maybe under the rug.

Ritchie's past directorial attempts have had interesting parts to them, and, quite frankly, were some of the best crime films of the 1990's. *Lock, Stock and Two Smoking Barrels* and *Snatch* were essentially the same movie, but they were good regardless. Both *Lock* and *Snatch* were interesting and compelling for what they were and I enjoyed them both. *Swept Away* was a mistake, and for many reasons, far too many to recount them all here.

In terms of the overall story, the 2002 *Swept Away* was very much like the original. The main character, Amber (Madonna), is the obnoxious wife of a patient millionaire. They are on a cruise on a private yacht from Greece to Italy with five other passengers, none of whom have any importance to the general plot. Amber mercilessly insults Giuseppe (Adriano Giannini—the son of Gianni Giannini who played the same part in the 1974 film) the deckhand because she has immediately decided he is ill-mannered and not very bright. Although this was the exact premise of the first film, Ritchie allows the script to just go too far. It becomes comical how petty and bitchy Amber becomes, quickly re-sulting in it seeming implausible beyond belief. In the original the bitchiness is kept in check and therefore the class bias seems more plausible and less vaudeville-like.

Amber bullies Giuseppe into taking her out in the yacht's dingy, even though Giuseppe thinks it is a bad idea. They run out of gas and begin to drift. Amber, through a series of temper tantrums and insults, puts a hole in the dingy. They drift at sea until they wash up on a deserted island; this is Giuseppe's time to shine. He may not have wealth but his common sense and survival skills are worth much more than Amber's money in this situation. He has the upper hand now.

Ritchie's film lacks the political motives and the social commentary of the Wertmuller film, and I really cannot understand how Ritchie could have deleted this from the script. What is the point of making *Swept Away* if you are going to whitewash it politically and miss the basic premise? To do so leaves a very ugly, misogynistic shell of a film.

Essentially without the political commentary of the original, the remake is a film relying on the chemistry of Madonna and Giannini. It is a sad reality that the two of them could not take this picture and run with it. It has all the makings of a sexy romp of a film—deserted island, lots of alcohol, and two attractive, tan, nude people romping on the beach. It should have been sexy and fun, but it was just painful to watch. Madonna is too forceful and bold for a film about a woman who is swept away by emotions. It seems implausible that Madonna, superstar sex woman, would ever allow this to happen. The casting of Madonna was all wrong and the casting of Adriano Giannini seems just a cheap trick.

The original film did not fall into the trap of conventional love attractions, while this one fell all over it. It just seemed so contrived and tried so hard, yet failed at every turn. Wurtmuller showcased a love film with such interesting themes as capitalism and Marxism; this watered-down version by Guy Ritchie takes all the politics out but doesn't replace them with anything interesting. This film is an empty shell, and I think we all know Ritchie is capable of better things and will patiently wait for him to make this up to us.

—Laura Abraham

CREDITS

Amber: Madonna
Giuseppe: Adriano Giannini
Marina: Jeanne Tripplehorn
Anthony: Bruce Greenwood
Michael: David Thornton
Captain: Yorgo Voyagis
Debi: Elizabeth Banks
Todd: Michael Beattie

Origin: USA
Released: 2002
Production: Matthew Vaughn; SKA Films; released by Screen Gems
Directed by: Guy Ritchie
Written by: Guy Ritchie
Cinematography by: Alex Barber
Music by: Michel Colombier
Sound: Simon Hayes
Editing: Eddie Hamilton
Art Direction: Damon Earnshaw
Costumes: Arianne Phillips
Production Design: Russell de Rozario
MPAA rating: R
Running time: 93 minutes

 REVIEWS

Chicago Sun-Times Online. October 11, 2002.
Entertainment Weekly. October 18, 2002, p. 91.
Los Angeles Times Online. October 11, 2002.
New York Times Online. October 11, 2002.
People. October 21, 2002, p. 44.
Variety Online. October 11, 2002.
Washington Post. October 11, 2002, p. WE47.

Swimfan

Ben Cronin had the perfect life until he met the new girl.
—Movie tagline

Obsession. Betrayal. Revenge. Some girls have all the fun.
—Movie tagline

His biggest fan just became his worst nightmare.
—Movie tagline

 Box Office: $28.5 million

One of the production companies that was behind the making of *Swimfan* was Further Films, Michael Douglas' company. It's kind of an odd match-up because *Swimfan* could be best described as *Fatal Attraction* for teens. Maybe it was that the times were different back in 1987 when *Fatal Attraction* was released; maybe it was that *Fatal Attraction* had the considerable acting talents of Douglas and Glenn Close to hold up the movie—but some-how *Swimfan* doesn't seem nearly as important or interesting as *Fatal Attraction*. It wasn't that the earlier film was a superb film or anything like that, but the female psycho-stalker was at least a novel concept. Plus director Adrian Lyne gave the film his typically stylish sheen.

Films like these are like two-hour infomercials for monogamy. The message is that one who cheats will be severely punished. Not only will the cheater have to tell their significant other, but they will also have their lives ruined by the one with whom they've cheated. The "other woman" is not a reasonable person who's making a decision, albeit not the best one, and accepting the consequences; but someone who's completely psychotic and ready to start going on a killing spree.

When *Swimfan* opens, Ben Cronin (Jesse Bradford) has his life together. He's a high school student who has a nice girlfriend, Amy (Shiri Appleby), and a bright future. His swim coach, Coach Simkins (Dan Hedaya), tells Ben that at the next meet—just eight days away!—there will be scouts from Stanford watching him. If Ben can shave a few seconds off of his time, he might get recruited by Stanford and get a chance to make the Olympic team. This means a lot to Ben because he's recently turned his life around. He was formerly a drug user and had gotten in trouble with the law for breaking and entering to support his habit. With the help of a new found passion for swimming, the support of Amy and his supportive mother (Kate Burton), Ben got his life back on track.

But there's going to be something that comes between him and his dream—the Evil Sexual Woman. The one here is Madison Bell (Erika Christensen), a new student in school who, oddly, dresses like a heroine from a 1940's movie. The rest of Ben's swim team is lusting after Madison, but Madison only is interested in Ben. He fixes her locker, gives her a ride home and soon ends up on a date with her at the local diner. He tells her he has a girlfriend, which in his mind seems to exonerate him from what else might happen during the rest of the evening, and Madison is undeterred.

She asks him for swim lessons and they end up at the school's pool in the late-night romantic light. (Too bad she doesn't pay better attention during the lessons because they could have come in mighty handy during the final fight scene in the pool.) The swim lessons turn into a kissing session which turn into sex. "It's okay, I want you to," whispers Madison. That's all the convincing Ben seems to need. He's agreeable that when Madison coos, "Tell me you love me. You don't have to mean it," Ben complies, although he's a little freaked out.

After they do the forbidden deed, the two agree that they won't tell anyone about it and that they will just be friends. But Madison idea of being friends is pretty intense. She shows up at Ben's house bearing flowers for his mother's birthday. "It's so nice to finally meet your mother," she says, even though she's only known Ben a few days herself. She pages him incessantly. And when he checks his e-mail, he has 82 messages from Swimfan, aka Madison.

Meanwhile, Ben is getting a bit freaked about Amy finding out. This isn't helped by her calling him up and saying stuff like, "I want you to know that I know" or "You're busted." In a stupid filmmaker's trick, Amy invariably is talking about some other benign thing. Finally Ben stops being nice to Madison and states his true feelings. "I think that you're misunderstanding our relationship in a very fundamental way," he tells her. This is unacceptable information to Madison. We can tell because, whenever Madison is feeling a little crazed, director John Polson jumps between cuts from multiple takes and puts crazy strings on the soundtrack. It's a self-conscious technique that doesn't work and, in fact, takes away from what could have been the natural drama of the moment.

Ben starts losing his focus as the spurned Madison turns vengeful. Madison comes to Ben's job as a hospital orderly and switches his pills so that he accidentally gives a lovable (of course) old man a nearly fatal dose. She steals his car and runs over good girl, Amy, making it look like he was the driver. And on the day of the Big Meet, she somehow makes Ben fail the urine test so that he tests positive for steroids. Since Ben has had a checked past, the police and his mother are somewhat doubtful of his claims of innocence. To try to clear his name, Ben has to enlist the help of Madison's weird, outcast cousin (James Debello). The action all has to end up back at the pool (instead of *Fatal Attraction*'s bathtub), and it involves hand-to-hand combat.

It's hard to say just why the film doesn't work. The best possibility is that maybe it was just a stupid idea and from the outset was unworkable. It's also not helped by the acting. Bradford, who looks like a cross between Donny Osmond and Freddie Prinze Jr., has as his main acting device a cocky smirk. It's difficult to feel any sympathy for a character who is smirking all the time. In fact, it's pretty easy to feel a bit of happiness that such a jerk is getting such a bad string of luck. Christensen is slightly better but not by much. Her idea of acting crazy is to get a faraway look in her eye and frown. She seems spacey and unreal. Appleby is bland and sort of clingy as the long-suffering girlfriend. The bright spots are Hedaya as the coach and Clayne Crawford as Josh, Ben's competitor on the swim team. Crawford is a charismatic bad boy, and it will be interesting to see if he gets some better roles from this film.

Critics did not seem like they'd be candidates to start stalking the film since there wasn't much of a love connection happening. Manohla Dargis of the *Los Angeles Times* wrote, "Ripped from the pages of the 'See Dick Run, See Jane Stalk Him' handbook, the thrill-less thriller *Swimfan* is as dumb as it gets." Jonathan Foreman of the *New York Post* wrote that the film "falls victim to sloppy plotting, an insultingly unbelievable final act and a villainess who is too crazy to be interesting." And Stephen Holden of the *New York Times* wrote, "Like *Cruel Intentions*, *Swimfan* is entertaining enough to be considered a guilty pleasure. but to transcend the teenage movie genre both movies would have needed a baby Glenn Close, and both came up short."

—*Jill Hamilton*

CREDITS

Madison: Erika Christensen
Ben: Jesse Bradford
Amy: Shiri Appleby
Carla: Kate Burton
Josh: Clayne Crawford
Randy: Jason Ritter
Rene: Kia Joy Goodwin
Coach Simkins: Dan Hedaya
Mr. Tillman: Michael Higgins
Detective John Zabel: Nick Sandow
Danta: James DeBello
Mrs. Egan: Pamela Isaacs
Aunt Gretchen: Phyllis Somerville

Origin: USA
Released: 2002
Production: John Penotti, Alison Lyon Segan, Joe Caracciolo Jr.; Greenstreet, Further Films, Cobalt Media Group; released by 20th Century-Fox
Directed by: John Polson
Written by: Charles F. Bohl, Phillip Schneider
Cinematography by: Giles Nuttgens
Music by: Louis Febre
Sound: Charles R. Hunt
Editing: Sarah Flack
Art Direction: Frank White III
Costumes: Arjun Bhasin
Production Design: Kalina Ivanov
MPAA rating: PG-13
Running time: 93 minutes

REVIEWS

Entertainment Weekly. September 20, 2002, p. 74.
Los Angeles Times Online. September 6, 2002.
New York Times Online. September 6, 2002.
USA Today Online. September 6, 2002.
Variety Online. September 8, 2002.

Madison (Erika Christensen) to Ben (Jesse Bradford) about his girlfriend: "She doesn't love you like I do, Ben! No one will ever love you like I love you. You love me, I know it!"

Tadpole

Everyone says he should date girls his own age. Oscar respectfully disagrees.
—Movie tagline

 Box Office: $2.8 million

Gary Winick's *tadpole* was a hit at this year's Sundance Film Festival, where it was awarded the prize for Best Director. The epitome of low-budget filmmaking, *Tadpole* was shot in two weeks with a hand-held digital camera and has the rough, grainy look common to movies shot on digital video. The screenplay by Heather McGowan and Niels Mueller revolves around a precocious 15-year-old prep school student who is in love with his stepmother. Played by Aaron Stanford, who was actually 23 when the film was shot but can pass for 15, Oscar Grubman fancies himself a sophisticate—he reads Voltaire, speaks fluent French, and loves to discuss literature and philosophy. When his friend and confidant, Charlie (Robert Iler), points out that one of their classmates, the pretty Miranda (Kate Mara), likes him, Oscar is dismissive. Her hands, he claims, are like those of a child. He prefers Eve (Sigourney Weaver), his father's wife, and he tortures himself over how to make his feelings known to her. *Tadpole* has a promising setup, and certain scenes are very funny, but the overall result is quite uneven, with the screenplay turning out to be as fuzzy as the camerawork.

A student at the exclusive Chauncey school, Oscar is heading home for the Thanksgiving break to his family's fashionable apartment on Manhattan's Upper East Side, where his father, a Columbia history professor named Stanley (John Ritter), is hosting a dinner attended mainly by fellow academics. Concerned by his son's apparent lack of interest in girls, Stanley tries to help him along by having Oscar escort home a cute girl named Daphne (Alicia Van Couvering). Their conversation tells us just about everything we need to know about Oscar—he is not interested in the pop music that appeals to kids his age, and Daphne concludes that he is "like a 40-year-old trapped in a 15-year-old's body."

That night Oscar gets drunk in a bar and staggers out, only to bump into Diane (Bebe Neuwirth), a family friend who takes him home to sober up. Using her skills as a chiropractor, Diane starts to give Oscar a massage, and very quickly his shirt and sweater come off. Because Diane is wearing a scarf she borrowed from Eve, Oscar starts to swoon over Diane, and a passionate kiss soon leads them to the bedroom. Oscar wakes up the next morning horrified, presumably because he feels that he has been unfaithful to Eve and is worried that she and his father will find out what has happened. This raises an odd question about Oscar, namely, why he would fall for the staid Eve over the sexy and fun Diane. Weaver's rather flat performance does little to make us understand Oscar's attraction to Eve, while Neuwirth's Diane is the best thing in the movie. Dressed in leather skirts and sporting a frisky, devil-may-care attitude, Diane has a flirtatious, lusty streak yet still possesses the culture and sophistication that seem to appeal to Oscar. Why he should suddenly be repulsed by what he has done and hold Eve as an ideal is more than a bit puzzling.

From here on, the big questions in *Tadpole* are when will everyone find out what happened between Diane and Oscar and how will he react when they do? Before these questions are addressed, however, the thin story is filled out with sequences that, while sometimes amusing, feel contrived and end up going nowhere. Trying to impress Eve, Oscar brings her lunch at work. She is a medical researcher, and they have a conversation about the heart as an organ and as a metaphor for love, but they talk at cross-purposes. Oblivious to his obvious affection for her, she tells Oscar, "The heart is simple; fixing it is complicated," and "Your heart can fit right in my hand"—lines that are too obvious in their double meaning.

There is also an odd scene in which Oscar tracks down Diane in a restaurant with some girlfriends, who immediately become smitten with him. One woman even gives him her phone number after he has dazzled her with his scholarly acumen. The film posits the dubious notion that sophisticated New York women have become so disenchanted with adult men that a precocious teenager expounding on French philosophy is just what they want. Most women, however, would probably, at best, be mildly amused by Oscar, who comes across as more pedantic than charming. Perhaps if this scene were played as farce, it would be more effective, but Neuwirth makes the scene work as well as it does because of the wicked satisfaction Diane takes in showing off her little conquest to her friends and watching them flirt shamelessly.

While *Tadpole*'s light comedy is genial enough, the film never really develops a point of view about Oscar's plight. It is hard to tell whether we are to take his desires seriously or laugh at his impossible lurch into early adulthood. When Diane tells him that Eve as a young woman loved Elvis Presley and fell for men with sideburns, Oscar tries to fashion fake sideburns to impress her. Could a boy who debates literature with adults really believe that fake sideburns could make him look anything other than silly? There is simply no consistency to Oscar's character, and, while Stanford is convincing in his earnestness, the screenplay does not give him more to do than act rather smug and suffer from an aching lovesickness.

The highlight of the movie is a tense but funny dinner involving Oscar, Diane, Stanley, and Eve. Hoping to ensure that Diane does not reveal what they did, Oscar tries to stop her from drinking too much wine and talks to her in French, while the clueless Eve and Stanley seem to be in their own world. Diane does her best to make Oscar uncomfortable, even putting her foot on his crotch under the table and later, when they are away from the others, planting a big kiss on him when she thinks that no one can see them. But Stanley notices their reflection in a mirror, and they are forced to admit that they have made love. The revelation scene is almost guaranteed to bring laughs, thanks largely to Neuwirth's snaky charm and the way she toys with the nervous Oscar. But in terms of the overall story, this scene (the best in the film) really becomes a stopping point. Oscar's exposure does not mean much since nothing is at stake—Oscar and Diane are not in love, and she is not going to be charged with a crime (that is never really an issue).

The angry Eve confronts Diane, but Diane's explanation that it was easy to fall for such a passionate, smart boy does not fit the reality that their lovemaking was virtually an accident, a chance encounter. Eve works through her anger at Oscar in a game of tennis when she conks him on the head with a tennis ball. When he finally declares his love at home, she simply walks away, but Oscar gets up the courage to give her a long kiss, which she returns in kind before abruptly leaving the room. The film has been working up to this climactic moment from the beginning and then, amazingly enough, does nothing with it.

Tadpole never develops its story beyond Oscar's adolescent crush and does not honestly deal with its consequences. Indeed, the most disappointing aspect of the film is its abrupt ending, which finds a suddenly transformed Oscar heading back to school. He seems to have gotten over his infatuation with Eve and his interest in Voltaire—he leaves his copy of *Candide* on a public bench—but his change is never explained. He and Eve seem fine with each other, so how they dealt with the kiss is never revealed. He has even encouraged his somewhat self-absorbed father to be more attentive to Eve. The last scene finds Oscar taking an interest in Miranda, who has had her eye on him from the beginning. Apparently, his interest in older women was just a phase that he has now grown out of, but one cannot really be sure what has happened. His last words to Charlie about Eve—"It wasn't as important as I thought it was"—leave us feeling that Oscar's core conflict was not very serious after all. For a film that runs a mere 77 minutes, surely more time

could have been spent spelling out how Oscar comes to accept his adolescence.

Tadpole is divided into chapters, with quotations from Voltaire appearing as inter-titles (an initially cute conceit that ultimately feels like an attempt to make the film seem more intellectual than it is). As Oscar is boarding the train back for school, Miranda speaks the last quotation to him: "If we don't find anything pleasant, at least we shall find something new." *Tadpole* itself, however, turns this idea around. Winick does not discover anything new in this story of teenage angst and heartache, but it is at times pleasant enough—that is, until the virtually missing final act, when it completely falls apart.

—*Peter N. Chumo II*

CREDITS

Oscar Grubman: Aaron Stanford
Eve: Sigourney Weaver
Stanley Grubman: John Ritter
Diane: Bebe Neuwirth
Charlie: Robert Iler
Jimmy: Peter Appel
Phil: Adam LeFevre

Origin: USA
Released: 2002
Directed by: Gary Winick
Written by: Heather McGowan, Niels Mueller
Cinematography by: Hubert Taczanowski
Sound: William Cozy
Editing: Susan Littenberg
Art Direction: Sara Parks
Costumes: Suzanne Schwarzer
Production Design: Anthony Gasparro
MPAA rating: PG-13
Running time: 77 minutes

 ## REVIEWS

Boxoffice. April, 2002, p. 174.
Chicago Sun-Times Online. July 26, 2002.
Entertainment Weekly. July 26, 2002, p. 44.
Los Angeles Times Online. July 19, 2002.
New York Times Online. July 19, 2002.
People. August 5, 2002, p. 34.
USA Today Online. July 18, 2002.
Variety. January 21, 2002, p. 33.
Washington Post. July 16, 2002, p. WE37.

Eve (Sigourney Weaver) to teenaged stepson Oscar (Aaron Stanford): "The heart is simple. Fixing it is complicated."

Talk to Her
(Hable con Ella)

 Box Office: $1.3 million

In the United States, *Talk to Her*, the film by Pedro Almodovar was one of the most acclaimed films of the year. It was named one of the best pictures of the year by over 100 of the nation's most prominent film critics, including those from *Time* and the *New York Times*. It won several awards, including a Golden Globe Award for best foreign language film and a best director award from the Los Angeles Film Critics Association.

Despite all the praise, there was no way *Talk to Her* was going to win an Academy Award for Best Foreign Language Film. The reason? It wasn't nominated. The way that the Oscars work in that category is that countries are in charge of choosing for themselves what film that will be entered from their country. Spain entered a film called *Mondays in the Sun*, which was about unemployed dock workers. The film was a big hit in Spain and won several Goya awards, but was virtually unseen in the U.S. An article in the *Los Angeles Times* noted that *Talk to Her*'s chances were also hindered by the fact that the film was controversial in Spain because one of the lead characters commits a serious crime. (Director Almodovar had won a best foreign language Oscar two years previous for *All About My Mother*.)

Talk To Her was seen as somewhat of a departure for Almodovar. He had become famous for non-conventional, often campy, over-the-top films. This film is more traditional, although it contains an almost unspeakable crime, bizarre love relationships and a lead character that's kind of a creepy stalker. And it does veer strangely at least once. In one scene, Almodovar has created an old black and white silent movie in which a man shrinks to about the size of a toothbrush. While in bed with his sleeping lover, he decides that the perfect way to be close to her forever is to climb up inside her sex organ. (Imagine the set designers working on that particular prop.)

Almodovar takes his time with the film, and it unfolds with a slow sort of inevitability. He lingers on scenes that aren't necessarily integral to moving the plot along and this gives the film a palpable presence that stays with you long after the closing credits have faded from the screen. One powerful scene like that is one in which Lydia (Rosario Flores) gets ready for a bullfight. She is a rarity in Spain, a famous female matador. As she is dressed for the fight, Almodovar lingers over the details of the process—the way the tights are pulled up, the manner in which the pants are fastened. The scene shows the power of a uniform and tradition. As the clothes go onto her, Lydia changes from Lydia the woman to the fierce matador. In another scene, the Brazilian artist Caetano Veloso sings a mournful song. It adds buckets of atmosphere, but it's also a nice touch that Almodovar lets the movie stop for a few moments while the audiences can take a brief break and enjoy the song.

Lydia has recently broken up with her famous matador boyfriend and started a relationship with Marco (Dario Grandinetti), a journalist who's trying to do a story on her. The couple's burgeoning romance is stopped abruptly when Lydia is gored by a bull during a fight. (A testament to the non-American origin of this film is that the camera does not linger lovingly over any gore.) Lydia goes into a coma and is pronounced brain dead. Marco does not know how to deal with his grief except to linger by her bedside, hoping that she miraculously will wake. He meets a kindred spirit down the hall when he spies Benigno (Javier Camara) tending to another coma victim, Alicia (Leonor Watling).

Benigno is a full-time nurse for Alicia and is devoted to her. He bathes her, fixes her hair the way she liked it and takes her outside to see the sky. The nerdy, slightly overweight Benigno talks to her as though she is his girlfriend and calls their relationship "better than most married couples" since they get along so well. In his grief, Marco finds himself somewhat jealous of their odd relationship.

As the story continues, Benigno's relationship with Alicia gets a bit more complicated. In flashbacks, we learn that Benigno tended to his ailing mother for years before she died. After her death, he spends his time staring out his window at a dance studio where Alicia is a student. To get closer to her, he finds out where she lives and schedules an appointment with her psychiatrist father who works out of the home. During his appointment, he pretends to be troubled by his sexuality. (It's ironic, since that is certainly a real problem he has.) After the appointment, he sneaks into Alicia's room and steals her hairclip. It's definitely a creepy move, but the strange thing about this film is that, in the context, it's almost an understandable move. Benigno is exactly on the border of being a sympathetic character and a despicable one.

It's even more creepy that after Alicia is in the auto accident that sends her into a coma, she is cared for by her stalker. In the brief encounters she had with him during her conscious life, she didn't care for him much. Would she want him to be massaging lotion into her legs? And in such a sensual fashion?

The love relationships in the film are all odd. Benigno and Alicia's relationship is intense and one-sided. Marco and Benigno's relationship has homoerotic overtones and the weird commonality of girlfriends in comas. And Marco is somehow more close to the comatose Lydia than he was with the conscious Lydia.

It's also interesting to see how a coma robs a person of their essence. When, in flashback, we see Alicia practicing as a ballerina, it is shocking to see her up and animated. She seems so alive and is so different from her comatose self. And Lydia is such a strong vibrant character before she is gored—she fills the screen. After, she has only a weak, wounded presence.

The acting is fine throughout the film. Grandinetti's Marco has a strong appealing presence and Flores' Lydia is exciting to watch. She is not beautiful in the traditional American way—she's too angular for that—but she's an arresting presence. Camara's Benigno is good in how he defies characterizations. He seems like he might be gay, but lives his life in dedication and love to one woman. He does a horribly violent thing, but somehow seems like a fairly gentle guy. Geraldine Chaplin shows up as Alicia's tightly-wound and emaciated dance teacher.

Most critics liked the film. Roger Ebert of the *Chicago Sun-Times* wrote, "*Talk to Her* combines improbable melodrama with subtly kinky bedside vigils and sensational denouements, and yet at the end, we are undeniably touched. No director since Fassbinder has been able to evoke such complex emotions with such problematic material." Elvis Mitchell of the *New York Times* wrote, "Like all great doomed affairs, *Talk to Her* is full of lovely, sweet suffering. And when it's over, the realization of how much the movie means to you really sinks in; you can't get it out of your heart." Lou Lumeneck of the *New York Post* wrote, "*Talk to Her* isn't quite as accessible or as deeply moving as his masterpiece, *All About My Mother*. It's a tad too self-consciously a work of art for that. But it's still a must-see for anyone who's halfway serious about film."

—*Jill Hamilton*

CREDITS

Benigno: Javier Camara
Marco: Dario Grandinetti
Lydia: Rosario Flores
Alicia: Leonor Watling
Katerina: Geraldine Chaplin

Origin: Spain
Language: Spanish
Released: 2002

Production: Esther Garcia; El Deseo; released by Sony Pictures Classics
Directed by: Pedro Almodovar
Written by: Pedro Almodovar
Cinematography by: Javier Aguirresarobe
Music by: Alberto Iglesias
Sound: Miguel Rejas
Editing: Jose Salcedo
Costumes: Sonia Grande
Production Design: Antxon Gomez
MPAA rating: R
Running time: 112 minutes

REVIEWS

Boxoffice. October, 2002, p. 55.
Chicago Sun-Times Online. December 25, 2002.
Entertainment Weekly. November 29, 2002, p. 80.
Los Angeles Times Online. November 3, 2002.
Los Angeles Times Online. December 13, 2002.
New York Times Online. October 12, 2002.
Rolling Stone. November 28, 2002, p. 98.
Sight and Sound. July, 2002, p. 25.
Sight and Sound. September, 2002, p. 76.
Variety. March 25, 2002, p. 38.
Washington Post. December 25, 2002, p. C1.

AWARDS AND NOMINATIONS

British Acad. 2002: Foreign Film, Orig. Screenplay
Golden Globes 2003: Foreign Film
L.A. Film Critics 2002: Director (Almodovar)
Natl. Bd. of Review 2002: Foreign Film
Nomination:
Oscars 2002: Director (Almodovar), Orig. Screenplay.

Texas Rangers

Count Your Bullets.
—Movie tagline
Before There Was Law, There Were The Rangers.
—Movie tagline

It is easy to get nostalgic about the Western, that dwindling and diminishing genre that once encompassed happy illusions about the Frontier as a testing place for manly virtues, Westward movement, progress, and a sort of paradigm for the American national character. The Western achieved the height of its popularity during the 1950s during the optimism of the Eisenhower era, before national goals were complicated by an undeclared war in Southeast Asia and powerful new notions about the morality of waging war outside our national boundaries, colonialism, and the exploitation of indigenous people. During the 1950s the Western dominated television networks, with series such as *Wagon Train, Gunsmoke, The Rifleman, Bonanza, Wyatt Earp,* and *Have Gun, Will Travel.* By the end of the decade, there had been such a glut of Westerns on the market that audiences began to tire of the genre formulas.

Things changed after Vietnam and the national bloodbath that saturated television screens, and the Western changed as well with Sam Peckinpah's *The Wild Bunch* (1969), a film with complicated characters that both began and ended with a bloodbath, involving the slaughter of innocent civilians. This so-called Post-Western, made during the twilight of the Vietnam war, suggested that violence might be justified if in the service of idealism, eradicating a dictatorial military regime in Mexico. A half-dozen years later, after the evacuation of Saigon, the national mood had no stomach for violence. The only successful revival of the Western was Don Siegel's *The Shootist* (1976), starring John Wayne as a dying gunfighter, determined to end his life in a blaze of glory in 1902, long after the Frontier had "vanished," and Clint Eastwood's *Unforgiven* (1992), an "Anti-Western" with Eastwood himself playing an anti-hero.

Meanwhile, a few Westerns continued to be made by younger talents, Lawrence Kasdan's *Silverado* (1985), for example, starring Kevin Kline, Kevin Costner, Jeff Goldblum, and Danny Glover, and, later still, the less successful *Young Guns* (1988), starring Emilio Estevez, Kiefer Sutherland, Charlis Sheen, and Lou Diamond Philllips. Steve Miner's *Texas Rangers* follows in this tradition, showcasing younger, television actors fighting bandits in the Texas Southwest in 1875, ten years after the American Civil War. It involves a "legendary" story of how the Texas Rangers were regrouped to establish law and order on the Mexican border. The screenplay by Scott Busby and Martin Copeland, was adapted from the book *Taming of the Nueces Strip: The Story of McNelly's Texas Rangers,* by George Durham, as told to Clyde Wantland. Although certainly a Western in terms of setting and geography, it is also a post-Civil War story. Like Ang Lee's *Ride with the Devil* (1999), another Civil War story involving the Kansas-Missouri Border Wars, it features an African-American "scout" riding with the outlaws (in the case of Lee's film) and with the Rangers (in the case of Miner's *Texas Rangers*).

During the Civil War, according to the film's opening credits, the only lawmen in Southern Texas were the Texas Rangers, who disbanded to fight for the Confederacy. Ranger Captain Leander McNelly (Dylan McDermott, the star lawyer of the ABC television series *The Practice*), a preacher from San Antonio, left his family and ministry to fight with his men. After the war McNelly returned to a defeated Texas, only to find his wife and three children gone,

taken by bandits. Ten years later the Governor of Texas wanted to re-commission the Texas Rangers under McNelly's command. The Governor's agents find McNelly, sick with consumption, digging his own grave. Why? Because, he tells them, if he waited until winter, "the ground will be froze." He expects to die; he has nothing to lose, and he is determined to avenge the deaths of his family. But McNelly is not the only avenger in the plot.

The source story was told from the perspective of George Durham (Ashton Kutcher in the film), but the central character is Lincoln Rogers Dunnison (James Van Der Beek), who goes to Brownsville to join the Rangers after his mother, father, and brother are shot down by John King Fisher (Alfred Molina) and his outlaw band. The Dunnisons have just arrived in Texas when a cattle auction is about to take place. Fisher and his men ride into town intending to steal the cattle. The Marshal challenges them and the slaughter begins. Lincoln Rogers Dunnison is saved only because his mortally wounded brother falls on top of him during the shoot-out. He then rides to Brownsville with George Durham, intending to become a Texas Ranger. When they arrive, a vigilante committee is being formed, just as McNelly and two deputies ride into town. McNelly tells the vigilante committee to disband, and when the leader refuses and draws on him, McNelly answers with guns blazing.

Dunnison becomes a Ranger, despite his inexperience, because he can write and is multilingual. McNelly dictates his reports to Dunnison, his scribe, and this device advances the plot as 30 raw recruits are trained. "The Lord is coming for me, Mr. Dunnison," McNelly explains. "Our mission is to stop the outlaw John King Fisher," who has killed 400 men while rustling cattle into Mexico and selling them to the Mexican army. Fisher advises the Mexicans to advance into Southern Texas, which he believes is inadequately defended. Fisher tells General Cortinas (Joe Renteria) that the Republic of Texas is theirs for the taking. But, meanwhile, McNelly is building an army of Rangers. Within weeks the Rangers are patrolling the Rio Grande. Their first campaign at Mesa Valley is successful, and two of Fisher's men are lynched (against Dunnison's protest, since he believes the outlaws were entitled to a trial). McNelly defends his harsh treatment by saying "The meek will inherit the earth, Mr. Dunnison, [but] somebody's got to get it ready for them."

McNelly then goes to the ranch of his friend Richard Dukes (Tom Skerritt) in Palo Alto, telling him he's "got twelve men to bury." They capture a Mexican woman named Perdida (Leonor Varela), who gives McNelly misleading information that takes the Rangers to the Logan ranch after they take on new recruits. But McNelly makes a mistake by trusting her, as he realizes when he asks himself, "why didn't they kill her?" McNelly concludes that "The raid can only be at the Dukes ranch," but by the time he gets back there, the raid has already taken place, and Richard Dukes has been taken hostage. The Rangers catch up with the Fisher gang at the Rio Grande, with Fisher and Richard Dukes safely on the Mexican side. McNelly agrees to exchange Perdida for Richard Dukes, but Fisher hangs Dukes anyway. Infuriated, McNelly is ready to shoot Perdida in reprisal, but is persuaded by the law-abiding Dunnison to send her back across the Rio Grande. She was coerced into betraying the Rangers because Fisher held her family hostage back in Mexico. Unlike the brutal Fisher, the Rangers are capable of mercy and decency, even though their commander is a dangerous man, not to be crossed.

On November 19th, McNelly dictates his Last Will and Testament to Dunnison, whom he designates as "a soldier fit to lead." The Rangers decide to ride into Mexico to attack Fisher's outlaw band. This results in a Mexican stand-off. Fisher has his gun on McNelly, Dunnison has his gun on Fisher, but he manages to rescue McNelly and shoots Fisher, avenging the murders of his family. McNelly is taken, wounded, back to the Dukes ranch, where he dies and is buried, along with Richard Dukes. The film ends with Lincoln Rogers Dunnison taking the command of the Rangers. As the film's promotional slogan proclaims, "In a land without justice, a few brave men fought back and became legends."

The plot is serviceable enough, and both Dylan McDermott and James Van Der Beek give convincing performances. The plot borrows one trick from the typical war film, in which raw recruits are trained to be killers and then sent into battle. McNelly is the strong, silent type, whose past is something of a mystery. The vigilante he kills in Brownsville identifies him as a preacher from San Antonio who lost his family and his faith. He never behaves like a preacher, however, even when his men are buried. But despite the reasonably good acting, the story is rather short on development. At one point one of the recruits, Sam Walters (Matt Keeslar), who seems harmless enough and speaks with a stammer, tells Dunnison that he has skills making and reading maps and asks to be taken into McNelly's tent to offer his special services. When he is taken to McNelly, however, he quickly loses his stammer and draws upon the Captain, intending to kill him for the bounty Fisher has put on his head. McNelly's knife is quicker than Walters's gun, however, and the assassination attempt is prevented. Dunnison feels guilty for having taken Walters to McNelly and offers to leave the Rangers, but McNelly wants him to stay on.

Beyond this instance, the plot has few surprises. It is, in short, a pretty ordinary Western, offering grand vistas but very little star talent. According to Scott Brown in *Entertainment Weekly*, the $35 million film "rode into the post-shoot sunset in July 1999," the same year that *Ride with the Devil*, a better Western, was produced and distributed. But *Ride* did not perform well at the boxoffice, grossing under $700,000. Originally scheduled for release in August 2000, *Texas Rangers* was first bumped to April 2001 and subsequently rescheduled for the spring 2002, but it was then released theatrically in December of 2001, against heavy seasonal competition. Brown reported that insiders felt the film "felt inauthentic and unreal," and "that's pretty deadly for a Western." Bob Weinstein of Dimension Films did not consider the film "a complete stinker," but admitted that Westerns are a "tough sell," despite a "marketable cast of young guns." For whatever reason, the release of the film was seriously delayed, and upon its release, it went quickly to video.

—*James M. Welsh*

CREDITS

Lincoln Rogers Dunnison: James Van Der Beek
Leander McNelly: Dylan McDermott
George Durham: Ashton Kutcher
Randolph Douglas Scipio: Usher Raymond
John B. Armstrong: Robert Patrick
Caroline Dukes: Rachael Leigh Cook
Perdita: Leonor Varela
Frank Bones: Randy Travis
Berry Smith: Jon Abrahams
Suh Suh Sam: Matt Keeslar
Ed Simms: Vincent Spano
Jesus Sandoval: Marco Leonardi
Pete Marsele: Oded Fehr
Mr. Dunnison: Joe Spano
Richard Dukes: Tom Skerritt
John King Fisher: Alfred Molina

Origin: USA
Released: 2001
Production: Alan Greisman, Frank Price; released by Dimension Films
Directed by: Steve Miner
Written by: Scott Busby, Martin Copeland
Cinematography by: Daryn Okada
Music by: Trevor Rabin
Sound: George Tarrant
Music Supervisor: Ed Gerrard
Editing: Peter Devaney Flanagan, Greg Featherman
Production Design: Herbert Pinter
MPAA rating: PG-13
Running time: 90 minutes

REVIEWS

Detroit Free Press. December 1, 2001, p. 2A.
Los Angeles Times Online. December 3, 2001.

New York Times Online. December 1, 2001.
Variety. December 10, 2001, p. 33.
Washington Post Weekend. December 7, 2001, p. 45.

QUOTES

Leander McNelly (Dylan McDermott): "Let them remember us not as men of vengeance but as men of law and justice."

13 Conversations About One Thing

Box Office: $3.1 million

In New York the average human prefers 18 inches of space between themselves and other humans according to the character Patricia (Amy Irving), who appears in Jill Sprecher's *13 Conversations About One Thing.* It's not surprising that these same characters would feel alienated and alone in a crowded city where one's life can be easily changed by a mugging or a winning lottery ticket. And New York itself has often been a setting where fateful encounters take place as is the case with such films as *An Affair to Remember* or even the 2001 release *Synchronicity.* Fate and karma happens everywhere in the world but is most dramatic set in a city that seems to be decaying and thriving at the same time. New York is full of romance and intrigue as well as criminal acts and desperation.

Sprecher's (*Clockwatchers*) latest release, co-written with her sister Karen Sprecher, splashes emotional paint onto New York's vast canvas. Sprecher came with the concept for *13 Conversations* after experiencing her own life-changing act. According to the press notes, Jill suffered a severe head injury as a result of a mugging in New York. The following year, a complete stranger walked up to her in the subway and slapped her in the head. As tears welled up in the director's eyes, she begun to hate people, that is until another stranger smiled. "This poor man just looked at me and smiled. I had a lot of bottled up anger because of what I had been through, and that smile just broke the spell." Later, Jill would share her concept of creating a film about life-changing events, fate and karma with her social worker-turned-filmmaker sister and *13 Conversations* manifested into reality.

Similar to *Clockwatchers,* *13 Conversations* consists mostly of interior shots and most of the scenes take place at the workplace. Again, the co-writer-sisters appear to be commenting on the social conditions of the workplace as well as the relationship between employees and their bosses and how those relationships play themselves out on the bigger canvas. The characters range from professionals such as an insurance claim department manager, attorneys, and professors to house cleaners and claim adjusters. All of characters seek happiness while battling with their lack of faith, feelings of guilt, envy or boredom. Specher asks "How can we know what effect we have on a passing stranger? What if the smallest gesture can change the course of someone's life?"

13 Conversations, with its multiple narratives and multiple timelines, proves to be a difficult film to describe. A professor (John Turturro) decides to change his life as he approaches middle age. A rising young lawyer (Matthew McConaughey), used to a life of ease and comfort, celebrates a victory only to soon experience a life-altering event that sends him plummeting. An innocent house cleaner (Clea Du Vall), once saved by a childhood miracle, experiences a dark night of the soul and is later saved by a stranger's smile. A woman (Irving) learns that her husband is having an affair so she moves on while trying to solve her fears of alienation. And finally, an envious businessman (Alan Arkin) seeks revenge on a cheerful worker that leads to surprising results. All of the above characters figure into each other's lives either indirectly or directly, leading us to philosophize about cause and effect.

Although all the performances prove to be capable, Arkin's cynical businessman, Du Vall's vulnerable childlike house cleaner, and Turturro's detached and fastidious professor stand out. All of the actors add just the right combination of emotions to the film with an equal blend of pathos and humor. However, most of the credit should go to the writers who created the humanistic characters and stories. *13 Conversations* places Sprecher on the map along with other talented international filmmakers. Her persistence has reaped rewards.

—*Patty-Lynne Herlevi*

CREDITS

Troy: Matthew McConaughey
Gene: Alan Arkin
Walker: John Turturro
Beatrice: Clea DuVall
Patricia: Amy Irving
Helen: Barbara Sukowa
Dorrie: Tia Texada
Dick Lacey: Frankie Faison
Wade Bowman: William Wise
Mickey Wheeler: Shawn Elliott
Owen: David Connolly

The Triumph of Love

Seduction, persuasion and utter confusion . . . a romantic comedy that aims for the heart.
—Movie tagline

Her Game Is Seduction, The Prize Is His Love.
—Movie tagline

Based on the 300-year-old classic romantic comedy play by Pierre Marivaux, this gender-bending, bodice ripper is the stuff Shakespearean humor is made of. Comely young lasses parading in drag, posing as sensitive young men while signals cross and miscommunication abounds, all for the sake of love. Set in a fictional European country, this period farce involves a lovelorn but determined princess who goes undercover as a boy to try to win the heart of an exiled prince. Guarded by a brother and sister, the prince is forbidden from romance, raised by the misguided siblings to disdain such emotion. The once placid villa which holds the hapless trio is soon turned upside-down when the pantalooned stranger enters their midst and inspires all kinds of messy, impassioned goings-on. Director/writer Clare Peploe's fourth feature film, *Triumph* is a light and stylish mannered piece which the acclaimed actors play out nicely against the lovely Tuscan backdrop.

The fairytale story begins as the beautiful princess (Mira Sorvino), going for a walk in the forest one day, happens upon the vision of a handsome young man emerging from a swim—in the buff and looking buff, naturally. It's love at first sight for the princess, even as she realizes that the young man is, in fact, her sworn enemy Agis (Jay Rodan), due to the fact that he is the rightful heir to the kingdom which her father has usurped. Realizing this trivial truth might keep them from getting along, let alone having an opportunity to be introduced, the daring princess formulates a cunning scheme for infiltrating the prince's lair, which is carefully guarded by the rational philosopher Hermocrates (Ben Kingsley) and his sister Leontine (Fiona Shaw), a spinster scientist whose only passion is her intense devotion to her brother.

To get close to the misogynist prince, living in exile in the secluded villa, she must first get past these two surrogate parents, who have raised Agis to avoid all things amorous and emotional. The film opens with a rollicking scene that shows the plot she has chosen in action. Riding through the forest in a carriage, the princess and her dutiful maid Hermidas (Rachael Stirling) begin doffing their girly garb and kitting themselves out as guys. The two have designs to penetrate Hermocrates' hide-out, ingratiating themselves to the brother and sister, and thereby get within arm's reach of the athletic prince. It is a risky plan, at best, as her charade could easily be exposed by any of the three at any moment, forever losing her beloved prince.

The princess decides the risk is worth it and, once inside the compound, does her best convincing all three of the occupants of her attraction and devotion to only them. Calling herself Phocion, she pretends to be a young student and sets about seducing all three occupants in order to ultimately win the heart of Agis. The wise Hermocrates, who staunchly stands against anything to do with women or love, is the first to seek through her disguise and quickly accuses her of being a female. She confesses that this is true, and in yet another ruse, tells him her name is actually Aspasie, and that she came to the estate just to be near him, Hermocrates. At first he refuses to believe—accusing her of desiring Agis—but is flattered when the young girl convinces him she is only there in order to be close to him. As she seductively crawls across the desk in his study, where he is want to pursue his daily scholarship, Hermocrates panics, telling her all this emotion has made him confused and doesn't want to get involved with the danger that is love. Even as he speaks, it is clear he is completely smitten with the girl who agrees with his dismal views of love and asks for his help in ridding herself of these nasty feelings. The seduction is complete and abundantly clear when the bald philosopher later materializes from his study draped in velvet, donning a long black wig and rouge. Naturally, though, he tells no one in the villa of his newfound relationship.

Seducing Hermocrates sister is the next order of business for the busy princess, as she gathers that Leontine feels threatened by her new place in Hermocrates' heart and wants her banished from the premises. In a particularly charming and funny scene, the princess picks her moment in a wooded area, and soon the straitlaced spinster's defenses are battered and then completely downed, as she revels in the belief that the young lad professing his love before her has come to the villa with the sole intention of being near her. Just as Hermocrates has taken a renewed interest in dressing more attractively, Leontine just as mysteriously shows up later dressed in her finest finery, an extremely tacky yellow ensemble, complete with hat. Just a Hermocrates, too, she keeps her dealings with Phocion to herself.

With all these romantic distractions, the princess, who has meanwhile become engaged to both brother and sister, must continue to focus on the actual object of her affection—Agis. With his ousted father in prison, Agis was taken as a child to the villa and taught by the philosopher and his sister to beware of women, she has quite a task on her hands. As Phocion, however, she is able to profess her friendly devotion to the prince, who craves an outside friendship with someone his own age. Realizing she will be unable to go as far as she'd like with the prince as Phocion, however, she eventually uses the Aspasie persona with him, as well, to reveal her inner female and work on overcoming his aversion to love. She tread lightly in revealing her actual identity, however, which becomes clear while he teaches her to use a bow, taking aim directly at the heart of the target, dressed to look exactly like the princess he despises and is actually her. With everyone in the throes of love after so long without it, the excitement builds within villa until it is impossible for the princess to keep her many secrets.

The acting is stylized and mannered, something now quite foreign in American cinema and certainly not found far beyond its theatrical, commedia dell'arte, roots. Star Sorvino seems to enjoy the more broad style, and plays this unfamiliar classical material deftly, nimbly switching between her male and female characters. Although certainly not convincing as a man in any realistic way, this film offers her as a man in the Shakespearean way—that is to say in the theatrical sense, with her voice lowered just a notch and looking less feminine. Sorvino's princess clearly enjoys the ruse, as well as getting everyone riled up in the process but also shows she feels for her unwitting victims of seduction, as well. Her performance within a performance, however, sometimes seems too scripted, as her character seems to anticipate the reactions of others a bit too well. Rodan's prince is sufficiently attractive and manly but has the least to do of all the characters in the villa. His role is to be somewhat naive yet curious and a foil for the farcical action of the others. Stirling, daughter of Diana Rigg, is a perfectly cast partner for the princess as Hermidas/Corine.

The best performances, however, are Kingsley's Hermocrates and Shaw's Leontine. Kingsley plays the curmudgeon of a scholar brilliantly, revealing that beneath his logical, emotionless exterior, beats the heart of a true romantic, capable of the most embarrassing displays of vanity and affection. His comedic timing (and Shaw's) is impeccable and keeps things rolling beautifully in his scenes. Shaw's self-deprecating Leontine is so adept at evoking both laughter and sympathy by falling in unrequited love that it threatens to undermine the audience's view of the princess. Shaw plays the transformation to a tee, and is delightful to watch in her scenes with Sorvino.

Director/writer Clare Peploe cut her teeth in feature films with renowned Italian director Michelangelo Antonioni on his classic *Zabriskie Point.* Following that, she worked with future husband Bernardo Bertolucci as assistant director on *1900* and *La Luna.* Her feature film debut was the notable *High Season,* a romantic serio-comedy set on a Greek Isle and she wrote/associate produced Bertolucci's 1998 *Besieged.* Here, Peploe fully embraces the classical comedy tradition, even letting the characters in the film have brief glimpses of the modern-day audience watching them. The premise is intentionally preposterous, the performances over-the-top, and the message appropriately lofty resulting in a farce that finds its depth in the subtlety of the able performances and its relevance in the modern camera-work and filmatic style Peploe employs to tell the ages-old story.

Legendary director Bertolucci takes on the rare role of producer on this film, as well as writer, when he became enchanted with the play, which his wife Peploe brought to his attention. Bertolucci, arguably most famous for helming the controversial *Last Tango in Paris,* starring Marlon Brando and Maria Schneider and briefly banned in his native Italy, also directed 1986's Academy Award winning best film, *The Last Emperor,* also winning eight other Academy Awards, including Best Director. His 1998 film, *Stealing Beauty,* was filmed in Italy, as well.

Filmed against the lush landscapes of Tuscany, Italy, cinematographer Fabio Cianchetti shot *Triumph of Love* in Super-16 to give it a jittery, contemporary cinematic feel. Cianchetti has worked with the married filmmakers on Bertolucci's *Besieged,* lauded for its photographic style. The movie's beautiful and sometimes whimsical costumes are courtesy of Metka Kosak, who has also worked with the couple since 1989, most recently on *Besieged.* The classical and playful baroque score was provided by Jason Osborn and aided by David Gilmour's talented guitar. *Triumph* premiered at the 58th Venice Film Festival, September 2001.

—Hilary White

CREDITS

Leonide/Phocion/Aspasie: Mira Sorvino
Hermocrates: Ben Kingsley
Leontine: Fiona Shaw
Agis: Jay Rodan
Hermidas: Rachael Stirling
Harlequin: Ignazio Oliva

Origin: Italy, Great Britain
Released: 2001
Production: Bernardo Bertolucci; Medusa Film, Recorded Pictures Company, Odeon Pictures, Fiction; released by Paramount Classics
Directed by: Clare Peploe
Written by: Clare Peploe, Bernardo Bertolucci, Marilyn Goldin
Cinematography by: Fabio Cianchetti
Music by: Jason Osborn, Jason Osborn
Sound: Maurizio Argentieri
Editing: Jacopo Quadri
Art Direction: Ettore Guerrieri
Costumes: Metka Kosak
Production Design: Ben van Os
MPAA rating: PG-13
Running time: 107 minutes

REVIEWS

Boxoffice. November, 2001, p. 136.
Chicago Sun-Times Online. April 19, 2002.
Entertainment Weekly. April 26, 2002, p. 122.
Los Angeles Times Online. April 17, 2002.
New York Times Online. April 17, 2002.
San Francisco Chronicle. May 10, 2002, p. D3.
Variety. September 10, 2001, p. 63.
Washington Post. April 19, 2002, p. WE53.

TRIVIA

The play was first performed in Paris in 1732.

The Truth About Charlie

Box Office: $5.3 million

The short way to describe *The Truth About Charlie* is that it's a bad movie but done well. It's fun, lovely to look at and filled with all kinds of in-joke film references. The problem is in the plot. It's hard to believe that one of the weak points of the film would be its story since it's a remake of the well-loved 1963 Stanley Donen film, *Charade*. *Charade*, which starred Audrey Hepburn and Cary Grant at the peak of their powers, has become a classic, and it seems like its story would be above reproach. But, although *Charade* had a twisty, tricky plot, it was one of the weaker points of the film. Perhaps it's heresy to say so, but the film's twists were more often incoherent than thrilling. The part of *Charade* that was good and remains good is Grant and Hepburn. It was their chemistry, their suave banter, and even their designer wardrobes.

The Truth About Charlie is stuck with the weakness of *Charade*—its plot—and lacks the strength of that film—Grant and Hepburn. *Charlie* is not completely lacking in charismatic star power. Thandie Newman (*Mission: Impossible II*), who plays the Hepburn role of Regina Lambert, can't replicate Hepburn's aura—who could, after all?—but she does a surprisingly good job. She shares Hepburn's grace, her slight figure and her ability to wear clothes well. It's the substitute Grant that's the problem. Mark Wahlberg plays Joshua Peters (which was Peter Joshua in the original) has proven himself to be a good actor in films like *Three Kings* and *Boogie Nights,* but here, he's just not up for the role. (According to the *Wall Street Journal,* Will Smith was originally supposed to take on the role but did *Ali* instead.)

Reportedly, Demme didn't want Wahlberg to play the role like Grant which seems reasonable and wise, since it would be foolhardy to try to match Grant's performance. But Wahlberg doesn't bring enough charisma of his own to the role. His character is supposed to be mysterious, but the young actor seems more blank and bland than mysterious.

In *The Truth About Charlie,* Regina is heading back to Paris after a vacation in Martinique. In Martinique, she has a brief, flirty meeting with Joshua on the beach. When she gets back home, she plans to divorce her husband, Charlie Lambert (Stephen Dillane) even though they've only been married a few months. Charlie is an art dealer who travels a lot for his job and Regina is feeling neglected. But when she arrives home, she is shocked to find Charlie missing and their apartment ransacked. Someone has gone through everything in their house, including knocking out the dry wall to search in between the wall. Oddly, Joshua keeps turning up. First he's at the airport, then after Regina's apartment is broken into, he shows up at her door. He is a supportive, kindly friend to Regina and she finds herself turning to him for support.

When she is called to the police station, she discovers that Charlie has been murdered. The police investigator (Christine Boisson) pulls out a bunch of Charlie's forged passports for different countries and under different names. Regina had had no idea about her husband's secret life. The police tell her that Charlie had been in possession of several million dollars and that Regina needs to find it.

It turns out that the police aren't the only ones who want the money. She's also pursued by a trio of apparent baddies, Li-Sang Lee (Joong-Hoon Park), Emil Zatapec (Ted Levine) and Lola Jansco (Lisa Gay Hamilton) The three claim to be former partners of Charlie who he has double-crossed. Regina also meets Mr. Bartholomew (Tim Robbins), the Walter Matthau character from the first film. Mr. Bartholomew says he's from the U.S. government and has been sent to help Regina find the money. He insists that she not tell anyone of their meetings.

The central question of *Charlie* is who should Regina trust. Mr. Bartholomew seems like a straightforward guy, but could he be tricking her? And Joshua seems like a nice person and Regina is half in love with him. Then she gets a mysterious phone call that puts doubt in her mind about Joshua's integrity. The idea of the film is that all this mystery is swirling around Regina as a backdrop to her romance with (or betrayal by) Joshua. The problem is that Joshua is not nearly as intriguing enough as a character. It seems if Regina has any doubt about his character, he would be easy to toss aside. He's just not alluring enough to risk one's life for. The romance between the two doesn't work and that's a big problem for the film.

But Demme (who has also directed films like *Something Wild* and *Stop Making Sense*) has a secret weapon, his long-time cinematographer Tak Fujimoto. Fujimoto makes the film look like a 1960's French New Wave film. His Paris is a beautiful place where well-dressed people do interesting things. (Wahlberg's succession of hats alone is an interesting diversion.) The film looks very glamorous with cool retro cars, music and a strong European feel.

Demme adds to the throwback feeling by adding cameos by some of the figures of French New Wave cinema like director Agnes Varda and actresses Anna Karina and Magali Noel. In one scene, the players of the film show up in a nightclub and, as they trade dances, share information with each other. It's a charged scene full of energy. And in another nice touches, Charles Aznavour from *Shoot the Piano Player* shows up in the frame to sing "Quand Tu M'Aimes" to the young lovers. *The Truth About Charlie* is a film made by a film buff for film buffs. Demme seems to be having quite a bit of fun making the film, and some of that fun is bound to translate to the audience. Even his music choices were obviously made with a lot of care. There's everything in there from the Soft Boys to Manu Chao.

Most of the major critics thought that the film wasn't what it could be. Kenneth Turan of the *Los Angeles Times* wrote, "*The Truth About Charlie* is excessively clever and minimally charming, so eager to demonstrate its undeniable cinematic skills that it ends up outsmarting itself, showing off for its own pleasure when it should be trying to satisfy the rest of us." Owen Gleiberman of *Entertainment Weekly* gave the film a C and wrote, "*The Truth About Charlie* isn't incompetent, exactly, yet it would be hard to think of a recent movie that has worked this hard to achieve this little fun." And Joe Morgenstern of the *Wall Street Journal* wrote, "*The Truth About Charlie* . . . contains so many reference to other films, particularly classics of France's New Wave, that it constitutes a treasure hunt for movie lovers who cherish the medium's history. What's missing is a new movie to love."

—*Jill Hamilton*

CREDITS

Joshua Peters: Mark Wahlberg
Regina Lambert: Thandie Newton
Mr. Bartholomew: Tim Robbins
Il-Sang Lee: Joong-Hoon Park
Emil Zadapec: Ted Levine
Lola Jansco: Lisa Gay Hamilton
Commandant Dominique: Christine Boisson
Charlie: Stephen (Dillon) Dillane
Cameo: Charles Aznavour
Cameo: Anna Karina

Origin: USA
Released: 2002

Production: Jonathan Demme, Edward Saxon, Peter Saraf; Mediastream Film, Clinica Estetico; released by Universal Pictures
Directed by: Jonathan Demme
Written by: Jonathan Demme, Stephen Schmidt, Jessica Bendinger
Cinematography by: Tak Fujimoto
Music by: Rachel Portman
Music Supervisor: Deva Anderson
Editing: Carol Littleton
Art Direction: Ford Wheeler, Delphine Mabed
Costumes: Catherine Leterrier
Production Design: Hugo Luczyc-Wyhowski
MPAA rating: PG-13
Running time: 104 minutes

REVIEWS

Chicago Sun-Times Online. October 25, 2002.
Detroit Free Press. October 20, 2002, p. J1.
Entertainment Weekly. November 1, 2002, p. 48.
Los Angeles Times Online. October 25, 2002.
New York Times Online. October 25, 2002.
People. November 4, 2002, p. 41.
USA Today Online. October 25, 2002.
Variety Online. October 22, 2002.
Washington Post. October 25, 2002, p. WE40.

TRIVIA

Peter Stone, screenwriter for *Charade*, is given credit as Peter Joshua for the remake, which was the name of Cary Grant's character.

Tuck Everlasting

If you could choose to live forever, would you?
—Movie tagline
A secret is about to be discovered. An adventure is about to begin . . .
—Movie tagline
A magical adventure is about to begin.
—Movie tagline

 Box Office: $18.8 million

Tuck Everlasting is based on Natalie Babbitt's cult 1975 children's novel of the same name. It's actually the second film to come from the novel. The first was a version made in 1980 that's a staple of cable television. Why two movies on this book? Well, perhaps it's the meaty subject matter. Immortality, growing up and, in this particular version, teen love. Director Jay Russell, who also did the kids' film *My Dog Skip,* has made a few changes from the book. He set the film in the early 1900's instead of the late 1800's so there are modernities like cars.

He also made lead girl Winnie Foster (Alexis Bledel of TV's *Gilmore Girls*) a 15-year-old instead of a 10-year-old. This was probably a demographic decision as much as an artistic one. One of the prime groups this film is aimed as is young teen girls. Making Winnie 15 instead of 10 allows her to do more than just get a crush on the handsome Jesse Tuck (Jonathan Jackson). And 17-year-old Jesse, who in the book is more interested in the philosophical implications of his life, finds Winnie a lot more interesting romantically as a 15-year-old. So expect some sigh-worthy chaste first kisses.

Winnie lives in Treegap, a small town in the West. It's a modest town and Winnie's family, the Fosters, are the town rich folk. Her mother, Mrs. Foster (Amy Irving), takes her position very seriously and has decorated their large house with the finest of furnishings. She has definite opinions on how a young lady should be raised and wants Winnie to be a proper young woman who is quiet, plays instruments and doesn't get dirty. Robert Foster (Victor Garber) lets his wife run the home and is content to continue making more and more money for the family.

When the Fosters decree that Winnie shall be sent off to a boarding school, the girl is horrified. The school has a reputation for being a terrible place. She runs off into the forbidden woods that adjoin her backyard. Of course, forbidden woods wouldn't be forbidden unless there were something mighty interesting in there, and indeed, something interesting is just what Winnie finds. While wandering around lost, she spies Jesse drinking from a spring beneath a tree. He sees her and makes the kind of guilty face that makes her feel like he's up to something. She asks for a drink from the spring and he nervously refuses her, saying that it's poison. "You just drank it," Winnie notes. "I'm starting to feel sick," answers Jesse, who's not the most gifted liar in the world. Jesse and Winnie have instant dislike for each other, which in the movies, is a sure sign that they will be madly in love in short order.

Just before they are about to discover this, Jesse's brother, Miles (Scott Barstow), shows up. Miles is, as his mother puts it, "as prickly as barbed wire." He insists that they need to kidnap Winnie and take her back to his parents until they decide what to do with her. The boys take Winnie back to their quaint little cottage (courtesy of set decorator Catherine D. Davis) in the middle of the forest. There Winnie meets sweet, salt-of-the-earth type Mae Tuck (Sissy Spacek) and the philosophically-bent dad, Angus Tuck (William Hurt). Both parents sport Irish accents, though it's not completely clear why.

While the Tucks decide what to do with Winnie, she starts becoming enchanted by the family and their lives, which is so different from her own cold and distant home. She is especially enchanted by the young Jesse, who introduces her to a world of exploring the forest, climbing rocks and swimming half-naked under the waterfall. It doesn't escape Winnie's attention that Jesse doesn't look half-bad swimming half-naked. In the narration by Elisabeth Shue, we hear that Winnie is noticing the way that the family takes their time doing things, like they have all the time in the world. As it turns out, they do have all the time in the world. Winnie slowly gains the family's trust and they share their big secret with her: the spring that Jesse drank out of is the source of eternal life. The entire family drunk from it and soon noticed that they became immune to physical pain and were unable to die. Jesse reveals that he is 104-years-old.

Winnie learns that eternal life is not all good. Miles tells of marrying and having children with the love of his life. When she found out the family's secret, she thought they were satanic, and took the boys and left. Even though his wife has been dead for years, Miles still pines for his lost family. And dad Tuck, Angus, tells Winnie that being immortal is kind of a weird way to live. "We're like rocks," he says gravely. "We just are." Angus also offers Winnie the moral of the story, "Don't be afraid of death," he says. "Be afraid of the unlived life." Jesse, on the other hand, is more upbeat about eternal life and urges Winnie to drink from the stream. After all, they are in love and if she was eternal too, they could truly love each other forever. (He doesn't seem to be realizing that it would be the rare marriage that actually could make it through eternity.)

But the Tucks have a bigger problem than whether or not Winnie should drink from the spring. The Man in the Yellow Suit (Ben Kingsley) has been trailing the Tucks for years. He hopes to take over the spring and makes lots of money from it. When he tells a priest of his plan, the priest hisses, "You speak blasphemy!" The Man in the Yellow Suit answers cooly, "Fluently."

Will he get them? Will civilization take the Tucks' woods away anyway? Will Winnie drink the water? Is eternal life something that's even desirable? These are the questions that *Tuck Everlasting* focuses on. But it doesn't require that much heavy thinking. After all, heavy thinking might lead audiences to wonder why, if Jesse is 104, how come he still behaves just like a 17-year-old. And, Jesse's a handsome guy. How is it that he hasn't managed to find a date in all those years? And if one drink from the spring causes eternal life, why the need to live by it and continuing to drink from it? And isn't mom going to get sick of cooking for her men after all these years?

Written by: Manoel de Oliveira
Cinematography by: Renato Berta
Sound: Henri Maikof
Editing: Manoel de Oliveira, Catherine Krassovsky
Art Direction: Maria Jose Branco
Costumes: Isabel Branco
MPAA rating: Unrated
Running time: 133 minutes

 REVIEWS

New York Times Online. October 1, 2002.
Variety. June 17, 2002, p. 25.

Under the Skin of the City
(Zir-e Poust-e Shahr)
(Under the City's Skin)

Chador-cloaked women bustling on crowded city streets have become synonymous with Iranian cinema. This proves no exception with Iranian cinema luminary Rakhshan Bani Etemad's latest release, *Under the Skin of the City.* Etemad's film also shares other aspects in common with notable Iranian features, including its documentary-style drama that revolves around the treatment of women, the relations between the sexes, the labor force and other political issues. And anyone expecting a happy ending hasn't seen the latest Iranian cinematic fare. Etemad's characters suffer under the weight of poor decisions, parental sacrifice, drug trafficking, domestic abuse, low wages and human misery. It's a cinematic Iran that comes as an embarrassment to the Iranian government during an era in which injustice will no longer be tolerated anywhere in the world.

Etemad is one of a handful of women directors producing films in Iran. She is considered a post-revolutionary filmmaker (1984 to present) and despite censorship and the curtailing of women's rights in a strict patriarchal society, Etemad has aired her society's dirty laundry. This is not an easy task when considering the threat of imprisonment, as in the case of filmmaker Tahmineh Milani who currently faces charges against the Iranian government for her latest film. Censorship is precarious and Iranian filmmakers never know what will tip their scales of fate.

According to a description of *Under the Skin of the City* that appeared in the Toronto International Film Festival program, "Etemad's characters are strikingly realistic and resoundingly sympathetic. As in her previous films *The May Lady* and *The Blue-Veiled,* the hero of *Under the Skin of the City* is forced to choose between herself and her family." The film portrays a family facing the travails of life in the midst of social upheaval. It's a film rife with tension, strife and turmoil that exists alongside hope for a brighter future, blooming romances, parental love and forgiveness. Focusing on an impoverished matriarch, this docudrama tackles various social ills that effect all cultures, then places one family's misery over the backdrop of a crumbling society. As the family's life falls apart, a city also threatens to explode.

A film crew interviews Tuba (Golab Adineh) and other factory workers about an upcoming parliamentary election. Tuba finds it difficult to articulate her concerns in front of the glaring camera lens, but soon we, the viewers, are shown the details of Tuba's wretched life. Tuba and her family live on hope and they try to surmount their collective woes. Tuba finds solace in a home that she owns while she suffers from a back ailment caused by her factory job. Her disabled husband is unable to work and Tuba is forced to carry the lion's share of supporting her family. Her son Abbas (Mohammad Reza Forutan) hopes to find employment in Japan so that he can win the hand of a beautiful office worker and improve his family's living situation.

Meanwhile, Tuba's oldest daughter endures abuse at the hands of her overworked husband and the youngest sister watches her best friend's life fall apart also due to domestic abuse. Finally, Tuba's youngest son attempts to make a name for himself as a politician through subversive means. Although the family already faces a variety of societal ills, their lives plunge further into hell and their dreams shatter after Abbas' sells his mother's house in order to pay for a visa to Japan only to later learn that he had been conned. Abbas accepts an offer to traffic drugs in order to save his mother's house, but his plans go awry, leading to his mother's ultimate sacrifice and an excruciating film climax. The film ends with Tuba shouting at the film crew out of frustration as she wonders who will see the film in which she appears.

Although the film proves painful to watch, the Toronto International Film Festival program described it as "an inspiring account of parental love and forgiveness and amazing determination as Tuba's perseverance and the bonds of family ultimately prove unbeatable." In some respects Etemad's feature recalls French director Laurent Cantet's gritty, realistic *Human Resources* with its focus on how economic hardship tears a family apart. But Etemad focuses mostly on women and the sacrifices they make for their loved ones. 🎞

—*Patty-Lynne Herlevi*

CREDITS

Tuba: Golab Adineh
Abbas: Mohammad Reza Forutan
Daughter: Baran Kosani

Origin: Iran
Language: Farsi
Released: 2001
Production: Rakhshan Bani Etemad, Jahangir Kosari; released by Farabi Cinema Foundation
Directed by: Rakhshan Bani Etemad
Written by: Rakhshan Bani Etemad, Farid Mestafavi
Cinematography by: Hossein Jafarian
Sound: Asghar Shahverdi
Editing: Mastafa Kherghehpaush
Production Design: Omid Mohit
MPAA rating: Unrated
Running time: 92 minutes

REVIEWS

Boxoffice. December, 2001, p. 54.
Variety Online. February 16, 2001.

Undercover Brother

He's All Action.
—Movie tagline

Box Office: $38.3 million

According to a short informational film that kicks off *Undercover Brother,* the pinnacle of black culture was sometime in the 1970s. Over a backdrop of various images of seventies black culture, like Martin Luther King giving a rousing speech, the film makes the case that black culture societal force was greatest during that time. And, according to the documentary, this was upsetting to The Man. The Man, who in *Undercover Brother* is an actual guy, didn't like white acceptance of black culture and embarked upon a campaign to wipe it out. The evidence of The Man's success, according to the mini-film were the fame of people like Mr. T, Urkel, and even worse, Dennis Rodman in a wedding dress.

The only thing standing between The Man and his plan to make America lily white again is a secret organization called the B.R.O.T.H.E.R.H.O.O.D. The organization is run by an all-star team of agents. There's The Chief (Chi McBride), a gruff, yet lovable team leader; Sistah Girl (Aunjanue Ellis), the sexy and smart agent who ends up doing all the actual work, and Smart Brother (Gary Anthony Ramsey), the guy who runs the computers and knows obscure facts. The team is rounded out by Conspiracy Brother (Dave Chapelle), who smokes a lot of pot and believes every theory out there. "Babe Ruth was black!" he reports passionately. "George Washington Carver made the first computer out of a peanut!"

Despite this kind of crack team, the organization realizes that they're going to need more help to foil The Man's biggest plan yet. It involves General Warren Boatwell (Billy Dee Williams), a "well-spoken" war hero with political aspirations who sure seems a lot like Colin Powell. At a big press conference in which Boatwell is expected to announce his candidacy for president, he instead informs the press that he's going to open a chain of fried chicken restaurants. The chain's slogan will be "We Do Chicken Right-On!" Boatwell goes on to announce the Nappy Hair Special which includes a 40-ounce Malt Liquor with every meal. The B.R.O.T.H.E.R.H.O.O.D figures out that The Man has drugged Boatwell with a brainwashing potion and, worse, plans to drug all black people using the General's chicken as the delivery device.

To stop this plan, the B.R.O.T.H.E.R.H.O.O.D recruits Undercover Brother (Eddie Griffin). Undercover Brother is, as Sistah Girl puts it, "a Soul Train reject with a Robin Hood complex." When we first meet Undercover Brother he's sporting a huge afro, wearing an outlandish seventies outfit and driving an early seventies Cadillac Coupe de Ville. This man is cool. He swerves to avoid another car and ends up spinning his car around. While the car is careening out of control, he takes a moment to sip some of his orange soda out of his big cup. Of course, he doesn't spill a drop.

The ultra-cool Undercover Brother has to go undercover as Anton Jackson, an uptight white man who works at one of The Man's many corporations. He gets a crash course in whiteness, including the forced viewing of a film about white culture that includes scenes of 'N Sync, polka music, and dancing from Riverdance. He is even forced to eat the wretched food of the white man, mayonnaise. (To counteract this particular condiment, Undercover Brother is given a special watch that can shoot hot sauce onto any meal, thus making it palatable.)

But Undercover Brother meets his biggest challenge yet when The Man, aided by his henchman, Mr. Feather (Chris Kattan), sicks the White She Devil (Denise Richards) on Undercover Brother. This super-sexy agent is so-called "black man's kryponite." (Of course it's completely racist to suggest that any black man would go ga-ga over this white woman, but the film deals so lightly with such stereotypes that they manage to get away with it. And it doesn't hurt that the film has the extra cred of being directed by Malcolm D. Lee, director of *The Best Man* and Spike's cousin.)

The White She Devil works her magic on Undercover Brother quickly. Soon he is buying bland clothes at a store called Khaki Republic, watching NBC's Must-See TV lineup and asking for extra mayo on his sandwiches. His acceptance of white culture reaches its lowest point when he willingly performs a soulless rendition of "Ebony and Ivory" with She Devil at a karaoke bar.

Will Undercover Brother be able to find the funk again? Will the B.R.O.T.H.E.R.H.O.O.D be able to stop The Man before he brainwashes James Brown? Will Undercover Brother's afro ever rise again? It really doesn't matter much, because the film is about the jokes, not the plot.

The film, based on an Internet comic series created by John Ridley (who wrote *Three Kings*), is much funnier than it looked like it would be based on the trailers. According to those, *Undercover Brother* looked like it wasn't about much more than a guy who can pin criminals against the wall using two afro picks and save himself from plummeting from a plane by creating a makeshift parachute out of his gigantic bell bottoms. But the film is much more clever than you'd guess from that.

Maybe it's that there are so many jokes of all types crammed into the film that at some point it just wears you down. The film uses it all: highbrow, lowbrow, slapstick, old jokes and fresh jokes. If a person doesn't think Undercover Brother's use of outmoded slang like "Solid!" is particularly funny, maybe they'll like Conspiracy Brother's rant that Hollywood is definitely against Spike Lee. "C'mon, even Cher got an Oscar!"he yells. If someone doesn't like the joke that there is a token white guy at B.R.O.T.H.E.R.H.O.O.D, Lance (Neil Patrick Harris), maybe they'll like the fight scene between Mr. Feather and Undercover Brother in which the two imitate the silly fighting moves of Michael Jackson's "Beat It" video.

Griffin is game as Undercover Brother. He wears his platforms like he means it and has the right kind of off-handed cool. He's better when he's goofing on white culture as the uptight Jackson. Chapelle brings his usual manic energy to the show, and it serves the film well. It's nice to have such a strong player in a supporting role. Richards is good-humored about her role, in which she is little more than a sexpot. (Actually, she is nothing more than a sexpot.) In a scene where she's having a cat fight with Sistah Girl that ends up, of course, in the shower, she puts on her best pornographic pouts. Also good is Williams, who seems to be having fun voicing such outrageous stereotypes as the chicken-loving black man.

More critics liked the film than didn't, which for a comedy like this, is a good reception. Many compared the film to the Austin Powers films. Owen Gleiberman of *Entertainment Weekly* gave the film a C + and complained

that the movie "traffics in the kind of prechewed racial cliches that have already been throughout the corporate stand-up-comedy mill." Renee Graham of the *Boston Globe* wrote: "*Undercover Brother* tries to wring laughs from just about every dusty stereotype about blacks and whites imaginable. But it's all cheap, lazy, and unoriginal." A.O. Scott of the *New York Times* wrote, "The one-liners are clever enough and the physical comedy and pop-culture goofing sufficiently dumb and broad to make *Undercover Brother* . . . a reasonably pleasant experience." And Jonathan Foreman of the *New York Post* wrote, "That *Undercover Brother* was made at all says something about the way race is lived in America today. This relaxed, frequently hilarious collection of clever jokes about race and American pop culture makes light of topics that were once dynamite."

—*Jill Hamilton*

CREDITS

Anton Jackson/U.B.: Eddie Griffin
Mr. Feather: Chris Kattan
White She Devil: Denise Richards
Conspiracy Brother: Dave Chappelle
The Chief: Chi McBride
Sistah Girl: Aunjanue Ellis
Lance: Neil Patrick Harris
General Boutwell: Billy Dee Williams
Mr. Elias: Jack Noseworthy
Smart Brother: Gary Anthony Williams
Himself: James Brown
The Man: Robert Trumbull
Narrator: J.D. Hall

Origin: USA
Released: 2002
Production: Brian Grazer, Michael Jenkinson, Damon Lee; Imagine Entertainment; released by Universal Pictures
Directed by: Malcolm Lee
Written by: John Ridley, Michael McCullers
Cinematography by: Tom Priestley
Music by: Stanley Clarke
Sound: Douglas Ganton
Music Supervisor: Bonnie Greenberg
Editing: William Kerr
Art Direction: Elis Lam
Costumes: Danielle Hollowell
Production Design: William Elliott
MPAA rating: PG-13
Running time: 85 minutes

REVIEWS

Entertainment Weekly. June 7, 2002, p. 46.
Los Angeles Times Online. May 31, 2002.
New York Times Online. May 26, 2002.
New York Times Online. May 31, 2002.
USA Today Online. May 31, 2002.
Variety. June 3, 2002, p. 20.
Washington Post. May 31, 2002, p. WE42.

QUOTES

Anton Jackson (Eddie Griffin) to Mr. Feather (Chris Kattan): "You mess with the 'fro, you got to go!"

Undisputed

One's fighting for freedom. One's fighting for greed. It's going to be war.
—Movie tagline

Box Office: $12.4 million

A no-nonsense action picture about boxing in a prison milieu, *Undisputed* teams up veteran action director Walter Hill (*The Warriors, 48 Hrs.*) with actors Ving Rhames and Wesley Snipes. It's the first feature for Hill since 1996's *Last Man Standing,* but the 60-year-old hasn't lost his touch for pounding, pulsating scenes. Hill wrote the screenplay for *Undisputed* with David Giler and was one of the producers.

Subtlety isn't Hill's style, and in keeping with his direct approach he decided to introduce the film's characters by putting their names (and the crimes for which they were imprisoned, if applicable) on the screen when they have their first scenes. He also uses titles to locate times and places, and occasionally does so egregiously (as in tagging a "5 P.M. MEAL" when it's obvious the prisoners are eating dinner).

The action takes place in California's maximum security Sweetwater Prison in the middle of the Mojave Desert. The prison has a boxing program that pits Sweetwater fighters against opponents from any facility in the state prison system. As the film opens, we witness the undefeated Sweetwater champion, Monroe Hutchen (Snipes), decimating a much bigger opponent as the prisoners cheer for their favorite son. The match takes place in a barbed-wire-topped cage amid a profane running commentary from a ringside announcer and vicious shouts from the prisoners on bleachers

surrounding the cage. Hutchen has been in the joint for 10 years, and nobody has come close to beating him.

But the heavyweight champion of the world, James "Iceman" Chambers (Rhames), might change that. The world-famous Iceman has been convicted of raping a showgirl who claims their sexual encounter wasn't consensual; Chambers vigorously denies he is guilty and claims the victim (Tawnee Rawlins) was simply out to destroy him and get his money; in fact, she's filed a multimillion-dollar civil suit against him. Not only that, but his business holdings are a mess and the Internal Revenue Service is asking questions about back taxes. His handlers tell Iceman that he'd better be on his best behavior so he can get early parole in 18 months rather than serve the full sentence of up to 10 years. Iceman already is 35, and he needs to continue fighting to pile up more big paydays to right himself financially.

For Iceman, however, keeping out of trouble in prison is asking a lot. He's used to calling the shots and being the king of the hill, and he doesn't like the idea that there's another fighter inside his new home who considers himself the reigning champion. Iceman slaps the face of Hutchen when he first encounters him in the dining room food line, and Hutchen slugs back. Because Iceman is so famous and the warden fears negative publicity, it's Hutchen who ends up being disciplined, placed in solitary confinement so that he doesn't stir up Iceman's wrath again.

After a couple more incidents, however, the prison authorities no longer look so kindly on Chambers. He's openly challenging them, but they still refuse to discipline him. Instead, the warden agrees to look the other way while backers arrange a showdown fight between Chambers and Hutchen. The idea is masterminded by Mendy Ripstein (Peter Falk), an aging mob boss who is a boxing aficionado and the most powerful inmate in Sweetwater because of his mob connections. Ripstein decides the two men should fight according to 19th-century British bare-knuckle rules, but later relents and allows them to wear gloves.

In one of the movie's better scene, Ripstein meets with the warden, who wants to cancel the fight after a near-riot in the dining room instigated by prisoners taunting Iceman. Ripstein tells a story about a mayor who refused to build a casino the mob wanted, and how he had the choice of dying or getting a large amount of money deposited in his bank account. Either way, Ripstein points out, the casino would get built. He didn't have to spell out that it was the same way with the boxing match. The warden is helpless to intervene. In fact, Ripstein's connections are so powerful that he promises to get Chambers released early if he agrees to fight, and he comes through on his promise.

For a prison drama, *Undisputed* doesn't have many, if any, surprising plot twists or turns. The tension in the film comes primarily from Rhames's bravura performance as the self-appointed baddest man on the planet. Rhames is fascinating in the role. He manages to spout invective and strut his oversized ego while still exuding a quiet, sympathetic magnificence. Is he, in fact, innocent of the charges? Hill does a good job of leaving that question open. Is he a pampered superstar? Well, yes, but he also seems to be a man of immense dignity. Is he a vicious villain? Rhames portrays him more as a man of conviction and honor. It's a fascinating role, full of sharp, profane dialogue and regal bearing, and it literally carries what would otherwise be a purely pedestrian film.

Snipes does well, in a quieter way, as an unemotional, patient man who spends his solitary confinement months building a pagoda out of toothpicks. But Snipes's character is less well drawn, not fully flushed out, and this leaves an imbalance of personalities leading up to their final showdown.

Hill makes overly excessive use of sharp fades into white, almost cinematic mini-explosions as scenes go up in smoke. He does a better job of interspersing old fight scenes, memory flashbacks, and interviews into the narrative. He keeps the story moving along so well that it's possible to forget for awhile that not much is really happening. Minor characters abound, but most of them don't get involved in any distinct or interesting subplots. There is no threat that the prisoners are going to riot or explode, no real tensions involving mob influence, and so all the sizzle must be carried by Rhames's magnificent Iceman and the prospect that he is eventually going to fight the rather colorless Hutchen.

When the fight finally takes place, Hill treats it almost reverentially. The boxing reenactments are mediocre but effective enough, though the sound effects used when punches land tend all to sound exactly the same. There are a lot of punches landed but very little finesse or footwork, and despite being pounded neither man really looks like he's had his face beaten to a pulp. The makeup department might have been put to better use here.

Rapper Master P has a small part, but the rest of the cast is filled out by virtual unknowns. They all do a competent enough job. Falk plays his typical character—street-wise, ancient, curmudgeonly, and vaguely threatening.

The best that can be said about *Undisputed* is that, because of the way Hill has defined the two competitors and because of the compelling stature that Rhames brings to his role, the outcome of the showdown is in doubt. Rhames's Iceman isn't a despicable villain, and even though the prisoners are rooting for one of their own, anything could happen. However, the ending of the film is a disappointment. The fight takes place, one man wins, and that's that. The plot doesn't have many ideas, and it runs out of them fast.

Audiences expecting an action flick will be disappointed. There isn't a whole lot of action in the film other than the boxing matches and some pushing and shoving. But there's plenty of rough language—Falk's character employs a familiar popular expletive in one of every three words

he speaks—and the dialogue and situations seem authentic. If it weren't for Rhames, however, *Undisputed* would hardly be of any interest except to fans of boxing.

—*Michael Betzold*

CREDITS

Monroe Hutchen: Wesley Snipes
James "Iceman" Chambers: Ving Rhames
Emmanuel "Mendy" Ripstein: Peter Falk
A.J. Mercker: Michael Rooker
Jesus "Chuy" Campos: Jon Seda
Mingo Pace: Wes Studi
Ratag Dolan: Fisher Stevens
Yank Lewis: Dayton Callie
Darlene Early: Amy Aquino
Vern Van Zandt: Nils Allen Stewart
Warden Lipscom: Denis Arndt
Tawnee Rawlins: Rose Rollins

Origin: USA
Released: 2002
Production: David Giler, Walter Hill, Brad Krevoy, Andrew Sugerman; Millennium Films, Amen Ra, Motion Picture Corporation of America, Hollywood Partners; released by Miramax Films
Directed by: Walter Hill
Written by: Walter Hill, David Giler
Cinematography by: Lloyd Ahern
Music by: Stanley Clarke
Sound: Jacob Goldstein
Music Supervisor: David Schulhof, Ashley Miller
Editing: Freeman A. Davies
Costumes: Barbara Inglehart
Production Design: Maria Caso
MPAA rating: R
Running time: 96 minutes

REVIEWS

Chicago Sun-Times Online. August 23, 2002.
Entertainment Weekly. September 6, 2002, p. 57.
Los Angeles Times Online. August 21, 2002.
Los Angeles Times Online. August 23, 2002.
New York Times Online. August 23, 2002.
People. September 2, 2002, p. 31.
USA Today Online. August 22, 2002.
Variety Online. August 18, 2002.
Washington Post. August 23, 2002, p. WE45.

Unfaithful

The end of the affair is only the beginning.
—Movie tagline

 Box Office: $52.8

Appropriately enough the action of this domestic melo-drama starts out on a windy, tempestuous day in West-chester County, near the Hudson River, and follows Constance Sumner, the wife of the owner of an armored car company, into New York City, where she is shopping. The wind is awful. Connie (Diane Lane) can't get a taxi, and in her haste and confusion she literally bumps into a handsome young Frenchman named Paul Martel (Olivier Martinez), knocking them both to the pavement, scuffing up her leg. Paul, a book dealer, lives nearby and invites her up to his apartment to bandage her bleeding leg. He also offers her a cup of tea. She finds him attractive, but she resists the temptation of falling into bed with him that day. She goes back, again, and again, until her obsession is out of control and her scruples melt away.

Connie has been married to her husband Edward (Richard Gere) for over 10 years. Certainly, rock-solid and dependable Ed does not neglect her or their young son, Charlie (Erik Per Sullivan), whom they both seem to care about. But Connie becomes increasingly obsessed with the handsome young stranger. She visits his SoHo apartment a second time, then a third, until a full-blown affair develops. One day on her way to Paul's apartment, she encounters two of her friends, who insist on having coffee with her at a café just around the corner from Paul's flat. One of them at-tempts to warn her of the perils of an extramarital affair, but the warning falls on deaf ears. Instead, Connie calls Paul to explain why she will be late, and Paul shows up at the café and seduces Connie in the rest room. They are both excited by the danger of it all. Paul courts disaster again when he takes Connie to lunch one day, and they are seen kissing by an associate of Connie's husband. Ed later fires the man for disloyalty, and is told that if loyalty is an issue, Ed should look to his own family.

Ed then hires a private investigator, Frank Wilson (Do-minic Chianese), to follow Connie. The investigator gets pictures of Connie and Paul together and gives Ed the address of the SoHo flat. When Ed then decides to pay Paul a visit, the attraction turns truly fatal. Ed is angry, frustrated, disoriented. Paul invites him in and offers him a drink. Ed gets sick, and before the viewer quite realizes what is hap-pening, Ed strikes Paul with a paperweight, killing him. Befuddled, Ed starts to call the police, as panic sets in. But before he can get to the telephone, he hears an incoming call from Connie being recorded, as she tells Paul that the affair cannot go on. Ed cleans up the apartment, wraps Paul's body in a Persian carpet, gets it into the trunk of his car, and disposes of it at a landfill. But first he goes to see his son perform in a school play, a truly bizarre domestic touch. The police later come to his Westchester County home to inves-tigate, since Connie's telephone number was found written down at Paul's apartment.

Gradually, Connie begins to realize that Ed murdered Paul. The murder weapon was a paperweight Ed had given her that she had, in turn, stupidly given to Paul. It's the sight of this paperweight that drives Ed over the edge. When the paperweight, wiped clean of fingerprints, appears back in its accustomed place at the couple's home, Connie knows what has transpired. She has betrayed Ed, and Ed has more than evened the score. She lies to the police about when and where she met Paul, and Ed backs up her lie, claiming that they both first met Paul together at a charity fund-raiser held at the Julliard School. They have betrayed and hurt each other. The adulteress turns out to be married to a murderer.

The film ends by leaving them in a car at night, stopped at a stoplight outside a police station. Will Ed the killer get away with murder? The answer is no, even though he may escape the police investigation, since he will have to live with his conscience and with a wife who has been demonstrably "unfaithful," whom he has said he "hates," not only for what she has done, but for what she has driven him to do. At the end of the film one gets an uncomfortable feeling akin to what was created in the final scene of *In the Bedroom,* which left the murderous conspirators to comfort each other "in the bedroom," though not too successfully. Both films have a powerful message to convey about the possible consequences of infidelity and jealousy.

The story takes place in two increments. The first part concerns the illicit affair (steamy enough, but far short of accusations of "soft" pornography, as some reviewers claimed); the second part involves the husband's investiga-tion, his confrontation with the lover, and the "fatal" conse-quences. The plot was lifted from French filmmaker Claude Chabrol, an early admirer and imitator of Alfred Hitchcock, whose film *La Femme Infidele* (1969) is credited as the source, giving the film what one critic called a "vaguely European" feel. But the film, adapted by Alvin Sargent and William Broyles, Jr., was directed by Adrian Lyne, famous for *Fatal Attraction* (1987), and capable of establishing his own distinctive sexual sizzle. Diane Lane told the *New York Times* she "knew that the subject matter and Adrian Lyne were made for each other." In his *Variety* review, however, Todd McCarthy was surprised by the director's restraint: "Just as he did with *Lolita* five years ago," McCarthy wrote, "Lyne again dares to pit his own work against that of a highly regarded filmmaker."

However, *Unfaithful* was more than simply an American remake of a better film from the French New Wave. Chabrol had studied the directorial style of the "master of suspense" and even co-authored with fellow director Eric Rohmer a book entitled *Hitchcock: The First Forty-four Films* (1979). *Washington Post* reviewer Stephen Hunter, who preferred Chabrol's version, protests that Lyne turns "Chabrol's coldbloodedness into a less blameworthy act of temporary insanity." He ridiculed the film's opening metaphor ("An ill wind blows no good") and accused the director of trying to replicate his earlier success with *Fatal Attraction,* calling *Unfaithful* an "unfathomable attraction." But this review was more cute than true. Todd McCarthy was more on target when he wrote that Lyne's film, more than simply a remake, had "a very American character of its own."

The principal acting talent was strong. Though unknown to Americans, 36-year-old Olivier Martinez was well known in Europe after starring with Juliette Binoche in *The Horseman On the Roof* in 1995. Writing in the *New York Times,* Dave Kehr considered Connie to be the "best role to date" for the 37-year-old Diane Lane. Richard Gere has grown into the role of Edward, the wronged husband. Todd McCarthy opined that the role might have been more interesting "had the actor's own reputation been called into service to suggest that Edward might once have been exactly the kind of man with whom his wife now is philandering," though a younger Richard Gere could not have conjured up the Continental flair that Martinez brought to the role. But McCarthy also demanded more of a backstory for the characters.

Owen Gleiberman's *Entertainment Weekly* review of this "more languid *Fatal Attraction*" was one of the most enthusiastic. He praised Lyne's "uncanny sensitivity to the hidden jagged byways of feminine desire," staged "with a slow, forbidden-game meditative savvy that allows the audience to linger over each dread-ridden secret and lie." Connie strays "into a fling because she's a sensual woman whose contentment is tinged with complacency, and because the opportunity presents itself in a way that's too sexy to resist." But, really, the film offers no background information about Connie and her husband, and the *Variety* review complained that there was no "psychological depth to the principal characters, especially the married couple." Perhaps that is why Lyne leaves them alone in the car at the end, where the camera cannot finally penetrate their privacy and shared misery. There is a quiet sort of elegance in that concluding shot that appears to provide a perfect conclusion to a film good enough to hold its own for adult audiences, even as the next *Star Wars* sequel was about to be released.

—James M. Welsh

CREDITS

Edward Sumner: Richard Gere
Connie Sumner: Diane Lane
Paul Martel: Olivier Martinez
Charlie Sumner: Erik Per Sullivan
Frank Wilson: Dominic Chianese
Detective Dean: Zeljko Ivanek
Tracy: Kate Burton
Bill Stone: Chad Lowe
Detective Mirojnick: Gary Basaraba
Sally: Margaret Colin

Origin: USA
Released: 2002
Production: G. Mac Brown, Adrian Lyne; Fox 2000 Pictures, Regency Enterprises; released by 20th Century-Fox
Directed by: Adrian Lyne
Written by: Alvin Sargent, William Broyles Jr.
Cinematography by: Peter Biziou
Music by: Jan A.P. Kaczmarek
Sound: Tod A. Maitland
Editing: Anne Coates
Art Direction: John J. Kasarda
Costumes: Ellen Mirojnick
Production Design: Brian Morris
MPAA rating: R
Running time: 123 minutes

REVIEWS

Baltimore Sun. May 10, 2002, p. E1.
Chicago Sun-Times Online. May 10, 2002.
Entertainment Weekly. May 17, 2002, p. 50.
Los Angeles Times Online. May 8, 2002.
New York Times Online. May 5, 2002.
New York Times Online. May 8, 2002.
New York Times. May 10, 2002, p. B29.
People. May 20, 2002, p. 38.
Rolling Stone. June 6, 2002, p. 84.
USA Today. May 10, 2002, p. D12.
Variety. May 6, 2002, p. 41.
Washington Post. May 10, 2002, p. C1.
Washington Post Weekend. May 10, 2002, p. WE42.
Washington Times. May 19, 2002, p. B5.

QUOTES

Paul (Olivier Martinez) to Connie (Diane Lane) on their affair: "There's no such thing as a mistake—there's what you do, and what you don't do."

N.Y. Film Critics 2002: Actress (Lane), Actress (Lane)
Nomination:
Oscars 2002: Actress (Lane)
Golden Globes 2003: Actress—Drama (Lane)
Screen Actors Guild 2002: Actress (Lane).

Very Annie Mary

about to be very big in a very small town
—Movie tagline

one can dream, can't one?
—Movie tagline

From its very cutesy title, one can tell *Very Annie Mary* will *not* be another Mike Leigh or Ken Loach kitchen-sink drama about the British. Rather, *Very Annie Mary* falls into what Stephen Holden of the *New York Times* dubs "the sentimental oh-those-wacky-Brits genre that was ushered in by *The Full Monty.*" Actually, this more popular genre could and should be traced back before *Monty,* though that 1997 sleeper transformed the working-class heroes and heroines of the Leigh-Loach pictures into more appealingly optimistic, if indeed "wacky," Brits.

The titular heroine of Sara Sugarman's entry into the field (played by Rachel Griffiths) shares with her *Full Monty* male counterparts, a desire to perform. Annie Mary is a repressed young woman working in the bakery of her father, Jack Pugh (Jonathan Pryce), but yearns to leave the cozy but cloistered village of Ogw, located in Garw Valley in South Wales.

Annie Mary puts her dreams on hold when her father suffers a stroke while he himself performs in a local pub. During Jack's rehabilitation, however, Annie Mary rediscovers her childhood calling—singing—and announces to her father that she is going to Cardiff to perform in a major talent contest (albeit a karaoke contest). Surprisingly, Annie Mary and her partners win the contest, and they donate the proceeds toward a fund for a teenager (Joanna Page) who is dying of leukemia back home.

Upon Annie Mary's return, Jack shows disapproval for his daughter's new-found independence, and demands she go back to the menial work in his bakery, but the awkward Annie finally stands up to her father and declares her life will be forever different—she even plans to move away and buy her own home.

If the brightly-colored opening titles weren't enough of a give-away of the film's tone, then certainly the opening sequence should be: Pryce, wearing a Pavarotti mask, pre-tends to sing as the maestro from *Turnandot* while driving his van through town, delivering bread and goodies (please note the working title of the film was *Pavarotti in Dad's Room*).

Clearly writer-director Sugarman wants to keep things amusing if schmaltzy, and she does a good job of balancing the eccentric and the serious. But never does the film surprise us: we've seen it all before—if it wasn't in *Stepping Out*(1991) then it was *Little Voice* (1998); if not *Four Weddings and a Funeral* (1994), then *The Englishman Who Went up a Hill But Came down a Mountain* (1995).

At least you don't have to love the cast to like the movie: the ubiquitous Rachel Griffiths may not be everyone's taste in *Me Myself & I* or the hit HBO cable-TV show, *Six Feet Under,* but she carries off Annie Mary, awkward footing, heavy accent, and all. The annoyingly arrogant Jonathan Pryce is well cast as . . . the annoying arrogant Jack. And there are a few nice touches from the supporting cast—Joanna Page doesn't overplay the sickly teen and Ioan Grufford (the dashing hero of *Horatio Hornblower*) plays a small, funny bit as a part of gay shopkeeper duo (Hob and Nob) who inspire Annie Mary to pursue her dreams (Matthew Rhys plays Nob).

For a production that probably cost less than the music rights (many different songs are heard or performed throughout the film), Sugarman uses the Wales countryside to perfection and technically gets things right. It's too bad, then, *Very Annie Mary* couldn't offer more originality or a deeper resonance. The film probably didn't deserve the boxoffice dismissal it received, but its failure is not that surprising, either.

—*Eric Monder*

CREDITS

Annie Mary: Rachel Griffiths
Jack Pugh: Jonathan Pryce
Hob: Ioan Gruffudd
Nob: Matthew Rhys
Minister: Kenneth Griffiths
Mrs. Ifans: Ruth Madoc
Bethan Bevan: Joanna Page
Mayor: Radcliffe Grafton

Origin: Great Britain, France
Released: 2000
Production: Damian Jones, Graham Broadbent; Le Studio Canal Plus, FilmFour, Arts Council of England, Dragon Pictures, Arts Council of Wales; released by Empire Pictures
Directed by: Sara Sugarman
Written by: Sara Sugarman

CREDITS

Julia: Laura Regan
Paul: Marc Blucas
Sam: Ethan (Randall) Embry
Terry: Dagmara Dominczyk
Billy: Jon Abrahams
Dr. Booth: Jay Brazeau

Origin: USA
Released: 2002
Production: Scott Kroopf, Tom Engelman; Focus Features, Radar Pictures; released by Dimension Films
Directed by: Robert Harmon
Written by: Brendan William Hood
Cinematography by: Rene Ohashi
Music by: Elia Cmiral
Sound: David Husby
Editing: Chris Peppe
Art Direction: Patrick Banister
Costumes: Karen Matthews
Production Design: Doug Higgins
MPAA rating: PG-13
Running time: 100 minutes

REVIEWS

Los Angeles Times Online. November 29, 2002.
New York Times Online. November 28, 2002.
San Francisco Chronicle. November 29, 2002, p. D5.
Variety Online. November 26, 2002.

QUOTES

Terry (Dagmara Dominczyk): "I'm 24 years old, and I walk into a dark room now, and it's like I'm five again."

White Oleander

Where does a mother end and a daughter begin?
—Movie tagline

Box Office: $16.4 million

Ingrid Magnussen (Michelle Pfeiffer) is not exactly a typical mother. What she is is a self-absorbed artist prone to emotional outbursts and inclined to forget things like parent's night at her daughter Astrid's (Alison Lohman) school. This is not to say Ingrid doesn't love Astrid, it's just that her kind of mother-love is not what one would normally expect. Cool, beautiful and controlling, Ingrid seems to live in a world of her own and Astrid is nothing more than an obscure little satellite orbiting her larger-than-life mother.

The teenage Astrid, on the other hand, is a blank canvas on which her mother has been drawing for years, and in light of who Ingrid is, it shouldn't be too unexpected that maybe Astrid is a young woman at a loss as to who she really is.

Although Ingrid is a very independent, outspoken woman, she still ends up having a boyfriend. His name is Barry (Billy Connolly) and he's a writer who's as independent as Ingrid. One day, after making love to Ingrid, Billy basically tells her to leave because he has another date. This sends Ingrid into a rage and although we can only infer that she has killed him, we do witness her being arrested by the police and marched out of her house right in front of her impressionable daughter.

The steely Ingrid is now sent to jail for 35 years to life and Astrid is sent on a journey through California's foster care system. Her first stop is at the small home of Starr Thomas (Robin Wright Penn) a one-time alcoholic, cokehead and topless dancer and now a born again Christian who's nonetheless still inclined to wear hot pink and spandex. Astrid shares a room with Starr's rebellious daughter and shares the house with Starr's two other foster children and her live-in boyfriend Ray (Cole Hauser)

Ray is a genuinely nice guy and he soon becomes a surrogate father to Astrid. This of course makes Starr jealous and she starts drinking again. It doesn't take long for Ray and Astrid to find solace in each other's arms and Starr ends up shooting Astrid in a drunken rage.

Now without a home, Astrid is sent to recuperate at McKinney Hall, a clearing house for foster children. There she isolates herself from everyone but eventually a young man, Paul Trout (Patrick Fugit), breaks through her barriers by using their mutual love of drawing. While Astrid sketches people, Paul draws sophisticated comic characters. Their friendship may not be close for long, though, for Paul will soon turn 18 and plans on moving to New York, and Astrid has just been assigned to a new family, the Richards.

Claire (Renee Zellwegger) and Mark (Noah Wyle) Richards are an actress and television producer with no kids of their own. They have a beautiful Malibu home and Astrid and Claire soon create a loving friendship. It's easy to see why, they're both missing something in their lives. Astrid is missing her mother who's in jail, and Claire is missing her husband who is more often on business trips than he is at home.

When Ingrid realizes that Claire and Astrid are bonding, she starts writing Claire and even arranges a prison visit with her. For the controlling Ingrid, Claire is a threat. As much as Ingrid hated that her daughter was baptized while under Starr's care, she hates even more that Claire might actually be replacing her as a mother and guide in Astrid's life. As a result, the wily Ingrid plants a few ideas in the impressionable and vulnerable Claire's mind and not long afterward Claire commits suicide.

As for Astrid, it's back to McKinney Hall. Astrid is now beginning to see her mother as the poisonous person she is and is also rebuilding the protective walls around herself after being "rejected" so to speak, by two foster families. In her disgust at herself and with her mother, even though she is offered another kindly family to live with, Astrid purposely picks Rena Grushenka (Svetlana Efremova) a Russian emigre and capitalist of the first order. Rena's foster girls are all older and instead of mothering them she mentors them in and uses them for making a living. Rena teaches the girls to pick through garbage and then take their findings to sell at flea markets.

In this environment Astrid goes through her rebel, goth stage. She darkens her blond hair and takes to wearing black and way too much makeup. One can only imagine how much this upsets Ingrid who constantly harps on their superior Viking heritage, but maybe this is Astrid finally breaking away from her mother. One just worries that it is a break that will have her going in the opposite direction to her own destruction, while also hoping that it will instead send her to find her own identity independent of her mother.

British director Peter Kosminsky, a former documentary filmmaker who is probably best known here for his television version of *Wuthering Heights,* featuring Ralph Fiennes and Juliette Binoche, has done a valid, even if abbreviated, job of bringing the best-selling book by Janet Fitch (and the May 1999 pick for Oprah Winfrey's book club) to the screen. Although he does avoid or play down some of the more sensational aspects of the book (such as a dog attack that leaves Astrid scarred), he is savvy enough to realize that this is a story about characters. By emphasizing psychology over melodrama, Kosminsky and screenwriter Mary Agnes Donoghue (*Beaches*) have created a movie that is segmented into separate vignettes as Astrid goes from family to family. However, by doing this the filmmakers have also managed to focus on character and avoid a lot of stereotypical situations that would have created that by-the-numbers melodrama.

White Oleander, for example, is not an indictment of the foster care system which could have been an easy target. That system is nothing more than a background against which the characters act and react. Similarly, Astrid is not exploited by her foster families. Even the sexual relation she has with Ray is consensual and initiated by Astrid as is her "employment" at the hands of Rena, which is something she undertakes willingly.

Similarly, Claire could have been painted as a smothering, too needy, childless woman, but she's not. No one beats Astrid or abuses her, and even when Starr shoots her it is in the context of her character's self-loathing and substance abuse.

Astrid, too, isn't the typical troubled foster child one might expect a filmmaker to create. Why? Because she is not a victim. She may be a little lost, but underneath is the strong woman the seeds for which her mother has planted. All she needs is a little self-confidence and to get out from under her mother's far-reaching control and we have no doubt she will truly bloom.

The film really tells two parallel stories. One involves the mother-daughter relationship and the other concerns Astrid's daily struggle to discover herself while being bounced around in the state's foster care system.

There have been several movies recently about mother-daughter relationships. Coming immediately to mind are *Anywhere But Here, Tumbleweeds,* and the recent *Divine Secrets of the Ya-Ya Sisterhood.* And while all feature daughters with ambivalent feelings towards their mothers and mothers who are, shall we say, a bit neurotic, the mother in *White Oleander* can be positively scary.

The film's title, by the way, comes from the delicate flower, the white oleander, which is beautiful but protects itself by making its own poison. It is suggested that it was the poison of the white oleander that Ingrid used to murder her boyfriend. Ingrid Magnussen is more than a bit like the white oleander, beautiful and lethal. She is a self-absorbed, strong-willed, and uncompromising artist. (Oddly enough, in Fitch's novel she is a poet.) Ingrid also will do whatever is necessary to keep her daughter from being anything other than what she wants her to be—which means being the same as she is.

Besides losing her daughter as a disciple, what Ingrid may fear most is that her daughter will become average. Consequently, as Astrid moves through the story, reflecting the average lives of the families she comes to live with, Ingrid uses the only weapon she has to control her daughter while behind bars, mind games. They are tactics that work well while her daughter is confused and impressionable and still loves her mother a lot, and they even work well on Ingrid's other victims, such as Claire.

Ingrid is an incredibly complex character who is brought to life in an amazing way by Michelle Pfeiffer. While she could have been nothing more than just another cinematic villain, in Pfeiffer's hands Ingrid is as fascinating as she is malevolent. It's almost mesmerizing to watch the cold calculations that are going on behind that dazzlingly beautiful face. It is to Pfeiffer's credit that she did not soften the character of Ingrid to try and make her more likable or sympathetic. In

Pfeiffer's capable hands, Ingrid's icy exterior—and even her icy interior—never cracks. It is a masterful performance.

The performance by relative newcomer Alison Lohman as Astrid is also well done. Known probably for her term on the short-lived television series *Pasadena* and her feature film debut in 1999's *The Thirteenth Floor,* Lohman's Astrid is unforgettable even though she is a chameleon, changing her appearance, her attitude, even her wardrobe to reflect whatever the major influence is in her life at that particular moment. Lohman convincingly plays Astrid from 15 to 18 (although she ages from 12 to 19 in the book) and we want to follow her on her compelling journey through a very tough period in her life.

We care about Astrid. We see how toxic her mother's love is and yet how much she wants and needs her. We feel her courage, her fear, her anger and, eventually, her grace. We willingly follow her on her quest to find a sense of belonging, to find love, to find herself.

Pfeiffer and Lohman are not the only stand-out performances in *White Oleander.* Robin Wright Penn as the born-again Starr Thomas infuses a character that could easily have become a laughable cliche with a degree of vulnerability and self-doubt. We see how her original topless dancing, alcoholic persona could have morphed believably into a fundamentalist Christian. In Wright Penn's hands Starr is both tough and tragic. For Starr, taking in foster children is both a source of income and a form of redemption.

Renee Zellwegger, too, takes a character who could have been shallowly drawn and gives her depth. As Claire, a woman who is married to a man she can't trust and fears she is losing, Zellwegger does not portray her has helpless and pathetic but instead as fragile and sympathetic. Claire becomes a very touching character whose very vulnerability and generosity may be just what Astrid needs. Claire nurtures Astrid, and Astrid gives Claire a purpose. That is why what the incredibly strong Ingrid does to innocent Claire is so horrific and tragic.

Even Patrick Fugit's relatively peripheral character of Paul Trout is well drawn and well acted. Best known as Cameron Crowe's alter ego in *Almost Famous,* Paul is the only person in Astrid's life who doesn't judge her, doesn't try to mold her and who loves her unconditionally because they are so similar. Paul provides a kind of objectivity to Astrid's cloudy perceptions about love.

White Oleander can also boast first-rate production values and beautiful cinematography (by Elliot Davis) which give the film a sharp visual style. In lesser hands it could have been nothing more than another chick-flick, another made-for-cable movie shown on the Lifetime channel. Instead it's a good-looking film featuring superb acting, and a smart story about survival and salvation that avoids mawkishness and gives us women who are complex and worth watching.

—Beverley Bare Buehrer

CREDITS

Astrid Magnussen: Alison Lohman
Ingrid Magnussen: Michelle Pfeiffer
Starr: Robin Wright Penn
Clair Richards: Renee Zellweger
Paul Trout: Patrick Fugit
Barry Kolker: Billy Connolly
Ray: Cole Hauser
Mark Richards: Noah Wyle
Miss Martinez: Amy Aquino
Rena: Svetlana Efremova

Origin: USA
Released: 2002
Production: John Wells, Hunt Lowry; Pandora Film; released by Warner Bros.
Directed by: Peter Kosminsky
Written by: Mary Agnes Donoghue
Cinematography by: Elliot Davis
Music by: Thomas Newman
Sound: Steve Bowerman
Music Supervisor: Debra Baum, Ann Kline
Editing: Chris Ridsdale
Art Direction: Anthony Rivero Stabley
Costumes: Susie De Santo
Production Design: Donald Graham Burt
MPAA rating: PG-13
Running time: 110 minutes

REVIEWS

Boxoffice. November, 2002, p. 147.
Chicago Sun-Times Online. October 11, 2002.
Entertainment Weekly. October 18, 2002, p. 89.
Los Angeles Times Online. October 11, 2002.
New York Times Online. October 11, 2002.
People. October 21, 2002, p. 43.
USA Today Online. October 11, 2002.
Variety Online. September 7, 2002.
Washington Post. October 11, 2002, p. WE47.

QUOTES

Ingrid (Michelle Pfeiffer): "Loneliness is the human condition. Love humiliates you, hate cradles you."

Nomination:
Screen Actors Guild 2002: Support. Actress (Pfeiffer).

The Wild Thornberrys Movie

Go Wild!!!
—Movie tagline
This could be the beginning of a beautiful adventure.
—Movie tagline
New Home. New Friends. No Powers.
—Movie tagline
You don't need extraordinary powers to do extraordinary things.
—Movie tagline

 Box Office: $38.8 million

A lot of trouble went into *The Wild Thornberrys Movie*. The film is based on the series that has run on kid cable channel Nickelodeon since 1988. Producers Arlene Klasky and Gabor Csupo, who created the series, and directors Jeff McGrath and Cathy Malkasian, have lined up a lot of talent and put enough work into the film so that it's not another cash-in-quick Nickelodeon film. For the soundtrack, they got music from the Pretenders, Peter Gabriel and Youssou N'Dour, and even Paul Simon's first original song for a film in 15 years, "Father and Daughter." And the cast list is filled with enough talent that it would be nearly impossible for the movie to be a complete dud. A partial list of the casting agent's big scores includes: Tim Curry, Alfre Woodward, Lynn Redgrave, Rupert Everett and Marisa Tomei.

Producers Klasky and Csupo paid extreme attention to making sure that the film was accurate in tiny ways. The film takes place on the Serengeti plain in Africa and the native plants are detailed faithfully. The animals that roam the plains there are the right kind of animals and the African tribespeople who show up in the film speak in the authentic Lingala dialect. It would be a rare kid who could note and appreciate the precision of the Lingala speakers, but it's nice to know that someone took some time on this film.

The animation hasn't been juiced up much for the film. It looks odd and offbeat on TV and it does on the big-screen, too. As Dave Kehr of the *New York Times* described it, "On screen, *The Wild Thornberrys* looks just as it does on television, only wider." The animators of the Thornberrys shun realism, and like to exaggerate features. Eliza Thornberry (Lacey Chabert) is little more than a giant head adorned with braces, freckles and braids. The whole deal is propped up precariously on a tiny neck and held up by a body with impossibly skinny legs. Her dad Nigel (Curry) has his Britishness emphasized by a pair of large, protruding buck teeth. This is not a pretty family.

Those who are unfamiliar with the brood will be brought up to speed in the first few minutes where all is explained. Eliza is the curious 12-year-old daughter of nature documentarians Nigel and Marianne (Jodi Carlisle) Thornberry. To film their series for public television, the couple travels the globe, while Nigel narrates and Marianne films. They take along Eliza and her big sister, Debbie (Danielle Harris), a teen who wishes for nothing more than to return to the civilized world of boys and malls. Also along is Donnie (voiced by Flea of the Red Hot Chili Peppers), a wild child who the family has adopted. The boy hasn't become too tame and communicates by grunting and doing the "wedgie dance." During their adventures, the family is joined by Nigel's very proper British parents, Grandmother (Redgrave) and Grandpa (Curry again) Thornberry.

We also learn that, after once saving a tribal priest who had been turned into a warthog, Eliza has been given the gift of being able to talk with the animals. The shaman warns that the only condition Eliza must follow is that she must never tell any human about her gift. If she does, she will lose it. At first it's not too hard to follow this rule since Eliza spends most of her time with animals. Her best friend and constant companion is Darwin (Tom Kane), a fussy and chatty chimp who speaks with the clipped accent of an upper-class Brit.

While on yet another of her explorations of nature, Eliza talks to a mom cheetah, Akela (Alfre Woodward) and convinces her to let her cubs come out to play with Eliza and Darwin. As they frolic, a helicopter manned by poachers swoops by and grabs one of the cubs. Eliza valiantly tries to save the cub and even grabs onto a ladder dangling down from the helicopter but it isn't enough to save the cheetah.

Her grandmother is horrified by such uncivilized behavior and insists that Eliza immediately be sent off to an English boarding school so that she can learn to become a proper young lady. It's one of the plot's flaws that her parents agree to this, against their better judgment, but then writer Kate Boutilier has to do something to stretch this episode to feature length. Big sister Debbie seethes with jealousy that Eliza gets to escape the Godforsaken plain. She moans, "We're headed to the abyss with no chance of teen interaction." But Eliza is devastated to leave her home in nature—

especially before she's had a chance to rescue the cheetah cub.

Eliza spends some screen time at her snooty boarding school and battles her even more snooty roommate and the headmistress, Mrs. Fairgood (Brenda Blethyn). All of this is filler until the real action—saving the cub. Eliza ditches school and returns to her family. On route to finding the poachers, she discovers more animals that she must save. She learns that the poachers are Sloan (Everett) and Bree (Tomei) Blackburn, two hipsters that have been posing as wildlife explorers. Their evil plan includes rounding up thousands of elephants when the animals gather by the river during an eclipse. They will kill the animals and take their tusks. Insert evil chuckle here. Also trying to help out are Debbie and her new friend, tribesman Boko (Obba Babatunde), who helps her track Eliza.

What makes this story rise above others of its ilk is its positive message and its humor. *The Wild Thornberrys Movie* teaches that nature is good, poaching is bad, a person should trust their own abilities and stuff like that, but it's done gently and is never strident. And there are lots of funny lines sprinkled through the movie, mostly provided by Eliza's oddball family, especially Valley Girl Debbie. After laying another of her biting comments on her father, Debbie quips, "Dad, have you completely lost your ability to recognize sarcasm?" He father answers cheerily and blankly, "I'm not sure I ever had it!" When a baboon does a dance that involves waving its hind quarters in Debbie's face, she says disgustedly, "That is SO wrong."

Critics gave the film mostly favorable reviews. Roger Ebert of the *Chicago Sun-Times* wrote that the film was "a jolly surprise" and that the "charm of *The Wild Thornberrys Movie* comes from its zany visual style, the energy of the voiceover actors and the fine balance of action that is thrilling but not too scary." Ann Hornaday of the *Washington Post* was particularly enthralled with Eliza. "Kids could not have found a better heroine than Eliza," she wrote, "a brave and sensitive little girl." Kevin Thomas of the *Los Angeles Times* wrote, "In a splendid animation transition from the Nickelodeon cable channel to the big screen, *The Wild Thornberrys Movie* makes a witty and delightful Christmas present for the entire family." Kehr of the *New York Times* was less enthralled. "Without the financial or creative resources of the Disney animators, *The Wild Thornberrys Movie* remains essentially an extended Saturday morning cartoon—which is to say, a series of hastily executed illustrations matched to a voice track."

—*Jill Hamilton*

CREDITS

Eliza Thornberry: Lacey Chabert (Voice)

Darwin: Tom Kane (Voice)
Nigel Thornberry/The Colonel: Tim Curry (Voice)
Cordelia Thornberry: Lynn Redgrave (Voice)
Debbie Thornberry: Danielle Harris (Voice)
Donnie Thornberry: Flea (Voice)
Marianne Thornberry: Jodi Carlisle (Voice)
Sloan Blackburn: Rupert Everett (Voice)
Bree Blackburn: Marisa Tomei (Voice)
Shaman Mnyambo: Kevin M. Richardson (Voice)
Boko: Obba Babatunde (Voice)
Akela: Alfre Woodard (Voice)
Sarah Wellington: Melissa Greenspan (Voice)
Jomo: Brock Peters (Voice)
Mrs. Fairgood: Brenda Blethyn (Voice)

Origin: USA
Released: 2002
Production: Arlene Klasky, Gabor Csupo; Nickelodeon; released by Paramount Pictures
Directed by: Jeff McGrath, Cathy Malkasian
Written by: Kate Boutilier
Music by: Drew Neumann
Sound: Eric Flickinger, Eddie Bydalek
Editing: John Bryant
Production Design: Dima Malanitchev
MPAA rating: PG
Running time: 88 minutes

REVIEWS

Boxoffice. November, 2002, p. 124.
Chicago Sun-Times Online. December 20, 2002.
Entertainment Weekly. January 3, 2003, p. 48.
Los Angeles Times Online. December 20, 2002.
New York Times Online. December 20, 2002.
USA Today Online. December 20, 2002.
Variety Online. December 14, 2002.
Washington Post. December 20, 2002, p. C5.

QUOTES

Debbie (Danielle Harris) to her younger brother: "Donnie, now is not the time for the wedgie dance!"

AWARDS AND NOMINATIONS

Nomination:
Oscars 2002: Song ("Father and Daughter")
Golden Globes 2003: Song ("Father and Daughter").

Windtalkers

Honor was their code.
—Movie tagline

"The Navajo Has The Code. Protect The Code At All Costs."
—Movie tagline

 Box Office: $40.4 million

As WWII was waged in the Pacific, the United States and its allies not only found the Japanese to be fierce fighters but also skilled code breakers, making an arduous struggle even more difficult. Time after time, Tojo's men were able to crack our codes, putting military operations and thousands of men in jeopardy. Then, in 1942, Philip Johnston, who grew up amongst the Navajo as the son of a missionary, approached the U.S. military with an idea to use that tribe's language as the basis for a new code. It ended up completely baffling the enemy and enabling the Allies to gain the upper hand in that theater of the war. Four hundred Navajo were recruited by the Marines to serve as code talkers or "windtalkers," each translating information into code and relaying it to another to be quickly and efficiently deciphered. The whole remarkable setup was veiled in such secrecy that the U.S. government kept it classified for a quarter of a century after the war had ended. These brave, indispensable Native Americans had to wait over 30 years after that to receive recognition and their nation's thanks, with Congressional Medals of Honor being awarded in 2001.

Even more time will have to elapse before their tale is truly told on the silver screen, despite the release of *Windtalkers,* a fairly run-of-the-mill, cliche-ridden war film in which the code talkers and their story is secondary to that of a tormented white soldier. Posters heralding the film's release, which prominently featured Nicolas Cage as that tortured soul, should have warned those interested in seeing a film focusing on the Native Americans that this was not going to be their film. While some surviving code talkers and their families praised the film, perhaps glad to finally receive at least some degree of recognition, others were disappointed that a production purporting to be a tribute to the Navajo felt the need to focus instead on one of the white Marines given the duty of protecting them. "Why does Hollywood find it impossible to trust minority groups with their own stories?" lamented Roger Ebert. "It's that white-guy problem, again," is how Leah Rozen began her review.

Windtalkers itself begins promisingly enough, looking for all the world like a John Ford film with its arresting epic longshots of the majestically-beautiful Southwest. Indeed, parts of the film were shot in Ford's beloved and oft-used Monument Valley, Utah. With its sun-drenched golden rock formations under an expansive sky, it is a place where nature predominates, an appropriate starting point for a film about a people tied so closely to nature. As the wind whistles, the camera practically caresses the landscape. Soon we see Navajo Ben Yahzee (Canadian native Adam Beach, actually a member of the Saulteaux tribe) leaving his wife, young son, and assorted relatives and friends to go off and serve his country. He heads off along with Charlie Whitehorse (Navajo Roger Willie, who inadvertently got the role when he accompanied two younger relatives to a casting call).

From this serene setting, the film takes a jolting jump to a horrific battle scene in the Solomon Islands, complete with grisly human carnage, dreadful screams, and deafening explosions. U.S. Marine Corps Cpl. Joe Enders (Cage, last in uniform in 2001's *Captain Corelli's Mandolin*) has been ordered to hold their position and vows to do so, resulting in the loss of all his men. (One soldier even damns him with his dying breath.) Enders, himself wounded, is sent to recuperate at a Naval Hospital in Hawaii, where he meets a sympathetic nurse named Rita (Frances O'Connor). She and the doctors do what they can to heal damage to his ear which has impaired his equilibrium, but it is clear that the wounds to the haunted, guilt-ridden man's psyche remain painfully raw. Rita helps falsify some test results so that Enders can rush back into action, fiercely determined to "kill Japs," but he is less than thrilled when told about the new, top-secret code talkers project and informed that his job will be to protect the Navajo recruit with whom he will be paired. Enders complains that he has no interest in "babysitting some Indians," but accepts his orders (and a promotion to Sergeant) to "protect the code talkers—at all costs."

Still emotionally drained and exhibiting a shell-shocked stare, Enders meets Pete "Ox" Anderson (Christian Slater), who will also be responsible for one of the talkers. Enders warns Ox not to get too attached to the Navajo, partly because he knows the pain of losing men in battle and partly because there is the unspoken order that if the talkers are about to fall into Japanese hands, they must be killed before the enemy tortures it out of them. (There does not appear to be any historical evidence to support this important element in the screenplay.) Enders is paired with Yahzee and Ox with Charlie. As the reluctant "babysitter" Sergeant Enders and the Marines under his command get to know their comrades from another culture, there are predictable scenes of uneasiness, and even brutal bigotry from a racist jerk named Chick (Noah Emmerich), who asserts that the Navajo look way too much like Japs for his liking.

At what seems like fairly evenly spaced intervals, *Windtalkers* proceeds to alternate between scenes showing interaction between the Marines and those featuring thunderous, ultra-violent and gory battles. When things seem too quiet for a stretch, we know that all hell is about to break loose again. Enders shoots the enemy with a crazed, gritted-teeth intensity that clearly startles his own men, and drowns his sorrows in saki. Yahzee is horrified by his first battle experience, and when he and a Japanese soldier point guns at each other, it is Enders who must pull the trigger. One of the more gripping scenes in the film is that in which Enders and Yahzee, mistakenly under fire from their own ships as well as by Japanese troops, hatch a successful plan to commandeer one of the enemy's radios when their own is destroyed.

There is a bonding which takes place between the men of both races, signified visually by shots of Ox and Charlie now playing flute and harmonica together harmoniously. Even Chick comes to admire Yahzee's bravery, and Charlie saves his life. This increased closeness, however, puts more pressure on the still-fragile emotions of Enders, causing him to demand that he be relieved of his duties. His request is refused, and the time inevitably comes when, in the midst of a brutal enemy onslaught, he has to decide whether he can bring himself to kill one of his own men. He does so when Charlie is about to be taken prisoner, lobbing a grenade in the Navajo's direction. During the last combat scenes in which Ox and others are killed, a battle also rages between Yahzee and Enders. The code talker not only mourns the loss of his friend, but also grapples with a burning anger when he discovers the circumstances surrounding Charlie's death. Finally, when Enders is fatally wounded as he self-lessly tries to save his remaining men, Yahzee forgives him and the two come to terms just before Enders expires heroi-cally in a dramatic death scene. The film ends with Yahzee back home amongst the Navajo, but the scene highlights none of his (or Charlie's) bravery and instead is devoted to giving thanks to the brave man who protected him. It is Enders' tags that Yahzee puts around his own boy's neck, and extolls the virtues of the fallen hero.

In *Entertainment Weekly*'s Summer Movie Preview is-sue, it stated that "this epic could either fill MGM's sails or knock the wind right out of 'em." The studio was already hurting from the disappointing showings of its two most recent big releases, *hart's War* and *Rollerball*, and it began to worry about *Windtalkers* as its ever-inflating budget rose to a whopping $115 million, and a longer than expected period of post production and September 11th publicity concerns pushed back its release for a full year. Their uneasiness turned out to be justified, as the film only grossed $40.9 million at the boxoffice, leading to a drop in the value of MGM stock and the firing of at least one executive.

Aside from the film's unfortunate shift of focus and its historical embellishment, it has other problems, as well. John Woo, the film's director, is known for his many violent action films and the immense, cacophonous combat scenes he carefully stages, complete with the use of slow-motion to highlight acts of bravery, are truly potent and ghastly. (He

used more than a dozen cameras, hundreds of explosives, and countless extras.) Woo said he hoped these scenes in *Windtalkers* would increase viewers' abhorrence of war. He succeeds in that endeavor, but the scenes overwhelm all else in the film.

Woo certainly seems more interested in them and, as usual, in the complex relationships between men, rather than in telling us much about the code talkers. What comes between the impressive battle scenes is fairly flat and features too much cliched material we have seen in countless other war movies. For example, there is the emotional goodbye to wife and child, the pretty nurse who takes a liking to the injured soldier, and the doomed character who says, "If anything should happen to me . . ." Beach is quite appealing, but the unabated, acute agony of Cage's character makes him hard to warm up to. Critical reaction to the film was more negative than positive. With only a disappointing sideways glance at the code talkers' efforts, *Windtalkers* ends up being just another war picture by subjugating the material that would have made it both distinctive and far more interesting.

—*David L. Boxerbaum*

CREDITS

Joe Enders: Nicolas Cage
Ben Yahzee: Adam Beach
Ox Henderson: Christian Slater
Chick: Noah Emmerich
Pappas: Mark Ruffalo
Hjelmstad: Peter Stormare
Harrigan: Brian Van Holt
Rita: Frances O'Connor
Major Mellitz: Jason Isaacs
Nellie: Martin Henderson
Charlie Whitehorse: Roger Willie

Origin: USA
Released: 2002
Production: John Woo, Terence Chang, Scott Kramer, Gregory Jacobs; Lion Rock; released by MGM
Directed by: John Woo
Written by: John Rice, Joe Batteer
Cinematography by: Jeffrey L. Kimball
Music by: James Horner
Sound: Richard Goodman
Editing: Tom Rolf, Steven Kemper, Jeff Gullo
Art Direction: Kevin Ishioka
Costumes: Nick Scarano
Production Design: Holger Gross
MPAA rating: R
Running time: 134 minutes

Boxoffice. October, 2001, p. 24.
Chicago Sun-Times Online. June 14, 2002.
Entertainment Weekly. June 14, 2002, p. 65.
Los Angeles Times Online. June 14, 2002.
New York Times Online. June 9, 2002.
New York Times Online. June 14, 2002.
People. June 24, 2002, p. 31.
Time. June 10, 2002, p. 64.
USA Weekend. June 7, 2002, p. 10.
Variety. June 10, 2002, p. 28.
Wall Street Journal. June 14, 2002, p. WE7.
Washington Post. June 14, 2002, p. WE41.

World Traveler

ever wander?
—Movie tagline

One woman wasn't enough. One road trip was.
—Movie tagline

Bart Freundlich's *World Traveler* is a moody road film that challenges us to follow the journey of a thirtysomething architect named Cal (Billy Crudup), who one day walks out on his beautiful wife and little boy, gets in the family's Volvo station wagon, and sets out to discover the freedom of the open road. Since we do not know at the outset what motivates Cal, the premise is puzzling, even frustrating, and the film's deliberate pace requires a certain amount of patience from the audience. However, *World Traveler* gradually develops a cumulative power through Cal's various encounters on the road before sputtering out at the end.

Cal seems to have a contented life—a good job and an adoring wife and son—so why he suddenly flees New York on the morning of his son's third birthday and heads West without so much as saying good-bye is a mystery. A man in his early 30s, Cal appears to be having a midlife crisis. No single event accounts for his malaise, but we gradually see that fatherhood and family life are weighing heavily on him. In Pennsylvania, he takes up briefly with a waitress named Delores (Karen Allen), who has had four failed marriages but no children and thus no reason to stay when things were tough, which may be a subtle warning to Cal against fleeing his stable life.

Cal soon gets a job at a construction site, where he makes friends with a fellow worker named Carl (Cleavant Derricks) and takes him on as a drinking buddy. Even though he knows Carl is married, Cal brings him along when he tries to pick up some gals in a bar. When Carl finally brings him home one night, Carl's wife (Mary McCormack) berates Cal for taking Carl drinking since he is

a recovering alcoholic. The irresponsible Cal, still drunk, even makes a clumsy pass at her. Cal, in effect, is not a very sympathetic protagonist; free from the constraints of home, he behaves recklessly, but Crudup gives him enough charm and humor so that we stick with him despite his sometimes reprehensible behavior.

Cal moves on and gives a brief ride to a hitchhiker, Meg (Liane Balaban), who fondly remembers cross-country trips with her mom before she died. Each person he meets, then, seems to offer Cal a glimpse into the varieties of family life and thus a reminder of what he is leaving behind.

Cal's next encounter is very funny and yet unsettling at the same time. When Cal takes Meg to the Minneapolis airport to pick up a bag, he meets an old high school classmate, Jack (James LeGros), who remembers Cal vividly even though Cal can barely recall him. Jack urges Cal to have a drink for old times' sake, and Cal goes along, even though Jack's oddly insistent manner is a bit strange. Jack is snarky and sardonic, and his overly chummy manner can barely mask a deep resentment that stretches back to high school. According to Jack, Cal stole his girlfriend, though Cal does not think that Jack and the girl were a couple to begin with. Jack is quite funny in the way he has harbored this grudge for years and is all set to spring it on Cal. Cal needs someone to challenge his complacency and smugness (after all, he does seem like a spoiled kid who has everything a man could want but does not appreciate it), but Jack's over-the-top anger over a high school slight also makes him an oddball himself. Nonetheless, his final accusation that "I bet you haven't done one good thing since I saw you last, and I bet you won't" gnaws at Cal and sets up the next encounter.

At a roadside bar, Cal happens upon a woman named Dulcie, who is passed out and about to be picked up by the police. Deciding to play Good Samaritan, he throws her over his shoulder and takes her to his motel room. Played by Freundlich's real-life partner, Julianne Moore, Dulcie claims to be fleeing from her ex-husband, who is trying to take half of her inheritance. She also wants to go pick up her little son, and Cal, determined to be a do-gooder for once, agrees to take her to him in Montana. First, however, they stop at a fair and ride the Ferris wheel, which becomes a brief respite from their troubles. While this interlude does not do much for the story, the scenes at the fair are beautifully shot and evoke a sense of freedom from the cares of the world and possibly an escape into childhood away from the grownup responsibilities that Cal is fleeing.

Sadly, however, Dulcie turns out to be mentally unhinged, a revelation that hits Cal very hard. The morning after she and Cal have made love, he discovers her talking to her little son, who of course is not with her. Whether or not Dulcie even has a child, we never learn. But her delusion that her son is right there with them is such a shock to Cal that he finally deserts her, leaving the crazed Dulcie running after his car and screaming for the son that she thinks Cal is kidnapping. Moore gives the film a burst of energy as the troubled Dulcie. Before we see the extent of her problem, she seems to be just what Cal needs—a fun, unpredictable traveling companion who needs saving. She appears to be the classic screwball heroine who can transform the hero's life, but then she becomes the embodiment of what may be Cal's worst nightmare for himself—the madness of a parent who has been separated from a child. Moore brings depth to both aspects of Dulcie, making her a complex, sympathetic character.

All of these encounters could feel like random meetings that do not add up to much were it not for the sense, gradually developed throughout the film, that Cal is facing different versions of himself. Carl represents the happy domestic life that Cal is fleeing (Carl even points out that their names differ by only one letter, which suggests that we are supposed to see them as alter egos), and Jack is a reminder of his past failings. But Dulcie is a kind of warning of what he could become away from home. Dulcie, after all, claims to have a child who is celebrating a birthday at the same time Cal's son is having a birthday, thus making them soul mates of sorts. Cal in effect is confronting his possible future through Dulcie, and he does not like what he sees. Cal's encounters thus grow increasingly bizarre as he travels further from the comforts of home, and the Dulcie episode is the scorching climax—the wake-up call that Cal needs to return to his wife and son.

Cal's last stop is in Oregon, where he sees his father (David Keith), who deserted him and his mother 22 years ago. Unfortunately, this last encounter is a big disappointment because nothing is really learned or resolved. Cal's father is hospitable but remote to the son he barely knows and says that he left Cal and his mother because he "wanted a better life," which really tells us nothing. This reunion should be the revelatory endpoint of the journey, but instead it falls flat, especially after the riveting climax with Dulcie. Cal's anguish throughout the film revolves around his role as a father, but, because Cal's visit with his own father is trite and ultimately pointless, it is hard to believe that it could assuage or at least address his fears and doubts.

And yet Cal somehow finds redemption. In a fantasy sequence, he rises off the ground and flies across the country, revisiting in his imagination many of the people he has met along the way. They smile at him, indicating that they are fine (Dulcie has even been reunited with her son). However, because we never learn what actually happened to any of these people, this sequence, albeit beautifully shot, ends up feeling like an easy way of letting Cal off the hook by allowing him to pretend that everyone he has hurt is fine. Soon Cal himself is back home and in the arms of the son who has missed him.

World Traveler may not be a fully realized piece—especially in the unconvincing way Cal finally comes to grips with his responsibility as a father—but it has some rich,

often funny moments as Cal makes his way across America. If one is left with the feeling that the whole does not equal the sum of the parts, that may be because Cal is such an enigma, we are never sure what he craves or what would constitute fulfillment in his mind at the end of the journey.

Still, the film is filled with small gems. Terry Stacey's wide-screen cinematography showcasing the beauty of America is stunning, and the ubiquitous Willie Nelson songs that seem to follow Cal wherever he goes lovingly evoke American myths of travel and freedom. There is even a glorious shot of the World Trade Center at the end that, in our post-9/11 world, makes Cal's homecoming sweeter and lends the film an added poignancy that it would not otherwise have.

—*Peter N. Chumo II*

CREDITS

Cal: Billy Crudup
Dulcie: Julianne Moore
Carl: Cleavant Derricks
Richard: David Keith
Margaret: Mary McCormack
Jack: James LeGros
Delores: Karen Allen
Meg: Liane Balaban

Origin: USA, Canada
Released: 2001
Production: Tim Perell, Bart Freundlich; Alliance Atlantis, Independent Film Channel (IFC); released by ThinkFilm
Directed by: Bart Freundlich
Written by: Bart Freundlich
Cinematography by: Terry Stacey
Music by: Clint Mansell
Sound: Judy Karp
Editing: Kate Sanford
Art Direction: Tony Grimes
Costumes: Victoria Farrell
Production Design: Kevin Thompson
MPAA rating: R
Running time: 104 minutes

REVIEWS

Boxoffice. December, 2001, p. 51.
Chicago Sun-Times Online. April 26, 2002.
Entertainment Weekly. April 26, 2002, p. 121.
Los Angeles Times Online. April 19, 2002.
New York Times Online. April 19, 2002.

Variety. September 24, 2001, p. 30.
Washington Post. May 9, 2002, p. WE44.

QUOTES

Carl (Cleavant Derricks) tells Cal (Billy Crudup) his wife (Mary McCormick) is angry about their bar trip: "She's mad about the drinking—and the objectification of women."

XXX

A New Breed Of Secret Agent.
—Movie tagline

 Box Office: $141.2 million

XXX was touted as a new kind of James Bond-like spy thriller with a new youthful hero, Vin Diesel. There would be no tuxedos, witty banter or finicky martini orders for this new Bond. Young teen boys, the audience that movie studios for some reason salivate over, don't care about martini-swigging old guys; they want someone they can relate to, is the way the studio logic goes. Xander Cage (Diesel) seems like the kind of hero that has been scientifically designed for this demographic. It's as though Columbia Pictures (related to Sony, makers of the Playstation video game systems which gets a big ol' plug in the film) entered the characteristics of young teen boydom into a computer program and came up with the elements of this film.

For the teen cred, there is currently cool music, modern stunts involving skateboards and a hero with lots of tattoos. (Diesel's are fakes, by the way. There's no use getting XXX tattooed on the back of your neck before you know if your film's going to be a bomb or not.) Other nods to the youth crowd include a minor bad guy who's against skateboarding, a hero who hosts a website, and not much icky romance to ruin the awesome stunts. One bit of failed connection with the youth market are some white partygoers who are speaking hip-hop slang. They could hardly be less cool.

The film is a team effort between Rob Cohen and Diesel. Cohen directed Diesel in *The Fast and Furious,* a street racing film with fast cars, hot women and a ton of adrenaline, that was a big summer hit. Even though that film had a hideously weak plot and many laughable moments of dialogue, Cohen showed that he knew how to make an exciting movie. Even though it was low-budget and plenty cheesy, *The Fast and the Furious* was a visceral experience, with screeching tires, daring stunts and a new fast pace that

was borrowed from video games. With his bald head and growly voice, Diesel was the alpha male of the picture, and he did a good job of it.

In *XXX,* Cohen and Diesel try to amp it up again. There is always something going on in this film. And if there's nothing too exciting happening onscreen, Cohen makes it seem exciting anyway by keeping his camera moving around like it's on the prowl. There is jolting music by aggressive German metal band Rammstein. There are a lot of scenes in nightclubs so that there can be more modern music and ladies with skimpy clothing. And things blow up.

Cage, also known as XXX (say Triple X), is a guy who likes extreme sports. He videotapes himself doing stunts, then posts them on his website, the Xander Zone. He poses as a valet at a posh country club and steals the car of a jerky senator. Cage videotapes the subsequent police chase, as well as himself driving the car off a really high bridge and jumping out with a parachute just . . . in . . . the . . . nick . . . of . . . time. His bad behavior catches the eye of Augustus Gibbons (Samuel L. Jackson), who works for the National Security Agency. We can tell he's tough because he has a big scary scar on the side of his face. Gibbons is looking for a thug like Cage to help him with a spy mission in Prague, in the Czech Republic. His idea is to find "the best and brightest of the bottom of the barrel. Instead of dropping a mouse in the snake pit," Gibbons tells his colleagues, "let's send our own snake to crawl in." Besides, Gibbons considers a guy like Cage to be expendable. If he dies, there are plenty more where he came from.

Some of the more entertaining segments of the film involve Cage's "training." Gibbons drugs Cage then sets him up in a fake diner with a fake robbery so that he can see how Cage reacts. Cage, naturally, has great instincts and passes the test. How did he know something was up with this particular diner? "The waitress," he growls cooly, noting his mother was a waitress and that she never would have worn high heels. It's fun to see how Cage can outwit the traps that the NSA set up for him.

Cage isn't interested in becoming a spy, but he's given a choice between that and going to jail. He decides on the spying, after Gibbons gives him a really lame speech about jail being like a cage for a wild animal like Cage. Cage's assignment: to infiltrate a group of Czech baddies, led by poorly shaven Yorgi (Marton Csokas), and, yawn, to save the world and whatnot. Apparently Yorgi is the leader of a group called Anarchy 99. They've developed a deadly chemical agent called Silent Night that they plan to carry in a submarine, which will release it on various cities until governments break down and the world's people are free to enjoy their freedom.

When we meet the Czechs, there are subtitles so that we can see what they are saying. It's kind of funny because in an action sequence, does anyone really care that the exact translation of the bad guy's words are, "Time to move"?

(Other goodies include: "Catch him fast! Kill him slow!") It seems like a line of dialogue should have a certain level of quality before it is subtitled.

Yorgi and friends let Cage into the group because they're fans of his website. Cage becomes a lot more interested in the case when he lays his eyes on Yorgi's girlfriend, Yelena (Asia Argento, daughter of Italian horror director Dario Argento). Is this the type of movie in which the villains take the time to explain their evil plan before killing the hero? You bet. It happens twice in *XXX*. Do bad guys never watch spy films?

Along the way are the stunts, which are the real stars of the movie. (A stuntman was killed doing one such stunt.) Cage leaps out of planes, drives really fast, and uses a dinner tray to slide down a banister. The biggest and best stunt is one in which Cage is being chased by, oh, who knows, someone. He is on a snow-covered mountain and he tosses a grenade to set off an avalanche. Cage snowboards just barely in front of the crash of falling snow. During the stunts, Cage says stuff like, "I live for this #$%$!" and "Welcome to the Xander Zone!" He also likes to put others down. Some of his bon mots: "Is this guy going to hump my leg?" (said to Yorgi about a security goon) or "If you're going to shoot somebody, shoot that monkey that sold you that shirt."

Critics didn't agree on whether *XXX* was a fun action flick or a dreary drag. Elvis Mitchell of the *New York Times* wrote, "This is perhaps the silliest movie to certify the arrival of a major star since, well, *The Fast and the Furious*." Mick LaSalle of the *San Francisco Chronicle* wrote, "In *XXX*, any time the filmmakers try to strike a note of sincere emotion, it sounds ridiculous. Any time they try to give an intellectual grounding for the action-movie plot, it becomes laughable. And the action set pieces are so outlandish as to be as unbelievable as a Roadrunner cartoon. So what?—In terms of adrenaline, *XXX* is one of the most satisfying entries this summer." Lisa Schwarzbaum of *Entertainment Weekly* gave the film a D and wrote, "Even in the summertime, the most restless young audience deserves the dignity of an action hero motivated by something more than franchise possibilities."

As it turns out, Yorgi didn't need Cage to foil his plan. As Roger Ebert of the *Chicago Sun-Times* pointed out, the idea of driving a poison submarine around the world had a major fault: "Where can a boat go in the landlocked Czech Republic?"

—*Jill Hamilton*

CREDITS

Xander Cage: Vin Diesel
Agent Augustus Gibbons: Samuel L. Jackson
Yelena: Asia Argento
Yorgi: Marton Csokas
El Jefe: Danny Trejo
Toby Lee Shavers: Michael Roof
Sen. Dick Hotchkiss: Tom Everett
Milan Sova: Richy Muller
Kirill: Werner Daehn

Origin: USA
Released: 2002
Production: Neal H. Moritz; Revolution Studios; released by Columbia Pictures
Directed by: Rob Cohen
Written by: Rich Wilkes
Cinematography by: Dean Semler
Music by: Randy Edelman
Sound: William B. Kaplan
Music Supervisor: Kathy Nelson
Editing: Chris Lebenzon, Paul Rubell, Joel Negron
Art Direction: Jonathan Lee
Costumes: Sanja Milkovic Hays
Production Design: Gavin Bocquet
Visual Effects: Joel Hynek
MPAA rating: PG-13
Running time: 111 minutes

REVIEWS

Chicago Sun-Times Online. August 9, 2002.
Entertainment Weekly. August 16, 2002, p. 43.
Los Angeles Times Online. August 9, 2002.
New York Times Online. August 9, 2002.
People. August 19, 2002, p. 33.
Variety. August 5, 2002, p. 19.
Washington Post. August 9, 2002, p. WE37.

QUOTES

Gibbons (Samuel L. Jackson) to Xander Cage (Vin Diesel): "I noticed that you got three X's on your neck. That's appropriate since you're looking at three strikes."

TRIVIA

Asia Argento's tattoos are real while Vin Diesel's were applied for the film.

Y Tu Mama Tambien (And Your Mother Too)

Box Office: $13.6 million

Mexican-born filmmaker Alfonso Cuaròn's release, *Y Tu Mama Tambien* might give film audiences the impression of a couple of spoiled mama's boys venturing into the adulthood, if only the protagonists ever saw their mothers. Part of the film's sad tone derives from the fact that the two boys, for different reasons, do not experience maternal love and only through a painful sexual rite of passage (a road trip with an older woman) do these boys begin to understand women. Co-written with his brother Carlos, *Mama* focuses on two young men from different backgrounds whose hormones are constantly in overdrive. However, despite the boys' vulgarity, masturbation sessions, pot smoking, and sexual escapades, this is not your typical teen sex movie. And instead, the writers emphasized a parallel between a young and restless Mexico and two teens growing up together.

This Mexican menage a trois opens with 17-year-old Tenoch (Diego Luna) engaging in sex with his girlfriend and then Julio (Gael Garcia Bernal) engaging in sex with his girlfriend before the girls take off for a summer trip to Italy. The director doesn't shy away from full-frontal nudity and brazenly portrays erotic scenes in a realistic fashion. The women promise that they will not sleep with any other men while in Italy, but somehow we already know they will never keep their promise and neither will the boys. After the girls leave, the boys hang out at a country club masturbating by the pool and smoking pot. They await a long and boring summer until they meet Luisa (Maribel Verdù) at a posh wedding. The drunken Julio and Tenoch hit on the already-married and older Luisa and ask her if she would like to go on a road trip with them to a beautiful beach. Although she teases the boys a bit, she rejects their offer.

Told through a narrator, we watch Luisa visit a hospital clinic and later we see her crying while she reclines on a bed. She receives a call from her husband, who confesses yet another love affair. After she breaks down, she decides to leave her husband and hit the road with the boys. Although the relationship between Luisa and the boys starts out chaste, she eventually engages in sex with both of them. And in fact, she throws herself into a new life of liberation. The boys confess to each other that they slept with each other's girlfriends and they vow to hate each other until Luisa sets some new house rules.

Midway point through the film, we begin to focus on Luisa more than the teens. We see her sadness when she plays with an indigenous couple's children and we watch her give herself like a willing sacrifice to sex-hungry men. Verdù's mesmerizing performance holds our attention as her character transforms from a shy and self-imposing wife to a near-goddess. She blossoms while finally engaging the life that once zoomed past her, only because she realizes that her days are literally numbered. Eventually, she parts with the boys while staying behind to spend her last days at the beach. The boys return to the city where they eventually split and grow into manhood.

The Cuaròn brothers veered away of writing a typical teen sex flick and in an interview with *RANT*, Alfonso reflected on this decision. "Our point of departure was that this was a movie about identity: two characters seeking identities as grownups; a woman seeking identity as a free, liberated woman; and a teenaged country trying to seek its identity as a grown-up country." The brothers brazenly reveal the political and social conditions of their home country with scenes of demonstrations and narration about the corroding government. Most of the story takes place before a liberal president replaced a 71 year conservative and corrupt leadership. The narrator also informs us of various subplots that involve displacement of indigenous fishermen. One fisherman in particular would lose his way of life near the sea and become a janitor at a resort hotel.

Luna, Bernal and Verdù take numerous risks when rendering their vulnerable characters. They engage in bold sex scenes, exposing their bodies and their souls. Bernal, who appeared in last year's Mexican hit, *Amores Perros,* returns to appear in another Mexican boxoffice hit and plays his final role as a teen. Verdù (*Belle Epoque*) delivers a stunning performance while defining a character that is both vulgar and dignified. Men of any age need a strong woman to help them mature.

—Patty-Lynne Herlevi

CREDITS

Julio Zapata: Gael Garcia Bernal
Tenoch Iturbide: Diego Luna
Luisa Cortes: Maribel Verdu

Origin: Mexico
Language: Spanish
Released: 2001
Production: Jorge Vegara; Producciones Anhelo; released by IFC Films
Directed by: Alfonso Cuaron
Written by: Alfonso Cuaron, Carlos Cuaron
Cinematography by: Emmanuel Lubezki

Sound: Jose Antonio Garcia
Music Supervisor: Liza Richardson, Anette Fradera
Editing: Alfonso Cuaron, Alex Rodriguez
Art Direction: Miguel Alvarez
Costumes: Gabriela Diaque
MPAA rating: Unrated
Running time: 105 minutes

REVIEWS

Boxoffice. November, 2001, p. 136.
Chicago Sun-Times Online. April 5, 2002.
Entertainment Weekly. March 22, 2002, p. 79.
Hollywood Reporter. October 23, 2001, p. 19.
Los Angeles Times Online. March 15, 2002.
New York Times Online. March 17, 2002.
RANT. March/April, 2002, p. 12.
Rolling Stone. April 11, 2002, p. 138.
Sight and Sound. April, 2002, p. 16.
US Weekly. March 25, 2002, p. 1.
Vanity Fair. March, 2002, p. 112.
Variety Online. June 24, 2001.
Washington Post. May 3, 2002, p. WE43.

QUOTES

Luisa (Maribel Verdu): "You have to make the clitoris your best friend." Tenoch (Diego Luna): "What kind of friend is always hiding?"

AWARDS AND NOMINATIONS

L.A. Film Critics 2002: Foreign Film
N.Y. Film Critics 2002: Foreign Film
Natl. Soc. Film Critics 2002: Foreign Film
Nomination:
Oscars 2002: Orig. Screenplay
British Acad. 2002: Foreign Film, Orig. Screenplay
Ind. Spirit 2003: Foreign Film.

Apes (1970), *Escape from the Planet of the Apes* (1971), and *Midnight in the Garden of Good and Evil* (1997).

Adele Jergens (November 26, 1917–November 22, 2002). Born in Brooklyn, New York, the actress played blonde bombshells and femme fatales in B movies during the 1940s and '50s. A New York showgirl, Jergens was the understudy for Gypsy Rose Lee in the Broadway show *Star and Garter,* when she was spotted by a Columbia Studios talent scout and offered a contract. She made her film debut in an uncredited role in 1944's *Together Again* and played her first lead in the serial *Black Arrow* (also 1944). Screen credits included *A Thousand and One Nights* (1945), *The Fuller Brush Man* (1948), *I Love Trouble* (1948), *Ladies of the Chorus* (1948), *The Treasure of Monte Cristo* (1949), *Armored Car Robbery* (1950), *Blonde Dynamite* (1950), *Side Street* (1950), *Abbott and Costello Meet the Invisible Man* (1951), *Sugarfoot* (1951), *The Big Chase* (1954), *The Day the World Ended* (1956) and *Girls in Prison* (1956).

Charles Martin "Chuck" Jones (September 12, 1912–February 22, 2002). Born in Spokane, Washington, Jones had a nearly 70-year career in animation and directed more than 300 films, winning three Academy Awards and being awarded a special lifetime achievement Oscar in 1996. After graduating from the Chouinard Art Institute, Jones got his first job in 1932 with Ub Iwerks, later working as an animator for Leon Schlesinger Studio, which was sold to Warner Bros. Jones remained with the studio until it closed its animation department in 1962. He directed his first cartoon, *The Night Watchman,* in 1938 and won a special award in 1940 for the patriotic cartoon *Old Glory.* During World War II, Jones worked with Theodor S. Geisel ("Dr. Seuss") on a series of army training films featuring the cartoon character Private Snafu; the two later collaborated on *Dr. Seuss's How the Grinch Stole Christmas* and *Horton Hears a Who.* Chuck Jones sketched Bugs Bunny for more than 50 years and created Wile E. Coyote and the Road Runner (who debuted in 1949) as well as Pepe Le Pew, Marvin Martian, Michigan J. Frog, and Gossamer. Jones's three Oscar-winning films were *For Scent-Imental Reasons* (1949), *So Much for So Little* (1949), and *The Dot and the Line* (1965). His autobiography, *Chuck Amuck: The Life and Times of an Animated Cartoonist,* was published in 1989, with a sequel, *Chuck Reducks,* in 1996.

Katy Jurado (January 16, 1924–July 5, 2002). Born Maria Christina Jurado Garcia in Guadalajara, Mexico, the actress made her movie debut in Mexico in 1943 and continued to act in films until 1998. Her first American film was 1951's *The Bullfighter and the Lady* and she received an Academy Award nomination as best supporting actress in the western *Broken Lance* (1954), although her best-known role was as Gary Cooper's former mistress in *High Noon* (1952). Screen

credits included *We the Poor* (1948), *The Brute* (1952), *Trapeze* (1956), *One-Eyed Jacks* (1961), *Barabbas* (1962), *Pat Garrett and Billy the Kid* (1973), *Under the Volcano* (1984), and *Hi-Lo Country* (1998).

Nathan "Jerry" Juran (September 1, 1907–October 23, 2002). Born in Austria, Juran's family emigrated to Minnesota in 1913. The art director and filmmaker graduated from the University of Minnesota School of Architecture and earned a master's degree from the Massachusetts Institute of Technology. He moved to Los Angeles and got a job with RKO, later moving to 20th Century Fox where his first job as an art director was on *How Green Was My Valley,* which won him an Academy Award in 1941. Other credits as an art director included *The Razor's Edge* (1946), *Body and Soul* (1947), and *Winchester '73* (1950). Juran made his directorial debut with *The Black Castle* (1952) and also directed *Hellcats of the Navy* (1957), *Good Day for a Hanging* (1958), *The 7th Voyage of Sinbad* (1958), and *First Men in the Moon* (1964). He also directed *The Brain From Planet Arous* (1957), *The Deadly Mantis* (1957), *20 Million Miles to Earth* (1957) and *The Attack of the 50-Foot Woman*(1958) under the name of Nathan Hertz.

Lee H. Katzin (April 12, 1935–October 30, 2002). Born in Detroit, Michigan, Katzin started his career in Hollywood in the late 1950s as an assistant television director and went on to direct hundreds of episodes of such TV series as *The Wild Wild West, Rat Patrol, Mannix, In the Heat of the Night, Miami Vice,* and *Walker: Texas Ranger.* His feature film credits included *Heaven With a Gun* (1969), *Whatever Happened to Aunt Alice?* (1969), *Along Came a Spider* (1970), *Le Mans* (1971), *The Salzburg Connection* (1972), and *The Break* (1995).

Ward Kimball (March 4, 1914–July 8, 2002). The Disney animator, who created Jiminy Cricket, was born in Minneapolis, Minnesota, and attended the Santa Barbara School of the Arts. An instructor urged him to submit his portfolio to Walt Disney Studio in 1934 and he remained with Disney until retiring in 1973. Kimball was one of the key animators known as the "nine old men," working on such films as *Snow White and the Seven Dwarfs, Pinocchio, Fantasia, The Three Caballeros, Dumbo, Cinderella, Alice in Wonderland, Mary Poppins,* and *Peter Pan.* He also directed the Oscar-winning shorts *Toot, Whistle, Plunk and Boom* (1953) and *It's Tough to Be a Bird* (1969).

Hildegard Knef (December 28, 1925–February 1, 2002). Born Hildegard Frieda Albertina Knef in Ulm, Germany, the actress studied at the Babbelsberg Film Institute and became a star for her role as a former concentration camp inmate in Germany's first postwar film, *Murderers Among Us* (1946). She appeared in more than 50 films, most made in made some 30 films between 1933 and 1939, including the serial *Pirate Treasure* (1934), the westerns *Range Warfare* (1935), *Rio Grande Romance* (1936) and *Timber War* (1936), and the Three Stooges shorts *Three Dumb Clucks* (1937) and *Healthy, Wealthy and Dumb* (1938). She quit acting in 1939 (her last film was *The Awful Goof*) after marrying and giving birth to two daughters.

Sihung Lung (1930–May 2, 2002). Born Hsiung Lang in mainland China, the actor joined the Nationalist army and was forced to flee to Taiwan in 1949 after the Communist victory. He began his acting career with an army theater troupe in Taipei and played numerous roles in Chinese-language films, on stage and on Taiwanese television. Lung had retired when director Ang Lee asked him to play the role of the conflicted father in *Pushing Hands* (1992) as well as in Lee's *The Wedding Banquet* (1993) and *Eat Drink Man Woman* (1994). Lung's last roles were in *Crouching Tiger, Hidden Dragon* (2000) and *The Touch* (2002).

Antonio Margheriti (September 19, 1930–November 4, 2002). Born in Rome, Italy, the director of more than 50 films specialized in low-budget science fiction, horror and adventures movies that were released under various titles and often with the name of Anthony M. Dawson as director. Margheriti began his career in the 1960s; films included *Space Men* (1960), *The Battle of the Worlds* (1961), *The Virgin of Nuremberg* (1963), *Killer Fish* (1978), *Cannibal Apocalypse* (1980), and *Hunters of the Golden Cobra* (1982).

Irish McCalla (December 25, 1929–February 1, 2002). Born in Pawnee City, Nebraska, the actress was best-known for her role as the female version of Tarzan in the 1956 TV series, *Sheena, Queen of the Jungle*. McCalla also appeared in several B movies, including *She Demons* (1958), *Beat Generation* (1959), *Five Gates to Hell* (1959), *Five Bold Women* (1962) and *Hands of a Stranger* (1962). She later gave up acting for painting.

Nobu McCarthy (November 13, 1934–April 6, 2002). Born Nobu Atsumi in Ottawa, Canada, the actress grew up in Japan and became a successful model. She married a U.S. Army sergeant and moved to Los Angeles where she was spotted by an agent in Little Tokyo and sent on an audition for the Jerry Lewis comedy *The Geisha Boy* (1958). McCarthy also appeared in the films *The Hunters* (1958), *Wake Me When It's Over* (1960), *Walk Like a Dragon* (1960), and *Love with the Proper Stranger* (1963). She later revived her acting career by joining the East West Players, the first Asian American theater company, in 1971 and became its artistic director from 1989–93. McCarthy later appeared in the TV movie *Farewell to Manzanar* (1976) as well as the films *Karate Kid II* (1986), *Pacific Heights* (1990) and *Last Chance* (1999). She collapsed on the set of the film *Gaijin II*.

Leo McKern (March 16, 1920–July 23, 2002). Born Reginald McKern in Sydney, Australia, the veteran stage and screen actor was best known to American audiences for his television role as the irascible British barrister Horace Rumpole in *Rumpole of the Bailey*, which he played for 44 episodes from 1975 to 1992. McKern was also notable as "No. 2" in the cult television series *The Prisoner* (1967). He made his stage debut in Sydney in 1944 and moved to England in 1946. McKern made his screen debut in *A Murder in the Cathedral* (1952). Screen credits included *A Tale of Two Cities* (1958), *The Mouse That Roared* (1959), *Scent of Mystery* (1960), *Help!* (1965), *A Man for All Seasons* (1966), *Ryan's Daughter* (1970), *The Omen* (1976), *The French Lieutenant's Woman* (1981), *Monsieur Quixote* (1985), *A Foreign Field* (1993), and *Molokai: The Story of Father Damien* (1999). McKern published his memoirs, *Just Resting*, in 1983.

Ivan Moffat (February 18,1918–July 4, 2002). Born in Havana, Cuba, the screenwriter was nominated for an Academy Award, along with Fred Guiol, for the adaptation of Edna Ferber's novel *Giant* in 1956. The drama was directed by George Stevens with whom Moffat had worked as part a documentary film unit during World War II. Moffat also served as associate producer of the Stevens films *Shane* and *A Place in the Sun*. Among Moffat's other screenwriting credits were *Black Sunday, The Wayward Bus, Tender Is the Night, Boy on a Dolphin, They Came to Codura*, and *Bhowani Junction*.

Dudley Moore (April 18, 1935–March 27, 2002). The diminutive comedian, composer, musician, and actor was born in Dagenham, East London, England and began studying piano at age six. He attended Oxford University on an organ scholarship and began composing for cabaret. Along with fellow Oxford graduates Peter Cook, Jonathan Miller and Alan Bennett, Moore would write and perform the comedy revue *Beyond the Fringe*. Opening in London in 1961, the show ran for four years; Moore then partnered with Cook for a TV series, another comedy revue, and five movies, including *The Wrong Box* (1966) and *Bedazzled* (1967). Moore became an unlikely sex symbol when teamed with Bo Derek in the 1979 hit *10*. In 1981, he received an Oscar nomination for best actor in the comedy *Arthur*. Other screen credits included *Foul Play* (1978), *Six Weeks* (1982), *Lovesick* (1983), *Romantic Comedy* (1983), *Best Defense* (1984), *Unfaithfully Yours* (1984), *Arthur 2: On the Rocks* (1988), *Crazy People* (1990), *Blame It On the Bellboy* (1992), and Moore's last film *A Weekend in the Country* (1996). Moore had been diagnosed with progressive supranuclear palsy, a rare brain disorder, in 1997.

Peggy Moran (October 23, 1918–October 25, 2002). Born Marie Jeanette Moran in Clinton, Iowa, the actress was known as the "shrieking violet" and "Queen of Scream" for her roles in such horror films as *The Mummy's Hand* (1940) and *Horror Island* (1941). A contract player with Warner Bros. and Universal, Moran made a number of mostly B movies during the '30s and '40s. Other films included *Rhythm of the Saddle* (1938), *Argentine Nights* (1940), *One Night in the Tropics* (1940), *Double Date* (1941) and *There's One Born Every Minute* (1942). Moran retired from films after her marriage to director Henry Koster in 1942.

George Nader (October 19, 1921–February 4, 2002). Born in Pasadena, California, the actor, known for his beefcake roles, made over 50 films, later turning to work in television and to writing. Nader signed a contract with Universal after studying at the Pasadena Playhouse; his first role was in 1951's *Monsoon*. Another of his early roles was 1953's *Robot Monster*, a boxoffice success that has become a cult classic after being named one of the 50 worst movies ever made. Among his other films were *Sins of Jezebel* (1953), *Four Guns to the Border* (1954), *Six Bridges to Cross* (1955), *Lady Godiva* (1955), *The Unguarded Moment* (1956), *Away All Boats* (1956), *The Second Greatest Sex* (1956), *Four Girls in Town* (1957), *Man Afraid* (1957), and *The Female Animal* (1958). Nader later made low-budget films in Europe and a series of action thrillers filmed in West Germany in the 1960s in which he played an FBI agent. His last film role was in *Beyond Atlantis* (1973); he retired from acting in 1974 after suffering an eye injury. Nader's cult science-fiction novel *Chrome* was published in 1978.

Joel Oliansky (October 11, 1935–July 29, 2002). Born in New York City, the writer and director earned a master's degree at Yale and was playwright in residence there before going to Hollywood in 1964. He directed *The Competition* (1980), *The Silence at Bethany* (1988), *In Defense of a Married Man* (1990), and numerous television shows. Oliansky received an Emmy for his work on the series *The Senator* (1970); Emmy, Writers Guild and Humanitas awards for the miniseries *The Law* (1975); and a Writers Guild award for the miniseries *Masada* (1981). He also wrote the screenplays for *Counterpoint* (1968), *The Todd Killings* (1971), and *Bird* (1988).

Bibi Osterwald (February 3, 1918–January 2, 2002). Born Margaret Virignia Osterwald in New Brunswick, New Jersey, the stage, film, and television actress grew up in Washington, D.C. She received a drama scholarship to Catholic University and was recommended to the Theater Guild in New York where Osterwald made her Broadway debut in 1944's *Sing Out, Sweet Land* and went on to work in such shows as *Gentlemen Prefer Blondes*, *The Golden Apple*, *Hello, Dolly!* and *42nd Street*. The actress began work in television in 1948 with *The Philco Television Playhouse*. Among her film credits were *Parrish* (1961), *The World of Henry Orient* (1964), *A Fine Madness* (1966), *The Tiger Makes Out* (1967), and *As Good As It Gets* (1997).

Bruce Paltrow (November 26, 1943–October 3, 2002). Born in Brooklyn, New York, the producer and director was best known for his groundbreaking television work in the series' *The White Shadow* and *St. Elsewhere*. He met his actress wife, Blythe Danner, while they worked on the 1969 Off-Broadway play *Someone's Comin' Hungry*. Paltrow's first work in television was producing and directing the 1973 ABC movie *Shirts/Skins*. His first theatrical film was 1982's *A Little Sex*. He also produced and directed the film *Duets* (2000), starring daughter Gwyneth Paltrow.

Bill Peet (January 29, 1915–May 11, 2002). Born William Bartlett Peed in Grandview, Indiana, the animator, illustrator and author began working for Walt Disney Studios in 1937. Peet worked on such Disney classics as *Fantasia* (1940), *Dumbo* (1941), *Song of the South* (1946), *Cinderella* (1950), *Alice in Wonderland* (1951), and *Sleeping Beauty* (1959). Peet's first screenplay was Disney's *101 Dalmatians* (1961) and he also wrote 1963's *The Sword in the Stone*. He left the studio in 1964. Peet published some 35 children's books, beginning with 1959's *Goliath II* and *Hubert's Hair-Raising Adventure*. His memoir *Bill Peet: An Autobiography* was published in 1989.

Julia Phillips (April 7, 1944–January 1, 2002). Film producer who made Hollywood history by becoming the first woman to co-produce a film that won a best picture Oscar with 1973's *The Sting*. Born Julia Miller in New York City, Phillips worked in magazine publishing and later at Paramount Pictures, Mirisch Productions and First Artist Productions. Working with her then-husband, banker and producer Michael Phillips, and actor/producer Tony Bill, the three optioned *Steelyard Blues*, which came out in 1972, and *The Sting*. Among her other credits were *Taxi Driver* (1976) and *Close Encounters of the Third Kind* (1977). She scandalized the industry with her best-selling autobiography *You'll Never Eat Lunch in This Town Again* (1990), which also detailed her long-running drug problems.

Sidney Pink (1916–October 12, 2002). Born in Pittsburgh, Pennsylvania, film producer Pink began his career as a film projectionist. He was first hired as a budget manager by Grand National Pictures and Columbia, later working for American International Pictures (AIP). He and partner Arch Oboler made film history with the first 3-D feature-length movie, *Bwana Devil* (1952). In 1959, Pink co-wrote and produced *The Angry Red Planet*, which was filmed in a print-processing technique known as "Cinemagic." Among his other films were *Reptilicus* (1961), *The Castilian* (1963), *The Drums of Tabu* (1965), *Madigan's Millions* (1965), and *A Candidate for a Killing* (1969).

Ernest Pintoff (December 15, 1931–January 12, 2002). Born in Watertown, Connecticut, the animator and director was nominated for an Oscar for the animated short *The Violinist* (1959) and won for 1963's animated satire *The Critic*. Pintoff directed such films as *Harvey Middleman, Fireman* (1965), *Dynamite Chicken* (1971), *Who Killed Mary What's 'Er Name?* (1971), *Jaguar Lives* (1979), *Lunch Wagon* (1980), and *St. Helens* (1981) as well as numerous television shows. Pintoff's memoirs were entitled *Bolt from the Blue.*

Scott Plank (November 11, 1958–October 23, 2002). Born in Washington, D.C., the actor, who worked on Broadway and in televisions and films, died from injuries suffered in a car accident. He had recurring roles on television on *Melrose Place* and *The Division.* Among his screen credits were *A Chorus Line* (1985), *The In Crowd* (1988), *Wired* (1989), *Panama Sugar* (1990), *Pastime* (1991), *Without Evidence* (1995), *American Strays* (1996), *Moonbase* (1997), *The Flying Dutchman* (2000) and *Holes* (2002).

Glenn Quinn (May 28, 1970–December 3, 2002). Born in Dublin, Ireland, the actor died from a suspected drug overdose. Moving with his family to the U.S. in 1988, Quinn had a recurring role as Mark Healy in the television sitcom *Roseanne* from 1990 to 1997 and as the semi-demon Doyle on *Angel* in 1999. Films included *Shout* (1991), *Dr. Giggles* (1992), *Campfire Tales* (1997), *Some Girls* (1999) and *RSVP* (2002).

Beulah Quo (April 17, 1923–October 23, 2002). Born in Stockton, California, the character actress was teaching sociology when she applied for work as a dialect coach on the 1955 film *Love Is a Many-Splendored Thing.* Instead, director Henry King hired Quo (she changed the spelling from Kwoh) for a role. She then went on to work in such films as *Flower Drum Song* (1951), *Chinatown* (1974), *MacArthur* (1977), *Into the Night* (1985), *Bad Girls* (1994), *Brokedown Palace* (1999), *Forbidden City* (2001), and the television films *The Children of An Lac* (1980), *Marco Polo* (1982), and *Forbidden Nights* (1990). She also played the recurring role of Olin on the ABC soap *General Hospital* from 1985–91. In 1965, Quo co-founded the nation's first Asian American repertory company, East West Players, and served as board president for eight years.

Karel Reisz (July 21, 1926–November 25, 2002). Born in Ostrava, Czechoslovakia, the director was sent to England in 1938 because of the Nazi threat; his parents died at Auschwitz. While a student at Oxford, Reisz co-founded the film magazine *Sequence* and also worked as a film critic for *Sight and Sound.* He directed only 11 films but was a leading director of the so-called British New Wave, along with Tony Richardson and Lindsay Anderson. His first film was the 1958 documentary *We Are the Lambeth Boys* and he found his first theatrical success with *Saturday Night and Sunday Morning* (1960) and *Night Must Fall* (1964), both starring Albert Finney. Reisz's other films included *Morgan!* (1966), *Isadora* (1968), *The Gambler* (1974), *Who'll Stop the Rain?* (1978), *The French Lieutenant's Woman* (1981), *Sweet Dreams* (1985), and *Everybody Wins* (1990).

Dean Riesner (November 3, 1918–August 18, 2002). Born in New York City, the screenwriter was the son of silent film director Charles Reisner, who worked with Charlie Chaplin. At age three, "Dinky" Dean Riesner was cast in the Chaplin film *The Pilgrim.* His first screenwriting credits were under the name Dean Franklin on *Code of the Secret Service* (1939) and *The Fighting 69th* (1940). Riesner wrote and directed the film short *Bill and Coo* for which he received a 1948 Academy Award for special achievement. Among Reisner's other credits were *The Helen Morgan Story* (1957), *Paris Holiday* (1958), *Coogan's Bluff* (1968), *Dirty Harry* (1971), *Play Misty for Me* (1971), *High Plains Drifter* (1972), *Charley Varrick* (1973), *The Enforcer* (1976), *The High Country* (1981), and *Fatal Beauty* (1987).

Herb Ritts (August 13, 1952–December 26, 2002). Born in Los Angeles, the photographer was best known for his work with celebrities, including a 1979 impromptu photo session with his friend, a then-unknown Richard Gere. Ritts was a contributor to *Vogue* for more than 15 years and he contributed dozens of cover images for *Vanity Fair* as well as working in fashion photography and as a director of television commercials and music videos. Ritts also published several books of his photographs, including *Men/Women* (1989), *Duo* (1991), *Notorious* (1992), and *Africa* (1994).

Yves Robert (June 21, 1920–May 10, 2002). Born in Saumur, France, the actor, director, writer and producer began his career with a theatrical troupe in Lyon in 1942. He appeared in dozens of movies and directed 23 films. His fifth film, *The War of the Buttons* (1961), was his first big success. Other films included *Very Happy Alexander* (1967), *The Tall Blond Man With One Black Shoe* (1972), *The Bit Player* (1973), *The Return of the Tall Blond Man With One Black Shoe* (1974), *Pardon Mon Affaire* (1976), *My Father's Glory* and *My Mother's Castle* (both 1989) and his last film *Montparnasse-Pondichery* (1993).

Reginald Rose (December 10, 1920–April 19, 2002). Born in New York City, the writer won an Emmy Award in 1954 for the television version of *Twelve Angry Men* and went on to received an Oscar nomination for the 1957 screenplay of the film version, which Rose produced along with its star Henry Fonda. He wrote the CBS pilot for the *The Defenders* and wrote for the series from 1961–65. He also wrote the television dramas *The Sacco-Vanzetti Story* (1960) and *Escape from Sobibor* (1987). Rose's other film credits include *Somebody*

Killed Her Husband (1978), *The Wild Geese* (1978), *The Sea Wolves* (1980), *Whose Life Is It Anyway?* (1981), and *Wild Geese II* (1985).

Frank P. Rosenberg (1914–October 18, 2002). Born in Brooklyn, New York, the producer ran the publicity office of Columbia Pictures in both New York and Hollywood. In 1951, Rosenberg decided to become an independent producer and worked on such films as *The Secret of Convict Lake* (1951), *King of the Khyber Rifles* (1953), *The Girl He Left Behind* (1956), *Madigan* (1968), and *The Reincarnation of Peter Proud* (1975). Rosenberg also produced the only film directed by Marlon Brando, 1961's *One-Eyed Jacks.*

Ted Ross (1934–September 3, 2002). Born in Zanesville, Ohio, the actor won a 1975 Tony award as best supporting actor in a musical for his role as the Cowardly Lion in the musical *The Wiz.* He also reprised the role in the 1978 film version and its sequel. Ross played the recurring role of Dean Harris on *The Cosby Show* and *A Different World.* Among his screen credits were *Arthur* (1981), *Ragtime* (1981), *Amityville II* (1982), *Arthur 2* (1988), *Stealing Home* (1988), and *The Fisher King* (1991).

Harold Russell (January 14, 1914–January 29, 2002). Born in North Sydney, Nova Scotia, and raised in Cambridge, Massachusetts, the disabled veteran lost both hands in an accident while serving in World War II. He made an Army training film for disabled soldiers, *Diary of a Sergeant* (1945), which was later seen by director William Wyler, who cast Russell in his first acting role as disabled sailor Homer Parrish in the 1946 film *The Best Years of Our Lives.* Russell won two Academy Awards for that role as best supporting actor and a second special achievement award. In 1992, Russell sold his best supporting actor Oscar in a New York auction despite protests from the Academy. After college, Russell started a public relations firm and worked as a consultant for various veterans' organizations. He had few other acting jobs, later appearing in the films *Inside Moves* (1980) and *Dogtown* (1997) and in various television series. Russell wrote two autobiographies: *Victory in My Hands* (1949) and *The Best Years of My Life* (1981).

George Sidney (October 14, 1916–May 5, 2002). Born in Long Island City, New York, the director came from a showbiz family. As a teenager Sidney got a job as a messenger at MGM and later became a film editor, assistant director, and a director of one-reel shorts beginning in 1936. His first features were B movies, including *Free and Easy* (1941), *Pacific Rendezvous* (1942), and *Pilot No. 5* (1943). Sidney directed a series of MGM musicals, including *Thousands Cheer* (1943), *Bathing Beauty* (1944), *Anchors Aweigh* (1945), *Holiday in Mexico* (1945), *Ziegfeld Follies* (1946), *The Harvey Girls* (1946), *Annie Get Your Gun* (1950), *Show Boat* (1951),

Kiss Me Kate (1953), and *Jupiter's Darling* (1955). He later became an independent producer on such films as *The Eddy Duchin Story* (1956), *Jeanne Eagels* (1957), *Pal Joey* (1957), *Who Was That Lady?* (1959), *Pepe* (1960), *Bye Bye Birdie* (1963), *Viva Las Vegas* (1964), *The Swinger* (1966), and *Half a Sixpence* (1967).

Darwood Smith (September 8, 1929–May 15, 2002). Born in Fort Collins, Colorado, he was a child actor under the name Darwood Kaye and starred as Waldo in 22 of the *Our Gang* film comedies from 1937 to 1940. He also appear in 1943's *Best Foot Forward* but quit acting as a teenager. Smith later became a Seventh-Day Adventist pastor.

Kevin Smith (March 16, 1963–February 15, 2002). Born in Auckland, New Zealand, the rugged actor was best known for his recurring role of Ares on the television series' *Xena: Warrior Princess* and *Hercules: The Legendary Journeys.* Among his film roles were *Mon Desir* (1991), *Desperate Remedies* (1993), *Channeling Baby* (1999), and *Jubilee* (2000). He died from injuries suffered in a fall while filming the martial arts film *Warriors of Virtue II* in Beijing.

Rod Steiger (April 14, 1925–July 9, 2002). Born Rodney Stephen Steiger in Westhampton, New York, the intense Method actor began acting in grade school. He lied about his age, enlisting in the Navy at 16 and serving in the South Pacific during World War II. Steiger used the GI Bill to study acting at the New School for Social Research and with Lee Strasberg at the Actors Studio. He appeared in over 250 live television productions between 1948 and 1953 and made his film debut in 1951's *Teresa.* Steiger received an Oscar nomination for *On the Waterfront* in 1954 and for *The Pawnbroker* in 1965; he won a best actor Oscar in 1967 for *In the Heat of the Night.* Screen credits included *Oklahoma!* (1955), *Cry Terror* (1958), *Al Capone* (1959), *Dr. Zhivago* (1965), *The Loved One* (1965), *The Illustrated Man* (1968), *No Way to Treat a Lady* (1968), *Waterloo* (1970), *W.C. Fields and Me* (1976), *F.I.S.T.* (1978), *Lion of the Desert* (1981), *The Specialist* (1994) *Mars Attacks!* (1996), and *The Hurricane* (1999).

Guy Stockwell (November 16, 1934–February 6, 2002). Born in New York City, the son of actor/singer Harry Stockwell and the older brother of actor Dean, Guy made his stage debut at five and his film debut at eight in *The Green Years* (1946). Stockwell was a regular on the television shows *Adventures in Paradise* and *The Richard Boone Show* and played numerous guest roles in his long career. He also began a career as an acting coach and stage producer in the early 1960s and helped create the Los Angeles Art Theater. Screen credits included *This Rebel Age* (1959), *Please Don't Eat the Daisies* (1960), *The Warlord* (1965), *And Now Miguel* (1966), *Beau Geste* (1966), *Banning* (1967), *Airport 1975* (1974), and *Santa Sangre* (1989).

Joe Strummer (August 21, 1952–December 22, 2002). Born John Graham Mellor in Ankara, Turkey, the musician and actor, who died of a heart attack, formed the punk band The Clash in 1976. The band made six albums before breaking up in 1986; Strummer then went on to release solo albums and later to form the band Mescaleros. He contributed songs to the soundtrack of *Sid & Nancy* and scored the films *Walker, Permanent Record,* and *Grosse Pointe Blank.* Strummer also acted in the films *Straight to Hell* (1986), *Mystery Train* (1988), *Walker* (1989), *I Hired a Contract Killer* (1990), and *Super 8 Stories* (2001).

Mary Stuart (July 4, 1926–March 3, 2002). Born Mary Houchins in Miami, Florida, and raised in Tulsa, Oklahoma, the veteran actress starred for 35 years as heroine Joanne Gardner Barron on the soap opera *Search for Tomorrow* (1951–1986). As a teenager, Stuart was spotted working at New York's Roosevelt Hotel by producer Joe Pasternak, who offered her a screen test. She then went on to play small roles in a number of Hollywood films, including *This Time for Keeps* (1947), *The Adventures of Don Juan* (1948), *Thunderhoof* (1948), and *The Girl from Jones Beach* (1949) before returning to New York. Stuart's last role was as Aunt Meta Bauer on the CBS soap opera *Guiding Light,* which she played from 1996 until her death. Stuart also wrote an autobiography entitled *Both of Me.*

Richard Sylbert (April 16, 1928–March 23, 2002). The production designer was born in Brooklyn, New York, and later attended the Tyler School of Art in Philadelphia, along with his twin brother, Paul, who also became a production designer. Sylbert's first work was painting scenery at NBC; he became an art director on the TV series *The Inner Sanctum* in 1954 and served as art director on his first feature film, *Patterns* in 1956. That same year, Sylbert and his brother worked together on the feature *Baby Doll.* Sylbert earned six Academy Award nominations and won two art direction Oscars for *Who's Afraid of Virginia Woolf* (1966) and *Dick Tracy* (1990). Among his other films were *Splendor in the Grass* (1961), *Long Day's Journey Into Night* (1962), *The Manchurian Candidate* (1962), *The Graduate* (1967), *Rosemary's Baby* (1968), *Carnal Knowledge* (1971), *Chinatown* (1974), *Shampoo* (1975), *Reds* (1981), *The Cotton Club* (1984), and *My Best Friend's Wedding* (1997).

John Thaw (January 3, 1942–February 21, 2002). The actor was born in Manchester, England, and attended the Royal Academy of Dramatic Arts. His first success came as a cop on the popular British television series *The Sweeney* (1975–78). Thaw was best known for his role as "Inspector Morse" in a mystery series that lasted for 33 episodes over a 15 year period beginning (in England) in 1985. The penultimate episode of the series ended with Morse's death. He also played the title role in the series *Kavanagh QC.* Films

included *The Loneliness of the Long Distance Runner* (1962), *Five to One* (1964), *The Bofors Gun* (1968), *Dr. Phibes Rises Again* (1972), *Cry Freedom* (1987), *Chaplin* (1992), and *Monsignor Renard* (1999).

J. Lee Thompson (August 1, 1914–August 30, 2002). Born John Lee-Thompson in Bristol, England, the director made more than 50 films, including nine with Charles Bronson. He worked as an actor and writer before directing his first film, *Murder Without Crime,* in 1950. Other films included *The Yellow Balloon* (1952), *Ice-Cold in Alex* (1958), *North West Frontier* (1959), *Tiger Bay* (1959), *The Guns of Navarone* (1961), *Cape Fear* (1962), *Taras Bulba* (1962), *The Chairman* (1969), *McKenna's Gold* (1969), *Conquest of the Planet of the Apes,* (1972), *Battle for the Planet of the Apes* (1973), *Huckleberry Finn* (1974), *The White Buffalo* (1977), *St. Ives* (1976), *The Greek Tycoon* (1978), *10 to Midnight* (1983), *Death Wish 4* (1987), *Messenger of Death* (1988), and his last film, *Kinjite: Forbidden Subjects* (1989).

Lawrence Tierney (March 15, 1919–February 26, 2002). The tough guy actor was born in Brooklyn, New York, and worked a series of odd jobs before being spotted by a talent scout and landing a contract with RKO Studios in 1943. Tierney achieved stardom in the title role of gangster *Dillinger* in the 1945 B movie. Other films included *Kill or Be Killed* (1946), *The Devil Thumbs a Ride* (1947), *Born to Kill* (1947), *San Quentin* (1950), *The Greatest Show on Earth* (1952), *Such Good Friends* (1971), *Gloria* (1980), *Arthur* (1981), *Prizzi's Honor* (1985), *Tough Guys Don't Dance* (1987), and as the leader of a gang of vicious criminals in Quentin Tarantino's *Reservoir Dogs* (1992). Tierney's career was marred by drunken brawls and run-ins with the law and acting work became sporadic before he rekindled it with television roles beginning in the early 1980s.

Kenneth Tobey (March 23, 1919–December 22, 2002). Born in Oakland, California, the character actor appeared in nearly 100 films, beginning with 1947's *Dangerous Venture.* He achieved cult stardom for his lead role in the science-fiction classic *The Thing from Another World* (1951) and for his co-starring role on the TV adventure series *The Whirlybird* (1957–59). Other films included *I Was a Male War Bride* (1949), *The Beast from 20,000 Fathoms* (1953), *It Came from Beneath the Sea* (1955), *Gunfight at the OK Corral* (1957), *The Candidate* (1972), *Airplane!* (1980), *The Howling* (1981), *Gremlins* (1984), *Innerspace* (1987), and *Gremlins 2* (1990).

Michael Todd Jr. (October 8, 1929–May 5, 2002). The son of Oscar-winning producer Mike Todd, Michael Jr. was born in Los Angeles and, after his father's death in 1958, took over as head of his movie production company. Todd Jr. produced the only film to be released in Smell-O-Vision with 1960's *Scent of Mystery.* He also wrote a biography of his father, *A Valuable Property: The Life Story of Michael Todd,* which was published in 1983.

Robert Urich (December 16, 1946–April 16, 2002). Born in Toronto, Ohio, the actor with the Everyman quality had roles in 15 TV series and more than 40 TV movies and miniseries, including playing detective leads in *Vega$* (1978–81) and *Spenser: For Hire* (1985–88). Urich won a football scholarship to Florida State University and received a master's degree in broadcast research and management from Michigan State University. Fellow FSU alumnus Burt Reynolds helped Urich get his acting break when he co-starred with Reynolds in a stage production of *The Rainmaker* (1972). Urich's first film was *Magnum Force* (1973) and other film credits included *Endangered Species* (1982), *Ice Pirates* (1984) and *Turk 182!* (1985). Among his TV movie work was the miniseries *Lonesome Dove* as well as *Blind Faith, The Defiant Ones, Captains Courageous,* and *Night of the Wolf.* Urich was diagnosed with the rare cancer synovial cell sarcoma in 1996 but continued to work; his last series was 2001's *Emeril.*

Raf Vallone (February 17, 1916–October 31, 2002). Born Raffaele Vallone in Tropea, Italy, the actor grew up in Turin and studied law. He was unexpectedly cast by director Giuseppe De Santis for 1948's *Bitter Rice* after being hired to do research for the film. Films included *The Road to Hope* (1949), *Therese Raquin* (1953), *No Escape* (1959), *Two Women* (1960), *El Cid* (1961), *A View from the Bridge* (1962), *The Cardinal* (1963), *The Secret Invasion* (1964), *Harlow* (1965), *Nevada Smith* (1966) and *Godfather Part III* (1990).

Henri Verneuil (October 15, 1920–January 11, 2002). Born Achod Malakian in Rodosto, Turkey, the director made France his adopted home and worked with some of the country's biggest stars. He began directing shorts in 1946 and turned to features in the early 1950s. Films included *The Hunting Ground* (1952), *Carnaval* (1953), *The Sheep Has Five Legs* (1954), *The Cow and I* (1959), *A Monkey in Winter* (1962), *Any Number Can Win* (1963), *The 25th Hour* (1967), *Guns for San Sebastian* (1968), *Night Flight from Moscow* (1973), *Mayrig* (1991), and his last film *588 Rue Paradis* (1992).

Josef von Stroheim (September 18, 1922–March 22, 2002). The son of legendary silent film director Erich von Stroheim was born in Los Angeles and became an award-winning sound editor. He started his career as a publicity photographer for MGM and served as a combat photographer for the Army during World War II. Von Stroheim won two Emmys for his work on *QB VII* and *The Immortals.* Film credits included *Carnal Knowledge, Day of the Dolphin, The Getaway, Three Days of the Condor, Jeremiah Johnson,* and *Alice Doesn't Live Here Anymore.*

Lew R. Wasserman (March 15, 1913–June 3, 2002). Born in Cleveland, Ohio, Wasserman became the protégé of Dr. Jules C. Stein, the founder of talent agency Music Corp. of America, in 1936 when he was hired as the director of advertising and public relations. Wasserman became MCA's president in 1946 and sold the company in 1990 to the Japanese firm Matsushita. He remained with a management contract until 1995 when Matsushita sold to Seagram Co., which renamed MCA Universal Studios. Wasserman had previously expanded MCA's clout by buying Paramount Pictures' pre-1948 film library in 1957 to license for television broadcasts. In 1959, he bought Universal Pictures back lot for film and television production, then acquired Universal Studios and Revue and Decca Records in 1962. He was forced to dissolve his talent agency in 1962 when the U.S. Justice Department filed an antitrust suit, charging that MCA couldn't represent talent while owning a studio and producing for television. Wasserman continued as a consultant to Universal until his death.

Billy Wilder (June 22, 1906–March 27, 2002). Born Samuel Wilder in Sucha, Austro-Hungary (now a part of Poland), the famed writer and director was given his nickname by his mother in honor of the Buffalo Bill Wild West show. At 18, he found a job as a tabloid reporter in Vienna and then moved to Berlin, where he worked as a ghostwriter for silent movies. His first credited script was 1929's *Der Teufelsreporter* (*The Demon Reporter*), which was followed by 1930's *Menschen am Sonntag* (*People on Sunday*). That film's success lead to Wilder being hired by UFA studio. When Hitler came to power in 1933, Wilder fled to Paris (where he co-directed *Mauvaise Graine*) and then to Hollywood in 1934 to work for Columbia studios, although he didn't speak English. Wilder received 12 Oscar nominations as a screenwriter, eight for directing, and one for producing. He first collaborated with Charles Brackett on the 1938 film *Bluebeard's Eighth Wife* and they wrote 13 screenplays together, including the Oscar-nominated films *Ninotchka* and *Hold Back the Dawn* before parting in 1950. Wilder received Oscars for directing and co-writing *The Lost Weekend* (1945) and for co-writing *Sunset Boulevard* (1950). He then worked with I.A.L. Diamond until his last film, *Buddy, Buddy,* in 1981. Wilder won Oscars as co-writer, director, and producer of 1960's *The Apartment.* His first Hollywood film as writer/director was *The Major and the Minor* (1942). Other films included *Five Graves to Cairo* (1943), *Double Indemnity* (1944), *A Foreign Affair* (1948), *Ace in the Hole* (1951), *Stalag 17* (1953), *Sabrina* (1954), *The Seven-Year Itch* (1955), *Love in the Afternoon* (1957), *Witness for the Prosecution* (1958), *Some Like It Hot* (1959), *One, Two, Three* (1961), *Irma La Douce* (1963), *The Fortune Cookie* (1966), *The Private Life of Sherlock Holmes* (1970), and *The Front Page* (1974).

Doris Wishman (April 23, 1920–August 10, 2002). The independent filmmaker wrote, produced, cast, directed, and edited some 30 films (including those made under pseudonyms) for the exploitation market. Born in New York City (possibly as early as 1912), Wishman studied acting but found a job in film distribution. After the courts relaxed censorship rules, Wishman decided to produce and distribute independent pictures. She started with eight films about nudist camps, including *Diary of a Nudist, Behind the Nudist Curtain, Blaze Starr Goes Nudist,* and *Nudie on the Moon.* Other films included *A Taste of Flesh, Bad Girls Go to Hell, Indecent Desires, Love Toy, Deadly Weapons, Double Agent 73, A Night to Dismember, Satan Was a Lady, Dildo Heaven,* and her last film, 2002's *Each Time I Kill.*

William Witney (May 15, 1915–March 17, 2002). Born in Lawton, Oklahoma, the director worked on numerous movie serials, including the Lone Ranger, Dick Tracy and Captain Marvel shows, and directed some 60 features. He became a studio messenger in 1931 and directed his first film at the age of 21 on the Republic Pictures serial, *The Painted Stallion.* He directed or co-directed 23 Republic serials between 1937 and 1946, 27 Roy Rogers westerns between 1946 and 1951, and nine Rex Allen westerns before Republic ceased production in 1956. Witney then went to work for American International Pictures, directing *The Bonnie Parker Story* (1958) among other films. His last film was *Darktown Strutters* (1975). Witney published his biography *Into a Door, Into a Fight, Out a Door, Into a Chase* in 1996.

Irene Worth (June 23, 1916–May 10, 2002). Born Harriet Abrams in Fairbury, Nebraska, she moved to California at a young age and graduated from the University of California at Los Angeles. Moving to New York, Worth (a producer suggested the name change) made her stage debut in 1942; she eventually won three Tony awards for *Tiny Alice* (1965), *Sweet Bird of Youth* (1976), and *Lost in Yonkers* (1991). In 1953, she was a founding member of the Shakespeare Festival Theater in Stratford, Ontario. Although best known for her stage work, Worth also appeared in films, including *Orders to Kill* (1958), *The Scapegoat* (1959), *King Lear* (1971), *Nicholas and Alexandra* (1971), *Eyewitness* (1979), *Deathtrap* (1982), *Lost in Yonkers* (1993), and *Onegin* (1999).

Selected Film Books of 2002

Aichele, George and Richard Walsh, editors. *Screening Scripture.*
Trinity Press International, 2002.

Essay collection on cinema and the Bible.

Allon, Yoram, Del Cullen and Hannah Patterson, editors. *The Wallflower Guide to Contemporary North American Directors.*
Columbia University Press, 2002.

Comprehensive listing of the most important and influential filmmakers with an extensive critique of their working methods and films.

Antonio, Sheril D. *Contemporary Black Cinema.*
Peter Lang Publishing, 2002.

Antonio's book is restricted to just six films—*Boyz N the Hood, New Jack City, Just Another Girl on the I.R.T., Menace II Society,* and *Clockers*—where the directors used media as a key element in the film's narrative.

Barrios, Richard. *Screened Out: Playing Gay in Hollywood from Edison to Stonewall.*
Routledge, 2002.

A look at sexuality in the movies and how depictions of homosexuality have—and have not—changed over the years.

Bart, Peter and Peter Guber. *Shoot Out: Surviving Fame and (Mis)Fortune in Hollywood.*
Putnam, 2002.

Two industry veterans offer their personal views of the economic, political and personal clashes involved in the mechanics of movie making.

Beck, Robert. *The Edward G. Robinson Encyclopedia.*
McFarland & Company, Inc., 2002.

Documents Robinson's every known public performance or appearance that the actor was involved in during his 60 year career.

Berry, Mark F. *The Dinosaur Filmography.*
McFarland & Company, Inc., 2002.

Covers works featuring prehistoric, reptilian, and non-humanoid creatures intending to represent a real or fictional dinosaur.

Borde, Raymond and Etienne Chaumeton. *A Panorama of American Film Noir (1941–1953).*
City Lights, 2002.

Study of film noir originally published in France and translated by Paul Hammond.

Boyreau, Jacques. *Trash: The Graphic Genius of Xploitation Movie Posters.*
Chronicle Books, 2002.

Celebrates the world of exploitation film posters from the 1950s through the 1980s.

Brode, Douglas. *Sinema: Erotic Adventures in Film.*
Citadel Press, 2002.

A look at movies' erotic elements from the silent era to the present.

Bubbeo, Daniel. *The Women of Warner Brothers: The Lives and Careers of 15 Leading Ladies, with Filmographies for Each.*
McFarland & Company, Inc., 2002.

Covers their personal and professional careers and includes interviews.

Budd, David H. *Culture Meets Culture in the Movies: An Analysis East, West, North and South, with Filmographies.*
McFarland & Company, Inc., 2002

Examines cultural differences in generally available American and European films.

Buhle, Paul and Dave Wagner. *Radical Hollywood: The Untold Story Behind America's Favorite Movies.*
New Press, 2002.

An account of the leftist influence in Hollywood from the 1920s to the 1950s, including capsule biographies of writers, producers, directors, and actors as well as an analysis of progressive politics in specific films.

Magill's Cinema Annual 2003
Indexes

Director Index

JEAN-PIERRE DENIS
Murderous Maids *315*

BRIAN DEPALMA (1941-)
Femme Fatale *155*

ARNAUD DESPLECHIN
Esther Kahn *146*

DANNY DEVITO (1944-)
Death to Smoochy *113*

TOM DEY
Showtime *421*

AGUSTIN DIAZ YANES
No News from God *335*

BOB DOLMAN
The Banger Sisters *34*

KEVIN DONOVAN
The Tuxedo *501*

CHRISTIAN DUGUAY
Extreme Ops *149*

CLINT EASTWOOD (1930-)
Blood Work *49*

ATOM EGOYAN (1960-)
Ararat *23*

ELLORY ELKAYEM
Eight Legged Freaks *129*

RAKHSHAN BANI
ETEMAD
Under the Skin of the
City *511*

CHRIS EYRE
Skins *427*

RICK FAMUYIWA
Brown Sugar *64*

LARRY FESSENDEN
Wendigo *526*

DAVID FINCHER (1963-)
Panic Room *344*

GARY FLEDER
Imposter *227*

JONATHON FRAKES
(1952-)
Clockstoppers *91*

CARL FRANKLIN (1949-)
High Crimes *206*

BART FREUNDLICH
World Traveler *536*

STEPHEN GAGHAN
Abandon *1*

CHRISTOPHE GANS
(1960-)
Brotherhood of the
Wolf *61*

JEAN-LUC GODARD
(1930-)
In Praise of Love *229*

SANDRA GOLDBACHER
Me Without You *291*

MICHEL GONDRY
Human Nature *214*

RAJA GOSNELL
Scooby-Doo *407*

ASHUTOSH GOWARIKER
Lagaan: Once upon a Time
in India *252*

PAUL GREENGRASS
Bloody Sunday *51*

PAUL GROSS (1959-)
Men with Brooms *295*

JOHN LEE HANCOCK
The Rookie *396*

MICHAEL HANEKE
Code Unknown *92*
The Piano Teacher *353*

CURTIS HANSON (1945-)
8 Mile *130*

ROBERT HARMON
Wes Craven Presents:
They *527*

HAL HARTLEY (1959-)
No Such Thing *336*

RYOSUKE HASHIGUCHI
Hush! *216*

PETER HASTINGS
The Country Bears *100*

ETHAN HAWKE (1971-)
Chelsea Walls *79*

TODD HAYNES (1961-)
Far from Heaven *151*

STEPHEN HEREK (1958-)
Life or Something Like
It *263*

CHARLES HERMAN-
WURMFELD
Kissing Jessica Stein *247*

WERNER HERZOG (1942-)
Invincible *233*

GEORGE
HICKENLOOPER
(1964-)
The Man from Elysian
Fields *281*

WALTER HILL (1942-)
Undisputed *514*

GREGORY HOBLIT
Hart's War *199*

MICHAEL HOFFMAN
The Emperor's Club *137*

NICOLE HOLOFCENER
Lovely and Amazing *274*

HOU HSIAO-HSIEN (1947-)
Millennium Mambo *298*

REGINALD (REGGIE)
HUDLIN (1961-)
Serving Sara *418*

KWON TAEK IM
Chihwaseon: Painted
Fire *86*

DAN IRELAND
Passionada *346*

JAMES ISAAC
Jason X *235*

PETER JACKSON (1961-)
The Lord of the Rings 2:
The Two Towers *270*

HENRY JAGLOM (1943-)
Festival at Cannes *158*

CHRISTINE JEFFS
Rain *373*

PETE JONES
Stolen Summer *460*

SPIKE JONZE (1969-)
Adaptation *10*

PAUL JUSTMAN
Standing in the Shadows of
Motown *450*

SCOTT KALVERT
Deuces Wild *115*

KAOS
Ballistic: Ecks vs. Sever *32*

SHEKHAR KAPUR (1945-)
The Four Feathers *163*

JAKE KASDAN
Orange County *340*

AKI KAURISMAKI (1957-)
The Man Without a
Past *283*

SETH KEARSLEY
Adam Sandler's 8 Crazy
Nights *8*

RICHARD KELLY
Donnie Darko *122*

CALLIE KHOURI
Divine Secrets of the Ya-Ya
Sisterhood *120*

DYLAN KIDD
Roger Dodger *391*

BRIAN KOPPELMAN
Knockaround Guys *248*

DOVER KOSASHVILI
Late Marriage *260*

PETER KOSMINSKY
White Oleander *529*

ROGER KUMBLE
The Sweetest Thing *472*

STANLEY KWAN
Lan Yu *254*

NEIL LABUTE (1963-)
Possession *358*

CLARA LAW
The Goddess of 1967 *183*

MARC LAWRENCE
Two Weeks Notice *507*

MALCOLM LEE
Undercover Brother *512*

SPIKE LEE (1957-)
25th Hour *503*

MICHAEL LEHMANN
(1957-)
40 Days and 40
Nights *161*

MIKE LEIGH (1943-)
All or Nothing *16*

MICHAEL LEMBECK
(1948-)
The Santa Clause 2 *405*

BRIAN LEVANT (1952-)
Snow Dogs *430*

DAVID LEVIEN
Knockaround Guys *248*

SHAWN LEVY
Big Fat Liar *41*

DOUG LIMAN
The Bourne Identity *59*

GEORGE LUCAS (1944-)
Star Wars: Episode II—
Attack of the
Clones *455*

ADRIAN LYNE (1941-)
Unfaithful *516*

CATHY MALKASIAN
The Wild Thornberrys
Movie *532*

WILLIAM MALONE
Feardotcom *153*

LUIS MANDOKI
Trapped *490*

ROB MARSHALL
Chicago *84*

CATHERINE MARTIN
Marriages *286*

PETER MATTEI
Love in the Time of
Money *273*

FINN TAYLOR
Cherish *81*

JULIE TAYMOR
Frida *168*

ANDY TENNANT
Sweet Home Alabama *470*

BETTY THOMAS (1949-)
I Spy *218*

MOUFIDA TLATLI
The Season of Men *413*

JAMES TOBACK (1944-)
Harvard Man *201*

BLAIR TREU
Little Secrets *269*

ROSE TROCHE
The Safety of Objects *402*

TUCK TUCKER
Hey Arnold! The
Movie *204*

ANDRE TURPIN
Soft Shell Man *432*

TOM TYKWER (1965-)
Heaven *203*

**RON UNDERWOOD
(1953-)**
The Adventures of Pluto
Nash *13*

JESSE VAUGHAN
Juwanna Mann *241*

GERARDO VERA
Second Skin *414*

GORE VERBINSKI
The Ring *386*

RANDALL WALLACE
We Were Soldiers *521*

JOHN C. WALSH
Pipe Dream *357*

WAYNE WANG (1949-)
Maid in Manhattan *279*

XIAOSHUAI WANG
Beijing Bicycle *40*

**DENZEL WASHINGTON
(1954-)**
Antwone Fisher *22*

CHRIS WEDGE
Ice Age *219*

CHRIS WEITZ (1970-)
About a Boy *3*

PAUL WEITZ (1966-)
About a Boy *3*

SIMON WELLS
The Time Machine *486*

KURT WIMMER
Equilibrium *145*

GARY WINICK
Tadpole *477*

**MICHAEL
WINTERBOTTOM
(1961-)**
24 Hour Party People *506*

DOUG WOLEN
Butterfly *67*

**M. WALLACE
WOLODARSKY**
Sorority Boys *442*

JOHN WOO (1948-)
Windtalkers *534*

DAVID WU
Formula 51 *159*

ZHANG YIMOU (1951-)
Happy Times *193*

RONNY YU
Formula 51 *159*

YANG ZHANG
Quitting *369*

JOEL ZWICK
My Big Fat Greek
Wedding *316*

Screenwriter Index

SCOTT ABBOTT
Queen of the
Damned *365*

PETER ACKERMAN
Ice Age *219*

JESSE ALEXANDER
Eight Legged Freaks *129*

SHERMAN ALEXIE
The Business of
Fancydancing *66*

WOODY ALLEN (1935-)
Hollywood Ending *208*

BRADLEY ALLENSTEIN
Juwanna Mann *241*

**PEDRO ALMODOVAR
(1951-)**
Talk to Her *479*

HOSSEIN AMINI
The Four Feathers *163*

PAUL ANDERSON
Resident Evil *383*

**PAUL THOMAS
ANDERSON (1970-)**
Punch-Drunk Love *362*

MARK ANDRUS
Divine Secrets of the Ya-Ya
Sisterhood *120*

VICENTE ARANDA (1926-)
Mad Love *278*

ALICE ARLEN
The Weight of Water *523*

BROOKS ARTHUR
Adam Sandler's 8 Crazy
Nights *8*

YVAN ATTAL (1965-)
My Wife Is an
Actress *320*

PAUL ATTANASIO
The Sum of All Fears *465*

JACQUES AUDIARD
Read My Lips *374*

BILLE AUGUST (1948-)
A Song for Martin *439*

**ROGER ROBERTS AVARY
(1967-)**
The Rules of
Attraction *398*

PASCALE BAILLY
God Is Great, I'm
Not *182*

JESSICA BARONDES
Little Secrets *269*

CRAIG BARTLETT
Hey Arnold! The
Movie *204*

JOE BATTEER
Windtalkers *534*

JESSICA BENDINGER
The Truth About
Charlie *497*

**ROBERTO BENIGNI
(1952-)**
Pinocchio *355*

DAVID BENIOFF
25th Hour *503*

RONAN BENNETT
Lucky Break *276*

**TONINO
BERANACQUISTA**
Read My Lips *374*

MICHAEL BERG
Ice Age *219*

**BERNARDO BERTOLUCCI
(1940-)**
The Triumph of Love *495*

CARY BICKLEY
High Crimes *206*

THOMAS BIDEGAIN
The Chateau *77*

FABIAN BIELINSKY
Nine Queens *334*

ANNE-SOPHIE BIROT
Girls Can't Swim *181*

CHARLES F. BOHL
Swimfan *475*

JACQUES BOON
Pauline and Paulette *347*

EMMANUEL BOURDIEU
Esther Kahn *146*

KATE BOUTILIER
The Wild Thornberrys
Movie *532*

PHILIPPA BOYENS
The Lord of the Rings 2:
The Two Towers *270*

TOM BRADY
The Hot Chick *210*

LARRY BRAND
Halloween:
Resurrection *191*

PATRICK BREEN
Just a Kiss *239*

JEREMY BROCK
Charlotte Gray *75*

ADAM LARSON BRODER
Pumpkin *361*

MARK BROWN
Barbershop *36*

MICHAEL BROWNING
Bad Company *30*

**WILLIAM BROYLES, JR.
(1944-)**
Unfaithful *516*

NICOLE BURDETTE
Chelsea Walls *79*

SCOTT BUSBY
Texas Rangers *480*

JEZ BUTTERWORTH
Birthday Girl *45*

TOM BUTTERWORTH
Birthday Girl *45*

STEPHANE CABEL
Brotherhood of the
Wolf *61*

**MICHAEL CACOYANNIS
(1927-)**
The Cherry Orchard *83*

BRANDON CAMP
Dragonfly *125*

JUAN J. CAMPANELLA
Son of the Bride *437*

ROBIN CAMPILLO
Time Out *489*

LAURENT CANTET (1961-)
Time Out *489*

JOHN CARLEN
Sonny *440*

JOE CARNAHAN
Narc *323*

DANA CARVEY (1955-)
Master of Disguise *287*

CAROLINE CASE
Imposter *227*

FERNANDO CASTETS
Son of the Bride *437*

VINCENZO CERAMI
Pinocchio *355*

GREGG CHABOT
Reign of Fire *381*

CLAUDE CHABROL (1930-)
Merci pour le
Chocolat *296*

ILYA CHAIKEN
Margarita Happy
Hour *285*

PEGGY CHIAO
Beijing Bicycle *40*

TINA GORDON CHISM
Drumline *127*

ELIE CHOURAQUI (1953-)
Harrison's Flowers *194*

TIEN-WEN CHU
Millennium Mambo *298*

RON CLEMENTS (1953-)
Treasure Planet *493*

JAY COCKS
Gangs of New York *174*

JON COHEN
Minority Report *299*

BILL CONDON
Chicago *84*

GREG COOLIDGE
Sorority Boys *442*

MARTIN COPELAND
Texas Rangers *480*

PAUL TREJO
Skins *427*

MICHAEL TRONICK
The Scorpion King *409*

BARBARA TULLIVER
Signs *423*

JEAN-PIERRE VIGUIE
God Is Great, I'm
Not *182*

DENNIS VIRKLER
Collateral Damage *93*

TRACEY WADMORE-
SMITH
Sweet Home Alabama *470*

CHRISTIAN WAGNER
Die Another Day *116*

WAYNE WAHRMAN
The Time Machine *486*

LESLEY WALKER
All or Nothing *16*
Nicholas Nickleby *332*

ANGUS WALL
Panic Room *344*

MARTIN WALSH
Chicago *84*

MARK WARNER
Abandon *1*

EDWARD A.
WARSCHILKA
13 Ghosts *484*

BILLY WEBER
Showtime *421*

ROSS WEBER
Last Wedding *258*

STEVEN WEISBERG
Big Trouble *43*
Men in Black II *293*

JULIETTE WELFING
Read My Lips *374*

NICK WENTWORTH
Second Skin *414*

DIRK WESTERVELT
Brown Sugar *64*

MONIKA WILLI
The Piano Teacher *353*

KATE WILLIAMS
The Goddess of 1967 *183*
Last Orders *256*

MICHAEL
WINTERBOTTOM
(1961-)
24 Hour Party People *506*

PAM WISE
Secretary *416*

JACQUES WITTA
Harrison's Flowers *194*

DOUG WOLEN
Butterfly *67*

CHRIS WOMACK
The Count of Monte
Cristo *97*

CRAIG WOOD
The Ring *386*

JOHN WRIGHT
Rollerball *393*

DAVID WU
Brotherhood of the
Wolf *61*

CHRIS WYATT
Max *289*

HONG YU YANG
Quitting *369*

WILLIAM YEH
Equilibrium *145*

DAVID ZIEFF
The Next Big Thing *330*

DON ZIMMERMAN
Dragonfly *125*

SERGIO ZOTTOLA
Nine Queens *334*

LUCIA ZUCCHETTI
Morvern Callar *308*

ERIC ZUMBRUNNEN
Adaptation *10*

Art Director Index

JASON GRAHAM
Bollywood/Hollywood *56*

STEVEN GRAHAM
Bad Company *30*
Changing Lanes *73*

ANDREW GRANT
Nicholas Nickleby *332*

T. ARRINDER GREWAL
K-19: The
Widowmaker *243*

TONY GRIMES
World Traveler *536*

ISABELLE GUAY
Confessions of a Dangerous
Mind *95*

ETTORE GUERRIERI
The Triumph of Love *495*

ALEXANDER HAMMOND
Men in Black II *293*

ROSWELL HAMRICK
Igby Goes Down *221*

GUY M. HARRINGTON
Cherish *81*

J. MARK HARRINGTON
Big Trouble *43*

SEAN HAWORTH
Men in Black II *293*

JON HENSON
Esther Kahn *146*

WILLIE HESLUP
Trapped *490*

MICHAEL HIGGINS
Borstal Boy *58*

BRUCE ROBERT HILL
The Time Machine *486*

RICHARD HOBBS
Ghost Ship *179*

GEOFF HUBBARD
Showtime *421*

DENISE HUDSON
Blue Crush *54*
Welcome to
Collinwood *524*

YVONNE HURST
40 Days and 40
Nights *161*

KEVIN ISHIOKA
Windtalkers *534*

PHIL IVEY
The Lord of the Rings 2:
The Two Towers *270*

HELEN JARVIS
Life or Something Like
It *263*

Rollerball *393*

JOHN R. JENSEN
Divine Secrets of the Ya-Ya
Sisterhood *120*

CAO JIUPING
Happy Times *193*

BO JOHNSON
I Spy *218*

RICHARD JOHNSON
Road to Perdition *388*

BRUTON JONES
Sorority Boys *442*

JOHN J. KASARDA
Unfaithful *516*

KEVIN KAVANAUGH
Clockstoppers *91*
8 Mile *130*

BARRY KINGSTON
Crossroads *108*

RAY KLUGA
Tuck Everlasting *498*
Two Weeks Notice *507*

SARAH KNOWLES
Simone *425*

CHRISTINE KOLOSOV
Hey Arnold! The
Movie *204*

GARY KOSKO
High Crimes *206*

MARK LAING
The Weight of Water *523*

ELIS LAM
John Q *237*
Undercover Brother *512*

NEIL LAMONT
Harry Potter and the
Chamber of Secrets *196*

SIMON LAMONT
Die Another Day *116*

DAVID LAZAN
Antwone Fisher *22*

TIBOR LAZAR
Max *289*

JONATHAN LEE
XXX *538*

TEMA LEVINE
Kissing Jessica Stein *247*

WENDY LUEBBE
Return to Never Land *384*

TATIANA LUND
Charlotte Gray *75*

NICHOLAS LUNDY
25th Hour *503*

DELPHINE MABED
The Truth About
Charlie *497*

DON MACAULAY
13 Ghosts *484*

MICHAEL MANSON
One Hour Photo *338*

MARTIN MARTINEC
Harrison's Flowers *194*

CATY MAXEY
The Banger Sisters *34*

ROD MCLEAN
Enigma *140*

DOUG MEERDINK
The Scorpion King *409*

ANDREW MENZIES
Enough *142*

DENIS MERCIER
God Is Great, I'm
Not *182*

YVON MORENO
Girls Can't Swim *181*

ANDREW MUNRO
Lucky Break *276*

JIM NEDZA
Dragonfly *125*

KEITH NEELY
Panic Room *344*

ANDREW NESKOROMNY
The Sum of All Fears *465*

KEI NG
Knockaround Guys *248*
My Big Fat Greek
Wedding *316*

YVAN NICLASS
Merci pour le
Chocolat *296*

SHELLEY NIEDER
Scotland, PA *411*

HARALDS EGEDE NISSEN
Elling *136*

TOM NURSEY
Queen of the
Damned *365*

JENNIFER O'KELLY
Juwanna Mann *241*

ANDREAS OLSHAUSEN
Extreme Ops *149*

ERIC OLSON
Equilibrium *145*

PADRAIG O'NEILL
Bloody Sunday *51*

STEFANO ORTOLANI
Gangs of New York *174*

JAMES OSWALD
Jason X *235*

ROB OTTERSIDE
The Lord of the Rings 2:
The Two Towers *270*

KEITH PAIN
The Four Feathers *163*

CLAUDE PARE
The Sum of All Fears *465*

MISSY PARKER
Lovely and Amazing *274*

SARA PARKS
Tadpole *477*

JAY PELISSIER
Sweet Home Alabama *470*

PIERRE PERRAULT
Abandon *1*

LAWRENCE PEVEC
Ballistic: Ecks vs. Sever *32*

FRANCIS J. PEZZA
Big Fat Liar *41*

MARK RAGGETT
The Hours *212*

NICK RALBOVSKY
Secretary *416*

TOM READ
Nicholas Nickleby *332*

SETH REED
Auto Focus *28*

JOHN REID
Crush *110*

DENIS RENAULT
Femme Fatale *155*

CARLO RESCIGNO
The Emperor's New
Clothes *139*

RICHARD RESEIGNE
Collateral Damage *93*

DEB RILEY
Real Women Have
Curves *376*

MARK ROBINS
The Lord of the Rings 2:
The Two Towers *270*

PHILIP ROBINSON
Formula 51 *159*

PETER ROGNESS
Far from Heaven *151*

STUART ROSE
Enigma *140*

JOSEP ROSELL
Mad Love *278*

Music Index

BRYAN ADAMS
Spirit: Stallion of the
Cimarron *447*

JOSEPH (JOEY) ALTRUDA
Slackers *428*

JEN ANDERSEN
The Goddess of 1967 *183*

PER ANDREASSON
Gossip *187*

MICHAEL ANDREWS
Donnie Darko *122*
Orange County *340*

CRAIG ARMSTRONG
The Quiet American *367*

DAVID ARNOLD (1962-)
Changing Lanes *73*
Die Another Day *116*
Enough *142*

SETH ASARNOW
Bartleby *39*

**ANGELO BADALAMENTI
(1937-)**
Auto Focus *28*
Secretary *416*

KLAUS BADELT
Equilibrium *145*
Invincible *233*
K-19: The
Widowmaker *243*
The Time Machine *486*

BADLY DRAWN BOY
About a Boy *3*

ROQUE BANOS
Second Skin *414*

SAN BAO
Happy Times *193*

JOSEPH BARDANASHVILI
Late Marriage *260*

JOHN BARRY (1933-)
Enigma *140*

PATRIK BARTOSCH
The Chateau *77*

CHRISTOPHE BECK
Stealing Harvard *458*
The Tuxedo *501*

BELLE & SEBASTIAN
Storytelling *461*

MARCO BELTRAMI
Blade II *47*
The Dangerous Lives of
Altar Boys *112*
Resident Evil *383*

**ELMER BERNSTEIN
(1922-)**
Far from Heaven *151*

**TERENCE BLANCHARD
(1962-)**
Barbershop *36*
25th Hour *503*

BERNARDO BONEZZI
No News from God *335*

ANOUAR BRAHEM
The Season of Men *413*

JON BRION
Punch-Drunk Love *362*

PAOLO BUONINO
The Last Kiss *255*

T-BONE BURNETT
Divine Secrets of the Ya-Ya
Sisterhood *120*

CARTER BURWELL (1955-)
Adaptation *10*
The Rookie *396*
Simone *425*

SAM CARDON
Little Secrets *269*

RON CARTER
The Guys *189*

TEDDY CASTELLUCCI
Adam Sandler's 8 Crazy
Nights *8*
Mr. Deeds *302*

MATTHIEU CHABROL
Merci pour le
Chocolat *296*

ERNEST CHAUSSON
Girls Can't Swim *181*

SANDEEP CHOWTA
Bollywood/Hollywood *56*

STANLEY CLARKE
Undercover Brother *512*
Undisputed *514*

**GEORGE S. CLINTON
(1947-)**
Austin Powers in
Goldmember *26*
The Santa Clause 2 *405*

ELIA CMIRAL
Wes Craven Presents:
They *527*

LISA COLEMAN
Juwanna Mann *241*

MICHEL COLOMBIER
Swept Away *474*

ERIC COLVIN
Bark! *38*

GIBA CONCALVES
Code Unknown *92*

**STEWART COPELAND
(1952-)**
Deuces Wild *115*

NORMAND CORBEIL
Extreme Ops *149*

JOHN DANKWORTH
Gangster No. 1 *177*

JEFF DANNA (1964-)
The Grey Zone *188*
The Kid Stays in the
Picture *245*

MYCHAEL DANNA (1958-)
Antwone Fisher *22*
Ararat *23*
Monsoon Wedding *303*

MASON DARING
Sunshine State *467*

DON DAVIS
Ballistic: Ecks vs. Sever *32*

JONATHAN DAVIS
Queen of the
Damned *365*

MARK DE GIL ANTONI
Cherish *81*

JOHN DEBNEY (1957-)
Dragonfly *125*

The Hot Chick *210*
The Scorpion King *409*
Snow Dogs *430*
Spy Kids 2: The Island of
Lost Dreams *449*
The Tuxedo *501*

ALEXANDRE DESPLAT
Read My Lips *374*

FREDERIC DEVREESE
Pauline and Paulette *347*

MICHELLE DIBUCCI
Wendigo *526*

ANDREW DICKSON
All or Nothing *16*

SEAN DINSMORE
Just a Kiss *239*

ANNE DUDLEY (1956-)
Lucky Break *276*

ANTOINE DUHAMEL
Safe Conduct *400*

FRED EBB
Chicago *84*

RANDY EDELMAN (1947-)
XXX *538*

CLIFF EIDELMAN
Harrison's Flowers *194*

DANNY ELFMAN (1953-)
Chicago *84*
Men in Black II *293*
Red Dragon *378*
Spider-Man *444*

MARC ELLIS
Adam Sandler's 8 Crazy
Nights *8*
Master of Disguise *287*

RAY ELLIS
Adam Sandler's 8 Crazy
Nights *8*

EMINEM (1972-)
8 Mile *130*

STEPHEN ENDELMAN
Evelyn *147*

JACK BOWDEN FAULKNER
American Chai *18*

LOUIS FEBRE
Swimfan *475*

WANG HSIAO FENG
Beijing Bicycle *40*

GEORGE FENTON
Sweet Home Alabama *470*

NEIL FINN
Rain *373*

JOHN (GIANNI) FRIZZELL (1966-)
Ghost Ship *179*
13 Ghosts *484*

PETER GABRIEL (1950-)
Rabbit-Proof Fence *370*

RICHARD GIBBS
I Spy *218*
Like Mike *265*
Queen of the
Damned *365*

PHILIP GLASS (1937-)
The Hours *212*

NICK GLENNIE-SMITH
We Were Soldiers *521*

ELLIOT GOLDENTHAL
Frida *168*

JERRY GOLDSMITH (1929-)
Star Trek: Nemesis *453*
The Sum of All Fears *465*

PAUL GRABOWSKY
Last Orders *256*

HARRY GREGSON-WILLIAMS
Passionada *346*

PAUL GROSS (1959-)
Men with Brooms *295*

YOSHIHIRO HANNO
Millennium Mambo *298*

HAL HARTLEY (1959-)
No Such Thing *336*

PAUL HASLINGER
Blue Crush *54*

REINHOLD HEIL
One Hour Photo *338*

JOHN HIATT
The Country Bears *100*

DAVID HIRSCHFELDER
The Weight of Water *523*

DAVID HOLMES
Analyze That *20*

JOSHUA HOMME
The Dangerous Lives of
Altar Boys *112*

R.M. HOOPES
Dirty Cop No Donut *119*

JAMES HORNER (1953-)
The Four Feathers *163*
Windtalkers *534*

JAMES NEWTON HOWARD (1951-)
Big Trouble *43*
The Emperor's Club *137*
Signs *423*
Treasure Planet *493*

ROBERT HURST
Brown Sugar *64*

ZAKIR HUSSAIN
The Mystic Masseur *321*

ALBERTO IGLESIAS
Sex and Lucia *420*
Talk to Her *479*

ANGEL ILLARAMENDI
Son of the Bride *437*

MARK ISHAM (1951-)
Imposter *227*
Moonlight Mile *306*

ALEXANDER JANKO
My Big Fat Greek
Wedding *316*

ADRIAN JOHNSTON
Me Without You *291*

DANIEL JONES
Max *289*

TREVOR JONES (1949-)
Crossroads *108*

DAVID JULYAN
Insomnia *231*

JAN A.P. KACZMAREK
Unfaithful *516*

JOHN KANDER
Chicago *84*

ROLFE KENT (1963-)
About Schmidt *5*
40 Days and 40
Nights *161*

WOJCIECH KILAR (1932-)
The Pianist *350*

KEVIN KINER
The Other Side of
Heaven *342*

JOHNNY KLIMEK
One Hour Photo *338*

AMANDA KRAVAT
Never Again *327*

JIM LANG
Hey Arnold! The
Movie *204*

NATHAN LARSON
The Chateau *77*
Storytelling *461*

ALEXANDER LASARENKO
Pipe Dream *357*

DAVID LAWRENCE
National Lampoon's Van
Wilder *325*

JEAN LE LOUP
Soft Shell Man *432*

JACK LENZ
Men with Brooms *295*

ROBERT LEPAGE (1957-)
Marriages *286*

CESAR LERNER
Nine Queens *334*

KRISHNA LEVY
8 Women *133*

MAX LICHTENSTEIN
Margarita Happy
Hour *285*

GIONG LIM
Millennium Mambo *298*

JOSEPH LODUCA
Brotherhood of the
Wolf *61*

DANNY LUX
Halloween:
Resurrection *191*
Stolen Summer *460*

DON MACDONALD
Last Wedding *258*

STEPHANE MAKA
God Is Great, I'm
Not *182*

HARRY MANFREDINI
Jason X *235*

CLINT MANSELL
Abandon *1*
Knockaround Guys *248*
Murder by Numbers *313*
Sonny *440*
World Traveler *536*

ANTHONY MARINELLI
The Man from Elysian
Fields *281*

CLIFF MARTINEZ
Narc *323*
Solaris *433*

MARK MCDUFF
The Crocodile Hunter:
Collision Course *106*

BOBBY MCFERRIN
Hush! *216*

STEPHEN MCKEON
Borstal Boy *58*

JOEL MCNEELY
Return to Never Land *384*

EDMUND MCWILLIAMS
Rain *373*

AALOK MEHTA
American Chai *18*

WENDY MELVOIN
Juwanna Mann *241*

MARCUS MILLER (1959-)
Serving Sara *418*

CHARLIE MOLE
The Importance of Being
Earnest *225*

MARK MOTHERSBAUGH (1950-)
Sorority Boys *442*
Welcome to
Collinwood *524*

DOMINIC MULDOWNEY
Bloody Sunday *51*

JOHN MURPHY
All About the
Benjamins *15*
City by the Sea *89*
Friday After Next *170*

DREW NEUMANN
The Wild Thornberrys
Movie *532*

DAVID NEWMAN (1954-)
Death to Smoochy *113*
Ice Age *219*
Life or Something Like
It *263*
Scooby-Doo *407*

THOMAS NEWMAN (1955-)
Road to Perdition *388*
The Salton Sea *403*
White Oleander *529*

LENNIE NIEHAUS
Blood Work *49*

JOSE NIETO
Mad Love *278*

STEFAN NILSSON
A Song for Martin *439*

JASON OSBORN
The Triumph of Love *495*

JOHN OTTMAN
Eight Legged Freaks *129*
Pumpkin *361*
Trapped *490*

JONATHAN PARKER
Bartleby *39*

Performer Index

AALIYAH (1979-2001)
Queen of the
Damned *365*

CAROLINE AARON (1952-)
Never Again *327*
Pumpkin *361*

IGNASI ABADAL
Nine Queens *334*

LIONEL ABELANSKI
My Wife Is an
Actress *320*

SIMON ABKARIAN
Ararat *23*

F. MURRAY ABRAHAM
(1939-)
13 Ghosts *484*

JON ABRAHAMS (1977-)
Texas Rangers *480*
Wes Craven Presents:
They *527*

VICTORIA ABRIL (1959-)
No News from God *335*

JOE ABSOLOM
Extreme Ops *149*

STEFANO ACCORSI
The Last Kiss *255*

JOSH ACKERMAN
American Chai *18*

JOSS ACKLAND (1928-)
K-19: The
Widowmaker *243*

AMY ADAMS
Catch Me If You Can *68*
Serving Sara *418*

EVAN ADAMS
The Business of
Fancydancing *66*

JANE ADAMS (1965-)
Orange County *340*

JOEY LAUREN ADAMS
(1971-)
Harvard Man *201*

MEAT LOAF ADAY (1948-)
Formula 51 *159*
The Salton Sea *403*

MARK ADDY (1963-)
The Time Machine *486*

MELYSSA ADE
Jason X *235*

GOLAB ADINEH
Under the Skin of the
City *511*

BEN AFFLECK (1972-)
Changing Lanes *73*
The Sum of All Fears *465*

SUNG-KI AHN
Chihwaseon: Painted
Fire *86*

JOUKO AHOLA
Invincible *233*

LIAM AIKEN (1990-)
Road to Perdition *388*

ANOUK AIMEE (1932-)
Festival at Cannes *158*

HOLLY AIRD (1969-)
Possession *358*

ADEWALE AKINNUOYE-
AGBAJE
The Bourne Identity *59*

JAVIER ALBALA
Second Skin *414*

DAMIAN ALCAZAR
The Crime of Father
Amaro *104*

NORMA ALEANDRO
(1936-)
Son of the Bride *437*

JANE ALEXANDER (1939-)
The Ring *386*
Sunshine State *467*

KALA ALEXANDER
Blue Crush *54*

MARY ALICE (1941-)
Sunshine State *467*

KAREN ALLEN (1951-)
World Traveler *536*

KEITH ALLEN (1953-)
My Wife Is an
Actress *320*
24 Hour Party People *506*

RAY ALLEN
Harvard Man *201*

TESSA ALLEN
Enough *142*

TIM ALLEN (1953-)
Big Trouble *43*
The Santa Clause 2 *405*

WOODY ALLEN (1935-)
Hollywood Ending *208*

JAMES ALLODI
Men with Brooms *295*

DAVID ALPAY
Ararat *23*

HECTOR ALTERIO (1929-)
Son of the Bride *437*

KAREN ALYX
Girls Can't Swim *181*

EVA AMURRI (1985-)
The Banger Sisters *34*

ELENA ANAYA
Sex and Lucia *420*

ANTHONY ANDERSON
(1970-)
Barbershop *36*

SAM ANDERSON
Slackers *428*

STANLEY ANDERSON
40 Days and 40
Nights *161*
Red Dragon *378*
Simone *425*
Spider-Man *444*

HARRIET ANDERSSON
(1932-)
Gossip *187*

PETER ANDERSSON
Gossip *187*

NAVEEN ANDREWS
(1971-)
Rollerball *393*

MICHAEL ANGARANO
Little Secrets *269*

JENNIFER ANISTON
(1969-)
The Good Girl *184*

MICHAEL APARO
Harvard Man *201*

PETER APPEL (1959-)
Tadpole *477*

SHIRI APPLEBY (1978-)
Swimfan *475*

CHRISTINA APPLEGATE
(1971-)
The Sweetest Thing *472*

ROYCE D. APPLEGATE
(1939-2003)
The Rookie *396*

AMY AQUINO
Undisputed *514*
White Oleander *529*

ANGELICA ARAGON
The Crime of Father
Amaro *104*

NATHANIEL ARCAND
Skins *427*

MANUELA ARCURI
Mad Love *278*

FANNY ARDANT (1949-)
8 Women *133*
No News from God *335*

KAREN ARDIFF
Evelyn *147*

BRUNO ARENA
Pinocchio *355*

ASIA ARGENTO (1975-)
XXX *538*

YANCEY ARIAS
The Time Machine *486*

ALAN ARKIN (1934-)
Thirteen Conversations
About One Thing *483*

PEDRO ARMENDARIZ, JR.
(1930-)
The Crime of Father
Amaro *104*

ALUN ARMSTRONG
(1946-)
Harrison's Flowers *194*

CURTIS ARMSTRONG (1953-)
National Lampoon's Van
Wilder *325*

DENIS ARNDT
Undisputed *514*

DAVID ARQUETTE (1971-)
Eight Legged Freaks *129*
The Grey Zone *188*

PATRICIA ARQUETTE (1968-)
Human Nature *214*

LIOR LOUI ASHKENAZI
Late Marriage *260*

ROGER ASHTON-GRIFFITHS
Gangs of New York *174*

LUKE ASKEW (1937-)
Frailty *166*

SEAN ASTIN (1971-)
The Lord of the Rings 2:
The Two Towers *270*

EILEEN ATKINS (1934-)
The Hours *212*

ROWAN ATKINSON (1955-)
Scooby-Doo *407*

YVAN ATTAL (1965-)
My Wife Is an
Actress *320*

K.D. AUBERT
Friday After Next *170*

PERNILLA AUGUST (1958-)
Gossip *187*
Star Wars: Episode II—
Attack of the
Clones *455*

ERIK AVARI
Mr. Deeds *302*

DAN AYKROYD (1952-)
Crossroads *108*

HANK AZARIA (1964-)
Bark! *38*

CHARLES AZNAVOUR (1924-)
Ararat *23*
The Truth About
Charlie *497*

ELOY AZORIN
Mad Love *278*

OBBA BABATUNDE
John Q *237*
The Wild Thornberrys
Movie (V) *532*

BURT BACHARACH
Austin Powers in
Goldmember *26*

STEVE BACIC (1965-)
Ballistic: Ecks vs. Sever *32*

KEVIN BACON (1958-)
Trapped *490*

DIEDRICH BADER (1966-)
The Country Bears
(V) *100*
Ice Age (V) *219*

JOLLY BADER
Bollywood/Hollywood *56*

MINA (BADIYI) BADIE
Road to Perdition *388*
Roger Dodger *391*

EDOUARD BAER
God Is Great, I'm
Not *182*

LORRI BAGLEY
Ice Age (V) *219*

ROBERT BAGNELL
We Were Soldiers *521*

CLAUDE BAIGNERES
In Praise of Love *229*

MARION BAILEY
All or Nothing *16*

ROBERT BAILEY, JR.
Dragonfly *125*

RACHEL BAILIT
Festival at Cannes *158*

SCOTT BAIRSTOW (1970-)
Tuck Everlasting *498*

DAVID AARON BAKER (1963-)
Kissing Jessica Stein *247*

DIANE BAKER (1938-)
Harrison's Flowers *194*

DYLAN BAKER (1958-)
Changing Lanes *73*
Road to Perdition *388*

KENNY BAKER (1934-)
Star Wars: Episode II—
Attack of the
Clones *455*

LIANE BALABAN
World Traveler *536*

LEONOR BALDAQUE
I'm Going Home *224*
The Uncertainty
Principle *509*

CHRISTIAN BALE (1974-)
Equilibrium *145*
Reign of Fire *381*

FAIRUZA BALK (1974-)
Deuces Wild *115*
Personal Velocity *348*

SAMUEL BALL
Pumpkin *361*

ANTONIO BANDERAS (1960-)
Ballistic: Ecks vs. Sever *32*
Femme Fatale *155*
Frida *168*
Spy Kids 2: The Island of
Lost Dreams *449*

LISA BANES (1955-)
Dragonfly *125*
Pumpkin *361*

ELIZABETH BANKS
Swept Away *474*

TYRA BANKS (1973-)
Halloween:
Resurrection *191*

CHRISTINE BARANSKI (1952-)
Chicago *84*

FRANCES BARBER (1958-)
Esther Kahn *146*

JAVIER BARDEM (1969-)
Second Skin *414*

NIKKI BARNETT
Turning Paige *500*

PEPPE BARRA
Pinocchio *355*

JULIAN BARRATT
Lucky Break *276*

MAJEL BARRETT (1932-)
Star Trek: Nemesis
(V) *453*

CHUCK BARRIS
Confessions of a Dangerous
Mind *95*

DREW BARRYMORE (1975-)
Confessions of a Dangerous
Mind *95*
Donnie Darko *122*

GARY BASARABA (1959-)
Unfaithful *516*

JOANNA BASCALSO
Snow Dogs *430*

KIM BASINGER (1953-)
8 Mile *130*

ANGELA BASSETT (1958-)
Sunshine State *467*

LINDA BASSETT
The Hours *212*

STEVE BASTONI
The Crocodile Hunter:
Collision Course *106*

LAURENT BATEAU
My Wife Is an
Actress *320*

JASON BATEMAN (1969-)
The Sweetest Thing *472*

ALAN BATES (1934-)
The Cherry Orchard *83*
Evelyn *147*
The Mothman
Prophecies *311*
The Sum of All Fears *465*

KATHY BATES (1948-)
About Schmidt *5*
Dragonfly *125*

PAUL BATES
8 Mile *130*

PATRICK BAUCHAU (1938-)
Panic Room *344*
Secretary *416*

NATHALIE BAYE (1948-)
Catch Me If You Can *68*

ADAM BEACH (1972-)
Windtalkers *534*

NIALL BEAGAN
Evelyn *147*

KATE BEAHAN
The Crocodile Hunter:
Collision Course *106*

JENNIFER BEALS (1963-)
Roger Dodger *391*

SEAN BEAN (1959-)
Equilibrium *145*

EMMANUELLE BEART (1965-)
8 Women *133*

JOHN BEASLEY
The Sum of All Fears *465*

MICHAEL BEATTIE
Swept Away *474*

GARCELLE BEAUVAIS (1966-)
Bad Company *30*

DAMIAN BECHIR
No News from God *335*

GERRY BECKER
Blood Work *49*
Spider-Man *444*

ED BEGLEY, JR. (1949-)
Auto Focus *28*

JAMIE BELL
Nicholas Nickleby *332*

RACHAEL BELLA
The Ring *386*

MINO BELLEI
Pinocchio *355*

MARIA BELLO (1967-)
Auto Focus *28*

MONICA BELLUCCI (1968-)
Brotherhood of the
Wolf *61*

MELANIE LYNSKEY
(1977-)
Abandon *1*
The Cherry Orchard *83*
Sweet Home Alabama *470*

NATASHA LYONNE (1979-)
The Grey Zone *188*

TZI MA
The Quiet American *367*

ERIC MABIUS (1971-)
Resident Evil *383*

SUNNY MABREY
The New Guy *328*

ERIK MACARTHUR
We Were Soldiers *521*

HUGH MACDONAGH
Evelyn *147*

ANDIE MACDOWELL
(1958-)
Crush *110*
Harrison's Flowers *194*

ANGUS MACFADYEN
(1964-)
Divine Secrets of the Ya-Ya
Sisterhood *120*
Equilibrium *145*

MATTHEW MACFADYEN
Enigma *140*

GABRIEL MACHT (1972-)
Bad Company *30*

GEORGIA MACKENZIE
Possession *358*

ANTHONY MACKIE
8 Mile *130*

KYLE MACLACHLAN
(1959-)
Me Without You *291*

TRESS MACNEILLE
Hey Arnold! The Movie
(V) *204*

WILLIAM H. MACY (1950-)
Welcome to
Collinwood *524*

RUTH MADOC
Very Annie Mary *518*

MADONNA (1959-)
Swept Away *474*

MICHAEL MADSEN (1959-)
Die Another Day *116*

MIA MAESTRO
Frida *168*

BENOIT MAGIMEL (1974-)
The Piano Teacher *353*

ANN MAGNUSON (1956-)
Panic Room *344*

TOBEY MAGUIRE (1975-)
Spider-Man *444*

CHRISTOPHER MAHER
Enough *142*

DEBORAH MAILMAN
Rabbit-Proof Fence *370*

AUSTIN MAJORS
Treasure Planet (V) *493*

LEE MAJORS (1940-)
Big Fat Liar *41*

LAWRENCE MAKOARE
Die Another Day *116*

ROMANY MALCO
The Chateau *77*
The Tuxedo *501*

RISHMA MALIK
Bollywood/Hollywood *56*

JOHN MALKOVICH (1953-)
I'm Going Home *224*
Knockaround Guys *248*

MATT MALLOY
Changing Lanes *73*

JENA MALONE (1984-)
The Dangerous Lives of
Altar Boys *112*
Donnie Darko *122*

AASIF MANDVI
American Chai *18*
The Mystic Masseur *321*

LOUIS MANDYLOR (1966-)
My Big Fat Greek
Wedding *316*

JOE MANGANIELLO
Spider-Man *444*

JEAN-PIERRE MANGEOT
Time Out *489*

MONIQUE MANGEOT
Time Out *489*

ALEX CRAIG MANN
Festival at Cannes *158*

GABRIEL MANN
Abandon *1*
The Bourne Identity *59*

LESLIE MANN (1972-)
Orange County *340*
Stealing Harvard *458*

SIMON MANN
Bloody Sunday *51*

TARYN MANNING (1978-)
Crossroads *108*
8 Mile *130*

CHRISTIAN MANON
Queen of the
Damned *365*

MICHAEL MANTELL
Secretary *416*

LESLIE MANVILLE
All or Nothing *16*

MIRIAM MARGOLYES
(1941-)
Harry Potter and the
Chamber of Secrets *196*

JULIANNA MARGULIES
(1966-)
Evelyn *147*
Ghost Ship *179*
The Man from Elysian
Fields *281*

ELI MARIENTHAL (1986-)
The Country Bears *100*

RICHARD "CHEECH"
MARIN (1946-)
Pinocchio (V) *355*
Spy Kids 2: The Island of
Lost Dreams *449*

MORGAN MARINNE
The Son *435*

JODIE MARKELL
Hollywood Ending *208*

GED MARLON
Safe Conduct *400*

MICHAEL MARONNA
40 Days and 40
Nights *161*
Slackers *428*

ADONI MAROPIS
Bad Company *30*

EDDIE MARSAN
The Emperor's New
Clothes *139*
Gangs of New York *174*
Gangster No. 1 *177*

MATTHEW MARSH
Bad Company *30*

GARRY MARSHALL (1934-)
Orange County *340*

KRIS MARSHALL
The Four Feathers *163*

FRANCOIS
MARTHOURET
The Lady and the
Duke *250*

ANDREA MARTIN (1947-)
My Big Fat Greek
Wedding *316*

DICK MARTIN (1928-)
Bartleby *39*

MARGO MARTINDALE
The Hours *212*

OLIVIER MARTINEZ
(1966-)
Unfaithful *516*

ANNA MASSEY (1937-)
The Importance of Being
Earnest *225*
Possession *358*

MICHAEL MASTRO
Kissing Jessica Stein *247*

HEATHER MATARAZZO
(1982-)
Sorority Boys *442*

KARI MATCHETT
Men with Brooms *295*

TIM MATHESON (1947-)
National Lampoon's Van
Wilder *325*

MARISSA MATRONE
Maid in Manhattan *279*

TERENCE MAYNARD
Reign of Fire *381*

DANIEL MAYS
All or Nothing *16*

DEBI MAZAR (1964-)
The Tuxedo *501*

MONET MAZUR
40 Days and 40
Nights *161*

RACHEL MCADAMS
The Hot Chick *210*

CHI MCBRIDE (1961-)
Narc *323*
Undercover Brother *512*

CARMEL MCCALLION
Bloody Sunday *51*

EDIE MCCLURG (1950-)
Master of Disguise *287*

MATTHEW
MCCONAUGHEY
(1969-)
Frailty *166*
Reign of Fire *381*
Thirteen Conversations
About One Thing *483*

CATHERINE
MCCORMACK (1972-)
The Weight of Water *523*

CIAN MCCORMACK
Gangs of New York *174*

MARY MCCORMACK
(1969-)
Full Frontal *172*
World Traveler *536*

WILL MCCORMACK
Abandon *1*

ALEC MCCOWEN (1925-)
Gangs of New York *174*

MARK MCCRACKEN
We Were Soldiers *521*

DAISY MCCRACKIN
Halloween:
Resurrection *191*

ELISE MCCREDIE
The Goddess of 1967 *183*

HELEN MCCRORY
Charlotte Gray *75*

**BRUCE MCCULLOCH
(1961-)**
Stealing Harvard *458*

JAMES MCDANIEL (1958-)
Sunshine State *467*

**DYLAN MCDERMOTT
(1962-)**
Texas Rangers *480*

**KATHLEEN
MCDERMOTT**
Morvern Callar *308*

IAN MCDIARMID (1947-)
Star Wars: Episode II—
Attack of the
Clones *455*

**GARRY MCDONALD
(1948-)**
Rabbit-Proof Fence *370*

**KEVIN MCDONALD
(1961-)**
Lilo and Stitch (V) *267*

**MARY MCDONNELL
(1952-)**
Donnie Darko *122*

ANDREW MCDONOUGH
Return to Never Land
(V) *384*

**NEAL MCDONOUGH
(1966-)**
Minority Report *299*

**FRANCES MCDORMAND
(1958-)**
City by the Sea *89*

**MALCOLM MCDOWELL
(1943-)**
Gangster No. 1 *177*
I Spy *218*

**NATASCHA (NATASHA)
MCELHONE (1971-)**
Feardotcom *153*
Solaris *433*

JOHN MCENROE
Mr. Deeds *302*

**GATES (CHERYL)
MCFADDEN (1949-)**
Star Trek: Nemesis *453*

PAUL MCGANN (1959-)
Queen of the
Damned *365*

BRUCE MCGILL (1950-)
The Sum of All Fears *465*

**JOHN C. MCGINLEY
(1959-)**
Stealing Harvard *458*

**PATRICK MCGOOHAN
(1928-)**
Treasure Planet (V) *493*

EWAN MCGREGOR (1971-)
Star Wars: Episode II—
Attack of the
Clones *455*

**STEPHEN MCHATTIE
(1947-)**
Secretary *416*

**TIM (MCINNERNY)
MCINNERY (1956-)**
The Emperor's New
Clothes *139*

JO MCINNES
My Wife Is an
Actress *320*

**MICHAEL MCKEAN
(1947-)**
Auto Focus *28*
Never Again *327*

GINA MCKEE (1964-)
Divine Secrets of the Ya-Ya
Sisterhood *120*

IAN MCKELLEN (1939-)
The Lord of the Rings 2:
The Two Towers *270*

**JACQUELINE MCKENZIE
(1967-)**
Divine Secrets of the Ya-Ya
Sisterhood *120*

KEVIN MCKIDD (1973-)
Max *289*

IAN MCNEICE (1950-)
The Cherry Orchard *83*

**MICHAEL MCSHANE
(1957-)**
Treasure Planet (V) *493*

GERARD MCSORLEY
Bloody Sunday *51*

ANNE MEARA (1929-)
Like Mike *265*

JULIO MECHOSO
Pumpkin *361*

AALOK MEHTA
American Chai *18*

RISHI MEHTA
The Emperor's Club *137*

BESS MEISLER
My Big Fat Greek
Wedding *316*

MURRAY MELVIN (1932-)
The Emperor's New
Clothes *139*

EVA MENDES
All About the
Benjamins *15*

JOSE MANUEL MENDES
The Uncertainty
Principle *509*

PETER MENSAH
Jason X *235*

RYAN MERRIMAN (1983-)
Halloween:
Resurrection *191*

DEBRA MESSING (1968-)
Hollywood Ending *208*
The Mothman
Prophecies *311*

LAURIE METCALF (1955-)
Treasure Planet (V) *493*

BRECKIN MEYER (1974-)
Pinocchio (V) *355*

DINA MEYER (1969-)
Star Trek: Nemesis *453*

HANS MEYER
Brotherhood of the
Wolf *61*

JESSICA KATE MEYER
The Pianist *350*

**GIOVANNA
MEZZOGIORNO**
The Last Kiss *255*

AMOL MHATRE
Leela *262*

OLIVER MILBURN
Me Without You *291*

ELAINE MILES
The Business of
Fancydancing *66*

**JOEL MCKINNON
MILLER**
Friday After Next *170*

OMAR BENSON MILLER
8 Mile *130*

VALARIE RAE MILLER
All About the
Benjamins *15*

SOFIA MILOS
Passionada *346*

HELEN MIRREN (1946-)
Last Orders *256*
No Such Thing *336*

DORIAN MISSICK
Two Weeks Notice *507*

JIMI MISTRY
The Mystic Masseur *321*

**DARRYL (CHILL)
MITCHELL**
The Country Bears *100*

**ELIZABETH MITCHELL
(1970-)**
The Santa Clause 2 *405*

RHONA MITRA
Sweet Home Alabama *470*

JEROD MIXON (1981-)
The New Guy *328*

ISAAC MIZRAHI
Hollywood Ending *208*

**RALPH (RALF) MOELLER
(1959-)**
The Scorpion King *409*

JAY MOHR (1970-)
The Adventures of Pluto
Nash *13*
Simone *425*

ALFRED MOLINA (1953-)
Frida *168*
Texas Rangers *480*

JORDI MOLLA
Second Skin *414*

SLOANE MOMSEN (1997-)
We Were Soldiers *521*

TAYLOR MOMSEN
We Were Soldiers *521*

DOMINIC MONAGHAN
The Lord of the Rings 2:
The Two Towers *270*

LAURA MONAGHAN
Rabbit-Proof Fence *370*

**RICARDO MONTALBAN
(1920-)**
Spy Kids 2: The Island of
Lost Dreams *449*

EDOUARD MONTOUTE
Femme Fatale *155*

JULIANNE MOORE (1961-)
Far from Heaven *151*
The Hours *212*
World Traveler *536*

MANDY MOORE (1984-)
A Walk to Remember *519*

MARGUERITE MOREAU
Queen of the
Damned *365*

LAURA MORELLI
Last Orders *256*

HEATHER MORGAN
Bark! *38*

JAYE P. MORGAN (1931-)
Confessions of a Dangerous
Mind *95*

TREVOR MORGAN (1986-)
The Rookie *396*

CATHY MORIARTY (1961-)
Analyze That *20*

**PHILIPPE MORIER-
GENOUD**
Safe Conduct *400*

CAROLINE MORIN
The Lady and the
Duke *250*

KATHRYN MORRIS
Minority Report *299*

TEMUERA MORRISON
(1961-)
Star Wars: Episode II—
Attack of the
Clones *455*

EDWIN MORROW (1980-)
We Were Soldiers *521*

ROB MORROW (1962-)
The Emperor's Club *137*

VIGGO MORTENSEN
(1958-)
The Lord of the Rings 2:
The Two Towers *270*

EMILY MORTIMER (1971-)
Formula 51 *159*
Lovely and Amazing *274*

JOE MORTON (1947-)
Dragonfly *125*

SAMANTHA MORTON
(1977-)
Minority Report *299*
Morvern Callar *308*

MONI MOSHONOV
Late Marriage *260*

GREG MOTTOLA
Hollywood Ending *208*

ANNA MOUGLALIS
Merci pour le
Chocolat *296*

MARY MOULDS
Bloody Sunday *51*

ANSON MOUNT
City by the Sea *89*
Crossroads *108*

SCOTT JAMES MOUTTER
Reign of Fire *381*

TAMERA MOWRY
The Hot Chick *210*

TIA MOWRY
The Hot Chick *210*

BRIDGET MOYNAHAN
(1972-)
The Sum of All Fears *465*

SUHASINI MULAY
Lagaan: Once upon a Time
in India *252*

KATE MULGREW (1955-)
Star Trek: Nemesis *453*

MEGAN MULLALLY
(1958-)
Stealing Harvard *458*

RICHY MULLER
XXX *538*

DERMOT MULRONEY
(1963-)
About Schmidt *5*
Lovely and Amazing *274*
The Safety of Objects *402*

OMERA MUMBA
The Time Machine *486*

SAMANTHA MUMBA
The Time Machine *486*

LILIANA MUMY
The Santa Clause 2 *405*

FRANKIE MUNIZ (1985-)
Big Fat Liar *41*
Deuces Wild *115*

GEORGE MURDOCK
(1930-)
Orange County *340*

AARON MURPHY
Rain *373*

BRITTANY MURPHY
(1977-)
8 Mile *130*

EDDIE MURPHY (1961-)
The Adventures of Pluto
Nash *13*
I Spy *218*
Showtime *421*

BRIAN MURRAY
Treasure Planet (V) *493*

GARIKAYI MUTAMBIRWA
Clockstoppers *91*

DWIGHT MYERS (1967-)
Big Trouble *43*

MIKE MYERS (1963-)
Austin Powers in
Goldmember *26*

PHILIPPE NAHON
Brotherhood of the
Wolf *61*
The Chateau *77*

AJAY NAIDU
American Chai *18*

DEEPTI NAVAL
Leela *262*

DYLAN NEAL
40 Days and 40
Nights *161*

KEVIN NEALON (1953-)
Adam Sandler's 8 Crazy
Nights (V) *8*

LIAM NEESON (1952-)
Gangs of New York *174*
K-19: The
Widowmaker *243*

CHRISTOPHER NEIMAN
Auto Focus *28*

NOVELLA NELSON (1939-)
Antwone Fisher *22*

TIM BLAKE NELSON
(1965-)
Cherish *81*
The Good Girl *184*
Minority Report *299*

FRANCESCA NERI (1964-)
Collateral Damage *93*

JAMES NESBITT (1966-)
Bloody Sunday *51*
Lucky Break *276*

THIERRY NEUVIC
Code Unknown *92*

BEBE NEUWIRTH (1958-)
Tadpole *477*

BARRY NEWMAN (1938-)
40 Days and 40
Nights *161*

PAUL NEWMAN (1925-)
Road to Perdition *388*

THANDIE NEWTON
(1972-)
The Truth About
Charlie *497*

THOMAS IAN NICHOLAS
(1980-)
Halloween:
Resurrection *191*
The Rules of
Attraction *398*

NICHELLE NICHOLS
(1933-)
Snow Dogs *430*

JACK NICHOLSON (1937-)
About Schmidt *5*

STEVE NICHOLSON
K-19: The
Widowmaker *243*

JUHANI NIELMELA
The Man Without a
Past *283*

CONNIE NIELSEN (1965-)
One Hour Photo *338*

LESLIE NIELSEN (1926-)
Men with Brooms *295*

BILL NIGHY (1949-)
Lucky Break *276*

NAJWA NIMRI
Sex and Lucia *420*

CYNTHIA NIXON (1966-)
Igby Goes Down *221*

GIMENA NOBILE
Son of the Bride *437*

MICHELLE NOLDEN
Men with Brooms *295*

TOM NOONAN (1951-)
Eight Legged Freaks *129*
Knockaround Guys *248*

SVEN NORDIN
Elling *136*

JEAN-GABRIEL
NORDMANN
Murderous Maids *315*

ZACK NORMAN
Festival at Cannes *158*

JEREMY NORTHAM
(1961-)
Enigma *140*
Possession *358*

ALEX NORTON
The Count of Monte
Cristo *97*

EDWARD NORTON (1969-)
Death to Smoochy *113*
Frida *168*
Red Dragon *378*
25th Hour *503*

JACK NOSEWORTHY
(1969-)
Undercover Brother *512*

MOUNA NOUREDDINE
The Season of Men *413*

MICHAEL NOURI (1945-)
Lovely and Amazing *274*

BEN NU
Happy Times *193*

MIGUEL A. NUNEZ, JR.
(1964-)
The Adventures of Pluto
Nash *13*
Juwanna Mann *241*
Scooby-Doo *407*

BILL NUNN (1953-)
Spider-Man *444*

SEAN O'BRYAN
Big Fat Liar *41*

FRANCES O'CONNOR
(1969-)
The Importance of Being
Earnest *225*
Windtalkers *534*

CHRISTOPHE ODENT
Safe Conduct *400*

SANDRA OH (1971-)
Big Fat Liar *41*

CATHERINE O'HARA
(1954-)
Orange County *340*

MICHAEL O'KEEFE (1955-)
The Hot Chick *210*

MATT O'LEARY
Frailty *166*
Spy Kids 2: The Island of
Lost Dreams *449*

LENA OLIN (1955-)
Queen of the
Damned *365*

INGRID OLIU
Real Women Have
Curves *376*

Roger Dodger *391*
24 Hour Party People *506*

OBSESSIVE LOVE
The Good Girl *184*
Mad Love *278*
Punch-Drunk Love *362*
Swimfan *475*

OCCULT
Brotherhood of the
Wolf *61*

ORGANIZED CRIME
Analyze That *20*
Death to Smoochy *113*
Deuces Wild *115*
Gangster No. 1 *177*
Harvard Man *201*
Knockaround Guys *248*
Road to Perdition *388*

PARENTHOOD
About a Boy *3*
The Banger Sisters *34*
Evelyn *147*
Maid in Manhattan *279*
Margarita Happy
Hour *285*
The Ring *386*
Turning Paige *500*
A Walk to Remember *519*

PARIS, FRANCE
The Bourne Identity *59*
Code Unknown *92*
CQ *102*
The Emperor's New
Clothes *139*
Femme Fatale *155*
I'm Going Home *224*
In Praise of Love *229*
The Lady and the
Duke *250*
My Wife Is an
Actress *320*
Safe Conduct *400*
The Truth About
Charlie *497*

PERIOD PIECE: 15TH CENTURY
Mad Love *278*

PERIOD PIECE: 16TH CENTURY
Mad Love *278*

PERIOD PIECE: 18TH CENTURY
Brotherhood of the
Wolf *61*
The Lady and the
Duke *250*
The Triumph of Love *495*

PERIOD PIECE: 19TH CENTURY
Chihwaseon: Painted
Fire *86*
The Count of Monte
Cristo *97*

The Emperor's New
Clothes *139*
The Four Feathers *163*
Gangs of New York *174*
The Importance of Being
Earnest *225*
Mariages *286*
Nicholas Nickleby *332*
Possession *358*
Spirit: Stallion of the
Cimarron *447*
Texas Rangers *480*
The Weight of Water *523*

PERIOD PIECE: 20TH CENTURY
Frida *168*
Lagaan: Once upon a Time
in India *252*
Me Without You *291*

PERIOD PIECE: 1900
The Cherry Orchard *83*

PERIOD PIECE: 1910
Max *289*
Tuck Everlasting *498*

PERIOD PIECE: 1920
The Cat's Meow *71*
Chicago *84*

PERIOD PIECE: 1930
Borstal Boy *58*
Invincible *233*
Murderous Maids *315*
Rabbit-Proof Fence *370*
Road to Perdition *388*

PERIOD PIECE: 1940
The Grey Zone *188*
The Hours *212*
The Mystic Masseur *321*
The Pianist *350*

PERIOD PIECE: 1950
Austin Powers in
Goldmember *26*
Deuces Wild *115*
Evelyn *147*
Far from Heaven *151*
The Hours *212*
The Mystic Masseur *321*
The Other Side of
Heaven *342*
The Quiet American *367*

PERIOD PIECE: 1960
Auto Focus *28*
Catch Me If You Can *68*
Confessions of a Dangerous
Mind *95*
CQ *102*
Gangster No. 1 *177*
K-19: The
Widowmaker *243*

PERIOD PIECE: 1970
Austin Powers in
Goldmember *26*
Auto Focus *28*
Bloody Sunday *51*
Catch Me If You Can *68*
Confessions of a Dangerous
Mind *95*

The Dangerous Lives of
Altar Boys *112*
The Emperor's Club *137*
Frailty *166*
Moonlight Mile *306*
Rain *373*
Scotland, PA *411*
Stolen Summer *460*
24 Hour Party People *506*

PERIOD PIECE: 1980
Donnie Darko *122*
Lan Yu *254*
Sonny *440*
24 Hour Party People *506*

PHILADELPHIA, PENNSYLVANIA
Like Mike *265*

PHOTOGRAPHY OR PHOTOGRAPHERS
Femme Fatale *155*
Harrison's Flowers *194*
One Hour Photo *338*
Soft Shell Man *432*
The Weight of Water *523*

PHYSICALLY CHALLENGED
Brotherhood of the
Wolf *61*
Pumpkin *361*
The Season of Men *413*
Son of the Bride *437*
Very Annie Mary *518*

PIRATES
Return to Never Land *384*
Treasure Planet *493*

POETRY
The Business of
Fancydancing *66*
Possession *358*

POLICE
Abandon *1*
City by the Sea *89*
Dirty Cop No Donut *119*
Enough *142*
Feardotcom *153*
Formula 51 *159*
Heaven *203*
Insomnia *231*
Murder by Numbers *313*
Narc *323*
The Salton Sea *403*
Scotland, PA *411*
Showtime *421*
Skins *427*

POLITICS
The Emperor's New
Clothes *139*
Gangs of New York *174*
Max *289*
The Mystic Masseur *321*

PORNOGRAPHY
Auto Focus *28*

POST APOCALYPSE
Equilibrium *145*
Reign of Fire *381*
The Time Machine *486*

POVERTY
All or Nothing *16*
Beijing Bicycle *40*
Code Unknown *92*
8 Mile *130*
The Man Without a
Past *283*
Nicholas Nickleby *332*
Under the Skin of the
City *511*

PREGNANCY
Barbershop *36*
The Crime of Father
Amaro *104*
Crossroads *108*
The Good Girl *184*
Gossip *187*
The Last Kiss *255*
My Wife Is an
Actress *320*
Personal Velocity *348*
Talk to Her *479*

PRISON OR PRISONERS
Catch Me If You Can *68*
Chicago *84*
The Count of Monte
Cristo *97*
Lucky Break *276*
The New Guy *328*
Red Dragon *378*
Undisputed *514*
White Oleander *529*

PROSTITUTION
The Man from Elysian
Fields *281*
Sonny *440*

PSYCHIATRY AND PSYCHIATRISTS
Analyze That *20*
Antwone Fisher *22*
Bark *38*
Solaris *433*
Wes Craven Presents:
They *527*

PUPPETS
Pinocchio *355*

RELIGION
Brotherhood of the
Wolf *61*
The Crime of Father
Amaro *104*
The Dangerous Lives of
Altar Boys *112*
Evelyn *147*
40 Days and 40
Nights *161*
The Other Side of
Heaven *342*
Stolen Summer *460*
A Walk to Remember *519*

THE RESISTANCE
Charlotte Gray *75*
Equilibrium *145*
Safe Conduct *400*

REVENGE
Changing Lanes *73*

Imagine 1988
Immediate Family 1989
Immortal Beloved 1995
Imperative 1985
Importance of Being Earnest, The 1995
The Importance of Being Earnest, The (Parker), pg. 225
Imported Bridegroom, The 1991
Impostor, pg. 227
Impostors 1999
Impromptu 1991
Impulse (Baker) 1984
Impulse (Locke) 1990
In a Shallow Grave 1988
In and Out 1997
In Country 1989
In Crowd, The 2001
In Custody 1995
In Dangerous Company 1988
In Dreams 2000
In Fashion. See Á la Mode.
In God's Hands 1999
In Love and War 1997
In Our Hands 1983
In Praise of Love, pg. 229
In the Army Now 1995
In the Bedroom 2002
In the Company of Men 1997
In the Heat of Passion 1992
In the Heat of the Night [1967] 1992
In the Land of the Deaf 1995
In the Line of Fire 1993
In the Mood 1987
In the Mood for Love 2002
In the Mouth of Madness 1995
In the Name of the Father 1993
In the Shadow of Kilimanjaro 1986
In the Shadow of the Stars 1992
In the Soup 1992
In the Spirit 1990
In Too Deep 2000
In Weiter Ferne, So Nah!. See Faraway, So Close.
Inchon 1982
Incident at Oglala 1992
Incident at Raven's Gate 1988
Incognito 1999
Incredible Journey, The. See Homeward Bound.
Incredibly True Adventures of Two Girls in Love, The 1995
Incubus, The 1982
Indecent Proposal 1993
Independence Day 1996
Indian in the Cupboard, The 1995
Indian Runner, The 1991
Indian Summer 1993
Indiana Jones and the Last Crusade 1989
Indiana Jones and the Temple of Doom 1984
Indochine 1992

Inevitable Grace 1995
Infinity 1991
Infinity (Broderick) 1996
Informer, The [1935] 1986
Inkwell, The 1995
Inland Sea, The 1995
Inner Circle, The 1991
Innerspace 1987
Innocent, The 1988
Innocent, The 1995
Innocent Blood 1992
Innocent Man, An 1989
Innocent Sleep, The 1997
Innocents Abroad 1992
Inside Monkey Zetterland 1993
Insider, The 2000
Insignificance 1985
Insomnia (Skjoldbjaerg) 1999
Insomnia (Nolan), pg. 231
Inspector Gadget 2000
Instant Karma 1990
Instinct 2000
Internal Affairs 1990
Interrogation, The 1990
Intersection 1995
Interview with the Vampire 1995
Intervista 1993
Intimacy 2002
Intimate Relations 1997
Into the Night 1985
Into the Sun 1992
Into the West 1993
Invaders from Mars 1986
Invasion! See Top of the Food Chain
Invasion of the Body Snatchers [1956] 1982
Invasion U.S.A. 1985
Inventing the Abbotts 1997
Invention of Love 2001
Invincible, pg. 233
Invisible Circus 2002
Invisible Kid, The 1988
Invitation au voyage 1983
Invitation to the Dance [1956] 1985
I.Q. 1995
Iris 2002
Irma la Douce [1963] 1986
Irma Vep 1997
Iron Eagle 1986
Iron Eagle II 1988
Iron Giant, The 2000
Iron Maze 1991
Iron Triangle, The 1989
Iron Will 1995
Ironweed 1987
Irreconcilable Differences 1984
Ishtar 1987
Island of Dr. Moreau, The 1996
Isn't She Great 2001
Istoriya As-Klyachimol. See Asya's Happiness.
It Could Happen to You 1995
It Couldn't Happen Here 1988
It Had to Be You 1989
It Happened One Night [1934] 1982

It Happened Tomorrow [1944] 1983
It Takes Two 1988
It Takes Two 1995
Italian for Beginners 2002
Italiensk for Begyndere See Italian for Beginners.
It's a Wonderful Life [1946] 1982
It's Alive III 1987
It's All True 1993
It's My Party 1996
It's Pat 1995
It's the Rage 2001
Ivan and Abraham 1995
I've Heard the Mermaids Singing 1987

Jack 1996
Jack and His Friends 1993
Jack and Sarah 1996
Jack Frost 1999
Jack the Bear 1993
Jackal, The 1997
Jackie Brown 1997
Jackie Chan's First Strike 1997
Jackpot 2002
Jack's Back 1988
Jacknife 1989
Jacob 1988
Jacob's Ladder 1990
Jacquot of Nantes 1993
Jade 1995
Jagged Edge 1985
J'ai épousé une ombre. See I Married a Shadow.
Jailhouse Rock [1957] 1986
Jake Speed 1986
Jakob the Liar 2000
James and the Giant Peach 1996
James Joyce's Women 1985
Jamon, Jamon 1993
Jane Eyre 1996
January Man, The 1989
Jason Goes to Hell 1993
Jason X, pg. 235
Jason's Lyric 1995
Jawbreaker 2000
Jaws: The Revenge 1987
Jaws 3-D 1983
Jay and Silent Bob Strike Back 2002
Jazzman 1984
Je Rentre a la Maison. See I'm Going Home.
Je tu il elle [1974] 1985
Je vous salue, Marie. See Hail Mary.
Jean de Florette 1987
Jeanne Dielman, 23 Quai du Commerce, 1080 Bruxelles [1976] 1981
Jeepers Creepers 2002
Jefferson in Paris 1995
Jeffrey 1995
Jekyll and Hyde ... Together Again 1982
Jennifer Eight 1992
Jerky Boys 1995
Jerome 2001

Jerry Maguire 1996
Jerusalem, 289
Jesus of Montreal 1989
Jesus' Son 2000
Jetsons 1990
Jewel of the Nile, The 1985
JFK 1991
Jigsaw Man, The 1984
Jim and Piraterna Blom. See Jim and the Pirates.
Jim and the Pirates 1987
Jimmy Hollywood 1995
Jimmy Neutron: Boy Genius 2002
Jimmy the Kid 1983
Jingle All the Way 1996
Jinxed 1982
Jit 1995
Jo-Jo at the Gate of Lions 1995
Jo Jo Dancer, Your Life Is Calling 1986
Joan the Mad. See Mad Love.
Jocks 1987
Joe Dirt 2002
Joe Gould's Secret 2001
Joe Somebody 2002
Joe the King 2000
Joe Versus the Volcano 1990
Joe's Apartment 1996
Joey 1985
Joey Takes a Cab 1991
John and the Missus 1987
John Carpenter's Ghosts of Mars 2002
John Carpenter's Vampires 1999
John Grisham's the Rainmaker
John Huston 1988
John Huston and the Dubliners 1987
John Q, pg. 237
Johnny Be Good 1988
Johnny Dangerously 1984
Johnny Handsome 1989
Johnny Mnemonic 1995
Johnny Stecchino 1992
Johnny Suede 1992
johns 1997
Joke of Destiny, A 1984
Joseph Conrad's the Secret Agent 1996
Josh and S.A.M. 1993
Joshua Then and Now 1985
Josie and the Pussycats 2002
Journey into Fear [1943] 1985
Journey of August King 1995
Journey of Hope 1991
Journey of Love 1990
Journey of Natty Gann, The 1985
Journey to Spirit Island 1988
Joy Luck Club, The 1993
Joy of Sex 1984
Joy Ride 2002
Joysticks 1983
Ju Dou 1991
Juana la Loca. See Mad Love.
Judas Kiss 2000
Judas Project, The 1995
Jude 1996
Judge Dredd 1995